Social Security Pension Reform in Europe

A National Bureau
of Economic Research
Conference Report

Social Security Pension Reform in Europe

Edited by **Martin Feldstein and Horst Siebert**

The University of Chicago Press

Chicago and London

Social Security Pension Reform in Europe

Edited by **Martin Feldstein and Horst Siebert**

The University of Chicago Press

Chicago and London

MARTIN FELDSTEIN is the George F. Baker Professor of Economics, Harvard University, and president of the National Bureau of Economic Research. HORST SIEBERT is president of the Kiel Institute of World Economics, chair of theoretical economics and professor at the Christian-Albrechts University, Kiel, Germany.

The University of Chicago Press, Chicago 60637
The University of Chicago Press, Ltd., London
© 2002 by the National Bureau of Economic Research
All rights reserved. Published 2002
Printed in the United States of America
11 10 09 08 07 06 05 04 03 02   1 2 3 4 5
ISBN: 0-226-24108-4 (cloth)

Library of Congress Cataloging-in-Publication Data

Social security pension reform in Europe / edited by Martin Feldstein and Horst Siebert.
    p. cm. — (National Bureau of Economic Research conference report)
    Papers presented at a conference held in Berlin, Germany, in March of 2000.
    Includes bibliographical references and index.
    ISBN 0-226-24108-4 (cloth : alk. paper)
    1. Social security—Europe—Congresses.   2. Pensions—Europe—Finance—Congresses.   3. Pension trusts—Investments—Europe—Congresses.   4. Privatization—Europe—Congresses.
I.   Feldstein, Martin S.   II. Siebert, Horst, 1938–   III.   Series.

HD7164.S62 2002
331.25′22′094—dc21

2002016569

Contents

Acknowledgments

This volume is part of a larger series of studies of Social Security reform conducted separately by the National Bureau of Economic Research and by the Kiel Institute. More information on these studies is available on the internet at [www.nber.org/socialsecurity] and [www.uni-kiel.de].

The papers in this volume were presented and discussed at a conference in Berlin in March 2000. The remarks by the discussant of each paper and a summary of the general discussion are also included in the volume. We are grateful to Klaus-Jürgen Gern and Oliver Lorz for preparing the summary of the general discussion.

We are grateful to the Ford Foundation, the Starr Foundation, and the Allianz Versicherungs AG for the financial support that made this project possible. We also want to thank individual staff members of the NBER and of the Kiel Institute for their help with the many aspects of the planning and execution of the research, the conference, and the volume. In addition to the researchers and the research assistants named in the individual papers, we want to thank Kirsten Foss Davis, Helena Fitz-Patrick, Norma MacKenzie, Jutta M. Arpe, and Hannelore Owe for logistic support of the meetings and assistance in the preparation of this volume.

Preface

The papers in this volume show the enormous variety of ways in which the European nations are confronting the public pension crisis that has been brought about by the combination of generous promises in the past and a changing demographic structure in the future. Some countries have made radical reforms to reduce the cost of future benefits while maintaining support for future retirees. Others have done very little.

These papers are the result of a project organized jointly by the National Bureau of Economic Research (based in Cambridge, Massachusetts) and the Kiel Institute of World Economics (based in Kiel, Germany). Although the volume makes no explicit recommendations, we think that the evidence on the alternatives pursued by different European countries should be helpful to policy officials and others who are contemplating future reforms in Europe as well as in the United States and elsewhere.

The ten separate country studies provide information on the demographic and economic facts that confront each country in dealing with its aging population; describe the reforms that have been adopted in recent years; and discuss the political and conceptual issues involved in those reforms. In addition, three essays deal with the broader context of social security reform: the economic aspects of reform, the social context of reform, and the implications of the European labor market. Two brief introductory essays—by Martin Feldstein and Horst Siebert—give American and European points of view, respectively. A summary survey of European social security programs written by Klaus-Jürgen Gern and a data appendix prepared by the Organization for Economic Cooperation and Development complete the volume.

Introduction
An American Perspective

Martin Feldstein

Financing the retirement income and health benefits of an aging population is the most significant fiscal problem facing the industrial countries of the world. Spending on these programs is already the largest part of the public budget in most industrial countries. The taxes to finance these outlays have an enormous impact on the economy. They raise the overall marginal tax rate of middle-income workers to more than 50 percent, reducing the incentive to work and increasing the incentive to take income in the form of fringe benefits and other nontaxable forms. These distortions cause large deadweight losses that reduce the standard of living of the working population.

The high tax cost of financing the current benefits for the aged reflects the pay-as-you-go nature of the existing programs. In pure pay-as-you-go (PAYGO) programs, there are no investments in private stocks and bonds in either government trust funds or in individual accounts to reduce the cost of providing benefits. In those countries that have previously adopted investment-based programs to supplement or replace PAYGO systems, the cost to the taxpayers is significantly less.

The aging of the population will make the problem substantially worse in the next several decades. Moreover, although the retirement of the baby boom generation will accelerate this process, the increase in the relative number of aged in the population is a permanent shift that will make the cost of PAYGO programs permanently higher. Actuaries estimate that this demographic change will raise the cost of financing existing benefit rules

Martin Feldstein is the George F. Baker Professor of Economics, Harvard University, and president of the National Bureau of Economic Research.

by about 50 percent or, if taxes are not to be raised, will require reducing benefits by about one-third. The provision of adequate retirement income and appropriate medical care for the aged is thus also one of the biggest social problems that industrial countries face.[1]

The Problems are Greater for Europe

Although the situation varies from country to country, the problem is generally more serious in Europe than in the United States. There are five reasons for this. First, the current benefit costs are substantially higher relative to gross domestic product (GDP) in Europe than in the United States. This primarily reflects earlier retirement and higher ratios of benefits to previous wages. The earlier retirement is due to a combination of the incentives built into the Social Security pension rules (see Gruber and Wise 1999, and chap. 2 in this volume) and the national labor market practices designed to encourage early retirement on the mistaken presumption that it will reduce unemployment among the young population. Because benefits are now a higher fraction of GDP in Europe than in the United States, the increase in benefits associated with any degree of aging will also be a greater proportion of GDP as well.

Second, the demographic trends in Europe will lead to a higher ratio of aged to young than in the United States. While the ratio of those over the age of sixty-five to the population aged fifteen to sixty-four is expected to increase from 19 percent now to 36 percent in 2050 in the United States, the same ratio is expected to rise in Germany from 24 percent now to 49 percent in 2050.

Third, overall tax rates are already substantially higher in Europe than in the United States. While taxes take one-third of GDP in the United States, the share in Europe is typically one-half or more. Since the deadweight loss of the tax system varies with the square of the marginal tax rate, adding each additional percentage point to the tax rate will cause a greater incremental deadweight loss in Europe than in the United States.

Fourth, in Europe these problems are exacerbated by the interaction of taxes and minimum net-of-tax wages. Because legal rules and national custom put a floor on net wages, the increased taxes raise the cost to firms of hiring low-skilled workers. Where custom forces relative wages to remain roughly unchanged, the increased taxes raise the cost of hiring more-skilled workers, as well. The result of these higher real-wage costs is an increase in unemployment and therefore in unemployment benefits and

---

1. The problem of financing health care for the aged is basically similar to the problem of providing general retirement income. We do not discuss these similarities here, but the reader can consult Feldstein and Samwick (1997).

welfare payments. Financing these unemployment benefits and welfare payments exacerbates the problem of high social insurance taxes. The consequence is a vicious spiral in which higher benefits for the aged lead to higher taxes, higher labor costs, more unemployment, and more unemployment benefits and welfare payments—and thus even higher taxes, more unemployment, and so on.

Finally, although a majority of American workers now participate in investment-based company pension plans or have private Individual Retirement Accounts (IRAs), in most European countries company pensions are generally unfunded and individual tax-advantaged retirement saving plans like the American IRAs do not exist.

European governments are, of course, acutely aware of these problems and are beginning to take steps to deal with them. Although European countries differ in their responses, the common feature of the response in almost every country has been a reduction in future benefits.[2] In some cases, this was achieved by changing inflation-indexing within the existing system; in others, by shifting the base for calculating benefits or the age of eligibility for full benefits, or by more radical changes associated with going from traditional defined benefit (DB) plans to notional defined contribution (DC) plans.

Some countries have shifted to investment-based systems to reduce the long-run cost of providing benefits. The Netherlands has had such a system for a very long time. As a result, the Netherlands and the United Kingdom have already substantially funded their future benefits and do not face the kind of problem that affects the others. Sweden now permits individuals to shift 2 percentage points of their payroll tax to investment-based individual accounts. Italy permits firms and their employees to agree to shift their currently unfunded private severance pension plans into regular investment-based pension accounts, although there are strong incentives that until now have limited the adoption of this possibility. The essays in this volume describe these changes as well as the more radical innovations that have been made in Poland, Hungary, and Romania. The German government has announced a plan, not yet enacted at the time of this writing, to reduce future retirement benefits while allowing workers to save in tax-advantaged accounts to make up for the lost retirement income.

---

2. This is particularly striking to an American observer because much of the emphasis in the current discussion about Social Security reform in the United States has been on how to avoid future benefit reductions. It is true, however, that the last major reform of Social Security in the United States in the early 1980s also involved substantial reductions in benefits achieved through increasing the retirement age, temporarily suspending indexing, and subjecting benefits to taxation. There are now a number of Congressional plans in the United States that would also resolve the future financing problem in part by a reduction in benefits.

Problems for an Integrated Labor Market

The enormous differences in social security systems among the European countries can create substantial problems for the attempt to develop an integrated labor market for Europe. Because the individual country systems are essentially DB systems, someone who works in a country for a short period of time may get nothing in exchange for the taxes that he and his employer paid during those years. Similarly, someone who works in several countries over the course of a lifetime will receive less than someone with the same earnings record who worked in a single country. Because these benefits are large, the current system may substantially discourage cross-border mobility.

An obvious resolution of this problem would be a system based on individual investment-based accounts. I have difficulty reconciling the French prime minister's recent rejection of such accounts on the assumption that maintaining the current unfunded DB system is crucial for national solidarity with the French government's emphasis on the need for a single market for labor in the European Union. What does national solidarity for employees mean in a single Europe-wide labor market?

A Life-Cycle Framework

As an economist, when I think about retirement income and the expenses of old age, it seems natural to think in terms of a life-cycle framework in which individuals save during their working years and dissave during their retirement. Because of the well-known problems of short-sighted planning and the ability of lower-income individuals to benefit by "gaming" the welfare state (i.e., undersaving in the knowledge that means-tested benefits will then be provided), retirement saving cannot be left completely to individual discretion. With these considerations in mind, it is surprising that individual DC accounts are not more commonly used or discussed as a way of dealing with the current and future problems of financing benefits for the aging population.

There is, of course, some use of such investment-based DC plans. Sweden has explicitly adopted this as part of its overall state pension system. The U.K. system also has such accounts as an option and it is one that is widely chosen.[3] The transition economies that were formerly under Soviet domination have moved further in this direction than have the major countries of western Europe.

Such individual investment-based accounts have much to recommend

---

3. In the United States a majority of the voluntary employer plans (i.e., the plans that are over and above the mandatory Social Security pensions) are now defined contribution plans. Some of the proposed reforms in the United States would also use personal retirement accounts.

them in comparison to alternative ways of financing income during retirement years. The most important advantage is that an investment-based plan (or a mixed plan that combines traditional PAYGO and investment-based components) has lower long-run costs than a PAYGO system. Calculations based on U.S. demographic data show that each 1 percent of wages saved in an investment-based system with a real return of 5.5 percent can replace about 3 percent of wages collected in taxes in a PAYGO system. This is a long-run property that reflects additional saving in the transition years. Although it is not a Pareto improvement that benefits all generations, the resulting change in the consumption stream has a positive present value because the marginal product of capital exceeds the net return that private savers receive after corporate and personal taxes.[4]

Individual Investment-Based Retirement Accounts

The cost-reducing advantage of an investment-based system (or a mixed system) could in principle be achieved regardless of whether the investments are in individual accounts or in a centrally managed government trust fund. However, the individual accounts do have several additional advantages.

First, an investment-based system automatically eliminates the existing early retirement incentives that raise the cost of the program. Although a PAYGO system can in principle be modified to make the present value of retirement benefits independent of the age of retirement, an investment-based system with individual accounts automatically achieves this because the funds belong to the individual.

Second, individual accounts avoid the risks of political control that would accompany a centralized pool of funds, a point emphasized in this volume by Assar Lindbeck (chap. 1). Avoiding the political control that might accompany a centralized account is not only desirable in itself but also could increase the rate of return on the accumulated funds and thus reduce the cost of providing any given level of retirement income.

Individual accounts that are provided competitively by private financial institutions are likely to lead to greater innovation in products and a higher standard of service than would be achieved with a government monopoly.

Assets accumulated in individual accounts could be bequeathed to spouses or other heirs if the individual died before reaching retirement age. Postretirement annuities could be designed to permit bequests conditional either on the age of death or on the size of the accumulated fund. All of this creates a greater sense of ownership than would be true in a centralized investment fund.

Although critics worry about the risks inherent in an investment-based

---

4. For a discussion of these issues, see the appendix to Feldstein (1998).

system, a number of studies show that the risk that individuals would face in a mixed system would be relatively low and could be eliminated or reduced by either government guarantees or by the guarantees that could be provided by private financial markets.[5]

Finally, although there is much debate about the administrative cost of a system of individual accounts,[6] the recent introduction by TIAA-CREF[7] of a saving and variable annuity plan with an annual cost of only 37 basis points is reassuring evidence. A program in which the government would collect the funds along with the Social Security payroll tax could be managed for an even lower annual cost.

Notional Defined Contribution Systems

The attractive features of a system with investment-based individual accounts have induced several European countries to adopt investment-based systems as part of their state pension programs. The transition to an investment-based system does, however, require some additional saving. The amount of this transition saving, although relatively low,[8] is one of the barriers to adopting any degree of investment-based funding. Sweden, Italy, and Poland have therefore adopted something of a compromise system in the form of notional defined contributions within the broader framework of a PAYGO system. The basic idea in such a system is that individual employees (or those employees and their employers) pay mandatory contributions and receive credits in individual accounts for the amounts contributed just as they would in any other DC plan. These contributions are not, however, invested in financial assets but are paid out as part of a PAYGO system. The notional accounts nevertheless keep track of the individual contributions and are credited with a rate of return equal to the growth rate of wages. In this way, the benefits that will eventually be paid are consistent with a PAYGO method of financing with a constant rate of tax.[9]

---

5. See Campbell and Feldstein (2001) for several studies of the risks of PAYGO and investment-based systems. Also see Feldstein and Ranguelova (2001b) for a discussion of risk in a pure investment-based system. Feldstein and Ranguelova (1998) discuss ways that the government could reduce the risk to retirees of the investment-based system, while Feldstein and Ranguelova (2001a) show how financial market instruments (a combination of buying a put and selling a call) might be used to guarantee retiree benefit levels.

6. See Shoven (2000) for several studies of the factors affecting the administrative costs of an individual account investment-based system.

7. Teachers Insurance and Annuity Association College Retirement Equity Fund, a very large U.S. insurer and mutual fund provider.

8. Feldstein and Samwick (1997) showed that the transition from the existing U.S. PAYGO system to a fully investment-based system could be done without ever increasing the payroll tax rate by more than 2 percentage points.

9. See the papers by Palmer on Sweden and Franco on Italy (chaps. 6 and 7 in this volume, respectively) for more details of how such systems will operate.

These notional DC accounts have three major advantages over traditional DB plans. First, by linking future benefits clearly and tangibly to the individual's contributions, they reduce the extent to which those contributions are perceived as a tax. Second, the focus on the "assets" in the individual account (even if they are only "accounting assets") reduces the distortion in retirement decisions. Third, notional DC accounts implicitly limit future benefits to the amounts that can be financed by the existing tax rates. And fourth, they provide an individual account framework within which an investment-based system could later be introduced or expanded.

It must be emphasized, however, that the notional defined contributions provide a lower rate of return than true investment-based accounts and therefore cannot achieve the full advantages of an investment-based system. The rate of return in a notional system can be only the rate of growth of the tax base that results from rising real wages and increasing numbers of employees (Samuelson 1958). This is now likely to be about 2 percent, substantially less than the real pretax rate of return on incremental capital, which may be as much as 9 or 10 percent. Even if individuals could receive a net-of-tax real return of only 6 percent, the difference between that and a 2 percent rate of return in notional accounts implies that the mandatory contributions to the notional system are effectively a tax of about three-fourths of the statutory tax rate.[10] This means that the distortions in labor supply during working years and at the time of retirement are reduced somewhat but are not changed substantially. The cost of funding future retirements is not reduced as it would be with an investment-based system.

For an American looking at social security pension reform in Europe, it is encouraging that many countries have made or are making fundamental reforms. Yet for several of the larger countries, including France, Germany, and Spain, the reforms are either very small or nonexistent. There is now, however, an opportunity for these countries to learn from the experiences of their European neighbors. Investment-based reforms can have substantial favorable effects but only over a long period of time. Because the demographic changes will exacerbate an already worrisome situation, Euro-

---

10. To see why the effective tax rate in the notional system is approximately three-fourths of the statutory rate, consider the following example. An individual earns an additional 500 kronor (SKr) and pays mandatory contribution of 100 SKr to a notional account, equivalent to a 20 percent tax rate. The value in the account grows at 2 percent per year. If we take age forty as the midpoint of the years of contribution and age seventy-five as the midpoint of the years during which benefits are withdrawn, the initial 100 SKr would grow to 200 SKr. If instead the 200 SKr of benefits had been financed by an investment-based plan that provided a real return of 6 percent, the 200 SKr could have been accumulated with an initial deposit of 25 SKr, equivalent to 5 percent of the 500 SKr of initial earnings. The 5 percent in the investment-based plan is not really a tax because the individual receives a full market rate of return. However, the excess tax (i.e., the difference between the 5 percent and the 20 percent in the notional system) is a tax. Thus three-fourths of the mandatory contribution to the notional system should be viewed as a tax.

pean governments must make major changes soon to keep their retirement systems viable and their overall tax burdens tolerable in the decades ahead.

References

Campbell, John, and Martin Feldstein, eds. 2001. *Risk aspects of investment-based Social Security reform.* Chicago: University of Chicago Press.

Feldstein, Martin, ed. 1998. *Privatizing Social Security.* Chicago: University of Chicago Press.

Feldstein, Martin, and Elena Ranguelova. 1998. Individual risk and intergenerational risk sharing in an investment-based Social Security system. NBER Working Paper no. 6839. Cambridge, Mass.: National Bureau of Economic Research, December.

———. 2001a. Accumulated pension collars: A market approach to reducing the risk of investment-based social security reform. In *Tax policy and the economy,* ed. James M. Poterba, 149–66. Cambridge, Mass.: MIT Press.

———. 2001b. Individual risk in an investment-based Social Security system. *American Economic Review* 91:1116–25.

Feldstein, Martin, Elena Ranguelova, and Andrew Samwick. 2001. The transition to investment-based Social Security when portfolio returns and capital profitability are uncertain. In *Risk aspects of investment-based Social Security reform,* ed. John Campbell and Martin Feldstein, 41–81. Chicago: University of Chicago Press.

Feldstein, Martin, and Andrew Samwick. 1998. The economics of prefunding Social Security and Medicare benefits. In *NBER Macroeconomics Annual 1997,* ed. Ben Bernanke and Julio Rotemberg, 115–47. Cambridge, Mass.: MIT Press.

Gruber, Jonathan, and David Wise, eds. 1999. *Social Security and retirement around the world.* Chicago: University of Chicago Press.

Samuelson, Paul. 1958. An exact consumption loan model of interest with or without the social contrivance of money. *Journal of Political Economy.*

Shoven, John, ed. 2000. *Administrative aspects of investment-based Social Security reform.* Chicago: University of Chicago Press.

Introduction
A European Perspective

Horst Siebert

The Issue

In the major continental countries of Europe, as the population ages, a larger proportion of gross domestic product (GDP) will have to be spent to finance pay-as-you-go systems. In Italy, which other than Germany has the most acute expected population decline (see appendix table A.1), the share of expenditures for the pay-as-you-go (PAYGO) system in relation to GDP is expected to reach a peak of 15.8 percent in 2032 (Organization for Economic Cooperation and Development [OECD] 2000, fig. 27). This figure holds even after the Dini and Prodi reforms, and while assuming constant contributions (see fig. 1 in this introduction). The gap between expenditures and (constant) contributions and the budget deficit in proportion to GDP illustrated the issue of financial viability. For Germany,[1] earlier estimates indicate a peak of 17 percent (OECD 1995, fig. 13; these estimates do not include the pension reform of 2001). For France, where the population decline will be somewhat less pronounced, the Charpin Report (Charpin 1999) expects the share of social security expenditures in GDP to rise to 15.8 or 16.7 percent in 2040, based on two different scenarios, both assuming constant contributions.

The required contributions to a mandatory public PAYGO system place a high burden on the young, who must also accumulate private funds for their old age because the official systems have lost the credibility regarding

Horst Siebert is president of the Kiel Institute of World Economics, professor at Christian-Albrechts University, Kiel, Germany (chair of Theoretical Economics), and member of the German Council of Economic Advisers.

The author appreciates critical comments from Klaus-Jürgen Gern and Jens Oliver Lorz.

1. The figures for Germany exclude statutory transfers from the federal government.

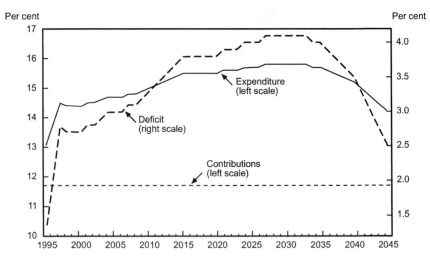

Fig. 1   Italy, postreform expenditures
Source: OECD (2000, Figure 27).

their ability to deliver their promised payments in the future. This situation does not appear to be sustainable. The younger generation are unlikely to be willing to give up such a large part of their income in the form of required contributions, and they are likely to renege on their generation's contract. This means that the existing old age systems are not politically viable. Moreover, the international competitiveness of jobs in countries having large future burdens because of required contributions to pension systems is severely affected, because, with the linking of system financing to the work contract, labor costs will be relatively high. All this implies that changes in the status quo are necessary.

The problem in Europe is more acute than anywhere else in the world, except Japan. There are two reasons for this: The aging of the population is more pronounced in Europe than elsewhere, and the welfare state has been extended throughout Europe more than in other parts of the world. Within Europe, the pension crisis is a continental problem; it is less a problem for the United Kingdom (with estimated social security expenditures of 6 percent of GDP by 2030; OECD 1995, fig. 13). Some smaller countries have old age assistance systems that are less prone to problems (for example, Denmark, the Netherlands, and Switzerland), whereas others (Sweden, for example) have introduced some of the necessary changes to their systems already. In Eastern Europe, some countries have made the same mistakes as Western European countries, and thus are under even greater pressure to change their systems.

In Europe, the problem of the PAYGO system is an issue not only of financial sustainability, but also of labor market distortions and resulting unemployment. Contributions to the pension system have an incidence similar to an explicit tax on labor; they weaken the demand for labor, which in turn implies a lower net wage. Where trade unions succeed in keeping the wage rate high, unemployment follows. The tax wedge between the producers' wage and the consumers' wage differs among European countries: Contributions are low in countries using tax finance (creating another tax wedge), but contributions paid by firms run as high as 64 percent of financing costs in France and 80 percent in Italy. As an additional distortion, there is an implicit tax on work before retirement, especially in the age group between 58 and 65; that distortion creates an incentive to retire early. This further aggravates the pension crisis.

The Illusionary Way Out: Other Avenues of Financing

As one way out of the looming crisis, European governments have attempted to find new sources of financing their public systems without really attacking the root of the pension crisis.

Because contributions to defined benefit (DB) types of systems are already high and cannot be increased without major opportunity costs, one of the practices followed is to enlarge the group required to contribute in the hope of increasing the financial means available—for instance, to include the self-employed. However, this forces more people into the governmental system to claim benefits in the future. It also means reducing the chances for a voluntary, privately funded system (i.e., for individual [retirement] saving).

In the search for new sources of finance, another option is general taxation. In this case, the future generation will have to carry the burden in the form of taxes. However, tax financing weakens the links between contributions and benefits in the pension system. It therefore represents a larger distortion of incentives and implies a larger deadweight loss if the given level of benefits is sustained. Shifting to a tax-financed general basic pension system (as in Denmark) or to a flat-rate benefit system with flat-rate contributions (as in the United Kingdom) would imply reducing the benefit level drastically. Even if it were desirable, it would not be politically feasible.

A related approach is to introduce into the public schemes a new basic pension for everyone, as a lower floor for old age income. Such a pension would be financed by general taxes. The motivation for a basic pension is to prevent old age poverty, especially for those who have not been regularly employed during their lifetimes and thus have "broken biographies." As discussed in Germany, this would introduce both an income floor and means-tested social welfare benefits. It could be expected to have distortionary effects that are stronger than those discussed for the existing PAYGO system financed by contributions.

An ecological tax is another alternative. The motivation behind it is to tax activities straining the environment and to use the tax receipts to finance pensions, thus lowering mandatory contributions and reducing the tax on labor. The theoretical hope is for a double dividend that could come from reducing the tax wedge that exists because we do not pay to use the environment. In Germany, such an ecological tax has been introduced by the new government, although it is merely an increase in the existing oil tax and a new tax on electricity, not a carbon dioxide emissions tax designed to help solve the global warming problem. Thus, its link to the environmental problem is weak. Moreover, the tax affects productivity negatively and lessens the competitiveness of environmentally intensive industries when applied unilaterally by only one country. Consequently, in Germany, exemptions were made for very pollution-intensive activities. Furthermore, it is questionable whether a country should link the financing of its pension system to the receipts of taxing a factor input that must be imported. All in all, making energy more expensive (by "fueling up for pensions") does not seem to be a promising way to solve the pension crisis.

The Mitigating Way Out: Changing the Supply of Labor

Another approach to mitigating the pension crisis is to change the supply of labor effectively.

Because the implicit tax on labor prior to retirement provides an incentive to retire early, doing away with this tax would help reduce the magnitude of the pension crisis by lowering expenditures and increasing the receipts from the tax system. This implies increasing both the statutory and the effective ages of retirement, in some countries by at least five years. Eligibility rules for early retirement would have to be tightened. In a number of countries (e.g., Germany, Italy, United Kingdom) this approach is already being applied.

Another realistic avenue for developing new financial proceeds for the PAYGO system is to increase immigration. Immigration of young people will add to the work force, and immigration of workers with high skills will raise productivity. This will increase the base for contributions to a pension system.

A Realistic Way Out: Reduce the Benefit Level

The PAYGO system is an implicit public debt, that should be made explicit. However, to consider explicitly the existing pension debt under an intertemporal budget constraint is not sufficient to solve the pension crisis. An automatic mechanism must be established that prevents an excessive rise in the implicit debt. That is, the system must adjust its benefits in accordance with the intertemporal constraint. This is the most important implication for ameliorating the future pension crisis in Europe: a reduction in the benefit level. Toward this end, governments so far have used an ad hoc approach, such as increasing the period of earnings referred to in the calculation of benefits (Belgium, Finland, France, the Netherlands, and Spain). Indexation rules also have been changed.[2]

The more systematic task, however, is to find a formula that expresses the intertemporal budget constraint. This requires a calculation of future contributions to and future payments by the system, one that links benefits to contributions with some smoothing between periods. This approach necessitates a forecast of the demographic development of a country. For instance, introducing a demographic factor for life expectancy into the pension formula will lower the increase in pensions in an aging population. Alternatively, a "generation factor" specific to each cohort can be selected so that reductions will apply only to new cohorts of pensioners. Either way, the benefit level of the PAYGO system is reduced.

This approach also requires a political decision about the acceptable level of the future burden.[3] In Germany, for example, the pension reform of 2001 reduces the benefit level of the PAYGO system from 70 percent of the previous net wage to 67 percent, while at the same time raising the overall benefit level (including private benefits) to 75 percent. Thus an aging society, amazingly, ends up with a higher benefit level. It is obvious that the political process has attempted to postpone the necessary marked reduction of benefits in the PAYGO system until far into the future.

The Attractive Way Out: Introduce a Funded Pillar

Reducing the pension level by making explicit the intertemporal budget constraint is not an appealing political solution because it only implies that pensioners will receive relatively less than they do today. A more appealing political solution would also make the old age insurance system more attractive. The answer, therefore, is to introduce a "funded pillar."

There are different ways to introduce a funded pillar (see the papers in this volume). Although in principle it can be achieved in a centrally funded governmental system, a privately organized system would be more robust against political seizure (see below). The continental countries are unlikely to switch to a completely funded system. As of now, a major shift (of, say, 20 percentage points or more) to covering a larger share of pensions will not likely occur. In either case, a mandatory funded insurance system would be required. Rather, the European countries probably will undertake only a marginal shift, so that the funded private pillar will account

---

2. Basic benefits have been made subject to an income test (Finland, Sweden; Gern 1998).
3. How far the pension will have to fall depends on the other instruments (such as increases in contributions and in the effective retirement age) being applied.

for a smaller percentage of the pension,[4] and will be built up by a voluntary additional private insurance, with a favorable tax treatment for contributions. Pensions then would be taxed as ordinary income. To make such insurance mandatory would be necessary only if a major shift occurred.

If Europe were to undertake a privately organized and funded system only marginally, then the pension crisis would not be solved in the most effective way. Europe would not get the full premium from making the systems more actuarially fair (Lindbeck, chap. 1 in this volume), and thus could not reduce its costs for financing old age pensions considerably. Thus, it can only be hoped that the comparison between the PAYGO system in the first pillar and the funded system in the second pillar eventually will prove that the funded system has higher efficiency. In the end, political pressure will work in favor of a funded system.

In changing partially to a funded system, maintaining clear-cut private property rights on the pension claims of individuals has an important advantage. For example, in the case of bankruptcy, such legally protected accounts strengthen the interest of individuals in their pension system and represent a safeguard against political seizure. Notional accounts within the PAYGO system are a first step in the direction of legally protected claims.

There are other risks, as well: Politicians are tempted to work for the benefit of the current generation and to neglect future generations. They may have specific groups of the electorate in mind, wanting to maximize political support for their own parties. For instance, they might want to ease the unemployment problem by using the revenues of the pension system. Finally, there is another relevant risk: Funds put aside for pensions can be used for industrial policy and for controlling the economy. At the extreme, funding pensions thus would lead to the socialization of firms.

Privately managed occupational pension schemes may represent another important avenue for helping to solve the pension crisis. In order to prevent political influence, they must be privately managed. They cannot be mandatory, either for firms or for employees, because they would otherwise represent a tax on labor. Finally, portability of the claims in such systems would have to be insured. Otherwise, labor mobility would be reduced.

One important aspect of shifting to a (partially) funded system is the uncoupling of the financing of the pension system from the work contract.[5]

4. Nevertheless, the intended 4 percent of the gross wage contribution in Germany (in 2008) for which favorable tax treatment is envisioned amounts to an increase in the benefit level of 8.5 percentage points of the previous wage in 2030 of the pensioners' cohort (and to 16 percent in 2050), assuming an interest rate of 4 percent.

5. Another implicit assumption was a single earner in a family with insurance coverage for the whole family. In this case, family breakups are a problem; furthermore, the labor participation rate of women has risen. The issue is to what extent insurance claims must be defined for the individual.

The old system has as its premise the full-time worker. This premise is no longer valid, however; socioeconomic change is affecting the basis of the European social insurance systems. Part-time workers are more typical; the time profile of the working life varies; and the self-employed play a more important role than before. Income from labor is not the only source of income, with personal wealth becoming more widespread. These sorts of change would suggest raising the net wage by the amount that firms pay and then giving individuals more choice in how much insurance they want.

Two major questions for Europe are: Which role should actuarial equivalence between contributions and benefits play, and which weight should be given to redistribution (from higher market income of individuals to lower market income) within the pension system? Redistribution has distorting incentive effects; a stronger link between contributions and subsequent pensions reduces these negative incentive effects and builds a strong vested interest in a funded system. If more equivalence is accepted as the guiding principle for the reorganization of the pension system, then distributional concerns will have to be taken care of outside the pension system by the tax-transfer mechanism (for instance, families with children may receive a tax break). When the pension level is not satisfactory at the end of a working life, welfare payments would fill the gap.

If the income floor of social welfare benefits cannot be reduced, the scope of European governmental maneuvering to lower the basic pension of the PAYGO system is limited. It seems difficult to reduce the public PAYGO system below the level defined by social welfare payments. However, the funded portion of pensions could be organized as a mandatory substitution for some of the current PAYGO portion.

Thus, restricting the PAYGO system in some of the European countries is related to rearranging the income floor provided by social welfare. However, this is a highly complex issue. We might redefine the criteria of eligibility for social welfare, not for the elderly, but for those who are able to work. We could reduce the benefit level for them, make it more difficult to receive social welfare, or reduce their option to say "no" to jobs offered. This would have no direct effect on welfare as an income floor for the pension system, however, but it would represent a psychological redefinition of the income floor and thus of the income level that individuals require from the government. This could have an indirect effect on behavior, by emphasizing the importance of self-reliance in preparing financially for retirement.

If the income floor of social welfare benefits could not be reduced, then European governments would have only a limited space within which to lower the basic pension under the PAYGO system. As a consequence, there would be little room for a funded system.

Some Additional Specific European Issues

There are also some specific issues of the pension system in an increasingly integrated Europe. The existing systems have developed as national insurance schemes. They differ considerably with respect to the levels of benefits, the rates of contribution, and the means of financing (contributions versus tax financing, and the role of funding relative to the PAYGO system). The issue is how these national systems cope with higher labor mobility in Europe. Moreover, national systems will be under pressure in a single market with higher capital mobility if the labor costs they generate impede the competitiveness of firms and reduce returns to mobile capital.

One basic question is whether membership should be mandatory, and if so, how mandatory membership in the different pillars should be defined—in other words, who must be a member of which system? Should membership be by nationality (where one was born) or by residence (where one works, where one lives)? Or should membership in old age insurance be left to individual choice? This issue corresponds to the problem of how to organize the systems.

It might be tempting to apply the country-of-origin principle (the Casis-de-Dijon verdict of the European Court of Justice) to the first pillar and to give individuals a choice of which national system they wish to join; thus national systems would compete with each other, which would put pressure on the national systems to adjust. With noticeable differences between existing national systems, however, huge (and unpredictable) adjustments would occur. It is unlikely that this approach will be taken.

The Europeanization of pension systems, that is, a harmonized European first pillar, may be considered by some as part of a social union. However, it does not appear to be realistic. It would have the severe disadvantage of introducing even more redistribution into the system, along with less equivalence and a greater risk of political seizure of accounts by a centralized Europe.

The pension system in Europe therefore must rely on the territoriality principle (*"cuius regio eius religio"*) for insurance, with residency being the criterion for membership in the first pillar.[6] To move toward a Europewide system is simply not a policy option.

One practical problem that must be addressed is portability; that is, what happens to the claims of individuals if workers switch from one national system in the first pillar to another because of cross-border mobility? European integration implies that we must move toward portable claims in the national systems. For example, a Belgian who has moved to

---

6. This would be in line with uncoupling social insurance from the work contract. Otherwise the workplace may be the criterion for membership.

France either continues to be covered by his original Belgian insurance, or his claim is made transferable to the French system.

The issue of portability is linked to the question of how much the PAYGO system can be pushed back and a privately organized, funded system introduced in its place. The more actuarial equivalence is established, the easier it is to solve the problem of portable claims. Therefore, the practical requirement of portability is yet another reason that it might be necessary to introduce more actuarial equivalence and to uncouple the financing of old age insurance from the work contract.

References

Charpin, J.-M. 1999. *L'avenir de nos retraites, rapport au premier ministre.* Paris: La Documentation Française.

Gern, K.-J. 1998. Recent developments in old-age pension systems: An international overview. Kiel Working Paper no. 863. Kiel, Germany: Kiel Institute of World Economics.

Organization for Economic Cooperation and Development (OECD). 1995. *Economic Outlook* no. 57. June.

———. 2000. *Economic Surveys: Italy.* May.

1

Pensions and Contemporary Socioeconomic Change

Assar Lindbeck

Contemporary pension systems in developed countries reflect economic, social, and political conditions in the 1930s and the first decades after World War II. Recently, new socioeconomic conditions have created both rationales and political forces for revisions of existing pension systems. Changes in demography, real wage growth, and real interest rates are obvious examples. Increased heterogeneity and instability of the family, higher labor force participation by women, increased diversity of individual life cycles, greater international mobility of labor and capital, and ambitions to encourage individual responsibility also have important implications for pension systems. Moreover, some socioeconomic changes have been induced by the pension system itself via (endogenous) behavioral adjustments of individuals, with feedback effects on the pension system.

When discussing these issues, it is useful to set up a more elaborate classification of pension systems than the usual distinction between defined benefit (DB) and defined contribution (DC) systems. The choice of an appropriate taxonomy depends, of course, on the issues to be raised. One question on which this paper focuses concerns the consequences of socioeconomic changes for the intergenerational distribution of income and the sharing of income risk among generations. The distinction between pension systems with exogenous and endogenous contribution rates (tax rates) then becomes crucial. However, when one is analyzing socio-

Assar Lindbeck is professor of international economics at the Institute for International Economic Studies, Stockholm University, and an associate of the Research Institute of Industrial Economics (IUI), Stockholm.

The author is grateful for comments on a draft of the paper from Jon Dutrieux Andersen, Peter Diamond, Martin Feldstein, Laurence Kotlikoff, Mats Persson, Dennis Snower, Kjetil Storesletten, and David Sundén.

economic changes that are induced by the pension arrangements themselves, other distinguishing features of pension systems must be taken into account. These include the degree to which the systems are pay-as-you-go (PAYGO) and funded, respectively; whether the systems have strong links between contributions and benefits with individual accounts; and whether pension payments are lump sum, a fraction of previous individual earnings or contributions, or a fraction of current average earnings.

Against this background, six generic pension systems are classified in section 1.1. Each system can be varied considerably, both by incorporating elements from other systems and by introducing restrictions on contributions or benefits. Section 1.2 turns to the consequences, in the context of each system, of socioeconomic changes for the intergenerational distribution of income, risk sharing, and macroeconomic balance. Endogenous behavioral adjustments in response to welfare-state arrangements, in particular via disincentive effects on work and saving, are also introduced. Such effects are discussed in more detail in subsequent sections, which examine alternative pension reforms aimed at mitigating disincentives. A few of these reforms are "marginal" in the sense that the existing pension system is modified (section 1.3). Such reforms include both ad hoc policy measures and various automatic adjustment mechanisms. Two radical reforms are discussed in section 1.4, namely, a shift to either a quasi-actuarial system characterized by a strong link between contributions and benefits, or to a fully funded pension system with a capital-market rate of return on the contributions. Adjustments of various pension systems to increased heterogeneity of individuals and households are considered in section 1.5, and section 1.6 concludes.

1.1 Classification of Pension Systems

I begin by considering two pension systems with exogenous contribution rates and, hence, endogenous pension benefits: (1) a fixed-fee PAYGO system with budget balance and (2) a fully funded system with individual accounts and a capital-market return on the pension contributions. I then turn to four PAYGO systems with fixed benefit rules and hence endogenous contribution rates: (3) a lump-sum benefit system, (4) an earnings-based system, (5) a contribution-based system, and (6) a fixed (intergenerational) income-ratio system. I use the following notations:

τ = payroll tax rate
y = average labor income
N = number of employed individuals (workers)
R = number of retired individuals
B = fixed (lump-sum) pension benefit per person
$G_t = (y_t \cdot N_t)/(y_{t-1} \cdot N_{t-1})$ = rate of growth factor for labor income (tax base)

i = real interest rate on financial markets
$I = 1 + i$ = real interest-rate factor
w^j = real wage rate of individual j
h^j = hours of work of individual j

I assume two overlapping generations, each living for two periods. For some purposes, however, it is important to divide each of these periods into several subperiods ("years"). The following schematic description of revenues and expenditures of various pension systems should be self-explanatory. The revenues of the pension system are denoted below, and the expenditures above the horizontal lines.

1.1.1 Exogenous Contribution Rate

System No. 1: Fixed-Fee System

In this pension system, there is a *fixed* contribution rate τ_t in each period, although the rate may vary from period to period. Because the system is PAYGO, aggregate pension benefits in period t are determined by the revenues of the system in the same period, $\tau_t y_t N_t$. Hence, the budget is balanced by definition.

	$(t-1)$	(t)	$(t+1)$
Expenditures		$\tau_t y_t N_t$	
Revenues	$\tau_{t-1} y_{t-1} N_{t-1}$		

$\tau_{t+1} y_{t+1} N_{t+1}$

$\tau_y y_t N_t$

Each pensioner in period t receives

(1)
$$\frac{\tau_t y_t N_t}{R_t}.$$

The implicit return factor is

(2)
$$\frac{\tau_t y_t N_t}{\tau_{t-1} y_{t-1} R_t}.$$

This factor is G_t if $R_t = N_{t-1}$ and $\tau_t = \tau_{t-1}$.

System No. 2: Actuarially Fair, Fully Funded System

As in the fixed-fee system, the contribution rate τ is exogenous in each period and the pension benefit is endogenous. The return on the individual's forced saving is determined by the return in capital markets, i. There is intertemporal budget balance for each cohort.

$\prime$ $\dfrac{\prime}{\tau_{t-1} y_{t-1} N_{t-1}}$ $\prime$ $\dfrac{I\tau_{t-1} y_{t-1} N_{t-1}}{}$ $\prime$

$\prime$ $\dfrac{\prime}{\tau_y y_t N_t}$ $\prime$ $\dfrac{I\tau_t y_t N_t}{}$ $\prime$

As is well known, a compulsory, fully funded pension system will influence the consumption of the individual only if he or she is liquidity constrained or unwilling to borrow or to reduce saving, and hence unable to offset government-induced reallocations of his or her cash flow. The return factor is IN_{t-1}/R_t.

1.1.2 Endogenous Contribution Rate

System No. 3: Lump-Sum Benefit System

This pension system provides the individual with an exogenously given *basic pension,* while the contribution rate τ is endogenously determined in each period to ensure balance in the budget of the pension system.

$\prime$ $\dfrac{\prime}{\tau_{t-1} y_{t-1} N_{t-1}}$ $\prime$ $\dfrac{B \cdot R_t}{}$ $\prime$

$\prime$ $\dfrac{\prime}{\tau_y y_t N_t}$ $\prime$ $\dfrac{B \cdot R_{t+1}}{}$ $\prime$

The balanced budget requirement is

$$BR_t = \tau_t y_t N_t.$$

The implicit return factor[1] is

$$(3) \qquad \frac{\dfrac{B}{y_{t-1}}}{\tau_{t-1}} = \frac{\tau_t y_t N_t}{R_t \tau_{t-1} y_{t-1}}.$$

This factor is G_t if $R_t = N_{t-1}$ and $\tau_t = \tau_{t-1}$. B/y_{t-1} is the replacement rate, which is inversely proportional to the individual's previous income.

$$(4) \qquad \text{Endogenous } \tau = \frac{B}{y_t} \cdot \frac{R_t}{N_t},$$

where $B/y_t =$ the intergenerational income ratio and R_t/N_t the dependency ratio.

---

1. The return is the same as in the fixed-fee system in equation (2) if the benefit is the same ($B = \tau_t y_t N_t/R_t$).

System No. 4: Earnings-Based System

In this system, the pension of an individual is determined as a fixed fraction (replacement rate) α of his or her previous earnings.

$$\begin{array}{ccc} ' & ' & \dfrac{\alpha y_{t-1} R_t}{} \quad ' \\[2ex] \tau_{t-1} y_{t-1} N_{t-1} & & \end{array}$$

$$\begin{array}{ccc} ' & ' & \dfrac{\alpha y_t R_{t+1}}{} \quad ' \\[2ex] & \tau_t y_t N_t & \end{array}$$

The balanced budget requirement is

$$\alpha y_{t-1} R_t = \tau_t y_t N_t.$$

The implicit return factor is[2]

$$(5) \qquad\qquad \frac{\alpha y_{t-1}}{\tau_{t-1} y_{t-1}} = \frac{\alpha}{\tau_{t-1}}.$$

This factor is G_t if $R_t = N_{t-1}$ and $\tau_t = \tau_{t-1}$.

$$(6) \qquad\qquad \text{Endogenous } \tau_t = \frac{\alpha y_{t-1} R_t}{y_t N_t}.$$

System No. 5: Contribution-Based System

The pension in this system is a fixed fraction, γ, of contributions previously paid by the individual. Such a system is sometimes called a *notional defined contribution* (NDC) system.

$$\begin{array}{ccc} ' & ' & \dfrac{\gamma \tau_{t-1} y_{t-1} R_t}{} \quad ' \\[2ex] \tau_{t-1} y_{t-1} N_{t-1} & & \end{array}$$

$$\begin{array}{ccc} ' & ' & \gamma \tau \cdot w_t \cdot R_{t+1} \quad ' \\[2ex] & \tau_t y_t N_t & \end{array}$$

The balanced budget requirement is

$$\gamma \tau_{t-1} y_{t-1} R_t = \tau_t y_t N_t.$$

The implicit return factor is

2. The return is the same as in a lump-sum benefit system if $\alpha = B/y_{t-1}$.

(7)
$$\gamma = \frac{\tau_t y_t N_t}{\tau_{t-1} y_{t-1} R_t}.$$

This factor is G_t if $R_t = N_{t-1}$ and $\tau_t = \tau_{t-1}$.

(8)
$$\text{Endogenous } \tau_t = \gamma \tau_{t-1} \left(\frac{y_{t-1} R_t}{y_t N_t} \right).$$

System No. 6: Fixed Intergenerational Income-Ratio System

In this system, the pension of an individual is a fixed fraction, μ, of the average earnings of *contemporary* workers (i.e., the system is based on an intergenerational income distribution target).

$$\frac{\mu y_t R_t}{\tau_{t-1} y_{t-1} N_{t-1}}$$

$$\frac{\mu y_{t+1} R_{t+1}}{\tau_t y_t N_t}$$

The balanced budget requirement is

$$\mu y_t R_t = \tau_t y_t N_t.$$

The implicit return factor is

(9)
$$\frac{\mu y_t}{\tau_{t-1} y_{t-1}}.$$

This factor is G_t if $R_t = N_{t-1}$ and $\tau_t = \tau_{t-1}$.

(10)
$$\text{Endogenous } \tau_t = \frac{\mu \cdot R_t}{N_t^3}.^3$$

To summarize, in a fixed-fee PAYGO system, the (endogenous) pension benefit to a representative pensioner must fall in proportion to a drop in average earnings of contemporary workers (y_t) and in the number of workers (N_t) relative to the number of pensioners (R_t); see equation (1). In lump-sum benefit, earnings-based, and contribution-based systems, the (endogenous) contribution rate must be raised in proportion to similar changes in the same variables; see equations (4), (6), and (8). In a fixed income-ratio system, the (endogenous) contribution rate must be raised in proportion to a fall in the number of workers relative to the number of

3. An alternative version of this pension system could be a fixed after-tax income ratio between generations, with the pension set to $\mu(1 - \tau_t) y_t$. The implicit return factor is now $\mu(1 - \tau_t) y_t / (\tau_{t-1} y_{t-1})$, but with a balanced budget the return will be identical to the case in the text: $\tau_t N_t y_t / (\tau_{t-1} R_t y_{t-1}) = G_t$ if $R_t = N_{t-1}$ and $\tau_t = \tau_{t-1}$. The endogenous τ_t required for a balanced budget is now $\mu(1 - \tau_t) R_t / N_t$.

retirees; see equation (10). In actuarially fair systems, neither the contribution rate nor the pension benefit is *directly* related to the number of pensioners or the aggregate earnings of workers.

Observe that the well-known result that the rate of return in a PAYGO pension system equals the growth rate of the wage sum ($G_t - 1$) holds only if $\tau_t = \tau_{t-1}$ and $R_t = N_{t-1}$. The intuition is obvious. So long as the contribution rate is raised over time ($\tau_t > \tau_{t-1}$), the return for contemporary pensioners is higher than $G_t - 1$; see equations above for the return factor. If some individuals die before retirement age (so that $R_t < N_{t-1}$), those who live long enough to receive pensions will get a higher return $G_t - 1$ on previously paid contributions.[4]

To highlight the incentive structure for individuals in different pension systems, it is useful to write aggregate contributions as $\tau_{t-1} y_{t-1} N_{t-1} = \Sigma \tau_{t-1} w_{t-1}^j h_{t-1}^j$. Suppose that the individual increases the number of hours he or she works, h_{t-1}^j, or raises his or her wage, w_{t-1}^j, by his or her own effort (including training). Both the individual's contributions and his or her pension benefits will then increase in the same proportion in a contribution-based system with individual (notional) accounts (i.e., an NDC system). I will call such a system *quasi-actuarial,* because there is a close link between the contributions paid earlier by the individual and the benefit that he or she subsequently receives. (The term *quasi* refers to the fact that, in general, the return differs from the return in financial markets.) In fixed-fee, fixed income-ratio, and lump-sum benefit systems, the individual pension depends only on *aggregate* contributions and earnings, not on the individual's own contributions or earnings. Thus, when the individual changes the number of hours he or she works (h_{t-1}^j) or influences his or her wage (w_{t-1}^j), there is no effect whatsoever on the individual's own pension.

The distinction between earnings-based and contribution-based systems is not brought out in the two-period framework above. To highlight this distinction, we must partition the period of work into a number of subperiods (at least two). In this case, only if the contribution rate τ is constant over time will the implicit return be the same in both systems (assuming the calibration $\alpha = \gamma \tau_{t-1}$[5]).

4. Both pension systems with exogenous contribution rates (systems no. 1 and 2) and contribution-based system (system no. 5) with endogenous contribution rates, could possibly be called defined contribution (DC) systems. The remaining systems discussed above would then be called defined benefit (DB) systems. Some authors, however, reserve the term *DC system* for actuarially fair, fully funded systems with individual accounts, while identifying a DB system as one in which pensions are tied to previous earnings (with lump-sum pensions regarded as a special case). The latter terminology is used, for instance, by Diamond (2001) and Thomson (1998).

5. Assume that the individual works in two periods and is retired in a third period. Retired individuals are then supported by two subsequent generations: one engaged in its second period of work and the other in its first period of work. Earnings of workers in periods $t - 2$, $t - 1$, and t are y_{t-2}, y_{t-1}, and y_t, respectively. The oldest generation, which starts work in period $t - 2$, consists of N_{t-2} workers; the two subsequent generations, which start work in

1.2   Effects of Socioeconomic Changes

Let us begin by looking at the effects of four types of socioeconomic change on the distribution of income between pensioners and workers, and hence on the risk-sharing properties of different pension systems: (1) a reduction in the number of workers (N_t); (2) lower average labor income (y_t) or a slower rate of increase in labor income (y_t/y_{t-1}); (3) a greater number of retired individuals (R_t); and (4) lower interest rates (i).

I begin with the direct impact on the income of workers and pensioners, that is, the ceteris paribus effect on income of a change in a socioeconomic variable, with given rules concerning benefits and fees, and with constant values for the other variables. Because the exposition is not based on a formal general equilibrium model, indirect effects (e.g., on product prices, wages, and asset prices) are treated heuristically.[6] A useful starting point then is to examine the consequences of various disturbances for the macroeconomic balance between aggregate demand and supply of output and financial assets. In this way, we are reminded of the fact that the macroeconomic costs of providing pensions for the elderly consist of the elderly's increased consumption, which reduces resources available for younger generations.

1.2.1   Reduced Number of Workers

An actual or expected fall in the number of workers (reduced N_t) for a prolonged period is one important factor behind recent concerns about the viability of existing pension systems. On a high level of abstraction the consequences are rather similar, regardless of whether such a decline is the result of emigration or of a fall (in the past) in the birth rate.

Under fixed-fee pension systems, pensioners must bear the entire (direct) burden of adjusting to such a change because the aggregate amount of pension benefits is constrained by the exogenously given contribution rate times the tax base. Disposable income of individual workers is unaffected. The benefit received by the average pensioner, $(\tau_t y_t N_t)/R_t$, and the implicit rate of return on previous contributions, $(N_t/R_t)(y_t/y_{t-1})$, are both reduced in proportion to the fall in N_t. It is therefore reasonable to assume that the aggregate consumption of pensioners will fall in (about) the same proportion. Because there is no reason that individual workers would change their consumption, the aggregate consumption of workers would also be expected to fall in that proportion. If aggregate output hap-

---

periods $t - 1$ and t, respectively, consist of N_{t-1} and N_t workers. In an earnings-based system, the implicit return factor is now $\alpha(y_{t-2} + y_{t-1})/(\tau_{t-2}y_{t-2} + \tau_{t-1}y_{t-1})$, whereas in a contribution-based system it is γ. If $\tau_{t-2} = \tau_{t-1} = \tau_t$, the return is the same in both systems if $\alpha = \gamma\tau_{t-1}$. The same condition ensures that the endogenous contribution rate is the same in both systems.

6. For formal general equilibrium analysis of pension systems, see Diamond (1977) and Bohn (1999).

pens to decrease by the same percent as employment, there would be no disturbance to the macroeconomic balance.

In all of the other PAYGO systems mentioned above, workers have to bear the entire (direct) burden of adjustment since fewer workers have to finance the same (fixed or predetermined) aggregate pension payments as before. Neglecting conceivable consequences for aggregate labor supply (i.e., assuming the income and substitution effects on labor supply approximately cancel), τ_t must be raised in proportion to the fall in the number of active individuals in order to balance the pension budget; see equations (4), (6), (8), and (10).[7] Workers' *aggregate* consumption tends to decrease as a result of both the fall in the number of workers and the reduction in after-tax income of each individual worker. Thus, if aggregate output (again) happens to decline in proportion to the reduction in the number of workers, then aggregate demand is likely to fall more than aggregate supply. If so, there will be macroeconomic scope for reduced taxes or increased government spending (or both).

Clearly, there is no (direct) risk sharing in any of the PAYGO systems listed above in response to a fall in the number of workers.

The consequences for various pension systems are about the same if employment falls as a result of increased structural unemployment. In this case, however, the government would be in a worse financial position due to higher expenditures for unemployment benefits. It is also worth noting that a rise in structural unemployment may to some extent be caused by the pension system itself because payroll taxes tend to raise labor costs for workers who are exposed to minimum wages (via legislation or collective bargaining).

In the context of an actuarially fair (fully funded) pension system, by contrast, the income of both individual pensioners and individual workers will be unaffected. After a fall in N_t, both have sufficient income to continue consuming as much as before—as long as indirect effects are neglected. There may be indirect effects, however. When pensioners begin unloading financial assets, there are fewer potential buyers of these assets than before due to the fall in the cohort size of workers. As a result, asset prices would fall and interest rates rise, except in the special case of a small open economy with capital markets that are completely integrated internationally.[8] By this indirect route, even under an actuarially fair pension system, pensioners may suffer from a fall in the number of workers. This argument assumes, of course, that asset holders do not rationally anticipate future changes in the demand for and supply of assets in connection with future demographic change. Moreover, because workers may also

---

7. The derivative of $\ln \tau_t$ with respect to $\ln N_t$ is -1.

8. If the same demographic change occurred simultaneously in other countries, pensioners would also be exposed to lower asset prices in small open economies with fully integrated international capital markets.

hold financial assets, some risk sharing with workers will take place via this indirect route (i.e., via falling asset prices).

Except for the case of a very large decline in asset prices when pensioners unload their securities, aggregate demand is likely to fall less than aggregate output in a society with an actuarially fair, funded pension system. If so, there would be excess domestic demand for goods and services, with increased inflation or deterioration of the current account of the balance of payments, or both. If pensions are not fully indexed to inflation (and they usually are not in fully funded systems), retirees will have to accept further downward adjustment of their per capita consumption. Pensioners may also be harmed by government attempts to combat the current account deficit with policy measures designed to reduce domestic aggregate demand. After all, the size of the current account of the balance of payment is often a policy target of the government—for good or bad reasons.

Determining the proportion of the reduction in consumption of workers and pensioners would require a quantitative general equilibrium model, which is outside the scope of this paper. In any event, a main point here is that even under an actuarially fair pension system, pensions may not be fully protected against the consequences of a drop in the number of workers—due to the eventuality of falling asset prices, to a deterioration in the current account of the balance of payments, and (without price indexation of asset return) to higher inflation.[9]

1.2.2   Reduced Labor Income Growth

The slowdown in the rate of growth of average labor income (a fall in y_t/y_{t-1}) since the early 1970s is another factor underlying today's concern about pension systems. This development might not be entirely regarded as an exogenous shock from the point of view of the pension system. To some extent, the slowdown may have been induced by labor market distortions due to marginal tax wedges associated with payroll taxes, resulting in negative substitution effects on both hours of work h^j and real wages w^j (the latter because of disincentives on investment in human capital and on work intensity).

In the context of a PAYGO pension system, the direct distributional effects are rather similar to those in the case of a fall in the number of workers; y and N enter in the same way in most PAYGO systems. One important difference, however, is that *individual* workers are now directly exposed to reduced earnings. This holds regardless of whether the fall in earnings is the result of lower wages, w^j, or of shorter hours of work, h^j (for instance, via work sharing).

Both a fixed-fee system and a fixed income-ratio system incorporate (automatic) risk-sharing devices between workers and pensioners in the case

9. Such mechanisms are discussed in Barr (1999).

of shocks in wages and hours of work, as opposed to the earlier-discussed case of a change in the number of workers.[10] In fixed-fee systems, a fall in workers' average disposable income by $\Delta y(1 - \tau_t)$ is accompanied by a fall in the average pension by $\tau_t \Delta y(N_t/R_t)$. Thus, income risk is shared between pensioners and workers in the proportion $[\tau_t/(1 - \tau_t)] \cdot (N_t/R_t)$. In the case of a fixed income-ratio system, a fall in average labor income is shared between representative agents in the two groups in the proportion μ. The consequences for macroeconomic balance are quite complex and depend partly on whether the fall in the real wage is related to a drop in productivity (and hence of output), or to a redistribution of income between labor and capital.

Again, the consequences are more complicated in an actuarially fair system. Because there is no direct impact on pensioners, individual workers must bear the entire direct burden of a fall in real wages. Meanwhile, the reduction in wage rates implies that workers have fewer resources available to buy unloaded assets from pensioners. Thus, asset prices may decline in this case as well, thereby reducing pensioners' resources for consumption—with the earlier reservation in the case of a small open economy with perfect capital mobility, or with rational expectations. If so, some of the wage risk for workers is translated into asset risk for pensioners. As in the case of PAYGO systems, it is a complicated matter to determine the consequences for macroeconomic balance and inflation.

The slowdown in real-wage growth from the mid-1970s in most developed countries may very well be reversed in the future, for instance, as a consequence of the emerging information and communications technology (ICT) revolution. This would strengthen the financial viability of existing PAYGO pension systems. However, the ratio between pensions and the wages of coexistent workers would then fall in the context of lump-sum benefit, earnings-based, contribution-based, and actuarially fair pension systems—with the possibility of distributional conflicts as a result.

1.2.3 Increased Number of Pensioners

Recent and predicted future increases in the number of retirees is a third important factor behind today's concern about pension systems. The consequences depend on how this change comes about, for instance, via immigration of elderly people, the aging of a particularly large cohort (such as the baby boomers), early retirement, or higher longevity after retirement.

In the first case—immigration of elderly individuals—the crucial issue is how immigrants are treated relative to native-born citizens.[11] The conse-

---

10. Merton (1983) was a pioneer in showing that PAYGO pension systems may pool labor and capital income risks between the young and the old.

11. If treated in the same way, immigrants would be entitled to a domestic pension under three of the generic pension schemes listed: fixed-fee, lump-sum benefit, and fixed income-ratio systems. In fixed-fee systems, domestic pensioners would have to accept a fall in their

quences are more clear-cut if the number of retired individuals increases as the result of the aging of a particularly large cohort, which may be described as a parallel increase in N_{t-1} and R_t with N_t unchanged. In fixed-fee systems, per capita pensions will fall in proportion to the rise in R_t (equation [1]), whereas contribution rates would have to be raised in the same proportion in lump-sum benefit, earning-based, contribution-based, and fixed income-ratio systems (equations [4], [6], and [8]). Again, there is no automatic risk-sharing mechanism. Assuming no differences in marginal propensities to consume, problems of macroeconomic balance would not be induced (except for labor supply effects of higher marginal tax rates).

If a rise in the number of pensioners is instead caused by an increase in the frequency of early retirement, the outcome would be a simultaneous rise in R_t and a fall in N_t. In reality, this type of change is often induced by the incentive structure of the pension system itself, including generous rules for early retirement. In the context of a fixed-fee system, pensions would have to be reduced in proportion to the fall in the ratio N_t/R_t, while in lump-sum benefit, earnings-based, contribution-based, and fixed intergenerational income-ratio systems, the tax rate would have to be raised in proportion to the rise in the ratio R_t/N_t.

In the context of an actuarially fair pension system, there will be no direct impact on the income flows. When a large number of pensioners sell assets to workers, however, the former may face falling asset prices in the same way as in the case of a reduced number of workers. This would imply that pensioners will be hit indirectly in fully funded systems as well—except with fully rational expectations or in a small open economy with fully internationalized capital markets.

The situation becomes more complicated if the number of pensioners instead increases because of greater longevity after retirement, so that R_t increases relative to both N_{t-1} and N_t. In fixed-fee systems, pensioners would have to accept a reduction in yearly pensions in proportion to higher longevity. More precisely, there will be a reduction in yearly pensions by the change in the factor N_{t-1}/R_t. By contrast, under lump-sum benefit, earnings-based, contribution-based, and fixed intergenerational income-ratio systems, τ_t would have to be raised in proportion to the increase in the ratio R_t/N_t, provided that each pensioner is guaranteed the

per capita pension by the factor N_{t-1}/R_t, whereas in lump-sum benefit and fixed intertemporal income-ratio pension systems, payroll taxes would have to be raised by that factor. Thus, there are no automatic mechanisms for risk sharing between workers and pensioners in any of these systems when the number of pensioners increases due to the immigration of elderly people. Problems of macroeconomic balance will not arise as long as the marginal propensity to consume is the same for all groups concerned. Income flows in the context of other pension systems—earnings-based, contribution-based, and actuarially fair—would be unaffected. Under these three systems, elderly immigrants would (in the real world) be financed either by relatives or by social welfare payments. The latter, of course, would require a general tax increase.

same annual pension as before. Again, there is no risk sharing between generations.

In principle, the situation is the same in the case of an actuarially fair system as in a fixed-fee system, if information about longevity is obtained exactly when a fixed annuity is determined (at the time of retirement); the annuity must be reduced in proportion to greater longevity. However, if such information is not obtained until *after* the annuity has been determined, the pension provider must cover the higher costs, while the annual income of pensioners is unchanged. In reality, however, information about higher (expected) longevity is usually available *before* retirement, during the course of working life. The insurance provider is then able to propose higher contributions, and workers are likely to accept such proposals. It has been argued that similar adjustments are difficult to achieve under PAYGO systems, because the link between what an individual pays and what he or she receives later on is usually rather weak. Because the fee in such a system functions as a tax wedge, higher fees may also be resisted by those who are anxious to avoid additional work distortions (Persson 1998).

1.2.4   Lower Real Interest Rates

The rise in real interest rates in recent decades, as compared to the 1950s and 1960s, is an important factor behind the increased popularity of actuarially fair, fully funded systems. Having already discussed shocks that create problems mainly for PAYGO systems, I now examine an interest shock that creates problems for actuarially fair, fully funded systems (i.e., a fall in real interest rates). A fall that takes place after retirement will either create financial difficulties for the pension provider (if the annuity is fixed) or force retirees to accept lower pensions (if the annuity is variable in the sense that it is gradually adjusted to realized asset returns also after retirement). In the first case, pension providers may try to shift the consequences of interest rate shock onto subsequent cohorts of pensioners.

At the individual-pensioner level, an obvious difference between a fixed and a variable annuity is that in the latter case the individual must accept higher income risk during the period of retirement. The reason, of course, is that with a variable annuity, the drawing down of previously accumulated pension capital takes place only gradually during the retirement period. The advantage to the individual is that he or she then has a further opportunity to enjoy the return on assets, such as shares, after having retired. A variable annuity also fulfills the role of reducing fluctuations in the relation (ratio) between replacement rates for consecutive cohorts of pensioners, because the capital value of the annuity will depend less on the prevailing financial-market situation at the time of retirement. This gives rise to a genuine trade-off problem. Although a fixed annuity provides greater income insurance in connection with uncertainty about longevity, a variable annuity furnishes relative income insurance in connection with uncertainty about asset prices at the time of retirement. The individual may alternatively opt for "revolving" annuitization for a number of years before retirement, or for a gradual shift (also before retirement) to less risky assets. This means, however, that the individual would miss out on the opportunity to enjoy the return on high-yielding assets after retirement on the basis of accumulated pension capital.

So far I have considered changes in real interest rates only at or after retirement. If real interest rates fell during the individual's working life and were expected to remain low for quite a while, he or she would probably agree to pay higher yearly contributions to a fully funded system in order to boost the future pension.

Even though there are no direct effects (as long as there are no buffer funds), PAYGO pension systems are not immune to changes in real interest rates. Both contribution rates and pension benefits may be influenced indirectly (general equilibrium effects). The most obvious indirect effect is that lower (higher) real interest rates would increase (decrease) future real wage rates by boosting (retarding) the real capital stock. However, it is also important to consider changes in factor prices that are induced by the pension system itself, an issue to be dealt with in subsequent sections.

1.3   Marginal Reforms

1.3.1   Ad Hoc Adjustment

Under all the stylized pension systems discussed earlier, well-specified rules guarantee budget balance—intertemporal balance in fully funded systems and balance in PAYGO systems, in the latter case via adjustments in either fees or pensions. In reality, however, adjustments in conformity with such rules often require explicit political decisions in the case of PAYGO systems. As a result, such adjustment may take considerable time, partly because of conflicts about the distribution of income. In the meantime, financial imbalances of a PAYGO pension system easily emerge after exogenous shocks. This is likely to initiate demand for ad hoc changes in contributions or benefits (i.e., changes outside the original rule system). In extreme cases, a PAYGO pension system may even break down, in the sense that large and rising deficits finally necessitate abrupt, unplanned cancellations of earlier promised entitlements.

For example, after a fall in the number of workers (N) or in average real earnings (y), workers may resist higher fees in lump-sum benefit, earnings-based, and contribution-based systems, and in fixed income-ratio systems after a fall in the number of workers. It is therefore tempting to speculate that workers may want to force contemporary pensioners to share the burden of adjustment in such cases. Indeed, doubts are often expressed in the political debate as to whether a majority of voters will grant promised pension entitlements to the elderly after such disturbances. If explicit changes in the rules for pension benefits (B, α, γ, or μ, above) are not politically feasible, obvious alternatives are higher taxes on pension income or partial punctuation of price indexation of pensions—illustrations of the role of "framing" in politics.

Because pensioners constitute only a minority among voters, it is perhaps less likely that workers could be forced to share the burden of adjustment (via an increase in τ) when the burden would otherwise fall on pensioners. (This occurs, for example, in the case of a fall in the number of workers in fixed-fee systems and in the case of reduced real interest rates in actuarially fair systems, unless a fixed annuity has been set.) Policy actions for this purpose may be released, however, if pensioners are an important swing group in the political arena, and if their voting behavior is particularly sensitive to the pension benefits offered. Pensioners may also find political support for their position among workers close to retirement.

Even though the benefits of contemporary pensioners have recently been cut to a considerable extent in some countries, and fees have been raised for workers, empirical evidence suggests that political authorities have mainly opted for a "third alternative": cuts in pensions for *future* pensioners (McHale 1999). As an explanation, McHale has hypothesized that today's workers are afraid of becoming exposed to even greater cuts in their own pensions in the future unless they agree to some cuts immediately. Another explanation, however, could be that the political price is higher if the government cuts current disposable income by means of higher fees or lower pensions today, than if it decides to reduce pensions far into the future. After all, myopic behavior is not unheard of; indeed, reference to such behavior (often interpreted as time inconsistency) is one of the most common arguments for having compulsory pension systems in the first place.

When a pension system encounters problems because of a fall in the number of individuals of working age relative to the number of individuals above retirement age (the ratio N_t/R_t), immigration of young workers may be a solution. This presupposes, of course, that such immigration is not expected to result in serious tensions and conflicts in society.

1.3.2   Automatic Adjustment Mechanisms

To introduce new types of automatic adjustment mechanisms within existing pension systems is an alternative to ad hoc policy interventions for dealing with the distributional consequences of exogenous socioeconomic shocks. One way of achieving this consists of shifting to a fixed income-ratio system (system 6 in the classification above). However, such a reform cannot be combined with ambitions to maintain strong quasi-actuarial elements in the pension system, which exist in contribution-based systems with individual accounts (system 5 in the classification above). However, it would still be possible to make relative pensions among individual pensioners proportional to each individual's accumulated earnings or contributions; thus, some relative quasi-actuarial element could still be achieved.

We may also want to modify redistributions of income among generations in the case of unexpected increases in longevity after retirement. Under lump-sum benefit, earnings-based, and contribution-based systems (i.e., systems 3–5), a technically simple way of avoiding placement of the entire burden of adjustment on wage earners is an automatic rule that makes annual pensions a declining function of remaining life expectancy after retirement. For example, when pension annuities in the new NDC-pension system in Sweden are determined, pension benefits will be inversely proportional to expected longevity after retirement. However, this means the entire burden of adjustment will be borne by the retirees—hardly a risk-sharing device, which has made Diamond (2001) question the wisdom of this element in the Swedish pension reform.[12]

Setting higher ages for both regular and earliest possible retirement is a natural response to a rise in the number of retirees as a result of improved health for individuals above today's retirement age. In terms of the notations above, the budget balance of the pension system then would be improved by a combination of higher N_t and lower R_t. (It may then also be important to implement stricter rules for disability and unemployment insurance, because these systems have in fact been used as alternative routes to early retirement even by individuals without serious health problems.[13]) Increased downward flexibility of relative wages for the elderly, as with a less steep age-wage profile, is one way to avoid sending a large fraction of the elderly toward unemployment if the retirement age were raised considerably. An alternative would be to reduce payroll taxes for the elderly. In most countries, union and government wage policies may be obstacles to both these solutions.

Because both health quality and preferences for work vary considerably among the elderly, one no doubt could make a strong case for a *flexible* retirement age. To avoid distorting work incentives, however, and to keep pension systems financially viable, there are also good arguments for combining such flexibility with actuarially fair adjustments of pensions under conditions of early retirement. Elderly individuals with health problems could then be referred to the sick-insurance system. It is curious that the

---

12. The new pension system in Sweden, however, does not include any automatic adjustment mechanisms if the remaining life expectancy of individuals of a given age rises during their retirement period. Such costs have to be covered by *ad hoc* adjustments via the braking mechanism mentioned in the text.

13. There are limits, of course, to what can be achieved by such a reform. Given current fees and benefit rules, the Organization for Economic Cooperation and Development (OECD) has calculated that the statutory retirement age would have to be raised, within a few decades, to no less than seventy-three to seventy-four years in many developed countries to keep pension systems financially viable. See Thomson (1998, 48, note 10) and OECD (1988).

designs of today's pension systems and labor market arrangements appear to turn higher longevity and better health among the elderly into serious social problems rather than into blessings. Such designs are hardly examples of good "social engineering."

A more crude way of making a pension system financially viable via automatic adjustment mechanisms, regardless of the type of disturbance, would be automatic reductions in benefits or increases in fees in response to an emerging or anticipated deficit in the pension budget.

1.4   Radical Reforms

1.4.1   Shifting to a Quasi-actuarial System (NDC System)

Lump-sum benefit systems and earnings-based systems (pension systems nos. 3 and 4) have served as the most common pension schemes during the second half of the twentieth century. Although the former are completely nonactuarial, there is some indirectly positive link between an individual's earlier contributions and his or her pension in earnings-based systems. The link is very weak in most countries, however, because pensions are often calculated on the basis of earnings during a limited number of years of work. It is not technically difficult to strengthen the link between benefits and previously paid contributions (also without prefunding). One obvious technique would be to increase the number of earning years used as a basis for the size of an individual's pensions.

The most straightforward way, however, would be to shift to a notional defined contribution (NDC) system with individual accounts (a pension system of type 5 with the average *and* marginal return $\gamma = G_t$ for the individual when $R_t = N_{t-1}$ and $\tau_t = \tau_{t-1}$). Buchanan (1968) may have made the first proposal along these lines. A basic argument for this reform involves reducing the implicit marginal tax wedge on work, hence raising the return on work. Because economic efficiency will then increase in the labor market, a Pareto improvement is possible in principle. There would also be less risk of undermining the financial viability of the pension system via an induced reduction in the number of employed workers (N) or a reduction in earnings per worker (y) due to a fall in hours of work or labor productivity. Under realistic assumptions, about 40 percent of the tax wedge implicit in the pension system may be removed by a shift from a completely nonactuarial to a quasi-actuarial, contribution-based pension system with individual accounts.[14] A prerequisite for favorable effects on

14. Assume that an individual starts working at the age of twenty, retires at sixty-four, and lives for another twenty years thereafter. On average, a worker pays his or her contribution at age forty-two, and receives his or her pension at age seventy-four. Thus, as an approximation, we may say that thirty-two years (74 − 42) elapse between the payment of the contribution and the enjoyment of the benefit. Let the contribution rate (τ) be 20 percent, so that if

work incentives, of course, is that an individual understands the connection between his or her own contributions (payroll taxes) and the subsequent pension benefits.

It is virtually impossible, however, to create a fully actuarially fair PAYGO system (i.e., a system without tax wedges) in a dynamically efficient economy (i.e., an economy in which the real interest rate is higher than the growth rate). If a PAYGO pension system would pay a higher return than the growth rate of the tax base, the system would wind up with an ever-rising deficit. In a dynamically *inefficient* economy, by contrast, it can be shown that an actuarially fair PAYGO system would automatically accumulate a fund of the same size as in a fully funded system (Hassler and Lindbeck 1997). However, there is then no point in choosing an actuarially fair system in the first place because the return on paid contributions would be higher in a traditional PAYGO system, in which it is equal to the growth rate of aggregate earnings.

Is it possible, or even desirable, to make a PAYGO system actuarially fair *only on the margin,* while maintaining a balanced budget by setting the average return equal to the growth rate of the economy? Intuition suggests that efficiency would be improved if the marginal return on pensions were set in such a way that the individual's marginal work decisions are indifferent between paying pension fees and investing on the capital market. The point would be that many economic distortions are associated with marginal rather than average tax wedges. It turns out to be technically possible to create such a system (Auerbach and Kotlikoff 1987; Hassler and Lindbeck 1997); owing to intragenerational distributional considerations, however, such a system is politically difficult to implement, because it requires a lump-sum tax (a "poll tax") in order to balance the pension budget.[15]

The financial viability of a PAYGO pension system, of course, requires that pensions are tied to the growth rate of aggregate earnings, hence the product $y_t N_t$, rather than to the growth rate of average earnings, y_t. When

---

an individual earns $500 more (due to more hours of work or higher work intensity), he or she pays $100 in pension contributions. In a quasi-actuarial PAYGO system in which the return is 2 percent (the growth of the tax base), this contribution will be worth $188 after thirty-two years. If the real rate of return in financial markets is 5 percent and this is used as a discount rate, the capital value of the $188 at average working age is $40 ($188/[1.05]^{32}$). This means that the marginal tax wedge on work is 12 percent ($[100 - 40]/500$). Thus, a shift from a completely nonactuarial to a quasi-actuarial system will reduce the tax wedge from 20 percent to 12 percent in this case. See Lindbeck and Persson (2000, 7). The marginal tax wedge would disappear in an actuarially fair system only if such a system were introduced from scratch, and thus without the need to honor pension claims of previous PAYGO pensioners. However, the mandatory nature of such a system may, by itself, distort individual behavior if borrowing is constrained in the capital market.

15. Moreover, for a given tax rate τ, it can be shown that the welfare gain of the increased efficiency of work would wind up entirely with the older generation. If the objective is to let all generations enjoy a welfare gain, however, the pension fee may be reduced (Hassler and Lindbeck 1997).

the new pension reform in Sweden in the late 1990s promised a rate of return on paid contributions equal to the rate of growth of average wage earnings, the system threatened to be unstable in the case of slow employment growth. It was therefore necessary to introduce a braking mechanism on pension benefits that will be automatically released in the case of slower employment growth.

1.4.2 Shifting to an Actuarially Fair, Fully Funded System

I have pointed out the efficiency gain of shifting from a PAYGO pension system with a weak (or nonexistent) link between contributions and benefits for the individual to a PAYGO system with a stronger link, for instance a quasi-actuarial system with individual accounts (system no. 5). A similar efficiency gain may, of course, be achieved by a shift to a fully funded pension system (system no. 2), because the marginal tax wedge falls in this case as well.

Yet, what is the gain, if any, of a shift from a quasi-actuarial pension system (with a strong link between contributions and benefits) to a fully funded system with a market rate of return? Neglecting (to begin with) conceivable behavior adjustments of individuals, it is easy to show that the capital value of the gross income gain for individuals participating in the pension system is the same as the implicit debt to the PAYGO pensioners. Thus, there is no aggregate income gain of such a shift because someone must serve this implicit debt (Feldstein 1995; Sinn 1999). Starting out with a quasi-actuarial pension system, a shift to a fully funded system will not result in a Pareto improvement in the labor market—assuming no distortion of the capital stock to begin with (Kotlikoff 1998; Fenge 1995; Lindbeck and Persson 2000). This conclusion assumes that all income streams are discounted by the market interest rate (which is not completely self-evident, because we compare incomes of different generations rather than incomes during different periods for a given individual).

There will, of course, be redistributions among generations. The signs and sizes of these redistributions depend crucially on how the claims of the old PAYGO pensioners are met. If the PAYGO pensioners are bailed out by taxes on a transitional generation, that generation will experience a sizeable income loss, whereas subsequent generations will experience income gains as compared to the alternative of retaining the PAYGO system. Our attitudes to such redistributions among generations, of course, depend on how we evaluate (i.e., discount) income of different generations. One argument for enforcing a redistribution to future generations may be that the previous introduction of the PAYGO pension system most likely reduced aggregate saving, and hence, the aggregate capital stock, to the disadvantage of future generations. Metaphorically speaking, because the grandparents of today's children originally received a gift at the expense of future generations, the grandchildren may ask their parents' generation to contribute to an increase in the capital stock via compulsory pension saving. Because lump-sum taxes hardly are politically feasible, a transition generation would also be exposed to higher marginal taxes, with lower economic efficiency of work as result. Subsequent generations would instead be able to enjoy smaller marginal tax wedges, with increased work efficiency as a consequence.

All this may give the impression that the issue of shifting from a quasi-actuarial PAYGO system to an actuarially fair, fully funded pension system is a problem only of intergenerational distribution of income (wealth), and of a trade-off between work incentives and aggregate saving among different generations. There is more to it than that, however.

First, in most countries, existing capital-income taxation distorts aggregate national saving and investment. This is another reason—distinct from the one that the gift to the first generation of PAYGO pensioners has reduced aggregate saving—that the capital stock is likely to be lower than it would have been otherwise. As a result, the discount rate (regardless of whether this is the market interest rate or the subjective discount rate) may be lower than the return on capital assets, a point made by Feldstein (1996). A shift to a fully funded pensions system, like a reduction in government debt, could then be regarded as a second-best policy designed to increase the distorted stock of aggregate wealth, including real capital assets, in society.[16]

Second, we also must look at the risk-return combination of alternative pension systems. Normally, the returns on PAYGO pension claims are not fully correlated with the returns on claims in an actuarially fair pension systems. For one thing, the growth rate of the tax base of a PAYGO system (i.e., aggregate earnings) and the return on financial markets are not fully correlated, particularly when pension funds hold foreign assets. The political risk is also likely to differ. (It is often assumed that claims on funded systems with individual accounts provide stronger property rights than do pension claims in PAYGO systems.) What all this boils down to is that a combination of a PAYGO and a fully funded system provides a richer portfolio of pension assets than either of these pension systems in isolation. This is an additional rationale for a partial shift to a fully funded system.

The most problematic aspect of any shift to a compulsory, fully funded pension system is, in my view, how to minimize the risks that such a reform will—sooner or later—result in politicization of the domestic economy. There is a serious risk that future politicians will use government-

---

16. However, in some countries, including a number of European countries, this negative effect on the aggregate capital stock may have been compensated for by various types of investment subsidies, although these may have distorted the allocation of investment.

controlled pension funds to allocate financial funds to politically correct industries and to those parts of the national economy where it is particularly tempting to buy votes. Politicians, or their subordinates, might also start using voting rights in firms to exert influence within firms, even though they may lack knowledge as to how firms should be run. Thus, the case against nationalizing pension capital is the same as the arguments against the Lange-Lerner proposal of market socialism.

Technically, it is possible to design institutions that isolate government-operated pension funds from political pressure, including party politics. The most obvious method is perhaps to require such funds to invest only in index funds, possibly global ones, and to give the managers of the funds instructions to exercise the voting rights in firms. Future politicians anxious to exercise economic power, however, are free to change such rules. It is much easier politically to change the rules of portfolio allocation and corporate governance in existing government-operated funds than to propose outright nationalization of an economy from scratch. Thus, those who are critical of market socialism have good reasons to be critical of government-operated pension funds as well. After all, proposals of market socialism also incorporate stringent rules instructing managers of government-owned firms to behave like profit miximizers under perfect competition. Clearly, it is naive to believe that politicians, who choose their profession to exert power, would accept such rules.

The most promising way to mitigate the risks for politicization of the national economy is probably to make pension funds privately owned and operated from the outset, and to allow individuals to choose fund managers. The higher administrative costs of decentralized (versus centralized) fund management is the price of limiting the risk of politicizing the national economy. There are also devices to limit these administrative costs, such as caps on fees, which would induce some managers of mandatory pension funds to choose index funds.

1.5   Adjustment to Increased Heterogeneity

Real-world pension systems have always, at least to some extent, granted (or exploited) the heterogeneity of the population. An obvious example is the overcompensation of early cohorts when PAYGO systems were introduced to bring about a rapid increase in living standards for the elderly or to create broad political support for the reform. This overcompensation was extended to a great number of cohorts by a gradual increase in the contribution rate (a rise in the ratio τ_t/τ_{t-1}).

An example of overcompensation *within* cohorts is redistribution in favor of low-income groups via either a basic (lump-sum) pension or a guaranteed pension with means testing on pension benefits. In most earnings-based pension systems in the real world (when fixed annuities are tied to earnings during a limited number of years of work), females are also favored because of fewer years of work and a larger number of years after retirement. However, there are also well-known regressive redistributional elements in most real-world pension systems, although it is difficult to say whether these effects are intentional. One example is redistribution in favor of the individual with a steep income profile over his or her life cycle (when the pension level is tied to earnings late in the individual's working life). Another example is redistribution to individuals with high expected longevity (in systems with fixed annuities). In both cases, the arrangements tend to favor highly educated individuals with relatively high lifetime income (wealth).

In recent decades, it is only natural that new types of heterogeneity in the population have given rise to proposals for pension reforms. An obvious example is increased instability of the typical family structure. Pension systems established in the early twentieth century were careful to provide support for widows and their children because the death of the (usually male) income provider was a major factor in the breakup of families. A strong trend toward the labor-force participation of married women has reduced the need for special pension claims for widows. It does not seem reasonable that widows should receive pensions based on both their own previous incomes (or contributions) and widowhood. A delicate issue, however, is what should be regarded a reasonable length of time to phase out the latter type of pension claim, if politicians decide about such an outphasing. The huge increase in part-time work, also largely a result of increased labor force participation of women, also raises the issue of whether the benefit rules in contribution-based and earnings-based systems should favor or disfavor part-time work of different durations.

Today, family instability is largely related to divorce and temporary cohabitation outside marriage. One way of adjusting pension systems to this new situation would be to give couples property rights on one another's pension capital, in the same way that the law stipulates such property rights for spouses regarding real estate and financial assets. Such arrangements may also solve the problem of pensions for survivors (including widows). After all, pension capital usually accumulates gradually over the working life of the family in a manner similar to that of other assets. A delicate issue here concerns how other forms of cohabitation than marriage should be treated.

The heterogeneity of the population has also increased as a result of changes in the traditional life cycle, characterized by the linear sequence of education-work-retirement. This sequence is currently being replaced by more complex and individually varied life cycles. The continuity of working life is often interrupted by education, retraining, periods of work at home (e.g., caring for children) and prolonged periods of leisure. This is an important background for contemporary proposals to replace existing welfare-state arrangements with compulsory saving accounts (possibly negative accounts early in life) and related drawing rights on claims accumulated before retirement.[17] Proposals of compulsory saving with drawing rights are based on the assumption that individuals can handle modest economic setbacks on their own by drawing on accumulated compulsory saving, for instance, in connection with short periods of unemployment or health problems. However, people would be obligated to reserve a certain minimum balance in their accounts for old age. Thus, proposals of this type may be seen as efforts to encourage individuals to take greater responsibility for their own income protection in the event of moderate strains on their economic situations. Of course, when having to deal with major income losses, the system of drawing rights must be combined with insurance; this point is also granted in most proposals. Another basic idea behind the scheme of drawing rights is to provide the individual with increased resources to shift among work, education, and leisure over the life cycle. Work incentives would then also be improved (via smaller tax wedges) and problems of moral hazard mitigated—two major problems of today's social insurance systems (evidenced by moral hazard in connection with unemployment, sick leave, and early retirement insurances).

It is also a commonplace that higher international labor mobility creates difficulties in assigning individuals to national pension systems. It will certainly become necessary to adjust pension rules in the future to deal with this issue and, in particular, to decide whether pensions should be provided on the basis of an individual's country of origin or of residence. Without some coordination of national rules, individuals may in some cases lose entitlements earned in one country, yet in other instances may end up with more favorable pensions by living part of their lives in one country and part in another. In the former case, the pension system would impede international mobility of labor in the same way that nontransferable occupational pensions among firms or sectors reduce domestic labor mobility. In the latter case, international labor mobility may, in fact, be subsidized. Shifts to quasi-actuarial or fully actuarial systems, or to compulsory saving with individual accounts, would mitigate or even eliminate such problems. Of course, ambitions to use pension systems as tools of redistribution would then be reduced. Increased international flexibility of the choice of residence of individuals also creates an increased need to unify the taxation principles for private pension policies, including occupational pensions. In some countries, governments permit tax deductions

---

17. An early proposal along these lines is Rehm (1961). More elaborate plans have been developed by Fölster (1999) and Orzag and Snower (1999).

for such insurance contributions while taxing subsequent pension benefits, whereas governments in other countries do the opposite, which clearly distorts residence decisions.

1.6 Concluding Remarks

As we have seen, the consequences for pension systems of various types of socioeconomic changes depend crucially on the detailed structure of the pension system.[18] For instance, there is no (direct) risk sharing in PAYGO pension systems in response to variations in the number of workers or the number of pensioners. By contrast, both a fixed-fee and a fixed income-ratio system incorporate automatic risk-sharing devices between workers and pensioners in the event of shocks in wages and hours of work. Although there is no direct risk sharing in the case of socioeconomic shocks in fully funded systems, I have argued that indirect effects of different types may create some risk sharing.

It is clear that several weaknesses of current PAYGO systems can be solved within the framework of existing systems. For instance, problems concerning financial vulnerability and unexpected redistribution may be mitigated by ad hoc increases in fees, cuts in benefits (often by way of less-favorable price indexing), or increased retirement age. At the same time, such interventions highlight the political risks inherent in government-operated pension systems.

If more-automatic risk sharing between generations is desired, an obvious reform is to shift to what have in this chapter been called fixed income-ratio systems, in which the relation between pensions and the earnings of contemporary workers is fixed. The consequences of increased instability of the family can also be alleviated, for instance, by legislation requiring spouses to share one another's pension claims. If enhanced work incentives were called for instead, then the actuarial elements of the PAYGO system could be extended by strengthening the link between contributions and benefits for each individual, possibly by shifting to what have here been called quasi-actuarial systems. In the context of such a system, it is also technically easy to have a flexible retirement age without individuals' being able to shift the costs of early retirement upon others. I have also mentioned that compulsory saving accounts with individual drawing rights, combined with compulsory insurance systems, provide an interesting response to increased heterogeneity among individuals and to demands for placing greater responsibility on the individual for his or her own economic security.

The most obvious argument for a shift to an actuarially fair, fully funded

---

18. This type of observation has been made about welfare-state arrangements in general by Freeman (1995) and Atkinson (1999).

pension system is perhaps to favor future generations at the expense of currently working generations—if such a redistribution is regarded ethically fair. One specific twist of this argument is to expand the capital stock in order to compensate either for reduced national saving when the PAYGO system was introduced or for distortions of saving and investment decisions via the existing capital-income tax system. If we start from a PAYGO system with a weak (or nonexistent) marginal link between contributions and benefits for individuals, a shift to a fully funded system will also result in an efficiency gain via smaller marginal tax wedges, in the same way as when such a PAYGO system is replaced with a quasi-actuarial system. However, it should be noted that a shift from a quasi-actuarial system to an actuarially fair system does not reduce the marginal tax wedge for any generation without raising it for some other generations. The reason is that a removal of an earlier existing PAYGO system must in reality be financed by distortionary taxes (Lindbeck and Persson 2000).

However, there is also a portfolio diversification argument for a *partial* shift to a fully funded pension system. The reason is that the returns on pension claims are not completely correlated among pension systems. A partial shift would provide individuals with more well-balanced portfolios of pension claim than would either a PAYGO or an actuarially fair system alone. This is an important point in a world with different types of market risks (risk in earnings versus risk in returns on capital markets) and different types of political risks (such as different strengths of property rights among types of pension claims). The most severe problem inherent in either a partial or complete shift to a fully funded system lies in finding ways to avoid politicizing the domestic economy. The most promising way to achieve this is probably to let pension funds be privately owned and operated from the outset, and to allow individuals to choose fund managers, possibly combined with caps on the administrative fees to pension fund managers.

References

Atkinson, A. B. 1999. *The economic consequences of rolling back the welfare state.* Cambridge, Mass.: MIT Press.

Auerbach, A., and L. Kotlikoff. 1987. *Dynamic fiscal policy.* Cambridge: Cambridge University Press.

Barr, N. 1999. A public-private partnership in pensions: Getting the balance right. In *Partnership in pensions? Responses to the Pensions Green Paper.* Case Paper no. 24. London: London School of Economics.

Bohn, H. 1999. Social security and demographic uncertainty: The risk sharing properties of alternative policies. University of California, Santa Barbara, Department of Economics, Working Paper.

Buchanan, J. 1968. Social insurance in a growing economy: A proposal for radical reform. *National Tax Journal* 21 (4): 386–95.

Diamond, P. 1977. A framework for social security analysis. *Journal of Public Economics* 8:275–98.

———. 2001. *Social security reform* (forthcoming). Uppsala, Sweden: Lindahl Lectures.

Feldstein, M. 1996. Would privatizing Social Security raise economic welfare? NBER Working Paper no. 5281. Cambridge, Mass.: National Bureau of Economic Research.

Fenge, R. 1995. Pareto efficiency of the pay-as-you-go pension system with intragenerational fairness. *Finanzarchiv* 52:357–63.

Fölster, S. 1999. Social insurance based on personal savings accounts: A possible reform strategy for overburdened welfare states? In Buti, M., Franco, D. and Pench, L. (eds.), *The Welfare State in Europe*, 93–115. Cheltenham, UK: Edward Elgar.

Freeman, R. 1995. The large welfare state as a system. *American Economic Review, Papers and Proceedings* 85:16–21.

Hassler, J., and A. Lindbeck. 1997. Intergenerational risk sharing, stability and optimality of alternative pension systems. University of Stockholm, Institute for International Economic Studies, Seminar Paper no. 631.

Kotlikoff, L. 1998. "Simulating the privatization of Social Security in general equilibrium. In *Privatizing Social Security*, ed. Martin Feldstein, 265–306. Chicago: University of Chicago Press.

Lindbeck, A., and M. Persson. 2000. What are the gains from pension reform? Research Institute for Industrial Economics (IUI), Working Paper no. 535. Stockholm: IUI.

McHale, J. 1999. The risk of social security benefit rule changes: Some international evidence. NBER Working Paper no. 7031. Cambridge, Mass.: National Bureau of Economic Research, March.

Merton, R. C. 1983. On the role of social security as a means for efficient risk sharing in an economy where human capital is not tradable. In *Financial aspects of the U.S. pension system*, ed. Z. Bodie and J. B. Shoven, 325–58. Chicago: University of Chicago Press.

Organization for Economic Cooperation and Development (OECD). 1988. *Aging populations: The social policy implications*. Paris: OECD.

Orzag, M., and D. Snower. 1999. Expanding the welfare system: A proposal for reform. In *The welfare state in Europe*, ed. M. Buti, D. Franco, and L. Pench, 116–35. Cheltenham, U.K.: Edward Elgar.

Persson, M. 1998. Reforming social security in Sweden. In *Redesigning social security*, ed. H. Siebert, 169–85. Tübingen, Germany: Mohr Siebeck.

Rehn, G. 1961. "Arbetsmarknadspolitik som samhällsidé" (Labor market policy as a vision of society). In *Femton år med Tage Erlander*, ed. O. Svensson. Stockholm: Tiden.

Sinn, H. W. 1999. Pension reform and demographic crisis: Why a funded system is needed and why it is not needed. CESifo Working Paper no. 195. Munich: CESifo.

Thomson, L. 1998. *Older and wiser*. Washington, D.C.: Urban Institute Press.

Discussion Summary

Martin Feldstein shared the worry expressed in the paper that a centrally managed, funded system would create problems of political interference. He cited some evidence from the United States in which state governments have pension systems for their workers and often have rules about investing the funds locally. He concluded that this could be avoided by having a system of individual accounts. *Rolf Langhammer* suggested that in making a relative assessment of the desirability of government versus privately operated pension funds, the probability of insolvency should also be taken into consideration. He brought up the American Orange County case, which shows that lower levels of state authority can also go bust.

A. Lans Bovenberg argued that Pareto improving transitions from pay-as-you-go (PAYGO) to funded systems are possible and that everyone can gain if there is a distortion in the economy. In Europe, more important than the capital income tax already mentioned by Martin Feldstein would be labor market distortions, and he suggested exploitation of this distortion for efficiency gains. He conceded, however, that this is a difficult task because many of these distortions are connected with intragenerational redistribution, which makes it much harder to come up with something like a Pareto improvement. Bovenberg concluded that the key challenge is to perform redistribution more efficiently. *Eytan Sheshinski* pointed out that the extent to which a fully funded system eliminates distortions depends on the details of the system with respect to provisions against idiosyncratic risks, individual risks, or macro risks, and that every kind of guarantee will involve some kind of distortion. He gave the example of government guarantees in case of bankruptcy, which will have distortive effects on the portfolio choices of the managers. As further distortions, which he suggested can be acceptable for distributional purposes, he mentioned mandatory pricing of annuities when there are different risks—for example, with respect to longevity.

Martin Feldstein argued that the potential gains from going beyond notional defined contributions to actually funded defined contributions are much greater than suggested in the paper, because differences in rates of return prevail for more than one year. He cited the example in which a defined contribution system produces the rate of growth in the economy of 2 percent and a funded system provides the real rate of return on capital of 8 percent, and assumed that the contributions would be in the accounts for an average of thirty years (put in at age forty-five in the middle of the working life and withdrawn at age seventy-five in the middle of the retirement life). In this case he calculated that the difference between a 2 percent growth rate and an 8 percent growth rate would be a factor of 5 or 6 leading to an enormous implicit tax wedge if one was forced to take the lower rate of return. *Assar Lindbeck* replied that there would effectively be less return than 8 percent if there was a PAYGO system to begin with because of financing of the inherited PAYGO pensions. He pointed out that in the case of starting from a PAYGO system, it is possible to gain from a move toward a funded system only when the rate of return is higher than the discount rate. *Pierre Pestieau* remarked that it is not clear that there is a gain from the move toward the stock market, at least in a general equilibrium framework, unless there are liquidity-constrained households.

The issue of risk sharing emphasized in the paper was stressed by *A. Lans Bovenberg,* who argued that it is particularly important in the European context, because Europeans tend to be particularly risk averse, due in part (as he suggests) to the fact that the less risk averse left the continent and went to the United States. He argued that in order to diversify risk it would be appropriate to combine various types of pension systems. Risk sharing is also behind the problems with portability in funded systems, according to Bovenberg, because in Europe funded plans tend to include many intergenerational transfers—meaning that they are not purely funded systems but contain, in a sense, elements of PAYGO systems. The element of intergenerational risk sharing in many funded systems actually enabled these systems to better exploit the equity premium, because they did not need to be particularly risk averse, as an individual would be (especially when nearing retirement age). As the population generally appreciates arrangements of this kind, it seems important to Bovenberg to look for ways to maintain them in the face of increasing competitive pressures. One of only a few available options would be to increase the use of the capital market and take advantage of capital market integration to improve risk diversification. Another option could be to go to a pan-European system, but he deemed this very difficult as well because of huge transaction costs. *Assar Lindbeck* endorsed the view that there is a strong case for a mixed system because the systems are associated with different risks that are not completely correlated. Therefore, it would be possible to achieve an improved portfolio. However, he warned that it might not be sensible to set up a very small funded system because of high fixed costs, and added that it might have been unwise for Sweden to relegate only 2.5 percentage points of the contributions to the fully funded system. With respect to the equity premium, he noted that it is has proven very difficult to explain it by mere consideration of risk. To the extent that this premium is higher than the compensation for risk, a fully funded system would give the entire population the chance to enjoy this equity premium. He argued that the possibility of investing on a voluntary basis was limited, given the high level of taxes.

Laurence J. Kotlikoff remarked that the prevailing notion that switching to a funded system would be neutral when the government would borrow money to pay for the funding and assess taxes to cover the interest overlooks the facts that the European pension systems are simply not sustainable, and that governments have only a few years left in which to make adjustments to prevent a complete collapse of the systems. This is, he reported, the conclusion of recent generational account exercises that suggest that tax rates will have to be raised dramatically in the future, beginning with tax rates that are already enormously high. He pointed out that the situation is that of drastically disadvantaging future generations so as to maintain the situation for current generations—the current elderly in particular—and concluded that a reasonable position on the question of whom to hurt is to share the harm across current and future generations. He argued that it would be insufficient to go to a notional account system and slightly improve the incentive system, but that it is necessary to do something major that addresses the intergenerational equity issue, and suggested that this would occur through a move to a funded system.

Edward Palmer raised the issue of the risk of longevity and noted that one advantage of notional account systems is that they put longevity into the equation and increase the transparency of the system with respect to the expected benefits. He noted that in a notional or financial-account defined contribution system it is clear that the worker bears the longevity risk, whereas this is not the case in a defined benefit system.

2

Different Approaches to Pension Reform from an Economic Point of View

Jonathan Gruber and David A. Wise

Most social security systems around the world are operated on a pay-as-you-go (or PAYGO) basis. Taxes collected from working people today are routed directly to pay the benefits of current retirees. Now these systems are faced with rapidly aging populations, increasing the number of retirees relative to the number of persons in the labor force. In addition, employees in most countries are leaving the labor force at younger and younger ages, further increasing the ratio of retirees to employed persons. The combination of these two trends, together with generous retirement benefits in many countries, has placed social security systems around the world under enormous financial stress. Most social security systems face large unfunded liabilities. Without changes in the systems, the prospect is for rapidly increasing tax rates on the young to pay for benefits for the old. What is more, in many countries the young are likely to receive benefits when they retire that are substantially lower than benefits promised today. It seems inevitable that the young will have to consume less to save for their own retirement while at the same time paying the benefits of current retirees. The goal of this paper is to explain the nature of the problem faced by social security systems and then to describe the various approaches that might be used to address the problem, commenting on the economic features of each.

Jonathan Gruber is professor of economics at the Massachusetts Institute of Technology and a research associate and director of the program on children at the National Bureau of Economic Research. David A. Wise is the John F. Stambaugh Professor of Political Economy at the John F. Kennedy School of Government, Harvard University, and director of health and retirement programs at the National Bureau of Economic Research.

The authors have benefited from the detailed and careful comments of Jeff Liebman and from data provided by Andrew Samwick.

2.1   What Is the Problem?

We first consider the demographic and labor force trends that have placed financial pressure on social security systems. We then discuss specific features of PAYGO systems that provide a background for discussion of reform proposals. We give particular attention to the critical provisions of most social security programs that induce employees to leave the labor force at increasingly younger ages. Removing these features can be an important component of almost any reform proposal.

2.1.1   Demographic and Labor Force Trends

Suppose that the social security taxes paid today are just enough to pay the benefits of today's retirees. As long as the number of retirees does not grow faster than total earnings of employees, the tax receipts can continue to pay the benefits of retirees. That is not the case today, however. Babies born after World War II—the baby boomers—are now approaching retirement age. The number of retirees is now increasing very rapidly relative to the number of younger persons in the workforce. In addition, persons are living longer, so that those who reach retirement age will be receiving benefits longer than they used to. The ratio of the number of persons aged sixty-five and higher to the number aged twenty to sixty-four is shown in figure 2.1, now and in future years, for ten countries.[1] The increase is striking in almost every country. In Japan, with the most rapid population aging, the ratio will more than double by 2020 and will almost triple by 2050. These demographic trends have placed enormous pressure on the financial viability of the social security systems in these countries.

This pressure is compounded by another trend: In virtually every country, employees are leaving the labor force at younger and younger ages. The labor force participation rates of men aged sixty to sixty-four for the years 1960 to 1996 are shown for each of the ten countries in figure 2.2. The decline was substantial in each country, but was much greater in some countries than in others. In the early 1960s, the participation rates were higher than 70 percent in all but one of the countries and higher than 80 percent in several countries. By the mid-1990s, the rate had fallen to less than 20 percent in Belgium, Italy, France, and the Netherlands. It had fallen to about 35 percent in Germany and 40 percent in Spain. Although U.S. analysts have often emphasized the "dramatic" fall in the United States, the U.S. decline from 82 percent to 53 percent was modest in comparison to the much more precipitous declines in these European countries. The decline to 57 percent in Sweden was also large, but modest when compared to the fall in other countries. Japan stands out with the smallest

---

1. These projected trends account for projected birth rates, which are slowing in many countries, and in future years will reduce the number of persons in the labor force.

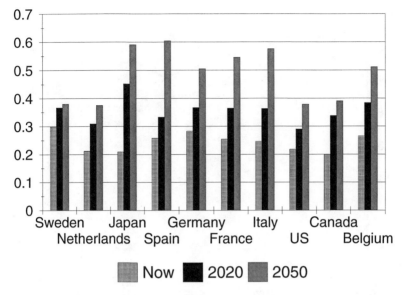

Fig. 2.1   **Ratio of individuals in the population aged sixty-five and up to those aged twenty to sixty-four**

decline of all the countries, from about 83 percent to 75 percent. Labor force participation rates of forty-five- to fifty-nine-year-old men, as well as those of men aged sixty and older, have also declined substantially. Below, we will emphasize that these declines in labor force participation can be attributed in large part to the provisions of the social security systems themselves.

In many countries, the aging population and early retirement trends come on top of very generous retirement benefits, further compounding the financial consequences of these trends. For example, in Belgium, France, Italy, and the Netherlands, the social security replacement rates— the benefit relative to final earnings—at the early retirement age average 77, 91, 75, and 91 percent, respectively. In contrast, the replacement rate at the early retirement age in Canada is only about 20 percent; in the United States it is about 41 percent.

2.1.2   Incentive Effects of Plan Provisions and Early Retirement

A critical feature of many social security systems is the incentive they provide for early retirement. As emphasized above, the financial pressure of aging populations on social security systems is compounded by younger and younger withdrawal from the labor force. Ironically, in many countries social security provisions themselves provide enormous incentive to leave the labor force early, thus by their very structure exacerbating the financial problems they face. Reducing the work penalty alone could improve the

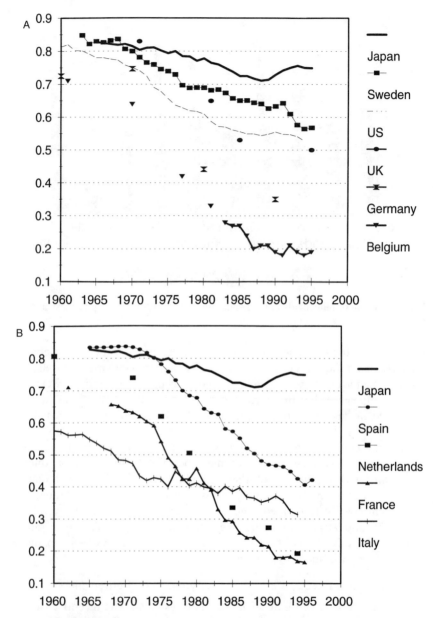

Fig. 2.2 Labor-force participation trends for men aged sixty to sixty-four. Panel A: Japan, Sweden, United States, United Kingdom, Germany, and Belgium; Panel B: Japan, Spain, the Netherlands, France, and Italy
Source: Gruber and Wise (1999b).

financial situation of social security systems in many countries, and we return to this issue in discussion of reform possibilities.

Consider two components of total compensation for working an additional year. One component is current wage earnings. The other component is the increase in future promised social security benefits. Consider a person who has attained the social security early retirement age (the age at which benefits are first available), and suppose that person is considering whether to work for an additional year. It is natural to suppose that if benefit receipt is delayed by a year, benefits when they are received might be increased, to offset the receipt of benefits for one year fewer. In most countries, however, this is not the case. Once benefits are available, a person who continues work for an additional year will receive less in social security benefits over his or her lifetime than if the person quit work and began to receive benefits at the first opportunity. That is, the present value of expected social security benefits declines. In many countries, this loss of social security benefits can offset a large fraction of the wage earnings a person would receive from continued work. Thus there is an implicit tax on work, and total compensation can be much less than net wage earnings.

Data for Germany—summarized in Gruber and Wise (1998, 1999a) and presented in more detail in Börsch-Supan and Schnabel (1999)—illustrate the importance of this "implicit tax on work." These data also illustrate two other important features of social security systems: One is the importance of the age of first eligibility for benefits; the second is that, in many countries, disability and unemployment insurance programs effectively provide early retirement before the explicit social security early retirement age. In considering social security reform, therefore, these programs must be considered in conjunction with the social security program itself.

Before 1972, the social security retirement age in Germany was sixty-five, except in the case of disability, and there was no social security early retirement age. However, legislation in 1972 provided for early retirement at age sixty for women and at age sixty-three for men (given the accumulation of required social security work years). In addition, liberal use of disability and unemployment benefits effectively expanded the early retirement option. In a large fraction of cases, social security early retirement benefits were made available with no reduction in benefits; benefits taken at the early retirement age were the same as those taken at the normal retirement age. This greatly increased the net tax on work because delaying retirement simply reduced the number of years that one could receive benefits, without increasing the annual benefit.

In fact, there was a dramatic response to this increase in retirement incentives. Over the next few years the mean retirement age of white-collar workers was reduced by five and one-half years, as shown in figure 2.3.[2]

2. The mean retirement age is the average age of persons retiring in a given year.

The correspondence between plan provisions and retirement can also be demonstrated by considering the relationship between retirement and social security provisions at a point in time. The detailed provisions of the 1972 legislation are mirrored in the retirement rates by age. Figure 2.4 shows the proportion of men employed at a given age who retire at that age—the *hazard* (or *departure*) rate. The ages of key plan provisions are also noted in the figure so that the correspondence between provisions and retirement is easily seen. Men who are disabled or unemployed at age sixty, and who have a certain number of years of employment under the social security system, are eligible for early retirement at that age. There is a large corresponding jump in the retirement rate at that age. Men who have been employed for thirty-five years are eligible for early retirement at age sixty-three and there is a corresponding jump in the retirement rate at that age. The normal retirement age is sixty-five and there is a corresponding spike at that age as well. By age sixty-five, however, fewer than 29 percent of men are still in the labor force. In addition, even before age sixty, liberal inter-pretation of disability and unemployment plan provisions effectively serves to provide early retirement benefits, a situation discussed in more depth later.

Retirement eligibility may not by itself induce retirement, however. In Germany, a high price is paid for not retiring if eligible. Consider, for ex-ample, the prospects faced by a man with median earnings whose wife is three years younger than he is. He—like 40 percent of older German

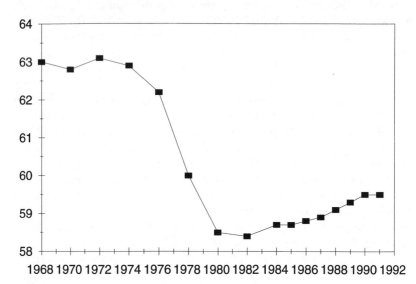

Fig. 2.3   Mean retirement age in Germany
Source: Gruber and Wise (1999b).

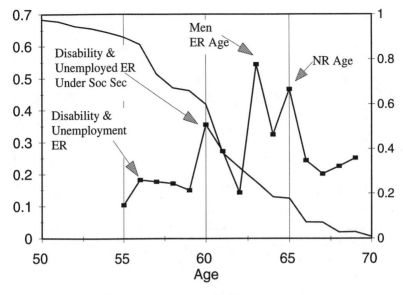

Fig. 2.4   Hazard and labor force participation rates for Germany
Source: Gruber and Wise (1999b).

workers—would be eligible for disability benefits were he to leave the labor force. Suppose he could retire at age sixty but was considering postponing retirement until age sixty-five. The receipt of benefits for five fewer years would not be offset by larger benefits. Indeed, the present value of benefits if taken at sixty-five would be much less than the present value of benefits if taken at sixty; that is, the social security accrual rate is negative. If retirement were postponed by five years, the present value of the benefits would fall by almost 18 percent. Delaying retirement from sixty to sixty-one would reduce the present value of future social security benefits by more than 4 percent. This large negative accrual rate implies a substantial tax on additional work. The 4 percent reduction in benefits from delaying retirement until age sixty-one is equivalent to a tax of roughly 35 percent of the net wage earnings from working an additional year. This represents an enormous disincentive to continued work, in addition to the already high earnings tax.

The tax rates on earnings for each additional year in the labor force from age fifty-five to age seventy are shown in figure 2.5. It is clear that the cost of postponing retirement is substantial; a large fraction of what would be gained in wage earnings if the person worked between sixty and sixty-five, for example, is lost by way of reduced pension benefits. Thus a large fraction of employees retire as soon as they are eligible.

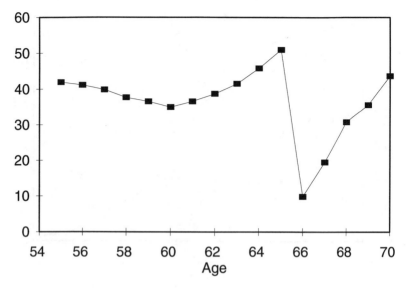

Fig. 2.5   Tax rates on work in Germany
Source: Gruber and Wise (1999b).

The net effect on labor force participation is illustrated by figure 2.6, which describes the labor force status of men by age.[3] Retirement under the social security plan begins at age sixty and labor force participation declines rapidly thereafter; by age sixty-five virtually all men are retired under the social security retirement system.

This figure also provides an illustration of the interaction of the social security system and other programs. The labor force participation of men begins to fall well before the social security early retirement age. Indeed, at age fifty-nine—just before the social security early retirement age— only about 50 percent of male employees are still in the labor force. The fall coincides with the increase in the proportion of men who are receiving unemployment benefits and the proportion receiving disability benefits. These programs, in effect, provide retirement benefits before the social security early retirement age. At age sixty, most of those who had been receiving unemployment, and many of those receiving disability benefits, switch to receiving social security benefits instead. At age sixty-five, all of those who had been receiving disability benefits switch to social security.

Gruber and Wise (1999a,b) show that there is a striking correspondence between the implicit tax on work and the proportion of older persons who

---

3. Note that the labor force participation figures here do not correspond exactly to the hazard rates shown earlier. The labor force status estimates are based on a nationally representative microdata survey, whereas the hazard rate estimates are from administrative data on pension receipts.

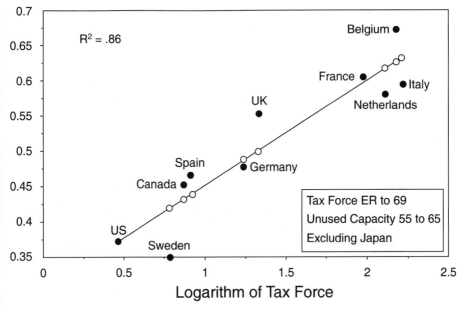

Fig. 2.6   Status of men by age in Germany
Source: Gruber and Wise (1999b).

have left the labor force. Figure 2.7 shows the relationship between the (logarithm of the) "tax force" to retire (the summation of annual implicit tax on work from the early retirement age to age sixty-nine) and "unused capacity" (the proportion of men aged fifty-five to sixty-five who are out of the labor force) in several countries. The correspondence between these two measures is striking: The variation in the tax force across countries can explain more than 80 percent of the variation in unused capacity. Although there may be other factors correlated with the tax force that are also driving work decisions at older ages, this enormous correspondence, taken together with case studies for Germany and other countries in Gruber and Wise (1999b), suggests strongly that social security incentives are an important determinant of work decisions.

2.1.3   Saving, Return, and Risk Features of the PAYGO System

A simple representation of the relationship between tax receipts and benefits in the PAYGO system will help emphasize the importance of the population and labor force trends and will also highlight other features of the PAYGO system. The relationship can be represented by

(Number in the Labor Force) · (Average Wage) · (Tax Rate)
= (Number of Retirees) · (Benefit per Retiree).

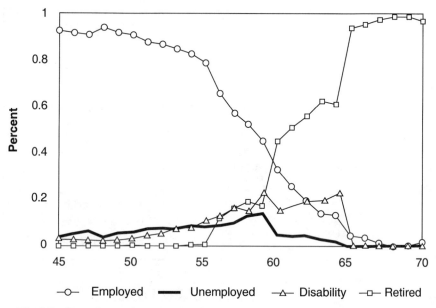

Fig. 2.7   Unused capacity versus tax force
Source: Gruber and Wise (1999b).

The left side represents tax receipts and the right side represents benefits paid. An aging population increases the number of retirees. Early departure from the labor force further increases the number of retirees and reduces the number of persons in the labor force. If receipts are to equal benefits, the tax rate is given by

$$\text{Tax Rate} = \left(\frac{\text{Number of Retirees}}{\text{Number in the Labor Force}}\right) \cdot \left(\frac{\text{Benefit}}{\text{Wage Rate}}\right)$$
$$= (\text{Dependency Ratio}) \cdot (\text{Replacement Rate}).$$

Thus, the larger the replacement rate, the greater the increase in the tax rate required to balance tax receipts and benefits paid when the dependency ratio increases. Both population aging (together with increasing life expectancy) and a declining retirement age increase the dependency ratio. With rapidly increasing dependency ratios, the prospect is for large increases in social security tax rates, unless benefits are changed. To put it another way, balancing the system requires that benefits be given by

$$(\text{Benefit per Retiree}) =$$
$$\left(\frac{\text{Number in the Labor Force}}{\text{Number Retired}}\right) \cdot (\text{Wage Rate}) \cdot (\text{Tax Rate}).$$

Thus, without changes in the tax rate, more retirees relative to persons in the labor force will mean lower benefits.

These relationships make clear additional features of PAYGO systems that are important in considering possible reforms. First, there is no national saving inherent in the PAYGO system, although current workers may think of promised future benefits as though they were personal saving. Unlike with private saving, no money is set aside today that can be invested and used to support consumption after retirement.

A second feature of PAYGO systems useful in evaluating potential reforms is the rate of return on contributions to ("investment" in) the social security system. The implicit rate of return is the rate of growth of the tax base, that is, the rate of growth of gross domestic product (GDP), which in turn is the product of the growth in the labor force times the real increase in the wage rate. To see this, note that current workers contribute an amount given by the left side of the first equality above, and current retirees receive that amount. However, when current workers are retired, they will receive benefits determined by the tax on future labor earnings. In a mature system, each generation of workers gives up a fraction of its earnings in exchange for the same fraction of earnings (hopefully larger) from the next generation. (In the United States, or example, the Social Security Administration now assumes a long-run GDP growth rate of 1.1 percent.) With a rapidly aging population, however, individual realized rates of return may differ substantially from this norm. Indeed, the future tax base may not be large enough to provide the same level of (future) benefits to current workers that today's workers are providing for current retirees.

Third, like other ways of saving for retirement, personal risk is associated with investment in the social security system. Benefits promised now may not in fact be available in the future. Demographic trends such as those emphasized above may be unanticipated, or may be inadequately accounted for in funding projections, and thus stipulated benefits may be incompatible with future population trends. Even in the absence of demographic changes, the vagaries of the political process can change benefits. Changes two or three decades ago typically increased benefits; more recent changes have typically reduced benefits. McHale (2000) shows that recent reform proposals in many Organization for Economic Cooperation and Development (OECD) countries will substantially reduce the benefits of future retirees in those countries. As explained in Wise (2000), true risk is likely to be greater than McHale's calculations demonstrate.

2.2 Reform

There is growing realization around the world that to avoid financial crisis, social security systems must be changed. How to change the systems, however, has been the subject of considerable debate in many countries. Here we consider different ways that the systems might be reformed, commenting on the economic implications of each. The goals of reform depend in part on the current circumstances in each country and in part on the individual preferences of political and economic leaders, or on the weight they place on specific goals. The following are a few prominent economic goals:

1. To correct the financial imbalance faced by social security systems. This is a goal shared by all reform proposals.
2. To increase national saving.
3. To increase the economic efficiency of the systems. Perhaps the most important inefficiency in current systems is the implicit penalty on work inherent in plan provisions.
4. To redistribute income, or to maintain income redistribution. This is an important goal in some countries but is much less important in others. Redistribution is a prominent feature of the U.S. system,[4] for example, but not of the German system.

The central economic goal might be put this way: It seems inevitable that the young will have to consume less than they otherwise would to save for their own retirement while at the same time paying the benefits of current retirees. What is the least painful way—the way that requires the least reduction in consumption—to accomplish this goal? With this general focus in mind, we consider three categories of reform: (1) removing the work penalty, (2) incremental reform, and (3) fundamental reform.

Removing the provisions that encourage early retirement could be considered either a specific reform or an important aspect of other reforms. We treat it separately. Incremental proposals, under our categorization, do not change the basic structure of the PAYGO system, but address the financial imbalance of the system by some combination of increased taxes and reduced benefits. Fundamental reform includes various proposals that would change the basic structure of the social security system. Proposals of this type typically involve at least some prefunding of the system, usually through the creation of personal accounts or through government purchase of financial assets on the part of the social security system.

2.2.1 Removing the Work Penalty

The early retirement incentives discussed above are implicit in the plan provisions that determine benefits. The key question is whether the increase in benefits if retirement is delayed is large enough to offset the loss in foregone benefits when their receipt is postponed. Reducing the penalty on continued work at older ages could substantially improve the long-run fiscal balance of social security systems in many countries. This aspect of social security provisions can be important under all reform proposals that maintain a defined benefit component. These incentive effects are largely

---

4. Liebman (2002), however, shows that features such as spousal benefits and differential mortality offset some of the redistribution implicit in the basic formula and lead to a wide range of rates of return for persons at any given level of lifetime earnings.

eliminated automatically through conversion to a defined contribution system, but may still be present to some extent if benefits are in the form of forced annuitization.[5]

The most important determinant of the tax on work is the early retirement reduction factor—the reduction in benefits if they are taken before the normal retirement age. At one extreme are systems, such as Germany's, in which early retirement (or disability or unemployment) benefits at age sixty are essentially the same as normal retirement benefits at sixty-five.[6] For those who are eligible for benefits at age sixty, there is a strong incentive to retire at sixty. A person who works for an additional year will receive no increase in subsequent benefits to offset the receipt of benefits for one year fewer. Because there is no early retirement reduction, there is also no increase in benefits if their receipt is delayed beyond the early retirement age. Thus the present discounted value of future social security benefits declines.

On the other hand, consider a system such as that in the United States: Benefits at the early retirement age of sixty-two are only 80 percent of benefits at the normal retirement age of sixty-five. In fact, the early retirement reduction is "actuarially fair"; that is, the present discounted value of benefits begun at the early retirement age is roughly equal to the present discounted value of benefits begun at the normal retirement age, or at any age in between. There is no incentive to retire early.

If one moved from a system like that in Germany to one with an actuarially fair early retirement reduction, the fiscal imbalance in the social security system would be improved in two ways: First, benefits for persons who continued to take them before the normal retirement age would be lower. Second, to the extent that persons would work longer—and the Gruber and Wise (1999b) analysis shows that they certainly would in many countries—social security tax receipts would be increased. Or, in terms of the equalities above, the dependency ratio is reduced, social security benefits are reduced, and social security tax receipts are increased. Moreover, by removing the large work penalty, actuarial reduction in early retirement benefits would yield clear gains in economic efficiency.

Many variants might remove the work penalty but do little to improve the financial imbalance of social security systems. For example, early retirement benefits could be maintained and normal retirement benefits in-

5. The reason that even a defined contribution system may have some work disincentives is that there may be forced annuitization of benefit payouts at some common rate. Forced annuitization would imply that the short-lived face lower return on their contributions, and the long-lived a higher rate of return, relative to a system without forced annuitization. This could in turn imply that social security is imposing a tax or a subsidy on work at all ages, including those ages near retirement, providing a small disincentive or incentive to additional work.

6. The German illustrations used in this paper are based on legislation under which most recent retirees left the labor force. Recent legislative changes have changed some provisions, including the early retirement reduction.

creased; or, early benefits could be reduced somewhat and normal benefits increased somewhat. Such reforms would have uncertain financial implications. On the one hand, individuals would work longer, as the evidence in Gruber and Wise (1999b) shows. On the other hand, benefits would be increased for some groups and perhaps lowered for others.

Similar incentives pertain to work beyond the normal retirement age. In this case as well, benefits often are not increased enough to offset their receipt for fewer years when retirement is delayed. That is, the benefit increase is not actuarially fair. This is currently the case in the United States, for example (although this deficiency will be addressed by delayed retirement increases that will be phased in by 2008). In this case there are two effects on the social security balance sheet: If benefits are increased when retirement is delayed, the increase in labor supply will reduce the dependency ratio, thus reducing the system financial imbalance. Benefits for those who delay, however, retirement will be higher. The net fiscal implications for the social security system depend on whether the additional work raises the receipt of social security taxes enough to offset the increase in benefits for those who work longer. However, just like the effect of removing the penalty on work after the early retirement age, economic efficiency is improved by removing the implicit tax on work beyond the normal retirement age. Older workers are free to choose the retirement age most beneficial to them.[7]

2.2.2   Incremental Reform

As emphasized above, actuarial reduction of early retirement benefits would eliminate the work penalty and reduce the financial liability of the social security systems in many countries, without changing the early or normal retirement ages. Suppose that the early retirement benefit reduction (as well as the delayed retirement benefit increase) are actuarially fair. Incremental reforms can reduce the system liability: Benefits can be reduced or tax receipts can be increased. We first consider reduction in benefits.

Reducing Benefits

Social security systems can be brought into financial balance by reducing benefits. In principle, all benefits could simply be cut by a given amount. In practice, however, most reform proposals are much less incisive, for several reasons: to reduce the transparency of reductions, perhaps increasing the political feasibility of reform; to use the reform to change

---

7. It is perhaps worth noting that a smaller step to reducing the work penalty is to allow recomputation of benefits to reflect possible higher earnings past the early retirement age. This is a feature of the U.S. system, for example, but not of most European systems. Earning at later ages is typically higher than at younger ages. In the United States, benefits are based on the thirty-five highest earning-years, so that additional work may mean higher average earning and thus higher benefits. Adding such a feature would also increase the return to work, and thereby increase work at older ages and reduce the dependency ratio.

the redistribution or incentive features of the system; or to assure that those most reliant on benefits are shielded from cuts.

Increase the Normal Retirement Age. Perhaps the most commonly proposed way to reduce benefits is to increase the normal retirement age. For example, the normal retirement age might be raised from sixty-five to sixty-seven (which is one of the currently planned revisions in the U.S. social security system, for example). In this case, benefits now available at age sixty-five would not be available until sixty-seven. Assuming that early retirement benefits are reduced actuarially, benefits at any age would be lower than they were. Thus, the increase in the normal retirement age is equivalent to a reduction in benefits with the normal retirement age left unchanged. In addition, the reduction in benefits is likely to induce later retirement: To maintain a given standard of living after retirement, a person would have to work longer. In this case, the dependency ratio would be reduced and tax receipts would be increased, assuming actuarial reduction in benefits.[8]

Increase the Early Retirement Age. It is clear from Gruber and Wise (1999a,b) that an increase in the early retirement age would delay the retirement of most individuals who now leave the labor force at the early retirement age. An increase in the early retirement age, from (for example) sixty to sixty-two, would delay receipt of benefits, but the present value of benefits would not change—assuming actuarial reduction in early retirement benefits. Because labor force participation would be prolonged, however, social security tax receipts would be increased.

If there were no early retirement benefit reduction, or the reduction were less than actuarially fair, an increase in the early retirement age would necessarily reduce total benefits. In Germany, for example, persons could receive the same annual benefit, but could not begin to receive benefits until age sixty-two rather than sixty.

Reduce Indexation of Benefits. Benefits are typically based on past wages, although not necessarily on lifetime wages. In most cases, past wages are used to determine benefits at the normal retirement age. Benefits taken at earlier ages are based on the benefits at the normal retirement age. In most countries benefits are indexed to accommodate increases in the cost of living; in the United States, for example, benefits are indexed to a consumer price index (CPI). Another way to reduce benefits is to reduce the

8. The increase in the normal retirement age in the United States, for example, will be accompanied by reduced actuarial adjustments from age sixty-two to sixty-four, put in place to minimize the benefit cut on those aged sixty-two and sixty-three. As a result, Coile and Gruber (2000) find only small net impacts on retirement from such a move, because the reductions in actuarial adjustment reduce the incentive for additional work at the same time that the reduction in benefits increases that incentive.

extent of indexation. Benefit increases might, for example, correspond to CPI increases, less 1 percentage point.

Increase Earning Years. Benefits might also be reduced by changing the formula used to calculate normal retirement benefits. How this might be done depends on the benefit formula. In Italy (before 1993), for example, benefits are based on the five years of earnings just before retirement. In the United States the highest thirty-five years of earnings are used to obtain average lifetime earnings, which are used to determine normal retirement benefits. Benefits can be reduced by increasing the number of years used in this formula. Because the top thirty-five years are used now, earnings in any additional years must necessarily be no greater than the lowest of the currently used thirty-five years. Thus average earnings can be no higher, and would typically be lower, than the current average.

Reduce Indexation of Earnings. Benefits can also be reduced by changing the way that earnings are indexed. In the United States, for example, average indexed monthly earnings are determined by indexing earnings to age sixty-two based on a nominal wage index. The wage index is essentially the sum of productivity gains and price increases, so indexation based on a price index would yield lower average indexed monthly earnings, and thus lower normal retirement benefits.

Increase the Tax on Benefits. Benefits can be reduced by taxing them more heavily. In the United States, for example, the tax on Social Security benefits depends on total income—families with incomes above a given level pay taxes on Social Security benefits. The income level at which Social Security benefits are taxed could be lowered.

Increasing Tax Receipts

Increasing the social security tax rate is a straightforward way to increase receipts. Another way to increase receipts is less direct. Taxes are typically based on wage earnings; but in some countries, such as the United States, earnings are taxed only up to the covered earnings limit. In the United States, this limit has increased substantially over time and continues to increase. If all earnings were taxed, for example, receipts would be increased.[9]

Equivalent to an increase in the social security tax rate is the use of other taxes to pay social security benefits. For example, in the United States there has been considerable discussion of using the budget surplus (which today

---

9. Although the financial implications for the social security system do not depend on the source of the revenue, the choice of tax used may have different efficiency implications for the economy as a whole. For example, raising the earning limit in the United States could lose revenue for the tax system as a whole.

is largely accounted for by a current surplus in the Social Security trust fund, but may be greater in the future) to add to the Social Security trust fund. Using other tax receipts to pay social security benefits is of course a substitute for increasing the social security tax rate. (Although the two approaches are dollar substitutes, they may be very different with respect to who pays the taxes.) Incremental reform proposals may include a combination of several of these methods of increasing taxes and reducing benefits.

2.2.3 Fundamental Reform

In principle, there are at least two ways to change the current PAYGO system fundamentally: prefunding or introducing individual accounts (or both; see table 2.1). The current PAYGO system incorporates neither change. In principle, the social security system could be taken off-budget and treated much like an employer-provided pension fund. Like private pensions funds, a social security fund could be funded in accordance with future expected benefit payments. Benefits could continue to be paid on a defined benefit (DB) basis, much as they are now—this would be a funded DB system. Similarly, as an accounting matter, individual accounts could be established without prefunding. The "amount" in an individual's account could be based entirely on social security taxes paid by or on behalf of that person; such accounts are sometimes called *notional individual accounts.* The most common fundamental reform proposals, however, involve both individual accounts and prefunding. Some approaches would convert the entire system to one of individual accounts and in so doing prefund the entire system. Other proposals would convert part of the system to one based on personal prefunded accounts, leaving some portion to operate as a PAYGO, DB system.

There are two related economic motivations for prefunding social security. One is that the expected rate of return on these accounts would presumably be much larger than the implicit rate of return on contributions to a PAYGO system. For example, the average real rate of return on equities in the United States since 1926 has been about 9 percent. The average real rate of return on a portfolio of 40 percent bonds and 60 percent equities has been about 5.5 percent. (The U.S. Social Security Administration

Table 2.1　　　**Reform Possibilities**

Individual Accounts	Prefunding	
	No	Yes
No	Current pay-as-you-go system	Funded defined-benefit system (increased trust fund balance)
Yes	Notional individual accounts	Individual accounts with defined-contribution component

assumes an implicit Social Security return of 1.1 percent.) This suggests that in the long run the system could be funded—and the same benefits provided—with a lower tax rate, if personal accounts were invested in private financial markets. To put it another way, many countries face the prospect of large tax rate increases to fund current PAYGO systems; the required tax increases would be much smaller if the increased tax revenues were invested in the market.

The second purpose suggested for personal accounts is to increase personal saving. As emphasized above, it seems evident that the young in virtually all countries will have to save more. A strictly PAYGO system involves no saving, unlike (for example) private employer-provided or individual retirement saving plans, which are funded by saving today to pay for future retirement benefits. Below we emphasize that at the outset of the transition to such a system, the increased saving (by the young) is used to pay for their own retirement while at the same time paying for those who are retired or will retire under the PAYGO system.[10]

Prefunding the Entire System: Illustrative Calculations

When considering prefunding of the social security system, the transition from a PAYGO to a funded system is a critical issue and has been the subject of substantial analysis. We begin first with a simple example that illustrates the potential gain after the transition, with a fully mature prefunded system in place. To get a picture of the eventual gain from a prefunded system with personal retirement accounts (or a system that is partially prefunded, with a defined contribution [DC] component), consider this simple example: Assume that individuals work from age twenty-five to sixty-five and live in retirement from age sixty-five to eighty-five. Suppose, to simplify further, that persons contribute to social security at age forty-five and receive benefits at seventy-five. If the gross domestic product (GDP) growth rate is 1.1 percent, $1.00 invested at age forty-five would grow to $(1.01)^{30} = \$1.39$ by age seventy-five. On the other hand, at a certain 9 percent rate of return, $1.00 invested in equities would grow to $(1.09)^{30} = \$13.28$ by age seventy-five. Using these values, $1.00 invested in equities yields 9.56 times as much as the PAYGO system would. Thus, to fund the system with equity investment (assuming this rate of return) would require only one-tenth as much as the PAYGO tax rate. Similar calculations show that to fund the system using a mixed stock-bond portfolio returning (for example) 6 percent would require less than one-fourth of the PAYGO tax rate. Of course, the market rate of return is uncertain; analysis of the potential risk from this uncertainty is discussed below.

In the transition from the current PAYGO system to a prefunded sys-

---

10. Feldstein and Samwick (2000) have proposed that under certain assumptions the transition could take place in the United States without an increase in the Social Security tax rate.

tem, however, current workers must pay both for current retirees and for their own personal accounts. To illustrate the transition to a prefunded system, Feldstein and Samwick (1996b, 1997) simulate a gradual phase-in of a funded system in the United States. Their illustrative personal account system provides the same aggregate benefits as the current system. They assume that persons begin to work at age thirty. The cohort that reaches age thirty in 1995 participates in the PAYGO system and begins to participate in the personal account system. Over the next twenty-five years, each cohort that reaches age twenty-five participates in both, but later cohorts participate only in the personal account component; they cease to accrue PAYGO benefits. They begin with a personal-account tax of 2.00 percent. As successive cohorts retire, increasingly larger fractions of benefits are provided by the personal component. The benefits that the personal-account balances provide replace some of the PAYGO benefits. This in turn permits a smaller PAYGO tax the next year, and so forth.

The stream of combined personal account and PAYGO taxes that would be required between 1995 and 2070 is shown in figure 2.8, along with the taxes that would be required to provide benefits under the current PAYGO system. During the transition period, the combined tax rate declines from 14.40 percent to 2.02 percent. Feldstein and Samwick assume that the current PAYGO tax rate would remain at the present 12.4 percent until the Social Security trust fund is exhausted; thereafter the rate increases to 18.25 percent by 2070, as projected by the Social Security Administration. The figure shows that between 1995 and about 2015, employees will pay more than the current tax rate. This area might be thought of as the cost

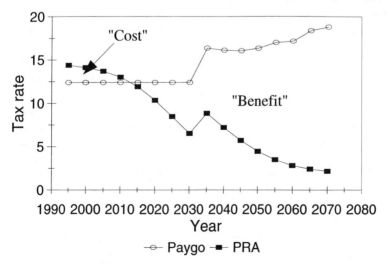

Fig. 2.8   PAYGO versus combined tax rate (by transition year)
Source: Feldstein and Samwick (1996a).

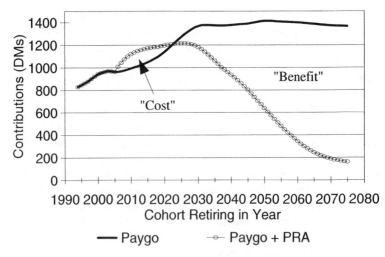

Fig. 2.9   Germany: Contributions (PAYGO versus transition to PRA)
Source: Börsch-Supan (1998).

of the transition to a prefunded system. Thereafter, the tax rate is lower; this area might be thought of as the benefit of the transition. (Whether the benefits outweigh the costs, of course, depends in part on the extent to which one discounts the benefits to future generations compared to the costs of current generations.) Additional discussion of prefunding is presented in Feldstein (1997).

Similar simulations describing the transition to a personal account prefunded system have been made for Germany by Börsch-Supan (1998). The German system is much more generous than the U.S. program and the social security benefits provide more than 80 percent of the preretirement income of retirees. The German population is also aging much more rapidly than the U.S. population. As a result, the unfunded liability of the German system is much greater than that of the U.S. system.

Figure 2.9 shows a transition scenario for German similar to the one above for the United States, but in this case, instead of the tax rate, average individual contributions are compared. The transition begins in the year 2005, when persons who retire (at age sixty, by assumption) will get a PAYGO benefit proportional to the share of their work lives that passed before 2005. The work life is assumed to be forty years; thus, for a person retiring in 2006, 39/40 of the retirement benefit will come from the PAYGO system and 1/40 from the personal account component. A person retiring in 2007 will obtain 38/40 from the PAYGO system and 2/40 from the personal account. From the year 2045 onward no worker will acquire new PAYGO pension rights. The simulated time path of contributions under these assumptions is shown in figure 2.9. A comparison of figures 2.8 and

2.9 shows that the pattern of required contributions (or tax rates) is very similar, reflecting the similar assumptions made in the two analyses. In the United States the ultimate personal account tax rate is about 2 percent compared to the projected PAYGO tax rate of 18.25 percent, a ratio of 0.11. In Germany, the ultimate personal contribution is 163 Deutsche marks under the personal retirement account (PRA) versus 1,368 Deutsche marks under the personal account system, a ratio of 0.12.

We take these calculations for the United States and Germany to be illustrative. Different assumptions would lead to different quantitative results. As long as the return in the market substantially exceeds the PAYGO rate of return, however, the qualitative results would not change. In addition to lower future costs to provide the same benefits, the more transparent relationship between personal account contributions and benefits is likely to dampen the labor supply reduction inherent in redistributive PAYGO systems. These illustrative calculations, however, do not address the importance of uncertain returns in the market; we return to that issue below.

Partial Prefunding and Personal Account Proposals

Several actual proposals combine a DC personal account component with a PAYGO DB component, creating a two-tier system. The contributions to the DC component—Tier 2—could be invested in the market. Some proposals begin by reducing the generosity of the PAYGO system and adding a DC component to it; an alternative is to maintain the current system as it is and add the DC component. We give one example of each, drawn from proposals in the United States. Both are motivated by the realization that future tax rate increases could be replaced by a smaller increase if market-invested personal accounts were introduced.

Among the plans proposed by the Social Security Advisory Council (1997) was a personal security account (PSA). This proposal sets a flat monthly benefit funded by the PAYGO system (Tier 1): $410 for single retirees and $615 for married couples for those with thirty-five years of earnings. These flat rates would be indexed to real wage earnings in the future. To fund the PSA (Tier 2), 5 percent of earnings would be placed in the PSA. The tax rate to support the Tier 1 benefits would be set at 8.92 percent. (Thus, the PAYGO payroll tax rate is reduced from 12.4 to 8.92 percent, and a mandatory 5 percent contribution to the PSA is instituted.) The proposal would be phased in, with gradual adoption of the PSA.[11]

Discussion of social security personal accounts typically refers both to contributions to fund the personal account component, and to taxes to fund the PAYGO component, as *tax rates*. There is a difference between

---

11. The proposal also includes other provisions to reduce benefits and to increase taxes. For example, the normal retirement age would be increased, and the early retirement age would also be increased gradually from sixty-two to sixty-five.

them, however. Perhaps a personal account contribution is better thought of as *forced saving,* if it is mandatory, or *personal saving,* if it is not. On the other hand, the PAYGO tax conforms more closely to a typical tax: It can be used to support a broader social program than the personal account component can.

Schieber and Shoven (1999) have suggested a variant of the PSA plan: lowering the current payroll tax rate to 9.9 percent and introducing a mandatory 5 percent contribution to an individual account. In addition, they set the flat Tier 1 benefit somewhat higher—$450 instead of $410. Feldstein and Samwick (1998a) have also proposed a two-tier system, which takes advantage of the current budget surplus to adopt personal accounts. In addition to the current PAYGO tax, individuals would contribute 2 percent of earnings—up to the U.S. Social Security limit—to a personal account. When benefits are taken, part of the gains from the personal account are offset by a reduction in the Tier 1 (current system) benefits. Their proposal is to guarantee benefits at least equal to those under the current system. The contribution is treated as a cashable income tax credit: if the contribution is greater than the tax bill, the excess is received as a tax refund from the Internal Revenue Service. The contributions are invested in the private market. The benefits from the personal account would be in the form of an indexed life annuity, such as the current U.S. Social Security benefits. However, for every dollar of Tier 2 benefits, Tier 1 benefits would be reduced by 75 cents. Thus the concept is that no one would receive lower benefits under this two-tier system than they do at present, and the government would capture much of the gain from market investment of personal accounts to support the current PAYGO system.

2.2.4 Summary of Economic Implications

We consider first the proposals discussed above. Then we comment on the possibility of investing PAYGO-system contributions in the market.

Proposals Discussed Above

An important feature (and perhaps the most important economic inefficiency) of most current PAYGO, DB social security systems is the work penalty. (As mentioned below, high social security tax rates have more-general labor supply reduction effects, an inefficiency made greater by the departure of older persons from the labor force, which increases the social security taxes on those still working.) The implicit tax on work can be eliminated by changing the benefit formula under the current DB structure. The most important change would be the introduction of an actuarially fair, early retirement benefit reduction. This inefficiency is largely removed under a DC (personal account) system. Indeed, even an unfunded notional account system would largely eliminate this inefficiency.

Removing the implicit tax on work reduces the future burden on the young; it reduces the future reduction in consumption that they will have to incur to pay future social security benefits. Indeed, longer participation in the labor force increases national output as well as national saving. Inducing older workers to leave the labor force—as current systems do—increases the tax on the young (workers) and may in fact induce them to work less, further reducing national output.

It is worth pausing to emphasize that *economies are not boxed.* Numerous anecdotal comments suggest that provisions to induce older workers to retire were introduced to make room for younger workers to enter the labor force. We have not, however, attempted to determine whether there is convincing evidence that this was in fact the motivation for current provisions. Regardless of whether the claim is true, reducing economic output by reducing the labor supply of older workers can only make the financial problems of social security systems worse. Economies grow and can absorb increasingly larger numbers of workers. Reducing the labor supply of older workers can only reduce economic output in the long run.

Incremental reforms—to reduce benefits and increase social security taxes—can alleviate the financial imbalance of the PAYGO system, but will do little to increase national saving. In addition, incremental reforms may be only a temporary fix, with the systems as open to future financial crises as the current ones are. On the other hand, redistribution is an important feature of some social security systems. A key feature of the U.S. system, for example, is that relatively higher benefits are given to persons with low lifetime earnings. Incremental reform maintains this redistribution.

Fundamental reform proposals, with a DB personal account component, would likely increase personal saving. Poterba, Venti, and Wise, in fact, have written a series of papers on the saving effects of 401(k) and individual retirement account (IRA) plans in the United States and find that the vast majority of contributions represent net new saving. Although some difference of opinion continues, we believe the weight of evidence heavily supports their conclusion, which they summarize in Poterba, Venti, and Wise (1998c). This evidence suggests that social security personal accounts would likely not substitute much for personal saving either. (Indeed, a large fraction of persons who would be covered by such accounts in the United States have no personal saving to reduce.)

In addition, funds in personal accounts are less likely than funds in a government trust fund to be offset by increases elsewhere in the government budget, and national saving would be increased as well. During the transition period, the new saving funds the transition. In a mature system, the PSA saving is used to provide individual retirement benefits. In addition, investment in the equity market would yield greater expected asset accumulation at retirement than the accumulation under the implicit return on current social security contributions. The expected cost of providing given benefits would be smaller—thus, the expected future financial burden on the young would be reduced.

There are two principle concerns about such plans: One is that the redistribution that is an important part of some PAYGO systems may not be maintained. The other is that the risk associated with market investments could reduce the benefits of some participants, compared to current PAYGO DB systems.

A good deal of conceptual and empirical work has been directed to these interrelated issues in the United States. In most cases the empirical evaluations and proposals consider the likelihood of maintaining benefits greater than those provided under the current system. Feldstein, Ranguelova, and Samwick (2001) show that for a typical person with average earnings, a personal account system with a 6 percent contribution rate would stand a very high chance of providing benefits higher than those provided by the current U.S. system. They show that this would also be true for the typical wage earner under a mixed system with a personal account system (with a 2.3 percent saving rate) on top of the current system.

Perhaps more relevant are the calculations that Feldstein and Liebman (2002) make for a representative sample of social security participants with essentially the full range of family status and earnings histories. They show that under a pure personal account system with a 9 percent contribution rate and historical rates of market return (5.5 percent), 94 percent of participants would have higher benefits than those provided by a 15.4 percent contribution rate to the current PAYGO system.[12] Qualitatively similar results are obtained under a politically more realistic system that maintains the current PAYGO tax rate, combined with a supplemental 3 percent contribution rate to a personal account. Even so, the relative increase of benefits would be greater for those with the highest earnings, and those with lower earnings would be more likely to receive lower benefits. Feldstein and Liebman then show that the Supplemental Security Income program puts a lower floor on benefits such that virtually no participants would receive benefits lower than those provided by the two programs together, and that, through government "redistributive" contributions to personal accounts, the mixed system can achieve the same level of progressiveness as the current system. They also show that under very low rates of return, based on historical standards, very few participants would receive benefits much lower than those provided by the current system.

The two proposed programs discussed above also rely on a benefit floor to maintain benefits at least as great as under the current system. Feldstein and Samwick (1998c) do this by explicitly guaranteeing benefits equal to those under the current PAYGO system. The Schieber and Shoven (1999) plan sets a floor on benefits, to be funded by a PAYGO DB system, but does not guarantee benefits above the floor. Schieber and Shoven show, however, that under historical rates of return a 5 percent contribution to a personal account would be very unlikely to lead to lower benefits than

12. This is the required tax rate projected by the Social Security Administration to fund Old Age Survivors Insurance (OASI) benefits for persons retiring in 2075.

under the current system. As emphasized above, in considering risk, it is important to keep in mind that current PAYGO systems present substantial individual risk as well.

The administrative cost of managing personal accounts could also be an important constraint on realized market returns. There has been a good deal of debate about this issue in the United States. Much of the available evidence is presented in Shoven (2000). Our evaluation of this evidence suggests that administrative costs are nontrivial, but would not be nearly large enough to offset the difference between market returns and the implicit return on Social Security contributions in the United States.

Trust-Fund Market Investment

An alternative to individual accounts is to invest social security contributions—under the DB system—in the market, much as is done with private pension fund contributions. (For example, such a proposal was for some time part of President Clinton's plan for the United States.) The hope is that the greater return from market investment of the trust fund would allow the system to meet future obligations with smaller tax rate increases than would otherwise be required.

In principle, such a plan could allow future liabilities to be met without increasing the social security tax rate, or without forcing the young to save more through personal accounts. In particular, it aims to avoid the transition cost of prefunding. It also would minimize administrative costs, which will presumably be considerably larger for a large number of small personal accounts.

Such proposals also try to address the difficult political trade-offs between individual control and government "protection." Consider annuitization. One motivation for social security is that individuals, left to their own ends, may not save enough for their old age, which also suggests paying benefits in the form of an annuity rather than as a lump sum. For perhaps similar reasons, personal account proposals also suggest annuitization of assets at retirement. This, of course, takes some control away from the individual, limiting the extent to which these accounts are strictly "personal." Similarly, typical personal account proposals have in mind that some limits would be placed on personal account investments. Investment of the trust fund in equities avoids these tensions.

Compared to personal accounts, however, this approach also presents important limitations. One is that it does nothing to increase national saving. Although such a scheme would likely increase the return on social security contributions, it would increase national saving for retirement only if resources that would otherwise be consumed are added to the trust fund—and retained in the fund until they are paid out as benefits. Otherwise, simply investing existing trust fund assets in the market would only induce asset swapping between the private sector and the social security trust fund, and would achieve no incremental saving. Unlike personal accounts, this proposal does not increase the saving that is set aside by today's workers to pay for future retirement benefits. That is, by trying to avoid the pain of increased saving—which might include the transition cost to a funded system—it also forgoes the gain.

A second important limitation of such a system is political intrusion. With investment of contributions in the market, the government could ultimately control an important fraction of the private capital market, providing an opening for politically motivated investment decisions. Additionally, with the accumulations kept in a trust fund rather than in personal accounts, there is significant risk that the trust fund would be "raided" during periods of future government deficit. That is, given the inherent difficulty that politicians have with leaving surpluses untouched, investing the trust fund could simply increase the amount of money they might be tempted to spend. Funds in personal accounts are further removed from the control of politicians and therefore less likely to be raided in times of budget pressures. In theory, of course, independent institutions (such as the Federal Reserve Board in the United States) might be established to deal with such problems. In practice, however, the effectiveness of this insulation is questionable, particularly in countries without a strong history of independent central banks.

2.2.5   Other Retirement Support

In many countries the social security system is the principle source of retirement benefits. In other countries the social security system is only one of the important sources of retirement support. In the United Kingdom and the Netherlands, for example, employer-provided pension plans are a key source of benefits. The same is true in the United States. In these countries, some retirees receive defined benefits in the form of annuities from employers as well as from the social security system. Indeed, in some countries—such as the United States—the employer-provided benefits are often integrated with social security benefits. The incentive effects of these private DB plans are very similar to those described above for social security programs, as shown by Kotlikoff and Wise (1988, 1989). Stock and Wise (1990a,b) Lumsdaine, Stock, and Wise (1990, 1991, 1992, 1994), and Wise 1997show that the effects on retirement are very similar as well. Indeed, Lumsdaine, Stock, and Wise (1997) show that social security and employer-provided DB systems may interact in important ways. Thus it may be important to consider public and private plans jointly.

The most dramatic change in retirement saving in the United States is the conversion to individual retirement saving plans (IRAs, 401[k] plans, and other), which are essentially the same as a voluntary version of personal social security accounts. Individuals must decide how much to contribute to the accounts, how to invest the contributions, and how to withdraw funds after retirement. In 1980, almost 92 percent of pension plan contributions were to traditional employer-provided plans, and about 64 percent of these contributions were to conventional DB plans. Today, almost 60 percent of contributions are to personal retirement accounts, including 401(k), IRA, and other plans. Including employer-provided (non-401[k]) DC plans, more than 76 percent of contributions are to plans controlled in large measure by individuals. Poterba, Venti, and Wise (1998a, b, 1999, 2000) show that for persons retiring three decades from now, personal assets in 401(k) plans alone are likely to be substantially greater than social security plan wealth. It is perhaps not an exaggeration to say that the personal control of retirement saving is progressing more quickly than any resolution of the debate about social security personal accounts. Universal 401(k) coverage would indeed look much like a social security system with personal accounts. The rapid spread of private personal accounts should inform and affect the discussion of social security personal accounts. A large fraction of employees already are used to and know a great deal about such accounts. In addition, the evidence on the saving effect of personal retirement accounts in the United States has been summarized by Poterba, Venti, and Wise (1998c) and shows that the vast majority of contributions to these accounts represents net new saving.[13] It is likely that personal social security accounts would have a similar saving effect.

2.2.6 Political Constraints on Action

Although social security reform has occurred in many countries—Chile and Mexico, for example—the political process in many countries makes reform extremely difficult. Although this is not the place to consider in detail the enormous importance and complexity of this issue, it seems important to at least highlight it. Political action seems difficult no matter how large the problem or how imminent the crisis. Although many proposals have been made by economists or legislators with varying political views, no reform is likely in the near future. In particular, no party wants to take the risk of proposing reduced benefits. In many European countries, where the financial crisis is much greater than in the United States, reform seems at least as difficult to obtain and perhaps no nearer to taking place. Here we have given little attention to this important matter, concentrating instead on potential reforms and their economic consequences.

References

Börsch-Supan, Axel. 1998. Germany: A social security system on the verge of collapse. In *Redesigning social security,* ed. Horst Siebert, 129–59. Tübingen, Germany: Mohr.

---

13. The referenced paper summarizes the results of a long series of papers on this issue. Others have put forth a different view, but we believe that the weight of the evidence supports the view expressed in this summary.

Börsch-Supan, Axel, and Reinhold Schnabel. 1999. Social security and retirement in Germany. In *Social security programs and retirement around the world,* ed. Jonathan Gruber and David A. Wise, 135–80. Chicago: University of Chicago Press.

Coile, Courtney, and Jonathan Gruber. 2000. Social Security incentives for retirement. NBER Working Paper no. 7651. Cambridge, Mass.: National Bureau of Economic Research, April.

Feldstein, Martin. 1997. Transition to a fully funded pension system: Five economic issues. NBER Working Paper no. 6149. Cambridge, Mass.: National Bureau of Economic Research, August.

Feldstein, Martin, and Jeffrey Liebman. 2002. The distributional effects of an investment-based social security system. Chicago: University of Chicago Press (forthcoming).

Feldstein, Martin, Elena Ranguelova, and Andrew Samwick. 2001. The transition to investment-based social security when portfolio returns and capital profitability are uncertain. In *Risk aspects of investment-based social security pension,* ed. John Campbell and Martin Feldstein. Chicago: University of Chicago Press (forthcoming).

Feldstein, Martin, and Andrew A. Samwick. 1996. The transition path in privatizing Social Security. NBER Working Paper no. 5761. Cambridge, Mass.: National Bureau of Economic Research.

———1997. The economics of prefunding Social Security and Medicare benefits. *NBER Macroeconomics Annual 1997,* 115–48. Cambridge, Mass.: MIT Press.

———. 1998a. Potential effects of two percent personal retirement accounts. *Tax Notes* 79 (5).

———. 1998b. The transition path in privatizing Social Security. In *Privatizing social security,* ed. Martin Feldstein, Chicago: University of Chicago Press.

———. 1998c. Two percent personal retirement accounts: Their potential effects on Social Security tax rates and national saving. NBER Working Paper no. 6540. Cambridge, Mass.: National Bureau of Economic Research, April.

———. 2000. Allocating payroll tax revenue to personal retirement accounts to maintain Social Security benefits and the payroll tax rate. Mimeograph.

Gruber, Jonathan, and David A. Wise. 1998. Social security and retirement: An international comparison. *American Economic Review, Papers and Proceedings* 88(2): 158–63.

———. 1999a. Introduction and summary. In *Social security programs and retirement around the world,* ed. Jonathan Gruber and David A. Wise. Chicago: University of Chicago Press.

———. 1999b. *Social security programs and retirement around the world.* Chicago: University of Chicago Press.

Kotlikoff, Laurence J., and David A. Wise. 1988. Pension backloading, wage taxes, and work disincentives. In *Tax policy and the economy,* vol. 2, ed. L. Summers, 161–96. Cambridge, Mass.: MIT Press.

———. 1989. *The wage carrot and the pension stick: Retirement benefits and labor force participation.* Kalamazoo, Mich.: W. E. Upjohn Institute for Employment Research.

Liebman, Jeffrey B. 2002. Redistribution in the current U.S. Social Security system. Forthcoming in *The distributional aspects of Social Security and Social Security reform,* ed. Martin Feldstein and Jeffrey Liebman. Chicago: Univerity of Chicago Press.

Lumsdaine, Robin, James Stock, and David Wise. 1990. Efficient windows and labor force reduction. *Journal of Public Economics* 43:131–59.

————. 1991. "Fenêtres et Retraites" (Windows and retirement). *Annales d'Economie et de Statistique* (20/21):219–42.

————. 1992. Three models of retirement: Computational complexity versus predictive validity. In *Topics in the economics of aging,* ed. David Wise, 19–60. Chicago: University of Chicago Press.

————. 1994. Pension plan provisions and retirement: Men and women, Medicare, and models. In *Studies in the economics of aging,* ed. David Wise, 183–222. Chicago: University of Chicago Press.

————. 1997. Retirement incentives: The interaction between employer-provided pension plans, social security, and retiree health benefits. In *The economic effects of aging in the United States and Japan.* ed. M. Hurd and N. Yashiro, 261–93. Chicago: University of Chicago Press.

McHale, John. 2000. The risk of social security benefit rule changes: Some international evidence. In *Risk aspects of investment-based social security pension,* ed. John Campbell and Martin Feldstein. Chicago: University of Chicago Press.

Poterba, James, Steven Venti, and David Wise. 1998a. 401(k) plans and future patterns of retirement saving. *American Economic Review, Papers and Proceedings* 90 (May): 297–302.

————. 1998b. Implications of rising personal retirement saving. In *Frontiers in the economics of aging,* ed. David A. Wise, 125–72. Chicago: University of Chicago Press.

————. 1998c. Personal retirement savings programs and asset accumulation: Reconciling the evidence. In *Frontiers in the economics of aging,* ed. David A. Wise, 123–24. Chicago: University of Chicago Press.

————. 1999. Pre-retirement cashouts and foregone retirement saving: Implications for 401(k) asset accumulation. NBER Working Paper no. 7314. Forthcoming in David A. Wise (ed.) *Perspectives in the Economics of Aging.* Chicago: University of Chicago Press.

————. 2000. Saver behavior and 401(k) retirement wealth. *American Economic Review Papers and Proceedings* 90 (2): 297-302.

Samwick, Andrew A. 1996. Tax shelters and passive losses after the Tax Reform Act of 1986. In *Empirical foundations of household taxation,* ed. M. Feldstein and J. Poterba, 193–226. Chicago: University of Chicago Press.

Schieber, Sylvester J., and John B. Shoven. 1999. *The real deal: The history and future of social security.* New Haven: Yale University Press.

Shoven, John B. 2000. The Personal Security Account 2000 plan, market outcomes, and risk. In *Themes in the economics of aging,* ed. David A. Wise, 59–90. Chicago: University of Chicago Press.

Social Security Advisory Council. 1997. *Report of the 1994–96 Advisory Council on Social Security. Vol. I: Findings and recommendations.* Washington D.C.: GPO.

Stock, James, and David Wise. 1990a. The pension inducement to retire: An option value analysis. In *Issues in the economics of aging,* ed. D. Wise, 205–29 Chicago: University of Chicago Press.

————. 1990b. Pensions, the option value of work, and retirement. *Econometrica* 58 (5):1151–80.

Wise, David A. 1997. Retirement against the demographic trend: More older people living longer, working less, and saving less. *Demography* 34 (1) 83–95.

————. 2000. Comment on "The risk of social security benefit-rule changes: Some international evidence." In *Risk aspects of investment-based social security pension,* ed. J. Campbell and M. Feldstein, 282–87. Chicago: University of Chicago Press.

Comment   Herbert Hax

Gruber and Wise present a clear and comprehensive analysis of the fundamental problems many pension systems face today, and of the political obstacles to farsighted reforms. In particular, they have worked out the two decisive shortcomings of a pay-as-you-go (PAYGO) system of the type practiced in Germany. The first is that such systems are highly sensitive to changes of the *dependency ratio* (number of retirees to number of participants in labor force); this problem is aggravated by the second weakness, the inherent incentive for early retirement.

In this case we are discussing pension systems with mandatory membership. At the risk of stating the obvious, I wish to make clear at the outset why mandatory membership in a pension system is regarded as necessary. The first and most convincing reason is that in a modern society no one is left to starve; everyone is guaranteed a certain subsistence level through public welfare. This concept is connected with moral hazard; individuals with low income in particular might neglect saving for old age and rely solely on welfare payments. A second reason may be that the pension system is used as an instrument of redistribution—for instance, by financing pensions of those with lower incomes in part through higher contributions of the more wealthy. The German system of redistribution favors families with children. A third reason may be that a PAYGO system is not viable without mandatory membership, although this is more an argument against PAYGO systems than one in favor of mandatory membership.

I will not discuss here whether the pension system is a suitable means for redistributing wealth, which is regarded as desirable. One of the reform models currently being discussed in Germany provides a high degree of redistribution by granting equal pensions to everyone, financed by taxes based on income; an advantage of this system is that it offers a solution for the moral hazard problem with a minimum of mandatory contributions. The present system in Germany is less redistributive insofar as pensions depend in some way on the contributions paid by retirees during their working lives.

Under certain circumstances, redistribution may have undesirable incentive effects, but in principle we should accept redistribution so far as it is explicitly wanted and is justified by a political value judgment. However, it seems that many people are unaware that some pension systems have unwanted distribution effects that are not based on any recognized value judgment; these intergenerational distribution effects are inevitably connected with a PAYGO system. In a stationary world in which the dependency rate and productivity are constant, each generation would during its working years pay, in form of contributions, the exact amount of pension

Herbert Hax is professor emeritus at Cologne University and is currently professor of business studies at the University of Vienna.

payments they would later receive; the rate of return would be zero. Because many relevant parameters change over the course of time, however, some generations may have high returns and others low or even negative ones. This not only is an offense to fairness, but may also have a negative effect on the political acceptance of the system when members of a generation feel that they are treated unfairly. This is why pension systems in several countries, including Germany, are facing a grave crisis.

Unwanted intergenerational distribution effects can be avoided only in a funded system. A pension system may be called *funded* if the implicit debt resulting from accrued pension claims is covered by a capital stock. A system may be fully or partially funded depending on the degree of coverage. A fully funded system is not necessarily actuarially fair. It may provide redistribution within each generation, even in the form of income-dependent contributions and equal pensions; it can, however, reliably preclude any unfair distortion of wealth among generations. In principle this is also possible in a partially funded system, to the degree that shifts in wealth from one generation to another can be avoided by fluctuations of the fund corresponding to fluctuations of implicit debt. In a partially funded system, however, the degree to which implicit debt is covered will always be arbitrary, and discretionary interventions from the side of short-term–oriented politicians cannot be ruled out.

To summarize my comments thus far, I add that, quite apart from other advantages of funded systems (such as positive effects on saving and capital formation), they have the merit of establishing fair intergenerational distribution and thereby safeguarding the pension system against potentially destructive stress.

Gruber and Wise refer to political constraints that, although reforms have been recognized as necessary and urgent, often stand in their way. To illustrate this, I will give some comments on the situation in Germany.

As Gruber and Wise point out, a grave default of the German system is that it provides false incentives for early retirement by penalizing continued work. It may seem paradoxical, but the widespread political opinion in Germany is that incentives for older workers to retire at younger ages are not wrong at all. The argument behind this opinion is that high unemployment in Germany is due to a shortage of jobs and that the adequate cure can only be a reduction of labor supply. More precisely, there are two related arguments:

- Because jobs are disposable only in a limited number, they should be distributed more evenly among applicants, which can be brought about by reducing individual working time (weekly or yearly working hours) as well as the working period during lifetime.
- Because older people are much more frequently affected by unemployment than younger people, early retirement may be preferable to (and, for the society as a whole, no more costly than) unemployment.

It is easy to detect the flaws in this kind of argument. The demand for labor is mistakenly regarded as constant, and one grave consequence is that policy measures to enhance labor demand—including legal reforms to provide more flexibility in the labor market—are neglected. Furthermore, the incentive to retire at an earlier age is established not only for those who would be unemployed in any case, but also for others: the still large majority of those who have jobs. This results in a waste of human capital, and may even have an adverse effect on employment if employees with special qualifications, who are not easily replaced, choose early retirement.

We should not deny that unemployment among older workers is a serious problem and cause for increasing concern. The main reason seems to be the accelerating process of technological and economic innovation, which goes along with more rapid obsolescence of human capital. In many professions, continuous renewal of human capital is essential for employees to meet changing demands. The problem of older workers is probably not so much that their ability to learn deteriorates, but that with approaching retirement the motivation to invest in new human capital is weakened. However, earlier retirement is not an adequate solution; its effect would only be an earlier onset of the weakening of motivation.

The solution of labor market problems is more than the pension system can cope with. The joint approach of labor market policy and reform in the pension system, as favored by influential institutions in Germany, leads down a wrong path, particularly if it takes place at the expense of other, more promising reforms in the labor market.

Although the merits of funded systems are recognized by the great majority of experts today, many politicians show great reluctance to accept this insight; they have a marked preference for a PAYGO system. The plausible explanation is that it is easy and (in the short term) very attractive to enter into a PAYGO system and very difficult and time-consuming to get out of it. At the beginning the PAYGO system seems to offer an easy solution for problems that otherwise might cause trouble. The German experience offers a good example: When East Germany joined the Federal Republic in 1990, some politicians were full of praise for the PAYGO system, into which East Germany could be integrated without further ado. Had there been a funded system, a long transition period would have been inevitable, and in the meantime it would have been necessary to find some other way to finance old age payments in East Germany.

Today we in Germany strongly feel the shortcomings of the PAYGO system, but politicians are repelled by the long period of transition into a funded system, during which (for some time at least) a higher load of contributions from taxpayers must be borne. The reaction of politicians is to resort to easier expedients, such as financing pension payments not only out of the contributions to the pension system but partly out of other taxes. This does not restore intergenerational fairness, of course, but it makes the system less transparent and can thereby lessen dissatisfaction and tension, at least in the short run. Only very recently there seems to be a growing insight that such expedients offer only a way from one crisis to the next. As the public is more aware than ever of the critical situation of the pension system, it may be that chances for fundamental reform are not as poor today as they were some years ago. There is some hope that the models discussed by economists will be of more than academic interest.

Discussion Summary

Jeroen Kremers remarked that all the suggestions in the paper lean in the direction of reform toward a funded system and posed the question of whether more funded is better, or whether one should be aiming for an optimal mix of a funded and a pay-as-you-go (PAYGO) system—for example, one that allowed smoothing tax rates over time. *Ignazio Visco* also inquired about the relevance of a multipillar system and asked what weights the authors would give to PAYGO mandatory, and voluntary funded elements, respectively. *David A. Wise* responded that it is difficult to define the optimal mix and that it would probably vary across countries. He suggested that a defined benefit system might be responsible for providing a floor of benefits that could contribute to the assurance that in converting to a partially funded system people would not lose. *Eytan Sheshinski* remarked that one problem with incremental reform is the lumpy nature of costs involved in reform for setting up personal accounts and the like. These costs would not be dependent on the size of accounts, and since they were significant (as could be seen from a number of countries like the United Kingdom and Chile), this called for a drastic change rather than an incremental one.

Pierre Pestieau raised the issue of redistribution and whether it will be possible to have redistribution in a system like the one the paper proposes. *Martin Feldstein* reported on work by Jeffrey Liebman that reveals that there is much less actual redistribution in the U.S. system than appears from the formulas, in significant part because low-income workers tend to die at relatively lower ages than higher-income workers, and they are therefore less likely to receive benefits at all or else will have fewer years of benefits. He suggested that the focus in the context of pension reform not be on redistribution per se but on reducing the risk of poverty in old age. *David A. Wise* remarked that one could achieve any amount of redistribution in a funded system by setting it up in a particular way.

Pierre Pestieau noted that the principal nature of the problem of pension reform is a political one. He held that the problem in itself is not aging, but all the entrenched interests that paralyze any kind of reform. He argued that there would be no problem with aging if there were a social planner who had all control over reform. *Axel Börsch-Supan* agreed that the political economy is the most conspicuously absent part of the framework presented in the paper. He referred to the debate in Germany on whether saving should be voluntary or mandatory in the transition to a funded pillar. On the one hand, the aim was to avoid myopia, adverse selection, and higher administrative costs related to a privately funded system; on the other hand, polls showed that the solidarity with the current system was very small, particularly among the young generations, and he argued that it is extremely important to increase support for the system. He concluded that it is arduous to design a voluntary transition without losing the advantages of decreasing costs and running into the problems that can be seen in the United Kingdom. *David A. Wise* acknowledged the importance of political issues and suggested that they be addressed by demonstrating that a funded system would produce benefits that will be no less than under the PAYGO system, and will likely be more.

Jeffrey Liebman commented on the proposition in the paper that a funded system is supposed to increase national saving, whereas changes within the PAYGO systems could not be expected to do so. He noted that from an economic perspective this is not entirely clear, because introducing some sort of individual accounts could cause people to shift much of their existing saving and not add to what is already saved. On the other hand, he said, the prospect of a deteriorating PAYGO system that ultimately will result in benefit cuts or higher taxes would also induce people to increase saving. *Rolf Langhammer* pointed to the possibility that the income effect of a higher rate of return dominates the price effect of current consumption relative to future consumption, and cited the experience of a number of emerging-market countries and developing countries where higher rewards per unit of saving have not fueled private saving but have lowered private saving.

Pierre Pestieau remarked that the emphasis on the effects of pension reform on national saving present in the writings of many North American authors is not adequate in the European context, where insufficient national saving is not much of a problem. *David A. Wise* replied that the required reduction in the consumption of the young in Europe is at least as great as it is in the United States and that, consequently, the question of how to accomplish this task with the least pain to the young applies at least as much in Europe as it does in other countries.

Horst Siebert pointed out that there is not only a link between the pension system and unemployment insurance but a much closer link between the pension system and the welfare state, resulting from the fact that there is an income floor provided by the social welfare system. The level of this floor was, of course, different across countries; in the case of Germany, it was around 50 percent of the worker's income for singles and around 70 percent for married couples. If in such a situation the relative benefit level—that is, the replacement ratio in the PAYGO system—were reduced to create room for a funded pillar, this income floor would quickly be hit. In that case, when benefits out of the pension system after forty or forty-five years of contribution were similar to those of social welfare payments, very strange incentive effects would result. According to Siebert, the problem of redesigning the old age pension system is also a question of redesigning the aspiration level that has been defined by the welfare state, part of which is the right to retire early without an actuarially fair cut in benefits. He concluded that part of the problem of pension reform in Europe is the history of the welfare state, which poses some severe restraints for an approach of switching to system which is at least partially funded.

Eytan Sheshinski asked whether there is a good argument not to increase the early retirement age at the same time that the nominal retirement age is increased, as has been the case in the United States. Another point he made in that context was that early retirement is only one of a number of options available to people. Others include disability and the welfare system, so that there is effectively a three-way margin. Accordingly, any analysis of the incentives to delay retirement should take all these other programs into account. *Ignazio Visco* reported that, according to OECD estimates, effective implicit tax rates on working beyond the age of 55 that take into account the cumulation of incentives inherent in the various welfare programs are generally high in European countries, at between 50 and 60 percent. In Italy before the recent reform it had even been 80 percent. *Laurence J. Kotlikoff* remarked that the U.S. House of Representatives has just voted to repeal the earnings test on the receipts of benefits for workers aged sixty-five to seventy and that also in the Swedish reform there is some evidence of reducing disincentives to work longer years, indicating the possibility of a trend here. While he stressed the importance of the notion that one of the major values of having a defined contribution system is that it naturally does not present these labor supply disincentives, he emphasized that going from an unfunded to a funded system is not sufficient in order to achieve a more generationally balanced system. Reforms of this kind often meant no more than a reduction in implicit debt and a simultaneous increase in explicit government debt, so that workers were left with lower payroll taxes in the future but higher taxes to cover the interest on the explicit debt. Such a policy would not lower the burden on future generations.

A. Lans Bovenberg wondered about the causality of the correlation between the effective tax rate on work and early retirement shown in figure 2.5. He pointed out that in many countries early retirement programs have been the result of a weak position of workers in the labor market, and that this suggests a correlation between labor market policies in general and early retirement programs. From that he concluded that without a general reform of inadequate labor market policies in Europe, early retirement programs will not lose their significance. As an example of developments moving in the right direction, he referred to the Netherlands, where labor market policies have improved and now, as a consequence of an increasingly tight labor market, people are starting to question these programs. He reported that the average retirement age is already moving up and the long-term trend is reversed, not so much because early retirement programs are changed but more because labor market policies in general have been improved. *Ignazio Visco* added that labor market reform that would increase the participation rates of older workers or the participation rates of other groups, like women, might contribute to the alleviation of the financial balance of the public pension schemes, at least temporarily. *David A. Wise* criticized the habit of taxing the old to remove them from the labor force in order to provide work for the young as being founded on the wrong assumption about the economy. He contended that unemployment should be addressed through macroeconomic policies and not the social security system. The latter policy would reduce the size of the economy and increase tax rates on the young, thus reducing labor supply further. Referring to the issue of causality, he noted that there is evidence of a significant relationship between changes in the rules and changes in retirement—for example, in Germany and France, where changes in the social security systems in the early 1970s had an enormous effect almost immediately. This, according to Wise, would be very difficult to explain by reversed causality.

A. Lans Bovenberg questioned the proposition that it would not matter greatly whether a pension system would be financed by a social security tax or other taxes. He maintained that there is an important difference in the sense that a social security tax tends to be paid by the young only, while all other taxes also tend to be shared by the elderly. Changing the way the social security system is financed would create the possibility of reducing intergenerational redistribution and actually enhance intragenerational redistribution by ensuring that the richer elderly also contribute to the PAYGO system. Such a reform, he argued, could make the system more sustainable.

George de Menil asked for a clarification with respect to figure F5, where he suspected some special factors at work, as it can be observed that the effective tax rate on work in Germany at age sixty-five drops from 40 percent to 5 percent before rising again with the retirement effects. On the whole, he argued, this would mean a huge incentive to work longer. *Laurence J. Kotlikoff* added the question of whether the numbers in this figure include only the implicit tax associated with the pension system or all taxes on labor supply. *David A. Wise* answered that the rates are relative to net earnings after income tax and the like. He added that the peculiarity in the German system was essentially of no relevance, merely a quirk in the system, and that no one in Germany works at age sixty-five in any case.

Labor Mobility, Redistribution, and Pension Reform in Europe

Alain Jousten and Pierre Pestieau

3.1 Introduction

The future of the public pension systems in the European (EU) is presently a widely discussed topic. Unfortunately, the debate can be qualified as a rather shallow one, because it addresses only a limited number of questions. In the United States, on the other hand, a great deal of writing—some of it quite influential—is devoted to the old age crisis even though the crisis there is much less severe than in most of the member states of the EU. To understand this statement, one should keep in mind that compared to the majority of European countries, the United States devotes considerably less resources to unfunded public pension systems. Also, U.S. Social Security—the main public retirement program—can rely on a non-negligible trust fund. Furthermore, private funded pension schemes are widespread, and people generally retire at a much higher effective retirement age. Even the most pessimistic forecast of the finances of the U.S. Social Security program seem rosy relative to what can be reasonably expected in a number of European countries. In that respect, Aaron (Aaron and Shoven 1999) notes that "even if no legislative changes were made, 70 to 75 percent of benefits provided under current law could be paid indefinitely," and adds, "To suggest that social security is in crisis is to engage in Orwellian doublespeak" (55). One surely could not write that about most EU countries.

On the issue of the viability of the public systems, European economists and politicians can be classified into two broad categories: those who

Alain Jousten and Pierre Pestieau are both professors of economics at the University of Liège.

The authors are grateful to M. Burda and H. Siebert for helpful comments.

think that the present systems are more or less fit for the future, and those who think that we are heading for serious financial trouble—if not in the short, at least in the medium run. On the face of this opposition, there seems to be little common ground between the two groups. However, most of the analysts seem to agree on at least one issue, namely, the neglect of individuals' mobility under future pension systems. Usually, critics tend to consider the future of an isolated pension system or, at best, of a given country's multiple systems while ignoring or underestimating the potential for increased intercountry and intersystem mobility. In so doing, the critics neglect an entire spectrum of issues that have the potential to induce large changes in the returns individuals can expect from their pension contributions. Furthermore, the consequences for the public systems themselves are also far from negligible.

In this paper, we discuss the main characteristics of European mandatory pension systems and the implications of increasing factor mobility for these systems. Although it is undoubtedly true that labor mobility between countries is rather limited, it is more than likely that it will increase. In the past, individuals' mobility was inhibited not only by cultural and language differences, but also (to a non-negligible extent) by regulatory and legal limitations. At present, these limitations on job mobility are being dismantled in the wave of reduction of public intervention and the creation of a true single European market. Obvious exceptions are some government jobs that we could call "strategic," as well as occupations in the legal profession. Cultural and language barriers are also becoming less relevant as people are exposed more frequently to foreign languages and cultures from a very young age.

The results of these changes can already be felt today, particularly in some segments of the workforce. For example, young college and university graduates are more mobile than their less-educated counterparts, for multiple reasons. First, they generally have better language training and more frequent exposure to other cultures (e.g., through the Erasmus and Socrates student exchange programs of the EU). Second, they generally hold jobs that are easier to relocate, due either to the characteristics of the job itself (e.g., a computer programmer telecommuting to work) or to an international working environment (e.g., a customer support machine-tool specialist with a European or even worldwide customer base).[1]

Hence, we must study not only the question of whether labor mobility will increase and thus will have an impact on the viability of the pension systems, but also the question of whether this mobility will continue to evolve differently for different population segments, and what the consequences of such an evolution will be.

In the present paper, we focus on the issue of mobility at the beginning

---

1. On the contrary, immigration from outside the EU tends to cater to unskilled workers (but this is not the concern of this paper).

of the working life. The questions we are mainly interested in are whether there is room for strategic relocation of individuals at the beginning of the working life, and whether such mobility has the potential to change the redistributive patterns (both inter- and intragenerational) of the various national pension systems.

Relocating at the beginning of the working life is not the only kind of mobility with implications for social security. A worker can relocate in the middle of the working life, and the portability of social security and other pensions schemes can foster or (more probably) restrict this type of mobility. One may also relocate at the end of one's working life. Retirees may be attracted to warmer weather or cheaper living expenses and accordingly move to another country. This type of mobility may have some consequence on public revenue, depending on the tax structure. Finally, there is the cross-border mobility, which occurs when an individual works and lives in two adjacent countries. We will also deal with these alternative types of mobility.

The structure of the paper is as follows. In section 3.2 we illustrate some of the core features of European pension systems and compare them to those of the United States when useful. We also discuss some issues relating to mobility in the middle and at the end of the working life. In section 3.3, we present some insights into which paths European governments can take toward reform. Section 3.4 represents the main thrust of the paper and deals with the direct implications of labor mobility on various provisions of pension systems. We use findings from the literature on fiscal federalism to illustrate some of the potential effects of mobility. Section 3.5 addresses the types of mobility within the life cycle other than that at the beginning of the working life. Finally, we conclude the paper with some comments in section 3.6.

3.2   Characteristics of the European Pension Systems

Before proceeding further, we must note four points that are worth emphasizing. They pertain to the differences between pension systems in the Federal United States and the Confederal EU. First, compared to the U.S. federal social security structure, pensions in the EU are the responsibility of national governments. Second, within the EU, there are important differences in the size and the organization of pension schemes across countries. Third, in the whole debate over the future of social security in the United States, the scope is limited to the national borders. In the EU, there is a well-founded concern that economic and political integration affects the survival prospect of each national pension system. Finally, labor mobility is known to be negligible within the EU; even within each national entity, interregional mobility is lower than across states in the United States.

The first and fundamental pillar of European pension systems is mandatory and unfunded. The systems are organized under the form of a pay-as-you-go (PAYGO) defined benefit scheme. Individuals contribute to the scheme today; in return they receive benefits when retired that are financed by future generations' contributions and based on some pension computation formula that is not necessarily a function of past contributions. Differing system characteristics across EU countries are their size and their redistributiveness. For example, the French and German systems are more than twice as important as the British system in terms of their share of gross domestic product (GDP)—close to 13 percent each, as opposed to 5.5 in the United Kingdom.[2] Furthermore, although in some countries these systems account for a large fraction of the total income of the elderly, in other countries they do not (see Disney and Johnson 2001).

Not surprisingly, the second pillar (occupational pensions) is quasi-inexistent in the countries that have a very strong first pillar; the same is also true of arrangements belonging to the third pillar (individual retirement savings). More generally, it is fair to say that the presence of private pension arrangements is an inverse function of the generosity of the public system. In the absence of public provision, individuals must try to secure their old age income through private market arrangements, be they compulsory or discretionary.

As opposed to the public PAYGO systems, occupational pensions are generally organized on a fully funded basis. A notable exception are the French unfunded second-tier pensions, which are both defined benefit and based entirely on a PAYGO principle, and hence belong to the first rather than the second pillar. Another characteristic of occupational pension plans is that they can be either defined benefit (DB) or defined contribution (DC), in which the pension is a direct function of past contributions. Third-pillar schemes, in turn, are generally fully funded and based entirely on DC basis.

From the point of view of redistribution, public pension systems are markedly different among the various EU countries. Two main levels of redistribution must be distinguished. The PAYGO nature of European public pension systems has lead to what is known as the *free lunch* given away to past and current generations of retirees. This free lunch implies an implicit government debt, the so-called *social security wealth,* which is particularly high in countries with generous pension schemes. In Germany and in France, this implicit debt is much higher than the explicit government debt. The French ratio of debt to GDP is just below the Maastricht ceiling of 60 percent. If the implicit government debt is added in, the overall ratio amounts to about 160 percent (Roseveare et al. 1996). This redistribution from younger to older generations clearly varies across European countries and is not without consequences as factor mobility increases.

---

2. The corresponding figure for the public Social Security retirement program in the United States is 4.6 percent.

Another source of variation across European countries is the extent of intragenerational redistribution. In some countries there is a tight link between contributions and pension benefits according to the insurance principle of getting an actuarially fair return. In some other countries this link is loose. Indeed, in countries (such as France and Germany) with contribution-related benefits, social security does not effect any redistribution; one sometimes speaks of a Bismarckian regime. On the contrary, in countries with redistributive benefit rules the replacement ratio declines as income increases. In these countries (such as the Netherlands or the United Kingdom), workers truly consider that their contributions are like taxes—namely, that the contributions do not entitle them to an equiproportionate benefit.

Intragenerational redistribution can take on different forms, however; for example, early retirement provisions can also cause major redistribution of income. Indeed, in countries such as Belgium, where implicit taxes on continuing work beyond the time of first eligibility for early retirement benefits is close to 80 percent, the system operates a clear redistribution toward individuals' retiring early (Pestieau and Stijns 1999).

The effective retirement age also varies across European countries. It is indeed striking to observe that in Europe, the current and expected demographic parameters are not terribly divergent. The statutory retirement ages are also quite similar. What varies more is effective retirement. To capture this notion, Gruber and Wise (1999) have introduced the concept of *unused labor capacity* between the ages of fifty-five and sixty-five. This capacity ranges from 67 percent for Belgium to 35 percent for Sweden (it is 37 percent in the United States and 22 percent in Japan). This is due mainly to a number of both implicit and explicit incentives to early retirement (so-called "actuarial" adjustments), which vary wildly among European countries. These incentives are pervasive in the social security programs of countries such as Belgium, France, Italy, and the Netherlands, where the effective retirement age is quite low.

Furthermore, some European countries have essentially opted for a universal national pension system, whereas others have preferred to set up multiple systems. As a consequence, the study of the question of inter- and intragenerational redistribution finds itself complicated by the sometimes quite opposing degrees of redistribution of the various national systems.

Altogether, the result of these features is that in most EU countries, elderly households experience an unprecedented standard of living relative to the other age groups and relative to the past. Poverty rates are also extremely low among today's retirees.

3.3 Reforming the Pension Systems

We have described the main characteristics of the European pension systems, which appear rather heterogeneous in four respects: size, burden on future generations, redistribution across households, and retirement age. These characteristics combined with population aging and declining productivity growth explain the old age crisis that is clearly more acute in countries with generous schemes. Until now, each national government has more or less successfully addressed this crisis. In Cremer and Pestieau (2000), it is argued that the old age crisis does not come solely from the combination of demographic aging and PAYGO schemes. By appropriately adjusting the key parameters of social security systems (namely, the replacement rates, the payroll taxes, and the retirement age) while fostering individual or collective saving for retirement, governments can avert the old age crisis. The real issue is also and mainly political. Reforms must go through the political process, in which majority voting and vested interests too often make impossible the implementation of reforms otherwise optimal from the standpoint of both intra- and intergenerational equity.

In that respect, two remarks are in order. In countries that have undertaken reforms, the approach has been to rely on the grandfathering formula, precisely to circumvent paralyzing interest groups. This can have an unbearable cost. Furthermore, it is well admitted that a total shift from PAYGO to a fully funded system is not feasible. If the transition generation is to be compensated for abandoning PAYGO by issuing an appropriate public debt, and if the benefit rule is unchanged so as to keep the extent of intragenerational redistribution constant, then such a shift would be neutral. The government that would undertake such a reform would run an increased deficit, which would be exactly offset by the increase in private savings from the surplus of the new pension plans. The national saving rate would not increase. In effect, the reform would simply convert an implicit obligation of the government to future retirees into explicit debt. That said, most reforms, whether implemented or contemplated, include the development of some fully funded schemes acting as supplement (and not a substitute) for the existing PAYGO first pillars.

Discussion of the viability of existing pension systems and alternative ways of reforming them is most often conducted in the setting of national borders with no or low labor mobility. The implicit assumption is that although physical capital has proven to be quite mobile, labor may not be so mobile. Language is often the most often-cited barrier to migration, but differing customs, traditions, and preferences matter as well. Governments themselves may implement policies that inhibit labor mobility: regulation of house prices and rents, subsidies of declining industries, residency linked social benefits. Inefficient property markets make moving an expensive proposition. One expects that these various barriers to mobility will progressively fall under the specific pressure of European integration and the more general pressure of economic globalization. It is therefore relevant to investigate the implications of labor mobility for the old age crisis.

We thus have an interesting question, namely, whether a shift from

PAYGO to fully funded systems has any effect in the face of increasing labor mobility. As already noted before, a "neutral" shift from a PAYGO to a fully funded system has no effect in the absence of mobility. The same proposition implies that, if before the reform there is what we call a *migration equilibrium,* after a neutral reform, this equilibrium is unchanged. Any individual will face the same lifetime utility before and after the reform; there are thus no reasons for moving.

Clearly, if the reform is not perfectly neutral from the viewpoint of inter- or intragenerational redistribution, then a migration equilibrium will result according to the argument developed in the next section. If the reform does not fully compensate the transition generation of retirees, the young generation of workers will face a lighter liability in the reform country (through lower implicit or explicit government debt). Retirees cannot move out but workers from other countries can be attracted by the reform country and move in. Hence, the changing intergenerational redistribution patterns induce mobility. Furthermore, recall that before the reform any individual worker was indifferent between staying in his or her home country and moving to the reform country. If the reform does not restitute the same redistributive pattern as that prevailing before (i.e., if it does not reduce the amount of intragenerational redistribution), high-wage workers can be attracted to move to the reform country and low-wage workers to move out of it.

3.4   The Implications of Labor Mobility in the European Union

As announced, we now turn to the expected effects of labor mobility on the way countries organize their social security systems. As already mentioned, we realize that we are far from smooth mobility across EU countries, although we believe that this will eventually be achieved. In any case, in a competitive market economy, capital mobility implies equalized rates of return and hence equality of wages for a given skill level. Yet— and this is important for the problem at hand—there is a difference between equal wage rates and equal lifetime utilities. That difference may arise from different factors, notably national indebtedness and unfunded pension systems that may benefit households when introduced and burden them thereafter.

We consider autarkic countries, each having its own specific pension policy, and see what happens when we allow for factor mobility. Two settings can be envisioned. In the first, countries are passive; they do not want to change their approach to financing (PAYGO vs. fully funding), the role of supplementary pension, or the type of benefit rule (Bismarckian or Beveridgean). As shown by Cremer and Pestieau (2000) in a two-country model, such passive behavior can have a pathological outcome, with all high-income individuals or all low-income individuals conglomerating in one country, depending on which group is mobile. In the second setting, countries react to migration and reform their pension systems according to their planners' social welfare function or through the political process.

We will adopt the latter setting and assume that each country has a social planner with a utilitarian objective. This seems to be the prevailing assumption in the literature. First we look at the effect of mobility on the intragenerationally redistributive dimension of pension provisions, and then at the effect of mobility on the intergenerationally redistributive dimension, namely, the size of the social security wealth.

3.4.1   Intragenerational Redistribution

The prevailing view is that a redistribution policy is best administered by the central government, in our case the EU. Accordingly, decentralized redistribution policies cause some kind of adverse selection. In a world of perfect mobility, we would expect individual countries with redistributive programs to attract poor households from less-redistributive neighboring countries and to repel rich households who must pay for the programs. These reactions eventually make it impossible to pursue any redistribution at the national level except through some kind of cooperation among the member states. We expect these general predictions to hold even in the presence of a limited mobility of individuals belonging to some income and social groups.

The canonical model used is naturally simple. It involves two countries producing an output using two types of workers, skilled and unskilled. Skilled workers are assumed to be mobile and unskilled workers are immobile (the opposite assumption does not change the resulting conclusion). There is a social security scheme that affects some redistribution between the two types of individuals. In the absence of mobility, each country implements the redistribution that fits its welfare criterion. When there is mobility, such a policy is bound by the constraint that the lifetime utility of mobile workers be identical. In other words, any move toward a more generous system in a country attracts migration from the other countries.

In the literature (Cremer, Fourgeaud, et al. 1996; Wellisch 2000) one usually contrasts redistributive social security conducted both without and with coordination. The former case reflects the current step of the EU; the latter a still far-fetched possibility. Three findings are standard. First, uncoordinated national redistributive policies result in migration distortions when countries are different. In other words, the efficiency required so that the marginal productivity of mobile workers be equated is violated; a corollary to this finding is that if one country values redistribution more than the other, it will end up with relatively less-skilled workers and less redistribution than in autarky. The second finding is that if both countries are identical in all respects, the equilibrium is symmetric and the allocation of mobile workers efficient; yet the suboptimal degree of redistribution remains. The third finding is that a coordinated increase in the redistributive payroll tax rate in the two regions increases social welfare. Note that the same conclusion holds if mobility is only partial. The only case in which mobility is neutral is that of an actuarially fair pension system.

3.4.2 Intergenerational Redistribution

Let us now look at differences in social security wealth, or, expressed differently, in intergenerational redistribution. The issue is the same as that of different levels of public debt. The Maastricht Treaty introduced a ceiling of 60 percent on the ratio of debt to GDP and adopted a narrow definition of public debt. It is clear, however, that the reasons that led to adopting that ceiling apply as well to the implicit debt generated by generous PAYGO pension systems. The major reason for imposing such a ceiling was the Economic and Monetary Union (EMU), which is independent of whether there is labor mobility. The rationale is simple: When a country deeply endebted through standard debt or through PAYGO social security joins a fully integrated economic union, it makes its partners partially pay for it.

If there is labor mobility, differentials in the net benefits that individuals can expect from public pensions along with other policies alter the payoff to migration and can influence the international allocation of labor. Wildasin (1999) estimates the change in the present value of lifetime wealth that results from switching from one public pension program to another for representative workers in seven EU countries. He shows that moving between certain countries can result in an increase of 15 percent or even more in lifetime wealth. As he points out, differentials in net benefits create fiscal incentives for inefficient labor allocation. We expect increased mobility to lead to a reduction in differences in intergenerational redistribution over time.

Consider two countries, identical in all respects, that contemplate adopting a PAYGO system for, say, compensating the current generation of retirees for hardship that prevented them from saving for retirement. It is clear that with mobility of the young generation, there will be a "race to the bottom," namely, toward a lower amount of such pension provision than decided in autarky. Naturally, we assume that the young generation anticipates that a PAYGO system relative to a fully funded system implies a cost that depends on the gap between the rate of return on capital and the rate of growth of the economy.

Consider an equally realistic setting in which two countries are identical in all respects but toward intergenerational redistribution. One relies more than the other on PAYGO to finance its pension system. What happens when their borders are open to possible migration of the young? One can expect an outflow from the more indebted country to the less indebted one.[3] The only way this outflow can be stopped is by decreasing the burden of such a debt, and this implies taxing the currently retired and immobile generation. Note that if on top of this, the population is aging and hence the dependency ratio is going up, so there is an additional incentive for the young generation to move out from PAYGO countries to fully funded ones.

As a consequence, countries with a population dedicated to the PAYGO principle and willing to resist even partial shifts toward fully funded schemes can be forced to reform their systems because of the mobility-induced tax competition.

Finally, let us analyze the implication of differences in retirement ages in European countries once we allow for increased labor mobility. Exactly as for the degrees of intra- and intergenerational redistribution, we would expect increased mobility to render social security systems less redistributive with respect to retirement age. By this, we do not understand that retirement ages will necessarily tend toward one identical age of retirement all across the EU. Rather, we would expect there to be a schedule of retirement ages and benefit packages that people of different survival probabilities could choose from. For example, early retirement would go together with reduced benefits, late retirement with increased monthly benefits. Individuals would then select the best package for themselves, depending on their own estimates of the survival probabilities they face.

3.4.3   Is There a Race to the Bottom?

In the two previous subsections, we have argued that with some factor mobility there would be convergence toward less spending on PAYGO provisions and less redistribution in retirement benefits. This expected evolution, often labeled a "race to the bottom," thus concerns PAYGO and flat-rate benefit systems. Do we witness such a race to the bottom?

When looking at the evolution of old age benefits (aggregate or per-beneficiary) over the last decades, it is surprising to see that they have not decreased in most EU countries. During the 1990–96 period, the ratio of old age benefits to GDP has increased everywhere but in the Netherlands. Does that mean that the danger of social dumping in the area of social security is not to be taken seriously? Not really. This question calls for a number of qualifications. First, it is possible that there are some lags in the reaction of mobile agents to increased mobility. Second, the cost of mobil-

---

3. This issue has lately received much attention. See Bräuminger (1999), Pemberton (1999), Meier (2000), Crettez, Michel, and Vidal (1996). If national governments are passive and the only factors of production are mobile labor and mobile capital, then the more indebted country disappears. To avoid such an extreme solution, one must introduce fixed factors such as land or real estate. Alternatively, one must allow for national government action toward a rapid reduction in the national debt or the PAYGO pensions at the expense of the immobile retirees.

ity might be higher than is often thought, and might not be restricted to the language issue or the financial cost of moving. The job market is still relatively closed. More importantly, the same reasons that explain why each country adopted a given type of social security (PAYGO or fully funded, Bismarckian or Beveridgean) can explain why people do not move. It is possible that they are attached to particular type of social protection, and in that respect, they are not as opportunist as assumed in models of fiscal competition. This point holds only for the mobility of net contributors and not for that of those benefitting from redistribution. Also, it noteworthy to consider recent work that identifies previously unrecognized beneficial effects of competition among governments. It can be shown that with imperfect competition (Wilson 1999) or with majority voting (Cremer and Pestieau 1998), public spending and redistribution can very well not decrease as a result of factor mobility. Finally, it is interesting to note that countries that redistribute intragenerationally quite often do not rely exclusively on PAYGO systems. The converse holds true for countries that do not redistribute intragenerationally. Hence, the two redistributive effects would offset each other.

These different arguments may explain why the effects of mobility on redistribution have so far been limited. It is, however, important to realize that in the future they can loose their strength. For example, the impediments to mobility induced by fiscal or social policies are likely to disappear in the future with the integration not only of European economies but also of national mentalities and cultures.

3.5 Mobility within the Life Cycle

In the previous sections, we implicitly assume that individuals contemplate migration at the beginning of their life cycles. At that early stage, they are supposed to be able to weight the pluses and minuses of alternative locations. In the real world, there are other types of mobility; workers can move within the working period or at the beginning of the retirement period. Exactly as for mobility at the beginning of the working life, such relocations can be triggered by factors pertaining to job offers on hand, family matters, health conditions, and health coverage—which are factors exogenous to the social security system—or, alternatively, by strategic considerations created by the social security system itself.

3.5.1 Mobility at Retirement

First we consider mobility at the beginning of the retirement period. Both public and private retirement schemes all across the EU allow individuals to receive their social security benefits independently of their place of residence in the EU, and sometimes even far beyond the reaches of the Union. In this respect, it is indeed not uncommon to observe retirees relocating from Germany or Sweden to Spain or Italy after retirement, be it for health reasons or simply because they want to see the sun. This is not uncommon but surely is not as widespread as in the United States (think of the situation currently observed in both Florida and Arizona). If a large number of retirees from Nordic countries would settle in southern countries, there would be a loss in the tax base for the former and a gain for the latter. This is so because the elderly essentially are taxed indirectly rather than directly. It is indeed well known that social security income is not as heavily taxed as labor income. Furthermore, interest income is hardly taxed in the EU. Value-added tax thus is frequently the only major source of tax income from the elderly. This effect on the tax base would be reinforced by the presence of differential mobility according to income. It is more than likely that the people moving south would have a higher average income than those staying behind in the north. Hence, this reduction of the tax base in northern countries would also be accompanied by a shift in the overall tax burden from the old to the young and from the rich to the poor, with all its consequences on the mobility of the young.

This finding is underlined when we introduce the welfare component of public pensions benefits—namely, means-tested old age benefits—into the picture. Eligibility for this type of income is based strictly on a residency criterion. Therefore, assuming a more generous system of means-tested benefits in the north of Europe, we would expect poor people to move north as a reaction to the more generous social security system. Again, this condition assumes that national governments do not react. Expectedly, they will not remain passive and will adjust their welfare systems and their tax structures to counter unpleasant effects of retirees' mobility.

3.5.2 Mobility during the Working Period

Turning to the concept of mobility within the working period, we must introduce several distinctions. First of all, we must distinguish the first from the second and third pillars. Second, we also must distinguish mobility concerning the workplace from mobility concerning the place of residence; here we consider the latter. Shortly after the Treaty of Rome, member states began to develop a system of multilateral coordination for social insurance legislation.[4] The coordination so achieved was aimed at establishing equality of treatment between nationals and nonnationals (but belonging to the EU) in social insurance. This has proved successful because it allows individuals to take up residence or employment in any country of the EU without undue loss of social insurance rights—that is, without being at significant disadvantage, compared with those who remained in their own countries throughout their entire working lives. This system of multilateral coordination applies to pension provisions, but only to the first pillar. When this system was developed, it was believed that, at a later

---

4. This is enacted through Regulation 1408/71 and 574/72; see EC (1994).

stage, a parallel multilateral scheme of coordination would eventually be put in place for supplementary pensions, whether based on legislation or on contractual arrangements. However, it quickly turned out that it was not easy to overcome the obstacles to freedom of movement posed by the pattern of existing supplementary pensions in the EU, which are both complex and diversified. Patterns are complex in the sense that even within a given country, there is a large diversity of pension schemes that are often interwoven with particular rules of the tax code. Furthermore, tax treatment of pensions is not necessarily stable, and thus introduces a high level of segmentation. The system is also diversified in the sense that, in some countries, private supplementary pensions represent the bulk of the pension rights of individuals, whereas in other countries they represent only a trickle. The distinction between defined benefit (DB) schemes and defined contribution (DC) schemes is also important here, because it is much easier to transfer balances of DC plans rather than accumulated pension rights in DB plans.

Over the last three decades, the Commission (as well as the private sector, the insurance industry, and the pension fund industry) have searched for some solutions, but obstacles remains today and hence freedom of movement of workers covered by supplementary pensions is restricted. For our purpose, the implication is clear: There is more freedom between countries with dominant mandatory social security plans than between countries with mixed arrangements. Let us add that in the latter, the first pillar is sometimes means-tested, implying that residency restrictions exist even after retirement (as already mentioned).

It is clear that when considering a pension system (both first and second pillars) that does not slow mobility, it is tempting to generalize DB approaches. In the first pillar, this would be made possible by adopting the so-called "national accounts pension system" that is now used in Italy and Sweden. Such a policy would clearly facilitate labor mobility in particular within an enlarged EU. Indeed, with a more and more heterogeneous economic union, the current arrangements concerning mandatory systems could become increasingly difficult to implement. At the same time, it is clear that a generalized move toward DC systems makes them less redistributive—a serious problem that assistance programs (means-tested minimal pensions) can solve only partially.

3.5.3   Cross-Border Mobility

We now turn to a frequently neglected issue related to mobility during the working life. Indeed, we must distinguish the mobility of workers with respect to their places of work from that with respect to their places of residence.[5] In Belgium, for example, the rules of the public social security

---

5. The first type of mobility is qualified as *travail frontalier* in French (i.e., people crossing the border to get to work).

program (the non–means-tested benefits) are not neutral with respect to the place of residence. Indeed, for workers changing both the residence and the place of work, the standard EU rules on cross-border mobility apply: The individual accumulates fractions of pension rights in different countries according to the proportion of his or her professional career spent contributing to a given system. Consider the case of a worker who instead of moving his place of residence to another country only commutes to work abroad. In this case, he still generates pension rights abroad in proportion to the time spent in every foreign system. However, in parallel, he accumulates fictive or imputed pension rights in the Belgian social security system: fictive wages—which are close to national average wages— are imputed into his Belgian earnings record, independently of the real observed earnings of the individual. If, at the time of retirement, the foreign pension is smaller than the fictive Belgian pension corresponding to the same period of time, the Belgian social security system then pays the difference to the individual. Hence, the Belgian system illustrates that it is possible to introduce an additional margin for maneuvering, namely, a separation of the choice of the residence and the workplace. This distinction is especially important for small countries such as the Benelux countries, where almost anyone can work in a different country than the one in which he or she resides. The same is obviously true for border regions of larger countries.

This particularity of the Belgian system, however, also reemphasizes one weakness of the entire current regulatory framework for mobility: namely, its focus on first-pillar pensions. To illustrate this point in the extreme, consider the case of a Belgian resident working in the Netherlands. At retirement, the worker will have significant Dutch pension entitlements, some large fraction of them under the form of occupational private pensions. However, in its computation of the potential pension complement, the Belgian social security administration does not take the Dutch occupational pension into account and hence pays out a much larger supplement than would have been the case had all kinds of pension income been taken into account.

3.6   Conclusions

We began this paper by showing that members of the EU have contrasting pensions systems, particularly with respect to redistribution. Such a setting is likely not sustainable, given factor mobility. Capital mobility that is high and labor mobility that is still negligible (except for highly qualified workers) imply that eventually there will be some convergence toward less redistribution, both between generations and across households. Pension systems, particularly generous ones, face a tough dilemma: adjust or perish.

Having some governments forced to reduce their debt, both explicit and implicit, is not a bad thing, particularly in view of the implications of aging for public finances. However, pressure to reduce the redistributiveness of social security, particularly toward low-income retirees, is by no means desirable. Even if the overall level of poverty among elderly people is quite low in the EU, there is a great deal of variability between member countries. One may therefore fear that a race to the bottom on social security benefits will lead all EU countries to experience the higher poverty rates among the elderly that we presently know only in countries such as the United Kingdom or Portugal.

In that respect, the idea of developing a European safety net for the elderly could be seriously envisioned. Indeed, there is little doubt that the elderly are the most vulnerable group of the population. This again raises the crucial question of whether European governments take the social dimensions of the EU seriously. As Atkinson (1995) points out, the main problems limiting individual national governments to provide effective social protection are "those arising from political pressure—a political economy, rather than a migratory, constraint on national policy" (9). One can easily speculate that such political pressure is much stronger at the level of the EU. To put it another way, one has the feeling that a number of national governments use the excuse of fiscal competition to explain their failure to push for effective social protection at both the national and Union levels.

The Maastricht Treaty implied a mandatory reduction of the public debt in countries such as Belgium and Italy. Another interpretation of this reduction is to consider it as a reaction to increasing mobility in Europe. Even if those countries are perhaps unwilling to abolish their PAYGO systems altogether, they still must lower the burden on their young, mobile workers in the face of increasing tax competition.

Two final remarks conclude: First, this paper has focused on labor mobility within the EU. There is an even more challenging mobility, that which results from immigration flows from outside the EU, particularly from Eastern Europe. The reality—or even more so, the *potentiality*—of these flows is likely to induce individual national government to reform their social security systems toward the insurance principal, with entitlements based on past work and past contributions (see Michel, Pestieau, and Vidal 1998). Finally, even for those concerned by the threat of economic integration on effective social protection, it is crucial to improve the portability of supplementary pension schemes within and across EU countries.

References

Aaron, H. J., and J. B. Shoven. 1999. *Should the United States privatize social security.* Cambridge, Mass.: MIT Press.

Atkinson, A. B. 1995. *Incomes and the welfare state: Essays on Britain and Europe.* Cambridge: Cambridge University Press.

Bräuminger, M. 1999. Generalized social security finance in a two-country world. *Scottish Journal of Political Economy* 46:287–302.

Cremer, H., V. Fourgeaud, M. Leite Monteiro, M. Marchand, and P. Pestieau. 1996. Mobility and redistribution: A survey of the literature. *Public Finance* 51:325–52.

Cremer, H., and P. Pestieau. 1998. Social insurance and labor mobility: A political economy approach. *Journal of Public Economics* 68:397–420.

———. 2000. Reforming our pension system: Is it a demographic, financial, or political problem? *European Economic Review* 44:974–84.

———. 2001. Social insurance competition between Bismarck and Beveridge. Unpublished manuscript.

Crettez, B., Ph. Michel, and J.-P. Vidal. 1996. Time preference and labor migration in an OLG model with land and capital. *Journal of Population Economics* 9:387–403.

Disney, R., and P. Johnson. 2001. *Pension systems and retirement incomes across OECD countries.* London: Edward Elgar.

European Commission (EC). 1994. Supplementary pensions in the European Union: Development, trends and outstanding issue. Report by the European Commission's Network of Experts on Supplementary Pensions, Brussels.

Gruber, J., and D. Wise, eds. 1999. *Social security and retirement around the world.* Chicago: University of Chicago Press.

Meier, V. 2000. Time preference, international migration and social security. *Journal of Population Economics* 13:127–46.

Michel, Ph., P. Pestieau, and J.-P. Vidal. 1998. Labor mobility and redistribution with evolving altruism: The case of a small economy. *Regional Science and Urban Economics* 28:363–77.

Pemberton, J. 1999. Social security: National policies with international implications. *Economic Journal* 109:492–598.

Pestieau, P., and J.-P. Stijns. 1999. Social security and retirement in Belgium. In *Social security and retirement around the world,* ed. J. Gruber and D. A. Wise. Chicago: University of Chicago Press.

Roseveare D., W. Leibfritz, D. Fore, and E. Wurzel. 1996. Aging population, pension systems and government budgets: Simulations for 20 OECD countries. OECD Working Paper no. 168. Paris: Organization for Economic Cooperation and Development.

Wellisch, D. 2000. *Theory of public finance in a federal state.* Cambridge: Cambridge University Press.

Wildasin, D. 1999. Public pensions in the EU: Migrations incentives and impacts. In *Environmental and public economics,* ed. A. Panagariga, P. Portney, and R. Schwab, 253–82. Cheltenham, U.K.: Edward Elgar.

Wilson, J. D. 1999. Theories of tax competition. *National Tax Journal* 52:269–304.

Comment   Michael Burda

This paper addresses a complex array of issues that has captured the attention of policy makers across Europe. In the domain of pension systems

Michael Burda is professor of economics at Humboldt University of Berlin.

and the pension crisis, Europe differs from the United States in obvious ways. First, unlike the United States, Europe does not yet constitute a nation in any practical sense of the word, and probably will not for at least another half-century. Second, although pensions remain a national responsibility, economic integration and labor mobility are already pan-European phenomena. Labor mobility has a direct impact on the way pensions function and are financed. Third, labor mobility is joined by increasing capital mobility and product market integration as potential mechanisms of economic integration. As Mundell (1957) argued, the latter two are generally substitutes for labor mobility and could, in principle, alleviate if not remove the urgency of labor mobility's threat to Europe's national pension systems.

Jousten and Pestieau describe the pension system of the representative European economy as primarily national pay-as-you-go (PAYGO), by virtue of its strong emphasis of the first pillar (public pensions, which have become increasingly easy to transfer across intra-European Union borders). Company pensions are fragmented and are difficult to vest. The authors' point is that the coming pension crisis in Europe, brought about by the same deteriorating demographics and declining productivity growth observed in the United States, will be exacerbated by heterogeneity in program generosity, burden on future generations, and degree of redistribution due to higher replacement rates and early retirement. The authors argue against a total shift to funded systems on the grounds that it is not feasible. Their main message is that, to the extent that pension reform is not neutral, mobility of labor in Europe may induce severe difficulties on its own. Marginal households will induce a forced convergence or even a race to the bottom among competing nations. This could eliminate redistributional aspects of pension systems, taken by the authors to be a desideratum. A central implication is that pan-European coordination of pension and, more generally, taxation policy is necessary to implement redistribution aims. The point is a familiar one, and applies to all available national mechanisms of redistribution, such as cash transfers and tax credits.

My first remark deals with the empirical, as opposed to the theoretical, relevance of labor mobility in Europe to the pension crisis. Implicit in the discussion is the Roy-Borjas model of mobility, in which heterogeneity of returns to spatial mobility lead agents to "vote with their feet" and choose those economies in which the net return is the largest. Generally, this means that low-skilled workers migrate to countries with generous safety nets and redistributive systems, whereas high-productivity workers migrate away from them. What I missed in the paper is empirical evidence that this is an important phenomenon. How important is (or was) "welfare shopping" in the United States? Using the Roy-Borjas model, one would conclude that European countries with more generous pension systems and social safety nets sow the seeds of their own destruction. However, is there enough variance of policies among European countries to induce such behavior? The fact that a number of European nations are parties to the Schengen Agreement without explicit convergence of social policy is evidence that the marginal worker is far from considering the decision to migrate, and the observed flows are too weak to matter. Merely asserting that marginal workers enforce an arbitrage condition is not enough, because a no-profit condition is observationally equivalent to an equilibrium in which no mobility occurs because no one wants to be mobile. Due either to fixed costs or option values of waiting, modern migration theory generally predicts a zone of inaction for wages, within which no migration occurs despite higher lifetime utility abroad; in this case, the marginal analysis, which gives rise to the results referenced by the authors, is of limited usefulness. A good example of this is East-West German migration, which remains a trickle despite a wage gap in 2000 of roughly 25 percent.

The overwhelming empirical evidence suggests that Europeans are immobile. Even in a fully integrated environment, Europeans simply do not move. This is due partly to their current demographic situation: Europeans are older and live in more homogeneous populations. Mobility declines sharply with age. Language differences militate against the migration decision. In addition to these factors, Europeans view local amenities as a strongly normal good, so that the income effect of local prosperity depresses migration considerably (see Faini and Venturini 2000). It is a red herring to attribute Europeans' behavior to institutions. European low mobility derives primarily from preferences, as intranational migration behavior clearly substantiates. In a democracy, economic institutions are a reflection of national tastes.

To illustrate how striking the differences can be, consider table 3C.1, which compares unemployment rates of cities (1995) in Louisiana with those in the Bundesländer (federal states) of Germany (1995). The rather tight homogeneity of rates in the former stands in stark contrast to the variance of the latter, and is remarkable, given substantial averaging-out of local labor market areas in Germany (for the states at least), and given that the public transport infrastructure is much more developed in Germany than in Louisiana.

An interesting question that is left unaddressed by the authors is the extent to which increased immigration from outside the European Union (EU) might change European "traditions." Guest workers are mobile almost by definition; once inside Europe and with the rights of EU citizens, they may become the enforcer of the marginal migrant equilibrium condition described by Jousten and Pestieau. It should be recalled, however, that older labor market participants tend unconditionally to be the least mobile and therefore pose the least threat to the redistributional element described (early retirement).

My second comment concerns the equivalence of product market inte-

Table 3C.1   **Regional Unemployment: German Federal States versus U.S. State of Louisiana, 1995**

Geographical Area	Unemployment Rate
German federal states	
City-states	
Berlin, West	14.3
Berlin, East	12.1
Bremen	14.0
Hamburg	10.7
Selected states	
Bavaria	7.9
Hessia	8.4
Mecklenburg-Vorpommern	16.1
Saxony	14.4
Schleswig-Holstein	9.1
Thuringia	15.0
Average	9.3
Louisiana	
Alexandria	7.3
Baton Rouge	7.6
Houma	7.1
Lafayette	7.5
Lake Charles	8.6
Monroe	7.5
New Orleans	7.7
Shreveport/Bossier City	7.5
Average	7.6

Source: Statistisches Jahrbuch der Bundesrepublik Deutschland (1999) and Louisiana Department of Labor.

gration and labor/capital mobility. Recalling Mundell, capital mobility and goods-market integration can be seen as substitutes for labor mobility. These two mechanisms can force labor costs into line with no active migration, and therefore with no additional fiscal burdens. If this does not happen, firms will exit and jobs will be destroyed until equilibrium is reached. It is useful to remind ourselves that the demand for labor is not inelastic in the medium to long run; the Marshall-Hicks rule predicts that capital mobility and product market competition increase the elasticity of labor demand, and put more pressure on governments to design employment-friendly social safety policies. Rather than as racing to the bottom, the examples of Italy and Belgium could be interpreted as prudent reactions to tightening fiscal constraints as tax-driven labor-cost wedges raise unemployment levels (increasing costs of social security) and lower the tax base (due to the destruction of jobs). It turns out, incidentally, that evidence for a race to the bottom in the EU remains scanty, as documented in Bertola, Boeri, and Nicoletti (2001).

Third, I thought the authors were not attentive enough to the growing importance of European pensions' third pillar (i.e., private provisions), which can be seen as (1) a tacit mechanism for scaling back redistribution in the system (first pillar), and (2) a driving force for the transferability of pensions. The third pillar may involve many more families in Europe than in the United States, because European household saving rates are significantly higher. One reason frequently given for the boom in European stock markets during the late 1990s is that households are taking note of these problems and are acquiring shares as insurance against future shortfalls in the public pension system.

Fourth, the authors focus too much on redistribution in my view and not enough on the size of the pie. The most important life-savers of pension systems are economic growth and concomitant labor force participation. David Wise, in his work with Gruber and others, documents a strong negative correlation between effective taxation and labor force participation, especially among older men just before retirement. Examples from Holland, Denmark, and Ireland support this point. The possibility that both could be jointly endogenous is real and has been demonstrated in Eastern Europe, where unemployment of older workers with unsuitable human capital for a market economy was reduced by massive early retirement (Hungary and East Germany are prominent examples). Governments faced limited financing options for this policy because the profits of state enterprises were no longer available and income taxes were not yet implemented. They ended up taxing labor at rates that correspond to the higher end of OECD (Organization for Economic Cooperation and Development) Europe (Boeri, Burda, and Köllö 1998). This makes it clear that early retirement as a mechanism of redistribution is a slippery slope that can lead to a low participation, high tax, and high unemployment equilibrium, making the region or nation a potential candidate for handouts from the EU—hardly a palatable option.

Finally, although the paper makes a number of important claims, I cannot hide my disappointment at the poor documentation of the empirical extent of migration's effect on pensions (i.e., the lack of hard tables and figures). The migration numbers, although low, must still provide some support for the authors' arguments about increasing mobility among the young, the educated, the non-EU nationals, and so on, which are presented in the paper without any quantitative evidence. It was disappointing that one of the key predictions of the paper—that mobility among economies with dominant first-pillar systems should be significantly higher than among less coordinated and harmonized countries emphasizing second-pillar systems—was never put to an econometric test, although this would have been rather straightforward.

References

Bertola, G., T. Boeri, and G. Nicoletti (eds.). 2001. *Welfare and employment in a united Europe.* Cambridge, Mass.: MIT Press.
Boeri, T., M. Burda, and J. Köllö. 1998. *Mediating the transition: Labor markets in Central and Eastern Europe.* EPI Report No. 4. London: CEPR.
Faini, R., and A. Venturini. 2000. Home bias and migration. Unpublished manuscript, University of Torino, Italy.
Mundell, R. 1957. International trade and factor mobility. *American Economic Review* 51:321–55.

Discussion Summary

Horst Siebert proposed to distinguish two organizational issues, namely, how to organize the schemes of insurance and how to define membership in these schemes. With respect to the first issue, he argued that especially in the first pillar the territoriality principle, that is, organization on a national basis, would be the only viable option, because a pan-European method of social insurance would be too complicated. As to the question of who should be a mandatory member in the first-pillar system, he suggested that one think of applying the Cassis-de-Dijon verdict to the national insurance schemes, at least as an intellectual device, in order to show the impact. Such a regime would mean that individuals could choose to which national systems they want to belong. This, according to Siebert, would probably result in adjustments of the national systems and reduced heterogeneity, because the systems could not stand the mobility of people. He added that uncoupling the pensions from the work contract, in the sense that pensions would be related to contributions and not to earnings, would increase the flexibility of the system under the European concept, provided contributors accrued rights in the first and second pillars that they can take along across national borders. Siebert noted that taking along the rights could require subsidies defined on the EU level, but that one should be careful not to open up a new category of subsidies in order to increase the mobility of people.

Martin Feldstein remarked that switching between two national systems seems to be a very complicated issue, partly because the systems are not proportional. He wondered why the solution toward a pan-European pension system is not to have defined contribution (DC) plans. As an illustration of how to avoid the problems of mobility, he argued that in a system with notional DC plans, people working in each country made contributions to their account and in the end each government would pay benefits based on the years that were contributed and on the notional rate of return that people are entitled to in their notional defined contribution system. *Pierre Pestieau* replied that the way benefits are computed in the case of cross-border mobility is quite fair and that there is not much room for strategic mobility. *Alain Jousten* added that, although portability would obviously be improved by introducing DC plans, problems would not be resolved altogether because DC plans are also usually interwoven with different parts of the tax code in the different countries.

Assar Lindbeck pointed out that the argument that grandfathers should pay because they were overcompensated confronts the dilemma that there is a trade-off between good rules and stable rules. Even if it was a mistake to design pension systems in a way that old generations receive six times what they paid in many countries, it would be problematic to change the rules when people reach sixty-five years of age, because many persons might have based their past economic decisions on those rules. He suggested one take into account the fact that rules may be bad, but stable rules have an advantage in society. *Edward Palmer* remarked that one reason for overcompensating old generations in our systems has been that many of them went through two world wars, a depression, and so forth. He noted that this era has passed and that Sweden has moved to notional accounts and financial accounts only, adding that he sees no reason why that type of combination could not be employed all over Europe. *Alain Jousten* responded that the focus should not only be justice toward the old generation, but also justice toward the young generation, which would justify levying at least some of the burden on the old generations as well. He agreed only to some degree to the argument of a free lunch as compensation for two world wars, as he noticed that in many countries high-income workers were compensated more for the war than low-income workers.

Assar Lindbeck questioned the proposition in the paper that redistribution should be centralized on a European level and suggested that people should be allowed to vote with their feet. *John McHale* remarked that in the real world the redistribution that takes place is determined in the political process, and that it is easy to write down political economy models in which the amount of redistribution taking place is excessive relative to any given social welfare function. In such a framework, he argued, mobility can act as a disciplining device, promoting a better social welfare outcome and, consequently, it is not self-evident that redistribution should move to the central level. *Pierre Pestieau* answered that the paper simply reproduces the state of the art in public finance and that he would not endorse any kind of harmonized social security system.

Axel Börsch-Supan argued that the problems of mobility are much easier to handle under a funded system than in a pay-as-you-go (PAYGO) system, simply because in a funded system there is capital that one can take along much more easily than the claims on human capital. He stressed that the current social security wealth in a funded system is always well defined, whereas the current social security wealth in an unfunded system is always ill defined even in a notional account system, essentially because the markets are different. He added some qualifications, namely that while portability of corporate pensions in the Netherlands was enforced recently, firm pensions in Germany are still often not portable at all, particularly in the reserve account system. He called for regulations to foster portability, because this could not be left to the market due to a complicated game of stick and carrot between employer and employees, as well as the interest employers have to bind workers to their company. *Ignazio Visco* also emphasized the importance of regulating the portability of pensions, which could be accomplished at the central European level, and stressed that increasing competition between open funds rather than closed occupational funds would have very positive effects. *Martin Feldstein* questioned the necessity of regulation and argued in favor of freedom of private agents to contract in any way they want.

David A. Wise noted that twenty years ago in the United States most firm pensions were defined benefit (DB) pensions with provisions not unlike those in the social security systems in Europe and with a considerable degree of variation. He reported that while these different provisions do not seem to have had a major impact on job choice, they seem to have been important with respect to mobility later on, typically encouraging employees to stay until some retirement age and giving an enormous incentive to leave afterward. Based on the evidence that twenty years later at least three-fourths of contributions to pension funds go to DC plans that have none of these incentive effects with respect to mobility, he concludes that limitations on the freedom of choice have been removed.

The importance of the federal issue was emphasized by *Georges de Menil,* who argued that it might become one of the major forces pushing European pension reform ahead. He noted that in a situation of system competition there is always the choice either to collude, which means centralized regulation, or to compete. Although, due to limited actual labor mobility, only a few people might be involved, he argued that the institution of the European Court of Justice can be expected to force governments to change regulations that represent obstacles to mobility and violate the European treaties. He added that labor mobility is not necessary to induce institutional competition but that it is sufficient to have capital mobility, which undisputably is realized, at least since the monetary union. *Assar Lindbeck* raised the issue that when looking at the low incidence of labor mobility in Europe it is necessary to look at the microeconomic incentives and that a situation is not reasonable in which contributions to a pension system in one country are lost when people move to another country. He proposed a system in which it is possible for an individual to carry his compulsory retirement savings with him. Lindbeck added that in his view the discussant underestimates the extent of labor mobility in the

United States in view of different welfare payments, as it is very difficult to explain the flooding from southern states in the United States to some northern large cities like New York from one unemployment situation to another without emphasizing that the welfare payments are five or six times as high in the state of New York as in Louisiana. The notion of very low labor mobility in Europe was challenged by *Axel Börsch-Supan,* who argued that in addition to the regional mobility—which might change in the future as well—there is the dimension of sectoral mobility within a region, which is of greater and increasing importance. Given that people are expected to move increasingly between different jobs, he argued in favor of a funded system, because patchwork life histories are much easier to accommodate here than in a PAYGO system.

As an illustration of what may come about in some countries in Europe, *Jeffrey Liebman* reported on the evidence in the United States with respect to the distributional implications of immigration, stating that the group that currently gets the highest rate of return in the Social Security system are Hispanic Americans, because disproportionally they are immigrants that come into the United States part of the way through their career. As a reaction to this, there had been a lot of pressure to reduce the benefits that are available to the immigrants. *Pierre Pestieau* observed that not only actual mobility but also the threat of mobility matters and noted that in a pure symmetric Nash equilibrium, mobility has an impact even if no one moves. He also endorsed the view that capital mobility is a kind of substitute, and underlined the conclusion in the paper that as a result there is a drive toward less PAYGO and less redistribution.

4

France
The Difficult Path to
Consensual Reforms

Didier Blanchet and Florence Legros

After more than ten years of quasi-continuous debate, some difficulties remain in reaching a consensus on how to adapt the French pension system to the expected demographic trends for the first half of this century. Some important steps have been taken, of course, especially for wage earners in the private sector; however, consensus is still lacking about the next steps in this long-term process.

One explanation of these difficulties is that some of the public remain skeptical about the magnitude of the pension problem. At the beginning, these doubts focused on the demographic diagnosis itself. The early 1990s were marked by controversy over the reliability of fertility indicators (cohort versus period measures), which cast doubt on demographers' ability to make reliable projections. This first stage of the pension debate is now more or less over. The view is now widely shared that below–replacement-level fertility is only one factor in the aging of the population, and not the most important one. Most of the process is due to heavier, irreversible trends, such as the graying of baby boom cohorts and the general rise in life expectancy. Disagreement has shifted to the problem of assessing the exact consequences of these demographic trends. At one end of the spectrum, some believe that their impact on pension systems is strongly overstated: They expect that general economic growth will largely offset the

Didier Blanchet is senior researcher at the Institut National d'Études Démographiques and head of the employment and labor income department at the Institut National de la Statistique et des Études Économiques (INSEE). Florence Legros is professor of economics at Dauphine University in Paris, France, and deputy director of Centre d'Études Prospectives et d'Informations Internationales (CEPII, Paris).

Views expressed are those of the authors, and do not necessarily reflect those of their institutions. The authors wish to thank both Martine Durand for helpful comments on a preliminary version of this paper and other participants at the Berlin seminar.

consequences of demographic changes, especially if it helps lower unemployment. The very good performance of the French economy and the fact that unemployment rates have declined rapidly since 1997 have significantly revived this optimistic view.

At the opposite end, those who are convinced that the pension problem is a real one argue either that economic growth is uncertain, or that it will be of only marginal help in solving pension imbalances. This group remains divided about solutions to this pension problem. Many actors of the French pension system (including trade unions, which are comanagers of most pension schemes) remain strongly opposed to developing the role of saving in retirement preparation. As a result, the only tools they have in hand are raising contribution rates, raising the retirement age, or accepting some relative decline of pensioners' standards of living. These groups can be differentiated according to the relative weights they implicitly or explicitly give to these three instruments. Back at the other end of the spectrum, some advocate the implementation of partial funding on top of existing pay-as-you-go (PAYGO) schemes, but (again) with some variance about the way this should be done: through traditional life insurance contracts, pension funds, employee saving plans, or the accumulation of reserves within existing PAYGO schemes.

The foregoing is, roughly stylized, a general map of existing positions in a field that remains politically very sensitive. We shall now consider the most important aspects of this landscape in more detail, examining the steps that led to its current state. We shall distinguish three main (and partially overlapping) stages of the pension debate. The first began around 1990, with the publication of *Livre Blanc sur les Retraites* (the *White Book on Pensions*), and finally led, in 1993, to the Balladur Reform concerning the general pension regime (which we shall discuss in section 4.1, where we will also recall the basic institutional facts about the organization of the French pension system).

The mid-1990s were then dominated by the debate on the implementation of pension funds. Supporters of pension funds made many propositions over this period; the last proposition (by Deputy Thomas) was adopted by Parliament in 1997. Section 4.2 summarizes the process that led to the adoption of this law, which nevertheless remained stillborn—political change in 1997 led to its abrogation. The new majority preferred to launch a new round of collaboration on pension reform, the first step of which was the Charpin Report, presented in the spring of 1999. Section 4.3 discusses the various developments concerning this report, which failed to promote a new consensus on pension problems. It instead revived the opposition between those with pessimistic and optimistic views of the consequences of aging, and revealed the extent to which the question of retirement age remains controversial. This also discusses how the question of partial funding remains open after the abrogation of the Thomas law and the publication of the Charpin Report.

4.1   Reform within PAYGO Schemes: From the Governmental *Livre Blanc* to the Balladur Reform

4.1.1   Institutional Background: The Main Characteristics of the
French Pension System in the Early 1990s

Let us first recall the major institutional facts about the organization of the French pension system. One characteristic is its almost exclusive reliance on PAYGO financing: French pension schemes did not accumulate more than marginal provisions, covering no more than a few months' worth of benefits. Another characteristic of the system is its relative complexity, due to the fact that it has not been possible, after World War II, to impose a normalized system to all existing socioprofessional groups, the interests of which were partly divergent. This element complicates the implementation of nationwide reform, as it will be discussed below.

One final characteristic of the system is that it globally offers a good average replacement rate, at a retirement age that is probably among the lowest in all developed countries. The net replacement rate is about 80 percent at the average wage, and varies from almost 100 percent at very low wages to 60 percent for higher wages (Charpin 1999). The male total labor-force participation rate in the fifty-five to sixty-four age bracket was 40 percent in 1999, corresponding to a median age at exit from the labor force of about fifty-nine years (Blanchet and Pelé 1999). This is partly the result of the introduction, in 1983, of retirement at age sixty (which was a political priority of the socialist government after François Mitterrand's election in 1981), but also of the development (by all successive governments) of paths to early retirement through either specific preretirement schemes or specific dispositions of unemployment insurance for older workers.

We shall not give here a full description of this system's complexity. The main point is that the French population is divided into three major groups (table 4.1):

- Wage earners from the private sector (about 68 percent of the labor force), who have a relatively homogeneous two-pillar scheme. The first pillar is the general regime (*Caisse Nationale d'Assurance Vieillesse des Travailleurs Salariés*, or CNAVTS). The second pillar consists of two complementary schemes: the *Association pour le Régime de Retraite complémentaire de Salariés* (ARRCO; for all workers) and the *Association Générale des Institutions de Retraite des Cadres* (AGIRC; for executives only).
- Wage earners belonging to the public sector or to large national firms, who have specific schemes that usually are more generous than the system for private-sector workers. This group represents about 21 percent of the labor force.

Table 4.1   Characteristics of the Main Pension Regimes

Pension Schemes	Contributors (thousands)	Demographic Ratio,[a] 1998	Benefits Paid, 1998 (billions of francs)	Benefits Paid, 1998 (% of GDP)	Effective Contribution Rate,[b] 1996
Wage earners, private sector					
CNAVTS (general regime)	14,249	1.7	349.5	4.08	17.0
ARRCO	14,000	1.7	163.1	1.90	10.0
AGIRC	3,030	2.4	83.9	0.98	24.7
Wage earners, public sector					
Civil servants' scheme	2,428	1.9	167.9	1.96	51.7
CNRACL (local administrations' pension scheme)	1,597	3.3	42.0	0.49	33.1
SNCF (railways)	175	0.9	16.8	0.20	38.5
IEG (electricity and gas)	149	1.7	28.8	0.34	63.6
Self-employed					
Farmers	725	0.4	49.9	0.58	n.a.
Organic	608	0.9	19.8	0.23	n.a.
Cancava	481	1.0	15.7	0.18	n.a.
CNAVPL	427	3.6	14.7	0.17	n.a.
Carmf	118	5.0	n.a.	n.a.	16.7

Source: Direction de la Sécurité Social (1999).

Notes: n.a. = not available. See text for explanation of other abbreviations.

[a] Contributors/pensioners, excluding widows and orphans.

[b] Ratio of total contributions (employers' + employees') to the wage bill.

- Self-employed workers, who also have specific schemes. These used to be less generous than the general scheme and ARRCO-AGIRC, and only progressively adjusted to the rules applying to the other schemes. This group represents about 11 percent of the labor force.

All these schemes are comanaged by social partners (trade unions and representatives of firms), with strong control of the basic schemes by the Ministry of Social Affairs.

Given that it comprises the largest part of the population, the general regime is the one for which we give details of the rules for computing pension levels. Workers (and their employers) contribute the fraction of wages below the social security ceiling (which is roughly equal to the average wage). Then they receive a pension proportional both to the number of years they have contributed to the scheme and to a reference wage. Before the 1993 reform, whose consequences will be detailed later, this reference wage formerly was the average gross wage of the ten best years of the pensioner's career (after truncation to the social security ceiling). The pension, at the maximum, was equal to 50 percent of this reference wage. Before 1983, an additional condition for pension-claiming was that the claimant be age sixty-five or higher. This threshold was lowered to age sixty in 1983, but only for people having contributed to the system for more than thirty-seven and one-half years. For people not fulfilling this condition, retirement between the ages of sixty and sixty-five was possible, but a strong penalty (a 10 percent pension reduction pension for each year of anticipation).

Complementary schemes are organized as systems of notional accounts, which provide pensions that are more or less proportional to the cumulative contributions paid by workers during their working lives. Workers buy "points" with their contributions when they are working, and receive pensions proportional to the number of points they have accumulated over their careers. Retirement is also possible at age sixty for individuals fulfilling the conditions for the full rate in the general regime. Special schemes are more generous in two respects: They generally allow retirement at age sixty or even lower without additional conditions, and pensions are often computed as a percentage of the most recent wage. Regimes for the self-employed, on the other hand, still have a retirement age equal to sixty-five and, at least for older cohorts, offer lower-level benefits than do other categories.

4.1.2   From the *Livre Blanc* to the 1993 Reform

Questions have been intensively raised about the long-term viability of this system during the 1980s. The end of the 1980s was marked especially by increasing pressure from private insurance companies to add the pension issue to the public agenda, with the explicit intention of developing their role in pension financing through the development of complementary funded schemes, in which they would have played a large role.

This lead to strong reactions by social partners and managers of PAYGO schemes who felt that their management of pensions was being unduly criticized, and who argued that, even if there were a real pension problem, funding would not be the right answer to the question. It was in this conflicted context that prime minister Michel Rocard ordered the preparation of a "white book," coordinated by the *Commissariat Général du Plan* (the General Planning Agency) and issued in 1991. The first purpose of this white book was to present basic facts and prospects about the pension system. Concerning prospects, it proposed a global projection for the aggregate pension system showing a need for increased contribution rates of 50 to 100 percent up to the year 2040, depending on fertility rates and employment rates. For specific regimes, it proposed detailed projections up to 2010 only. At this horizon, without changes in contributions rates, deficits were projected to be 374 billion francs for the main basic schemes, including 342 billion francs for the general regime, and 49 billion francs for ARRCO and AGIRC (the total amount of pension expenditures in France, at this time, was about 900 billion francs, or 12 percent of GDP).

The *Livre Blanc* then explored various solutions. It ruled out a few radical scenarios, such as a transition to a fully funded system (an announcement that was essentially rhetoric, because no one, in fact, advocated such a radical change) or a shift to a system of universal lump-sum pension benefits completed by private saving or pension funds. The *Livre Blanc* clearly favored adaptations within PAYGO schemes, with a quantification of some particular scenarios for the general regime: a modification of conditions necessary to receive a pension at the full rate at age sixty, changes in the rules for computing the reference wage, and indexation of pensions on prices. According to its evaluation, such measures could at least help solve potential imbalances up to the year 2010.

The publication of this white book was not immediately followed by any political decision. Rocard himself was replaced just after its publication. It was only in 1993 that some consequences were drawn from this report. The Balladur Reform (after the name of the prime minister of the conservative government between 1992 and 1995) was enforced during the summer of 1993. It applied to the general regime and assimilated schemes, and consisted of three major points directly inspired by the *Livre Blanc:*

- Indexation of pension on prices instead of indexation on average wages, but with a *clause de rendez-vous,* (regular adjustment meeting clause); that is, the possibility of discretionary increases of pensions in case of excessive divergence from average wages.
- Computation of the pension on the basis of a wage averaged over

twenty-five years instead of over ten. This is currently taking place progressively, with a one-year increase for each successive cohort between the 1933 and 1948 cohorts.

- An increase in the number of years spent in the workforce necessary to receive full pension benefits at age sixty. This number will progressively shift to forty years instead of thirty-seven and one-half. The increase is one-fourth year for each cohort, so that the new final condition should apply to the 1943 cohort.

Presently, these measures are the only formal reforms implemented in the French pension system. Some parallel adjustments have been introduced, however, in complementary schemes for wage earners (i.e., for ARRCO and AGIRC), especially in 1993, 1994, and 1996. In the first steps, some additional resources were collected through increases in contributions in order to face current deficits implied by the 1993–94 economic recession. Later, more restrictive measures—such as increases in the purchasing price of points, and moderation of the evolution of the nominal value of these points—were introduced.

How far did the Balladur reform and the adjustments performed by complementary schemes go toward solving the pension problem? Concerning the general regime, simulations show that the Balladur reform may help limit the progression of the equilibrium contribution rate, which should increase, until 2040, by only 11.7 percentage points (i.e., a 70 percent increase), while the demographic ratio is divided by two. The lengthening of the conditions necessary to receive the full rate do not play a large role in this result, at least in the medium run. Most of the members of cohorts leaving during the current decade and the next one will have accumulated a sufficient number of years of contribution at age sixty to remain unaffected by this aspect of the reform. It is rather the two other attributes that are likely to generate reductions of the total pension bill. Of course, this would result from declines in replacement rates, both at liquidation (table 4.2), and after liquidation (because of indexation on prices instead of on wages). This raises two concerns:

- The relative reduction in total pension is mechanically linked with the rate of economic growth. The reform's contributions to solving imbalances will be low if economic growth is very slow.
- The choice of solving imbalances through reductions in pensioners' relative standards of living has not been really debated, because the reform has in general been presented in technical terms that are not very explicit. In any case, this choice increases, rather than rules out, the need for complementary savings for individuals who wish to maintain their standards of living after retirement. This leads directly to the question of partial funding.

The same kind of observation can be made of reforms in complementary schemes. The downward adjustment of pension levels could even be stronger if these schemes were to follow literally the scenarios they have themselves provided for the Charpin Report, as shown in tables 4.2 and 4.3. These projections assumed a progression of the purchasing price of pension points parallel to the average wage, meaning that all successive cohorts, from now on, would accumulate a similar number of points over their careers. If we assume that the nominal value of these points would change only according to prices, this means a complete stagnation of pensions in real terms. Combined with a doubling of real wages over the next forty years, this plan indeed neutralizes almost completely the impact of demographic change (table 4.3), but with very severe consequences for replacement rates (table 4.2).

The contrast with expected changes for civil servants is striking. Because no change is planned for their replacement rates, the equilibrium contribution rate increases in parallel with the demographic dependency ratio. Two questions are thus raised: (1) How can we avoid the large declines of relative pension levels for the private sector, through complementary funding or by relying more on an upward adjustment of the retirement age? and (2) Is it possible to reduce the expected inequality of treatment between the private and the public sectors? We shall first discuss the role of complementary funding, which has been hotly debated since the 1990s.

Table 4.2   Projections of Gross Replacement Rates for Four Typical Cases

Pension Schemes	1996	2020	2040
Blue-collar workers, private sector[a]			
General regime	45.7	41.1	40.9
ARRCO	22.4	15.4	10.3
Total	68.1	56.5	51.2
Executive workers, private sector[b]			
General regime	22.9	20.6	20.6
AARCO	11.7	8.2	5.4
AGIRC	24.4	16.7	11.9
Total	59.0	45.5	37.9
Civil servants			
Total	57.8	57.8	57.8
Physicians			
Total	54.5	41.5	29.8

Source: Charpin (1991).

Notes: Includes the impact of the 1993 reform for the general regime and of planned indexation rules for ARRCO and AGIRC. See text for explanation of abbreviations.

[a]Individual reaching the social security ceiling after twenty years of contributions.

[b]Individual at the 90th percentile of wage earners affiliated to the general regime.

Table 4.3 Projections for a Selection of Pension Regimes

Pension Schemes	Demographic Ratio[a]			Current and Expected Balance[b]		
	1998	2020	2040	1998	2020	2040
Wage earners, private sector						
CNAVTS (general regime)	1.7	1.1	0.8	−0.1	−5.5	−11.2
ARRCO	1.7	1.1	0.7	0.3	−0.5	−1.1
AGIRC	2.4	1.3	0.9	−1.7	−5.3	−3.9
Wage earners, public sector						
Civil servants' scheme	1.9	1.1	0.9	0.0	−26.4	−40.9
CNRACL (local administrations' pension scheme)	3.3	1.4	1.0	9.2	−16.7	−28.9
Self-employed						
Carmf	5.0	1.6	1.3	1.7	−6.1	−7.0

Source: Charpin (1991).
Notes: See text for explanation of abbreviations.
[a] Contributors/pensioners, excluding widows and orphans.
[b] Before compensation transfers, in contribution points.

4.2 Implementing Pension Funds: From the Insurer's *Livre Blanc* to the Stillborn Thomas Law

4.2.1 A Multiplicity of Proposals with Fragile Political Support

Proposals for developing the role of saving in retirement preparation were made well before the pension debate rose to its current level of importance. It was already the topic of a book cowritten by Kessler and Strauss-Kahn (1982). The debate intensified and radicalized, however, when Kessler became president of the *Fédération Française des Sociétés d'Assurance* (FSSA, the French federation of insurers) and published the *White Book of Insurers* (FFSA 1991) as an echo to the one prepared by the government.

In their white book, insurers argued that the burden of the public pension scheme from 2005 to 2010 would lead to intergenerational inequity. They advocated stopping the revalorization of pensions in order to limit the implicit debt for future generations, and the creation of pension funds as additional pension schemes. Insurers' pension funds were to be sponsored by firms or branches, to benefit from strong fiscal incentives, and to be managed as life insurance, leading to the payment of annuities supplementing the PAYGO pension. This proposal was followed by two alternative proposals:

- Bankers and mutual societies (governed by the mutual insurance code) proposed the creation of *Fonds d'Epargne Retraite* (Retirement Pension Funds), whose major difference from the insurers' proposal was that it would allow a choice, upon retiring, between an annuity and a one-time payment of capital (a solution that met people's preferences, according to surveys).

- Provident institutions (*Institutions de Prévoyance* [contingency funds], closer to PAYGO pension schemes) proposed an organization in which trade unions would be involved in the management of funds (*Fonds à Gestion Paritaire;* i.e., funds managed with equal representation of partners). This proposal, too, offered the possibility of transforming the annuity into capital, but with restrictive conditions.

To be implemented, such propositions needed a legal basis. Many laws were proposed during the period. All came from the most liberal side of the political spectrum, the socialist party and trade unions having developed strong resistance to this trend (partly for historical reasons—the failure between WWI and WWII of fully funded basic schemes—and partly for political reasons). Their suspicion of these projects was generally reinforced by the fact that the projects were sponsored by professional lobbies potentially interested in the development of such funds.

The first proposition, written in 1993 by Senator Marini, aimed at creating a saving instrument designed to correct the historical weakness of the French equity market; it did not include any fiscal incentive. This proposition was never discussed by Parliament. The next proposal was written by two members of Parliament, Thomas and Millon, between the end of 1993 and the beginning of 1994. It proposed the creation of *plans d'épargne-retraite d'entreprise* (or firm retirement saving plans; the term *pension fund* had been ruled out because of the negative connotation generated by the Maxwell affair). This project proposed that 20 percent of the funds should be invested in the sponsoring firm. It was more strictly oriented toward retirement than was the Marini proposal. The next draft was by Minister Barrot (who returned to the term *pension fund*) and was characterized by generous fiscal incentives.

Finally, the Thomas law, voted-in in 1996, was a mix of all these drafts: It allowed the choice between exit with a rent or with a lump-sum capital, proposed generous fiscal incentives, and allowed internal management within the firm. It was precisely the last two points that raised problems for the new socialist majority following the political switch in 1997, and that led to the abrogation of the law.[1]

4.2.2   A Lack of Consensus among Economists Themselves

More generally, political arguments against pension funding (and partial privatization of the pension system) are

---

1. Moreover, the fact that the minister in charge of applying the law was the ministry of the economy and not of social affairs was considered additional proof that social concerns were absent from this law.

- Inability of saving vectors to cover the whole population;
- Risk linked with financial markets;
- Inequality provided by fiscal incentives in a country where only half the population pays income tax;
- Risk of resource evasion for mandatory PAYGO schemes, if payments to pension funds are exempted from social contributions; and
- Governance conflicts between wage owners and equity holders.

In this still inconclusive debate about the opportunity of developing pension funds, the economic profession, itself, did not speak with a unique voice (Blanchet and Villeneuve 1997). Part of that voice shares the public defiance of pension funding that was inherited from the failure of funded schemes around the time of WWII.

First, it was easy for opponents of funding to recall that funding is not intrinsically better-insulated from demographic risks than are PAYGO schemes. This is especially true if population aging is due to an increased life expectancy (this argument has been widely used by managers of PAYGO schemes); but it is also the case if aging is due to a slowdown or contraction of the active labor force, even if we take into account the possibility of exporting capital to countries where the labor force is apparently more dynamic.[2]

These points forced partisans of funding to adopt other arguments. The central one is the fact that, even when demographic shocks affect funding and PAYGO in parallel ways, a structural advantage may remain for funding if the economy is constantly evolving below the golden-rule savings rate. This remains only theoretical, however, and is itself subject to the following objections:

- The first well-known objection is that even if shifting toward partial funding is more efficient in the long run, it involves a short-term consumption loss, which is generally irreversible and is politically hard to impose on the current generation.

2. Artus (1999), for instance, argues that the demographic cycle that will begin in 2005–2010 will paradoxically favor the PAYGO schemes, especially if these funded schemes are invested in fixed-income assets (such as government bonds, which have been the favorite vector of insurance companies to date). The explanation is that the active population has been high during the past years, thus involving high rates of unemployment, low levels of wages, low levels of consumption, and weakness in the economic growth in Europe and Asia where the saving rates—pushed up by the high life expectancies—are high relative to the investment rates. When the numbers of the active population flatten out or even decrease after 2005–2010, wages will rise, consumption will be more dynamic, and inflation will be higher. In addition, currently active cohorts who bought expensive assets will have difficulties selling them back to subsequent, less-numerous cohorts. High wages, low yields, and higher inflation rates will create a yield gap between PAYGO and funded schemes; this gap will be higher for funds invested in fixed-income assets and cannot be reduced by the exporting of saving flows excedents, because life expectancy is also increasing in the emergent countries, where the induced effects are the same as in the developed countries. Thus saving rates exceed investment rates.

- The mechanisms through which this loss could eventually be compensated in the future are considered either as lacking empirical support (e.g., arguments involving endogenous growth mechanisms), or as not being adapted to the French context. This is the case for the idea that shifting to funding would boost growth by correcting distortions implied by the PAYGO scheme: Such distortions are generally considered limited in the French pension system, which is essentially contributive and generates little intracohort redistribution.
- There is also some dissent about the part of the current gap between equity yield and economic growth that results from a low saving rate, and about the part of this gap that is either a pure risk premium or the result of a transitory and unsustainable financial bubble.

On the whole, even if economists frequently agree about the benefits that would result from a lower financial intermediation (Artus and Legros 1992), many still doubt the ability of funded systems to resist demographic and economic fluctuations more than a PAYGO scheme could. This debate remains more or less open, but the difficulty of providing indisputable economic arguments in favor of funding certainly plays a role in the continuing hesitation to develop this tool for solving pension problems.

4.3   The Charpin Report and After

4.3.1   The Charpin Report

While movements were going on around the implementation of pension funds, some problems specific to PAYGO schemes remained unresolved. One problem was the question of the transposition of the Balladur reform to special regimes. An attempt to deal with this was the Juppé Plan in 1995, developed by the newly elected conservative government. Pensions were not the central aspect of the ambitious Juppé Plan, which was expected to foster regulation of social expenditures in France with a particular emphasis on health insurance. However, it also included the proposal to align pension rules in the public sector with those of the post-1993 general regime. This proposal is among those that led to a strong social contest in November 1995, which resulted in the withdrawal of the plan and a new period of uncertainty.

Not long afterward, new polls were organized, which allowed the arrival of a new socialist government. We mentioned earlier that this new majority abrogated the Thomas law; the failure of the Juppé Plan also showed that at least one faction of public opinion was not ready for further reforms within the PAYGO scheme. The pedagogical preparation that had apparently been successful with the first *Livre Blanc* was no longer effective.

This situation suggested the need for further collective thinking about the future of pensions in France. As had been the case for the first *Livre Blanc,* the organization of this collective reflection was entrusted to the *Commissariat Général du Plan,* the traditional forum for nationwide dialogue among the administration, academics, and social partners on long-term economic policies. The result was published in spring of 1999, and is now known as the Charpin Report, after the name of the head of the *Commissariat Général du Plan.*

The basic diagnosis is the same as the one of the *Livre Blanc,* but more emphasis has been put on very long-term perspectives (2040). The report made no recommendations, but explored various scenarios. The main ones were the following:

- A further increase in the duration of the working life needed to reach the full rate in the general regime before age sixty-five, beyond the increase instituted by the Balladur reform (i.e., forty-two and one-half years of contributions instead of forty). Given the current distribution of ages of entry into the labor force for younger generations, this should *de facto* raise the normal age at retirement to sixty-five, except for those entering the labor force very early, who are also those with the lowest qualifications and the lowest life expectancies. The suggestion therefore indirectly took into account considerations of intragenerational equity.
- Compensation for the problem above, by reducing penalties currently associated with anticipated retirement. As explained above, anticipation by one year for people who do not have the full rate currently implies a 10 percent loss in the level of pension, which is more than that requested by actuarial neutrality. This penalty could be reduced to 5 percent per missing year to receive the full rate.
- Development of reserves within PAYGO schemes in the interest of progressive adjustment.
- The need for continuous follow-up of pension regimes and for adaptive management of any future reform.[3]

Despite its very cautious approach, the report has been perceived as excessively pessimistic by a large fraction of the public, as attested by reactions of social partners annexed to the report, and reactions expressed in the news media.

This led to two more recent reports that adopt a more optimistic view of the pension problem. The first is the Taddei report, prepared within the *Conseil d'Analyse Economique* (CAE, or Council of Economic Analysis)

---

3. This recommendation recently led to the creation of *Conseil d'Orientation des Retraites,* directly attached to the prime minister, including representatives of trade unions, government, and academics. Note, however, that the Medef (large firms union) refused to join this council.

which concentrated on conditions for allowing a more progressive transition from activity to retirement. The second (and the most openly optimistic) is the Teulade report, written by a former minister of social affairs and prepared in the context of the *Conseil Economique et Social* (Economic and Social Council), where it received strong support from a number of trade unions (except the reformist *Confédération Français Démocratique du Travail* [CFDT], who joined the Medef in considering that the optimism of this report was excessive).

4.3.2   A New Focus on Retirement Age

Most of the dissent around the Charpin Report concentrated on this scenario of further restricting the conditions of access to full retirement before age sixty-five. There are two aspects of this problem; the first to determine whether an increase in the retirement age is realistic in the context of high unemployment rates.

We know, of course, that the relationship between age at retirement and unemployment is not a simple one. In particular, it is widely admitted that the lowering of the age of exit from the labor force over the last twenty years did not help reduce significantly the unemployment rate—quite the contrary, in fact, which supports the idea that changes in labor supply have no significant impact on unemployment rates. This view is the one generally promoted in theories of the equilibrium unemployment rate. Some models of equilibrium employment even predict that an excessively low retirement age increases rather than lowers unemployment, because of its positive impact on the tax wedge. If this is true, the case can be made for raising the retirement age without waiting for any improvement of the labor market situation.

However, the accuracy of such theories remains uncertain. One contributing factor could be the existence of an asymmetrical reaction. It is one thing to observe that reducing the age at retirement did not help lower the unemployment rate; to *prove* that postponing this same age would not raise the unemployment rate (at least in the short run) however, is another. This was certainly the reason that the Charpin Report was cautious in saying that increasing the age at retirement should not take place before the unemployment rate had durably returned to significantly lower levels.

When might this new context appear? Many expect it will result naturally from the expected downturn in labor force growth around 2005, precisely when baby boom cohorts will arrive at retirement. This raises once again the question of the impact of changes of labor supply on employment rates, the answer to which is unclear. The element of optimism, if any, thus comes from another point, which is the fact that unemployment rates already have begun to decline in recent years without the help of a more favorable demographic context. This new trend was still very recent at the time the Charpin Report was prepared, but has been confirmed since. Between mid-1997 and mid-2001, the unemployment rate declined from 12.3 to 8.7 percent. This same period has seen the greatest level of private-sector job creation in several decades (since at least 1970). This is the result both of good general economic performance and of a significant increase in the impact of growth and job creations. Although it is too soon to say how long this favorable trend will last, it does suggest that the level of unemployment could progressively become less of an obstacle to policies intended to increase retirement ages.

Dissent in this case will not concern the feasibility of the policy, but the intensity with which it should be developed. This presents several questions. First is the idea (developed, e.g., in the Teulade report) that full employment will, in itself, be sufficient to solve the pension problem, without need of further increase in the size of the occupied labor force through delayed retirement. We know, however, that this idea is only partially true, even under the assumption of full redirection of social expenses from unemployment insurance toward pension financing. Detractors may also object that these resources would be better used if directed toward other (non-pension) kinds of social expenditures.

Further potential cause for dissent is the idea that if we return to a situation of full employment and labor shortages appeared after 2005, we could reactivate the immigration policy. This option is not realistic in the long run,[4] but may be used for a few decades before the pension system is fully adapted to the new demographic context (a position developed in the Taddei report). Finally, many will ask whether this policy should be differentiated across social groups (whose life expectancies differ considerably) and how much flexibility should be permitted around this delayed normal retirement age. This question was at the center of the Taddei report; as mentioned earlier, however, the Charpin Report already dealt with these issues very carefully, with particular emphasis on the idea of promoting free choice of retirement age within systems, in a manner closer to rules of actuarial neutrality (a point bypassed by many of its detractors).

4.3.3   Reserves versus Pension Funds after the Charpin Report

These recent developments show that the question of age at retirement should become more central to the pension debate in France than it has been for years, probably because the shift to retirement at age sixty was too recent to be questioned yet. In this new context, the question of pension funding has been relegated somewhat to future discussion but has not been completely abandoned. Thus we turn now to the current state of opinion on this subtopic.

In the Charpin Report itself, the only reference to funding is the pro-

---

4. Immigration, in the long run, can compensate only for the part of the aging process that may be due to permanent, below-replacement fertility levels; it cannot compensate for the part of this process that is due to increased longevity. Such a compensation would require unrealistic migration rates, generating a path of rapid and continuous population growth, which would be unsustainable in the long run.

posal to develop reserves within PAYGO schemes. This option had been proposed earlier by some experts (Davanne and Pujol 1997), and such a reserve fund has been implemented for 1999 by the Social Security Finance Law and is expected to be funded by income from privatization and by exceptional receipts. This raises two questions. The first concerns the specificity of this reserve fund, because there is no fundamental macroeconomic difference between allocating income from privatization to this fund versus using that income to reduce any other component of public debt, even without invoking considerations of ricardian equivalence. The second concerns the amount to be invested in the fund. If the purpose is to reduce permanently the total cost of pension financing, the reserves must be much higher, although their final magnitude remains sensitive to assumptions concerning rates of return. For instance, reserves requested to structurally reduce the contribution rate by 1.5 points would vary between 14 and 55 of total gross domestic product in the long run, for real rates of return varying between 5.5 and 2.5 percent. This raises again the question of the sustainability of large gaps between rates of return and economic growth, and the problem of implied costs for the current generations of workers.

How is this policy perceived by social partners? The *Union Professionnelle Artisanale* (UPA; independent workers), the *Confédération Générale des Petits et Moyennes Entreprises* (CGPME; small firms), and the Medef (formerly the *Conseil National du Patronat Français* [CNPF]; larger firms) unambiguously express their opposition to reserves that they view as no more than a source for new increases in contribution rates, with the associated consequences for labor costs and competitiveness. They continue to ask for funded facultative plans with important fiscal incentives, promoted at the firm, branch, or interprofessional level.[5]

The professional lobbies have not changed their attitude since 1995. This attitude is very close to that of Medef (D. Kessler, still president of FFSA, is also vice-president of Medef). Insurers are critical of the PAYGO reserve fund: They consider that the measure is too late, that there will be too much temptation for the government to invest these reserves in public debt assets, and that investing in equities is not the government's role.

At the other end of the spectrum, reserves are not more welcome by trade unions, who remain more or less hostile to any form of funding, whatever its context. This is the case for the *Confédération Générale du Travail* (CGT), the *Fédération Syndicale Unitaire* (FSU), and *Force Ouvrière* (CGT-FO), whose membership rate is rather important in the public sec-

---

5. In a document called "Propositions of the Medef to Insure the Future of the Retirement Pensions in France" (April 1999), the Medef expressed two proposals: on the one hand, to increase the length of careers necessary to obtain a full pension to forty-five years (i.e., two and one-half years more than in the scenarios examined in the Charpin Report); and on the other hand, to divert 8 percent of the gross wages to a pension fund (this 8 percent being the level necessary to maintain the current generosity of the system). In fact, these two measures can be considered as partially redundant.

tor. The *Confédération Générales des Cadres* (CGC, a middle-executives' trade union) is opposed to individual funding but not to reserves. Finally, reformist trade unions are unopposed both to these reserves and to a certain development of pension funds or individual funding; these unions are the *Confédération Française des Travailleurs Chrétiens* (CFTC), and, more importantly, the CFDT.

4.3.4   Toward Employees' Saving Schemes

Assuming that individual funding will develop, we now ask what the form for this development will be. After the abrogation of the Thomas law, many feel that pension funds are less in favor and doubt the need for any new instrument for retirement preparation. This is partly the result of the demobilization of professional lobbies, especially insurers, whose interests in pension funds declined somewhat, and who preferred going back to more traditional activities, especially life insurance. Life insurance has been a very successful saving tool during the last decade and now represents 55 percent of French saving flows. It is probably one element of spontaneous answer to fears concerning the future of PAYGO replacement rates.

Reflecting another such perceived solution is the recent shift in interest toward another form of saving: employee saving schemes (Balligand and De Foucauld 2000). This interest has been stimulated by the observation that 40 percent of French enterprises are owned by nonresident investors (due, in part, to fiscal incentives for foreign investors). This weakness of the ratio owned by French investors created unusual movements in equities prices in 1999, and—together with a debate over the fiscal status of stock options—induced increasing interest in these employee saving schemes. This interest received support from different segments of the political spectrum. Trade unions have expressed different positions: CFDT expressed interest in strong development of employee saving schemes with links to retirement pension funds, whereas CGT—in an ambiguous position—contends that the two problems are different.

It was in this context that a law was voted-in in February 2001 with the aims of allocating saving to the firms' investment (with fiscal incentives), of favoring a better repartition of economic growth between employees (particularly by increasing the portability for wage earners in small firms), and of allowing employees to use these saving schemes for medium-run (ten-year) projects. For these purposes, the *Plans d'Epargne Interentreprises* (PEI, for small firms, with high portability) and the *Plan d'Epargne Salariale Volontaire* (PPESV, mainly medium-run projects) were created while the existing employee saving schemes were deeply renewed. All these schemes now include guaranties and rights for wage earners, such as portfolio-allocation rules and improved roles for ad hoc supervision committees.

However, although the ability to invest a significant part (one-third of the assets) in the sponsoring firm is expected to lead to strong incentives for wage earners, the law still puts apart the link with retirement pension financing.

4.4 Conclusion

To summarize briefly, positions with regard to the pension problem have evolved considerably since the early 1990s. Several reports on the topic have played their pedagogical roles. The first steps toward a moderation of pensions were taken by the Balladur reform in 1993; the debate about funding, even though consensus is still lacking, has become less ideological and less dramatized since then.

Yet some stumbling blocks remain. The matter of the alignment of special schemes with the general regime is still far from being resolved. Another matter—how far policies aimed at underindexing pensions should go (Sterdyniak, Dupont, and Dantec 1999)—is still insufficiently debated. These policies can give one the sense that the pension problem is solved— which is true, from the point of view of projected aggregate imbalances for PAYGO schemes. Those who will be pensioners in the future, however, may not understand that these policies are enacted at the expense of future replacement rates, and that they will result in large income losses for the oldest pensioners at ages in which their needs are not necessarily declining. The pension problem should, in this respect, be closely linked to reflections on the future of old age dependency and on the way we plan to finance its coverage.

Finally, the articulation between age at retirement and partial funding is still unclear. One solution would be to maintain relatively high replacement rates at low ages for low-income workers, arguing that these workers also benefit from shorter life expectancies and, on the whole, began working earlier. Higher-income workers, on the other hand, would have to choose between two options: relying essentially on their human capital by preparing themselves to work until a relatively advanced age; or relying on financial capital accumulated either through life insurance, employee saving schemes, and (if they are finally implemented) pension funds or any of their substitutes.

References

Artus, P. 1999. "Le vieillissement de la population est mondial: La génération active présente sera sacrifiée" (Population aging is a worldwide phenomenon: Currently active cohorts will be sacrificed). Caisse des Dépôts et Consignations, Working Paper no. 1999-03.
Artus, P., and F. Legros. 1992. Les fonds de pension et l'équilibre financier (Pension

funds and macroeconomic financial equilibrium). *Revue d'Économie Financière,* special issue: "Le financement des retraites."

Balligand, J. P., and J. B. De Foucauld. 2000. "L'épargne salariale au cœur du contrat social" (Employees' saving schemes at the heart of the social contract). Rapport au premier ministre. Paris: La Documentation Française.

Blanchet, D., and L. P. Pelé. 1999. Social security and retirement in France. In *Social security and retirement around the world,* ed. J. Gruber and D. Wise, 101–33. Chicago: University of Chicago Press.

Blanchet, D., and B. Villeneuve. 1997. "Que reste-t-il du débat répartition-capitalisation?" (What remains of the funding/PAYGO debate?) *Revue d'Économie Financière,* special issue: "Systèmes de retraite: Structure(s), défis et perspectives."

Charpin, J.-M. 1999. *"L'avenir de nos retraites"* (The future of our pensions). *Rapport au premier ministre.* Paris: La Documentation Française.

Commissariat Général du Plan. 1991. *Livre blanc sur les retraites: Garantir dans l'équité les retraites de demain* (White book on pensions: Warranting fairness for future pensions; with a foreword by M. Rocard). Paris: La Documentation Française.

Davanne, O., and T. Pujol. 1997. "Le débat sur les retraites: Capitalisation contre répartition" (The debate on pensions: Funding versus PAYGO). *Revue Française d'Economie* 1: 57–115.

Direction de la Sécurité Sociale. 1999. "Comptes annuels" (annual figures). Paris: Ministry of Employment and Solidarity.

Fédération Française des sociétés d'assurance (FFSA). 1991. *Contribution aux réflexions en cours sur les retraites* (Contribution to ongoing reflections on pensions). Paris: Risques.

Kessler, D., and D. Strauss-Kahn. 1982. *L'épargne et la retraite: L'avenir des retraites préfinancées* (Saving and retirement: The future of prefinanced pensions). Paris: Economica.

Sterdyniak, H., G. Dupont, and A. Dantec. 1999. "Les retraites en France: Que faire?" (Pensions in France: What should be done?). *Revue de l'OFCE* 68:19–81.

Taddei, D. 1999. *"Retraites choisies et progressives"* (Chosen and progressive retirement). Rapport pour le Conseil d'Analyse Economique no. 21. Paris: La Documentation Française.

Teulade, R. 2000. *"L'avenir des systèmes de retraite"* (The future of pension schemes). Avis présenté au Conseil Economique et Social. 12 January, Paris.

Comment   Martine Durand

The paper by Didier Blanchet and Florence Legros provides a very good overview of how the debate on pension reforms has evolved over the past decade or so in France. In particular, it highlights the political difficulties the various governments in place during this period encountered in attempting to introduce these reforms. The analysis presented in the paper

---

At the time of this writing, Martine Durand was counselor to the head of the economics department of the Organization for Economic Cooperation and Development.

provides an excellent background to understand both the present state of the debate and the direction of future reforms.

Some Institutional Features of the French Pension System and the Lack of Reform So Far

The paper emphasises the political context that has framed the pension reform debate in France, and implicitly argues that this context is at the root of the difficulties encountered in the push for the reform agenda. However, one should not underestimate some of the institutional features of the French pension system as another major explanation for the lack of reform so far. Three such features are worth mentioning.

The Complexity of the French Pension System

The authors give a broad outline of the present institutional arrangements, but the system is in fact much more complex. It consists of (1) a basic compulsory public scheme; (2) numerous compulsory complementary occupational schemes, some of which have fewer than 20,000 contributors; (3) mechanisms to ensure some level of redistribution between these two schemes; and (4) a separate scheme for public-sector employees. Although some progress has been made toward the unification of the major private-sector employee schemes, there remains a striking difference between the public- and private-sector schemes. The public-sector scheme is more generous and has remained unaffected so far by either past or proposed reforms. This complexity is undoubtedly a major source of rigidity.

The Management of the French Pension System

The private pension schemes are managed according to bi- or tripartite arrangements involving trade unions, industry confederations, and the government. This form of management is not unique in Europe, but it requires consensus building to undertake reform. In the case of France, it probably constitutes another reason for the lack of reform, given that French industrial relations are notoriously prone to conflicts.

The Various Conceptual Approaches to Pensions

Historically, French pension systems have been built on various conceptual approaches. Private-sector schemes were based on insurance principles; self-employed or occupational schemes were based on wealth accumulation; and public-sector schemes were based on deferred income. These different concepts have given rise to very different institutional arrangements across regimes with respect to the way contributions and benefits are determined. This contributes not only to the complexity of the system but also to the difficulty in harmonizing the various schemes, as the different philosophies underlying their setups has presented very different underlying technical characteristics.

What Is the Extent of the Aging Shock in France?

As mentioned in Blanchet and Legros's paper, another important element of the relatively slow progress in implementing reform has been a long-standing lack of consensus on the diagnosis on the French pension problem. It is true that there now seems to be a broad sense of agreement on the extent of the shock facing the overall system. However, what is probably still lacking is the sense of urgency. The French situation is indeed generally worse than in most other large countries in the Organization for Economic Cooperation and Development. This sense of urgency should perhaps have been given more prominence in the paper.

The Demographic Shock Will Be Larger in France
Than in the European Union

Based on Eurostat or United Nations projections for French demographics, by 2040 the old age dependency ratio might be about 80 percent relative to employment, and about 50 percent relative to the population aged twenty to sixty-four. These ratios are higher in France than in either the European Union (EU) or the OECD, indicating that France is in a worse situation than most other industrialized countries.

The Effects of Specific Labor Market Problems

An important factor of the French pension problem that also needs to be emphasized relates to the very low participation and employment rates of males aged fifty-five to sixty-four in France. Participation for this group is less than 40 percent in France, compared with close to 50 percent on average in the EU and more than 60 percent in the OECD. This difference is even more pronounced for employment rates. A continuation of these trends would have important implications for future dependency ratios in France.

Implications for Public Finances and Intergenerational Equity under a Business-as-Usual Scenario

The Less-Favorable Starting Point for Public Finances in France

Social expenditures on old age pensions are on a rising trend in France. These expenditures represented more than 12 percent of gross domestic product (GDP) in 1997, implying that, apart from Italy and Austria, France owns the largest share of GDP spent on pensions among OECD countries.

Poor Prospects for Public Finances in the Absence of Pension Reform

Simulations based on unchanged assumptions for the retirement age, productivity growth, immigration, unemployment rates, and institutional arrangements imply an unsustainable path for French public finances. The detailed simulations conducted in the context of the Charpin Report, also shown in the paper, confirm the earlier findings of an OECD study (see Leibfritz et al. 1995; OECD 1998) estimating that the net present value of French public pension liabilities amounted to 60 to 200 percent of GDP, depending on the assumptions made for the discount rate (7 percent and 2 percent, respectively). This estimated figure is among the highest in Europe.

Intergenerational Issues

Another aspect of unsustainability is illustrated by the results of intergenerational accounting models. Recent studies show (e.g., Doré and Levy 2000) that French generations born after 1995 will have to pay on average about 60 percent more than all generations born after 1995, if public finances are to remain in balance. Although these results usually depend in a crucial way on underlying assumptions regarding productivity growth and the discount rate, sensitivity analysis indicates that, whatever the assumptions, there remains a large intergenerational imbalance in France.

What is the Scope for Reform?

The above remarks underscore the pressing need for pension reform in France. However, it is also clear that, given the existing complexity and rigidities in the current system, any reform will require strong political will. At the outset, however, it should be noted that the current upswing should provide an opportunity to improve the starting point for reform in terms of public finances.

Current Proposals

Blanchet and Legros tell us that it is likely that upcoming reforms will center mainly on two aspects: increasing the retirement age and providing additional funding through the introduction of a specific reserve fund.

Other Options for Reform

There is, however, a number of other options for reform that are not discussed in the paper but that could be considered within the PAYGO system, while at the same time other forms of additional funding could be envisaged.

Simplifying the Overall System

This is probably politically difficult, but the experience of other countries shows that it is not impossible. Unless everyone sees what are the benefits and costs incurred by all, it will be difficult to implement reform. Transparency regarding who gets what now and who would get what after the reform of the various schemes is important. Otherwise, entrenched attitudes will persist. This transparency is particularly important if the issue of the widening divergence between private and public employee schemes is to be addressed.

Increasing the Labor Supply of the Elderly

As mentioned by Blanchet and Legros, and as seen above, an increase in French labor supply is desirable in order to lower future old-age dependency ratios. This can be achieved either through an increase in the statutory retirement age or through an increase in the number of years of contributions needed to receive full pension benefits. However, a further way to increase the labor supply is to remove existing incentives to early retirement and to disability and unemployment schemes for older people.

There are several avenues for reform in this area. In France, as rightly mentioned in the paper, the debate on whether to continue working at older ages has been very much linked to that of unemployment. However, the idea that an increase in the retirement age may translate into higher unemployment is generally unsubstantiated. Studies conducted in the context of the OECD Jobs Study (OECD 1999), for example, show that (1) lower employment rates at one end of the age spectrum have not translated into higher employment rates at the other end (i.e., the withdrawal of the elderly from the labor market as a way to create jobs for the young did not work), and (2) countries that have high employment rates are also those where the labor force has increased most.

As mentioned in the paper, the Balladur Reform, which will be fully effective in 2008, provides strong incentives to work until the age of fifty-nine because the penalty for retiring before fifty-nine is, in principle, very high. However, even with such a penalty, early retirement remains high in France, because there is still the option to retire *via* specific early retirement or unemployment benefit schemes. Of course, increasing the labor supply, especially for the elderly, will require measures to improve their employability.

Apart from indirect incentives toward early retirement, factors affecting the retirement decision depend on the replacement rate, accrual rates (i.e., the increase in pension wealth from working for an additional year), and the implicit tax rate on this extra year's earnings. The earlier reforms, including the Balladur Reform, have not reduced significantly the generosity of the French system, as mentioned in the paper. Based on a somewhat simplified but comparable methodology, OECD calculations show that the French replacement rate is among the highest in the major OECD countries (see Blondal and Scarpetta 1998).

Regarding accrual rates, the penalty for working after the retirement age (or after the earliest age at which pensions become available) is currently rather large in France. An extra year of work implies foregoing one year's pensions and often paying pension contributions for an additional year with little or no increase in acquired pension rights. Work done at the OECD shows that the drop in old age pension wealth (i.e., the discounted value of future pension streams minus pension contributions), is among the highest in France as a percent of gross income (see Leibfritz et al. 1995).

Finally, the implicit tax rate in France also provides an incentive to retire early. This tax on an extra year's earnings compares the difference in pension loss from working an additional year after the age of fifty-five with the increase of earnings during the additional year. If this tax rate is positive, the system discriminates ceteris paribus in favor of early retirement, because pension wealth decreases the longer the individual remains in employment. In France, the implicit tax rate remains at about 50 percent, among the highest in the OECD (see Blondal and Scarpetta 1998).

Modifications to Retirement Income

An important way to encourage people to work longer would be to move toward an actuarially neutral system. This option is not explicitly discussed in the paper, although other countries (e.g., Italy) have recently moved in this direction. Such a system would imply switching from a defined benefit system to an almost–defined contributions system, where the sum of the benefits an individual receives in retirement is linked to the contributions the individual made over his or her lifetime. Under such a system, individual choices toward retirement are better satisfied and less likely to be influenced by other factors.

Of course, pension revaluation remains an important issue. Although price indexation goes a long way toward reducing public deficits, it raises other issues such as those mentioned in the paper (e.g., equity problems between active and retired individuals, and declining standards of living for retired people). To a certain extent, switching to an actuarially neutral system would contribute to solving some of these problems, for instance, by indexing pensions on some moving average of real GDP growth, such as is done in Italy.

In addition, other forms of retirement income might be developed. Indeed, even in countries that have moved toward a more actuarially neutral system, additional funding is still necessary to maintain the living standards for the elderly. The authors discuss the proposal made by French economists Davanne and Pujol (1997) to introduce within the PAYGO system a reserve fund that could serve either to smooth contributions or to reduce pension costs permanently. However, whatever the purpose of the reserves, a major issue remains that of finding the necessary resources. A possibility in this respect might be to promote the development of private employees' saving schemes. At present, as mentioned in the paper, these schemes are still in their infancy and are only remotely linked to pensions. However, any form of private saving for pension purposes is likely to meet with trade-union resistance, because unions typically consider these private saving schemes as American-style pension funds, to which most of them are vehemently opposed.

Concluding Remarks

In conclusion, there exist a number of avenues for reforming the French pension system that go beyond the measures proposed in the paper, namely the retirement age and the introduction of reserves. Several other options might be contemplated both within the PAYGO system (in particular, increasing the labor supply of the elderly) and through the introduction of additional funding elements (whether in PAYGO or fully funded schemes).

These will require a large consensus, however, but one thing is certain: they need to be addressed without delay.

References

Blondal, S., and S. Scarpetta. 1998. The retirement decision in OECD countries. OECD Economics Department Working Paper no. 202. Paris: Organization for Economic Cooperation and Development.

Davanne, O., and T. Pujol. 1997. "Le débat sur les retraites: Capitalisation contre répartition" (The debate on pensions: Full funding versus PAYGO). *Revue Française d'Economie* 1:57–115.

Doré, O., and J. Levy. 2000. "Une comptabilité intergénérationelle pour la France: Les implications des retraites préfinancées" (Intergenerational accounting for France: Implications of prefinanced pensions). In *Fonds de pension: Aspects économiques et financiers,* ed. C. Bismut and N. El-Mekkaoui-de Freitas, 155–84. Paris: Economica.

Leibfritz, W., D. Roseveare, D. Fore, and E. Wurzel. 1995. Ageing populations, pension systems and government budgets: How do they affect savings? OECD Economics Department Working Paper no. 156. Paris: Organization for Economic Cooperation and Development.

Organization for Economic Cooperation and Development (OECD). 1998. *Maintaining prosperity in an ageing society.* Paris: OECD.

———. 1999. *Implementing the OECD jobs strategy.* Paris: OECD.

Discussion Summary

Didier Blanchet agreed with the discussant's view that there is no systematic connection between early retirement of the elderly and a reduction of unemployment of the younger. He pointed out that the paper refers to common beliefs about this connection, not to what this connection actually is.

Horst Siebert remarked that it appears difficult to change a system, such as the French, that is comanaged by social partners. In his view, social partners have vested interests in the existing system, and they have been given power to administer the system and to distribute administrative and political positions. He compared the French case with the case of Germany, where it is already extremely difficult to change the system. In his view, France will be the last of the three major continental countries—Italy, Germany, and France—to change its social security system.

Laurence Kotlikoff noted that the paper and the comments were very clear and that he had a deeper concern about France after hearing the paper than he had before. He asked whether it makes sense to set up an account for every French citizen who is invested in a global index fund at very low costs. On the one hand, that might give the average French citizen an opportunity to invest cheaply in a diversified global system. On the other hand, it might be a way of pointing out how desperate the current situation is.

Jeroen Kremers raised the issue of transparency in the French social security system. Given that the French system is so complex, he wondered whether French citizens can fairly easily get an assessment of their individual pension rights. He asked whether it might be useful at least to improve transparency of the system, because in his view confidence is an important aspect of the history of the policy debate in France. *Martine Durand* responded by mentioning her own experience studying the French pension system. She said that she had to do a lot of reading to understand the system and conjectured that the man in the street is probably not aware of his individual pension rights—despite all the reports that have been published. She noted that the announced reform of the pension system will not contribute greatly to an increase in transparency. *Didier Blanchet* reported that the complexity of the pension system is generally one of the first points raised in the different reports issued over the last decade. The recent history, especially in 1995, showed the difficulty of reforming some specific segments of this complex system, with the result of slowing down the general reform process. The problem with the reform of the French pension system may be, for one part, a political problem resulting from a "blocking minority."

Referring to the Charpin Report, *David A. Wise* asked why only early retirement benefits are going to be reduced but not the special unemployment provisions. The latter have to be reduced substantially to make them actuarially fair. *Martine Durand* agreed that any reform that does not address the special early retirement and unemployment schemes would be insufficient. *Didier Blanchet* mentioned that some changes were introduced in unemployment or preretirement provisions after the Balladur reform in

1993: This reform was accompanied by parallel changes of minimal ages necessary to claim preretirement benefits or the specific nondegressive benefits applying to unemployed people near the retirement age.

Martin Feldstein noted that the outcome of the public debate about pension reform in France is not to change the system, although a variety of educational reports have been issued in this respect. He asked whether there are projections of social security contributions for the next twenty or thirty years and whether the public understands these projections. *Didier Blanchet* responded that the evidence concerning the effects of the reports is mixed. In 1993, the reform was passed without major difficulties, and there was a feeling that the first *Livre Blanc* had actually contributed to developing a better understanding of pension problems. The social contest after the Juppé Plan in 1995 suggested the contrary. On the other hand, the increase of the savings rates during the second half of the 1990s may prove again that at least one part of the population tries to anticipate the impact of demographic changes on future pension levels.

David Blake raised the question of issuing recognition bonds to acknowledge unfunded pension liabilities. He remarked that no country would have been eligible to enter the Euro as part of the Maastricht criteria if the unfunded pension liabilities had been officially included as a part of national debts. In this sense he called the Euro one of the most dishonest games played in twentieth-century European politics. *Michael Burda* pointed out that pension liabilities and government bonds are not the same and they are perceived differently by the public. He mentioned that the government in Germany has reneged on a pension adjustment for two years now and that many people are saving for their retirement to supplement their promised pension benefits.

5

The German Pension System
Status Quo and Reform Options

Bert Rürup

5.1 Introduction

The German pension system, more so than any other in the world, is connected with the name *Bismarck*. Although it has changed a great deal since its establishment more than 100 years ago, some of its elements still resemble the 1889 version. The changes within the German pension system, which was originally organized as an investment-based fully funded system, were mostly results of political developments. The most drastic changes occurred after World War II: Because most of the capital stock in Germany was destroyed in the war, a way to provide income to the elderly was needed, and the only solution was to establish a pay-as-you-go (PAYGO) pension system. Between 1945 and 1957, the German pension system was still organized as an investment-based fully funded system, which could not be sustained because of a lack of physical assets in the German economy. In 1957 the fully funded system was replaced by an *Abschnittsdeckungsverfahren,* which is a special type of a PAYGO system[1]; in 1969, the entire system in West Germany was replaced by a completely PAYGO-financed system.[2] In the East, the flat-rate pension system installed in 1949 remained in place.

Since 1957, when the calculation of benefits was linked to gross wages, the system basically has worked well. No serious problems occurred until the end of the 1980s. Thus the pension reform of 1992 was the first major

Bert Rürup is professor of economics at the Darmstadt University of Technology.

1. The *Abschnittsdeckungsverfahren* is a PAYGO financed pension that is based on a constant contribution rate within a certain time period, which is called *Abschnitt.*

2. The difference between the pre-1969 and the post-1969 PAYGO financed systems is the yearly adjustment of the contribution rate depending on the level of expenditure. Between 1957 and 1969, the contribution rate was constant for any fixed time period beyond one year.

intervention into the pension system since 1957. It was passed by all political parties in the German parliament in 1989 and took effect in 1992. In between its passage and its enactment, however, a drastic political change occurred in Germany in the form of reunification. When the West German pension system was extended to East Germany, many problems occurred. In addition to demographic changes, these problems made further reform necessary. In 1997, the Minister of Social Affairs, Norbert Blüm of the Christian Democratic Party (CDU), designed the pension reform for 1999. After the 1998 election, however, the main governing party changed from the CDU to the Social Democratic Party; as a result, the main parts of the 1999 pension reform were abolished. However, the debate about the final reform of the system is not yet finished. So far there have been many proposals and discussions by all political parties in the parliament, the trade unions, and the employer associations.

In this paper, I focus on the changes within the German pension system. Section 5.2 briefly describes the institutional settings of the German pension system; section 5.3 describes the changes that occurred with the pension reform of 1992. Section 5.4 examines the most important elements of the pension reform of 1999. In section 5.5, I investigate the latest reform proposals by the German government, and in section 5.6, I summarize the existing situation of the German pension system.

5.2 The Institutional Settings of the German Pension System

The German pension system as it is constituted today is based to a great extent on the ideas of Bismarck. More precisely, the German pension system includes the former West German system, which was adopted by East Germany after reunification. Before that time, there was a flat-rate PAYGO system in East Germany.

The German pension system is a completely PAYGO, financed, defined-benefit system. Because it is mandatory for every employer, and with some exceptions for the self-employed as well, it is almost universal. The German system is financed mainly with contribution payments, which are shared equally by employers and employees and currently amount to 19.3 percent of the employees' gross wage up to a limit of approximately double the average income. Unlike a tax-based, flat-rate system, which insures that individuals will not fall below the poverty line when they are old, the German pension system aims at providing individuals a secure living standard.

Discussing the German system as one discrete pension system would be inaccurate, however. The German system is organized into several different units, the statutory pension system being the largest. Other units, ranked by size as indicated by the total amount of benefit payments and the share of participation, are shown in table 5.1.

Table 5.1   The Share of Old Age Security Systems in Programs for the Elderly
                     (measured according to volume of benefits)

Old Age Security System	Pensions 1998 (DM billions)	Share (%)
Statutory pension insurance	353.0	86.8
Civil servant provision	34.5[a]	8.5
Additional provision for public servants	11.0	2.7
Farmers' old age insurance	5.2	1.3
Occupational provisions	3.0	0.7
Total	406.7	100.0

Source: Schmähl (1998).
[a] Estimation from German Federal Parliament (Deutscher Bundestag 1996).

The most important old age security system in Germany is the statutory pension system, which has the largest share of participants and the highest benefit expenditure. The old age security system for civil servants is somewhat different: It also provides a secure living standard by paying a certain fraction of preretirement income, but unlike the regular pension system, its pensions are financed by the government budget and not by individual contribution payments.

Compulsory insurance covers approximately 28 million people at present. Of these, about 27 million workers are subject to compulsory insurance, and 160,000 are self-employed and have mandatory insurance. Payments from the statutory pension insurance system and the Social Miners' and Mine Employees' Insurance can be divided into pension payments (inclusive of payments for health insurance for pensioners of about 350 billion deutsche marks in 1998) and rehabilitation payments (approximately 7.6 billion deutsche marks in 1998).

The legislation differentiates among old age, disability, and surviving dependents' pensions. *Old age pensions* can be described as follows:

1. *Normal old age pension.* Entitlement to this pension is automatic at reaching the normal retirement age of sixty-five and fulfilling the general qualifying period (the minimum period subject to compulsory insurance) of five years.

2. *Old age pension for the long-term insured.* Eligibility before reaching age sixty-five occurs if the insured have reached the age of sixty-two and have fulfilled the qualifying period of thirty-five years.

3. *Old age pension for the severely handicapped.* If they are recognized as being severely handicapped, the insured are entitled to this pension after their sixty-third birthday[3] and after a qualifying period of thirty-five years.

3. An early claim for such an old age pension is possible from the sixtieth birthday.

In addition, *disability pensions* (pensions for those with a limited ability to work) are further distinguished as either *invalidity pensions* (pensions due to inability to work) or *vocational disability pensions* (pensions due to inability to follow one's occupation). A prerequisite for the payment of a pension due to an inability to work is the fulfillment of the qualifying period of five years and payment of mandatory contributions for at least three of the five years before the disability begins. These prerequisites are invalid if the cause of inability to work or to follow one's occupation was an accident at work, or an injury during military service. As a rule, pensions because of a limited ability to work are not limited until the worker reaches the normal old-age pension age of sixty-five. If there is a possibility of recovering the ability to work within a foreseeable period, then payments will be limited to three years or fewer (after the fifty-eighth birthday, payments are always unlimited). If the ability to work has not been recovered by the end of this period, then the insured again has a right to a (limited) pension. The difference between a pension for not being able to follow one's occupation and one for not being able to work is that the former is tied to the insured's measurable remaining ability to perform and thus to obtain further income. The latter, on the other hand, replaces a wage because it is granted only when the insured, over a foreseeable period, cannot pursue regular employment, or can pursue only low-paying employment, because of a handicap or severe illness.

The *surviving dependents' pensions* (pensions after death) grant the relatives of the deceased entitlement to a pension from the remaining pension payments. The size of such a pension is based on the relationship of the surviving dependents to the insured. Widows' and widowers' pensions are different, as are the education pension, the orphan's pension, and the pension for survivors of someone presumed but not proven dead.

The amount of the monthly pension to be paid is calculated according to the annual benefits accrued by the contributions made during the life of the insured. In addition, time of entry into the pension scheme and the type of pension are taken into account.

In accordance with these various grounds for the payment of a pension, the amount of the pension is calculated based on a formula (shown in fig. 5.1) that has been used since 1992.

The income index is based on the relationship in a calendar year between the individual benefit earner and the average benefit for all insured. Therefore, it takes into account individual contributions made and the length of insurance. The insurance period is usually longer than the period in which contributions were made. For example, contribution-free periods would be taken into account if they served to compensate for times when it was not possible for the insured to work, subject to compulsory insurance. There is a differentiation in the law between *fictitious qualifying periods* (e.g., military and civilian service), *credit periods* (e.g., disability, rehabilitation, raising children, occupational training periods), and *attribution*

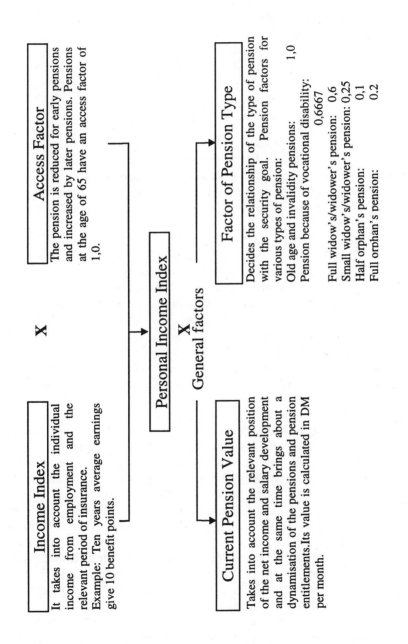

Fig. 5.1　The pension formula

periods (in terms of inability to work or to follow one's occupation). The regulations vary with regard to compensation and valuation of contribution-free periods. In addition to the contribution-free times, there are also *allowance periods* (for child care) and *contribution-reducing periods.* Periods of unemployment belong to both the contribution-reducing and the contribution-free periods.

The entrance or access factor is set according to the time of the insured's receipt of the pension, reducing the pension for early retirees and increasing it for late retirees. In the example of a claim for an early old age pension, the pension is reduced by an access factor of 0.003 for each month before the relevant, definitive age limit. This corresponds to a reduction in the pension of 0.3 percent (3.6 percent per annum) for each month of early pension payment. Pension reduction first became important in 2000, when the age limit for an early retirement old age pension rose. The *personal income index,* the product of the income index and the access factor, represents the individual portion of the pension formula. In addition to this, there are two general factors: the pension type factor and the actual pension value.

The *pension type factor* weights individual pensions according to their security goals. Pensions with full income replacement have higher weights than pensions with income-supplement or income-maintenance functions.

The standard benchmark pension, which is used to establish living standards security, is the level that an insured person with forty-five years of insurance at the average wage has attained. This "benchmark pensioner" has acquired 45 benefit points. The pension type factor is one. With an actual pension value of 48.29 for West and 42.01 for East Germany, a gross monthly pension of about 2,144 deutsche marks (West) and 1,839 deutsche marks (East) is calculated. After deducting contributions for health and nursing insurance, the net standard pension is 2,007.90 deutsche marks for West Germany and 1,741.11 deutsche marks for East Germany. The net standard pension is related to the net employment income of all insured; from this standard, the net benchmark level of 71.1 percent is calculated.

Comparing the German social insurance pension system to statutory old age protection systems that, like Germany's, aim to guarantee living standards and not simply to guarantee the avoidance of poverty—and, in terms of net replacement rates, the relationship between the average net pension and the average net wage—puts the German system in a somewhat ungenerous light. In Austria and Italy, the net replacement rate is 80 percent, whereas the German pension insurance scheme has a net pension level of about 70 percent. Yet despite the limited generosity of German old age pensions, the system is generous in terms of early retirement pensions and disability pensions.

However, it is noteworthy that in many countries, although the old age pension systems differentiate among individual occupational groups, it is almost impossible to set one net pension standard.

Figure 5.2 shows public pension expenditures[4] as a percent of gross domestic product (GDP). It shows that expenditures rose from below 6 percent at the beginning of the 1970s to slightly below 9 percent in 1998. Until 1990, these figures are valid only for West Germany. If the reunification had not happened, the ratio of public pension expenditure to GDP would be below 8 percent. This can be explained by the comparatively low GDP but high expenditures in East Germany.

5.3   The 1992 Pension Reform

The expression "1992 pension reform" is somewhat misleading. This reform was designed in 1989 just before the fall of the Berlin wall, and was planned to take effect on 1 January 1992. At the time, politicians from all parties represented in the German parliament had discussed what to do to avoid a worsening of the situation of the (West) German pension system. Although the situation was not nearly as serious as it is today (in fact, the system almost produced surpluses without substantially increasing the contribution rate), it was also foreseeable that such a situation could not hold if demographic development was taken into consideration. The system had to be reformed for the following reasons:

- A shift toward a disadvantageous contributor-per-pensioner ratio was expected after the year 2000.
- Average age of retirement was low.
- Longevity was increasing.
- Patterns of employment were changing.
- Fertility was low.

To insure that these developments would not worsen the situation for the pension system, changes had to be made. It was not planned that funded elements be introduced into the system, merely that some changes be made within the existing PAYGO system. In order to achieve stability of the system, four measures were installed.

To begin, in response to the increasing longevity, the government decided to increase the age of retirement. The first step in that direction was a step-by-step increase in the regular age of retirement from sixty-three to sixty-five for men, beginning in the year 2000 and ending in 2001; for women, the age rose from sixty to sixty-five, beginning in the year 2000 and ending in 2006. Because an increase in the regular age of retirement is not necessarily connected to an increase in the actual age of retirement, however, an additional change was made. To give workers an incentive to postpone retirement, the pension formula was raised by an enlargement factor, which reduced the individual pension by 0.3 percent per month for retirement before the regular age and increased the individual pension by

---

4. Including disability and orphans' pensions.

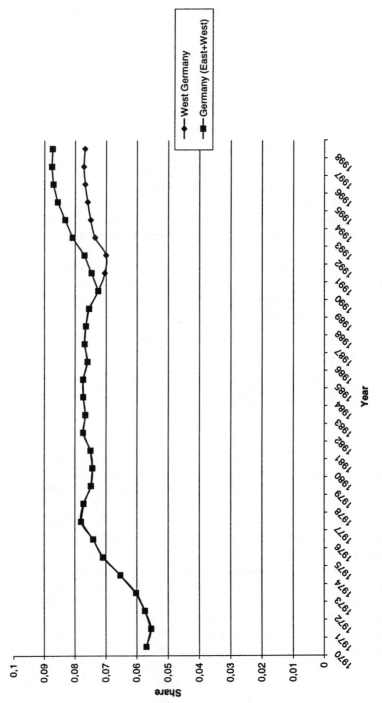

Fig. 5.2 Public pension share of gross domestic product in Germany

0.5 percent per month for retirement after the regular age. Both measures were put in place to increase the actual age of retirement. As useful as both of these measures may be, however, an increase in the actual age of retirement can be achieved only when *no other conditions* counteract it. Because a high average age of retirement also depends on the situation in the labor market, any measure for increasing the average age of retirement will have no effect when the labor market situation is unfavorable. In other words, all these measures will work only when the situation in the labor market is positive.

The second important element of the 1992 reform was a switch from adjusting pensions by the growth rate of *gross* wages to adjusting by the growth rate of *net* wages. This was conceived as a built-in stabilizer. Because any increase in the contribution rate for the pension system decreases net wages, pension will grow at a slower rate; this will have the effect of further reducing increases in the contribution rate. Besides this rather important effect, pensions will grow at a slower rate because net wages have increased less than gross wages over the past four years.

For intergenerational reasons, however, this cannot be considered fair. It is difficult to argue that there should be a more rapid increase in pensions (and therefore in the disposable income of pensioners) than in net wages, which are the disposable income of employees. In other words, for intergenerational reasons it cannot be considered fair that those who receive benefits will realize higher growth rates in their income than will those who finance the benefits. Finally, this measure has another effect connected to the growth of net and gross wages. By adjusting pensions by the growth rate of net wages, every change in the overall tax burden on wages, or any increase (decrease) in the contribution rates for other social insurance, such as health insurance or unemployment insurance, will affect pensions. For example, an increase in the contribution rate for health insurance or unemployment insurance will decrease net wages; therefore, the growth of pensions also will decrease. By indexing pensions to the growth of net wages, pensioners also indirectly finance social insurance.

If providing old age income as the German pension system does is considered socially desirable, then it is unreasonable that some groups of workers (such as civil servants) be excluded from financing it. This is why there is a transfer from the government budget to the otherwise separate budget of the pension system. This transfer makes the German pension system not solely contribution-based. Because transfers from the government budget are tax financed, it also has a tax-financed element; and because the German pension system covers more risks and more benefits than the old age income provision alone, a tax-financed element is justified. In the 1992 pension reform act, an increase in transfers from the government budget was undertaken. This increase had the estimated effect of lowering the contribution rate in the year 2030 by 1.7 percent.

Besides these main elements, the 1992 pension reform act had two additional components:

- A shortening of the contribution-free periods (e.g., military service and education), and
- A higher transfer from the Federal Employment Office (*Bundesanstalt für Arbeit*) for the unemployed.

The 1992 pension reform thus had three main elements: an increase in the regular age of retirement connected to incentives toward postponing retirement via the introduction of an access factor; a switch from adjustment by the growth of gross wages to adjustment by the growth of net wages; and an increase in transfers from the government budget. As Boll, Raffelhüschen, and Walliser (1994) showed, this pension reform would have been sufficient to keep the German pension system in generational balance.

5.4   The 1999 Pension Reform

In 1989, when the 1992 pension reform was formulated, the Berlin wall came down quite unexpectedly; and after one year of negotiations among the allied nations and East and West Germany, German reunification occurred. Before the actual reunification took place, an agreement was reached concerning economic and social union between the two states. The most important element of this agreement was East Germany's adoption of both the West German currency and the West German system of social insurance. The West German pension system was thus expanded to East Germany, and the consequences of this decision have been substantial. The 1992 pension reform was predicted to have a stabilizing effect, but one crucial point—reunification—was not taken into account.

After reunification the greatest problem was high unemployment. There are many reasons for unemployment in East Germany,[5] but the most important was the unfavorable situation in the East Germany economy. As far as firms there were concerned, it was the authorities rather than entrepreneurs who were the decision-making units. The consequence was nonmarket factor allocation. Most East German firms were faced with too many employees and too little capital (see Burda 1991). Overnight, these firms saw a completely new situation. Suddenly it was recognized that the productivity of the labor force was too low, mostly because the per capita endowment of capital was too low. Nevertheless, a political decision was made to equalize Eastern and Western wages rather than market forces decide wages. This political decision was justified only insofar as politicians were afraid that people would "vote with their feet" against Eastern

---

5. Some of them are discussed in detail by Sinn and Sinn (1991).

wages, according to Tiebout's (1956) model. In addition to the wage policy, there was uncertainty about property rights in East Germany; that and the position of the *Treuhandanstalt,* as described by Sinn and Sinn (1991), led to substantial unemployment in the East.

To improve the labor market situation, the German government decided to use the pension system and its possibility of early retirement. The result was an easing of the labor market situation and the related strain on unemployment insurance, a negative effect on the pension system.

For a number of reasons, the labor market problems that arose in East Germany after reunification affected the financial stability of the German pension system. Most importantly, the system had to provide benefits to many new people with a comparatively small quantity of additional contributions because of high unemployment among the system's contributors. The government, in fact, used the pension system as a labor market instrument: Getting the unemployed part of the labor force as well as old employees of the labor market via early retirement was believed to be helpful to younger people in search of jobs. However, because the unemployment was unrelated to age structure but was rather a structural problem for the East German economy, early retirement did not help younger people gain employment. Instead, the government managed to improve its unemployment figures compared to what they would have been otherwise, but the costs of unemployment were placed on the pension system. Thus the burden of unemployment shifted from unemployment insurance to the pension system, counteracting the intentions of the 1992 pension reform. Furthermore, because of demographic developments, the pension system lost intergenerational balance; therefore, further reform was needed.

The 1999 pension reform was the government's reaction to demographic developments and to the situation created by the effects of reunification. The German pension system had developed from a more or less intergenerationally balanced system (as shown by Boll, Raffelhüschen, and Walliser 1994) in 1989 to a system with much intergenerational redistribution—because future generations were in danger of being left with the burden—in 1995 (as shown by Jagob and Scholz 1998). The political agreement reached during the negotiations over pension reform was to maintain the PAYGO system. The problem was to find a solution that would both maintain the living-standard function of the PAYGO-financed German pension system and redistribute the burden of demographic development in a fair way.

One cannot blame all the problems of the pension system on reunification, which in fact is only one reason the 1992 pension reform did not work as designed. There were other problems with the German pension system, as well, which can be summarized as follows:

- A low average age of retirement, as described by Börsch-Supan and Schnabel (1999).

- Demographic changes, including a low fertility rate and, for the elderly, increasing life expectancy.
- High unemployment, only partly a problem of the pension system. On the one hand, because of unemployment, the pension system receives only reduced contribution payments by the *Bundesanstalt für Arbeit*. On the other hand, because of the institutional settings of the German old age income system, the pension system will be forced to lower expenditures in the future because of lower contribution payments today.

The 1999 pension reform was the political compromise designed to counteract these tendencies. The government decided to keep the PAYGO system mainly as it was, without introducing any funded elements. The main elements of the 1999 pension reform, therefore, were to install a demographic factor, to take education periods into greater account, and to change the disability system.

In adding a demographic factor, the government's goal was to reduce the overall pension level in correspondence with an increase in life expectancy, as a means of distributing the additional cost of longevity equally across those who much pay contributions and those who receive benefits. Except for the demographic factor DF_t, the pension formula is the same as described in section 5.2. It consists of the income index IP_a, the access factor AF, the current pension value cPV_t, and the factor of pension type PT. The only difference is that the individual monthly pension will be adjusted by the overall demographic factor DF_t, which takes account of the evolution of the average life expectancy, LE:

$$R(t) = \sum_{a=0}^{A} IP_a \cdot AF \cdot cPV_t \cdot PT \cdot DF_t,$$

where

$$DF_t = \left(\frac{LE_{t-2}}{LE_{t-1}} - 1 \right) \cdot \frac{1}{2} + 1.$$

The German and Swedish ways of adjusting the pension level for the increase in life expectancy differ in their treatment of the generations affected. As Jagob and Sesselmeier (2000) point out, the Swedish reform treats different generations differently: The costs of living longer are always imposed on those generations that create them, which also makes the retirement age more flexible to some extent.[6] The German pension reform had another approach in mind when it added a demographic factor, which was linked to life expectancy. As can be seen in the equation above, the adjustment was half of the increase in life expectancy over time. According

---

6. The limit of this flexibility is given by the occupational pension scheme.

to estimates, this would have reduced the pension level from about 70 percent currently to approximately 64 percent in 2030. The government chose to adjust the pension level by life expectancy, and this made possible a smooth decrease in the pension level over time. Although other factors, including average age, were discussed, life expectancy was chosen because it is the dominant factor in the pension system, as Rürup (1998) and Schmähl (1999) point out. It has changed most drastically over the years and, as far as actuarial calculations are concerned, is the most relevant factor.

The 1999 pension reform also took education periods into account more than the earlier system had. The idea was to create an incentive for raising children, which had been associated with high opportunity costs, mainly for women. Empirical analyses by Gustafsson, Wetzels, and Kenjoh (2000) show that in Germany, the probability of reentering the labor force is very low for women after they have children. Only those employed in the civil sector, where there is a high concentration of female employees, tend to return to work. Outside the civil sector, even if women reenter the labor force, they do so under conditions that are worse than they would have been if they had not had children and had remained in the labor market.

These indirect costs, the direct costs of lost income during the child-rearing time at home, and factors in the pension system worked in the same direction (i.e., time off for having children was taken into consideration only to a small extent by the 1992 pension formula). Taken together, these effects explain the low fertility rates in Germany over the past few years. To lower those opportunity costs a bit, and to create within the pension system an incentive for bearing children, these "education periods" were rewarded with higher entitlements under the 1999 pension reform.

To reduce the possibility of using early-retirement disability pensions as a labor market instrument, the government decided to set legal conditions for strict differentiation between *disability* and *unemployment*. Someone capable of working a maximum of three hours per day would receive a complete invalidity pension; someone working between three and six hours per day would receive half an invalidity pension. Anyone capable of working at least 6 hours per day had no entitlement to an invalidity pension. Furthermore, the level of the individual's invalidity pension would be adjusted to equal the individual's old age pension when retiring at age sixty. Furthermore, these new regulations had to work hand in hand with a new kind of labor market policy.

To summarize, after the 1992 pension reform was designed, the German reunification took place, which changed the situation for the pension system overnight. In addition, demographic changes and a decreasing actual age of retirement threatened the financial stability of the pension system. Therefore, further reforms had to be made. In 1997, the German government designed the 1999 pension reform. The major elements of this reform were the addition of a demographic factor, the change in disability pensions, and systematic consideration of education periods. The demographic factor was designed to distribute the costs of longevity equally across all persons covered by the public pension system. Taking education periods into greater account created an incentive for having children, reducing the opportunity costs somewhat. Finally, a reform of disability pensions, in addition to new regulations concerning labor market policy, created a stronger differentiation between labor market policy and the pension system.

5.5   The Latest Reform Proposals by the German Government

When the new government was formed in 1998 by the Social Democratic Party (SPD), the demographic factor from the 1999 pension reform was abolished almost immediately. It was considered unfair for those who were already retired. The new government decided instead to change some institutional settings. At the time, some exceptions were available to the self-employed in terms of being members of the statutory pension system; as a result, a new kind of self-employed worker emerged. Like regular employees, these self-employed workers depended exclusively, or at least to a very high degree, on the firm for which they worked. Some individuals chose this kind of self-employment to avoid making contributions to the pension system. Therefore, the government decided to expand the public pension system to those self-employed who depended on a single firm. It also decided to take into account those people who worked in the lowest earning sector.[7] Additionally, a decision was made to transfer tax expenditures to the newly introduced green tax on fossil fuels.[8]

In addition to these new regulations, which were developed by the government almost immediately after the election in 1998, a much more substantial reform is planned. To insure that this reform creates a higher degree of political confidence and stability, it is meant to be a common agreement of the political parties in Parliament and the relevant social groups in German society. So far, nothing has been finalized, but some approaches have been discussed. One element in common among all the serious approaches is that the German public pension system needs to be more fully funded; the following section presents four scenarios for this. The first scenario is the status quo, which shows what will happen if the pension system is not changed at all. The second shows the development of the pension system if the contribution rate is changed. The third scenario shows an equal distribution of the costs of aging within the PAYGO

---

7. A standard term in Germany used to be the *630–deutsche mark job*. Every job that did not exceed the upper limit of 630 deutsche mark was free of contributions to the pension system.

8. Note that the tax would have been introduced anyway.

system. Finally, the fourth scenario investigates what would happen if the third scenario were expanded by the addition of fully funded elements, reflecting the latest proposal by the Federal Minister of Social Affairs.

If a society—for example, in Germany—is aging, then a defined benefits system is associated with increasing costs. Taking as a base the demographic and economic presumptions that were accepted at the "pensions peak," and keeping the statutory retirement age constant, a status quo projection leads to the contribution and benefit development curves in figures 5.3 and 5.4. If policy changes nothing within the pension system, the contribution rate[9] will rise from the current 19.5 percent to a level of 24.2 percent in 2030. Because it is typical for a defined benefit system, the pension level stays constant at around 68 percent. The standard pension—which is the pension of an employee who worked forty-five years and earned exactly the average income—will increase from the current 2,173 deutsche marks to nearly 5,000 deutsche marks in 2030. Within the same time period, the total expenditures for the pension system will rise from about 336 billion to 1,062 billion deutsche marks.[10]

As usual, however, such a status quo scenario is neither the economically nor the politically desirable one. It is calculated simply as a benchmark for further scenarios. The next scenario shows what happens if the contribution rate is held constant at 20 percent. Such a policy has the effect of a switch from a defined benefit system to a defined contribution system. In the status quo scenario, the pension level is a more or less exogenously given variable that stays constant at a certain level, and the contribution rate must be determined endogenously and changes over time. When the contribution rate is fixed, the pension level must change as figure 5.5 shows. It decreases from its current level of 71 percent to a level of 56 percent in 2030. At the same time, the standard pension amount will grow. Compared to the status quo scenario, it will reach a much lower amount of 4,193 deutsche marks. At the same time, one goal will be achieved, as can be seen in figure 5.6; the total expenditures of the public pension system will still increase, but the increase will be lower than in the status quo scenario.

In the third scenario there is a switch from a defined benefit system to a defined contribution system. Unlike in the second scenario, however, the contribution rate will not be fixed at 20 percent—instead, there will be slight increase up to its maximum amount of 22 percent in 2030. This means that the contribution rate of the PAYGO-financed pension system

9. The contribution rate is levied on the gross wage of the employee whose employment is subject to mandatory insurance. It is shared equally by the employee and the employer; that is, having a contribution rate of 20 percent means that 10 percent is paid by the employer and another 10 percent by the employee.

10. All the calculations are in current prices with an assumed inflation rate of 1.7 percent per annum.

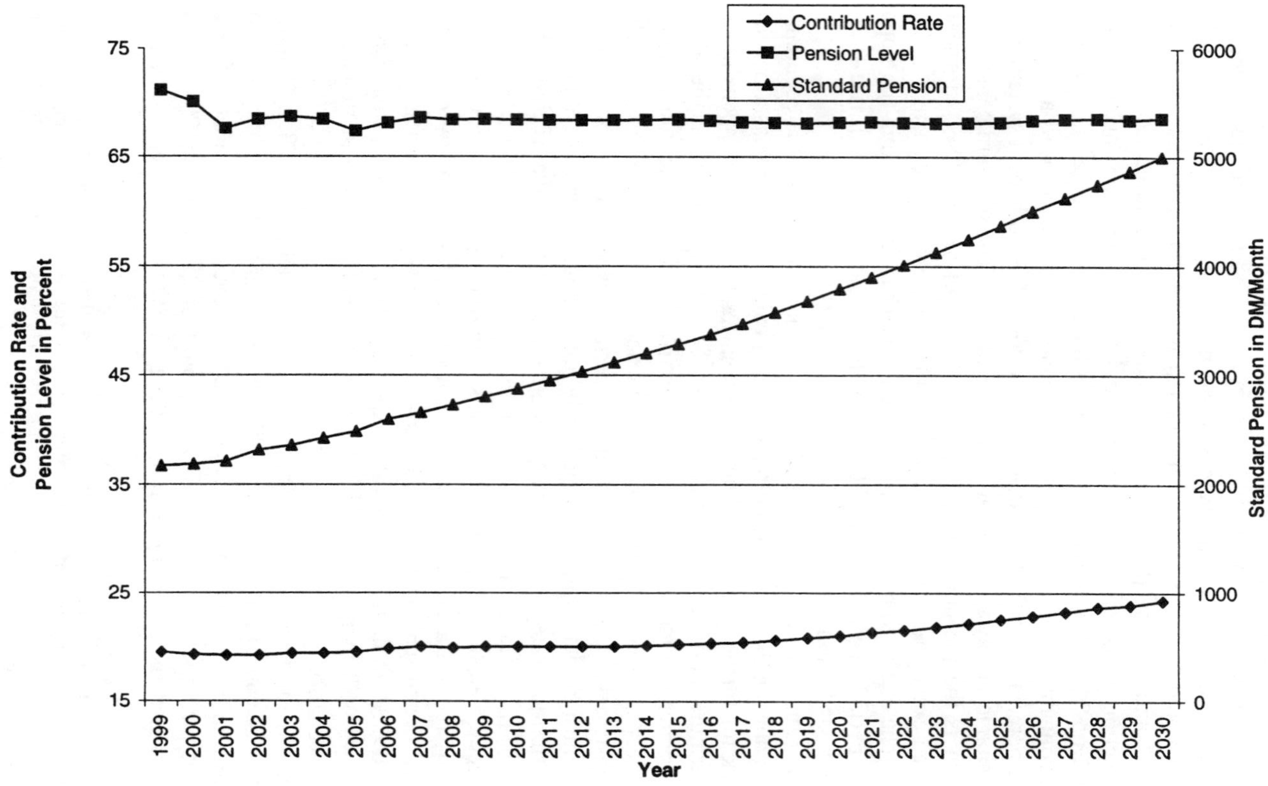

Fig. 5.3   Status quo contribution rate, pension level, and standard pension

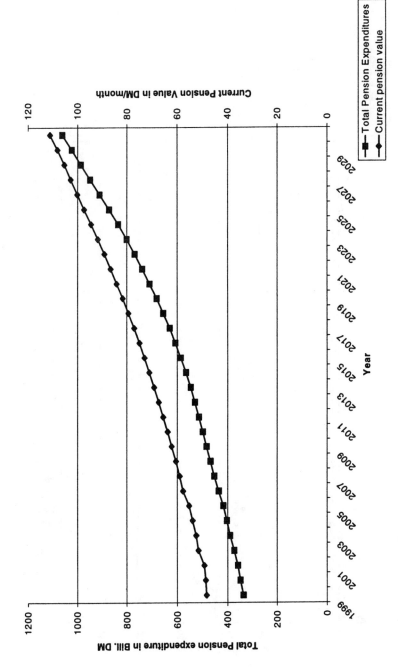

Fig. 5.4   Status quo total pension expenditure and current pension value

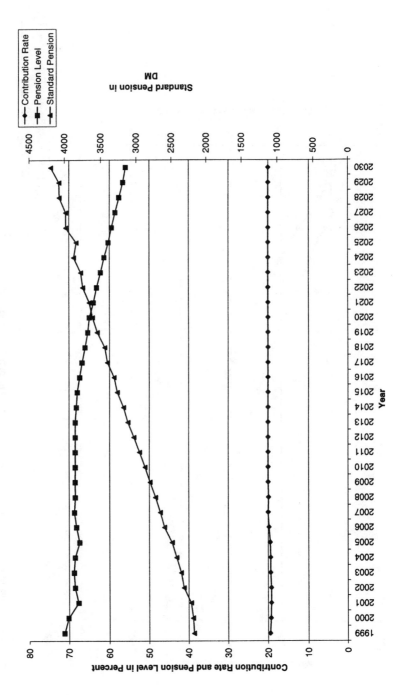

Fig. 5.5 Fixed contribution rate, pension level, and standard pension

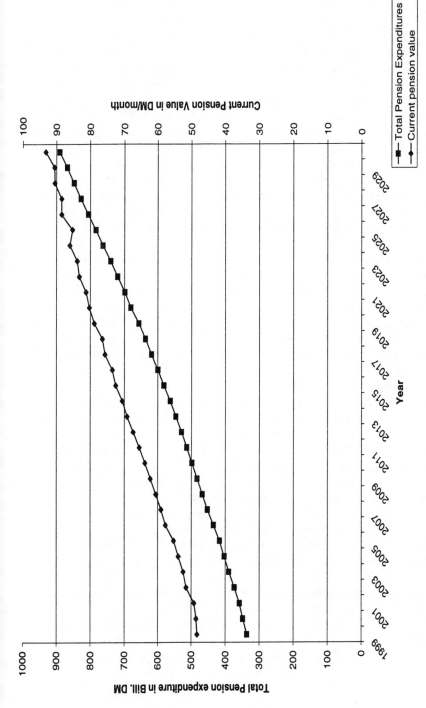

Fig. 5.6 Fixed contribution rate, total pension expenditure, and current pension value

will lie exactly between the first and second scenarios. The same is true for the standard pension: Its value in 2030 of 4,500 deutsche marks lies between the comparable values of the first two scenarios. The exact patterns of the contribution rate, the pension level, and the standard pension can be seen in figure 5.7. Total expenditures of the pension system in the scenario can be seen in figure 5.8. The intention of this policy alternative is to split the costs of aging. As can be seen, the contribution rate increases more than the fixed contribution rate, but less than in the status quo scenario. The opposite is true for the standard pension. This means that the costs of aging are distributed between both groups: on the pensioners by a reduced increase in their standard pensions, and on those who pay contributions by a slightly higher increase in the contribution rate.

If the political objective is to raise the contribution rate—in the sense of an equal division of the aging costs and, as more or less expressed by the proposal of the Minister of Social Affairs, to 22 percent at the maximum by the year 2030—then this objective can be achieved by the third scenario. It is also the minister's objective to guarantee future pensioners a high level of pensions with a comparatively low burden for the younger generations. It is commonly agreed by all political parties in Germany that they will maintain a PAYGO-financed pillar to guarantee that all additional risks that are currently covered by the pension system will still be covered. To satisfy all the demands of the politicians, the third scenario would have to be in place: The PAYGO-financed part is maintained, with an equal distribution of aging costs over all members of the public pension system.

To achieve a system that is (as much as in the third scenario) PAYGO-financed but that, at the same time, avoids a high burden for future generations and maintains a high level of pensions for future recipients, fully funded elements must be built into the system. One of the ways to introduce funded elements has been explained in a recent proposal: by starting the old age savings plan at 0.5 percent of the gross wage in 2003 and increasing it annually by 0.5 percent up to the amount of 7.5 percent in 2017, then keeping it at a steady 7.5 percent rate.

In such a case, the pension level would remain nearly constant at 68 percent, and the standard pension would be lower than the status quo scenario of 4,570 deutsche marks in 2030 by 427 deutsche marks. However, the overall benefit level, including a PAYGO pension and a capital pension—with a presumed interest rate of 5.5 percent—would be at 5,719 deutsche marks, substantially higher than the standard pension of 4,998 deutsche marks under the status quo scenario. Moreover, the PAYGO system would have developed into a mixed-funded provision system. In 2060, when this fully funded supplementary system reached its state of equilibrium, the overall benefit level would be about 90 percent. The effects of this approach are described in much more detail in table 5.2.

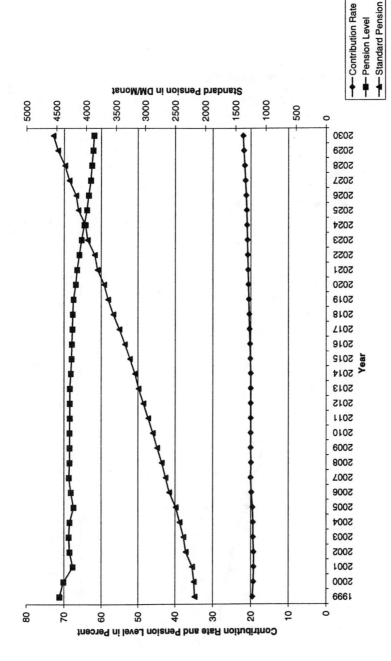

Fig. 5.7 Contribution rate, pension level, and standard pension

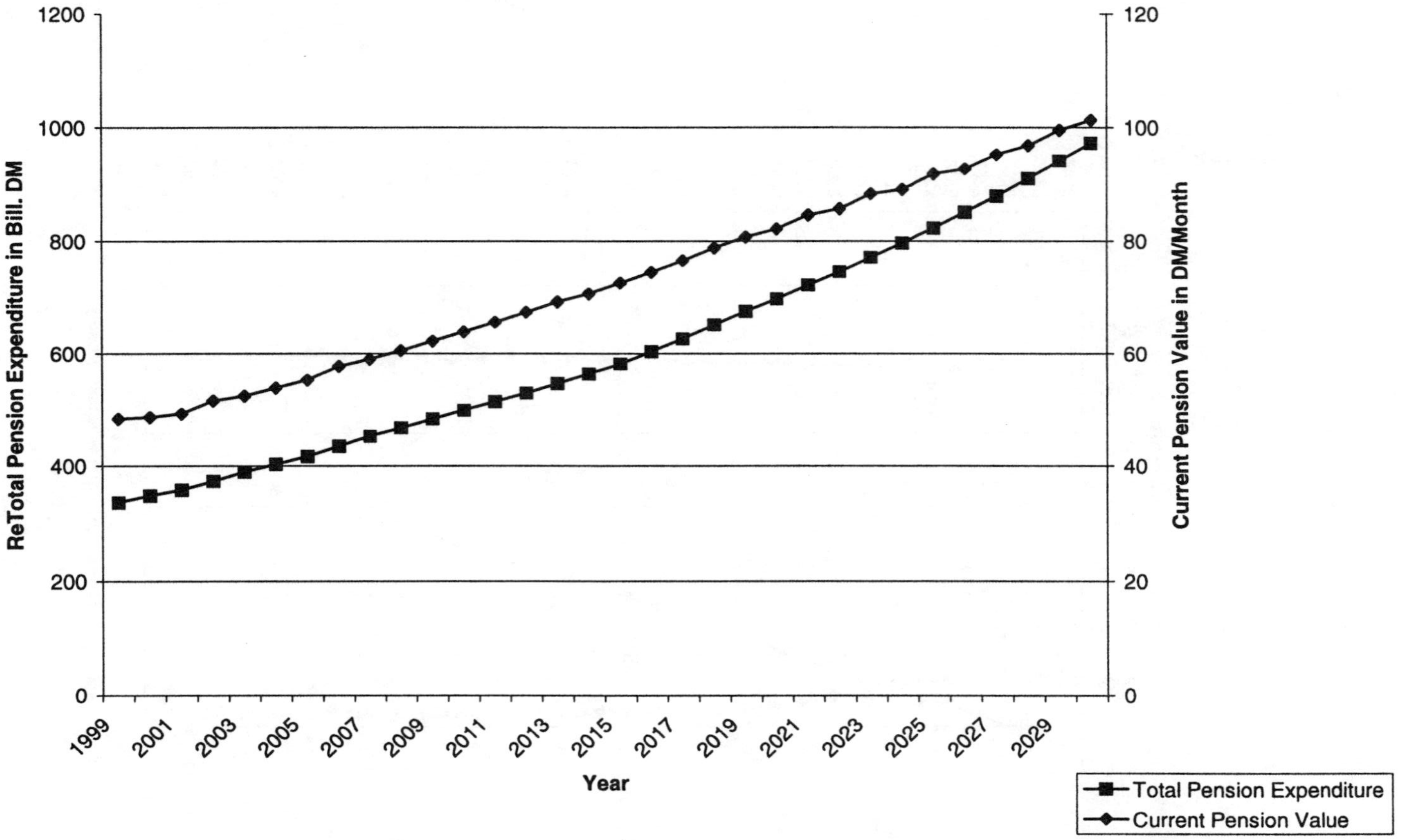

Fig. 5.8 Total pension expenditure and current pension value

Table 5.2   **The Funded Pillar of the Pension Reform**

Year	Contribution for Funding[a]	Pension per Month (in DM) in the Starting Period[b] for Retirees in Corresponding Year		Gross Standard Pension	Overall Supply (DM)	
		4.0% Annual Interest Rate	5.5% Annual Interest Rate		4.0% Annual Interest Rate	5.5% Annual Interest Rate
1999	0.0	0.00	0.00			
2000	0.0	0.00	0.00			
2001	0.0	0.00	0.00			
2002	0.0	0.00	0.00			
2003	0.5	1.13	1.33	2357.55	2358.68	2358.88
2004	1.0	3.50	4.14	2407.50	2411.00	2411.64
2005	1.5	7.23	8.58	2456.55	2463.78	2465.13
2006	2.0	12.45	14.83	2549.25	2561.70	2654.08
2007	2.5	19.30	23.06	2593.80	2613.10	2616.86
2008	3.0	27.93	33.48	2646.00	2673.93	2679.48
2009	3.5	38.48	46.28	2701.35	2739.83	2747.63
2010	4.0	51.12	61.69	2757.60	2808.72	2819.29
2011	4.5	66.04	79.95	2814.75	2880.79	2894.70
2012	5.0	83.40	101.32	2873.25	2956.65	2974.57
2013	5.5	103.42	126.06	2935.35	3038.77	3061.41
2014	6.0	126.31	154.48	2996.10	3122.41	3150.58
2015	6.5	152.28	186.87	3056.40	3208.68	3243.27
2016	7.0	181.58	223.59	3118.05	3299.63	3341.64
2017	7.5	214.45	264.97	3187.80	3402.25	3452.77
2018	7.5	249.41	309.33	3261.60	3511.01	3570.93
2019	7.5	286.55	356.84	3360.15	3646.70	3716.99
2020	7.5	326.00	407.68	3463.20	3789.20	3870.88
2021	7.5	367.86	462.06	3564.00	3931.86	4026.06
2022	7.5	412.26	520.18	3665.70	4077.96	4185.88
2023	7.5	459.33	582.25	3776.40	4235.73	4358.65
2024	7.5	509.20	648.51	3891.15	4400.35	4539.66
2025	7.5	562.01	719.20	4002.75	4564.76	4721.95
2026	7.5	617.90	794.57	4121.55	4739.45	4916.12
2027	7.5	677.03	874.88	4232.25	4909.28	5107.13
2028	7.5	739.56	960.44	4335.75	5075.31	5296.19
2029	7.5	805.66	1051.52	4452.75	5258.41	5504.27
2030	7.5	875.49	1148.45	4570.65	5446.14	5719.10

Source: Bundesministerium für Arbeit und Sozialordnung

[a]In percent of gross wage. Ten percent of the capital coverage will be deducted for administrative costs; an average income earner with constant contribution payments is considered.

[b]Assuming a pension period of eighteen insurance years and ten years of dependent's pension, the pension will increase each year during the period of payment by 2.6 percent. The pension of the corresponding retirees on 1 July of the corresponding year are shown.

In order to see what any of these approaches would really cost German society, one must consider the share of gross national product (GNP) in public pension expenditures. Figure 5.9 shows this for each of the first three scenarios. Not surprisingly, the status quo scenario leads to an increase in the ratio of public pension to GNP, whereas the third scenario leads to a rather constant ratio. If the ratio of pension expenditure to GNP is the target, then holding the contribution rate fixed yields the best result. Many facts must be considered, however, in making pension policy, so there is no one optimal way. The circumstances and the political point of view are always what decide the direction of pension policy.

5.6 Conclusions

The German pension system has developed from a more-or-less stable PAYGO system to a system that is threatened by the demographic changes within German society. As has been described, the German pension system recently had to be reformed for the first time in almost forty years. At that time, it was still in a more-or-less generationally balanced situation. The first problems occurred shortly after the 1992 pension reform was enacted. Reunification took place, with all of its economic consequences for the German pension system. The expansion of the German pension system was possible only because it was a PAYGO-financed system. A fully funded system never would have been able to manage a socially sound transition such as the one that took place.

In addition to reunification and its economic consequences, demographic change has made further reform necessary. In 1997 the German government enacted the 1999 pension reform, which was largely abolished by the new government after the 1998 election. So far, no other reform has enacted; yet there is a great need for reform because the demographic changes have not ceased, and, with the abolition of the demographic factor, the most important way to avoid an increasing burden on the pension system has disappeared.

Since 1998, the debate has centered on the question of funding versus no funding. As in most debates, both sides have good arguments for and against complete funding of the public pension system. The general arguments against a complete and fully funded system are summarized by Heller (1998), Orszag and Stiglitz (1999), and Barr (2000). At least for Germany, many calculations have been suggested to figure the cost of a transition toward a fully funded system, including one by Börsch-Supan (1998) showing that such a transition would be cheaper than expected. On the other hand, calculations by Eitenmüller and Hain (1998) show that such a transition is very costly. Agreement with either argument depends mostly on one's political viewpoint and social values.

The recent debate in Germany more or less represents a compromise

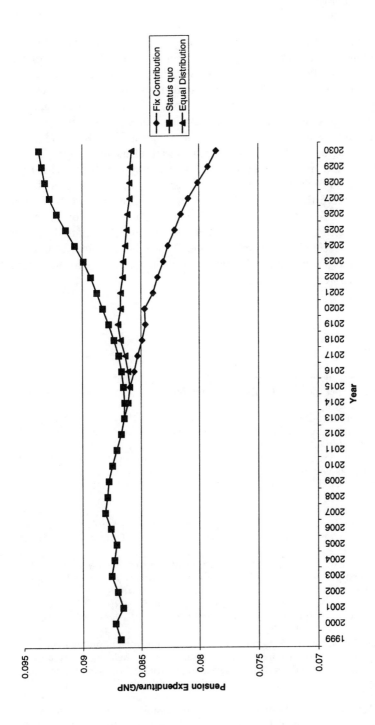

Fig. 5.9   Ratio of pension expenditure to gross national product

between points of view, with the intention of introducing a more funded element into the existing PAYGO system. This is not merely a compromise designed to keep both sides quiet, however; there are also convincing reasons for a mix of a PAYGO and a fully funded system (these are discussed in detail by Sinn 1999a, b). These arguments, and the attempt to enact a reform that can cope with the demographic change and survive the next election, are why such a partially funded system is likely to be adopted. Beyond demographic change, the decreasing actual age of receipt of benefits is the largest problem the German pension system faces. The 1992 pension reform took the first step toward creating incentives to postpone retirement. Nevertheless, the age of retirement has decreased, both as a consequence of the situation in the labor market and because of the incentives of the pension system itself. Recent reform plans attempt to deal with the problems created by the demographic change, but any reform that can be regarded as a solution for the problems of the German pension system must deal with early retirement as well.

References

Barr, Nicholas. 2000. Reforming pensions: Myths, truths, and policy choices. IMF Working Paper no. WP/00/139. Washington, D.C.: International Monetary Fund, August.

Boll, Stephan, Bernd Raffelhüschen, and Jan Walliser. 1994. Social security and intergenerational redistribution: A generational accounting perspective. *Public Choice* 81:79–100.

Börsch-Supan, Axel. 1998. A contribution to the German debate on a transition from a pay-as-you-go to a fully funded public pension system (in German). Diskussionspapier des Sonderforschungsbereichs 504 der Universität Mannheim, no. 98-41.

Börsch-Supan, Axel, and Reinhold Schnabel. 1999. Social security and retirement in Germany. In *Social security and retirement around the world*, ed. Jonathan Gruber and David A. Wise, 135–180. Chicago: University of Chicago Press.

Breyer, Friedrich. 1989. On the intergenerational pareto efficiency of pay-as-you-go financed pension systems. *Journal of Institutional and Theoretical Economics* 145:643–58.

Burda, Michael. 1991. Labor and product markets in Czechoslovakia and the ex-GDR: A twin study. CEPR Discussion Paper no. 548. Washington, D.C.: Center for Economic and Policy Research.

Deutscher Bundestag. 1996. Report of the Federal government on the benefits for employees in civil service in the calendar year 1993, as well as the development of the expenditure in the next fifteen years (in German). Social car report, Information of the Federal Government, 13th electoral period. Printed vol. no. 13/5840, 17 October.

Eitenmüller, Stefan, and Winfried Hain. 1998. Possible efficiency benefits versus transition costs: A calculation of the burden due to a change of the financing system of public pensions (in German). *Deutsche Rentenversicherung* (9–10): 634–54.

Gustafsson, Siv, Cecile M. M. P. Wetzels, and Eiko Kenjoh. 2000. Can postponement of maternity in the 1990s be explained by changes in time spent out of market work? Paper presented at the European Institute for Social Security conference, 6–10 September, Gothenburg, Germany.

Heller, Peter S. 1998. Rethinking public pension reform initiatives. IMF Working Paper no. WP/98/61. Washington, D.C.: International Monetary Fund, April.

Jagob, Jochen, and Oliver Scholz. 1998. Reforming the German pension system: Who wins and who loses? A generational accounting perspective. Discussion Papers in German Studies no. IGS98/12. University of Birmingham, U.K., Institute for German Studies.

Jagob, Jochen, and Werner Sesselmeier. 2000. Demographic change and partial funding: Is the Swedish pension reform a role model for Germany? Darmstadt Discussion Papers in Economics no. 100. Darmstadt, Germany: Darmstadt University, Department of Economics.

Orszag, Peter R., and Joseph E. Stiglitz. 1999. Rethinking pension reform: Ten myths about social security systems. Paper presented at conference, New Ideas about Old Age Security, 14–15 September, Washington D.C., World Bank.

Palmer, Edward, 1999. The Swedish pension reform model. Framework and issues. Forthcoming in World Bank volume. Washington, D.C.: World Bank.

Rürup, Bert. 1998. Considering the life expectancy within the public pension system (in German. *Deutsche Rentenversicherung* 5:281–91.

Schmähl, Winfried. 1998. *The whole system of old age security* (in German). In *Handbuch zur altersversorgung,* ed. Jörg-E. Cramer, Wolfgang Förster, and Franz Rutland, 59–83. Frankfurt am Main, Germany: Fritz Knapp.

———. 1999. Increasing life expectancy and social security: Tendencies, effects, and reactions (in German). Zentrum fuer Sozialpolitik (ZeS) Working Paper no. 4/99. University of Bremen, Center for Social Policy.

Sinn, Hans-Werner. 1999a. The crisis of Germany's pension insurance system and how it can be resolved. CESifo Working Paper Series no. 191. Munich: CESifo.

———. 1999b. Pension reform and demographic crisis: Why a funded system is needed and why it is not needed. CESifo Munich. Paper presented at the 55th annual meeting of the International Institute of Public Finance. 23–26 August, Moscow, Russia.

Sinn, Gerlinde, and Hans-Werner Sinn. 1991. *Kaltstart (Jumpstart).* Tübingen, Germany: Mohr.

Tiebout, Charles. 1956. A pure theory of local expenditures. *Journal of Political Economy* 64:416–24.

Comments   Axel Börsch-Supan

Commenting on Bert Rürup's paper was not an easy task because it was a moving target—it still is. It probably also was a difficult exercise for him to write this paper. When he wrote the first version in early 2000, the pen-

Axel Börsch-Supan is chair of macroeconomics and public policy at the University of Mannheim, and a research associate of the National Bureau of Economic Research.

sion reform discussion was still dominated by a great deal of optimism among politicians—notably Walter Riester, German Secretary of Labor—as well as academics, sharing the hope that a substantive reform would be politically feasible even in reform-resistant Germany. At the end of March, when Bert presented the second version of his paper during the NBER-Kiel Institute Conference, the German government's pension reform plan was in the middle of becoming a concrete proposal, very much with the help of Bert Rürup. The proposal was launched early that summer and entered the gruesome process of the political discussion—with the unions opposing the plan equally as much as quite a few leading figures of the opposition, although for very different reasons. During this process, Bert submitted this carefully packaged and cautiously worded third version of the paper. Not much later, in December 2000, the core of the reform proposal collapsed under the attack of the unions within a few days of hearings in Berlin. Now, in January 2001, when I am writing these comments, the remaining pieces of the original reform will be written into law, and there might be further changes in the days ahead—changes that are utterly unlikely to resuscitate the original "Riester plan."

Bert Rürup's paper begins with a description of the German pension system, then tells the stories of two past pension reforms in 1992 and 1999, before he sets out a range of reform options that seemed feasible in the late summer of 2000. Without much further ado, let me take issue with Bert's view of the economics and the history of German pension reform. Indeed, the 1992 reform was overshadowed by the German unification—I should say, *beamed* upon by this fortunate event—but its main failure was not the increasing costs of East German pensions, as suggested several times in the paper (despite a brief disclaimer to the opposite in one place). Rather (and this will is a recurring theme in these comments), overly optimistic assumptions about fiscal sustainability, an astounding ignorance of economic incentive effects, and the desire to shift hard political decisions farther into the future made the 1992 reform only a timid one.[1]

A reform of the reform was soon necessary, and indeed, the 1999 reform was more incisive by introducing an automatic adjustment to the impending demographic change. Then, however, came the change of government. Populist arguments identical to those that had made the 1992 reform so timid allowed the newly elected government in 1999 to revoke this reform of the reform, only to let the government discover a year later that something had to be done anyway. Discussing the options for this "reform of the reform of the reform" is the core of Rürup's paper.

Of course, first describing a system and then telling its history is not an

---

1. Projections beyond the year 2010 were not published because they revealed that the 1992 reform could not stabilize the system during 2020–2040, the peak of population aging in Germany.

entirely innocent exercise if options for reform are to follow. Careful readers inspect the foundations before they appraise the building erected on them. Three ingredients are downplayed or not mentioned at all in Rürup's description of the German pension system and its reforms. First, the system is substantially more expensive, as suggested by the description. It costs not only 19.3 percent of gross earnings (the direct contributions paid by employers and employees) but an additional 9.5 percent (roughly) of gross earnings in indirect contributions. These indirect contributions consist of an earmarked part of the value added tax, of the new tax on fossil fuel, and of general revenues. Thus, total contributions are more than two and one-half times as high as in the United States (to take an example). Second, the system has massive incentive effects to evade and to retire early. Part of these negative incentive effects are the high tax-like costs just mentioned, which suppress labor supply and drive a substantial portion of workers into the gray or even the black market. Rürup describes the surge of "self-employment" but fails to appreciate this as a serious warning signal of negative incentives. In addition, the early average retirement age mentioned by Rürup is not an accident—it is systematically generated by the incentives created through the lack of actuarial fairness in the adjustment of benefits to retirement age, as in many other countries described in the Gruber and Wise (1999) volume. Third, the German pension system has no independent board of trustees; rather, it is essentially part of the German bureaucracy. It is important to realize this feature in order to understand the political dynamics of the German system, which lacks any independent control similar to the actuaries in the United States, who oversee projections of fiscal sustainability. Even the relevant demographic forecasts are made by the government and are subject to political compromises. Projections of longevity in the 1999 reform process were tailored to the perceived maximal politically sustainable contribution rate, and not drawn from the best available epidemiological and demographic knowledge. At times, this approaches the bizarre: the Labor Ministry's official fiscal sustainability projections differ between the domestic version and the one delivered to the Commissioner for Economic and Financial Affairs of the European Union (EU; Economic Policy Committee 2000).

In appraising Bert Rürup's reform options, it is crucial to understand the significance of these three points. I proceed here in the reverse order. First, the demographic and employment projections underlying the reform options in section 5.4 of the paper seriously downplay the financial strain on the German pension system. The status quo projection is an increase in pension expenditures from 8.7 percent of gross domestic product (GDP) in 2000 to 9.4 percent in 2030 (see figure 5.8 in the paper). According to the official estimate delivered by the German government to the EU, however, the projected increase is from 10.3 to 14.6 percent of GDP. Rürup uses a different base, omitting substantial parts of the

PAYGO system;[2] the main difference, however, is the severity of the relative increase: Rürup projects an 8 percent increase, whereas the EU figures imply a 42 percent increase of the fiscal burden. Underestimating the fiscal strain of the PAYGO system makes timid parametric reforms within the PAYGO system appear more feasible.

Second, the different reform options—status quo, freezing the current contribution rate, and equally sharing the burden—have very different microeconomic side effects because they imply very different tax rates. Unfortunately, the resulting incentive effects are completely ignored in this paper, although they are at the center of the current debate on labor market policy in Germany. The wedge between net and gross wages in Germany is one of the largest in the world, due to high labor taxes and social security contributions. The government has vowed to reduce these, being aware of the incentive effects on employment; indeed, a tax reform has already taken a first step this year. The same rationale applies for social security contributions, which are overwhelmingly perceived as taxes—as evidenced by surveys as well as actual evasion (Boeri, Börsch-Supan, and Tabellini 2001). The government has a good reason for ending the steady increase in taxes and contributions, but this implies freezing or even reducing contributions, not raising them further in the equal-sharing scenario.

Third, shifting a part of the contribution burden to non–labor-related taxes might be a great temptation, but would amplify the incentive effects insofar as it would reduce the link between benefits and contributions even farther. Few German drivers appreciate the fact that they support the social security system by refueling their cars. As mentioned earlier, about a third of the social security budget is already financed indirectly—and this means by a pure tax.

Because Germany has to shoulder the large pension burden in the decades ahead one way or another, the main goal of a pension reform must be to make this burden as light as possible. First, the actual burden can be reduced by abolishing the incentive effects of early retirement. Average retirement age in Germany is currently about fifty-nine years; a shift by two years alleviates the burden by about 10 percent. Simply making the system actuarially fair (in the sense of equalizing the present discounted value of pension benefits across retirement ages) is estimated to shift the retirement age by about two and one-half years (Börsch-Supan 2000b). Second, taxes create deadweight losses on top of the actual burden. Thus, it is imperative to minimize the tax character of social security contributions. Notional defined contribution accounts that show the workers the link between their contributions and their pension rights are a big step in that direction; they also minimize the well-known political economy problems of public pension systems and make the system more "tinker proof" (Browning 1975). Third, a burden is easier to shoulder if it is dis-

---

2. Such as pensions to civil servants and various supplements; see table 5.1 in the paper.

tributed more evenly over time. This is true of a substantial role of funded pensions: They smoothen the pension burden over time, simultaneously providing automatically actuarial fairness and a tight link between benefits and contributions. Freezing the current contributions to the PAYGO system while also retaining the total replacement rate in a mixed system implies a division of labor between the PAYGO and the funded pillar of about 2 to 1—much in line with the ratios in Switzerland, the Netherlands, and the Anglo-Saxon countries.

This is not the place to discuss a transition to such a reformed multipillar system in detail (Börsch-Supan 2000a). Let me remark only that the discussion in Germany—partially reflected in Bert Rürup's paper—treats the structural aspects of pension reform like a stepchild. Adverse selection, pension fund and annuity market regulations, administrative costs of a mixed system—all these are important issues that deserve much more thought and economists' attention in the German discussion of pension reform options, in addition to a thorough understanding of the true costs of the system, of the incentive effects it exerts, and of its political exposure due to its lack of independent actuaries and overseers. Particularly in this last respect, the failure of last year's reform attempt (the original "Riester Plan") is a sad but instructive show-piece of economics and the political economy.

References

Boeri, T., A. Börsch-Supan, and G. Tabellini. 2001. Who wants to shrink the Welfare State: The Opinions of European Citizens. *Economic Policy* 32: 7–50.
Börsch-Supan, A. 2000a. A blue print for Germany's pension reform. Paper Presented at the Workshop on Reforming Old Age Pension Systems. 25–26 May, Herbert-Giersch-Stiftung, Magdeburg, Germany.
———. 2000b. Incentive effects of social security on labor force participation: Evidence in Germany and across Europe. *Journal of Public Economics* 78:25–49.
Browning, E. K. 1975. Why the social insurance budget is too large in a democracy. *Economic Inquiry* 13:373–88.
Economic Policy Committee. 2000. Impact of ageing populations on public pension systems. Report to the ECOFIN-Council no. EPC/ECFIN/581/00-EN.
Gruber, J., and D. Wise, eds. 1999. *Social security and retirement around the world.* Chicago: University of Chicago Press.

Discussion Summary

Martin Feldstein inquired whether the notion of the discussant that there was scope for a Pareto-improving transition because of reduced labor market distortions had taken into account that someone had to pay more tax. When *Axel Börsch-Supan* indicated that he had not considered that,

Feldstein concluded that there is no Pareto-improvement, as those early taxpayers would be worse off. Börsch-Supan replied that, indeed, someone has to pay more, but not necessarily more taxes, because whether contributions are viewed as taxes or as insurance premia is a question of perception and not one of economic theory. He reported on polls that allow the conclusion that if money is funneled through the pay-as-you-go (PAYGO) system it is considered taxes and if it is funneled through savings plans it is considered premia, so that the former has distortionary effects and the latter has not, even if both are actuarially fair. In such a world, a switch toward funding would remove distortions that it otherwise would not and would therefore permit Pareto-improvements. *Assar Lindbeck* added that some cohorts are necessarily worse off because of the assumption that old pensioners have to be bailed out by tax. Lindbeck asked whether it is really not allowed in the European Monetary Union (EMU) to issue recognition bonds that make implicit pension debt an explicit government debt. *Axel Börsch-Supan* responded that with Germany near both the 60 percent limit for government debt and the 3 percent limit for net borrowing set by the Maastricht and Amsterdam treaties, there is little scope for additional debt financing. Regarding the idea of having escape clauses whenever there is a past debt for former generations, he was positive that the European Commission would not like to open this Pandora's box because of the probable repercussion of all kinds. He concluded that for all purposes the bond financing of transition is infeasible.

Laurence J. Kotlikoff pointed out that neutrality of going from a PAYGO to a funded system means that the change is a zero-sum game in present value; that is, if a generation benefits today by 100 euros, in present value, some other generation has to be hurt by 100 euros. He made the example of a policy that hurts current old people by 100 euros today in order to help the generation of fifty years from now by 100 euros in presentvalue. While the future generation's benefit was only 100 euros in present value, however, it would be a lot more in fifty years: approximately 700 euros using a risk-free rate of 4 percent. He concluded from this that sacrifices today are relatively small because of "the money-making machine called capital, which can have a large impact on the actual welfare and utility of future generations. Kotlikoff challenged the view advocated by many participants that a mixed system consisting of a funded component and PAYGO component is superior with respect to risk sharing because of more diversification. He contended that the PAYGO mechanism increases risk rather than reduces it because it does not resolve problems early and therefore does not indicate how they will be resolved. In contrast, in a funded setting it was clearer exactly how resolutions of these problems arose. Kotlikoff further pointed out that there is no evidence of intergenerational risk sharing from tests based on consumption data, at least in the United States. He reported that the data reveal that over time in cohorts that do very poorly in terms of their income, consumption goes down, and the consumption of cohorts that do well goes up, indicating that little intergenerational risk-sharing is apparent, whether through the extended family or through the government. He suggested that the PAYGO system may be exaggerating the risk that it is supposed to reduce.

Bert Rürup remarked that he observed a broad consensus that it is necessary to shrink the PAYGO system in order to reduce its cost but that the critical question is how to compensate for the reduced provision. As to the issue of whether there should be a mandatory individual savings plan or mandatory occupational pensions, he stated that the answer is a normative one depending on the interpretation of what is called the "Sozialstaatsgebot" in the German constitution and, ultimately, the confidence in the responsibility and sovereignity of individuals regarding their requirements in old age. He expressed his belief that every society should be sovereign in deciding the degree of old age protection organized by politics. The task for economists, in Rürup's view, is in part to identify positive and negative incentives of the system, but also to show alternatives with respect to financing a politically defined pension level.

6

Swedish Pension Reform
How Did It Evolve, and What Does It Mean for the Future?

Edward Palmer

6.1 Introduction

Mandatory public pension systems constitute a large and important public commitment to the aged. They are typically constructed on the pay-as-you-go (PAYGO) principle and are designed to provide a defined benefit from a specific pension age—in countries in the Organization for Economic Cooperation and Development (OECD), this is typically age sixty-five. In practice, the actual age at which individuals leave the labor force is much lower due to older workers' high take-up of disability and occupational benefits. Not infrequently, mandatory public or occupational benefits provide little opportunity to combine work with a benefit, and as a result, older workers must choose between being in or out of the workforce. At the same time, PAYGO systems are being threatened by increasing costs due to increasing dependency ratios.

The financial instability of PAYGO systems can be resolved by changing system design to encourage a higher ratio of years of work and contributions to benefit years. More generally, pension systems should be actuarially neutral in individual choices between work and leisure. They should not be designed so that they effectively tax those who choose to work longer, although systems in the OECD presently do this very thing (Gruber and Wise 1999). An advantage of defined contribution (DC) systems over defined benefit (DB) systems is that they are actuarially fair. Beginning with the mandatory public system and followed by major occu-

Edward Palmer is Professor of Social Insurance Economics at Uppsala University and head of the division for research and development at the National Social Insurance Board in Sweden.

The author is grateful to Laurence J. Kotlikoff and the editors for comments.

pational schemes, Sweden converted its earnings-related schemes from DB to DC in the 1990s. The process and implications of this process for future benefits and financial stability are the topics of this paper.

Most OECD nations' pension schemes originated during the 1930s or later. Since that time the nature of the labor market and the character of work and the workplace have changed dramatically. Health has improved vastly due to improvements in medical technology, lifestyles, and working environments. As a result, longevity has been increasing by about one year for every ten years that pass, and is expected to improve at least at this pace in the coming century. In spite of this, male workers worked fewer years in the mid-1990s than they did in the mid-1970s. In the mid-1990s, workers in most of the OECD worked only four to five years after the age of fifty-five, while life expectancy from age sixty was eighteen to twenty years, depending on the country (Palmer 1999b). In the next quarter-century, life expectancy from age sixty will rise by at least another two to two and one-half years if it simply follows the trend of the past half-century. Some believe that improvements in medical technology will lead to a more spectacular change.

At the other end of the life span, people are devoting more time to schooling, which leads to later entry into the workforce. If present trends continue, individuals entering the workforce now will work about thirty-five years and will be pensioners for about twenty-five years. The DB systems of the OECD countries were not designed for this environment, but for one in which the typical worker entered the workforce at about age twenty and worked into his or her sixties (i.e., more than forty years), with a life expectancy from age sixty of about fifteen years. No wonder we see so many pension systems in crisis when we examine what is in store in the coming twenty years (see, e.g., Disney 1999).

Should countries continue with PAYGO systems, or do individual financial-account systems provide a better alternative? Defined contribution systems with full advance funding, by definition, deal with demographic risks: Individual rights depend on individual contributions and life expectancy is factored into the individual annuity. This has led many experts and politicians to the conclusion that a complete or large-scale transition to full funding is the best path for the future. Countries in the OECD have been reluctant to make this transition, however, due not only to the high initial cost for the transition generation, but also to the financial risk involved. The potential advantage to the transition generation would be that the return on financial accounts would surpass the tax required to implement the transition. Future generations would gain if the rate of return on financial assets continued to surpass the rate of economic growth.

The final tally on whether any generation will end up as winners or losers in terms of future rates of return, all else being equal, requires us to have the facts in hand. In fact, neoclassical wisdom as initially formulated by Samuelson (1958) and Aaron (1966) suggests that all the clothes may come out the same color in the end—yet they are not all the same color in the beginning, or even during the whole wash, as history has shown us. If rates of return were to remain at their average levels of the past half-century for another half-century, and if individual funds obtained an index return at this rate, then the prophecy of the proponents of funding (e.g., Feldstein and Samwick 1997) would come true.

On the plus side of the account for more advance funding stands the conventional wisdom that it is not wise to put all one's eggs into one basket. A mixture of PAYGO (with its dependency on economic growth) and funded (with financial returns) systems could be the best medicine of all. For example, the Polish reform has recently been implemented under the banner of security through diversity (Góra and Rutkowski 1997). Elsewhere in Eastern European, Hungary (Palacios and Rocha 1998) and Latvia (Fox and Palmer 1999) have taken similar steps. The Swedish reform, which is the focus of this paper, moved in this direction with the 1994 reform legislation (see Palmer 2000 for a more detailed discussion), although the step is smaller than in these Eastern European countries. In Europe, Italy (e.g., Castellino and Fornero 1999) and Germany (e.g., Börsch-Supan, chap. 5 in this volume) are discussing ways of introducing or promoting individual financial accounts. In the reform debate in the United States, increased advance funding has been one of the main alternatives discussed.

In Sweden, the discussion moved in the direction of lifetime accounts in the early 1990s. Official actuarial calculations presented by the National Social Insurance Board (Allmänna Tilläggspension [ATP] 1987) showed that the old DB system was financially unsustainable with low economic growth and continued improvements in longevity. In addition, for a long time it had been considered desirable to find a way to move the large buffer fund in the public system into the private financial market. It had been clear for some time that individual financial accounts with contribution-based rights would be a way to do this. It was also clear that in the coming quarter-century, public (demographic reserve) funds would be needed to help the retirement of baby boomers born in the 1940s, as well as to buffer future demographic cycles.

Three principles emerged in the reform discussion in Sweden: First, benefits should be based on contributions from lifetime earnings. Second, indexation should be based on the growth of the contribution wage base. Third, annuities—even in the PAYGO system—should reflect changes in life expectancy. These principles were put together in the concept presented by the government's Pension Reform Group in 1992, and with this Sweden's notional defined contribution (NDC) PAYGO scheme emerged in print. The idea of NDC, which had been around conceptually in the economic literature since Buchanan (1968), was given a face for the first time. In addition, the 1992 concept called for individual financial accounts for a segment of the system, although the actual scale of the financial account system was left open at that juncture.

In 1994, Swedish Parliament passed legislation on an NDC PAYGO first pillar, supplemented by a second pillar with privately managed individual financial accounts. One year later (in 1995), the Italian Parliament passed similar legislation (see, e.g., Tumbarello 2000 for a description). The ideas and their construction in the Italian and Swedish legislation are similar, although the Swedish transition into the new system is much faster,[1] thus avoiding the need for further reform for financial purposes.

The details of the Swedish reform are available from many sources.[2] In this paper I will focus on how the reform evolved and what it means for individuals and for society at large. The whole reform package in Sweden represents in my mind a paradigm shift in thinking about public pension provision, and to examine how the Swedish reform evolved is a valuable exercise in itself. The NDC idea spread quickly, first to Latvia and Poland, then to a number of other countries perhaps leading one to ask, What is so enticing about this PAYGO system? In my mind, what is new is that it is a *thoroughbred.* It goes all the way in introducing defined contribution into the PAYGO framework.

The NDC PAYGO system with lifetime accounts, the appropriate index-ation, and annuities based on life expectancy move the system in the direction of advance-funded systems when it comes to dealing with risk (as discussed in Palmer 1999). What remains different compared with advance funding, needless to say, is the potential difference in rates of return and possible differences in the impact on savings and growth. The reform of the PAYGO system also opened the door in Sweden for individual financial-account DC schemes within occupational schemes, and this is the path they have begun to take. Generally, it can be argued that the paradigm shift embodied in the Swedish reform is well suited to meet the foreseeable future. One of the aims of this paper is to give the reader a better understanding of why this can be the case.

6.2   Overview of the Reform

Sweden has combined NDC PAYGO with a mandatory and universal advance-funded DC component, with a total contribution rate of 18.5 percent. Due to the DC design of the public system, participants can expect

---

1. In Sweden, persons born in 1938 will receive 20 percent of their benefit according to the new rules and 80 percent according to the old rules. The percentages for persons born in 1939 are 25 and 75 percent, respectively, and so on through persons born 1954, who receive the entire benefit according to the new rules. Persons born between 1946 and 1953 will receive more than half their benefits from the new system.

2. Extensive overviews of the entire reform are available from [http://www.pension/nu] and [http://www.ppm.nu].

this contribution rate to remain unchanged in the future. This shifts the risk of financing benefits from future to current workers. Because annuities in both systems are directly related to increasing longevity, there are actuarial advantages to working longer. There is no longer the "full-benefit" age that is typical of many OECD public DB schemes. Individuals may continue to work and contribute to a higher lifetime annuity as long as they desire. The reform also abolishes the special tax credit for pensioners, and puts pension income on an equal footing with earnings.

Both components of the public scheme are based on individual lifetime accounts; the difference is that in PAYGO system, accounts are not financial but notional (in the sense that there is no financial backing). The money contributed to the NDC system finances the benefits of current pensioners. Money contributed to the financial account system is invested in individually chosen funds. In both cases, however, the account is illiquid until the individual claims an annuity at retirement. For this reason, the principal difference between the systems from the point of view of the individual is the rate of return. From the point of view of the economy, there is a potential macroeconomic difference in the effect on national saving. In fact, one of the motives behind the introduction of the funded component of the Swedish system was to help create (forced) saving in Sweden in the future, which will be discussed in some depth below.

The reform of the mandatory universal public schemes had repercussions for occupational schemes, as well, during the 1990s. Sweden has had quasi-mandatory, centrally negotiated, sector-based (occupational) pension schemes for 80–90 percent of the workforce since the mid-1970s. With the announcement of the public reform, the schemes for private blue-collar and local government employees, which together comprise more than half of Sweden's workforce, were transformed into advance-funded DC schemes.

In sum, with the reform, all workers in Sweden pay a 16 percent contribution rate to the PAYGO scheme and 2.5 percent to the mandatory advance-funded scheme. In addition, the blue-collar and municipal employees contribute 2.5 to 4.5 percent[3] to a quasi-mandatory DC scheme. This gives many workers a total contribution rate of 5–7 percent in an individual financial account DC system. In addition, the occupational schemes for private white-collar workers are also funded, but they are DB rather than DC schemes.

6.2.1 NDC Accounts and Annuities

Table 6.1 provides an example of how the NDC system works.[4] It depicts an individual with slightly higher than average full-time earnings,

---

3. The blue-collar scheme began with a contribution rate of 2 percent but is now at 3.5 percent. The rate varies for municipal workers.
4. Palmer (2000a) describes the options available in constructing an NDC system.

Table 6.1   Example of Notional Defined Contribution

Age	Earnings ($US)[a]	Capital Index ($US)[b]	Capital Balance ($US)[c]	Unisex Life Expectancy[d]	Annuity ($US)[e]	Replacement Rate (%)[f]	Annuity with Real Return = 1.6%		
							Unisex Life Expectancy[d]	Annuity ($US)	Replacement Rate (%)[f]
22	27,061	1.000	5,006						
23	27,602	1.020	10,213						
24	28,154	1.040	15,626						
60	57,432	2.122	414,368						
61	58,580	2.165	433,493	24.24	17,096	0.30	19.69	21,043	0.37
62	59,752	2.208	453,217	23.41	18,516	0.32	19.14	22,654	0.39
63	60,947	2.252	473,557	22.59	20,061	0.34	18.58	24,397	0.41
64	62,166	2.297	494,528	21.78	21,746	0.36	18.02	26,287	0.43
65	63,409	2.343	516,150	20.97	23,588	0.38	17.45	28,342	0.46
66	64,677	2.390	538,438	20.16	25,603	0.40	16.88	30,580	0.48
67	65,971	2.438	561,411	19.36	27,814	0.43	16.30	33,024	0.51
68	67,290	2.487	585,088	18.55	30,262	0.46	15.72	35,716	0.54
69	68,636	2.536	609,488	17.76	32,944	0.49	15.14	38,654	0.57
70	70,009	2.587	634,629	16.96	35,927	0.52	14.54	41,906	0.61

Source: Palmer (2000).

Notes: The sample subject is an individual who begins work at age twenty-two and works every year until he or she decides to retire fully, sometime between age sixty-one and seventy. Contribution rate on earnings = 18.5 percent.

[a] Individual earnings growth rate of 2 percent per annum.

[b] Two percent per annum.

[c] End of year.

[d] For Swede born in 1975.

[e] Based on life expectancy at retirement.

[f] Percent of earnings last year.

with values expressed in U.S. dollars. The NDC system is a typical account system. Contributions based on a certain percentage of earnings (in the example, 18.5 percent) are noted in an account. The account balance increases with indexation from one year to the next, and with new contributions from the current year. In Sweden, accounts are indexed with the per capita wage. In the example, individual earnings increase at the same rate as the per capita wage for an individual who enters the workforce at the age of twenty-two and continues to work every year until he or she claims a benefit. A benefit can be claimed from age sixty-one in Sweden. The example illustrates how the combination of additional earnings and contributions, the continued growth of the notional capital balance with indexation, and the change in life expectancy from retirement enhance the benefit—and the earnings replacement rate.

The benefit is calculated in the table in two ways. First, it is calculated by dividing the capital balance at the time of retirement by unisex life expectancy for persons the age of the person retiring. This is not how it is done in Sweden, but is how it is done in other countries that have followed the Swedish model (e.g., Latvia and Poland). In the Swedish system, as in the Italian reform legislated a year after the Swedish reform, the annuity also includes an imputed real rate of growth. In Sweden, this rate is 1.6 percent. (In Italy the rate is set at 1.5 percent.) A second example in the table shows what this means for the individual's annuity at retirement, compared to the use of life expectancy alone.

The annuity is indexed annually to the consumer price index (CPI). The annuity calculated with real growth of 1.6 percent implies real wage indexation over the lifetime at this rate. What happens if real long-term growth falls short of 1.6 percent? To maintain financial stability, given this form of front loading, this index is supplemented with an additional index that is based on the difference between actual growth and 1.6 percent. If actual growth is higher than 1.6 percent, the benefit is indexed upward according to the difference, and if it is lower, the benefit is adjusted downward according to the difference. Over the lifetime, this form of indexation of pensions gives the same result as straightforward wage indexation.

The front-loaded annuity shifts a part of the expected value of the total benefit stream, given life expectancy and the real return of 1.6 percent, from the future to the present. Compared to straightforward indexation of a benefit providing the same total income in retirement, this gives pensioners more money when young, but less when older. The Swedish annuity thus assumes that individuals discount future consumption in favor of present consumption. This method also provided a smooth transition from the old ATP system with its price-indexed benefit that, with real wage growth, declined in value over time relative to a current average wage.

The system as it has been implemented in Sweden is not perfectly financially stable under all circumstances, for at least two reasons. The estimate of life expectancy used to compute the annuity is derived from the outcome of the immediate past, and is not based on a forward-looking projection. Imbalance can occur if the contribution base (wage sum) grows slower than per capita earnings (used for indexation in Sweden), or if longevity turns out to be greater than the estimate used in calculating the annuity.

In order to deal with this, yet another indexation mechanism was introduced into the Swedish system to brake downward pressure that can arise with a declining labor force or deviations from actual longevity. This balance mechanism is based on the development of system debt relative to the debt that would arise in equilibrium and corrects for all technical imperfections in the actual construction of the system.[5] The system will be endowed from the beginning with a buffer fund having significant starting capital from a similar fund from the old system. The fund will be used, however, as was originally intended when the system was conceived in the 1950s: as a demographic buffer. It will be drawn on to finance the baby boomers in 2010–25.

6.2.2   Is the Swedish Scheme an Innovation?

Boskin, Kotlikoff, and Shoven (1988; hereafter BKS) and the French point system are probably alternative schemes that bear the closest resemblance to the Swedish model, but they differ in principle in that they are faithful to the DB genre in various ways. In the French system, points are calculated by dividing an individual's contributions in a given year by an amount based on a reference wage. Workers receive extra points when they are sick, injured, or unemployed, or when they have three or more children. These are "free of charge," which means that there is redistribution within the system. There are also free points covering the working period before the creation of the scheme. A worker thus receives a yearly benefit increment expressed as points. A full pension is paid at age sixty or sixty-five, depending on circumstances. When the individual chooses to retire, points are added up and multiplied by the current value of a point.

The value of points is determined by a board on the basis of an estimate of the resources of the system. In determining available resources, the board takes the interests of employers, workers, and pensioners into consideration. In sum, the system differs considerably from the Swedish system. It attempts to remain faithful to the DB genre by defining points and a full-benefit pension age. Redistribution is financed from within the

5. Other imperfections have to do with information lags in general because pure equilibrium requires spontaneous adjustment, and with the fact that the system has a demographic fund earning a financial market rate of return that may surpass the notional (economic) rate, thereby helping the system with liquidity.

system, so part of a contribution can be viewed as a tax rather than an insurance premium payment, as in the Swedish NDC scheme. The Swedish system is a pure insurance model, with "extra credits" financed separately. Finally, in the French point system, the value of a point is determined by a discretionary process. In the construction of the Swedish model, autonomy from discretionary decisions and from the risk of manipulation for political gain were deemed necessary to maintain the credibility of the system.

In the BKS model life expectancy in the year the contributions are paid is used to determine the incremental value of that year's contributions toward a pension. To achieve system balance, a weighting factor is used. This factor is calculated from a projection of future retirement behavior and from survivor and disability take-up. In other words, the rate of return in the BKS model depends on the performance of the overall system for old age, disability, and survivors. The aim is to maintain financial stability within the *entire* system. An increase in the frequency of disability or number of survivors would yield lower old age pensions, but decreased disability take-up or fewer survivor years in the system would enhance old age benefits.

From the point of view of the participant, the yearly points derived in the French and BKS systems do not give a clearer picture of the future than does the Swedish system. In the Swedish system, individuals can follow the development of life expectancy and benefits as the National Social Insurance Board sends out its annual benefit projections.[6] In other words, there seems to be no information advantage in aspiring to define benefit increments, as in the French and BKS models.

An important feature of the Swedish reform is that it divorced the disability and survivor benefit systems from the old age system, in order to create a pure insurance system covering old age only. Neither the French point system nor the BKS proposal for the United States do this. The Swedish model moves disability out of the system, but calculates the cost of providing old age benefits to the disabled from age sixty-five and transfers the resources needed to finance these costs to the old age scheme. Direct application of the BKS model transfers disability costs to all current workers by reducing their future pensions, whereas the Swedish model claims the resources from the present consumption of workers. Moreover, the Swedish model sets the spotlight directly on the problem.

Separating the old age and disability systems also makes it possible fo-

---

6. In the Swedish NDC and financial account systems, individuals are informed on an annual basis of the development of their accounts, and are given a benefit projection using current life expectancy and alternative assumptions about their retirement ages and about economic growth, and using current life projections.

cus on the costs and problems of disability per se, which in Europe have tended to be driven by "moral hazard." Moral hazard results because employers know they can let older workers drift into sickness and then disability without taking adequate measures at the workplace (e.g., adapting work tasks and work hours, providing necessary breaks, giving physical and vocational training with new technology, etc.) to prevent this. There also must be acceptance of the possibility that wages for older workers do not need to keep up with those of younger workers.

Proponents of the Swedish model (including the present author) claim that it is important to distinguish clearly the merits, problems, consequent design, and hence, the messages of the design of the old age system from those of the disability system. The Swedish model separates social policy from social insurance. The earnings-related old age system is set up as an insurance system, and redistribution is moved into social policy. Social policy—which includes a minimum guarantee for old age pensioners, credits for childbirth, and more (to be discussed below)—is financed from the state budget with general tax revenues.

Finally, as opposed to DB systems that focus on retirement as an event, DC-based systems put the spotlight on work and on the rewards associated with a longer working life. With the prospects of declining numbers in the workforce it now appears that older workers will have to be viewed as an asset and kept on in order to meet the overall demand for labor. Defined contribution systems combined with tax (and other) rules that are neutral between work and retirement go a long way toward reducing the distortions between work and leisure for older workers. The transition to DC systems erases impediments for continued work, and may help increase the age at which individuals leave the workforce as improvements in health and longevity continue. It will nevertheless be important to adjust the *minimum* age at which a benefit can be claimed as life expectancy improves.

6.2.3   The Funded Second Pillar of the Mandatory System: Individual Financial Accounts

The funded second pillar of the mandatory public system can best be viewed in terms of an accumulation period and an annuity period. For the accumulation period, Sweden has developed what has come to be called the *clearing-house model,* as opposed to a more traditional insurance model. During the accumulation period, individuals can choose freely among one or more funds registered with the system. In the first year of choice, 2000, about 500 funds were registered in the system. Although there will be no funds dealing solely with derivatives, there are in principle no restrictions on fund portfolio composition. This means that the individual chooses his or her own combination of risks and returns.

This construction can be compared with an alternative that is based on one or on a small number of index funds. For persons with the same accumulation period, an index fund will yield similar benefits; however, there still may be considerable differences between persons (and especially between age cohorts) who do not have the same accumulation period. The index fund idea was not adopted. The logic behind the alternative chosen is that, generally speaking, all funds can be expected to produce positive long-term returns, albeit of varying size. With unrestricted choice, persons can move freely between funds. No one is locked in a disadvantageous fund against his or her will.

The rate of return in the second pillar is thus determined by financial market development and individual choice of funds. In principle, table 6.1 is also a way to illustrate how the second-pillar financial accounts work, if one interprets the rate of return on the capital balance as a financial rate of return. Upon retirement, individuals can claim a fixed- or variable-rate annuity in the system. A variable-rate annuity is the result of leaving money in the individual's fund(s), as the annuity will reflect changes in fund values. A fixed-rate annuity is obtained by transferring individual capital at retirement to the state (monopoly) annuity provider. Annuities are based on unisex life expectancy.

The choice to limit the publicly managed component to a contribution rate of 2.5 percent was the result of a political compromise between the Social Democratic Party's position that the whole public system should be PAYGO, and the governing parties' preference for a larger advance-funded component. In addition, there was an agreement not to increase the scale of the entire public system, taking into consideration the fact that the vast majority of employees are also covered by supplementary occupational schemes. The supplementary system for blue-collar workers was also converted into an individual financial account DC system with a contribution rate of 3.5 percent. As has already been noted, the outcome for this and other groups is that the sum of the public mandatory and quasi-mandatory occupational contribution rate for old age coverage is approximately 22–23 percent, of which 5–7 percent goes to advance funding, depending on the sector in which they are employed.

Finally, the funded component of the public system was fit into the cost restriction (contribution rate of 18.5 percent) of the overall system without creating a new tax for future generations, by tightening up the system for those generations instead.[7] Younger workers traded future benefit rights in the PAYGO system for rights in the financial account system. If a higher portion of the 18.5 percent earmarked for the total system had been channeled into the financial account system, it would have had to be tax financed. Taxes had been increased during the deep recession in the early 1990s in order to restrict the size of the deficits. At the same time as the

---

7. Increasing life expectancy gradually decreases the size of the annuity, all else equal.

reform was being discussed and introduced, there was an agreement among all the major parties not to increase taxes any further, but instead to decrease them once budget balance had been achieved.

6.2.4   The New Paradigm and Social Policy

As the Swedish welfare state was being constructed in the 1960s and 1970s, there was a general feeling among policy makers and scholars that it was not important to identify the uses of funds in the government budget. Although the type of taxation might matter for individual decisions, the connection between a source of funds and a benefit was not considered to be important. The NDC PAYGO paradigm is based on the idea that it does matter. In principle, the NDC system is a pure insurance system: Individual lifetime contributions, and a return on these, determine an individual's capital when it is time to calculate an annuity at retirement. The individual is not paying a tax but is making a mandatory contribution to provide for his or her own future retirement.

Social policy is still important, but in making the above distinction, one is now arguing that the *tax-transfer* system *per se* is to be used for social policy. Redistribution is separated from the insurance system. Redistributional policy takes two primary forms: First, the main instrument of social policy is the guarantee pension for persons aged sixty-five and older. This is paid for through the tax-transfer system—that is, the state budget. Second, credits can be given to notional and financial accounts in the insurance system as long as they are accompanied by external financing. Without the external financing, the system would no longer be in financial equilibrium.

The Swedish system contains generous credits in conjunction with childbirth, which go almost exclusively to mothers and which can in total be the equivalent of a contribution rate of an additional three-fourths of one percent, but fluctuating with the number and timing of births.[8] There are also credits for time spent in military conscription and in pursuing higher education. Insured periods with benefits from sickness insurance, disability insurance, and unemployment insurance also give credits, and these credits are accompanied by money that is transferred into the pension system.

The guarantee pension is the primary safety net for pensioners. Individuals aged sixty-five and older can qualify for a guarantee benefit. The guarantee tops-off the two earnings-related benefits up to a specified ceiling.

---

8. Credits are given for a maximum of four years per child, and for one child at a time. Two children born two years apart give a credit of six years. The claimant (usually the mother) is entitled to the most advantageous of (a) an amount equal to 75 percent of average earnings for all covered persons; (b) 80 percent of her own earnings the year prior to childbirth; and (c) a supplement consisting of a fixed amount, indexed over time to the (covered) per capita wage.

For a single person, the guarantee by itself amounts to about 75 percent, after tax, of what is needed to reach the level set by the social authorities to obtain social assistance. The lifetime poor with no or only a very small earnings-related benefit will also qualify for a means-tested housing allowance, which normally is sufficient to bring him or her up to the national *minimum standard* for a pensioner. If this is still not enough, the individual has a right to means-tested social assistance.

In sum, the insurance system is separated from the social policy instruments in the new Swedish system. The insurance system links benefits directly to contributions and is designed to be financially stable over all generations. Social policy vis-à-vis the pension system is an entirely external affair. Credits backed by money can be voted upon in Parliament and transferred into the pension system. They can also be changed at some future date without affecting rights acquired and financed in the past. This gives Parliament latitude to change its mind on distributional issues without going back on its earlier promises, which have already been financed. One of the problems with the old system was that transfers built into the DB formula were not targeted; these turned out, upon close examination, to be arbitrary, and it was realized that they generally did not do what people believed they did or should do. Namely, they tended to benefit persons with steep earning careers. The reform has changed this.

6.2.5   The Outcome of the Reform for the Individual

A popular public misconception was that the old system replaced 60 percent of earnings at retirement, because the ATP formula was based on 0.6 times the individual's highest fifteen-year average earnings. Everyone with ATP and residing in Sweden also received the flat-rate *folkpension*— which was the floor in the system—and as a result could expect a replacement rate higher than 60 percent. Exactly how much higher depended on individual earnings levels, because the flat-rate supplement gave a higher replacement rate the lower individual earnings were. In sum, a pension in the old system could give varied replacement rates.

For most individuals, with average individual earnings growth of 1 percent, replacement was 60 percent—and with average individual earnings growth of 2 percent, replacement was 56 percent—of the final year's earnings before retirement. However, as we know, replacement rates in terms of final earnings may make little sense anyway because final earnings may not represent normal earnings. With the occupational supplement, which provided about 10 percent more, the replacement rate from the mandatory public systems and the occupational schemes was about 65–75 percent, depending on individual earnings growth during the fifteen years prior to retirement.

How does the new system compare with this? Pensions for the typical Swede are composed of the two components of the mandatory system—

Table 6.2   Replacement Rates (annuity as percentage of last earnings)

Age	NDC Only (contribution rate 16%)	Return for Public Second Pillar (2.5%) + Group Occupational (3.5%)			Return for NDC + Public Second Pillar + Group Occupational		
		2%	5%	8%	2%	5%	8%
61	0.32	0.12	0.23	0.47	0.44	0.55	0.79
62	0.33	0.13	0.25	0.52	0.46	0.58	0.85
63	0.35	0.14	0.27	0.57	0.49	0.62	0.92
64	0.37	0.15	0.29	0.63	0.52	0.66	1.00
65	0.39	0.15	0.31	0.69	0.54	0.70	1.11
66	0.42	0.16	0.33	0.76	0.58	0.75	1.18
67	0.44	0.17	0.36	0.83	0.61	0.80	1.27
68	0.47	0.18	0.39	0.92	0.65	0.86	1.39
69	0.50	0.19	0.42	1.01	0.69	0.92	1.51
70	0.53	0.20	0.45	1.12	0.73	0.98	1.65

Source: Based on Palmer (2000).

Notes: The individual's earnings are assumed to grow at a real rate of 2 percent per annum throughout the earning career. The rate of growth used for indexation of capital in the PAYGO system is 2 percent. The PAYGO, second-pillar, and group occupational annuities are all based on unisex life expectancy and a real rate of return on capital from retirement of 1.6 percent.

the NDC PAYGO component and the second pillar with individual financial accounts in the public system—and a group occupational scheme. Table 6.2 illustrates how all three of these work together.

The group occupational scheme for blue-collar workers was converted into a DC system with individual financial accounts in line with the reform of the public system. For the blue-collar worker, a total contribution rate of 6 percent (2.5 percent public + 3.5 percent occupational) goes to financial accounts. All calculations assume a rate of return of 1.6 percent per annum during the annuity period. The life expectancy is for persons born in 1975. Table 6.2 shows that with a rate of return of about 5 percent in the financial account systems, under the assumptions used here a replacement rate of 70 percent can be reached at age sixty-five.

As the example in table 6.2 illustrates, the financial rate of return is crucial. Financial rates in the range of 2–5 percent provide a replacement rate in line with traditional Swedish expectations about income replacement at retirement. Historically, from 1919 to 1996, the average real rate of return on Swedish stocks has been 8.6 percent while the real yield on bonds has been 3.1 percent (Frennberg and Hansson 1992; *Lag om premiepension* 1997). A mixed portfolio of stocks and bonds would yield about a 6 percent real rate of return, and a portfolio with a greater share of stocks would move upward to 8–9 percent if history were to repeat itself. In fact, if the financial rate of return is about 8 percent, these calculations suggest that Swedes are overinsured, because earnings replacement rates of more than 100 percent by age sixty-five overshoot by far what most people believe is necessary. With this perspective, it would be possible to reduce PAYGO commitments in the future.

A final word of caution is in order. Replacement rates are difficult to work with because earnings profiles are usually more complicated than those used in the examples here. Earnings grow every year, and at a constant rate, in table 6. 2. Empirical evidence shows that earnings profiles for older workers flatten and may even decline. As a result, if we were to assume no earnings growth after age sixty (or some other age prior to sixty), replacement rates based on earnings the year prior to retirement would become much higher than those reported in the table. In sum, table 6.2 provides a basis for understanding how the combined systems work, but indicates only *relative* differences in replacement rates based on the assumptions employed.

6.3   Why Reform?

The 1994 reform replaced a DB system consisting of the flat-rate *folk-pension* and the earnings-related ATP scheme introduced in 1960. The latter provided a full benefit at age sixty-five (age sixty-seven until July 1976), with thirty years of contribution history and based on an average of the best fifteen years of reported earnings (indexed to the CPI). Why did it become necessary to reform this system?

There were three major reasons for the reform. First, the old system was unfair: To a considerable extent, it transferred money from persons with lower lifetime resources to persons with higher lifetime resources. Second, it was financially perverse: It transferred a larger percent of resources from workers to pensioners when economic growth was low and less when real growth was high. Together with an increasing trend in life expectancy, a scenario with low real growth threatened to create an increasing burden on the working generation. The cost of the old age system could have increased from 18 percent to as much as 30 percent by 2030, with a low rate of growth. Few believed that future workers would regard this as tolerable, and thus most agreed that something had to be done.

A third reason for reform was the observation that, when the baby-boom cohort were to become pensioners, the large pension fund that had been accumulated since 1960 (equal to roughly 40 percent of GDP in the 1990s) would be depleted at the latest by around 2020. Although there was less consensus around this point, many believed it was important to create new "replacement" saving, but that any new form of forced saving should be managed through private-sector investment decisions.

The ATP system had served its original purpose well during its first three decades. It had been designed to provide significant benefits to persons born around 1905 to 1920, whose lives—and human capital—had been affected by two world wars and a depression. The system began with a generous transition rule requiring only twenty years for a full benefit for persons born before 1915, twenty-one years for persons born in 1915, and so on, up to thirty years for persons born in 1924 and after. Not surprisingly, then, Ståhlberg (1990) finds that pensioners born between 1905 and 1914 could expect to receive lifetime benefits six times greater than their contributions. The return falls for younger cohorts. Persons born in 1944 and later were covered during all their (potential) working careers from age sixteen by the ATP system. Ståhlberg shows that persons born between 1944 and 1950 and later could expect at retirement to get back only 80 percent of what they paid in contributions.

A system that returns less than a Krona for every discounted Krona paid in could be defended on the grounds that it is intended to redistribute money from the rich to the poor, and thereby constitutes a part of a country's redistribution policy. With current patterns of work, however, Ståhlberg's study showed that the system transferred lifetime resources from the lower to the upper classes: from wage earners with long earnings careers and flatter lifetime earnings profiles to professionals and others with increasing earnings profiles.

The thirty-year rule worked against the typical blue-collar worker, whose earnings career is long but can be relatively flat. At the other extreme, it worked in favor of the white-collar worker with a longer period of education and later entrance into the labor market, but with a rising earnings career throughout almost all his or her working life and generally higher lifetime earnings. The fifteen-year rule was clearly to the advantage of persons with good earnings growth toward the ends of their careers, which is the case for any DB system in which benefits are based largely or wholly on career-end earnings.

The major claim for the thirty-year rule was that it was to the advantage of women, because women work part-time during a significant portion of their working careers. This claim received some support from Ståhlberg's work on the redistribution effects of the old system, based on the fact that the negative return on contributions for upper- and middle-class women was slightly less than the negative return for males born in the same period. This implies an intergender transfer. This transfer was very small, however, and did not hold for working-class women, who were, in fact, the group who could expect to get the least out of a Krona put into the old system. In sum, the old Swedish system was hard to justify on social redistribution grounds.

On top of this, the system was financially unstable. Actuarial calculations produced by the National Social Insurance Board showed that the contribution rate would have to continue to increase in the future, and considerably so, if long-term real economic growth were to fall well below 2 percent. Viewed over any 20-year period, benefits were largely determined by acquired rights of both pensioners and older workers, which were price indexed and hence immobile in the face of changes in real growth.[9] Growth affected benefits slowly through increased wages and new acquired rights of younger workers. With acquired rights in the coming twenty years already nearly established, the contribution rate required to pay for them was determined almost exclusively by the real rate of growth of the contribution base. With real economic growth of 1 percent per year, the contribution rate would increase to about 27 percent. On the other hand, real growth of 3 percent would be sufficient to maintain a constant contribution rate.

It is noteworthy that when the old system was being constructed, toward the end of the 1950s, economists were using a 3 percent real growth rate as their pessimistic scenario for the long-term future. At that time, real growth was around 4–5 percent in Sweden. It would have been difficult in the 1990s to find a Swedish economist who believed in permanent real growth as high as 3 percent. Most believed that Sweden would do well to produce long-term growth of 2 percent. In fact, some believe that hourly wages are already so high that new entrants into the workforce could be more interested in working fewer hours in order to have more leisure time, and that growth as high as 2 percent would soon become history.

When the ATP reform was introduced in 1960, economists argued that the improvement in benefits would replace some private saving, and that national saving was likely to decrease as a result of the reform. Later, studies by Markowski and Palmer (1979), Palmer (1981), and Berg (1983)[10] provided empirical evidence that through 1980, private saving had indeed decreased. The saving rate of households would have been 2–4 percent higher in the absence of the reform, according to these studies. However, from 1960 to 1982, contributions to the earnings-related ATP pension system were higher than was needed to pay for benefits. In fact, during this period, this was more than what was needed to counteract the estimated decline in household saving (Markowski and Palmer 1979).

Sweden's sizable public pension funds (about 40 percent of GDP) have been surrounded by considerable political controversy during most of their forty years of existence. Here, there has always been a clear dividing line between, on one hand, the Social Democratic Party and the left, and on the other, the parties to the right of the political spectrum. The agreement that was reached and strictly upheld through 1974 (and then moderated only slightly) was that the funds should be invested only in bonds and direct loans to companies—not in equities. In spite of this, in 1974 an

---

9. This is demonstrated in the analytical work performed for the reform (*Reformerat pensionssystem: Kostnader och individeffekter* 1994, 40).

10. Both Palmer (1981) and Berg (1983) included variables to capture demographic as well as transitory inflationary and unemployment effects on savings.

equity fund was created and allocated a small portion of the total reserves, and this was supplemented with additional equity funds as time passed. The share in the total portfolio of the market value of equities[11] in the 1990s has been under 15 percent.

The financial market was highly regulated in Sweden into the 1980s. This meant that the public pension fund was required to hold a large share of its portfolio in government and mortgage-backed bonds at a lower than market value. Regulation is estimated to have held down bond yields by at least one percentage point. In practice, this meant that consumption possibilities were shifted from the future to the present, subsidizing mortgages and government debt. The financial market was gradually deregulated in the 1980s, and these restrictions were lifted.

It is also likely that many politicians have viewed the pension fund as a part of the consolidated financial balance of the public sector, leading to less discipline regarding public expenditures. Beginning with the second crisis involving the Organization of Petroleum Exporting Countries (OPEC), from 1978 through 1982, and then once again during the first half of the 1990s, following a financial crisis, Sweden combated deep recession with heavy government borrowing. Following recovery in the 1980s, politicians were more inclined to increase rather than decrease expenditure commitments. Perhaps a new order with public pension funds held in individual financial accounts instead of in central public funds will have a sobering effect on future political expenditure decisions.

Whereas there was broad agreement from the beginning regarding the problems with the old system, political interests diverged considerably on the issue of funding. The non-socialist parties had never supported a large public fund within a PAYGO framework. For them, if there was to be substantial social security funding in the future, this would have to be funneled into the private market. The Social Democratic Party, with the support of the large blue-collar labor organization *Landsorganisationen* (LO), were satisfied with a public fund and were not worried about its size. At the time the pension reform was to be formulated, saving in Sweden was at an all-time low; household saving had been declining steadily, and widespread concern about this trend transcended political interests. Given the more general goal of creating new forced saving, it appeared logical for the Social Democratic Party to open itself to the position of the parties to the right in this issue. In addition, with this concession it would be possible for the parties to the right to agree on a larger mandatory system than they otherwise were prepared to concede. This opened the door for the introduction of a system with mandatory, privately managed, individual financial accounts.

11. The pension "fund" actually consists of six funds with separate boards of directors and managers.

6.4   The Reform Process

The ATP reform of 1960 was the flagship of Social Democratic social policy rhetoric and of the social policy of the welfare state that emerged under a series of Social Democratic governments from after World War II through 1976. What is more, the political intentions behind the 1960 reform had been fulfilled. Persons retiring in the 1970s and 1980s were doing better and better. From 1970 to 1989, more than half of an increase of 1.8 percent in real wages—prior to deductions for contributions—was redistributed through employer contributions to the social insurance system, mainly to finance the increase in pension benefits.[12] Old age pensioners have been the redistribution winners from the mid-1970s (see, e.g., Gustafsson and Palmer 1997). By the early 1990s, the average standard of an ATP pensioner was not much below that of someone living in a household with children, once the weighted consumption needs of all family members were taken into account.

The success of the system in improving pensioners' standard of living was not generally associated by the public, with the low rate of growth of take-home pay over the same period. Even had it been recognized, it is not clear that this alone would have created intergenerational friction, as long as younger generations of workers could expect the intergenerational commitment to be honored. The question was, could they? From 1977 into the mid-1980s, the welfare state had been held up on credit. This was not what its architects had had in mind. As the 1980s rolled out, substantial pension debt (promises) was being augmented by a large increase in the state budget debt. This came at a time when the economic literature was focusing on this issue, and the discussion filtered quickly into the public debate. In addition, the National Social Insurance Board published an actuarial report in 1983 revealing the extreme dependence of the system on good economic growth to maintain financial stability.

It was logical, then, that in October 1984, as Sweden pulled out of its first deep and prolonged post–World War II recession, a new Social Democratic government initiated a Pension Commission. In its directives to the commission, the government expressed concern about the long-term viability of the whole package of welfare promises to the elderly—health and community care as well as pensions. The instructions from the government to the commission were to examine all of these, with particular emphasis on the financial stability of the pension system and the interaction between the pension system and the economy.

By 1990, when it was dissolved, the commission had published well over 1,000 pages of analysis and discussion. It had made few proposals, although the two that had been made were also passed in Parliament. First,

---

12. The commission's final report (Ståhlberg 1990, 66).

the commission had been instructed to examine how the survivor benefit available only to women in the old system could be made equal in status to that for men. The commission proposed that the survivor benefit for women born after 1945 should be abolished, arguing that men and women born after the war were participating on equal terms in the labor market, and that hence, there was no need to provide for a special benefit for women. This proposal was legislated by Parliament and went into effect in 1990. Here, it can be claimed, a political desire to promote gender equality in all aspects of life shadowed the potential need for a little extra insurance for elderly survivors of both genders. In practice, this measure had the effect of privatizing survivor insurance, while it saved considerable money for the public sector in the long run.

The commission's second proposal was to abolish a right to be converted from unemployment to disability insurance for persons who had been unemployed from 58.3 years of age. This mechanism had been used in consensus between employers and unions to get around the seniority rules for older workers when redundancies were declared.[13] The commission expressed concern over the fact that the disability system was being used to remedy unemployment, and when this decision was being made (in 1988) unemployment was at a historical low in Sweden. The change was also logical because demographic projections pointed toward a future shortage in the supply of labor. Given this perspective, it seemed unnecessary to give employers and unions the continued opportunity to use the disability system to minimize the need to let younger workers go—by pushing older workers into disability—when trimming down businesses.

The Pension Commission of the 1980s made no proposals about reforming the old age system per se. It had been impossible for the political parties and interest groups that formed the commission to agree on anything. To the public, the chairman of the commission explained this by claiming that the commission saw no acute need for reform because the economy was doing so well and could be expected to do so for a long time to come. Seemingly in defiance of this bold optimism, the economy began its downward spiral within a year after this statement was made. According to usual procedure in Sweden, the report was sent to political organizations, interest groups, government agencies, and academic institutions to provide them with the opportunity to comment formally. In this way, the report, which analyzed clearly the shortcomings of the system, signaled the start of serious debate about reform.

In 1991, Skandia, a large private insurance company in Sweden, presented calculations for a proposal for a partial transition to a system with

---

13. Once this was abolished, the next threshold (i.e., the age at which a person can go from work to an unemployment benefit that lasts until a full old-age benefit can be claimed at sixty-five) became 63.3 years.

privately managed individual financial accounts. These calculations showed that a transition to more advance funding would be expensive for younger workers. With an estimate of costs in hand, some supporters of a transition to a large-scale advance-funded system with privately managed individual financial accounts toned down their claims. Proponents of privately managed financial accounts also directed their efforts toward restricting the size of the PAYGO mandatory commitments. To this end, they focused on maintaining a low ceiling on covered earnings and holding down the size of the contribution rate.

Another problem with the old system that entered the public discussion around 1990 was that average yearly full-time earnings were already very close to the ceiling on covered earnings (about 80 percent). On the other hand, since 1982, contributions had been paid on *all* earnings. Without indexation of the ceiling for real growth, it was easy to show that average earnings would surpass the ceiling and that, eventually, the system would evolve into a flat-rate system anyway. The speed of this process would depend on the rate of real wage growth.

A scenario in which covered earnings came close to the ceiling had considerable political support from the right because it implied gradual retrenchment of the public commitment and future privatization. At the other extreme, Social Democratic voters and voters to the left of this party still believed that the old ATP system should be kept intact with minimal changes. The joker in the deck, just as in the 1950s,[14] was the large white-collar union, *Tjänstemannens Centralorganisation* (TCO). In the spring of 1990, TCO had managed to kill a switch to a 20-40 rule being considered by the Pension Commission in the final hours of its work, by leaking the idea to mass media and then claiming that it would be to the extreme disadvantage of women. Many of the members of this union had much to gain by an increase in the ceiling, because many of those with earnings above the ceiling were white-collar managers represented by TCO. Their employers were paying both the "tax" on earnings above the ceiling, while at the same time they were required to finance occupational pension insurance to cover the *same* earnings, because the tax did not give social insurance rights.

Interestingly, for a long time there was a natural alliance around the ceiling issue between the blue-collar union (LO) and the Employer Confederation. Because ATP was financed by employer contributions, letting the

---

14. The rules of the ATP reform were set out in a proposal presented by the metal-workers within LO (Martin 1984). The 15–30 rule, with a factor of 60 percent of historical average (fifteen-year) earnings, resembled closely the scheme in existence for white-collar workers in TCO. Given this choice of construction, as opposed to a lifetime earnings scheme proposed by the Pension Commission of the 1950s, the Social Democratic Party hoped to gain the open support of TCO. This attempt went in vain, however, when TCO chose not to take sides in the pension debate of the 1950s.

system evolve slowly into a flat-rate system (i.e., with a gradual decline in acquired rights per Krona paid) implied limiting employer contribution increases for the public system, but higher costs for the occupational schemes. From the mid-1980s the Swedish Employer Confederation (*Svenska Arbetsgivarförening,* or SAF) had opposed overall increases in the employer contribution rate, including changes needed to finance the ATP system.[15] The view of LO was that as long as their own members were not seriously affected by the ceiling on covered earnings, this progressive tax should be kept. This view was also shared by the Social Democratic Party, whereas the parties to the right wanted to eliminate this form of tax on higher earnings.

A new four-party coalition government took office after the election in autumn 1991, and around the start of the new year the government formed a Working Group with a mandate to reform the old age pension system. The minister heading the reform committee, and the minister responsible for the reform, was Bo Könberg, who represented the liberal party. All seven parties in Parliament at that time were given a place in the Working Group, and, together with a handful of experts, they began their work in 1992. Anna Hedborg, who had represented the Social Democratic Party in the Working Group, became the new Minister for Social Insurance with the next change in government in 1996, ensuring the continuation of the reform process.

From the outset, there was political agreement on the principles to be followed: There should be a mandatory system providing coverage for *all* persons residing and working in Sweden. There should also be an adequate safety net, similar in coverage to that already in existence. Finally, the system should be designed to secure intergenerational trust, with general agreement that this could be achieved only by a financially stable system.

Generally speaking, the proposals emerging from the public debate and submitted by the various interest organizations and government agencies favored a reform approaching or adopting lifetime accounts. This idea was not new in the Swedish pension literature. In fact, the backbone of the first proposal made by the Pension Commission of the 1950s was a system with lifetime accounts.[16] The public discussion that emerged between 1990 and 1992 focused on the issues of PAYGO versus advance funding (and individual choice), and, generally, on private versus public management of funds and accounts.

15. Note, however, that empirical research indicated that, historically, increases in employer contributions through the mid-1980s were passed over almost wholly to wage earners through increased inflation and lower real wage increases (Palmer and Palme 1989).

16. The 15-30 rule that eventually emerged at the end of the 1950s was a political construction proposed by the Social Democratic Party aimed at giving high benefits within a decade after the reform was introduced. This was facilitated by a transition rule requiring only twenty years for persons retiring up to 1980.

The starting position of the political parties was more or less the same as in the 1950s. The Conservative and Liberal Parties favored lifetime accounts and a stronger element of privately managed financial accounts. The Center (previously Farmers) Party and Christian Democratic Party favored a large increase in the flat rate at the bottom, with private insurance on top (i.e., the original Beveridge model). These were the four parties that formed a government coalition in the autumn of 1991.

The Social Democratic Party, now in opposition, favored a PAYGO plan, but reconstructed to create more financial stability. This could be interpreted as moving more in the direction of lifetime accounts and maintaining a public fund as a demographic reserve. Nevertheless, the greatest opposition to reform also came from the rank and file of the Social Democratic Party: Many still wondered why they could not keep the old system that had served older workers so well. On the other hand, the blue-collar union, LO—a staunch supporter of the Social Democratic Party—was among the earlier supporters of the reform because they could see that lifetime accounts generally favored their members, and that more financial stability was needed to guarantee future benefits.

The framework for the reform to come was presented for public scrutiny in the autumn of 1992 (*En Promoria* 1992), with the vision presented being shared by the five political parties just discussed (two others will be discussed later in the paper). This proposal was based on a system with lifetime accounts, with a certain portion going to individual financial accounts. The systems would otherwise be similar in that the annuity would be based on lifetime account values at retirement, life expectancy, and a real rate of return on accounts. There would be a guarantee and credits in conjunction with childbearing, military service, and pursuit of higher education, and payments made into the system for insured periods of sickness, unemployment, and disability. Already suggested at this point was that the overall contribution rate would be 18.5 percent, about what old age pensions cost at the time. The political parties followed up this published proposal with information and discussion materials distributed throughout the country.[17] Many important details of the reform remained to be worked out and there still appeared to be room to maneuver for all interest groups.

By the autumn of 1992 the Swedish economy had almost hit rock bottom. Sweden was forced to let its currency depreciate and float. Unemployment had risen to a record postwar high, and once again the government found itself undertaking massive debt financing of welfare-state transfers to hold up current consumption. With the fall of the Krona and the generally precarious economic situation, and with seemingly no end in

---

17. The two Working Group members representing the Social Democratic Party published a debate book outlining the questions and proposals that were being put forward.

sight, the government established an Economic Commission, to be led by economics professor Assar Lindbeck. The commission was charged with examining the state of the economy from a structural perspective, and to make proposals for change. The Lindbeck Commission, as it came to be called, presented its report in early 1993. The commission proposed a long list of structural changes for the pension system, in line with the general framework for the reform proposed by the Pension Commission.[18]

This was the setting as the reform legislation was being ironed out in 1993. The Working Group on Pensions presented its proposal to the Parliament in the spring of 1994 (Working Group on Pensions 1994). The reform had the support of the four parties in government and the Social Democratic Party. These five parties represented more than 80 percent of the voters and included the two largest parties in Swedish politics. Two of these together, the conservative *Moderata samlingsparti* and the Social Democratic Party, held approximately 60 percent of the seats in Parliament.

In sum, at the outset powerful groups in Swedish society were promoting just about every conceivable scenario for change; reflecting back on the discussion and positions taken in 1991, perhaps the common denominator was lifetime accounts. Given this point of departure, it was possible to discuss both nonfinancial and financial accounts; exactly how to enter life expectancy into the PAYGO system; how to index in order to maintain financial stability; and finally, given that part of the system would be based on financial accounts, what form this system should take in practice. Directives were created for a new working group, composed mainly of persons with experience in finance and insurance together with some of the experts from the main working group, to work on this problem.

The main political lesson of Swedish reform is that without ownership of the reform across party lines, it would not have been possible to do more than simply tinker with the old system—and even this would have been difficult, as was witnessed by the futile attempt in the 1980s. The consensus arose out of the shared view of the old system's problems and a sense of a mission to implement a structurally sound reform that would provide sufficient mandatory benefits, without impeding the performance of the economy.

6.5   Financial Affordability: The Record up to the Reform and the Future

6.5.1   Events Preceding the Reform

In 1976, Sweden's "golden period" of postwar growth had just come to an end, although politicians at the time did not know this. The general

---

18. A separate analysis of social insurance was performed as a part of the commission's work (Palmer and Scherman 1993).

feeling in the mid-1970s was still one of economic optimism, and having just experienced two decades of 3–4 percent real growth in the economy, many believed this would be the path of the future. In 1976, the full-benefit age in the public old age pension system was decreased from sixty-seven to sixty-five. In addition, all the major collective labor agreements were eventually formulated to make sixty-five an obligatory pension age. This seemed to be an order of things that was suitable to both employers and collective labor. In effect, to remain in the labor force after age sixty-five, a worker had to become self-employed and contract out his or her services. At the time, collective labor pushed the idea that a retirement benefit at age sixty-five was an integrated part of the overall employment agreement.

These labor-management agreements remained in place, and in spite of the new reform, which is designed to enable individuals to work past the age of sixty-five. Both employers and unions are reluctant to change. There was a political consensus that this reluctance to change centrally negotiated labor-management agreements would result in new legislation, establishing the right of individuals to keep their employment to the age of sixty-seven. This came in 2001.

Behind this emerging shift in how the political system views "the" retirement age is the trend in improved health and increased life expectancy, and the question of who should pay the cost of increased life expectancy for pensioners. Should it be future workers, as in the typical DB framework, or workers before they retire—by working longer—which the DC system encourages.

The major driving force behind the political consensus to remove impediments to remaining active for older workers has been the increase in life expectancy. On top of this, concern developed in the 1990s about the trend in employment of persons older than fifty-five. Let us examine briefly the history, in this respect, of the four decades since the ATP reform in 1960. The labor force increased by more than 50 percent, from about 2.7 million workers in 1960 to about 4.1–4.3 million in 1980, a level at which it has remained since then. The increase was mainly a result of the full-fledged entrance of women into the workforce, with participation rates for women born after 1945 equaling those of men. In addition, younger persons now spend more time getting an education, and thus delay their entrance into the labor force.

The increase in the labor force has been somewhat mitigated by an increase in disability claims, which doubled from about 150,000 to 300,000 between 1960 and 1980. In the 1990s the number of disability recipients appears to have leveled out at around 420,000 persons, or about 9 percent of the (potential) workforce. The ATP reform improved earnings replacement for disability, and disability take-up increased as benefits improved and as criteria were applied more liberally. Since 1960, individuals have also been able to claim an actuarially reduced benefit from the old age system from age sixty, and about 4 percent do so. In the 1990s, 22–25 percent of persons age sixty to sixty-four had a full disability benefit,[19] which means that about 25–30 percent of persons aged sixty to sixty-four have either a disability or an old age benefit from the public system.

Gendel (1998) has recently compared the median age of exit from the labor market with a social security benefit in four countries, including Sweden. For Sweden, this age declined from 65.9 for men and 65.0 for women in 1965–70 (before the decrease in the pension age from sixty-seven to sixty-five), to 62.3 for men and 62.4 for women in 1990–95. Gendel shows that American and Japanese women exited at about the same time as Swedish women in the early 1990s, but that Japanese men waited more than two years longer than Swedish men to claim a benefit.

The age at which people *leave the labor force* is lower than the age at which they claim an old age benefit from the public system. In Sweden, this age is influenced by the possibility for some workers to retire early with an occupational benefit and for other older workers to obtain severance pay from their employers. Presently, we have no good data to study these phenomena, especially that of severance with pay, because this remuneration is lumped together with earnings in the nation's income statistics.

What we can do is study employment among a cross-section of people in a specific age group at different points of time. Using this method (see Palmer 1999b; Wadensjö and Sjögren 2000), and examining employment of persons aged fifty-five to sixty-four, we find that in the mid-1990s men on average worked 6.5 out of a possible 10.0 years, implying an average exit at age 61.5. The picture was better as recently as 1990 for men, who worked an additional year, that is, about 7.5 of a possible 10.0 years between ages fifty-five and sixty-four. Unemployment among older men was around 2–3 percent until 1993, then increased to more than 10 percent in 1997, after which it began to decline.

Using the same approach, women worked on average a little more than four of ten possible years, for an average of four years of work out of ten possible and an implicit exit age of fifty-nine. By 1998, with an improving labor market, women were working about one year longer: five years with an implicit exit at sixty (Wadensjö and Sjögren 2000). In addition, since 1994, about 10 percent of women over age sixty have been unemployed. In an international comparison Sweden nevertheless does well in employing older workers. Within the OECD, only Iceland, Switzerland, Japan, and Norway employ a greater percentage of persons over fifty-five years of age (Wadensjö and Sjögren 2000). One of the reasons for Swedish success in keeping older workers employed may be that even the old system was designed with the goal of keeping employable persons in the labor

19. Unemployment among older workers was low—around 3 percent—until 1993, when it increased to more than 10 percent at its height in 1997.

Table 6.3   Life Expectancy from Age Sixty-Five

	1960	2000	2010	2020	2030	2040
Men	13.9	17.9	18.7	19.3	19.7	19.9
Women	15.4	21.3	21.9	22.4	22.7	22.9

Source: Statistics Sweden.

force up to age sixty-five. Palme and Svensson (1999) explain why, and as it turns out, the "tax" pressure to leave the labor force is lower in Sweden than in many other OECD countries (Gruber and Wise 1999).

In a DB system of the type Sweden had prior to the reform, the benefit formula did not reflect increasing life expectancy. In the 1950s, when the ATP reform was being considered, a man who was sixty-five years old then was expected to live about fourteen years past age sixty-five. For a woman who was sixty-five at that time, life expectancy was around fifteen years. In the year 2000, a man who was sixty-five was expected to live 17.9 years, and a woman, 21.3 (see table 6.3).

Life expectancy from age sixty-five increased by four years for men and six years for women between 1960 and 2000: on average, more than one year for every ten years. In the light of this, the official forecast (from 1998) is very cautious. Life expectancy is expected to continue to increase, but the rate of increase is assumed to be much slower in the forecasts. With the life expectancy increase in table 6.3, a DB pension for a new entrant (born in 1975) into the workforce will cost, in 2040, 11 percent more for a male and 7.5 percent more for a female than for a person retiring in the year 2000 at the same age. What would happen if life expectancy were to increase instead at the same rate as during the past forty years? The same DB pension would cost 22 percent more for a person becoming a pensioner in the year 2040 (person born 1975) compared with a person born in 1935 and retiring in the year 2000.

In sum, the record in the four decades following the 1960 ATP reform includes a decrease in the age at which Swedes claim a public pension and a strong increase in the life expectancy of pensioners. In principle, the reform has addressed this issue straight-on by strengthening the link between additional work and pension size, by rewarding older workers for foregoing early retirement, and by making the annuity a direct function of life expectancy. In practice, the final link in the reform is to create legislation for the right of workers to remain employed until the age of sixty-seven.

6.5.2   Who Should Pay the Bill for Increasing Life Expectancy?

The conflict of interests among politicians, employers, and unions has its origin in the paradigm shift in thinking about the rights and obligations of workers and pensioners in collective PAYGO pension schemes. The old view, as it is revealed in the design of most PAYGO schemes in practice, is that the risk of pensioners increasing longevity should fall on current workers. This view is anchored in the principle that it is not right to change the main source of income (i.e., pensions) for persons (pensioners) who cannot react to this by adapting their own labor supply. With this view there is no choice other than to charge current workers with the bill for increasing life expectancy, given the rules created by preceding generations as well as—at worst—the work and retirement decisions of the persons who were following those oftentimes too-generous rules.

The new paradigm, embodied in the NDC reform adopted in Sweden, is based on the insurance principle. The rules of the game are still set in advance, but the principle maintained is that the fairest system is one in which most—if not all—of the risk of increasing longevity is shifted to individuals while working and away from future workers or the pensioners themselves when they are retired.[20] In this way, expectations of future longevity become one of the determinants of our private decisions about work and leisure, and about consumption and saving, *before* we retire completely.

The Swedish reform uses the NDC PAYGO model to implement full decision flexibility for older workers and makes it easy to *exit gradually* from the work force. Because the system is actuarially fair and benefits have, in principle, the same form of indexation before and after retirement, the increment to lifetime resources that arises is derived from working longer and paying more contributions.

In the old system, under which future workers were assumed to pay the bill for increasing life expectancy, an implicit transfer was built into the system. In the end, however, future workers would always have the alternative to vote for forms of indexation or changes in tax schedules that shift resources back to themselves. The NDC PAYGO system as it has been formulated in Sweden substantially reduces this transfer, and the associated future political risk.[21] With increasing life expectancy, and all other things equal, an individual will have to work longer in order to maintain a given level of lifetime consumption. The alternative is to choose less

20. It is not possible to shift all the risk in a PAYGO system without having exact knowledge or perfect forecasts of longevity in advance. Most of the risk can be shifted, however, and the remaining nonrandom risk can be distributed as it becomes known. In the new Swedish system, the cost of any remaining change in life expectancy after retirement will be shared between workers and pensioners, to the extent that financial stability requires this. See the discussion below on indexation.

21. Diamond (1997) and others have argued that advance-funded schemes with privately managed individual accounts have an advantage compared with PAYGO systems in that they minimize political risk. The NDC formulation, with correct indexation for financial stability and with annuities based on life expectancy, can be claimed to remove much of the political risk inherent in typical PAYGO schemes.

consumption. In economic terms, there is no reason the pension system should be set up with a contract under which future workers subsidize early exit from the labor force for current workers. In insurance terms, the legitimate reason to shift the cost of early exit to others in the insurance collective is reduced working capacity owing to poor health or functional handicap.

What individuals clearly lose in the new Swedish system is a "subsidy" to retire early in a world with improving health and increasing life expectancy. In this new paradigm for social security, the individual chooses between work and leisure after reaching the minimum retirement age, with two new advantages: First, work or leisure can be combined with partial benefits (claimed at different times) from one or both of the two public systems. Second, covered work always yields contributions that produce higher benefits; that is, the system is fair. Because future workers bear the cost of the subsidy in the old system it is in the interests of organized labor to create a neutral system in this sense.

In a free market setting without protective employment legislation or strong union interests promoting the right of older workers to keep their jobs, individuals and employers freely negotiate individual contracts. In countries having strong employment legislation to protect individual rights, but also collective agreements beyond those needed to restrict rights for reasons of functional capacity with regard to certain work tasks, an additional step may have to be taken. The remaining question is whether the employment legislation should establish the right of older workers to remain until a certain age. In Sweden, politicians say yes, and this age has been set at sixty-seven. In practice, at least in the near future, most Swedes will probably prefer to exit earlier anyway; but as time goes on and as health continues to improve and life expectancy to increase, this will provide the opportunity for more people to choose to work longer.

6.5.3   The Swedish Reform and Affordability

Trends in the numbers of pensioners and contributors, along with the construction of the benefit formula, determine pension costs and the share of wages workers must pay to maintain the PAYGO system commitments. The contribution rate that must be paid to maintain a DB PAYGO system is simply the ratio of benefit payments to the covered wage bill. Breaking down benefit payments into the product of the average benefit (b) times the number of beneficiaries (P) and the wage bill into the average wage (w) times the number of workers contributing (W), we have

$$c = \frac{b \times P}{w \times N}.$$

This simple formula demonstrates the constraints on the system. For example, with two workers per pensioner, ($P/N = 0.5$), and with a policy goal to maintain a contribution rate of 18.5 percent, the ratio of an average benefit to an average wage will be 0.37. With three workers per pensioner ($P/N = 0.33$), the average PAYGO benefit can be about 56 percent of an average wage. The difference between three and two workers per pensioner means a lot, then, and this simple example illustrates that a country has a lot to gain by keeping people in the work force.

Table 6.4 shows how the dependency ratio has developed in Sweden since the ATP reform in 1960. The ratio of both old age and disability pensioners to contributors was 33 percent in 1960 and about 50 percent at the time of the reform. In other words, there were three workers per beneficiary in 1960 but only two by the mid-1990s. In terms of the simple equation above, a pretax old age benefit amounting to 65 percent of an average contributor's wage required a contribution rate of a little more than 18 percent in 1960 and almost 25 percent in 1997. With the 1997 dependency ratio, the contribution rate required to maintain, for *both* old age and disability, an average benefit level of 65 percent of a contributor's average wage would be 31 percent.

When the reform was being discussed in the early 1990s, the official demographic forecast indicated Sweden would have about 2 million persons over the age of sixty-five in 2025, an increase of about 25 percent since the turn of the century. The number of contributors will be about the same, however. In fact, the number of pensioners would be larger because there are also persons living abroad who have worked in Sweden and have earned the right to some portion of an earnings-related benefit. If we continue with the above example, it would require a contribution rate in the old age system of 31 percent to maintain an average benefit amounting to 65 percent of an average wage, and of 37 percent for old age and disability together.

The old Swedish system was not as expensive as this exercise might suggest, however; benefits did not keep up with real wage growth because

Table 6.4   Dependency Rate (pensioners [P] as a percentage of contributors [N])

	1960	1970	1980	1990	1997
Old age benefits	754	969	1,382	1,554	1,592
Disability benefits	145	212	303	361	417
Contributors	2,692	3,422	4,126	4,387	4,160
Dependency = old age benefits/ contributors	0.28	0.28	0.33	0.35	0.38
Dependency = (old age benefits + disability benefits)/contributors	0.33	0.35	0.41	0.44	0.48

Source: Swedish National Social Insurance Board.

Table 6.5   Contribution Rate Needed for Balance without a Fund

	2000	2020	2040	2060
Old system				
1% growth	16	24.1	28.7	29.8
2% growth	16	20.6	22.5	22.9
New system				
Per capita wage indexation				
1% growth	16	19.5	19.9	20.0
2% growth	16	18.8	19.4	19.6
New system				
Wage sum wage indexation				
1% growth	16	19.5	19.3	19.1
2% growth	16	18.9	18.8	18.8

Notes: Ratio of pension expenditures to the contribution base.

they were indexed with prices, not wages. The result is similar to multiplying the equation above with a reduction factor based on expected real growth and the survival rates for beneficiaries.

6.5.4   Projected Financial Costs

Finally, what happens to costs with and without the reform? To compare the new system with the old, the funded second pillar of the mandatory public system can be treated as an NDC component by setting the rate of return equal to the rate assumed for the NDC system. This has been done in table 6.5, in which the contribution rate upon which capital is accredited to accounts is 18.5 percent.

The ceiling has been indexed with real growth in the old-system scenarios to make them comparable. With real growth and a fixed ceiling, increasingly more wage earners would have larger and larger proportions of their earnings above the ceiling. Because of this, in the very long run the system would evolve into a flat-rate system with the same benefit for all. In the 2 percent growth alternative, this process would have reduced costs by about 5–10 percent in 2025 compared to the scenario with an indexed ceiling, and by 15–20 percent by 2050.[22] Of course, one of the alternatives to the reform had been to let this process simply continue, pushing future commitments increasingly into the occupational schemes, which before the reform were DB schemes. In terms of financial consequences for the public sector, the major problem with this strategy was that it worked much too

22. Calculations are presented in *Reformerat pensionssystem: Kostnader och individeffekter* (1994). The result depends on what one assumes about the future development of the distribution of earnings. The distribution used in these calculations reflects that of the first half of the 1990s. In the second half of the 1990s, renewed growth was unevenly distributed in favor of high-income earners. This distribution would have led to a higher percentage of earnings above the ceiling.

slowly in low-growth scenarios—precisely the scenarios that became much too expensive by 2020–30.

One of the problems with the old system was that the development of benefits poorly reflected the ability of the system to bear costs. In any given twenty-year period the cost of benefits were largely determined by past events. The ability to pay was a function instead of the growth of the contribution base. The system was designed for 3 percent growth, worked adequately with 2 percent growth, but became very expensive with 1 percent growth or less. This is illustrated in table 6. 5. Without reform, and with yearly per capita wage growth of 1 percent, pension costs would have increased by about 50 percent, from over 18 percent to over 26 percent by 2020. In the new system, the guarantee costs about 2 percent in the first decade, but since it is price indexed, its cost declines slowly with time.

For a long time, pension costs will continue to reflect old-system commitments. Beginning in 2003, when persons born in 1938 turn sixty-five, the new system will begin to go into effect in the sense that the first cohort will receive benefits based partially on the new rules. It will take until 2019 for all newly granted benefits to be calculated entirely with the NDC formula. The reform also strikes a deal with persons born before 1938, who are almost all retired by the year 2000. The deal is that even their benefits will be indexed with the same index used to adjust NDC annuities when they diverge from actual real growth of 1.6 percent. Thus, from the beginning of 2002, if growth falls below 1.6 percent the benefits of existing pensioners are reduced by the difference between actual growth and 1.6 percent. It is this process that—together with the gradual introduction of the NDC benefit—holds down costs in 2000–20. With 1.0 percent wage growth, costs are reduced to a contribution rate of 19.5 percent, instead of 24.1 percent without the reform. This was also part of the Swedish pension discussion in the early 1990s, when the National Social Insurance Board first proposed this mechanism.

The other side of the deal is that pensioners' benefits are increased by the difference between actual growth and 1.6 percent when wage growth is higher. This still costs less than the downside scenario with 1.0 percent growth, expressed in terms of the contribution rate needed to support benefit payments. This gives pensioners partial wage indexation, but the contribution base increases more quickly with the full rate of growth of average wages.

By 2040 almost all pensioners will have NDC benefits. The new system never fully reaches its equilibrium of 18.5 percent, because the calculations include the cost of the guarantee. Table 6.5 shows the difference between per capita wage indexation of NDC benefits and wage-sum indexation. There is a difference because the labor force is slowly declining in this demographic scenario: for any given rate of per capita wage growth, the contribution base will grow at a slower rate, and wage-sum indexation holds costs in line with the equilibrium rate of 18.5 percent. In the Swedish reform the balance index will perform this function.

Part of the remaining gap between actual costs and 18.5 percent has to do with the way life expectancy is entered into the NDC formula in practice in the Swedish reform. Life expectancy is calculated in terms of an average of the four last known years prior to a benefit claim. A strict actuarial procedure would be based on a projection, and with increasing life expectancy there would be less to mop up.[23]

Swedish Parliament decided to use per capita wage indexation and to calculate life expectancy as it is entered into the calculation of the annuity using ex post data. On the other hand, the NDC system begins with a large fund, and yields on this will be used to help finance benefits. (In fact, a larger portion will be invested in equities in the future.) In order to remedy the threat to financial equilibrium, a balance index has been created, based on the ratio of the actual pension debt to the theoretical debt using wage-sum indexation. When this index falls below unity, benefits are indexed downward, with the same effect as that of wage-sum indexation (see Settergren 2001).

In sum, the reform has also introduced an indexation mechanism for the transition period that will keep the system in financial balance. In the long run, the system moves toward financial equilibrium. There will always be imperfections in the actual engineering of systems until we have the facts in hand, because (for example) of the uncertainty about life expectancy and perhaps for other reasons that also have to do with how life expectancy enters the annuity. For this reason, some of the risk of increasing life expectancy may still have to be shifted to pensioners to achieve balance, but this effect will be very small if it occurs at all.

6.6   Conclusions

The first conclusion from Swedish pension reform is that political interests representing a broad spectrum of interests can be brought together in consensus. Second, although there are usually options at each point along the road in engineering reform, the framework of the reform consisted of principles for which there was broad agreement. This is what held the reform effort together. Third, the reform that developed appears to have central elements that should keep it resilient in the future. The most important of these are the transition to lifetime accounts (notional and financial) and the use of life expectancy throughout in the mandatory public system, with the resultant shift in the financial cost of aging to workers while they are working. Financial stability has been achieved even in the near future—the next twenty years—with the introduction of wage indexation

23. Note that this is the way it is done in the Latvian version of the NDC reform.

with a norm of 1.6 percent rather than zero. This means that, even with poor economic growth, the system will make it through the transition into the new NDC and advance-funded systems, and thereafter should remain financially stable.

References

Aaron, Henry. 1966. The social insurance paradox. *Canadian Journal of Economics* 32:371–74.
Allmänna Tillaggspension (ATP). 1987. *ATP och dess finansiering i det medel: Och långsiktiga perrspektivet.* RFV Anser 1987: 9. Stockholm: Riksförsäkringsverket.
Berg, Lennart. 1983. *Konsumtion och sparande: En studie av hushållens beteende.* Uppsala: Uppsala University.
Boskin, Michael, Laurence J. Kotlikoff, and John Shoven. 1988. *A proposal for fundamental social security reform in the 21st century.* Lexington, Mass: Lexington Books.
Bröms, Jan. 1990. *Ur askan av ATP* (From the ashes of ATP). Stockholm: SACO.
Buchanan, James M. 1968. Social insurance in a growing economy: A proposal for radical reform. *National Tax Journal* 21:386–95.
Castellino, Onorato, and Elsa Fornero. 1999. From PAYGO to funding in Italy: A feasible transition? *Geneva Papers on Risk and Insurance* 24 (4). Geneva: Blackwell Publishers.
Diamond, Peter. 1997. Insulation of pensions from political risk. In *The Economics of Pensions,* ed. S. Valdés-Prieto. Cambridge, UK: Cambridge University Press.
Disney, Richard. 1999. OECD public pension programs in crisis: An evaluation of the reform options. The World Bank Social Protection Paper no. 9921. Washington, D.C.: World Bank.
Feldstein, Martin, and A. Samwick. 1997. The economics of prefunding Social Security and medical care benefits. NBER Working Paper no. 6055. Cambridge, Mass: National Bureau of Economic Research.
Frennberg, P., and B. Hansson. 1992. Swedish stocks, bonds, bills and inflation. *Applied Financial Economics* 2:3–27.
Fox, Louise, and Edward Palmer. 1999. Latvian pension reform. Social Protection Discussion Paper no. 9922. Washington, D.C.: World Bank.
Gendel, Murray. 1998. Trends in the retirement age in four countries, 1965–1995. *Monthly Labor Review* 121 (8): 20–30.
Góra, Marek, and Michal Rutkowski. 1997. *Social security through diversity: Reform of the pension system in Poland.* Warsaw: Office of the Government Plenipotentiary for Social Security Reform.
Gruber, Jonathon, and David Wise. *Social security and retirement around the world.* National Bureau of Economic Research Conference Report. Chicago: University of Chicago Press.
Gustafsson, Björn, and Edward Palmer. 1997. Changes in Swedish inequality: A study of equivalent income 1975–1991. In *Changing patterns in the distribution of economic welfare,* ed. P. Gottschalk, B. Gustafsson, and E. Palmer. Cambridge: Cambridge University Press.
Lag om premiepension (Legislation for the Premium Pension). 1997. Sweden's Official Publications 1997, no. 131. Stockholm: Norstedts.

Markowski, Alexander, and Edward Palmer. 1979. Social insurance and saving in Sweden. In *Social security versus private saving in post-industrial democracies*, ed. George von Furstenberg. Cambridge, Mass.: Ballinger.

Martin, Andrew. 1984. Trade unions in Sweden: Strategic responses to change and crisis. In *Unions and economic crisis: Britain, West Germany, and Sweden*, ed. P. Gourevitch. London: Allen and Unwin.

Lindbeck Commission. 1993. *Nya villkor för ekonomi och politik: Ekonomikommissionens förslag.* Sweden's Official Publications 1993, no. 16. Stockholm: Norstedts.

Palacios, Robert, and Roberto Rocha. 1998. The Hungarian pension system in transition. Social Protection Discussion Paper no. 9812. Washington, D.C.: World Bank.

Palme, Mårten, and Ingemar Svensson. 1999. Social security, occupational pensions and retirement in Sweden. In *Social security and retirement around the world*, ed. J. Gruber and D. Wise. National Bureau of Economic Research Conference Report. Chicago: University of Chicago Press.

Palmer, Edward. 1981. *Determination of personal consumption: Theoretical foundations and empirical evidence from Sweden.* Stockholm: Almqvist and Wicksell International.

———. 1999a. Individual decisions and aggregate stability in the NDC system. mimeograph.

———. 1999b. Exit from the labor force for older workers: Can the NDC pension system help? *The Geneva papers on risk and insurance* 24 (4). Geneva: Blackwell Publishers.

———. 2000. The Swedish pension reform model: Framework and issues. World Bank, forthcoming.

Palmer, Edward, and Mårten Palme. 1989. A macroeconomic analysis of employer-contribution financed social security. In *The political economy of social security*, ed. B. A. Gustafsson and N. A. Klevmarken. Amsterdam: North-Holland.

En Promoria av Pensionsarbetsgruppen (Working Group on Pension). 1992. Promomoria: En Promomoria av Pensionarbetsgruppen (A proposal of the Working Group on Pensions). Socialdepartementet 89. Stockholm: Norstedts.

Reformerat pensionssystem (The Pension Reform). *Betänkande av pensionsarbetsgruppen* (Proposal of the working group on pensions). 1994a. Sweden's Official Publications 1994, no. 20. Stockholm: Norstedts.

———. 1994b. *Kostnader och individeffekter* (The financial consequences for individuals). Special Report of Sweden's Official Publications 1994, no. 21. Stockholm: Norstedts.

Samuelson, Paul. 1958. An exact consumption loan model of interest with or without the social contrivance of money. *Journal of Political Economy* 66:467–82.

Scherman, K-G., and Edward Palmer. 1993. *En ny socialförsäkring.* Stockholm: National Social Insurance Board.

Settergren, Ole. 2001. The automatic balancing mechanism of the Swedish Pension System. *Wirtschaftspolitische Blätter* 4:339–49.

Ståhlberg, Ann-Charlotte. 1990. *The ATP system viewed in a redistributional perspective* (in Swedish). In Sweden's Official Publications 1990, no. 78. *Allmän Pension.* Expertrapporter. Stockholm: Allmänna förlaget.

Tumbarello, Patrizia. 2000. The reform of the Italian pension system: A case for notional accounts. World Bank, forthcoming.

Wadensjö, Eskil, and Gabriella Sjögren. 2000. *Arbetslinjen för äldre i praktiken.* Stockholm: Institutet för social forskning.

Comments   Laurence J. Kotlikoff

Edward Palmer has written an insightful account of the very important and interesting notional defined contribution (NDC) redesign of the Swedish pension system. According to Palmer, the Swedish reform will keep the current 18.5 percent Swedish payroll tax rate used to finance the pension system from rising by roughly one third; that is, if future economic growth is modest. With more rapid economic growth, the reform will have a smaller impact in mitigating future payroll tax hikes. However, in that case, the requisite tax hike is itself rather modest.

In addition to limiting future payroll tax increases, Palmer praises the Swedish reform for improving benefit-tax linkage, eliminating capricious redistribution, providing an automatic financial stabilizer to deal with longevity increases, and introducing a small funded component to the state's compulsory pension system.

Although I agree with much of Palmer's assessment and believe he and his Swedish colleagues deserve a great deal of credit for steering the country away from what might, and I stress *might,* have been a calamitous policy path, my job is to play devil's advocate—and the devil here has much to say.

The first and most important concern is that the reform made a pay-as-you-go (PAYGO) financed state pension scheme a permanent component of Swedish fiscal policy when it could otherwise have been phased out through time. Under the old system, benefits were paid up to a time-invariant ceiling. Thus, had no reform occurred, the system would have naturally disappeared as an ever larger share of workers found their benefits were capped by this ceiling. The notional account reform, in linking state pension benefits to accumulated past contributions, has effectively indexed the pension system to the size of the economy, making it impossible for Sweden ever to outgrow this fiscal albatross.

Now Palmer believes that outgrowing the old system would have been impossible because Swedish governments would have responded, over time, to the natural shrinking of the pension system by periodically raising the benefit ceiling. This belief carries over to Palmer's analysis of the gains from reform. For example, in his table 6.5 comparison of payroll tax rates under the new and old pension systems, Palmer assumes that absent the reform, growth of the ceiling would have equaled growth in real wages. Although Palmer may be right, at least historically, the ceiling was never raised. Table 6.5 would benefit from showing how much the payroll tax would have declined had pension reform never occurred and the ceiling never been raised. This addition to the table would likely show that the

Laurence J. Kotlikoff is professor of economics at Boston University and a research associate of the National Bureau of Economic Research.

reform may have significantly raised long-run payroll tax rates and squandered a golden opportunity for getting out from under a PAYGO system once and for all.

A second concern involves transparency and benefit-tax linkage. The new system says that a thirty-year-old worker will receive marginal benefits in old age in exchange for his or her marginal contributions at age thirty. The precise amount of these future benefits, however, is highly uncertain because it depends on the following three factors: (1) economy-wide real wage growth, because contributions accumulate each year based on annual per capita real wage growth; (2) longevity improvements, because annual benefits are actuarially determined; and (3) a hard-to-understand "balance index adjustment" that adjusts benefits to maintain a certain size pension reserve fund.

These three factors leave workers with a claim to future pension benefits that is highly uncertain and very hard to comprehend. Contrast this way of establishing an NDC with the detailed NDC proposal I formulated with Michael Boskin and John Shoven in 1980 (Boskin, Kotlikoff, and Shoven 1988; hereafter BKS). The BKS plan, which we presented to the 1983 Greenspan Commission on U.S. Social Security reform, determined for the worker each year the marginal benefit he or she would receive in retirement for that year's contribution. The BKS scheme uses actuarial formulas to connect future retirement, survivor, and disability benefits to current contributions. The plan also specified the use of the very latest survival probabilities in calculating the amount of additional future pension benefits to be "purchased" each year in exchange for that year's contributions. The single discount rate used each year to discount all future amounts in these actuarial calculations is, in the BKS plan, chosen to produce present value financial balance in the overall pension system. Specifically, a lower rate of return is used in the actuarial formulas if the present value of system-wide future benefits, discounted at the then-prevailing term structure of market-determined government bonds rates, exceeds (1) the present value of system-wide future contributions, where these contributions are also discounted using the latest term structure of rates of return on government bonds, plus (2) the system's current reserves.

In choosing each year's NDC discount rate to keep the system in present-value balance, and in using the latest survival probabilities in the calculation, the BKS NDC plan, like the Swedish plan, makes automatic adjustments for longevity changes and long-term financial imbalances. However, it does so in a way that does not make a worker's annual future benefits highly uncertain right up to the moment he or she retires. Rather than foisting so much risk on new retirees, the BKS plan spreads that risk across all current workers. In so doing, it appears to provide better intergenerational risk sharing than does the Swedish plan.

A third concern one can raise with the Swedish reform involves the 2.5

percent funded pillar. Workers are forced to save 2.5 percent of their wages in the marketplace, ostensibly to help ensure that they do not end up with lower living standards in old age. Thus a social goal underlies this policy. Yet in permitting workers to (1) choose whatever portfolios of assets they like, (2) try to beat the market, (3) try to time the market, and (4) pay whatever loads, fees, and commissions investment companies can induce them to absorb, the Swedish government has, in effect, forced workers to play the lottery collectively with 2.5 percent of their lifetime incomes. Contrast this with the proposal Jeff Sachs and I put forward for a funded pillar in which all workers' contributions are invested in a single, market-weight, global index of stocks and bonds. By requiring that workers invest in the same fully diversified portfolio, the Kotlikoff-Sachs (1998; hereafter KS) plan ensures that all workers receive the same rate of return. In addition, competition to sell this single portfolio would drive fees and commissions down to very low levels.

The presumed response to the KS plan is that workers have different tolerances for risk and should, therefore, be permitted to invest in light of their own risk preferences. The counterargument has three elements. First, a social plan to guarantee old age income support should not promote old age income disparities among otherwise identically situated workers. Second, differences in risk preferences do not necessarily imply that workers should hold different portfolios of risky assets. Indeed, this is the key point of the capital asset pricing model and other models of portfolio allocation. Third, many households choose what appear to be patently inappropriate investments, either far too conservative (e.g., investing all assets in certificates of deposit) or far too risky (e.g., investing all assets in a single stock). If governments feel they need to force their constituents to save, they must believe that many of them lack the capacity to formulate and carry out appropriate saving plans. Why, then, should such governments presume these same constituents will be able to formulate and undertake appropriate portfolio choices? David Blake's paper (chapter 10 in this volume) provides ample evidence of the problems incurred when inexperienced investors are set upon by experienced money managers.

My final concern with the Swedish reform and Edward Palmer's defense of it is that the financial viability of that program must be considered in light of the financial viability of the entire Swedish fiscal enterprise. A recent generational accounting study of Sweden's long-term finances suggests that Sweden, like most other developed countries, faces significant fiscal stresses with the impending retirement of the baby boom generation (Raffelhüschen and Kotlikoff 1999). In light of the substantial imbalance in Swedish generational policy, one must ask whether future Swedes can really afford to pay close to 20 percent of their lifetime incomes to the pension system when their taxes for so many other programs are already high and likely to rise dramatically. Stated differently, although the Swedish reform appears to have greatly reduced the long-term fiscal problems facing that nation, it is unclear whether it went far enough in that direction.

References

Boskin, Michael, Laurence J. Kotlikoff, and John B. Shoven. 1988. Personal security accounts: A proposal for fundamental social security reform. In *Social security and private pensions: Providing for retirement in the 21st century,* ed. Susan Wachter, 179–206. Philadelphia: Lexington Books.
Kotlikoff, Laurence J., and Jeffrey Sachs. 1998. Privatizing Social Security the right way. Testimony before the Subcommittee on Social Security of the House Committee on Ways and Means. U.S. House of Representatives, 3 June. Available at [http://www.econ.bu.edu/kotlikoff].
Raffelhüschen, Bernd, and Laurence J. Kotlikoff. 1999. Generational accounting around the globe. *American Economic Review* 89 (May): 166–67.

Discussion Summary

In his reply to the discussant, *Edward Palmer* explained that in Sweden people receive an account statement every year. This account statement shows the value of the individual account converted into an increment to the benefits—given today's projection of life expectancy. Palmer said that he does not see a substantial difference between the benefits calculated in the Swedish notional defined contribution system and an annuity computed by a private insurance company. The only difference is the existence of funds in the one system but not in the other. Palmer emphasized that necessary adjustments are automatic and as explicit as possible in the Swedish system. According to *Laurence J. Kotlikoff,* there is a difference between the Swedish notional defined contribution (NDC) system and his own proposal. In the NDC system, the benefits in the annual account statement change from year to year with changes in the underlying parameters. In Kotlikoff's proposal, the benefits in the account statement do not change through time. Edward Palmer disagreed and said that he does not see a difference between the two proposals.

Palmer reported that during the debate about pension reform there were some proposals to let the old system die by having the "ceiling take its toll," as the discussant suggested. However, these proposals were not put on the table by the major political parties. Palmer said that the problem would be that the ceiling would take its toll on different groups in different ways and at different times. Concerning the survivor benefits, he noted that the goal in the 1989 part of the reform process was to eliminate the survivor benefits. The excuse for that was that the safety net was adequate without them. He raised doubts about this assessment. He also reported that there was a discussion about keeping overall balance in the whole public sector. He expressed his skepticism about the success of these plans. Referring to the discussant's proposal of introducing an index fund instead of the large number of funds, Palmer said that he expects that many index funds are going to be offered and that people can choose such a fund if they want to.

Axel Börsch-Supan raised three questions about the notional accounts. First, he asked whether intertemporal or interpersonal transfers are possible in the notional accounts system. Second, he noted that notional accounts may make pension reform harder in the future, because it will be harder to adjust the system if it is in trouble. He asked whether this effect has been taken into consideration in the Swedish reforms. Third, he referred to some rumors concerning troubles in managing the notional accounts. He wanted to know what these rumors are about. *Edward Palmer* answered that transfers would be possible in principle, and in the beginning of the reform process there were thoughts about introducing transfers between spouses. However, it was then decided to let divorce law legislation take this into consideration. The management problems mentioned by Börsch-Supan had to do with delays in the introduction of the information technology system for the second pillar. The system began in September 2000 instead of September 1999.

Assar Lindbeck called the Swedish pension reform progress, because the system now includes automatic adjustment mechanisms that adjust the system to increased longevity or changes in the tax base. Lindbeck called it one of the greatest advantages of the Swedish system to increase the freedom of choice and to return some responsibility to the individuals.

Jeffrey Liebman referred to concerns that the introduction of notional accounts reduces the amount of redistribution in the social security system. In his view, that does not have to be the case, because the governments can collect taxes proportional to earnings and contribute to the notional accounts in a redistributive way. With respect to redistribution in the Swedish system, he asked whether there is still a flat benefit in addition to the means-tested anti-poverty program. Liebman also wanted to know whether during the debate about setting up the new program there were discussions of funding the notional accounts in progressive manners. *Edward Palmer* answered that there is no longer a flat benefit but instead a guaranteed benefit, which very much resembles the Finnish system. The guaranteed benefit, however, is not enough to live on, so that some people need housing supplements or means-tested social assistance in addition to the guaranteed benefit.

Italy
A Never-Ending Pension Reform

Daniele Franco

7.1 Introduction

In recent years the reform of public pension systems has been called for in most western countries. Despite differences in institutional arrangements, most of the underlying reasons are common. The most important considerations are demographic: It is feared that present pay-as-you-go (PAYGO) retirement provisions, many of which originated long ago, are not financially sustainable in rapidly aging societies. It is also argued that today's programs direct too many resources to the elderly, thus preventing adequate income support to the social groups in which poverty is now prevalent.

These problems are especially acute in Italy. Pension spending is proportionally higher than in any other western industrial country (15.7 percent of gross domestic product [GDP] in 1999)[1] and the fertility rate is among the lowest (1.2 children per woman of child-bearing age). The ratio of the elderly to the working-age population is expected to increase from 21 percent in 1990 to about 30 percent in 2010 and 48 percent in 2030; thus it will be among the highest in the world. These problems are compounded

Daniele Franco is director of the public finance division, research department, Banca d'Italia.

The views expressed in this paper are those of the author and do not commit the Banca d'Italia. The author wishes to thank F. Balassone, F. Peracchi, R. M. Marino, S. Zotteri, and the participants at the Berlin conference for helpful comments and suggestions.

1. International comparisons of pension expenditure are influenced by differences among the definitions of pension benefits. They are also affected by the structures of national social protection systems. For example, in the case of Italy, pensions have been used extensively to substitute for other benefits. Moreover, the net burden on public-sector finances depends on the tax regime of pensions.

by the high public debt, which requires Italy to run sizeable primary surpluses in order to comply with the Stability and Growth Pact.

The reform of the pension system in Italy is at the core of the effort to ensure fiscal consolidation and long-term fiscal sustainability. It is also an important component of any policy aimed at improving the functioning of the labor market, namely, at increasing the present low participation rate. Because the incidence of pensions on total social spending is very high (70 percent), pension reform is also a precondition for implementing policies that may increase public support for the nonelderly groups of citizens and to finance additional spending on long-term care.

The reform process began in 1992. After decades of myopic policy making, about one-fourth of perspective public-sector pension liabilities was abruptly cancelled. A second major reform was introduced in 1995. These reforms were supplemented by numerous minor changes in legislation. The process is not yet completed. There is a widespread consensus that additional changes should be introduced in the PAYGO pillar. New reforms are also envisaged for the supplementary funded schemes, which are at present rather underdeveloped. Even if a supplementary funded pillar has been considered a necessary component of the reform since 1992, its development has been extremely slow. This lengthy reform process generates uncertainty, limits the microeconomic benefits of the actuarial approach introduced by the 1995 reform, and induces elderly workers to retire from the workforce as soon as they are allowed to for fear of possible cuts in benefits.

This paper examines the reforms implemented so far and considers the problematic aspects of current arrangements. It presents the main policy options under consideration and examines the issue of funding. The paper argues that in spite of the reversal of pension policy in 1992, in terms of expenditure control, there is considerable continuity in the Italian policymaking style. The same incremental and short-sighted approach that determined the extraordinary expansion of pension expenditure up to 1992 continued to work in the following years. The reforms implemented in recent years under the pressure of budgetary constraints largely reflect the demands of some specific groups. They have been introduced without adequate analysis of their implications and include solutions that may prove unsustainable in the long run. This also made the reform process longer and determined lengthy transition periods.

Section 7.2 outlines the main features of the development of the Italian pension system. Section 7.3 and 7.4 examine the reforms implemented in 1992 and 1995, respectively. The role of funded schemes is considered in section 7.5, whereas section 7.6 considers some critical aspects of the framework set up by the recent reforms. Section 7.7 examines the main additional reforms under consideration at present. Section 7.8 presents some general considerations about the reform process in Italy. Section 7.9 concludes.

7.2   History up to the 1980s: Growing Imbalances and Chaotic Distribution

The history of the Italian pension system is in many ways similar to that of other continental Europe systems.[2] The first pension plans were established for public employees in the second half of the nineteenth century. A voluntary pension scheme for private employees was introduced in 1898 and was made compulsory in 1919. The scheme, which was a funded one, was managed by the National Institute for Social Security (*Istituto Nazionale della Previdenza Sociale,* or INPS). It was financed by a payroll tax and provided old age and disability benefits based on paid contributions. Pensions were calculated on the basis of rules that worked in favor of workers with relatively short contribution records and lower earnings. Survivors' benefits were introduced in 1942.

In the aftermath of World War II the funded schemes were unable to sustain the costs of pension benefits. This was due to the effects of inflation and to the use of pension fund assets to support government finances. Only a small part of assets was invested in shares and real estate (about 5 percent in 1939; see Beltrametti and Soliani 1999). Out of necessity and in haphazard fashion, Italy shifted to the PAYGO system. The transition came to an end in 1952, when new rules were eventually introduced. A guaranteed minimum pension level was also introduced (Franco and Morcaldo 1989).

The resulting regulatory framework remained comparatively stable for a number of years. However, as the system gradually approached its full application there was a considerable increase in the number of pensions. By the end of the 1950s a period of far-reaching and frequent changes began, setting the stage for the rapid expansion of expenditure experienced in the following decades. Public pension coverage was extended to the self-employed,[3] to work-disabled citizens (in 1966), and to elderly persons with low incomes (in 1969). Also in 1969, pension entitlements for private-sector employees shifted from the old contribution-based formula to an earnings-based one. The change was a decisive step toward guaranteeing

2. For a general view of the development of the Italian social security system see National Council for Economic and Labor Issues (CNEL; 1963), Fausto (1978), Ferrera (1984), and Ascoli (1984); for the pension system see National Institute for Social Security (INPS; 1970), Castellino (1976), Morcaldo (1977), and Pizzuti (1990).

3. Special schemes (managed by INPS) were introduced for self-employed farmers in 1957, for artisans in 1959, and for other self-employed businesspersons (mainly shopkeepers) in 1966.

pensioners a standard of living correlated with that of active workers. Seniority (long-service) pensions, which can be taken at any age provided that the worker has a minimum contributory period, were established in 1956 for public-sector employees and in 1965 for private-sector employees and self-employed workers.[4] No evaluation of budgetary costs was carried out while these reforms were being introduced; these have been estimated altogether to involve a net transfer to living generations of about 80 percent of GDP (Castellino 1996).

The innovations of the 1970s were less sweeping, affecting mainly the indexation mechanisms, which had been introduced in 1969 and put into force in 1971. On account of the unequal protection afforded by the various indexing systems, the effects of the decade's high inflation on purchasing power varied form one class of pensioners to another. The recipients of higher benefits were hardly hit[5]; the failure to adjust the ceiling on pensionable earnings (introduced in 1968) generated additional disadvantages for high-income workers.

During the 1960s and the first half of the 1970s the social assistance functions of the pension system were extended. Pensions were used to provide income support to individuals working in agriculture, to those in the country's poorer regions, and to elderly workers with short contributory periods. Pension expenditure helped in easing social conflicts, first when the farming and the South were unable to keep up with the growth in industry and in the northern regions (see Becchi Collidà 1979; Fausto 1983), and later when the slowdown in economic growth exacerbated conflicts over income distribution. This enlargement of the welfare aspect was achieved partly through the introduction of new entitlements (welfare benefits for persons over the age of sixty-five who lacked adequate means of support, and for the disabled) and partly through the abuse of existing ones (such as, e.g., social security disability pensions[6]). However, the improper use of disability pensions, which also came to serve as a substitute for adequate unemployment benefits (Regonini 1984), produced uncontrolled redistributive effects, especially because of (1) the possibility of drawing multiple pensions or cumulating pensions and earned income, (2) the lack of strict eligibility requirements for benefits, and (3) the lack of

---

4. For public-sector male and female workers the required period was set at twenty-five and twenty years, respectively. In 1973 the period was reduced to twenty and fifteen years. For private-sector workers it was set at thirty-five years.

5. These effects were primarily due to the indexation mechanism involving lump-sum increases, rather than proportional increases, for private-sector employee pensions above the minimum level and for public-sector pensions. Each pensioner received the same increase in nominal terms, whatever the level of the pension (see Morcaldo 1977).

6. It should be noted, in particular, that the possibility of obtaining a disability pension often depended less on a real inability to work than on the inability to earn an income, to be assessed in the light of the socioeconomic conditions of the applicant's province of residence (see Franco and Morcaldo 1990).

requirements linked to effective participation in the labor force. Citizens' efforts to reap disability benefits found the authorities basically receptive. There was no systematic, attentive examination of applications nor any regular use of the instruments available to help beneficiaries find jobs. Several studies assert that disability pensions have long been a tool of political patronage (see Ferrera 1984). Between 1965 and 1975, disability pensions represented 40 percent of the new pensions paid to private-sector employees and 70 percent of those paid to the self-employed.

The 1980s saw the first steps toward rationalizing the rules, prompted by increasing expenditure on retirement provisions, the difficulties of the public finances, and certain glaring inequities in the distributive effects of pension plans. In 1983, means testing was introduced for eligibility to the minimum pension level and to disability pensions, and administrative verification of continued entitlement to welfare old age benefits was initiated. In 1984, the eligibility requirements for disability pensions were tightened: The criterion for eligibility was changed from loss of earning capacity to work disability. The flow of new disability pension was rapidly reduced.[7] In the same year the indexation system was made uniform.[8] The ceiling on pensionable earnings was abolished in 1988. However, lower accrual factors were applied for earnings above the former ceiling.

In 1990 the pension schemes for self-employed farmers, artisans, and other businesspersons were reformed. Although these groups previously could not receive pensions higher than the guaranteed minimum level, under the new rules they were gradually granted pensions proportional to their average earnings over the last ten years of their work, with the same accrual factor (2 percent) applied to employees. The reform increased by about 75 percent the expenditure level expected for the year 2010 (INPS 1989, 1993) and accelerated the increase in the equilibrium contribution rates of the three schemes. For instance, the rate of the artisans' scheme was expected to increase from 12.7 percent in 1992 to 33.7 percent by 2010.

In spite of frequent calls for a general reform of the pension system, no large-scale reform containing expenditure growth was introduced in the 1980s. Prospective expenditure was further increased by the decision to raise the benefits for the self-employed. Frequent changes in the rules con-

---

7. The number of new disability pensions paid by INPS went down from 0.4 million per year in the early 1970s to 0.1 million in the mid-1980s (see Franco and Morcaldo 1990).
8. In 1984 the mechanisms of price indexation were standardized. Since that year, coefficients for price indexation have varied with the size of the pension: Up to twice the guaranteed minimum pension, benefits are raised in line with the change in prices; for those between two and three times this minimum level, the increase is equal to 90 percent of the change; for those above three times the minimum level, the increase is equal to 75 percent of the change. From 1984 to 1992, all pensions awarded to employees were also linked to real wage increases (from 1988 to 1992 for the pensions of self-employed workers). Welfare pensions were not adjusted to the dynamics of earnings.

cerning initial pension awards introduced additional disparities: Persons with the same work histories but who had retired in different years often had substantially different benefits. Moreover, as mentioned above, the previous indexation system in a period of high inflation had increased the purchasing power of some pensions and severely reduced that of others. This situation prompted a decision to increase the level of the latter category of pensions. This action substantially contributed to increased expenditure levels and was not unproblematic from an equity point of view.

7.3   The 1992 Reform

The situation changed radically in 1992, when the pension formula and the eligibility conditions were extensively modified under the pressure of the exchange rate crisis and the urgent need to curb the deficit.[9] Before examining the main features of the reform, it is useful to overview briefly the three main factors underlying the reform: the increase in projected outlays, the adverse effects of the pension system on the labor market, and its widespread distributive anomalies and inequities (see Banca d'Italia 1991; Franco and Frasca 1992).

1. *Expenditure trends.* Pension expenditure increased from 5.0 percent of GDP in 1960 to 7.4 percent in 1970, 10.2 percent in 1980, and 14.9 percent in 1992, far outstripping the growth of the other items of social spending, which increased only from 5.1 to 6.7 percent of GDP between 1960 and 1970 and from 6.7 to 7.3 percent between 1980 and 1992 (fig. 7.1).[10] Only a limited part of the increase in pension expenditure can be imputed to demographic factors, the larger part being accounted for by the extension and the maturation of the system.[11] Expenditure was expected to increase further, approaching 25 percent of GDP by 2030. According to *Ministero del Tesoro* (the Ministry of Treasury, 1994a), the equilibrium contribution rate for private-sector employees was set to increase from 44 percent in 1995 to 50 percent in 2010 and 60 percent in 2025. The pension formula, the eligibility conditions, and the indexation rules granted rates of return that were considerably higher than the rate of growth of the social security tax base (Ministry of Treasury 1994b; Padoa Schioppa Kostoris 1995).

9. The role of external constraints in Italian fiscal and labor-market policies is examined in Ferrera and Gualmini (1999).

10. According to Rossi and Visco (1995), about 50 percent of the decline in the Italian private-sector saving ratio in the period 1954–93 can be attributed to the extensive development of the pension system.

11. Demographic changes accounted for about 20 percent of the increase of the GDP ratio of total pension expenditure, and for about 40 percent of the increase in the GDP ratio of the old age pensions during the 1960–90 period. The eligibility ratio increased by 60 percent, the dependency ratio by 47 percent, and the transfer ratio by 18 percent (Franco 1993a).

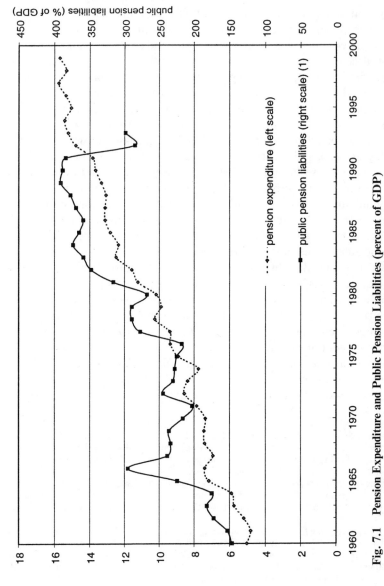

Fig. 7.1 Pension Expenditure and Public Pension Liabilities (percent of GDP)

Source: Beltrametti (1996). Estimates refer to the present value of pensions to be paid in the future on the basis of accrued rights to pensioners and existing workers, net of the contributions that the latter will pay under current rules.

2. *Labor market*. The provisions for seniority pensions and the noncumulability of pensions with labor income tended to foster "underground" employment and retirement. The lack of an actuarial correlation between the size of the pension benefit and the age of retirement was an incentive for the earliest possible retirement; in other words, there was a high implicit tax on continuing to work (Brugiavini 1999). This situation was reflected in the low employment rates of older men and women.[12] The lack of a strict correspondence between contributions paid and entitlements accrued also encouraged evasion and avoidance of contributions. The segmentation into several funds, each one operating with its own rules, hampered the mobility of workers both between and within the public and private sectors.

3. *Equity considerations*. The rate of return on contributions was extremely uneven for several reasons (Gronchi and Aprile 1998). The reference period for calculating pensionable salary (the last paycheck for public employees, the last five earning-years for the private sector) worked in favor of those whose earnings had risen the most rapidly toward the ends of their careers. On the other hand, low pensions were raised to the guaranteed minimum level while high-income workers were attributed lower accrual factors. Public-sector employees and the self-employed had very advantageous rules.[13] The standards for the means testing of certain benefits and the rules on cumulability of more than one pension had conflicting effects on income distribution. Because of the structure of the pension formula, other things being equal, the purchasing power of private-sector employees' pensions was inversely proportional to the inflation rate in the year prior to the year of retirement. After the initial award, medium-level and larger pensions lost purchasing power in proportion to inflation, which thus continued to affect the relative value of retirement benefits. Although the increase in outlays was accompanied by a sharp improvement in the economic conditions of the elderly and of pension beneficiaries in general,[14] it also constrained the resources available for other social policies.

12. In 1990, only 32 percent of individuals in the fifty-five to sixty-four age group were employed. In 1995, this percentage was down to 27 percent and was far below the percentages recorded in most other Western countries (see Organization for Economic Cooperation and Development [OECD] 2000; Peracchi 1998a).

13. See the estimates presented in Castellino (1996) and in Peracchi and Rossi (1998). The latter authors estimate that the rates of return on the contributions paid by the self-employed were two to three times higher than those on the contributions paid by private-sector employees.

14. The poverty rate for households headed by individuals older than sixty-five had steadily declined over the 1970s and 1980s. Although households headed by a pensioner remained slightly more likely to be poor—13 percent in 1987 versus 11 percent for other households. The difference between actual income and the poverty line was smaller for the former households (a gap of 19 percent in 1987, versus 28 percent); see Cannari and Franco (1990). These trends continued in the following years; see Cannari and Franco 1997. On the distribution of pension benefits, see Baldacci and Inglese (1999) and Peracchi (1999).

In this situation, expenditure control was closely linked to the reduction of differences in the rules applying to the different groups of workers. For instance, private-sector employees would not have accepted a reduction in entitlements if the special provisions granted to public sector employees had not been limited. The issue of harmonization remained at the core of the policy debate throughout the 1990s, when the debate gradually shifted from harmonization across workers of different sectors to harmonization across different age groups.

The main features of the reform, which aimed at limiting the ratio of public pension expenditure to GDP at its 1992 level, were the following:[15]

1. The age of retirement was raised (over the course of ten years) from fifty-five to sixty for women and from sixty to sixty-five for men in private employment.

2. The reference period for calculating pensionable earnings was lengthened (over the course of ten years) from five to ten years; for younger workers—those with fewer than fifteen years of contributions in 1992—it was extended to the whole working life; past earnings were to be revalued at a rate equal to the rise in the cost of living plus one percentage point per year.

3. The minimum number of years of contributions giving entitlement to an old age pension was raised (over the course of ten years) from fifteen to twenty.

4. The reference index for pension benefits indexation was changed from wages to prices; government was allowed to introduce discretionary additional adjustments through the budget.

5. The minimum number of years of contributions required for public-sector employees to be entitled to a seniority pension was gradually raised to thirty-five (i.e., to the requirement already in effect for private-sector workers' seniority pensions).

Moreover, in order to restrain public expenditure immediately, the adjustment of pensions to price dynamics was temporarily limited and the disbursement of new seniority pensions was curtailed.[16]

The parametric reform implemented in 1992 substantially changed the outlook for pension expenditure. At least one-fourth of net pension liabilities was cancelled. According to Beltrametti (1994), total outstanding liabilities were reduced from 389 percent to 278 percent of GDP (a 29 per-

15. The reform is examined in Franco (1993b and Vitaletti (1993). Baldacci and Tuzi (1999) examine the impact on public expenditure of the reforms implemented in the period 1992–97.
16. Additional reforms were introduced in the following years. In particular, they accelerated the gradual increase in retirement age and restricted the special eligibility conditions applying to public-sector employees.

cent cut).[17] Rostagno (1996) estimates that the liabilities of the scheme for private-sector employees were reduced by 27 percent. The cuts were unevenly distributed; Rostagno estimates reductions of 8 percent for pensioners, 42 percent for male workers, 94 percent for female workers, 37 percent for workers with long contributory records, and 42 percent for those with short or discontinuous records.

The reform also began a gradual harmonization of pension rules, and, by relating the pension levels of younger workers to lifetime contributions, it strengthened the link between contributions and benefits. However, it did not tackle the issue of seniority pensions. This substantially reduced the impact on effective retirement age of the increase in the age limit for old age pensions. Moreover, the exclusion of individuals with at least fifteen years of contributions from changes in the pension formula implied a long transition period and an uneven distribution of the reform burden.

By breaking the deadlock of Italian pension policy and immediately restraining expenditure increases, the reform set the conditions for better-planned and more systematic changes.

7.4   The 1995 Reform

In spite of the 1992 reform, expenditure prospects remained rather worrying. In 1995, both INPS and the Ministry of Treasury released projections that were more worrying than those carried out in the two previous years.[18] These expenditure prospects and the high level of equilibrium contribution rates pointed to the need for a new major reform,[19] which was introduced in 1995.[20]

Although the 1992 reform primarily aimed at cutting pension expenditure, the new reform had a wider range of objectives. It aimed at stabilizing the incidence of pension expenditure on GDP, at reducing distortions in the labor market, and at making the system more fair (see Rostagno 1996).[21] A tighter link of pensions to individual contributions was instru-

17. Beltrametti (1994) takes into consideration different definitions of pension liabilities. The estimates presented in this paper refer to the present value of pensions to be paid in the future on the basis of accrued rights to pensioners and existing workers, net of the contributions that the latter will pay under current rules.

18. INPS projections are reported in Senate of Italy (1995); see also Ministry of Treasury (1995).

19. See Aprile, Fassina, and Pace (1996), Artoni and Zanardi (1996), Banca d'Italia (1995), Castellino (1995), Centro Europa Ricerche (CER, 1994), Istituto Ricerche Sociali (IRS, 1995), Padoa Schioppa Kostoris (1995), Peracchi and Rossi (1998).

20. Further changes were introduced in legislation in the following years. In particular, the 1998 budget measures speeded up the harmonization of the rules governing the different pension systems, raised the age threshold for seniority pensions for some categories of workers, postponed the retirement dates for new seniority pensions due to take effect in 1998, and temporarily reduced the cost-of-living adjustments for larger pensions (Onofri 1998).

21. Most expenditure cuts were achieved through the tightening of the eligibility conditions for seniority and survivors' pensions.

mental in achieving the latter objectives. It was expected that contributions would have been more clearly perceived as deferral of earnings, thereby reducing the distortionary effect of labor income taxation. The reform aimed at equalizing the yields of the contributions paid by all workers of the same sex and the same pension cohort (i.e., those beginning to work and retiring in the same years). It removed the favorable treatment previously granted to workers with short or dynamic careers. Under the new rules, which apply to all categories of workers, the level of the pension wealth of each individual would not be affected by the age of retirement. The main features of the 1995 reform are the following:

1. Old age pension are related to the contributions paid over the whole working life (capitalized at a five-year moving average of GDP growth) and to retirement age.[22] Each worker holds a notional social security account. On retirement the pension is determined by multiplying the balance of the account by an age-related conversion coefficient. Coefficients, which make the present value of future benefits equal to capitalized contributions,[23] can be revised every ten years on the basis of changes in life expectancy and a comparison of the rates of growth of GDP and earnings assessed for social security contributions.

2. Workers are allowed to choose a retirement age between fifty-seven and sixty-five years.[24] Pensions are related to the average life expectancy at the age of retirement via the conversion coefficients on the basis of an actuarial discount. Seniority pensions will be gradually abolished.

3. The minimum number of years of contributions required for an old age pension is reduced to five. The guaranteed minimum pension level will be abolished. Welfare pensions for elderly citizens are to be reformed.

The reform, which was probably inspired by the reform process undertaken in Sweden in 1994, envisaged the shift from a defined benefit (DB) to a defined contribution (DC) system in which the notional accumulated contributions are transformed into an annuity at retirement. As noted by Castellino (1996), the actuarial approach underlying the reform represents

---

22. The formula used to calculate the initial pension award is $P_t = \beta c W_0 \Sigma_{k=1}^{a-1} (1 + g)^k (1 + w)^{a-k}$, where β is the conversion coefficient; c is the contribution rate; W_0 is the entry wage; a is the number of years of contribution; g is the average annual rise in the workers' earnings over the entire career; and w is the average rate of increase in real GDP. The conversion coefficients, which are determined on the basis of average life expectancy—including the probability of paying benefits to survivors—and of a 1.5 percent rate of return on accumulated contributions, range from 4.7 percent (for those retiring at fifty-seven years of age) and 6.1 percent (for those retiring at sixty-five years of age).

23. Contributions are proportional to earnings. However, the rate at which contributions are imputed to the notional accounts (33 percent for employees and 20 percent for the self-employed) is higher than the rate actually paid by individuals (32 percent and 15 percent, respectively). The latter rates have been increased after 1995.

24. Provided the pension is at least 1.2 times higher than the guaranteed minimum pension level.

a structural break in Italian pension policy-making, because in previous decades actuarial considerations had not had any significant role.

Most of the potential benefits and distributive effects of the new DC system could have been achieved by adapting the old DB system (Cichon 1999).[25] Pizzuti (1998) notes that the latter solution would have made changes more visible. The introduction of a new pension formula, which avoided the need to explicitly modify the old parameters, could contribute in making cuts in benefits more acceptable.

In spite of the change in the design of the pension system, the 1995 reform did not significantly affect the long-term expenditure trends determined by the 1992 reform. Rostagno (1996) estimates that the reform increased the liabilities of the private-sector employees' pension scheme by 4 to 9 percent of GDP,[26] depending on the rate of growth of GDP.

Moreover, the implementation of the reform will be extremely gradual. Workers with at least eighteen years of contributions in 1995 will receive a pension computed on the basis of the rules applying before the 1992 reform. Those with fewer than eighteen years of contributions in 1992 will be subject to a *pro rata* regime: The 1995 reform will apply only to the contributions paid after 1995.[27] Only individuals beginning to work after 1995 will receive a pension computed only on the basis of the new rules.

The length of the transition phase and other aspects of the reform may significantly reduce its expected microeconomic benefits (see section 7.6).

7.5   The Role of Supplementary Funds

The role of pension funding has been very limited in Italy since World War II.[28] This situation reflects the impact of the crisis of funds related to the war, the limited development of Italian capital markets, the lack of a favorable tax framework, and, especially, the extensive development of the public pension system and the existence of severance-pay provisions.[29]

---

25. The equalization of yields on contributions and the strengthening of the link between contributions and benefits could have been achieved by applying the same pension formula to all categories and computing pensions on the basis of lifetime earnings (see Pizzuti 1998).

26. The higher the GDP growth, the greater the increase in liabilities, because—in contrast to the pre-1995 regime—contributions are adjusted to GDP growth.

27. The pensions paid to individuals in the pro rata regime will be computed on the basis of two components: the pre-1995 contributions, and the contributions paid from 1995 onward.

28. At the end of 1998 the assets managed by social security funds (mostly by the pension schemes of the public-sector employees and of some categories of self-employed workers) and by pension schemes of the banking sector amounted to 5.5 percent of GDP. Shares represented about 3 percent of total assets (see Banca d'Italia 1999).

29. In order to fund the severance-pay benefits, employers must set aside 6.9 percent of each worker's gross earnings. These funds are disbursed to the employee upon the termination of the employment contract. While this severance entitlement is accruing, the worker has a secure but uncollectable credit with his or her employer, who retains full discretionary power over the funds—a very advantageous form of financing. Each year, contributions are to be revalued by 1.5 percent plus 0.75 percent of the inflation rate. If inflation is at 2 percent, the worker gets a 3 percent return in nominal terms.

Large public benefits reduced both the demand for supplementary plans and the resources available to finance them. The severance-pay provisions reinforced both these effects.

In the late 1980s, although it had become clear that Italy's public pension system would have inevitably experienced serious financial imbalances, the potential room for supplementary private pension plans was further reduced. As mentioned in section 7.2, in 1988 the ceiling on benefits for high-income employees was eliminated. In 1990 the self-employed were granted eligibility for more than the minimum pension.[30] Because the contributions of the self-employed were much lower than the long-term equilibrium rate, the yield on them was high.[31]

Only in the 1990s was a consensus reached on the need to develop private supplementary pension funds. The growth of such funds was viewed not only as a means to adjust retirement provisions to the different needs of the citizens and to allow workers to offset the reduction in replacement rates resulting from reforms of PAYGO schemes, but also as a way to strengthen the role of institutional investors in the capital market (see Pace 1993).

However, high contributory rates and large public finance imbalances, respectively, reduced the scope for additional contributions and for supporting the transition to funding via budgetary transfers or large-scale tax deductions. The contributions allocated to severance-pay funds (about 1.5 percent of GDP for private-sector employees) were therefore considered the only sizeable source of funds to develop the second supplementary pillar.[32] This was not unproblematic for either employers or employees. For the former group, severance-pay funds represented a source of cheap credit. For the latter, they represented an important form of liquidity during unemployment and for the purchase of the primary residence (see Aronica 1993; Ministry of Treasury 1994c; Fornero 1999; Messori and Scaffidi 1999).

Legislation was enacted in 1993 and in 1995 with a view toward increasing the role of funding by modifying the destination of severance-pay contributions and allowing additional contributions to be tax deductible. Employers and workers can unilaterally or jointly set up "closed" funds for workers of particular industries, companies, areas, and so on. Banks, insurance companies, and other financial institutions can set up "open"

---

30. An alternative solution to enhance the role of funding would have been the introduction of a ceiling on contributions.

31. The contribution rate was set at a level that was sufficient to finance current pensions—which had been awarded on the basis of previous rules—and not on a level consistent with the benefits that would be paid in the future on the basis of the new rules.

32. Under the assumptions that only new entrants into the labor market shift their severance-pay contributions to pension funds, (a) only these contributions are paid into the funds; (b) contributions are not drawn for any reason, and (c) the rate of return is 3 percent. Castellino and Fornero (1997) estimate that pension fund assets would represent 3 percent of GDP after ten years, 12 percent after twenty years, and 50 percent after forty years.

funds, for which anyone can sign up. However, workers can enroll in an open fund only if a closed company or industry fund is unavailable. Funds are usually based on DC criteria.

The development of supplementary pension funds has been rather slow.[33] Employers have been unenthusiastic because of the loss of the cheap credit source. Trade unions and the government have supported the development of contractual funds, limiting the possibility of joining "open funds." This may have negatively affected the employees' willingness to invest in pension funds. In a situation in which PAYGO pensions still guarantee relatively high replacement ratios for elderly workers and young workers are rather uncertain about the reliability of long-term commitments, many employees may have preferred to avoid the loss of liquidity determined by the shift from the severance-pay provision to supplementary funds. Moreover, tax incentives have been rather limited (Fornero 1995).[34]

The government is now considering further action to accelerate the development of pension funds. Tax deduction thresholds for contributions to the funds are to be increased. In order to benefit from the tax deductions, individuals would have two options: (1) joining the closed fund of the company or industry to which they belong; or (2) retaining the severance-pay provision, in which case the contributions would no longer be managed by the employer.

7.6 Critical Aspects

The reforms introduced in the pension system in the 1990s substantially contributed to changing the outlook for Italian public finances. Generational accounting studies highlight this change. On the basis of 1990 public accounts, the gap between the net taxes paid by the last newborn generation (on the basis of current policies) and those paid by future generations (taking into account policy actions to restore government solvency) was estimated at 198 million lira. On the basis of 1998 accounts, it was esti-

33. Up to 15 March 1999, only ninety-six new supplementary pension funds had been set up. About 400,000 workers were enrolled in these funds. Assets represented only 0.015 percent of GDP (Banca d'Italia 1999).

34. Some decisions made about the tax treatment of pension funds may have negatively affected their development. In particular, when legislation concerning funded supplementary pension schemes was introduced in 1992, contributions to funded schemes were subjected to a 15 percent withholding tax. Tax credits proportional to the tax levied on contributions were granted on future pensions. Tax credits were to be calculated on the basis of the rate achieved by each pension fund on the remaining 85 percent of the contributions paid to pension funds. The scheme, which aimed at increasing revenues in the first period of the development of pension funds (CER 1993), was abolished in 1995. Although the scheme would not have affected the pensions eventually paid by the funds, it introduced some additional uncertainty about these pensions: Although the tax was immediately levied, the credit was to be redeemed after a long time.

mated at 100 million lira.[35] In the latter case, in order to ensure the long-term sustainability of public finances, a 5 percent increase in the taxes paid by all generations would be required. Without the pension reforms introduced in the 1990s the required tax increase would have been 9 percent.

In spite of the important reforms introduced in the 1990s, there is a widespread consensus that further changes are required. The nature of the changes to be introduced still remains controversial. Before examining the main reforms under consideration (section 7.7), in the following section some critical aspects of the present arrangement are highlighted.[36]

7.6.1 The Lengthy Transition

The rules introduced in 1992 and 1995 will become fully operational only after a long transition period. This depends on the decision to exempt individuals with fifteen years of contributions from some important changes. About 40 percent of those currently employed will retire with the pre-1992 pension formula. For these people, the incentive to retire early will even be increased by the expectation that retirement conditions might be tightened (Porta and Saraceno 1996). This implies that, in spite of the increase in the age limit for old age pensions, the effective retirement age will not significantly increase over the next fifteen years. Moreover, during the same period, replacement rates will not decline.

The sharp difference in the treatment of workers who in 1992 and 1995 had small differences in contributory records raises an equity problem. There is also a budgetary problem. According to the Ministry of Treasury (1999), the ratio of public pension expenditure to GDP, which despite the reforms introduced during the 1990s reached 16 percent in 1999, is likely to rise by another 1.4 percentage points by 2015. Because the Stability and Growth Pact requires close-to-balance budgets and revenue increases are problematic, primary nonpension expenditure will have to be substantially squeezed if the transition is not sped up.

7.6.2 Long-Term Expenditure Levels

The Ministry of Treasury (1999) estimates that the ratio of pension expenditure to GDP will rise by an additional 0.2 points between 2015 and 2031. Subsequently, even though the ratio of pensioners to workers is forecast to rise sharply, expenditure should stabilize in relation to GDP for some years and is expected to decline significantly thereafter. According to INPS projections, the equilibrium contribution rate of the private-sector

---

35. Estimates are expressed in 1998 prices (see Franco et al. 1992; Istituto di Studi e Analisi Economica (ISAE), 1999; Cardarelli and Sartor 2000).

36. Extensive statistical information about the structure of the pension system and recent developments are provided in ISTAT (1997 and 1999) and *Nucleo di valutazione della spesa previdenziale* (1998, 1999).

employees' pension fund will rise from 45 percent in 2000 to 47.8 percent in 2010 and 48.5 percent in 2025. The corresponding rate of the artisans' pension scheme is projected to increase from 21.3 percent to 28.2 percent and then to 30 percent, and that of the shopkeepers' pension scheme from 18.5 percent to 25.4 percent and then to 33.9 percent.

These expenditure trends imply either larger transfers from general taxation or a further increase in social security contribution rates, which are already higher than in the other leading industrial countries. Both these solutions conflict with the need to reduce the burden of tax and contributions in view of growing international economic integration. They also appear problematic in the context of growing mobility of tax bases, which accentuates the distortionary effects produced by taxation in the markets for goods and factors of production.

Although the system is based on a close link between contributions and benefits for each individual, it is still vulnerable to demographic and economic shocks (Aprile, Fassina, and Pace 1996; Rostagno 1996; Hamann 1997; Gronchi and Aprile 1998; Cichon 1999). Furthermore, the system is vulnerable to increases in the dependency ratio determined by reductions in birth rates, because these increases would not affect the amount of accumulated contributions and the pensions already awarded. Increases in life expectancy automatically reduce new pension benefits via the conversion coefficients. However, it will take a long time before the impact of increases in life expectancy on the number of pensions is fully offset by the reduction in the average amount paid to each pensioner. This depends on the fact that reductions in mortality rates that take place after a pension is awarded do not affect its level. The ten-year interval between revisions in coefficients further increases the adjustment lag.[37]

A decline in the rate of GDP growth would not affect the amount of accumulated contributions and the pensions already awarded. A lasting decline in the ratio of GDP to earnings assessed for social security contributions can affect new pension benefits, via the conversion coefficients. As in the case of changes in life expectancy, financial equilibrium would be restored very slowly.

In the face of adverse demographic and economic events, as in the case of traditional PAYGO systems, cash deficits can be avoided only by ad hoc cuts in pensions and changes in the pension formula. Increases in contribution rates would have only temporary effects because they would translate into higher benefits.[38]

37. Baldacci and Tuzi (1999) estimate that the new mortality ratios would already imply a 1 percent cut in the benefits paid to those retiring at fifty-seven and a 3 percent cut for those retiring at sixty-five.
38. The need for a built-in equilibrating mechanism operating via the indexation of pensions was highlighted in a study carried out at the end of 1994 for the main parliamentary group supporting the reform (see Aprile, Fassina, and Page 1996). For instance, the study

Gronchi and Aprile (1998) argue that the predetermination of the rate of return on accumulated contributions (1.5 percent) introduces unnecessary inflexibility in the system. If GDP growth were lower than 1.5 percent, there would be financial problems. In any case, the interest rates imputed to workers and pensioners would be different. Giarda (1998) takes a sterner view and argues that problems will occur whenever GDP growth is lower than 2.5 percent. This position reflects two considerations: (1) Price indexation might be supplemented by ad hoc increases in pension levels; and (2) growth rates higher than 1.5 percent are required to offset the effects of some exceptions introduced in the general rules (e.g., the higher rates of return on contributions paid before eighteen years of age). Nicoletti-Altimari and Rostagno (1999) point to the risks related to the predetermination of the rate of return on the contributions paid to the pension system. They demonstrate that the ensuing rigidity reduces the capacity to absorb shocks and may generate persistent generational imbalances.

Moreover, the conversion coefficients have been computed without taking part of the expenditure for disability and survivors' pensions into consideration. More specifically, it has not been considered that disabled workers will receive benefits in excess of those awarded on the basis of their contributions.[39] Pensions paid to survivors of deceased workers have also been disregarded. These benefits have been implicitly considered welfare benefits to be financed by the government budget. This solution is questionable because the provision of a guaranteed minimum pension to disabled workers and survivors may be considered a component of social insurance, particularly considering that the contribution rates are relatively high (see Giarda 1998).

7.6.3 The Composition of Expenditure Cuts

The plan for bringing the pension system back into balance relies primarily on reducing the average pension in order to curb expenditure; limiting the number of pensions plays a relatively modest role. According to Ministry of Treasury (1999), the ratio between the pensions paid by the main pension funds and the total number of persons in work will rise from 92 percent in 1998 to 100 percent in 2015, 119 percent in 2030, and 130 percent in 2050.[40] The ratio of the average pension to per capita GDP would remain constant at 15.5 percent up to 2015, and then would decline to 13.3 percent in 2030 and 10.1 percent in 2050. These projections assume

---

advocated the introduction of a coefficient offsetting the effects of changes in working-age population. Aprile and colleagues, in an addendum to their original study, point to some drawbacks in the design of the reform from the financial equilibrium point of view.

39. Gronchi (1998) tentatively estimates that this expenditure may represent 2 percentage points of earnings.

40. See also the similar results obtained by Baldacci and Tuzi (1999).

that pensions will remain indexed exclusively to prices and that the conversion coefficients used to relate new pensions to the contribution record of each individual will be revised every ten years on the basis of demographic trends.

This situation depends on two decisions taken in 1995:

1. In spite of the increase in longevity, individuals will still be allowed to obtain a pension at age fifty-seven; an actuarially discounted old age pension will provide individuals with a greater incentive to delay retirement than previous rules. However:

   a. The conversion coefficients embody a discount rate that may still provide an incentive to quit the labor market (Brugiavini 1998) or may fail to discourage individuals from claiming a poor, actuarially reduced pension at an early age (Palmer 1999).

   b. Even an actuarially neutral pension system may not be sufficient to achieve a large increase in the activity rate of elderly individuals. Changes in the demand side of the labor market may also be required. More specifically, the wage structure for the different age groups should be consistent with their productivity.

2. The reform was designed to achieve a replacement rate at retirement that, for individuals retiring at age sixty-two after thirty-seven years of service, was close to the prereform rate; a full or a partial indexation to increases in real wages would have implied a reduction in the replacement rate at retirement (Banca d'Italia 1995; Castellino and Fornero 1997; Giarda 1998). Price indexation, which is adopted in several countries, implies that the purchasing power of each pensioner declines over time in comparison with that of workers and younger pensioners.[41] Two aspects may make this solution problematic in Italy over the long run. First, individuals are allowed to retire rather early. Most of those retiring at age fifty-seven may receive a pension for at least twenty-five years. Moreover, the adjustment to price increases of pensions that are twice as high as the minimum pension level is only partial. These factors may generate sizeable disparities among pensioners depending on the year of retirement.

The reliance on the reduction in the transfer ratio, instead than on increases in retirement age, may create political pressure for discretionary increases of pension in real terms (Gronchi and Aprile 1998; Peracchi and Rossi 1998).[42] Moreover, revisions of conversion coefficients at ten-year

---

41. Assuming a 1.5 percent yearly growth in real wages, other things being equal, a newly awarded pension would be 43 percent higher than a pension awarded twenty-five years earlier. The gap would increase to 61 percent with a 2 percent rate of growth and to 81 percent with a 2.5 percent rate of growth (see April, Fassina, and Pace 1996).

42. Rostagno (1996) points to the possibility that pensions (which implicitly include an adjustment to real wage dynamics), since the conversion coefficients have been computed

intervals may produce large differences in the treatment of contiguous generations of pensioners. This also may also be politically problematic.

7.6.4 The Expected Microeconomic Effects

The strengthening of actuarial principles in social security systems has been recently advocated to limit some of the negative effects of the system on the labor market and employment (Folster 1999; Orszag and Snower 1999). Contributions are often loosely related to benefits, so that they are largely regarded as a tax; expenditure controls frequently rely on administrative constraints rather than on built-in incentives; redistribution and insurance features are frequently mixed; and insurance schemes are utilized for inappropriate distribution objectives. In several countries, proposals have been put forward to redesign social security schemes along lines that are less distortive of individuals' choices and more transparent in their distributive effects.[43] The strengthening of the contribution-benefit link is a crucial factor. It increases the incentive to work and, more specifically, to stay on in regular jobs (because benefits depend on work record), to delay retirement, to move from benefits to work.[44] In the case of pension schemes, this implies increasing the role of funded schemes (where the contribution-benefit link is typically very strong), or shifting PAYGO schemes from DB systems (which base pensions on earnings in the final period of work) to DC systems (which base pensions on contributions paid over the whole working life). Since 1995, Italy has taken both routes.

However, a tight link between social contributions and benefits at the individual level may be effective only if the link is transparent, easy to grasp, and perceived as stable by citizens. Workers should be informed about their benefit entitlements (e.g., accrued pension rights). Welfare benefits should be separated from insurance benefits and funded from general revenues.

Several factors may reduce the immediate impact of the rules introduced in 1995 on the behavior of individuals:

1. An important component of the workforce is not affected by the reform.

---

assuming a 1.5 percent returns on residual accumulated contributions, may in the end be increased by ad hoc decisions prompted by the political pressure of pensioners. Pizzuti (1998) criticizes the elimination of indexation to real wage dynamics on the grounds that it breaks a long-established intergenerational contract and makes the pension system less credible.

43. See, for instance, Ministry of Health and Social Affairs (1994).

44. Making workers more aware of the value of the benefits for which they are paying contributions could also affect wage negotiations, for, if workers are unaware of the value of nonwage benefits, they are unlikely to trade lower wage increases for the continuation of present benefits. In this respect, the U.S. case, in which contributions to company-based health and pension schemes are an important part of wage negotiations, is particularly relevant.

2. The younger workers may expect that further changes will be introduced and therefore may have the perception that the return to their contributions is uncertain. This perception has probably been reinforced by
recent measures taken to curtail pension expenditure.[45]

3. There is a gap between the effective contribution rate and the (higher)
imputed rate used in the computation of benefits.

4. There is some lack of clarity about the way the system works. No
official document has explained the working of the new system; individuals
do not receive a statement of their contributory accounts presenting their
future pension entitlements; the formula underlying the conversion coefficients has not been published; and the methodology envisaged for the
revision of the coefficients has not been specified.

More generally, one can question whether, in a quickly-evolving economic
and demographic situation, the rate of return on contributions may remain
sufficiently stable and provide the microeconomic benefits expected from
strengthening the contribution-benefit link.[46]

7.7   Policy Options

As considered in section 7.6, present expenditure trends imply further
increases in contribution rates or general taxation, or cuts in other expenditure items. The latter may not be feasible in a situation in which pension
expenditure already represents a very large share of social expenditure and
of total primary expenditure (16 percentage points of GDP out of 23 and
42 points, respectively. Moreover, the pension system set up in 1995 does
not fully exploit some of the major positive aspects of notional DC systems
(i.e., the reduction of distortions in the labor market, the built-in incentive
to postpone retirement, and the self-equilibrating mechanism). This failure
may depend on the lack of an in-depth analysis of the implications and
requirements of these systems. The reform was defined and introduced
over the course of a few months with little preliminary work (Gronchi and
Aprile 1998).

Several proposals for further changes have been formulated in recent
years. They can be classified into three broad categories: faster implementation of the 1995 reform; tightening of the steady-state regime established
by the 1995 reform; and acceleration of the developments of the funded
pillar.

The transition to the new regime can be accelerated by the extension of
the formula introduced in 1995 to all workers and by the elimination of

---

45. This is the case of the temporary reduction in the adjustment to price changes of
pensions above a certain threshold that was introduced in 1997.

46. See the more general point made in Tamburi (1999) about the need for periodic adjustments of pension provision.

seniority pensions (see Giarda 1998). According to Ferraresi and Fornero (2000), these actions would reduce pension expenditure by about 0.8 percent of GDP in 2020. These proposals are technically simple, because they do not call into question the architecture of the pension system. However, they are politically sensitive, because they immediately affect a large number of older workers.

Several modifications of the 1995 regime have been contemplated in the large number of studies that have recently examined the reform. The extensive ex post analysis of the reform is in stark contrast to the lack of preparatory work. Among the main proposals[47] are the following:[48]

1. A shift in the old age retirement bracket (e.g., from between fifty-seven and sixty-five years to between sixty-two and seventy years)

2. A steeper curve of conversion coefficients, providing an incentive to postpone retirement

3. More frequent revisions of the conversion coefficients

4. An increase in the number of factors considered in the revision of the coefficients

5. A reduction in the pensions awarded at retirement that is associated with the introduction of an adjustment to real GDP growth or real earnings dynamics, and that takes into account the demographic and economic changes.[49]

Change (1) would increase the minimum age at which retirement is allowed and provide an incentive to postpone retirement beyond the age of sixty-five. It would move the Italian retirement bracket close to the one introduced in Sweden. Change (2) would remove any implicit tax on continuing work, and would take the negative externalities of retirement on public accounts into consideration. These changes should increase the effective retirement age and shift the focus of expenditure control from the reduction of replacement ratios to the reduction of the ratio of pensioners to workers.[50] The margins for this policy action are very large: In 1995, the

---

47. See *Commissione per l'analisi delle compatibilità macroeconomiche della spesa sociale* (1997), Giarda 1998; Gronchi 1997, 1998; Gronchi and Aprile 1998; Hamann 1997; Padoa Schioppa Kostoris 1996; Peracchi and Rossi 1998; Sartor 2000.

48. It has also been suggested that (a) effective contribution rates should be equal to the rates taken into account to determine the accumulated contributions, and (b) disability and survivors' pensions should be fully financed out of the contribution rate.

49. Gronchi (1998) suggests a reduction of the conversion coefficients by 15–20 percent. Giarda (1998) considers different options: (a) Coefficients could be computed every year assuming a rate of return on accumulated contributions equal to real GDP growth minus 1 percent; (b) whenever GDP growth is lower than 2.5 percent, indexation to price dynamics could be accordingly reduced; and (c) the rate of return on accumulated contributions could be reduced from 1.5 percent to 1 percent, while at the same time pensions could be increased in real terms if GDP growth exceeds 2 percent.

50. This strategy is in line with the policy response to population aging, advocated by OECD, that is centered on increasing the average number of years individuals spend active in the labor force and guaranteeing adequate income to pensioners (see Visco 1999).

average retirement age was about sixty years for males and fifty-seven for females; in 1998, about 25 percent of pension expenditure was paid to individuals below sixty-five years of age on old age pensions (Italian National Statistical Institute [ISTAT] 2000). In order to ensure an increase in the effective retirement age, these changes should probably be supplemented by reforms in the labor market, such as changes in the age profile of wages, more training for elderly workers, and more flexibility in work arrangements.[51] Gronchi (1998) argues that only an increase in the effective average retirement age would allow a reduction in payroll taxes: If retirement age remains low, high payroll taxes would still be required to provide politically adequate replacement rates, which he estimates in the 60–65 percent range.

Changes (3) and (4) would accelerate the adjustment of the system to demographic and economic shocks and broaden the range of shocks taken into consideration, respectively. Change (5) would reduce the political pressure for discretionary increases of pension in real terms, stemming from sizeable disparities among pensioners depending on the year of retirement. It would also introduce a second built-in equilibrating mechanism in the system: Adjustments in the conversion coefficients would offset the effects of changes in life expectancy, and the indexation mechanism would take cyclical aspects and birth-rate changes into account. These devices, which were considered in the preparatory work for the reform (see Aprile, Fassina, and Pace 1996), would make the pensioners share the burden or take advantage of negative and positive shocks, respectively.

The modifications considered above are probably sufficient to ensure the financial equilibrium of the pension system. They would still leave in place a situation in which the compulsory old age provisions require employees to pay a contributory rate of at least 40 percent (33 percent for the PAYGO scheme plus at least 7 percent for the supplementary schemes). Workers with long contributory periods would have relatively high replacement rates.

Several recent studies have explored the possibility to reduce PAYGO contribution rates and widen the role of funded schemes.[52] These studies generally move from the consideration that, taking returns and riskiness into account, a mixed system is superior to either a fully PAYGO system or a fully funded system. In the analysis of the implications of different balances between the two systems, the studies point to a trade-off between the benefits of a larger share of funding—in terms of higher rates of return or lower contribution rates—and the budgetary cost.

---

51. Sartor (2000) estimates that the reforms introduced in the 1990s do not necessarily reduce lifetime earnings significantly because the increase in labor earnings caused by the delay in retirement almost offsets the decrease in pension benefits. This condition applies if individuals can actually work longer.

52. Messori and Scaffidi (1999) formulate proposals about the tax treatment of pension funds and the reassignment of severance-pay contributions to pension funds.

Castellino and Fornero (1997) consider a reduction of the contribution rate of 8 percent (from 33 to 25 percent) only for the new entrants into the labor market. They estimate that it would take sixty years for the ensuing reduction in benefits to offset fully the cut in contributions. The government would have to cover a deficit that would peak after forty years at about 2 percent of GDP. Brugiavini and Peracchi (1999) consider the implications of reducing the PAYGO contributions of new entrants by 20 percent (5.6 points out of 28.3 points paid on average by all workers) and paying this amount into a pension fund. Revenue losses for PAYGO schemes will reach a peak of 1.7 percent of GDP after forty years.[53]

Forni and Giordano (1999) show that the replacement rates guaranteed by the PAYGO system to newly insured workers contributing for forty years range between 50 and 90 percent, depending on the career profile. Assuming that severance-pay contributions are fully used to finance supplementary funded schemes, replacement rates range between 60 and 120 percent. They argue that a 10 percentage point reduction in the contributions paid by employees to PAYGO would still guarantee adequate replacement rates: about 70 percent for a worker with an average career profile, working forty years and retiring when sixty-five years old. They consider two main scenarios: one in which the rate reduction applies only to new entrants; and another in which it also applies to the workers who are subject to the 1995 pension formula (those with fewer than eighteen years of contributions in 1995). In the first scenario, revenue losses would reach 0.4 percent of GDP in 2010 and peak at 1.8 percent by 2045. In the second scenario, revenue losses would increase more quickly (1.5 percent in 2010) and peak earlier (1.8 percent in 2025).[54]

Modigliani and Ceprini (1998) take a different approach and suggest a gradual transition to a fully funded system. They suggest the creation of a new fund financed by an additional contribution of 2 percent of earnings. Workers would receive the same pension benefits paid by the PAYGO schemes. The fund would gradually pay an increasing part of these benefits, allowing a reduction of PAYGO rates, which in the end would be 0 percent. In the process, the contributions to the funded scheme would be increased up to 6 or 7 percent of earnings. The funded scheme would operate on DB criteria, with the government guaranteeing a minimum rate of return on assets and benefiting from returns above this minimum. This solution would raise some problems of compliance with the Stability and

---

53. Assuming a 5 percent return on capital, workers receive higher pensions than in the no-change scenario. With a 33 percent reduction in PAYGO contributions, revenue losses would peak at 3 percent of GDP.

54. Forni and Giordano (1999) show that the cost of the transition would be substantially reduced if the payroll tax reduction induced positive effects on labor productivity and employment. If the unemployment rate were gradually reduced to half its current level, and if labor productivity growth were 0.5 percent higher each year, in the first scenario the impact on the budget would be positive by 2025.

Growth Pact. If the government were called to pay part of the pensions, the deficit could easily exceed the 3 percent threshold set by the Maastricht Treaty.

In conclusion, there is considerable consensus among pension experts that a comprehensive package including a faster implementation of the 1995 reform, some parametric changes in the pension regime established by that reform, and an acceleration of the development of funded schemes would avoid the expected rise of the pension expenditure to GDP ratio and reduce the negative effects of the systems on the labor market and employment. The acceleration of the implementation of the 1995 reform would provide some budgetary margins for a gradual reduction of the contributions to the PAYGO system, which could be implemented in parallel with the development of funded schemes.[55]

The optimal mix of PAYGO pensions and funded pensions remains open to discussion. High present contribution rates and budgetary constraints limit the speed of the transition to funding. It is likely that the Italian pension system will remain for a long time predominantly based on PAYGO criteria. However, it is likely that, if funding were to assume an important role, the structure of the PAYGO system would be discussed again. More specifically, the optimality of coupling a funded DC system and a PAYGO DC (rather than a DB) system could be questioned.

The introduction of the DC pensions aimed at mimicking the incentive effects of funded pensions, while avoiding the need to prefund future liabilities. For this reason, the 1995 reform clearly separated social insurance pensions (to be awarded on the basis of individual contributions) and welfare support for the elderly (to be financed out of general revenues). In a context in which the PAYGO DC pensions were significantly scaled down via a reduction in contribution rates, the levels of the pensions awarded to many individuals would be close to the minimum income guaranteed to all elderly citizens. The incentive effects of the PAYGO DC pensions would no longer be relevant. This might suggest reconsidering the separation of the social insurance and welfare functions, as well as the structure of the PAYGO benefits.

7.8   The Reform Process

This section considers four issues related to the pension reform process in Italy: the reasons underlying the critical situation of the Italian pension system in the early 1990s; the difficulties met in introducing reforms; the role of forecasts in the reform process; and the changes introduced into Italian policy-making in the pension domain during the 1990s.

---

55. Pizzuti (1998) takes a critical position on the development of supplementary pension funds, pointing to their costs and effects on income distribution.

7.8.1   How Italy Got into the Critical Situation of the Early 1990s

Even though Italian public pension expenditure is relatively high, the ratio of social expenditure to GDP is lower than the European Union (EU) average (24.6 percent, versus 28.5 percent in 1995). This depends on Italy's having an extraordinarily pension-biased social protection system: Old-age and survivors' benefits represent 63 percent of social expenditure in Italy, versus 42 percent in the EU.[56] The pension bias depends on the decisions to increase pension benefits and soften eligibility conditions that were made until the mid-1970s, and on the inability to reform the system in the following years. The other social benefits were crowded out.

The extensive role of pensions in the Italian social protection system is the result of a number of unrelated concurring factors and incremental decisions rather than of deliberate government plans. In the main report by public institutions on the future of the social protection in Italy, prepared by the National Council for Economic and Labor Issues (*Consiglio Nazionale dell'Economia e del Lavoro*, or CNEL) in 1963, expenditures for old age, survivors', and disability pensions were expected to increase— under constant policies—from 42 percent of total social expenditure in 1960 to 58 percent in 1980. These ratios were considered too high. In the "optimal" scenario outlined by CNEL, the ratio would have remained constant.

CNEL probably underestimated the inertial effects of decisions that had already been made. According to Beltrametti (1996), net pension liabilities increased from 0.66 percent of GDP in 1951 to about 2.20 percent in 1960. In 1960, pension expenditure was relatively low, but commitments were already very high. In a context in which the demographic structure was rather favorable and the Italian economy was growing fast, there was a strong pressure to extend and increase the benefits. When the system became more mature and dependency ratios increased, pension expenditure grew rapidly. Partly because short-run savings on pension outlays are politically impracticable, curbs on social spending concentrated more heavily on health services, unemployment benefits, and family allowances.

The expansion of pension expenditures also depends on the segmentation of the system in several industry-based schemes and on the ensuing segmentation of policy making. Maestri (1986, 1987), in examining the role of pensions in Italian politics, points to the existence of a political cycle in pension lawmaking and notes that competition between parties in a segmented pension system determined higher expenditure levels. Ferrera

---

56. In Italy, old age expenditure includes severance-pay benefits, only a part of which is paid to workers taking retirement. Excluding these benefits (about 1.5 percent of GDP), the ratio of old age and survivors' benefits to total social expenditure remains very high (see Ferrera 1997; Peracchi 1998b).

and Gualmini (2000) note that a highly fragmented social insurance system allowed the distribution of differentiated entitlements to selected party supporters. Pension schemes with temporarily low dependency ratios could provide high returns on the contributions paid by workers, whereas schemes with high dependency ratios were subsidized by government (Castellino 1998). The lack of evaluations concerning the long-term consequences of the decisions made and the limited role of actuarial principles also contributed indirectly to increased expenditure levels (Castellino 1996).

In the 1970s, when the demographic and economic conditions became less favorable to PAYGO systems, pension policies were carried out in a context of growing budgetary imbalances. As high deficits and rapidly growing public debt were politically accepted, there was no appreciation of the long-term implications of decisions that improved benefits or loosened eligibility conditions.

The problems that the tax administration met in assessing income, in particular that of the large number of self-employed workers, and the lack of social services also concurred in increasing the role of the pension system. These factors hampered the development of a welfare system comparable to those of most other EU countries and of an extensive unemployment support system. Universal welfare benefits were not considered viable from a budgetary point of view. Pensions were therefore used extensively for income distribution and for checking social tensions (Maestri 1986). Disability pensions surrogated welfare benefits in agriculture and in poor regions. Seniority pensions and early retirement schemes were used in place of unemployment benefits. In the 1990s welfare disability pensions were also used extensively to compensate for the lack of services to disabled citizens.

7.8.2   Why Was the Reform Delayed up to 1992?

The reforms introduced in the 1990s could have been introduced ten or even fifteen years earlier, when the coming imbalance of the system had become apparent. Even at that time, it should have been evident that the benefit and demographic structures were mutually incompatible and that gradual cuts in benefits would have eased the burden of the reform (in terms of changes in citizens' expectations) and, hence, softened the opposition to it.

The need to reform the Italian pension system had actually been recognized in the late 1970s. In 1981 this need was stressed in a report of the Ministry of Treasury, which also outlined some reform guidelines. The first long-term forecast of Italian pension expenditure carried out in the same years pointed to substantial increases in the ratio of pension expenditure to GDP (see Morcaldo 1977; Ministry of Treasury 1981). However, no

action was taken for a long time, in spite of high expenditure, large prospective imbalances, and rapid aging.

Several factors delayed the implementation of the pension reform: the
long-term nature of pension contracts, the short-term perspective of Italian politics, the lack of uncontroversial projections and of agreement on
the direction of reform, the segmentation of the Italian pension system,
and the high level of pension wealth.

The long-term nature of implicit pension contracts and the large number
of elderly citizens make difficult the introduction of pension reforms in
any country. However, reforms can be implemented gradually, avoiding
abrupt reductions in expected benefits. This approach, which limits opposition to changes, may work only if both government and public opinion
take a long-term view of budgetary issues and if long-term expenditure
projections are available and provide unequivocal indications.

This was not the case in Italy. Due to a number of political reasons—
among others, the frequent changes in government—policy makers took
a short-term view of public finance developments (see Sartor 1998). Moreover, for some time there was also no general agreement on pension expenditure trends and on the size of the prospective deficits of pension schemes
(see section 7.8.3). According to some projections the pension system was
already approaching maturity and the aging process could be partially
offset by a large increase in female labor force participation. Therefore, it
was argued that the need for corrective measures was limited. Only in
the early 1990s did all available projections concur on the seriousness of
the situation.

Moreover, during the 1980s there was no agreement on the direction of
reform. Some proposals supported a radical move from the public PAYGO
system to a privately funded system. These proposals met with the intim-
idating problems of transition and with the lingering uneasiness about
funded systems stemming from their crisis in the 1940s. Proposals were
also made to abandon the rule of proportionality between pension and
salary and to introduce a system in which each elderly citizen would receive the same benefit financed out of general revenues (Paci 1987). Such
a reform would have required a difficult switch from social security contributions to other sources of revenue. It would also have represented a complete reversal of the traditional role assigned to Italian pensions. In the
end, all plans for radical changes met strong opposition and were rejected.

The reform process was also hampered by the segmentation of the Italian pension system. As mentioned in sections 7.2 and 7.3, the system involved sizeable differences in benefits between categories of recipients.
Categories with less favorable treatment (e.g., private-sector employees)
accordingly opposed any reduction in their benefits in the absence of an
even more pronounced reduction in the benefits of the more privileged

categories (e.g., public-sector employees; see Vitaletti 1990). This meant that pension reform should have imposed different burdens on different categories and should have abrogated a large number of special benefit programmes set up over the years. The reform proposals got lost in the intricacies of the system till financial constraints developed a strong pressure for harmonization.[57]

The size of citizens' pension wealth and the large number of pensioners may also have contributed to stop the reform process. Trade unions were particularly active in defending pensioners and prospective pensioners. This situation was closely related to the increasing weight of pensioners in trade unions. In 1980, pensioners represented 18 percent of total union members; in 1991 their numbers were up to 40 percent with a peak of 48 percent in the main union (Peracchi and Rossi 1998).

7.8.3 The Role of the Forecasts

Long-term forecasts have played an important role in the Italian pension reform process. The analysis of the projections produced over the last twenty years suggests that this has been a two-way relationship: Forecasts have affected reforms, but at the same time political decisions to accelerate or postpone reforms may have influenced the forecasts as well. It also shows that expenditure forecasts have been frequently revised upward. In particular, sizeable changes in estimates took place over short periods of time with no adequate effort to explain the reason for the change.

As mentioned in section 7.8.2, the first long-term forecasts of Italian pension expenditure were carried out in the late 1970s and pointed to substantial increases in the ratio of pension expenditure to GDP. Several new projections were carried out in the second half of the 1980s, and the forecasting methodology was gradually improved. However, for some time there was no agreement on expenditure trends. Franco and Morcaldo (1986) projected a large rise in the equilibrium contribution rate of the private-sector employees' scheme, whereas Alvaro, Pedullà, and Ricci (1987), INPS (1989), and Ministry of Treasury (1988) projected a limited increase.[58] According to the latter projections, there was no urgent need to introduce major reforms in the pension system.

In the early 1990s it became gradually apparent that this optimistic view was inconsistent with actual expenditure trends. All projections now concurred on the seriousness of the situation. Both INPS (1991) and Ministry of Treasury (1991) pointed to alarming trends. Later projections, carried out after the 1992 pension reform, presented even more worrying prereform expenditure trends. INPS (1993) estimated that without the reform,

---

57. See *Commissione per l'analisi delle compatibilità macroeconomiche della spesa sociale* (1997). The governmental committee, in examining the reform of the Italian welfare state, noted that the harmonization was a prerequisite for pension reform.

58. On this debate, see Gronchi (1989).

the equilibrium contribution rate of the scheme for private-sector employees would have risen from 42 percent in 1992 to 54 percent in 2010. Ministry of Treasury (1994a) forecast the rate to be 50 percent in 2010 and 60 percent in 2025.[59]

However, these projections provided a reassuring postreform outlook. INPS (1993) projected a decline in the equilibrium contribution rate for the private–sector employees' scheme (from 42 percent in 1992 to 40 percent in 2010). Ministry of Treasury (1994a) was even more optimistic for this scheme (41 percent in 1995, 36 percent in 2010, 37 percent in 2025).[60] As a percentage of GDP, total pension expenditure was expected to decline slightly up to the year 2005, and then to increase gradually thereafter.[61]

In 1995 both INPS and the Ministry of Treasury released more unfavorable projections. In spite of the 1992 reform, INPS expected the equilibrium contribution rate for private-sector employees to remain stable at its 1995 level (49 percent). According to Ministry of Treasury (1995a), this rate would decline from 47 percent in 1995 to 42 percent in 2010 and then increase to 46 percent in 2030.[62]

Ministry of Treasury (1995a) also estimated the long-term effects of the 1995 reform. In the baseline scenario, the equilibrium contribution rate for the private-sector employees was moderately lower than in the prereform scenario (40 percent in 2010 and 45 percent in 2030). The GDP ratio of these pensions would decline from 7.3 percent in 1995 to 6.2 percent in 2010 and then increase to 7.0 percent in 2030.

The baseline scenario of Ministry of Treasury (1996) was significantly worse. The expenditure for the pension of private-sector employees was expected to increase from 8.3 percent of GDP in 1995 to 8.4 percent in 2010 and to 9.8 percent in 2030. In the new forecasts, the total expenditure of the main schemes was expected to increase from 13.6 percent in 1995 to 14.1 percent in 2010 and to 16.0 percent in 2030.

In Ministry of Treasury (1997) expenditure levels higher than in the 1996 projection were projected up to 2020, whereas they were expected to

59. It is also estimated that the equilibrium rate for public-sector employees' schemes would have risen from 40 percent in 1994 to 73 percent in 2010.

60. Ministry of Treasury (1994a) projected a moderate increase in the average rate for public-sector employees' schemes (from 42 percent in 1994 to 46 percent in 2010). The projections concerning the main schemes for self-employed workers were less reassuring. The equilibrium rates were expected to more than double by the year 2010 (INPS 1993). Quite strikingly, the equilibrium rates projected for the self-employed workers, taking the effects of the reform into account, were higher than those projected before the 1992 reform (INPS 1991).

61. This profile is obtained by summing up the expenditure-to-GDP ratios estimated by the Ministry of Treasury for the pensions of public-sector employees, and by INPS for the pensions of private-sector employees and the self-employed.

62. The equilibrium contribution rates of the schemes for the self-employed workers were also revised upward.

be lower thereafter.[63] Further changes along the same lines were introduced in Ministry of Treasury (1998), which expected total expenditure to increase to 15.0 percent of GDP in 2010 and to 15.8 percent in 2030.[64]

These developments emphasize the need for regular revisions of pension expenditure projections. The reasons underlying changes in assumptions and results with respect to previous exercises should be explained in each revision. The attribution of the responsibility for producing the projections could also be reconsidered. Indeed, an autonomous agency responding to Parliament or to the *Corte dei Conti*[65] would be more independent and less affected by the policy debate than the Ministry of Treasury and the National Institute for Social Security.

7.8.4   Has Policy-Making Changed?

As was argued in the previous sections, 1992 represents a turning point in Italian pension policy in terms of expenditure control. With a sudden change with respect to the previous decades, the policy debate since 1992 has been basically about the control of pension expenditure. This section considers whether this change affected the way policies are defined and implemented.

One major change regards the governmental departments in charge of developing pension policy proposals. Responsibility rapidly shifted to the Office of the Prime Minister and the Ministry of Treasury. They developed both the 1992 and 1995 reforms, whereas the Ministry for Labor and Social Protection had a very modest role. As in other countries (Tamburi 1999) the change is related to the reasons underlying the reforms, which were economic and financial in nature rather than social.

The role played by the different pressure groups changed in several respects. Although in the pre-1992 period both public-sector employees and self-employed workers had relatively advantageous rules with respect to those of private-sector employees (Castellino 1996), in the following years the cut in benefits was proportionally higher for them than for private-sector employees; public-sector employees lost more than the other groups in relative terms (Sartor 2000). Although private-sector employees managed to retain the right to take seniority retirement with thirty-five years of contributions, public-sector employees lost their preferential conditions for seniority retirement. Self-employed workers fared relatively better: As already mentioned, in 1995 their contribution rate was set at 15 percent whereas their pensions would be calculated on the basis of a 20 percent contribution rate.

63. In the new baseline scenario, which referred to new demographic projections, total expenditure was expected to increase from 13.7 percent of GDP in 1995 to 14.6 percent in 2010 and to 15.7 percent in 2030.

64. Only marginal changes were introduced in the latest projections (Ministry of Treasury 1999).

65. This is the independent court responsible for auditing government accounts.

With the gradual harmonization of rules, the division between pressure groups gradually shifted from employment characteristics to generational characteristics. In this context, the rules to be applied in the transition to the new regime became the main issue.

In other respects, the policy process did not significantly change. The following aspects are particularly relevant:

1. Reforms were introduced without adequate preliminary work. This deficiency was understandable in the emergency situation of 1992; it was less so in later years, however, when the focus shifted from expenditure control to a wider range of objectives. Gronchi and Aprile (1998) relate some deficiencies of the 1995 reform to the swiftness of its introduction, which prevented the reflection necessary to understand its implications (see also Aprile, Fassina, and Pace 1996).

2. No government document was ever presented in the 1990s illustrating the case for reform, the alternative changes taken into consideration, the objectives, and the expected outcomes. In particular, it is remarkable that the 1995 pension formula was never officially published (Gronchi 1997). This creates some ambiguity for future revisions of conversion coefficients.

3. Policy making remained both largely incremental and affected by short-term considerations. Changes were frequently introduced under external pressure. The effort to minimize the reactions of the more vocal groups led to solutions that may prove unsustainable in the long run. Most expenditure cuts came from changes in the indexation mechanisms, which are perhaps more acceptable to public opinion because they are less visible and more gradual. As mentioned in section 7.6, the 1995 reform avoided showing cuts in replacement rates at the cost of increasing pressures from pensioners in the future.[66] It also envisaged extremely long and complex transitory arrangements that will substantially reduce the expected incentive effects of the reform. Some important exceptions were introduced in the actuarial approach underlying the 1995 reform. In particular, the gaps between actual and imputed contribution rates are in stark contrast with this approach.

4. The distribution of the burden of reform between generations and groups of workers is uneven. The cut in the pension wealth of pensioners and elderly workers is very limited with respect to that imposed on younger workers. Generational disparities have replaced industry-based disparities. Moreover, workers with long contributory records have retained their seniority pensions, whereas those with shorter records have faced a sudden increase in the minimum age for obtaining an old age pension (a five-year increase over an eight-year period).

---

66. Pizzuti (1998) remarks that this decision, which relies on the short-sightedness of individuals, is in stark contrast with one of the main roles of public action in retirement provision, which is that of compensating for individuals' short-sightedness.

In the end, there is considerable continuity in Italian policy making in the pension domain. The same incremental and short-sighted approach that determined the extraordinary expansion of pension expenditure up to 1992 continued to work in the following years. Changes in benefit and eligibility conditions have again been introduced without adequate analysis of their implications.

7.9 Conclusion

The reforms introduced in the 1990s have significantly changed the outlook of the Italian pension system. Prospective expenditure growth has been contained, and the harmonization of the different schemes is well underway. The incentives for early retirement have been reduced.

The reform process is not yet complete, however. Faster implementation of the 1995 reform and some parametric changes in the pension regime established by that reform would avoid further increases in payroll taxes and make some resources available for other social benefits. An increase in effective retirement age would shift the focus of expenditure control from the reduction of replacement ratios to the reduction of the ratio of pensioners to workers, and would make the pension system more sustainable. Moreover, it is important to exploit fully the incentive effects and the self-equilibrating mechanism of the new, actuarially based system. An acceleration of the development of funded schemes would allow a gradual reduction of PAYGO contribution rates. The system would remain predominantly PAYGO, but it would be better suited to deal with different shocks. Some changes in policy making may also be required, in terms of preliminary work, communication with the public, and forecasts. It is important that further changes reduce uncertainty about the future prospects of the pension system, and that pension rules are perceived by public opinion as long lasting.

Italian experience provides some indications concerning the issue of pension reform:

1. Late reforms are necessarily less gradual and more painful than would be desirable. The delay in introducing a reform has imposed high costs on Italian pensioners and prospective pensioners in terms of unexpected reductions in purchasing power (e.g., those produced by the partial suspension of price indexation in 1993) and sudden changes in expectations (e.g., those related to the fast increase in the standard retirement age).

2. A lengthy reform process introduces additional burdens. The widespread perception that more adjustments are required increases uncertainty and induces elderly workers to retire at the earliest possible date. This increases public expenditure and negatively affects the labor market. Figure 7.2, for example, shows that the employment rates of Italian males

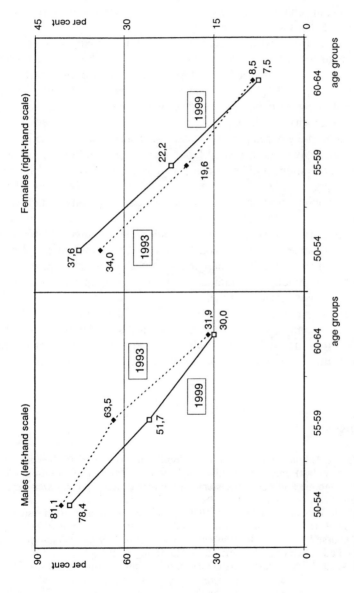

Fig. 7.2 Employment rates

in the fifty-to-sixty-four age brackets significantly declined during the 1990s in spite of the increase in minimum age for old age pensions. Moreover, although most experts consider that further changes are required, public opinion is experiencing "adjustment fatigue."

3. The segmentation of the pension system may hamper the reform process. Important changes in pension rules were introduced in Italy only when a process of harmonization was begun.

4. Some groups of workers accepted large cuts in their pension rights without major negative reactions. This is particularly the case for public-sector employees. Private-sector employees who lack long contributory records also accepted large cuts in their entitlements. On the other hand, workers with long contributory records resisted changes and retained entitlement to seniority pensions.

5. An actuarially based pension system, such as that introduced in Italy in 1995, can deliver the expected labor market benefits only if the link between contributions and benefits is transparent, easy to grasp, and perceived as stable by citizens. This may not be the case in Italy, where a large number of workers are unaffected by the new pension regime and further reforms are expected by public opinion.

6. Projections are very important to guide policy changes. The lack of regular and reliable projections contributed to the postponement of pension reform in the 1980s. Transparent and regular revisions of projections can contribute greatly to guiding the reform process and smoothing changes over long periods of time.

7. There is a trade-off between the need to make use of political windows of opportunity and the production of in-depth preliminary analysis of pension reforms. In Italy, the swiftness of the introduction of the reforms prevented adequate reflection on their designs and implications.

References

Alvaro, G., G. Pedullà, and L. Ricci. 1987. "Sull'evoluzione del sistema economico italiano e dei trattamenti pensionistici agli inizi del 2000" (The evolution of the Italian economic and pension systems in the new century). In *Il futuro del sistema pensionistico italiano,* ed. INPS, 161–222. Rome: INPS.

Aprile, R., S. Fassina, and D. Pace. 1996. "Equilibrio ed equità in un sistema a ripartizione: Un'ipotesi di riforma" (Equilibrium and equity in a PAYGO system: A possible reform). In *Pensioni e risanamento della finanza pubblica,* ed. Fiorella Padoa Schioppa Kostoris, 272–323. Bologna: Il Mulino.

Aronica, A. 1993. "Il trattamento di fine rapporto: Dall'autofinanziamento al mercato finanziario" (Severance pay: From self-financing to the financial market). In *Il risparmio previdenziale e i fondi pensione,* ed. D. Pace, 265–314. Milan: Franco Angeli.

Artoni, R., and A. Zanardi. 1996. The evolution of the Italian pension system.

Milan: Mission Interministerielle Recherche Experimentation (MIRE). Mimeograph.

Ascoli, U. 1984. "Il sistema italiano di welfare" (The Italian welfare system). In *Welfare state all'italiana,* ed. U. Ascoli, 5–51. Bari: Laterza.

Baldacci, E., and L. Inglese. 1999. "Le caratteristiche socio-economiche dei pensionati in Italia: Analisi della distribuzione dei redditi da pensione" (The socioeconomic characteristics of Italian pensioners: An analysis of the distribution of pension income). Paper presented at the Riunione Scientifica Gruppo MURST. 22–23 November, Messina, Italy.

Baldacci, E., and D. Tuzi. 1999. "Gli effetti delle riforme degli anni '90 sull'evoluzione della spesa per pensioni" (The effects of the reforms of the '90s on the evolution of pension expenditure). Paper presented at the eleventh Riunione Scientifica della Società di Economia Pubblica. 8–9 October, Pavia, Italy.

Banca d'Italia. 1991. The pension system: Reasons for reform. *Economic Bulletin* 13 (October): 68–70.

———. 1995. The 1995 pension reform. *Economic Bulletin* 21 (October): 65–70.

———. 1999. *Relazione annuale* (Annual report), May. Rome: Banca d'Italia.

Becchi Collidà, A. 1979. *Politiche del lavoro e garanzia del reddito in Italia* (Labor policies and guaranteed income in Italy). Bologna: Il Mulino.

Beltrametti, L. 1994. "Su alcuni aspetti redistributivi della riforma del sistema previdenziale" (On some redistribution aspects of the reform of the pension system). In *Secondo rapporto CNEL sulla distribuzione e redistribuzione del reddito in Italia,* ed. N. Rossi, 194–99. Bologna: Il Mulino.

———. 1996. *Il debito pensionistico in Italia* (Public pension liabilities in Italy). Bologna: Il Mulino.

Beltrametti, L., and R. Soliani. 1999. "Il sistema pensionistico italiano nel periodo 1919–39: Alcuni effetti macroeconomici e redistributivi" (The Italian pension system from 1919 to 1939: Some macroeconomic and redistribution effects). University of Genova, Department of Economics and Quantitative Measurement. Mimeograph.

Brugiavini, A. 1999. Social security and retirement in Italy. In *Social security and retirement around the world,* ed. J. Gruber and D. A. Wise, 181–238. Chicago: University of Chicago Press.

Brugiavini, A., and F. Peracchi. 1999. Reforming Italian social security: Should we switch from PAYGO to fully funded? Paper presented at the sixth annual conference on "Le nuove frontiere della politica economica." 7 June, Rome.

Cannari, L., and D. Franco. 1990. "Sistema pensionistico e distribuzione dei redditi" (The pension system and the distribution of income). In *Contributi all'analisi economica,* vol. 6, 121–61. Rome: Banca d'Italia.

———. 1997. "La povertà tra i minorenni in Italia: Dimensioni, caratteristiche, politiche" (Poverty among minors in Italy: Size, characteristics, policies). *Temi di discussione* no. 294. Rome: Banca d'Italia.

Cardarelli, R., and N. Sartor. 2000. Generational accounts for Italy. Paper presented at the Banca d'Italia Workshop on Fiscal Sustainability. 20–22 January, Perugia, Italy.

Castellino, O. 1976. *Il labirinto delle pensioni* (The pension labyrinth). Bologna: Il Mulino.

———. 1986. "Il futuro del sistema previdenziale italiano" (The future of the Italian pension system). *Rivista di politica economica* 76 (8): 1163–85.

———. 1995. "La previdenza sociale dalla riforma Amato alla riforma Dini (The pension system from the Amato reform to the Dini reform). *Rivista Internazionale di Scienze Sociali* 103 (3): 457–72.

———. 1996. "La redistribuzione tra ed entro generazioni nel sistema previdenziale italiano" (Redistribution between and within generations in the Italian pension system). In *Pensioni e risanamento della finanza pubblica,* ed. Fiorella Padoa Schioppa Kostoris, 59–146. Bologna: Il Mulino.

———. 1998. There is nothing either good or bad. *Politica Economica* 14 (1): 21–30.

Castellino, O., and E. Fornero. 1997. "Privatizzare la previdenza sociale? Condizioni, modalità e limiti" (Privatizing the pension system? Conditions, methods and limits). *Politica Economica* 13 (1): 3–25.

Centro Europa Ricerche (CER). 1993. "Fondi pensioni: Una legge da riformare" (Pension funds: A law to be reformed). *Rapporto CER* no. 2, monograph. Rome: CER.

———. 1994. "Pensioni: E ora la riforma" (Pensions: And now the reform). *Rapporto CER* no. 6, monograph. Rome: CER.

Cichon, M. 1999. Notional defined-contribution schemes: Old wine in new bottles? *International Social Security Review* 52 (4): 87–105.

Consiglio Nazionale dell'Economia e del Lavoro (CNEL). 1963. *Relazione preliminare sulla riforma della previdenza sociale* (A preliminary report on the reform of social protection). Rome: CNEL.

Commissione per l'analisi delle compatibilità macroeconomiche della spesa sociale. 1997. *Relazione Finale* (Final report), 28 February.

Fausto, D. 1978. *Il sistema italiano di sicurezza sociale* (The Italian social security system). Bologna: Il Mulino.

———. 1983. "La diffusione delle pensioni di invalidità: Una piaga non esclusiva del Sud" (The spread of disability pensions: a problem not limited to the South). *Mezzogiorno d'Europa* 1:53–75.

Ferrera, M. 1984. *Il welfare state in Italia* (The welfare state in Italy). Bologna: Il Mulino.

———. 1997. "La spesa sociale italiana in prospettiva comparata" (Italian social spending from a comparative point of view). Documento di base no. 1. *Commissione per l'analisi delle compatibilità macroeconomiche della spesa sociale, relazione finale,* 28 February.

Ferrera, M., and E. Gualmini. 1999. Rescue from without? Italian social policies 1970–1999 and the challenges of internationalisation. European University Institute Working Paper no. 13. Florence: European University Institute.

Ferraresi, P. M., and E. Fornero. 2000. "Costi e distorsioni della transizione previdenziale ed effetti correttivi di alcune proposte di riforma" (Costs and distortions in pension transition and the corrective effects of some reform proposals). *Politica Economica* 16 (1): 3–48.

Folster, S. 1999. Social insurance based on personal savings accounts: A possible reform strategy for overburdened welfare states? In *The welfare state in Europe,* ed. M. Buti, D. Franco, and L. Pench, 93–115. Cheltenham, U.K.: Edward Elgar.

Fornero, E. 1995. Totally unfunded versus partially funded pension schemes: The case of Italy. *Ricerche Economiche* 49:357–74.

———. 1999. *L'economia dei fondi pensioni* (The economy of pension funds). Bologna: Il Mulino.

Forni, L., and R. Giordano. 1999. Can Italy fund its social security system? Banca d'Italia, Rome. Mimeograph.

Franco, D. 1993a. *L'espansione della spesa pubblica in Italia* (The expansion of public spending in Italy). Bologna: Il Mulino.

———. 1993b. "Il sistema pensionistico fra provvedimenti di emergenza e riforme di struttura" (The pension system between emergency provisions and structural reforms). In *La finanza pubblica nel 1993,* ed. L. Bernardi, 105–40. Milan: Franco Angeli.

Franco, D., and F. Frasca. 1992. Public pensions in an ageing society: The case of Italy. In *The future of pensions in the European Community,* ed. J. Mortensen, 69–95. London: Centre for European Policy Studies, Brassey's.

Franco, D., J. Gokhale, L. Guiso, L. Kotlikoff, and N. Sartor. 1992. Generational accounting: The case of Italy. In *Saving and the accumulation of wealth,* ed. A. Ando, L. Guiso, and I. Visco, 128–60. Cambridge: Cambridge University Press.

Franco, D., and G. Morcaldo. 1986. *Un modello di previsione degli squilibri del sistema previdenziale* (A model for forecasting the imbalances in the pension system). Rome: Istituto Poligrafico e Zecca dello Stato.

———. 1989. The origins, functions and planned reform of some features of the Italian pension system. In *Social security and its financing,* ed. Ministero del Lavoro e della Previdenza Sociale, 45–92. Rome: Istituto Poligrafico e Zecca dello Stato.

———. 1990. *La spesa per la tutela degli invalidi in Italia* (Public expenditure for the care of the disabled in Italy). Milan: Franco Angeli.

Giarda, P. 1998. "La revisione del sistema pensionistico nel 1997: Come avrebbe potuto essere" (The 1997 revision of the pension system: How it could have been). *Economia Politica* 15 (2): 267–94.

Gronchi, S. 1989. The long-term outlook for the Italian social security system. In *Social security and its financing,* ed. Ministero del Lavoro della Previdenza Sociale, 131–201. Rome: Istituto Poligrafico e Zecca dello Stato.

———. 1997. "Un'ipotesi di correzione e completamento della riforma delle pensioni del 1995" (A proposal for correcting and completing the 1995 pension reform). *Studi e Note di Economia* 2:7–40.

———. 1998. "La sostenibilità delle nuove forme previdenziali ovvero il sistema pensionistico tra riforme fatte e da fare" (The sustainability of the new pension reforms: the pension system between completed and prospective reforms). *Economia Politica* 15 (2): 295–316.

Gronchi, S., and R. Aprile. 1998. The 1995 pension reform: Equity, sustainability and indexation. *Labour* 12 (1): 67–100.

Hamann, A. J. 1997. The reform on the pension system in Italy. IMF Working Paper no. WP/97/18. Washington, D.C.: International Monetary Fund.

Istituto Nazionale della Previdenza Sociale (INPS). 1970. "Sviluppi dell'assicurazione obbligatoria per l'invalidità, la vecchiaia ed i superstiti nel suo primo cinquantennio di applicazione" (The development of the compulsory insurance for disability, old age and survivors in its first fifty years). In *Settant' anni dell'Istituto Nazionale della Previdenza Sociale: Cinquant'anni dell'Assicurazione Generale Obbligatoria per l'Invalidità e la Vecchiaia,* ed. INPS, 321–34. Rome: Raccolta di Studi.

———. 1989. *Il modello INPS e le prime proiezioni al 2010* (The INPS model and the first projections up to 2010). Rome: INPS.

———. 1991. *Il nuovo modello previsionale INPS per le pensioni: Caratteristiche generali e risultati di sintesi della proiezione al 2010 del Fondo pensioni lavoratori dipendenti* (The new INPS model for pension expenditure forecasting: General characteristics and a synthesis of the projections of the employees' pension fund through 2010). Roma: INPS.

———. 1993. *Le pensioni domani* (The future of pensions). Bologna: Il Mulino.

———. 1995. "Relazione del Presidente Gianni Billia" (Report of the president, Gianni Billia). In *Crisi del sistema previdenziale italiano e confini tra pubblico e privato,* 25–39. Rome: Senate of Italy.

Istituto Ricerche Sociali (IRS). 1995. *Vecchie e nuove pensioni: La proposta Dini* (Old and new pensions: The Dini proposal). Milan: IRS.

Istituto di Studi e Analisi Economica (ISAE). 1999. *Rapporto trimestrale: Finanza pubblica e redistribuzione* (Quarterly report: public finance and redistribution). Rome: ISAE, October.

Italian National Statistical Institute (ISTAT). 1997. *Il sistema pensionistico italiano: Beneficiari e prestazioni* (The Italian pension system: pensioners and benefits). Rome: ISTAT.

————. 1999. *I trattamenti pensionistici: Anno 1998* (Pensions: year 1998). Rome: ISTAT.

————. 2000. *I beneficiari delle prestazioni pensionistiche: Anno 1998* (Beneficiaries of pensions: year 1998). Rome: ISTAT.

Maestri, E. 1986. "La politica delle pensioni in Italia fra ciclo elettorale e competizione interpartitica" (Pension policy in Italy between the electoral cycles and political party competition). *Quaderni di Sociologia* 33 (7): 47–73.

————. 1987. "La regolazione dei conflitti redistributivi in Italia: Il caso della politica pensionistica (1948–1983)" (Redistribution conflicts in Italy: The case of pension policy [1948–1983]). *Stato e Mercato* 20 (August): 249–79.

Messori, M., and A. Scaffidi. 1999. "Lo sviluppo dei fondi pensione 'chiusi': Il possibile ruolo del Trattamento di Fine Rapporto e del regime fiscale" (The development of "closed" pension funds: The possible role of severance pay and the tax regime). Rome: Società Per Lo Sviluppo Del Mercato Dei Fondi Pensione (MEFOP). Mimeograph.

Ministry of Health and Social Affairs. 1994. Pension reform in Sweden: A short summary. Proposal of the 1994 Working Group on Pensions, Stockholm.

Ministry of Treasury. 1981. *La spesa previdenziale e i suoi effetti sulla finanza pubblica. Relazione della Commissione di studio istituita dal Ministro del Tesoro* (Pension expenditure and its effects on public finance. Report of the committee appointed by the Minister of Treasury). Rome: Istituto Poligrafico e Zecca dello Stato.

————. 1988. *Metodi per la previsione a lungo termine degli squilibri previdenziali* (Methods for long-term forecasting of pension imbalances). Rome: Istituto Poligrafico e Zecca dello Stato.

————. 1991. *Fondo pensioni lavoratori dipendenti: Una proiezione al 2025* (Employees' pension fund: A projection through 2025). Rome: Istituto Poligrafico e Zecca della Stato.

————. 1994a. "Audizione del Ragioniere Generale dello Stato Andrea Monorchio" (Audit of State Comptroller General Andrea Monorchio). Camera dei Deputati, XI Commissione Permanente Lavoro pubblico e privato. 7 September, Rome.

————. 1994b. "I rendimenti impliciti della previdenza obbligatoria: Un'analisi delle iniquità del sistema" (The returns implicit in compulsory insurance: an analysis of the system's iniquities). *Conti pubblici e congiuntura economica*, vol. 2, monograph. Rome.

————. 1994c. "La previdenza complementare: Problemi e prospettive per il decollo" (Complementary insurance: Problems and prospects for its take-off). *Conti pubblici e congiuntura economica*, vol. 1, monograph. Rome.

————. 1995a. "Il progetto di riforma del sistema pensionistico pubblico presentato dal governo: Le tendenze di medio-lungo periodo del Fondo Pensioni Lavoratori Dipendenti" (The reform of the public pension system presented by the government: Trends in the medium and long term for the Employees' Pension Fund). Rome: Ministry of Treasury.

————. 1995b. "Il progetto di riforma del sistema pensionistico pubblico presentato dal governo: Le tendenze di medio-lungo periodo del Fondo Artigiani e Commercianti" (The reform of the public pension system presented by the government: Trends in the medium and long term for the Artisans' and Retailers' Funds). Rome: Ministry of Treasury.

————. 1996. "Tendenze demografiche e spesa pensionistica: Alcuni possibili scenari" (Demographic trends and pension spending: Some possible scenarios). *Quaderno Monografico: Conti Pubblici e Congiuntura Economica,* vol. 9, monograph. Rome.

————. 1997. "Sanità, scuola e pensioni: Le nuove previsioni basate sugli scenari demografici ISTAT" (Health, schools, and pensions: New forecasts based on ISTAT demographic scenarios). *Quaderno Monografico: Conti Pubblici e Congiuntura Economica,* vol. 13, monograph. Rome.

————. 1998. Italy's convergence towards EMU, January. Rome: Ministry of Treasury.

————. 1999. "Aggiornamento del modello di previsione del sistema pensionistico della Ragioneria Generale dello Stato: Le previsioni '99" (An update of the state comptroller general's pension system forecast: The 1999 forecast). June, monograph. Rome.

Modigliani, F., and M. Ceprini. 1998. Social security reform: A proposal for Italy. *Review of Economic Conditions in Italy* 2 (May–August): 177–201.

Morcaldo, G. 1977. "Analisi della struttura dei trattamenti pensionistici e della sua evoluzione" (An analysis of the structure of pensions and its evolution). *Contributi alla ricerca economica* 7:77–162.

Nicoletti-Altimari, S., and M. Rostagno. 1999. The *dis*-advantages of tying one's hands: Yield rate flexibility in unfunded pension systems. Paper presented at conference, "Le Nuove Frontiere della Politica Economica," 7 June, IGIER, Rome.

Nucleo di valutazione della spesa previdenziale (Pension Expenditure Evaluation Committee). 1988. "Analisi del Sistema Pensionistico Obbligatorio: I dati base e gli indicatori di gestione" (Analysis of the compulsory pension system: Data and indicators). Rome, May.

————. 1999. "Nota sugli andamenti della spesa previdenziale" (A note on the development of pension expenditure). Rome, April.

Organization for Economic Cooperation and Development (OECD). 2000. *Labor force statistics, 1978–1998: Part III.* Paris: OECD.

Onofri, P. 1998. "Nonostante tutto, un altro pezzo di riforma del sistema pensionistico" (In spite of everything, another step in the pension system reform). *Politica Economica* 1 (April): 5–19.

Orszag, J. M., and D. J. Snower. 1999. Expanding the welfare system: A proposal for reform. In *The welfare state in Europe,* ed. M. Buti, D. Franco, and L. Pench, 116–35. Cheltenham, U.K.: Edward Elgar.

Pace, D. 1993. "I fondi pensione e la previdenza obbligatoria in Italia" (Pension funds and compulsory insurance in Italy). In *Il risparmio previdenziale e i fondi pensione,* ed. D. Pace, 25–48. Milan: Franco Angeli.

Padoa Schioppa Kostoris, F. 1995. "A proposito dei tassi di rendimento interno per i neopensionati italiani: 1995–2001" (Concerning the rates of return for newly pensioned Italians: 1995–2001). In *Le pensioni difficili,* ed. O. Castellino, 143–64. Bologna: Il Mulino.

————. 1996. "La riforma italiana delle pensioni anzianità e vecchiaia del 1995 e gli effetti di finanza pubblica" (The Italian reform of seniority and old age pensions in 1995 and its effects on public finance). In *Pensioni e risanamento della finanza pubblica,* ed. F. Padoa Schioppa Kostoris, 399–480. Bologna: Il Mulino.

Palmer, E. 1999. Exit from the labor force for older workers: Can the NDC pension system help? *Geneva Papers on Risk and Insurance* 24 (4): 461–72.

Peracchi, F. 1998a. "Demografia, mercato del lavoro e spesa per la protezione sociale: Un confronto fra i paesi dell'Unione Europea" (Demographics, labor market, and social protection spending: A comparison among the countries of the European Union). CEIS Working Paper no. 45. Rome: Centro Interdipartimentale di Studi Internazionali sull'Economia e lo Sviluppo.

————. 1998b. "La spesa per la protezione sociale nei paesi dell'Unione Europea" (Social protection spending in the countries of the European Union). *Politica Economica* 14 (1): 31–63.

————. 1999. "Lavoro, retribuzioni e pensioni: Un confronto tra generazioni di italiani" (Work, salaries and pensions: A comparison between generations of Italians). Paper presented at conference on "Metodi quantitativi per l'analisi economica." December, Banca d'Italia, Perugia.

Peracchi, F., and N. Rossi. 1998. "Nonostante tutto, è una riforma" (In spite of everything, it is a reform). In *La costituzione fiscale*, ed. G. Tabellini, 63–155. Bologna: Il Mulino.

Pizzuti, F. R. 1990. *La sicurezza sociale tra previdenza assistenza e politica economica* (Social security between insurance, assistance and economic policy). Naples: Liguori.

————. 1998. Pension reform and economic policy constraints in Italy. *Labour* 12 (1): 45–66.

Porta, P., and P. Saraceno. 1996. The mandatory pension system in Italy: Country report of the Phare-Ace, Research project P95-2139-R. *Contributi di Ricerca IRS* no. 37.

Regonini, G. 1984. "Il sistema pensionistico: Risorse e vincoli" (The pension system: Resources and constraints). In *Welfare state all'italiana*, ed. U. Ascoli, 87–117. Bari: Laterza.

Rossi, N., and I. Visco. 1995. National saving and social security in Italy. *Temi di discussione* no. 262. Rome: Banca d'Italia.

Rostagno, M. 1996. "Il percorso della riforma: 1992–1995. Nuovi indicatori di consistenza e sostenibilità per il Fondo Pensioni Lavoratori Dipendenti" (The path of reform: 1992 to 1995. New consistency and sustainability indicators for the employees' pension fund). In *Pensioni e risanamento della finanza pubblica*, ed. F. Padoa Schioppa Kostoris, 325–97. Bologna: Il Mulino.

Sartor, N. 1998. *Il risanamento mancato: La politica di bilancio italiana, 1986–90* (A consolidation that failed: Italian budgetary policy, 1986–1990). Rome: Carocci.

————. 2000. The long-run effects of the Italian pension reforms. *International Tax and Public Finance* 8 (1): 83–111.

Senate of Italy. 1995. "Crisi del sistema previdenziale italiano e confini tra pubblico e privato" (The crisis in the Italian pension system and the borders between public and private sectors). *Incontri di studio a Palazzo Giustiniani, 21 February 1995*, no. 8, monograph. Rome.

Tamburi, G. 1999. Motivation, purpose and processes in pension reform. *International Social Security Review* 52 (3): 15–44.

Visco, I. 1999. Welfare systems, ageing and work: An OECD perspective. Paper presented at conference, "New Welfare and Social Security in Europe," 10–11 September, University of Brescia, Italy.

Vitaletti, G. 1990. "I conflitti di interesse sulla riforma pensionistica" (Conflicts of interest in pension reform). In *Il sistema pensionistico: Un riesame*, ed. F. R. Pizzuti and M. R. Rey, 281–88. Bologna: Il Mulino.

————. 1993. "Apparenza e realtà degli effetti dei provvedimenti di riforma pensionistica" (Appearance and reality in the effects of pension reform provisions). *Economia Pubblica* 23 (11): 491–99.

Comment   Franco Peracchi

The paper by Daniele Franco provides an excellent overview of the recent process of pension reform in Italy. The message of the paper is not very optimistic:

> In spite of the reversal of pension policy in 1992, in terms of expenditure control, there is considerable continuity in the Italian policy-making style. The same incremental and short-sighted approach that determined the extraordinary expansion of pension expenditure up to 1992 continued to work in the following years. The reforms implemented in recent years under the pressure of budgetary constraints largely reflect the demands of some specific groups. They have been introduced without adequate analysis of their implications and include solutions that may prove unsustainable in the long run. This also made the reform process longer and determined lengthy transition periods.

In my comment, I would like to strengthen Franco's conclusions by arguing that, at least so far, the Italian process of pension reform has missed the four main objectives it was originally supposed to achieve, namely, (1) stabilizing the ratio of public pension expenditure to gross domestic product (GDP), (2) reverting the trend toward early retirement, (3) increasing equity and fairness, and (4) promoting the creation of a two-pillar system. To this end, I will also present some additional statistical evidence that supplements the wealth of information provided in the paper.

The Expenditure-GDP Ratio

Figure 7C.1 shows the historical trends in the number of pensions (top left panel), average pension amounts (top right panel), pension expenditure (bottom left panel), and the ratio of pension expenditure to GDP (bottom right panel) as measured by the Italian National Statistical Institute (*Istituto Nazionale di Statistica,* or ISTAT). For simplicity, I consider only data on old age, disability, and survivors' pensions, thus excluding noncontributive pensions. Monetary amounts are at constant 1998 prices.

Between 1975 and the beginning of the reform process in 1992, the number of pensions outstanding grew by 34 percent, from 12.5 to 16.6 million, while the average pension doubled in real terms. As a result, expenditure increased by nearly three times and the ratio of pension expenditure to

Franco Peracchi is professor of econometrics at Tor Vergata University.

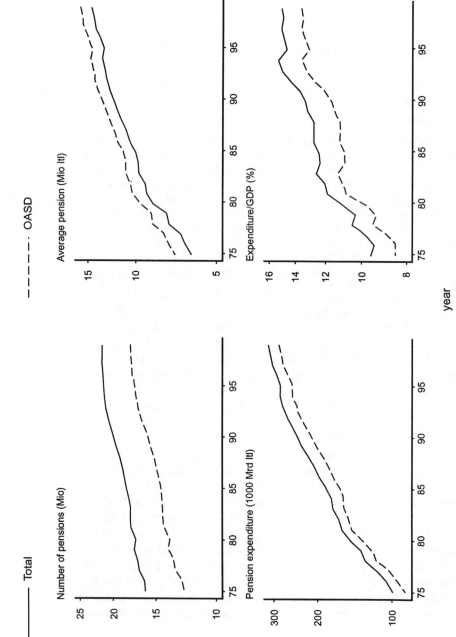

Fig. 7C.1 Number of pensions, amount of pension expenditure, average pension, and pension expenditure-GDP ratio, 1980–98 (log scale) for Old age, survivors', and disability pensions

Source: Author's calculations based on raw data from the Italian National Statistical Institute (ISTAT) and the Statistical Office of the European

GDP rose by more than 4 percentage points, from 8.4 percent to 12.8 percent. The increase in the number of pensions outstanding reflects the progressive aging of the Italian population and the steady reduction of the average retirement age, largely due to workers' taking advantage of the possibility of retiring with a seniority pension (*pensione di anzianità*) after thirty-five years of contributions (or even fewer for public-sector employees) without any actuarial reduction. On the other hand, the rise of average pensions is due to the sharp increase of lifetime earnings of successive cohorts of workers, a number of legislated changes that made the system progressively more generous, and the fact that outstanding pensions were *de facto* linked to productivity growth.

Between 1992 and 1998, pension expenditure increased by about 20 percent in real terms and the ratio of pension expenditure to GDP increased from 12.8 to 13.5 percent, as a result of a 6.6 percent increase in the number of pensions outstanding (from 16.6 to 17.7 million) and a 12.9 percent increase in the average pension. This slowdown of pension expenditure growth is often presented as a major achievement of the 1995 reform. In fact, the objective of stabilizing the ratio of pension expenditure to GDP (explicitly stated in the 1995 reform law) has not yet been reached, and pension expenditure has been growing at rates that, although lower than in the past, are still higher than GDP growth rates. Furthermore, the slowdown of expenditure growth is largely the result of decisions made in 1992, namely, the elimination of the double-indexing of pensions to price inflation and productivity growth, the introduction of limitations to early retirement, and the gradual increase of the normal retirement age from sixty to sixty-five for men and from fifty-five to sixty for women. Of the three, the elimination of double-indexing has been by far the most important.

Labor Market Trends

According to Istat baseline projections of the resident population for the period 1996–2050, the working-age population (persons aged twenty to fifty-nine) is expected to shrink from 32.5 million in 1996 to 20.9 million in 2050, with a loss of 11.6 million units. During the same period, the elderly population (persons aged sixty and older) is expected to increase from 12.9 to 17.4 million, gaining 4.5 million units. As a result, the elderly dependency ratio (the ratio between the elderly population and the working-age population) is expected to more than double, increasing from 40 percent in 1996 to 83 percent in 2050.

Although these demographic prospects have attracted considerable attention, the crucial issues of labor market trends and labor market incentives have been largely neglected in the policy debate. In fact, one of the most striking developments of the Italian labor market during the last three decades is the dramatic drop in labor force participation and employment rates in the age range between fifty and sixty years, as measured by the ISTAT quarterly labor force survey. This trend toward early retirement from the "official" labor market has contributed to a worsening of the financial situation of the social security system, above and beyond that caused by the unfavorable demographic trends and the generosity with which pensions have been awarded in the past.

Figure 7C.2 compares the employment rates of Italy (by sex and age) with those for the rest of Europe. It focuses on the eleven countries that, together with Italy, were part of the European Union in the early 1980s (EU-11). Between 1983 and 1997 Italy has lost its advantage in terms of higher male employment rates relative to the other countries. In the mean time, the gap between Italy and the EU-11 in terms of female employment rates has widened. Figure 7C.3 compares the average annual variation of employment rates, by sex and age, for Italy and the EU-11 between 1983 and 1997. Italy distinguishes itself by its much sharper decline in male employment rates before age thirty and in the age range of fifty to sixty, and by its more limited expansion of female rates.

Figure 7C.4 shows the average annual variation of Italian employment rates by sex and age separately for the two subperiods 1983–92 and 1992–98. Consider first the period 1983–92. Male employment rates have been falling at all ages, but the decline has been especially strong before age thirty and between ages fifty and sixty. Female employment rates have also been falling at these ages, but they have been rising at all ages between twenty-five and fifty. The drop in employment rates of young men and women reflects the increase in school attendance and the rise of youth unemployment. On the other hand, the available evidence shows that current social security regulations played a major role in the decline of employment rates among older men and women. Two aspects of the system appear to have had strong negative incentive effects on labor supply. One is the high implicit tax on continuing to work, through the benefit formula currently in use and the availability of seniority pensions. The other is the negative effect on human capital investment, through the early retirement option and the highly progressive taxation of earnings.

With regard to the first aspect, one should note that seniority pensions are the main escape route into retirement. Other escape routes, such as unemployment benefits or disability pensions, appear to be much less important. Eligibility for disability pensions has been tightened up considerably in the 1980s, whereas unemployment benefits have never played an important role.

Turning to the second aspect, it is a fact that schooling levels in Italy are lower than the European average, especially among women and older workers. This, by itself, may help explain about one-third of the differences in employment rates between Italy and the other countries. Increases in the education level of the Italian workforce may therefore go a long way in reducing the gap with respect to the rest of the EU.

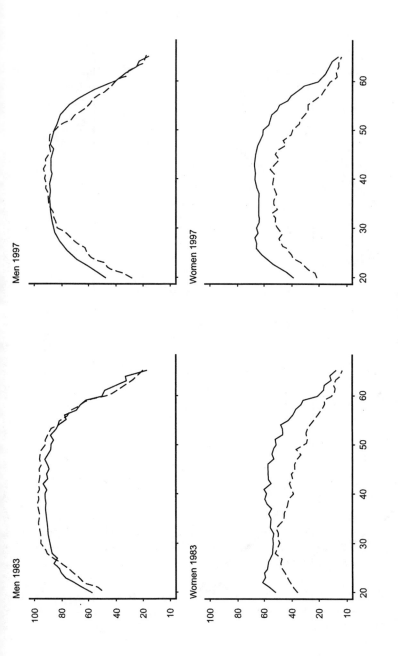

Fig. 7C.2 Employment rates by sex and age in 1983 and 1997: Italy versus EU-11

Sources: Author's calculations based on raw data from the Italian National Statistical Institute (ISTAT) and the Statistical Office of the European Communities (Eurostat).

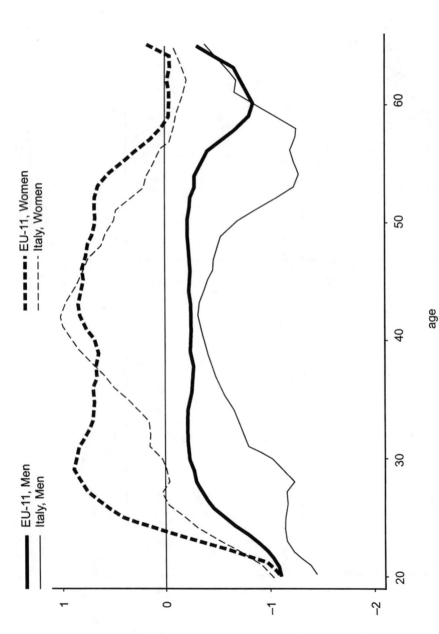

Fig. 7C.3 Average annual variation of employment rates by sex and age, 1983–97: Italy versus EU-11

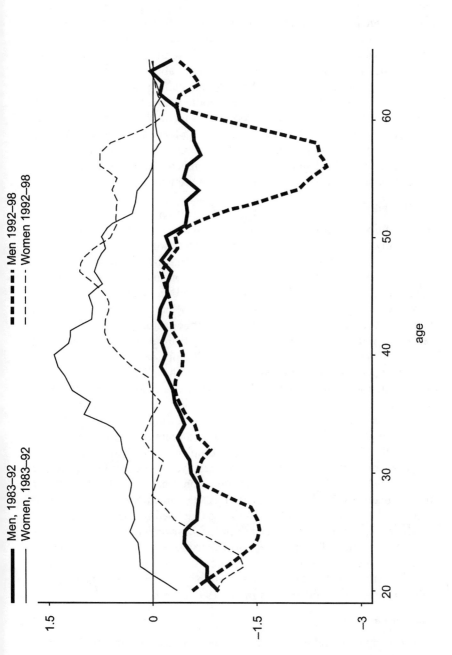

Fig. 7C.4 Average annual variation of employment rates by sex and age in Italy, 1983–92 and 1992–98

Sources: Author's calculations based on raw data from the Italian National Statistical Institute (ISTAT) and the Statistical Office of the European Communities (Eurostat).

As shown in figure 7C.4, the trend toward early retirement intensified after 1992, especially among male workers. Whereas male employment rates in the age range of fifty to sixty have been falling by a little less than 1 percentage point per year during the period 1977–92, during the period 1992–98 they have been falling by about 2 percentage points per year. From the viewpoint of labor market incentives, therefore, the recent process of social security reform has been remarkably unsuccessful, at least so far. As discussed by Daniele Franco, the main reasons for this are the extremely generous transitional rules adopted, coupled with uncertainty about a further tightening of the system and the fear of losing the benefits associated with the current regime. The lack of a similar effect for female workers is due to the presence of strong cohort effects and the fact that early retirement through a seniority pension is open only to workers with uninterrupted work histories, few of whom are women.

Equity and Fairness

Once fully phased-in, the 1995 reform will imply a more transparent and actuarially fair pension system. The reasons are twofold. First, benefits are more clearly linked to contributions and residual life expectancy than was the case with the previous "final-salary" type formulas, thus reducing negative incentive effects on labor supply. Second, most of the workforce is now covered by essentially the same system, thus reducing incentives in favor of certain types of employment (public-sector employees and the self-employed). The system is not completely neutral, however, and several provisions remain that tend to favor the self-employed.

Although equity and fairness of the system have been improved along some dimensions, the burden of the reform has been spread very unevenly. The problem arises because of the different treatment of workers depending on their seniority in 1992. The prereform rules apply, with only small changes, to workers with at least fifteen years of contributions at the end of 1992. These workers have been completely sheltered by the reform process. For workers with fewer than fifteen years of contributions at the end of 1992, the provisions for the transitional period allow the rules of the old regime to hold for the fraction of years in employment under that regime, whereas the remaining fraction is regulated by the new rules. As a result, workers will retire under the pre-1992 regime until about the year 2015. During the following fifteen to twenty years, an increasing fraction of a retiree's pension will be computed on the basis of the new system. It will be around 2030 that a significant number of workers will start retiring fully under the rules introduced by the 1995 reform.

The Second Pillar

In principle, the reform process also envisages a partial move toward a two-pillar system. At least so far, this does entails no reduction in the contribution to the public pay-as-you-go (PAYGO) system, but only a gradual rechanneling of the funds currently accruing to a separate severance-pay fund, known as *Trattamento di fine rapporto* (TFR). The TFR is managed directly by the employer and has been, until now, an important source of cheap credit to firms. Its annual contribution of 7.41 percent of gross earnings is retained by the employer (except for a small fraction that goes to the PAYGO system) and paid out as a lump sum when the worker quits or is laid off. TFR contributions are capitalized at an annual real rate of return equal to 1.5 percent minus 25 percent of the annual inflation rate.

Converting the TFR into a proper pension fund may increase its expected rate of return but has some disadvantages for the worker, mainly the loss of liquidity and the increase in risk. These disadvantages, along with the limited tax incentives and the excessively strong role given to trade unions in promoting pension funds, may explain why so few workers have decided to take this option.

Conclusions

Despite recent reforms, the long-run prospects for the Italian public PAYGO system remain worrisome. Even the official forecasts by the Ministry of Treasury acknowledge that, in the absence of further changes in policy, the ratio of public pension expenditure to GDP will keep increasing till about 2030. Given current demographic trends, stabilizing the expenditure-GDP ratio (as prescribed by the 1995 reform) requires a sharp increase in employment rates and a substantial reduction in the generosity of the system, as measured by the ratio between average pension and labor productivity.

The system designed by the 1995 reform goes a long way in both directions, by reducing the current implicit tax on continuing to work and by cutting benefits with respect to the current level. However, the new system will be introduced only very gradually. Furthermore, the high level of social security contribution represents a powerful negative incentive to employment creation and limits the attractiveness of complementary pension plans. So far, the main positive effect of the reform process has been the slowdown in the growth of the pension-GDP ratio, due largely to severance of the automatic link between productivity and pension growth. There are many signs that the resulting gap between new and old cohorts of pensioners is becoming politically unsustainable.

As argued by Daniele Franco, a faster implementation of the 1995 reform, the fine-tuning of several of its parameters, and the availability of regular and reliable projections to guide policy are necessary. The two unresolved questions are (1) whether this is enough, and (2) whether this is politically viable. The available demographic projections imply that the age of the Italian median voter will increase rapidly: It was between forty-four and forty-five in 1995, and is expected to grow to fifty in the year 2016 and fifty-five in 2032. It is unlikely that this will ease the reform process.

Discussion Summary

Ignazio Visco pointed out that the problems of the Italian pension system are no larger than elsewhere in Europe. He quoted an earlier paper of the discussant, saying, "after all, this is a reform." Visco highlighted the long transition period in the new system as an important point mentioned in the paper. In the transition period, around 40 to 50 percent of the labor force still retires according to the old rules. Visco reported that there is currently a debate about whether everyone has to retire according to the new rules, and he projected that this will be the outcome of the debate. Visco agreed with the author of the paper that the main problem in Italy is the labor market problem and that labor market reforms still have to show their effects if they are introduced at all.

Visco mentioned that the group of self-employed people, which accounts for one third of the labor force, is one of the most vocal groups in the political process. This group had ridiculously low contribution rates. The contribution rates have been raised, but Visco wondered whether this is enough. *Daniele Franco* added that the case of the self-employed is very interesting from a political economy point of view. He reported that the self-employed benefited greatly from the pension system in relative terms up to the 1992 reform. Even in 1990 there was a reform increasing the benefits of the self-employed. In the pension reform process of the 1990s, the self-employed lost with respect to what they were promised in 1990, but still they managed to have some benefits compared to private-sector employees.

Visco also referred to the second pillar in the Italian pension system, the advance-funded severance pay system. He noted that the fund in this system provides only an extremely low rate of return, currently of about 1 percent. He asked about the possibility of transforming the severance pay into open pension funds, which offer a higher rate of return, and of reducing the contribution rates of the firms with a part of the difference in the rates of return. *Daniele Franco* called the 7 percent of earnings paid to severance benefits are a pot of gold that other countries do not have. It was an obvious target for any government policy to develop a supplementary pension, because it was not possible to even consider having the pay-as-you-go (PAYGO) pension, the severance pay benefits, *and* the supplementary pension. Franco said that although in theory it appears to be simple to move money from severance pay to the supplementary pension, in practice it is more difficult to get the supplementary scheme started.

John McHale asked whether there is evidence that people in Italy have increased their savings, either because they do not believe that they will get their promised pension benefits or as a reaction to pension reforms that have take place already. McHale also noted that there does not seem to exist a natural obstacle to the pension system's getting larger if the birth rate declines: A decline in the birth rate leads to higher contributions and to higher benefits in a notional defined contribution (NDC) system, because benefits are linked directly to contributions. In his answer to McHale, *Daniele Franco* said that shocks in the birth rate were not taken into account in the 1995 reforms. He agreed with McHale that discretionary adjustments should not take place on the contribution side but rather on the conversion coefficients that affect future benefit payments.

McHale was puzzled that the second Italian pension reform went through so well, although the reform had such starkly contrasting distributional effects—especially with respect to the distribution between women and men. Franco noted that women lost more than men in the reforms in the 1990s. This is basically because many men can still retire with seniority pensions, for which they need thirty-five years of contributions, whereas women have a more irregular work pattern and typically do not have this opportunity. As a result, the five years' increase in the retirement age over the last eight years mostly affected women. However, the conversion coefficient introduced in 1995 is the same for men and women, although women have a higher life expectancy than men.

Martine Durand wondered why so much emphasis is put on the average retirement age of fifty-seven. Given the fact that Italy has moved to an NDC system, she asked why the retirement age is seen as a problem for the pension system and not as a matter of pure individual choice. *Daniele Franco* responded that some economists argue that the conversion formula is not completely neutral, so that the retirement age matters. In addition, even if coefficients are neutral with respect to the pension system, they are not neutral with respect to the whole public sector. A person retiring at age fifty-seven pays lower taxes but draws higher benefits from services of the public sector. In addition, if workers retire at fifty-seven, there is a higher likelihood that some of these people will ask for welfare benefits.

With respect to the allocation of labor, Durand asked why, if the reform is actually unifying all systems of retirement provision, there still exists the problem of reallocation of labor across industrial sectors.

Martin Feldstein asked whether individuals choose the opportunity to substitute for the severance accounts in any significant way. *Daniele Franco* reported that about 400,000 workers are involved in the new supplementary pension fund, which is about 2 percent of manpower.

Prefunding in a Defined Benefit Pension System
The Finnish Case

Jukka Lassila and Tarmo Valkonen

8.1 Introduction

The pension system of Finland consists of earnings-related pensions that cover almost all paid work, and a residence-based national pension. There has been considerable rivalry, even battle, between these two parts, with the former now the undisputed winner. The Finnish earnings-related system has some rather unique features: It is statutory by law but largely privately run, and it has collected funds to smoothe the contribution increases due to aging in the future. Despite the severe challenges caused by aging, it seems likely that the system will be changed from within, rather than simply replaced with a new system. It is difficult to foresee, however, what the changes will be and how the existing funds and future prefunding will be used.

Under the first comprehensive pension arrangement, the 1937 National Pension Law, the national pension was earnings related. In this arrangement there were personal retirement accounts, which were fully funded. Contributions began in 1939; but then came the war, inflation ate half of the accounts, and unfunded but indexed supplementary benefits became dominant. What was left in the personal accounts was never paid to the contributors,[1] but was used instead as starting capital for a new system,

Jukka Lassila is research director of The Research Institute of the Finnish Economy (ETLA). Tarmo Valkonen is head of unit at ETLA.

1. This decision was, of course, bitterly criticized by many of the contributors. For many others, however, especially those who had participated in the wars in 1939–40 and 1941–44, the accounts were small even nominally, and they felt that more redistribution was needed. Thus, new and bigger PAYGO pensions were lucrative. The decision was also shadowed by other urgent economic questions, such as the gradual abolishment of war-related regulations

enacted by the 1956 National Pension Law. The views of the rural population dominated, and the national pension became a means-tested, flat-rate pension.

The Employees' Pensions Act (TEL) came into force on 1 July 1962. It was created during negotiations between trade unions and employers' organizations, and supported politically by social democrats and conservative parties. To reduce political risks, administration was given to several private pension institutes. During the 1960s there were attempts in the form of law initiatives to combine TEL with the national pension system, but they failed to receive a majority. TEL is now by far the largest private-sector pension system in Finland, and has served as a model for several other earnings-related systems in that country.

After the 1960s, the growing importance of an increasingly united trade union movement was further reflected in the relative roles of the earnings-related and national pension systems (see Niemelä 1994). The former became the dominant pension arrangement, and plans to develop the national pension into a universal retirement provision, without means testing, were abolished.

This article proceeds as follows. Section 8.2 contains a description of the main features of the Finnish pension systems, and section 8.3 describes the current situation and future prospects. Section 8.4 discusses the reforms made during the last decade. Recent policy proposals are surveyed in section 8. 5. Section 8.6 concludes with some views on future changes.

8.2   The Present Old Age Pension System in Finland

The Finnish pension system consists of two main parts: The earnings-related pension system aims to provide retirement income sufficient for consumption comparable both to that of working years and to current workers' consumption. The national pension guarantees a minimum income in cases where the earnings-related pension is absent or insufficient. Both systems are mandatory. Voluntary pensions, whether employer-based or industry-wide supplementary pensions or personal pension arrangements, are of minor importance in Finland.

8.2.1   Statutory Earnings-Related Pension

The statutory earnings-related pension covers almost all paid work. It covers risks related to old age, disability, long-term unemployment of aging workers, and death of family earners.

Every employment contract and self-employment period adds to the

---

and the general strike in 1956, which, in itself, prevented the trade unions and employers from defending the earnings-related accounts in unison.

pension (after age twenty-three). The pensionable wage is aggregated over the last ten years of each contract. The accrued pension right is vested, even when the worker is changing employers or stopping work.

The target level of benefits is 60 percent of wages. This accrues in about forty years: 1.5 percent per year between ages twenty-three and fifty-nine and 2.5 percent per year between sixty and sixty-five. There is no upper absolute limit to benefits, but an upper percentage limit is 60 percent of the highest pensionable earnings. Pensions accrued under different systems are integrated. The disability pension is projected to the retirement age. Pension rights and benefits are index-linked, with 50–50 weights on wages and consumer prices, respectively, during working years and 20–80 weights after age sixty-five.

Contributions are collected from both employers (16.8 percent of wages in 2000) and employees (4.7 percent). Future changes have been agreed to be shared equally between employers and employees (see figs. 8.1 and 8.2).

The private-sector earnings-related system is partially funded. Funding is collective but based on individual pension rights. Currently, the main prefunding rules are as follows:

- *Old age pensions.* A part of old age pension benefits, payable after age sixty-five, is funded for each employee. Funding takes place between ages twenty-three and fifty-four, so only benefits accrued during those years are (partially) funded. The degree of funding is below one-third.[2] Of the 1.5 percent (of wage income) pension right accruing every year between the ages of twenty-three and 54, 0.5 percent is funded. The present value of accrued rights is calculated using a 3 percent discount rate. No funding is done for benefit increases due to indexation. Several additional detailed assumptions and rules are used to calculate the amount to be put in the fund.
- *Disability pensions.* Funding takes place when the case occurs. Funding was full for large firms, but beginning in 2000 the maximum funded share is 80 percent. The disability pension is paid, and funded, only until age sixty-five. After that the pensioner receives the old age pension. Again, no funding is done for benefit increases due to indexation. Similar funding rules apply to the unemployment pensions.
- *Both.* The rate of return also affects the size of the fund; see section 8.2.3.

2. There is no specified target for the share that is funded. Before 1997, funding between the ages of twenty-three and fifty-four was "full," in the sense that, had there been no wage inflation, the 5 percent nominal yield requirement of the funds would have resulted in funds sufficient to pay out (with no PAYGO financing) exactly the amount of benefits one had accrued between the ages of twenty-three and fifty-four. Needless to say, there was inflation both in prices and in wages, and funding was far from full. The changes made in 1997 (described later) were calibrated so that the required funding would stay at the prevailing level; 0.5 percent is a result of that calibration.

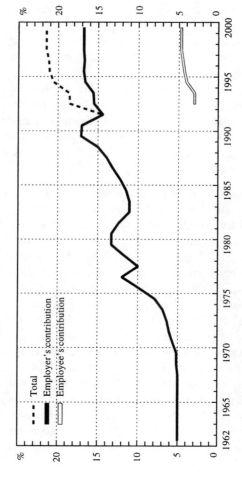

Fig. 8.1 TEL contributions
Source: Data from Central Pensions Institute.

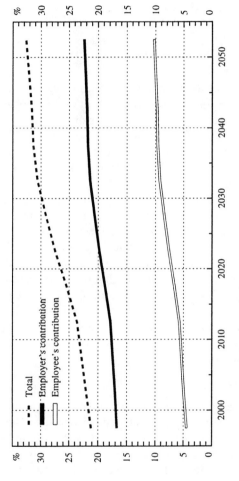

Fig. 8.2 Projected TEL contributions
Source: Lassila and Valkonen (2000b).

The funds are collective: Individual pension benefits do not depend on the existence or yield of funds. Funds affect contributions only. When a person receives pensions after the age of sixty-five, his or her funds are used to pay that part of the pension benefit that was prefunded. The rest comes from the pay-as-you-go (PAYGO) part, the so-called "pooled component" in the contribution rate.

The statutory earnings-related system was created in cooperation with labor market organizations, which are represented in the administrative bodies. The administration is decentralized among several pension institutes. The largest of these are private pension insurance companies and the Local Government Pensions Institution. These institutes collect the contributions, pay the pensions, and invest the retained funds. The Central Pension Security Institute maintains the central register, compiles statistics, and redistributes among the other institutions the pooled component of contributions collected in the private pension scheme.

The labor market organizations occupy at least half of the seats in the administrative bodies of the pension institutes. They also negotiate with the representatives of the central government about the future development of the pension scheme.

The earnings-related pensions in the public sector are very similar to those in the private sector, described above. The amount of annual funding, however, is discretionary and is not formally based on any formula concerning accrued pension rights or future expenditures. The Local Government Pensions Institution, handling the earnings-related pensions for municipal employees, has funds amounting to 137 percent of the sector's annual wage bill in 1999, roughly comparable to the TEL system. The pension fund of the central government is still small, but there is an agreement to raise the funding rate to the same level as in the private sector by the year 2010 (table 8.1 describes the distribution of pension fund assets among the general groups).

8.2.2 National Pension

The residence-based national pension guarantees a minimum pension to those without a sufficient earnings-related pension. The benefits also include survivors' pensions for widows, widowers, and children, housing allowances, care allowances, and veterans' supplements. The benefits are indexed to consumer prices. The national pension system is administered by the Social Insurance Institution (Kela), under the supervision of Parliament.

Before 1996, the basic national pension amount was paid to all pensioners over sixty-five years of age. For new retirees whose earnings-related pensions exceed a certain limit, a national pension is no longer paid, and for those retired before 1996 with a similar earnings-related pension, the

Table 8.1   **Assets of Pension Funds in 1999**

	Amount (in euros)	In Relation to GDP
Private sector	52.4	43
Local government	11.7	10
Central government	2.8	2
Total	67.0	55

Sources: Authors' tabulations from various databases.

basic part of the national pension is gradually reduced and will be abolished in 2001.

8.2.3   Experiences from the Finnish Prefunded Defined Benefit System

The main justification officially presented for partial prefunding was to alleviate the burden due to the aging baby boom generation. The expressed aim was to use the funds to lower the projected peak in the contribution rate. The current population forecasts imply, however, that there will be no marked reduction in pension expenditures after the large cohorts have died. This has created a situation in which there is no general agreement about the future funding rates.

The original reason for funding, however, was not necessarily to serve as a precautionary tool for future aging. Short-term tactical considerations may well have dominated. Employers' representatives could have favored partial funding for two reasons: First, it provided a way to have low actual contributions initially. Unions demanded higher pensions immediately, which would have meant high contributions. Funding allowed raising contributions with only small liquidity effects, because firms were entitled to borrow back most of the funded part of contributions. Second, in the aftermath of the 1956 National Pension Law, there were fears of a political takeover of the earnings-related pension system. Employers thought that trade unions would be more willing to defend the TEL system when there was money in the funds. That turned out to be correct: Even though socialists and communists in general favored national pensions, in trade unions they—along with social democrats—supported TEL.

During the first twenty-five years of the pension scheme, the allocation and even the yield of the funds were strictly regulated. The Insurance Companies Act and the instructions given by the Ministry of Social Affairs and Health restricted the risk content of portfolios by determining how assets with various risk characteristics were considered in the solvency calculations. These regulations were not, however, the most binding. The portfolio allocation was dominated by the privilege of firms to borrow most of the contributions paid. These premium loans were guaranteed mostly by banks and were therefore risk free for the pension institutions. The justification expressed for the low interest rate premium loans was to give preference to the strengthening of the contribution base by promoting investments.

The role of the Bank of Finland as a regulator of monetary and currency policy was also important. The direct methods to affect the pension fund portfolios were to give instructions for lending, to agree with the pension institutions about the lending rate, and to restrict foreign investments to an insignificant amount. Indirectly, the regulations of the central bank and the capital income tax code ensured that the domestic financial markets remained undeveloped and that savings were transmitted from households and the public sector to firms almost totally by promissory note loans. The control of lending rates, together with the high inflation rate, also lowered the real rate of return of the pension funds. Because part of the nominal yield was distributed back to employers in the form of lower contributions, the actual real yield affecting the size of the prefunded amount was negative until the year 1983.

After the liberalization of financial markets at the end of the 1980s, the real interest rate rose in the economy. The demand for loans decreased and the markets of other assets boomed. During the recession in the beginning of 1990s it became evident that the regulatory rules were not in line with the new investment environment. The solvency of the pension institutions was too weak to benefit the higher yield of the growing markets fully.

The investment regulations were amended according to the life assurance directive when Finland joined the European Union (EU; Tuomisto 1999). Another important decision was to join the Economic and Monetary Union (EMU), which allowed international diversification of investments without breaking the rules of uncovered currency positions. The pension system was nevertheless slow to react to the new investment environment, and it was not until 1997 that the new prefunding rules allowed more risky portfolio allocation.[3] In between, there has been a very favorable trend in stock markets, which has not been utilized until lately. The reform reduced the minimum rate of return on the funds and directed extra funds to the solvency margin of the pension institutions for three years. The impacts of the new rules and the growth of stock market prices have raised the share of domestic and foreign stocks in the private-sector pension fund portfolios from 11.9 percent in 1997 to 27.7 percent in 1999.

The new prefunding rules of the old age pensions can be described as follows. The funded component of the pension contribution is determined so as to give the individual a pension right of 0.5 percent of his or her yearly earnings between ages twenty-three and fifty-four. In the calculation

---

3. The earlier nominal minimum yield of 5 percent was also harder to generate by low-risk assets when inflation was subdued.

it is assumed that the observed mortality rates apply and the invested amount yields nominal interest rate of 3 percent. The impacts of inflation and the growth of wages to the final pension are not considered. The actual funding is supported by transferring the investment yield corresponding to the *TEL-calculated interest rate* (5.75 percent in 2000) to the individual's account. The TEL-calculated interest rate is the required rate of return on the invested funds and is determined by the Ministry of Social Affairs and Health. A working group is currently reconsidering whether this yield requirement should be linked to some combination of financial market indexes.

If the yield of the assets is higher than the TEL-calculated interest rate, the pension institution can either use the funds to strengthen its solvency or distribute the surplus to customer employers. The new solvency rules set both a minimum zone and a target zone for solvency. The higher the risks in the portfolio, the higher the required position inside the zone. If solvency of an institution falls below the target zone, the opportunities to distribute the surplus yield to employers are limited.

The supervisory board of a pension fund, in which the social partners are represented, is obliged to draft an investment plan and to supervise its implementation. This plan defines the aims of the investment policy, including, for example, the targeted average yield, diversification, and the security of assets and their convertibility into money. The fund's aims must be in line with the rules outlined in the relevant paragraphs of the Insurance Companies Act. In practice, the investment departments of pension funds have many degrees of freedom to operate within the given limits. The portfolio shares at the end of 1999 were roughly as follows: 41 percent in bonds, 28 percent in stocks, nearly 10 percent in both money market instruments and real estate, and the remainder in investment and premium loans.

The importance of prefunding to the pension system can be evaluated by noting that according to the recent forecasts, when the funds are stabilized at their equilibrium level around the year 2050, the yield will lower the private-sector contribution rate by 5 percentage points. This calculation assumes that the real rate of return on the pension fund assets is 3 percent.

Assuming that the incidence of employers' contributions has been mainly on labor, the mandatory prefunding has increased total saving and thereby investments as well. The efficiency of resource allocation was, however, subject to doubts during the period of strict regulation. Since the liberalization and development of financial markets, the allocation has improved, but the savings-investment link has lost its importance in the small open economy. Nevertheless, the beneficial impacts of saving on national wealth and on the intergenerational distribution of the aging burden remain.

8.3   The Financial Prospects of the Pension System

The overall prospects of the current Finnish pension system are dominated by rapid aging. The ratio of the population aged sixty and older to that aged twenty to fifty-nine is expected to increase from the current 0.35 to 0.66 in 2030. The stochastic population simulations of Alho (1998) challenge even this gloomy base scenario. These simulations, based on previous forecasting errors in fertility, mortality, and migration, show that uncertainty is higher than usually recognized. The 80 percent confidence interval of the age dependency ratio is 0.61–0.79 in 2030. The lower limit (0.61) results mostly from nonincreasing life expectancy, and the upper limit (0.79) from declining fertility and emigration.

The age dependency ratio does not comprehensively describe the ratio of pensioners to employees. The other often-used measure is the economic dependency ratio, which takes into account labor market conditions. Several contradictory trends affect the future labor force participation rate in Finland. First is the expected reduction in the unemployment rate from the current level of 9 percent. Another is the already high female participation rate, which does not allow much potential for improvement. Yet another is the fact that the average retirement age, although expected to rise somewhat, is as low as fifty-nine years and only 10 percent of each cohort retire at the statutory retirement age of sixty-five years.

Furthermore, the pension system is still maturing. The first employees in the private sector have just reached the right to retire with full pension (after contributing for the required number of years to the system), and it will take approximately thirty years until this is possible for all pensioners.

There are also two features that postpone the effects of the beneficial impacts of the recent reforms on pension expenditures. The first is the generous grandfathering rule followed in the reforms. Although most of the privileges in the public-sector scheme were abolished, it was decided that the new, higher retirement age (from sixty-three to sixty-five years) apply fully to the new entrants of this scheme only. Second, the likely positive impacts of a higher return on pension funds, facilitated by the 1997 reform, are not reflected in contributions until the corresponding cohorts retire.

The Central Pension Security Institute calculates long-term scenarios primarily for the private-sector scheme, but also for the public-sector pensions and the national pensions. The latest is published in Klaavo et al. (1999). According to the baseline scenario, the ratio of all pension expenditures to GDP rises from 11.7 percent in 1998 to 16.4 percent in 2034. After that the ratio declines somewhat due to the means testing of the basic pensions, the passing away of the baby boom generation, and the growth of income. The average private-sector pension contribution rate rises from the current 21.5 percent of wages to 32 percent in 2050. During the same period, the private-sector pension funds rise from 132 percent of the corresponding total wage bill to 250 percent in 2050.

Lassila and Valkonen (2000b) show that this baseline scenario is very sensitive to demographics. If the previously mentioned upper-limit (0.79) scenario of the confidence interval of the age ratio is followed, the private-sector contribution rate exceeds 50 percent in 2060. Scenarios with different assumptions exist in abundance. Increasing the retirement age by one year lowers the contribution rate by 1.5–2.0 percentage points. A 1 percent rise in the rate of return on the existing funds would lower (in the short term) the contribution rate by 1.3 percentage points. In the long term, the corresponding reduction would be 2.5 percentage points. If the growth rate in productivity and real wages is 2.0 percent, instead of the baseline assumption of 1.5 percent, the ratio of pension expenditures to wages will decline more than 2 percentage points in the long run (Klaavo et al. 1999). The contribution rate would decline by half of that amount under current funding rules.

8.4   Recent Reforms

Until the severe recession in the beginning of the 1990s, the trend in pension reforms was to raise the benefit level and to loosen the rules for eligibility to early pensions. The recession created an urgent need to cut labor costs both in the private and in the public sector and emphasized the problems of long-term sustainability of the pension system. In addition to the necessary expenditure cuts, the following reforms were aimed at several other objectives, such as a more stable ratio of pension expenditures to total wages during business cycles, a higher actual retirement age, and a higher yield on pension funds.

The first policy reaction was to introduce the employees' pension contribution and to agree that future hikes in the contribution rate would be divided 50–50 between the employers and employees. Furthermore, the generous benefit rules of the public-sector pension system were scaled down in line with those prevailing in the private sector. Later, the pension benefits were cut by tightening several times the rules for early retirement and by introducing a bent pension index. In the bent index, the weight of earnings is smaller and the weight of consumption prices larger after age sixty-five.

The introduction of the bent index implies that the discussed possibility of using the index system as means of adjusting the expenditures to variations in total wages was ruled out and that preference was given to expenditure cuts. The objective of dampening the impacts of business cycles was not, however, totally rejected. The labor market parties agreed in 1997 on the introduction of buffer funds both in the unemployment insurance system and in the private pension system. The special buffer reserve in the pension system is about 2.5 percent of the corresponding total wages.

Another major reform during the latter part of the decade was a shift in the funding rules. The separation of pension contribution determination from the same-period yield of the pension funds provided an opportunity for a more efficient portfolio allocation. Because the funding rate in the new system depends partly on the yield of the investments, the real value of the assets can be sheltered more efficiently from inflation than in the old fixed interest rate system. This becomes true if the TEL-calculated interest rate follows market rates.

There is a wide consensus that workers should not retire as early as they now do. The average retirement age is currently somewhat below sixty years. For instance, the current government aims to increase the average age of exit from the labor force by two to three years in the long term. There is a National Program on Aging Workers for the years 1998–2002, organized by the ministries of social affairs and health, labor, and education, aiming to help older workers to stay in work. The measures include increasing the physical and mental condition of aged workers, designing specific services to be provided by employment agencies, and in general making attitudes more favorable to elderly workers. Moreover, the economic incentives to retire early have been reduced, as discussed above.

These reforms have had a profound impact on the pension expenditure scenarios. Table 8.2 summarizes the main features of the Finnish pension reforms. Table 8.3 presents in more detail the contributions of the various reforms to the total 8.4 percentage point cut in expenditures in the long term.

8.5   Proposals and Discussion

8.5.1   Employers' Proposed Reduction in Contributions

Although there seems to be no disagreement about the necessity to raise the contribution rate in the future, a serious discussion concerning whether to decrease the current rate for a few years has emerged. The employer side proposed a reduction in the fall of 1999. The size of the measure for the year 2000 was not specified, but it could have been about one percentage point.

The proposed cut is based on two things. First, the cut could be seen simply as a result of following current rules. There is room for the contribution decrease because the EMU buffer stock fund target (2.5 percent of the respective annual wage bill), agreed upon in 1997, has been reached more quickly than originally planned. Second, if the reduction would not immediately result in wage increases of equal magnitude, labor costs

Table 8.2   The Main Features of the Pension Reforms, 1990–2000

Year Implemented	Measure Undertaken
1990	Eligibility rules for surviving spouse's pension were tightened.
1993	Employee's pension contribution was introduced.
	The public-sector pension scheme was curtailed in line with the rules of the private-sector scheme: The retirement age was raised from 63 to 65 years and the yearly accrual rate of pensions was lowered from 2.2 percent to 1.5 percent. For new employees the replacement rate drops from 66 to 60 percent. For current workers the rate will be somewhere in between.
1994	The index adjustment (1.3 percent) in pensions was not implemented.
	Agreement to divide the future hikes in the contribution rate equally between employers and employees was reached.
	The decision was made to deduct the employee's pension contribution from the pensionable wage.
	The minimum age for individual early retirement pensions was raised from 55 to 58 years and was lowered for part-time pensions from 60 to 58 years.
	The accrual rate for employees aged 60–64 was raised from 1.5 percent to 2.5 percent.
1996	The way in which pensionable earnings are calculated was changed so that the wages of the last 10 years in every employment contract are used, instead of the last 4 years. The implementation has been gradual; the transition period ends in 2005.
	The accrual rate for the post-contingency period in early retirement pensions was lowered from 1.5 percent to 1.2 percent if the retiree is 50–60 years old, and to 0.8 percent if the retiree is 60–65 years old.
	A two-index system was introduced. During working age an index consisting of an average of consumer prices and wages (halfway

(continued)

Table 8.2 (continued)

Year Implemented	Measure Undertaken
	index) is used, as earlier, but in the index of paid pensions the weight of wages was reduced from 0.5 to 0.2 and the weight of consumer prices was raised from 0.5 to 0.8 (bent index). When calculating either of the indexes the change in employee's pension contribution is reduced from the change in earnings.
	Means testing for eligibility to the national pension was extended.
1997	The rules of pension funding were changed. The link between current contributions and the current yield of pension funds was cut. This enables an increase in risky investments without changing the forward-looking funding principle.
	The lower age limit for additional days in unemployment benefits was raised from 55 to 57 years. This means, in practice, that the long-term unemployed can receive earnings-related income transfers either as unemployment allowances or as unemployment pensions from age 55 to 65. This "unemployment tube" began earlier, from the age of 53.
1998	The lower age limit for part-time pension was lowered temporarily from 58 to 56 years.
2000	The unemployment pension was cut.
	The prefunding of unemployment pensions was increased and the prefunding of the disability pensions was reduced in order to equalize the costs for the employer of using these alternative channels to reduce its labor force.
	The lower age limit for individual early retirement pensions was raised from 58 to 60 years.

Sources: See table 8.1.

Table 8.3   The Expenditure Impacts of the Main Pension Policy Measures (1990s)

Measure	Implementation	Change in Expenditures[a]
Surviving spouses' pensions	1990	−0.8
Public-sector pensions	1993	−2.7
Eligibility ages	1994	−0.7
Pensionable wages	1996	−0.4
Accrual rate for the post-contingency period	1996	−1.5
Bent index	1996	−1.5
Means testing of national pension	1996	−0.8
Total		−8.4

Source: Central Pension Security Institute (1999).
[a]As percent of total wages in 2030.

would be lower and the still-sizeable rate of unemployment could be reduced. This would also benefit the pension system.

The employee representatives have opposed the cut. Trade unions believe that the inevitable sharp increase in contributions, after the few years with lower rates, would strengthen the case for benefit reductions. The rate reduction did not take place for the year 2000. Instead, the social partners agreed that the need for funding shall be assessed before the rates are reduced. The issue reappeared in the fall of 2000, and the social partners agreed to suggest to the Ministry of Social Affairs and Health a cut of 0.4 percentage points. These suggestions are seldom turned down.

8.5.2 Ceiling for Pensions

An absolute ceiling for earnings-related pensions is recurrently, although not often, suggested for both cost-saving and distributive reasons. The system responds by saying that the ceiling would increase private voluntary arrangements, which would increase total costs. The effects of a pension ceiling on income distribution may also be counterintuitive. Palme (1999) shows that although the distribution of pensions in Finland is very wide in international comparison, the overall distribution of pensioners' income is one of the narrowest in Europe. He contrasts the Finnish case to those of countries that try to narrow the distribution of public pensions, thus leaving more room for the private pensions market and eventually having a more uneven distribution in total income.[4] High-income earners in Finland are satisfied with the current earnings-related pension system because it has no ceiling, and resort to private arrangements only to a minor degree.

4. Palme argues against means testing, but the same arguments can be used against pension ceilings.

8.5.3   Bent Index

Pension benefits are index-linked to both wages and consumer prices. After age sixty-five a bent index is used: The weight of earnings in the pension index is reduced from 0.5 to 0.2 and the weight of consumption prices increased from 0.5 to 0. 8. This "bending" reduces the increase in benefits that results from rising real wages. The bent index was introduced in 1996 and remains a disputed political issue. Pensioners' organizations speak of age discrimination and create political pressure, but their efforts seem unlikely to change matters. A law initiative was signed by 155 of the 200 members of Parliament in 1997, aimed at abolishing the bent index and returning to the use of a halfway index for all pensioners. Although there seemed to be a clear majority, Parliament managed with little difficulty to postpone the issue, and the initiative was automatically dismissed when a new Parliament was elected in 1999. The cost-saving effect of the bent index, compared to that of the halfway index, is about 1.5 percent of total wages (see table 8.3).

8.5.4   The Active Population's Share

Administrators of the pension systems argue that increasing pension expenditures and rising contributions will not necessarily be a problem. An oft-used argument is that the increase in productivity will probably be rapid enough to allow the living standards of the working-age population to increase, despite the growing share of the elderly. The opponents argue that growth in incomes does not necessarily make high contribution rates any more attractive.

8.5.5   Propositions by Hautala and Tuukkanen

The main ideas of the pension reform suggested by Hautala and Tuukkanen (1999) are to strengthen the link between pension contributions and benefits, to reduce the options for early retirement pensions, and to introduce an individual pension account for middle-aged workers. In the proposed pension scheme, old age pension contributions are paid entirely by employees, benefits are based on paid contributions, the retirement age is flexible, and early retirement reduces pensions actuarially. The system is financed mainly by the PAYGO principle until age fifty-four. After that, the employee moves to a fully funded, defined contribution pension scheme. The funds in the accounts are invested collectively, which reduces risks and administrative costs. The transition to the new individual account system requires little new financing because the labor force participation rate in that age group is low. The average retirement age is expected to rise markedly due to the improved incentives and due to the abolition of the current unemployment pension system. The reform is aimed at increasing efficiency and equity in both the earnings-related pension scheme and the unemployment insurance system.

8.5.6   Information Account Proposed by Lundqvist

The Lundqvist (1999) proposition takes as a starting point the diversified needs and the willingness of individuals to secure their old age incomes. Therefore, employees should be able to get information continuously about the amount of accrued pension entitlements in both the mandatory and voluntary schemes. The created information system also would make the links between contributions and benefits more transparent. According to the proposition, it is also necessary to enhance the possibilities to save for old age outside the earnings-related pension scheme.

8.5.7   Simplification of the Pension System

Representatives of the pension institutions and labor-market parties are currently discussing a package of measures aiming to simplify the pension system and to foster its transparency. The initiative for the reform can be traced back to the present government's program. Most of the issues in this discussion have already come up some time earlier. The main ideas are to improve the link between benefits and contributions and to simplify the administration of the overall pension system by unifying the rules of various private-sector pension schemes. In more detail, the proposed changes are to unify the accrual rate from age eighteen to age sixty-five to be 1.5 percent of corresponding wages; to use the wages of the whole working career to determine the pensionable wage; and the link the amount of early retirement pensions to the length of the working career. The initial idea is to implement the reform so that it does not change the amount of future expenditures. The adjusting variable is possibly indexation during working age, which could be made more generous because the other elements of the reform generate savings.

The outcome of the preliminary discussions is unclear because, even though industrial workers support the ideas, clerical workers and others with long employment records or with seniority rules in wage determination (or both) are against some of the proposed changes.

8.5.8   Adjustment of the Benefits and Prefunding
as a Reaction to Demographic Trends

The reformed Swedish pension system reduces pension benefits if life expectancy increases. The updated Finnish population forecasts assume that life expectancy will continue to rise for several decades, implying higher pension expenditures. These two starting points have generated a discussion about whether the Finnish pension system should adopt a similar life expectancy adjustment (see Lindell 1999).

Another suggestion is to link the prefunded amount of contributions in Finland to current birth rates. This idea is based on the observation that, from the point of view of pension expenditures, uncertainty about future birth rates is much more important than uncertainty about longevity.

Therefore, intergenerational insurance against unfavorable trends in the birth rate is necessary (see Lassila and Valkonen 1999). The corresponding adjustment on the benefits side could be, for example, indexation of the pensions to total wages (see Lassila and Valkonen 2000a).

8.6 Conclusions

The statutory earnings-related pension system has a strong position in Finland. It is generally accepted and widely supported. Besides its basic role of providing retirement income, it gives economic power to labor market organizations. It is flexible in the sense that changes have been (and are) made often. Its financial position is good in international comparison, due especially to partial prefunding and the high yield on these funds in recent years.

The other main part of the Finnish pension system, the national pension, also has an undisputed role. It provides basic subsistence for those with insufficient or no earnings-related pension. Thus, it is clearly secondary to the earnings-related pension. Its size may diminish relatively in the future, depending on how the concept of "basic subsistence" will be interpreted politically.

It seems likely that in the future, reforms will be made within current systems rather than through the establishment of new systems. The developments in the 1990s have created confidence that changes can be made when required. On the other hand, this positive attitude may reduce precautionary and far-sighted policies such as increasing prefunding.

Voluntary pensions have only a small role in Finland at this time. It is likely that supplementary pensions will become more common. This may have far-reaching consequences, because TEL cannot offer many choices even if in the future it would like to, due to EU competition rules. TEL is now an accepted exception in competition, but probably cannot expand the limits. Within TEL, more efficiency is sought.

Contributions will rise in the future. Although prefunding makes the Finnish position better than that of many European countries facing the aging problem, it may be that the contribution increase required to keep current benefit promises are deemed too high. The question, then, is how much and in which way the benefits will be reduced.

Partial pension funding has increased the domestic saving rate, thereby contributing markedly to the relatively high investment rate in Finland. However, the previous investment policy of the funds, which was linked to the then-strongly regulated financial system, may not have reached the standards of efficient resource allocation. Furthermore, the real yield generated by the funds was negative during the periods of high inflation rates.

Furthermore, adjustment to the new investment environment has been slow. Therefore, the possible benefits of a virtuous circle of increasing profitable investments, developing financial markets, and high investment yields were largely missed. With better coordination of financial market liberalization and reforms in solvency regulations and other investment rules, the pension funds could have profoundly contributed to the development of financial markets. Currently, there is no lack of financial resources in the small open economy; therefore the saving-investment link is weaker. The existing pension funds use modern investment-allocation methods and the funds' yields follow the market indexes rather closely.

One of the future challenges of the system is how to increase competition while ensuring the long-term solvency of the institutions. There are positive returns to scale in both the insurance and investment operations, which tends to lead to centralization. At the moment, the main means of competition is the repayment of pension contributions to the customer firms, facilitated by successful investment policy. If the smaller institutions cannot keep up in the competition, they will lose customers. Another related challenge is how to determine the minimum required rate of return on investments so that it is as high as possible, while still leaving room for a sufficient number of institutions to survive and develop.

Appendix
Old Age Pension Prefunding Rules in the TEL System

We first describe the prefunding of the average employee's future old age pension benefits, and how the fund is run down in the retirement age. Then we aggregate to the total population level and give a simplified presentation of the dynamics of total funds, the mechanism of contribution determination, and the use of the yield of funds.

Prefunding at the Individual Level

Every year, a new pension right accrues for each worker, and a part of the present value of the right is prefunded. For someone already retired, part of the money prefunded in his or her working years is used to pay a part of his or her pension. Equations (1) and (2), below, describe these funding rules for the average worker and pensioner in each age group i in period t. The gross labor income of the average worker in age group i is denoted by g.

(1) $$h_{t,i} = a \frac{\sum_{j=65}^{M} kg_{t,i} S_{t,ij}}{(1 + r^h)^{j-i}} \qquad i = 23, \ldots, 54$$

individual accumulation rule

$$(2) \qquad w_{t,i} = \sum_{j=23}^{54} h_{t-i+j,j}(1 + r^{\text{TEL}})^{i-j} \qquad i = 65, \dots, M$$

individual decumulation rule

According to equation (1), a share a of the present value of the pension right accruing in period t to workers aged twenty-three to fifty-four is put in the funds. The present value includes all old age pension years from sixty-five to a maximum age denoted by M. The labor income g creates a pension right for each year from age sixty-five onward. For prefunding purposes, the magnitude of this right is evaluated ignoring all future changes due to wage or price developments. Thus the value of the right is simply kg for each retirement year. Currently, k is 1.5 percent.

The discount factor includes both an interest rate and survival probabilities. The fund rate of interest, used in this calculation, is administratively set. We denoted it by r^h. The term S in equation (1) describes the expected effects of mortality. Only a share S of those in age group i in period t are expected to be alive in age j.

Equation (2) states that, for a retired person, the amount prefunded earlier (when the current pensioner was between ages twenty-three and fifty-four) for periods t's pension, and the interest accrued to those funds, is used to pay a part of the person's pension (the rest comes from the PAYGO part). The interest accrued is calculated using another administratively set interest rate, the so-called *TEL-calculated interest rate* (assumed constant here for a simpler exposition).

Equations (1) and (2) are, in practice, interesting only to pension companies because they are used in calculating the companies' pension liabilities. Each company is responsible for the prefunded parts of the pensions of those insured in the company. The companies are jointly responsible for the rest of the pensions. Of course, the equations are also important for the aggregate dynamics of the pension system, especially for the level and the time path of the contribution rate.

Aggregate Pension Funds and the Contribution Rate

The total amount of new funding in period t is obtained by multiplying the average individual funding in age group i, described in equation (1), by the number of workers n in the age group, and summing over all age groups. This is done in equation (3). The total amount withdrawn from funds is obtained analogously (equation [4]). Two other aggregates are defined in equations (5) and (6): the total wage bill, from which the pension contributions are collected, and the total amount of old age earnings-related pension expenditure, where the average individual pensions are denoted by z.

$$(3) \qquad A_t = \sum_{i=23}^{54} n_{t,i} h_{t,i} \qquad \text{new funding total}$$

(4) $$W_t = \sum_{i=65}^{M} n_{t,i} w_{t,i}$$ withdrawals from funds, total

(5) $$G_t = \sum_{i=14}^{64} n_{t,i} g_{t,i}$$ contribution base (wage bill)

(6) $$Z_t = \sum_{i=65}^{M} n_{t,i} z_{t,i}$$ total old-age pension expenditure

The dynamics of the total amount of funds, H, follow from equation (7), and the contribution rate is determined as a residual from equation (8).

(7) $$H_t = H_{t-1}(1 + r^{\text{TEL}}) + A_t - W_t$$

(8) $$(\tau_t^I + \tau_t^e)G_t = Z_t + A_t - W_t$$

The employer's contribution rate (τ^I) and the employee's contribution rate (τ^e) must bring receipts sufficient to cover the part of pension expenditure that does not come from withdrawals from funds, plus new funding. The employer's contribution rate is higher than the employee's, but they move hand in hand.

Actually, employers usually pay less than the nominal contribution rate. If the actual yield on funds exceeds the TEL-calculated interest rate, the difference is paid back to the employers. This yield difference varies among pension companies and is the main factor in their competition for customers, which are firms and other employers providing pension insurance for their workers. The employer's ex post contribution rate $\hat{\tau}^I$ is determined according to equation (9).

(9) $$\hat{\tau}_t^I = \tau_t^I - H_{t-1}(r - r^{\text{TEL}})$$

The presentation above is still simplified. We have ignored disability and unemployment pensions and the funds related to them, and other transfers the pension system pays.

References

Alho J. 1998. *A stochastic forecast of the population of Finland.* Statistics Finland, Review no. 1998/4. Helsinki.

Central Pension Security Institute. 1999. TELA-TIETOA newsletter, June.

Hautala, U., and J. Tuukkanen. 1999. The Finnish application of individual accounts (in Finnish). In *Personal social accounts: An efficient way to finance social insurance?* ETLA Series B, no. 157, ed. J. Lassila and T. Valkonen, 113–70. Helsinki: Research Institute of the Finnish Economy (ETLA).

Klaavo, T., J. Salonen, E. Tenkula and R. Vanne. 1999. *Pension expenditures, funds and contributions to the year 2050.* Central Pension Security Institute Papers no. 1999:29. Helsinki: Central Pension Security Institute.

Lassila, J., and T. Valkonen. 1999. *Pension prefunding and ageing in Finland* (in Finnish). Central Pension Security Institute Study no. 1999:2, and ETLA Series B no. 158. Helsinki: Central Pension Security Institute.

———. 2000a. *Pension indexing, longevity adjustment, and ageing in Finland* (in Finnish). Central Pension Security Institute Study no. 2000:2, and ETLA Series B, no. 172. Helsinki: Central Pension Security Institute.

———. 2000b. Pension prefunding, ageing, and demographic uncertainty. ETLA Discussion Paper no. 741. Helsinki: Research Institute of the Finnish Economy (ETLA).

Lindell, C. 1999. *Life expectancy increases: How about retirement age?* (in Finnish). Central Pension Security Institute Report no. 1999:18. Helsinki: Central Pension Security Institute.

Lundqvist, B. 1999. The Finnish individual pension accounts: A question of will or a necessity? (in Finnish). In *Personal social accounts: An efficient way to finance social insurance?* ETLA Series B, no. 157, ed. J. Lassila and T. Valkonen, 113–70. Helsinki: Research Institute of the Finnish Economy (ETLA).

Niemelä, H. 1994. *The development of Finland's overall pension system* (in Finnish, with English summary), 2nd ed. Helsinki: Publications of the Social Insurance Institution.

Palme, J. 1999. Pensions and the fight against poverty and inequality in old age. In *Economic survey of Europe* no. 3, 80–82. Geneva: United Nations Economic Commission for Europe.

Tuomisto, T. (ed.). 1999. *The Finnish statutory earnings-related pension scheme for the private sector.* Helsinki: Central Pension Security Institute.

Comment   Reijo Vanne

Jukka Lassila and Tarmo Valkonen have done pioneering work on models of overlapping generations in the Finnish economy. The sustainability and intergenerational effects of the pension system have been among their subjects of research. During the course of their work, they have acquired a profound knowledge of the Finnish pension system, and I regard their text as a good description of both the system and its problems, and of the reform proposals presented. Below, I will introduce a few additional points, mainly on the history of the ideas and arguments behind the present system.

Although the Finnish earnings-related pension system is based on agreement among the social partners, it has formally been statutory from the very beginning. However, private companies and funds run the schemes. In the national accounts, the pension institutions and their assets are nowadays included in the general government figures. Nevertheless, pension funds make their own decentralized investment decisions, like any other private funds.

Pension reform ideas and their acceptance have typically come up in

Reijo Vanne is chief economist at the Central Pension Security Institute in Helsinki, Finland.

negotiations among representatives of the social partners. Technically, the design of the system has been the responsibility of mathematicians and lawyers; economists have played a minor role.

Before the 1990s, the driving forces behind reforms were concepts of the Nordic-type welfare state. During the 1990s, these forces were, as the authors state, the recession and a growing awareness of an aging population.

The Original Ideas of an Original System

The authors offer a good presentation of the history of the Finnish pension system, which consists of the national and the earnings-related pension schemes. However, some of the first ideas of the earnings-related system and contemporary conditions may be worth mentioning. The committee that designed the prefunded defined benefit pension system worked from 1956 to 1960 under the chairmanship of Professor Teivo Pentikäinen (Report of the Pension Committee 1960).

The topical problem that had to be solved was poor and high-risk living standards in old age and in the event of disability. I suppose this was the reason behind the two main features of the plan. First, it was not possible to wait for decades until the first sufficiently high benefits could be paid. This fact recommended a pay-as-you-go (PAYGO) solution. Second, the designers emphasized that the fundamental purpose of a pension plan is to guarantee a targeted living standard after retirement. This view recommended a defined benefit system.

The committee also dealt with the issue of intergenerational distribution in the spirit of overlapping generations and possible political majorities in the future. It stated that a fully funded system would not sustain any intergenerational redistribution or political tension. Rather, the long transition period and the committee's view of the risks of the fund returns led them to recommend only partial funding. Inflation was regarded as the main threat to the real value of the funds. This view should be understood against a background of the regulated markets of that time. Also, thoughts related to the later Aaron's principle (Aaron 1966) were presented. The workforce would be expanding in future years due to the baby boomers, although the total fertility rate was declining rapidly.

Lassila and Valkonen state that prefunding is officially seen as a vehicle for smoothing the effects of baby boom generations on contribution rates. It is true that a couple of common views in Finland during, say, the last twenty-five years have been that prefunding is due to baby boomers and that funding should be a transitory phase. In spite of increasing longevity (which has either materialized or is expected) and other factors that recommend continued prefunding, this view is still widely shared in Finland, although not among experts. However, the baby boomer problem was not originally the main argument for partial prefunding, and nowadays better arguments are clearly available again.

The committee noted that no decent market for voluntary pension schemes had emerged and the fact that the advantage of the first generation in a PAYGO system may make later generations withdraw from the system. It therefore recommended a statutory scheme.

The Main Reforms before the 1990s

The real growth rate of the Finnish economy was fairly high in the 1960s and 1970s. The working-age population, productivity, and the wage sum were growing rapidly. There seemed to be room for a rise in the living standard of the elderly. The targeted replacement ratio was raised from 40 to 60 percent in 1975. Naturally, this had to be done by lowering the funding rate and by increasing the PAYGO part of the implicit liabilities. At the time of the decision, a few peaks and valleys had just been reached: an all-time low in the fertility rate, and all-time high in the growth rate for human capital in terms of expected real earnings due to the age structure, and a bottoming-out of relative oil prices. It appeared that the target level was too ambitious. The contribution level more than doubled in the 1970s, and the index link between pension benefits and accrued rights to the real wage level was reduced to 50 percent from the former 100 percent.

Rapid economic growth and changes in economic structure resulted in depreciation of the skills of aging workers in certain industries. The educational level of the older generations was very poor compared with that of younger generations. I suppose that the magnitude of this difference is one of the world records held by Finnish society. The pension system based on support form the social partners was in a sense a natural agent for internalizing the costs of human capital depreciation, and early retirement legislation was passed in the 1970s and 1980s.

At the beginning of the 1980s, the national pension scheme was thoroughly overhauled. Up until then, the benefits had been means tested against the total incomes of the beneficiaries. Since then, reform benefits have been means tested against the earnings-related pension benefits.

The problem of an aging population has been well known, at least since the beginning of the 1980s. The first exhaustive, long-run social expenditure projections had been presented in 1980 (Report of the Working Group for Evaluating the Expenditures and Goals of Social Security 1980). A mechanical projection based on a deterministic population forecast is still the most popular method for approaching the problem of aging populations all over the world. Even with hindsight, one cannot find the reason that the issue of aging populations was not emphasized when the decisions were made.

The Recent Past and Recent Future Projections

Lassila and Valkonen give a clear picture of the economic and demographic background, and of the nature and extent of the reforms in the 1990s.

Since 1994, the real annual growth rate of the Finnish economy has been nearly 5 percent, on average; the average real returns on the pension funds have been even higher, at 7–8 percent, although pension institutions have held low-risk portfolios. If the recent productivity growth rates and rates of return were those of the stationary state of the economy, we would not need to raise contribution rates by the year 2050 according to the baseline population forecast, even if ever-increasing longevity were included.

Although the present contribution rate of 21.5 percent has not been an obstacle to rapid growth, in the event of modest real returns we will have to raise contribution rates. According to the projections of the Central Pension Security Institute (Klaavo et al. 1999) as well as those of Lassila and Valkonen (1999), a balanced path can be found with (for example) a real return rate of 3 percent, a labor productivity growth rate of 1.5 percent, and a contribution rate rising to 32 percent by the year 2050. The risk is that the calculations underestimate the growth slowdown or the political effects of raising contribution rates, not to mention the risk included in the population forecasts described by Lassila and Valkonen.

The funds' rate of return has a crucial role to play in defining the funding rate and thus the future contribution rates. The funds are run mainly by private companies and foundations; investment decisions are made by the portfolio managers of these institutions, while in the national accounts the wealth of funds running statutory schemes is included in the general government coffers. Finland is thus one of the very few countries in which the net financial wealth of the general government is positive. I expect public net financial wealth at the end of the year 2000 to be approximately 50 percent of the year's gross domestic product (GDP). Generational accounting with 1995 as the base year showed that the net intertemporal liabilities of the Finnish general government were among the highest in Europe, 2.50 times the 1995 GDP (Feist et al. 1999). Using the year 2000 as the base year, the net liabilities are no more than 1.25 times the 2000 GDP according to my estimate. The reasons behind the improvement are forced saving to pension funds, high returns, expenditure cuts, and favorable economic development.

Advantages of a Mixed System

First, mixed decision making has worked well so far. The social partners have designed the reforms, but the political decision makers have also accepted them and passed the laws. The prerequisite for the success of this procedure is that both social partners have an interest in taking part in the process. With respect to fiscal-policy decision making, the Finnish pension system is also a mixed one. Both rules and discretionary decision making have been present. Lassila and Valkonen propose to link benefits or contributions to longevity or fertility rates. These proposals give more weight to rules compared with the present procedure, in which contribution rates are decided annually and longevity is to be managed by adjusting benefits and employers' costs so that incentives to continue working are strong enough.

Second, for several reasons there would not have been any opportunity to accumulate wealth to cover the liabilities of the aging population if the funds had been run by public institutions. It is very unlikely that political decision makers could have resisted the temptation to raise present expenditures or cut present taxes. Finally, it would have been unacceptable for politicians or the authorities to manage such vast wealth.

Third, partial prefunding represents a kind of risk sharing, in which the explicit part of the liabilities is covered by financial capital and the implicit part by human capital (i.e., by the PAYGO part of contributions). A mixed strategy may be a good one, for example, when it is unclear whether the benefits of the "new economy" will materialize in human capital or financial capital returns.

References

Aaron, H. 1966. The social insurance paradox. *Canadian Journal of Economics and Science* 32 (3): 371–74.

Feist, K., B. Raffelhüschen, R. Sullström, and R. Vanne. 2000. Finland: Macroeconomic turnabout and intergenerational redistribution. In *Generational accounting in Europe, European Economy Series, Reports and Studies* no. 1999:6, pp. 163–78. Brussels: *European Commission Directorate-General for Economic and Financial Affairs.*

Klaavo, T., J. Salonen, E. Tenkula, and R. Vanne. 1999. *Pension expenditures, funds and contributions to the year 2050.* Central Pension Security Institute Paper no. 1999:29. Helsinki: Central Pension Security Institute.

Lassila, J., and T. Valkonen. 1999. *Pension prefunding and aging in Finland* (in Finnish). Central Pension Security Institute Study no. 1999:2 and ETLA, B:158. Helsinki.

Pension Committee. 1960. Report of the Pension Committee. Committee Reports no. 11 (in Finnish).

Working Group. 1980. Report of the Working Group for Evaluating the Expenditures and Goals of Social Security (in Finnish). *Finnish Journal of Social Policy* 3:1–80.

Discussion Summary

According to *Horst Siebert,* a remarkable feature of the Finnish pension system is that social partners were able to build up a sufficient pension fund and that they did not use the fund for their own purposes. He asked whether there is any secret behind this outcome. *Georges de Menil* pointed out in this respect that in 1956 the government took money from the pension fund. He asked why this might not be a likely outcome again. *Jukka Lassila* answered by noting that it is not easy to find the secret behind decision making in the Finnish pension system, because the process of decision making is not clearly established but has come out of practice. The Finnish system appears to be rather effective right now, but a situation like that in 1956 is not totally inconceivable. Lassila interpreted the Finnish system as a division of labor between the political parties and the social partners, in which decisions on the pension system are separated from other political decisions. However, some kind of political consensus between the social partners and the main political parties is necessary in his view. *Reijo Vanne* added that in the beginning of the reforms the social partners did not want to rely on the state and tried to keep the state away from the pension system. This may also explain why the social partners made their decisions so rapidly, because they feared state intervention if they did not come to an agreement.

Martin Feldstein inquired about the statement of the authors that the pension system gave the trade unions more power. Feldstein wanted to know in which sense this was true. *Tarmo Valkonen* responded that the power of the social partners mainly results from the tripartite decision making in the development of the pension system, and from the seats in the administration of the pension institutes.

Laurence J. Kotlikoff asked the discussant whether he has redone the generational accounting for Finland recently and how the results have changed. *Reijo Vanne* responded that the generational accounts have not been redone yet, but his preliminary guess is that the true public debt including social security has declined from 2.5 times the GDP in 1995 to 1.5 times the GDP in 2000.

A. Lans Bovenberg asked whether there is any evidence for Finland that low income earners are supplying less labor as a consequence of means testing. He regarded this as an important issue, because there is a great deal of pressure in many countries to target pension funds to lower income levels, and the key question is whether this leads to more distortions. In his answer, *Jukka Lassila* noted that most people do not understand the workings of the pension system, so that the labor supply disincentives resulting from the integration of the national pensions into the earnings-related pensions are probably not very high. However, the disincentive effects will be more important if people become aware of the high marginal tax effects of the pensions. He added that work incentives for low-income earners are generally very low, because many transfer systems are means tested and have high marginal tax rates of more than 100 percent in some cases.

A. Lans Bovenberg wondered whether the public in Finland is concerned about the increasing level of equity investments of pension funds, because this might lead to problems of politicization of the equity holdings. *Assar*

Lindbeck estimated that pension fund holdings make up only 5 or 10 percent of the Finnish stock market so that their influence should be rather small. *Jukka Lassila* added that the increasing share of equity holdings of Finnish pension funds results from the increases in the prices of the equities and not from new investments in equities. In addition, a large part of equity holdings of the pension funds is held in foreign stocks. *Tarmo Valkonen* emphasized the importance of investments in new information technologies, which have yielded a great deal in Finland. According to *Reijo Vanne,* the pension funds follow a strategy of passive portfolio investing rather than strategic investing, so that their influence in the economy is also limited by this fact.

9

Pension Reform
Issues in the Netherlands

Jeroen J. M. Kremers

9.1 Introduction

The pension system of the Netherlands consists of three pillars: (1) a state-financed basic pension at minimum wage level, supplemented by (2) a collective pension financed by employees and employers typically at a level of 70 percent of prepension gross earnings (compulsory pension funds); and, on top of that, (3) an old age provision financed by an individual person (free choice of saving, investment, and life insurance products). The basic pension is financed on a pay-as-you-go (PAYGO) basis through premium payments as well as through the general government budget, while the financing of both of the supplementary pension components is funded on a capital basis. The basic features of this three-pillar pension system were established immediately after World War II.[1] Soon after, large part of the labor force was participating in premium payment and the accumulation of pension saving began.

The mix within this three-pillar system is such that the Netherlands currently boast what is perhaps the most funded collective pension system in the world. Although the country may thus seem relatively well placed to cope with the prospective increasing of the pension burden, several as-

Jeroen J. M. Kremers is deputy treasurer general and director for financial market policy at the Netherlands Ministry of Finance and professor of economics at Erasmus University, Rotterdam (OCFEB).

With thanks to Jaap D. Flikweert for comment and support, to A. Lans Bovenberg, Maarten R. P. M. Camps, Erik Jan van Kempen, and NBER conference participants for useful suggestions, and to Carla J. J. M. Kokshoorn for secretarial support.

1. See Tulfer (1997) and Lutjens (1999) for the history of pensions and pension reform in the Netherlands.

pects of the Netherlands pension system remain that would benefit from reform.

This paper first summarizes, from an international perspective, the financial challenges for the Netherlands pension system given the prospective population aging (section 9.2). Subsequently, in section 9.3, the main features of the three-pillar system are explained in more detail. Issues for reform are the subject of section 9.4.

9.2   Aging and the Costs of Financing Old Age Income

This section investigates the extent to which the aging of the population is expected to lead to deficiencies in the financing of pension benefits. It describes the level and composition of current benefits, and subsequently assesses potential difficulties in continuing to finance this benefit system in the future. First, however, the prospective population aging itself is placed in an international perspective.

Projections indicate that the Netherlands will be confronted with a substantial aging of the population (table 9.1). In 2000, the number of persons older than age sixty-five relative to those aged twenty to sixty-five stands at about 22 percent. This is roughly expected to double to something in the order of 40 percent or higher in 2050.[2]

Will such a substantial aging of the population pose major financing difficulties? That depends on the level of benefits, their composition between funded and nonfunded components and the degree to which each component's financing source is adequate in view of the prospective aging.

Given myriad institutional differences it is difficult to make precise international comparisons of the level of benefits. Nevertheless, some indication can be gleaned from replacement ratios, defined as disposable income during retirement as a percentage of disposable income preretirement. For most countries within the Organization for Economic Cooperation and Development (OECD) area, this ratio typically is on the order of 70–80 percent. Recent computations tend to place the Netherlands at the high end of this range (e.g., OECD 1998, 1999).

Can these benefits be financed when recourse to them rises with the increasing number of pensioners? The prospects in the case of the Netherlands are as follows.

2. Population projections may fluctuate over time; compare the numbers of table 9.1 with (for example) Kotlikoff and Leibfritz (1998, quoting *World Bank Projections* 1994). Table 9.1 for the Netherlands is based on Central Bureau voor de Statistiek (CBS; 1999), the most recent national population forecast, also used in recent studies such as Ministerie van Financiën (2000) and Ewijk et al. (2000). Employing different methodologies, Eurostat (2000) see the ratio of persons aged sixty-five and older to those aged twenty to sixty-five increasing from 22 percent in 2000 to 45 percent in 2050, and United Nations (1998) see it increasing even to 55 percent. The former projection lies within the 95 percent confidence band of the CBS projection; the latter does not.

Table 9.1   **Population Aging**

	2000	2050	Increase
Europe			
Spain	27	66	39
Italy	29	67	38
Germany	26	53	27
France	27	51	24
Belgium	28	50	22
United Kingdom	26	46	20
Netherlands	22	40	18
Denmark	24	42	18
Sweden	30	46	16
Other OECD			
Japan	27	64	37
Canada	21	44	23
Australia	20	40	20
United States	21	39	18

Sources: CBS (1999) for the Netherlands and Eurostat (2000) for other Europe; United Nations (1998) for other OECD.

Notes: Persons above age sixty-five relative to persons aged twenty to sixty-five; in percent.

9.2.1   The First Pillar

Until a few years ago, the first pillar (*Algemene Ouderdoms Wet* [AOW], the general old age law) was financed exclusively on a PAYGO basis. Premiums were paid by employees at a rate of about 17–18 percent of the first two brackets of income taxation (see the next section for more detail). Without further policy action, this rate would be set to rise considerably with the upward trend of the number of benefit recipients relative to the active labor force. This would place upward pressure on the wedge between gross and net earnings, and thus erode incentives to work.

The government has taken two initiatives to help avoid this. First, as of 1998 it has embarked on a temporary, earmarked reduction of the public debt until 2020 that will subsequently be used up for financing the AOW peak of 2020–50. This is the so-called AOW Fund, a "virtual" fund within the government budget and economically meaningful to the extent that it is reflected in declining public debt. In 2000 the fund's size is a mere 1.8 percent of gross domestic product (GDP); in years to come it will be fed with annual contributions on the order of 0.6 percent of GDP. This is projected to add up to a size sufficient to absorb the *temporary* hump of AOW costs during 2020–50. Current estimates show that the accrual of the AOW Fund during 1998–2002 indeed goes hand in hand with (much more substantial) debt reduction; the ratio of public debt to GDP is projected to fall from 70 percent in 1997 to 50 percent in 2002.

Second, as of 1998 the AOW premium rate is maximized (at a level of 18.25 percent of the first two income tax brackets). AOW costs rising above this level, corresponding with about 5 percent of GDP, will be financed by contributions from the central government budget. Current projections indicate that such contributions will have to begin from about 2010, climbing to a permanent level equal to 3 percent of GDP as of about 2030.[3] This may be financed by permanently reducing the public debt to GDP ratio before then, making permanent room in the budget through lower interest payments. Recent estimates show that a permanent raising of the annual budget balance by about 0.6 percent of GDP as of today and accordingly a reduction of the debt to GDP ratio to zero within twenty-five years would suffice to absorb both the permanent increase of the AOW burden and the similar rise of public health care expenditure also associated with the aging of the population (Ministerie van Financiën 2000; Ewijk et al. 2000). Alternatively, the structurally higher AOW contributions may have to be financed from higher taxation. The effect of the latter would be that AOW costs will be financed in part by AOW recipients themselves—thereby reducing net benefits in the first pillar. With this premium cap, therefore, there will be less upward pressure on labor tax rates and less adverse incentive and employment effects emanating from rising costs in the first pillar—the more so to the degree that the public debt to GDP ratio can be reduced by more than what is accounted for by the AOW Fund.

As background at this point it is also relevant to note that, more generally, taxes and social premiums have declined significantly in recent years and are set to decline further with the tax reform and reduction package of 2001. Relative to a high in the early 1990s, their total has come down by several percent of GDP and is projected to reach a level below 40 percent of GDP in 2001 (Centraal Planbureau 2000). Having started from a position with one of the highest tax burdens in the world, the Netherlands will begin facing the aging challenge with tax and premium levels below those of most other European countries—(although still substantially higher than those of many competitors in the rest of the world. This is relevant with an eye toward maintaining employment and GDP growth as a basis for financing the costs of an aging population.

9.2.2   The Second Pillar

The second pillar of old age income provisions is already fully prefunded through pension funds, taking into account to an important degree the prospective aging of the population. Furthermore, given the relative im-

---

3. On top of this, the temporary hump of AOW costs is projected to peak at 1.5 percent of GDP in 2035; see Ministerie van Financiën (2000).

Table 9.2   **Pension Fund and Life Insurance Assets in Europe (% of GDP, 1997)**

	Pension Funds	Life Insurance	Total
Netherlands	111	33	144
United Kingdom	78	22	99
Denmark	26	65	91
Sweden	42	23	65
Ireland	53	8	61
Finland	17	17	35
Germany	7	8	15
Portugal	12	1	13
Belgium	5	8	12
Italy	3	5	8
France	6	1	7
Spain	5	0	5
Greece	3	1	4
Austria	2	0	2

Source: Data provided by Pragma Consulting, Brussels.

portance of this pillar, it is not surprising that Dutch pension funds are among the largest in the world (table 9.2).

Taken together, the first and second pillars in the Netherlands account for a collective old age income provision typically totalling a level of about 70 percent of gross earnings before retirement (higher when measured net of taxes). This collective provision covers a very high share of the workforce (table 9.3), currently more than 90 percent.

9.2.3   The Third Pillar

Persons not fully covered by the first two pillars may take life insurance provisions for their old age income. Beyond that, such provisions may also serve to supplement the first two pillars at an individual level. As indicated in the introductory section, it is difficult to compare internationally the adequacy of individual old age income provisions. As far as life insurance provisions are concerned, available data suggest that here again the Netherlands stand out, with a relatively high level of accumulated savings (table 9.2). This may reflect in part the advantageous tax treatment of life insurance for old age income, as further explained in the next section.

9.2.4   Summary

As an overall conclusion, the Netherlands' old age system at present is fully and therefore adequately funded as regards the (relatively large) second and third pillars. The (relatively small) first pillar is unfunded, and (taking into account the temporary AOW budget fund) its annual

Table 9.3   **Coverage of Second-Pillar Pensions (mid-1990s)**

	Employees Covered (%)		Employees Covered (%)
Europe		Other OECD countries	
Finland	90	Australia	89
Sweden	90	United States	50
Netherlands	85	Canada	41
Denmark	80	Japan	37
United Kingdom	70		
Germany	46		
Belgium	31		
France	10		
Italy	5		
Austria	4		

Sources: Stanton and Whiteford (1998), Kohl and O'Brien (1998).

financing burden is projected to rise from 2010, to a level permanently higher by 3 percent of GDP as of 2030. Coping with this financing requirement in the years to come, preferably by achieving public
debt reduction and thus making budgetary room through lower interest payments, is the remaining challenge in financing retirement income
as the population ages. Current estimates show that a permanent raising of the annual budget balance by about 0.3 percent of GDP would
suffice.

Finally, it must be noted that all of these quantitative indications can be
quite sensitive with respect to underlying assumptions. For instance, Ewijk
et al. (2000) computed that a one-year-longer life expectancy would double
the required budgetary adjustment.

9.3   The Present Pension System

This section further explains the system consisting of three pillars: basic
collective, supplementary collective, and supplementary individual. The
third pillar, by its nature, can differ widely by individual; this pillar can be
taken to include not only insurance-type products (lifetime annual benefits
after retirement) but also more broadly any other types of capital accumulation contributing to income after retirement (saving, investments including owner-occupied housing). Comparisons of its features and relative
importance—both between pillars and internationally—are therefore difficult to make.

The sum of the first two pillars is the collective pension. In the Netherlands this typically totals 70 percent of final earnings before retirement,

when retiring at the age of sixty-five after forty years of employment. Precise international comparisons are difficult to come by, but nevertheless this seems to be a fairly usual profile (see Willemsen 1999; OECD 1995, 1998). Within this collective pension total, the first pillar in the Netherlands provides a state pension at the level of the minimum wage.

More specifically, the three pillars are organized as described in sections 9.3.1–9.3.3.

9.3.1   The First Pillar

The first pillar consists of the state social security pension scheme (so-called AOW). Participation is compulsory for all who reside or work in the Netherlands. Its purpose is to guarantee an income from the age of sixty-five. The benefit is flat rate and is linked to the statutory net minimum wage. The accrual rate is 2 percent a year. A full-fledged pension is built up between the ages of fifteen and sixty-five. The contribution is currently 17.9 percent of income (with a general exemption for taxes and social security contributions for tax payers under age sixty-five in the first two tax brackets). Since 1998, the AOW premium has been maximized at 18.25 percent. As soon as AOW costs rise, the remainder will be financed through the central government budget.

The benefit is independent of labor history, contributions paid, wealth, and other old age income. Since 1985, the first pillar benefits for couples have been individualized due to European Commission (EC) legislation. The benefit for a person with a partner is 50 percent of net minimum wage if that person is over sixty-five years of age. If both persons are over sixty-five years, the benefit for a couple is 100 percent. The benefit for a single person over sixty-five years of age is 70 percent of net minimum wage. A benefit is seen as a remuneration for labor in a former period and is taxed accordingly. The gross replacement rate of the national old age scheme amounts to 45 percent of average earnings. The state pension scheme disbursements currently amount to about 5 percent of GDP.

The first-pillar scheme is financed on a PAYGO basis. Additionally, the government has set up a support fund with yearly contributions from the government budget. This AOW Fund, including accumulated interest, will be used to contribute to first-pillar benefits from 2020 onward (see section 9.2).

9.3.2   The Second Pillar

The second pillar concerns labor-related pension schemes, which have an essential social function in the Netherlands because of the limited level of first-pillar provisions. Pension schemes are administered outside the company either by insurance companies (group life insurance) or by industry-wide or company pension funds. Membership by employees is compulsory whenever an employer offers a pension scheme. Employers within a branch of industry are obliged to take part in an industry-wide pension scheme, whenever participation in these schemes is made compulsory by the Minister of Social Affairs at the request of social partners (representative organizations of employers and of employees) in that branch. More than 90 percent of the working population is currently covered by occupational pension schemes, of which 77 percent belong to mandatory industry-wide pension funds (civil servants included; Verzekeringskamer 2000).

About 9 percent of the working population does not participate in a second-pillar scheme. Of that group, 2 percent are with employers that do not offer such a scheme (e.g., very small companies or new companies in as-yet unorganized sectors, such as areas of information technology), and 7 percent are not eligible (e.g., those who hold small and temporary part-time jobs). The government is currently preparing policy to broaden participation in second-pillar schemes.

These schemes offer many different provisions: old age pension, widows' and widowers' pension, partners' pension (in case of enduring cohabitation), orphans' pension, invalidity pension, bachelors' pension (if the pensioner is single), temporary old age pension (from the retiring age until the statutory age of sixty-five), temporary survivors' pension (until the age of sixty-five of the survivor), and lump-sum disbursement. Of all employees covered by second-pillar provisions, nearly all are insured against the consequences of old age and premature death. About 75 percent also have insurance against loss of income due to invalidity. Many have the prospect of early retirement on a PAYGO basis, under the so-called VUT (*Vervroegde UitTreding*) system.

Old age, survivors', and invalidity pensions are usually compulsory. However, recent measures to reduce first-pillar benefits due for invalidity pensions respectively survivors' pensions have created a need for more flexibility within the second pillar. The result is that pension funds gradually offer more optional provisions, not only for survivors' and invalidity pensions, but also for repairing old age pension.

As for old age pensions, 70 percent of employees have an accrual rate of 1.75 percent per year, which gives defined benefits at a level of 70 percent after forty years of service, mostly related to some final pay system (average gross salary of some recent years, or no past service costs for career development after the age of fifty-five). Twelve percent of employees have accrual rates of less than 1.5 percent per year, mostly belonging to an average salary system. Defined contribution systems are rare in the Netherlands. Only about one-half of one percent of employees have such a provision, often in addition to a defined benefit scheme. Pensioners usually receive an adjustment for the cost of living.

As for early retirement, the PAYGO VUT systems were developed by social partners (employers and employees) in the beginning of the 1980s to advance employment opportunities for the younger generations. A typical condition for early retirement was an uninterrupted span of employment lasting at least ten years before the moment of early retirement. Initially guaranteeing a replacement rate of at least 80 percent from the age of sixty onward (incidentally, even at an earlier age) and without any contribution of the employees, PAYGO VUT systems proved to be very popular. Obviously, they also became very expensive for the employer. In combination with an easily accessed state invalidity pension in the first pillar, the system of early retirement is an important reason for the low labor participation rates for elderly people in the Netherlands. Government therefore currently promotes a transformation into a capitalized flexible pension system. The friendly tax treatment of the PAYGO early retirement systems (contributions exempt and benefits taxed, often at a lower rate) will be phased out in the longer term.

Tax legislation is offering more possibilities for building up pensions than are generally used by pension funds. An accrual rate of 2 percent per working year on a final-pay basis (2.25 percent if based on average salaries), with a maximum of 100 percent of the final salary, is legally accepted. The retirement age in the pension scheme should be between sixty and seventy in order to be eligible for tax facilities. Retirement at an even earlier age is possible, but only with an adequate actuarial reduction of benefits.

In the board of pension funds, employers and employees are represented equally. Types of group life insurance, administered by insurance companies, are contracted by the employer. Pension funds themselves may reinsure (part of) their portfolios with insurance companies. This concerns about 45 percent of the schemes, for a total of less than 10 percent of employees, so reinsurance appears to be especially interesting for smaller pension funds.

Medical checks for entrance are forbidden. The level of contribution is different for each scheme, depending on the ambition of the scheme, the composition of membership, the different risks that are covered, the adjustment of pensions, the returns on investments, and the financial position of the fund. Usually both employer and employee pay part of the contribution for group provisions. In some schemes, only the employer pays. Individual provisions usually will be paid entirely by the employee.

The regulatory body for pension funds is the Ministry of Social Affairs, and for life insurance companies, the Ministry of Finance. The supervisory body for both pension funds and life insurance companies is the Insurance Supervisory Board. Schemes in the second pillar are fully funded under supervision of this board. Investments must be made according to the so-called "prudent person" principle. There are no quantitative restrictions on the portfolio investments of pension funds, except the limitation to a maximum of 10 percent of assets invested in the sponsoring company. This restriction limits the employer's influence with the board of company pension funds. There is no currency-matching requirement. Investments by insurance companies are governed by the rules of the Third Life Directive of the European Union (EU).

The tax treatment of second-pillar schemes is similar to the EET system: Contributions are *e*xempt, returns on investments are *e*xempt, and benefits are *t*axed. Pension funds are exempt from corporation tax. Insurance companies pay corporation tax on profits. Tax facilities, as mentioned, cover the provision of old age, survivors', and disability pensions.

Particularly relevant from a labor market perspective, finally, is how second-pillar benefits are treated when workers are mobile between firms. Until the mid-1990s this treatment was cumbersome, in many cases causing a significant disincentive to labor mobility. Since 1994, however, every employee has had a legal right to take along the capital corresponding with his or her accrued rights to a new employer and pension fund. Transfer takes place according to rules of calculation set by the government. The transferred value of pension rights, accrued under the old scheme until the moment of mobility, is converted into actuarially equivalent pension rights under the new scheme. In this sense, all second-pillar benefits are individually portable within the Netherlands, even the vast majority that are based on defined benefits. Portability of pensions between EU member states (other than in the case of a temporary assignment abroad for the same employer) is generally difficult for everyone, not just for workers from the Netherlands. The difficulty is due to very large differences in pension and taxation regimes between member states. These differences should be placed prominently on the European policy agenda.

9.3.3   The Third Pillar

As mentioned before, this pillar can be taken to include all parts of old age income provisions. In the Netherlands, individual life insurance products (up to a limit) enjoy favorable tax treatment similar to that of collective pension schemes in the second pillar. Beyond that, saving, investment, and other vehicles are liable to normal income and wealth taxation.

9.4   Pension Reform

Thanks to a long postwar tradition, the Netherlands boast a relatively soundly financed pension system, offering a good starting position for coping with contemporaneous policy challenges. These challenges can be summarized with two questions: (1) Do old age income schemes offer sufficient room for individual choice? and (2) are these schemes efficient? The preliminary challenge—safeguarding the financial solidity of old age income at the macro level—has been dealt with in section 9.2.

9.4.1 The Room for Individual Choice

Within the three-pillar system, equilibrium is sought between solidarity and individual choice. The first pillar offers every citizen a basic old-age income provision at minimum wage (and is thus income independent). This is solidarity at a national level. The PAYGO premium is compulsory and income dependent (within the first two brackets of income taxation). The second pillar offers employees a supplement, usually up to 70 percent of some definition of prepension gross income, collectively within the industry sector or the company. This is solidarity at the industry or company level. The premium to fund the second pillar is compulsory and paid by employers and employees (and, again is income dependent). The third pillar is voluntary and individual. In itself, this three-pillar system offers a suitable setup for balancing solidarity and individuality. In part, this is a question of economic efficiency. Boender et al. (2000) have shown that a collective pension for the commonly preferred pension component is economically efficient (i.e., it is more efficient in reducing risk than is individual saving). Finding the right equilibrium is also a political matter; it concerns the demarcation between the second and third pillar, and the scope for differentiation within the second pillar. The latter offers room for choice insofar as it is permitted by the collective (industry or company) wage agreement.

Since the 1990s there has been a growing interest in making room for individual choice. Factors behind this trend have been growing differentiation in household and labor participation patterns (more singles and working spouses), and growing labor mobility (changing employers, exit and reentry according to family circumstances, self-employment).

In principle there are three ways to offer more room for individual choice. The first is quite drastic: Allow individuals to opt out of collective arrangements and to invest their accrued capital individually. This road has been followed in the United Kingdom, leading to pension-misselling difficulties. Many persons have been ill advised and have taken risks with their basic pensions that subsequently turned sour. This road has not been considered in the Netherlands. Second, the room for individual choice can be enlarged by reducing the size of the second pillar in favor of the third pillar, with the total favorable tax treatment kept (see section 9.3) intact. Third, more room for choice can be offered to some extent within the second pillar itself. Of these three options, the latter two can be more gradual ways to accommodate shifting societal preferences.

However, there has been no policy of systematically reducing the size of the second pillar. Employers' and employees' organizations have not, in the context of their collective wage agreements, adopted such an approach. This is remarkable, given that surveys indicate time and again that there is demand for more individual choice.[4] Individual modules have been introduced *within* the second pillar, however. This can be explained by tax considerations and by incentives for the parties (employers' and employees' organizations, pension funds) involved.

In the current tax system, a reduction of the second pillar does not automatically lead to more tax-favored room within the third pillar. This is an important factor. There has been discussion during recent years about introducing tax neutrality between the second and third pillars (e.g., Kremers and Flikweert 1998). This has led to a move in the direction of, but not quite reaching, such tax neutrality in the new tax regime. As of 2001, all accrued non–tax exempt savings will be taxed at a low rate of 1.2 percent (applying a uniform tax rate of 30 percent to an assumed return of 4 percent, independent of actual investment returns). This will mitigate the relevance of the tax exemption for old age provisions.

Incentives of employees' and employers' organizations may be relevant as well. The organizations are the "social partners" deciding on collective wage agreements, of which second-pillar schemes are a part; they also form the boards of directors of pension funds active within this pillar. I am unaware of any systematic empirical research into the degree to which premium payers' preferences are reflected in their decisions. The scope for opting out of collective industry schemes is very limited for participating employers, and nonexistent for employees. Can it be expected that these organizations actively reduce the scope of "their" second pillar, even if warranted by participants' preferences?

It is indicated in this respect that more room for choice *has* been created *within* second-pillar schemes. This concerns, for instance, prepension options. Collective pension funds have also begun to offer individual third-pillar products; the demarcation between collective, tax-favored, second-pillar schemes and the free-market segment of the third pillar is blurring. This has raised important but still unresolved issues of fair competition (taxation, use of personal data) and of privacy in using personal data from collective schemes for making individual offers (see Kremers, van Kempen, and de Groot 1999).

Finally, of specific labor market relevance is the question of whether the pension system is amenable to individual choice regarding pension age. As noted above, the system hitherto has, in effect, contributed to early retirement and to low labor participation of the aged. With an eye both toward financing the costs of an aging population and toward fully utilizing the available labor capacity, it will become increasingly important that

---

4. See, for example, the Vos and Alessi (1998) research report commissioned by the Ministry of Finance.

people remain economically active and productive as long as they wish to and they reasonably can. Here again, the system's incentives will need to be adjusted and more flexibility will be required. To this end, it may be of interest to consider moving from a final-pay pension anchor toward a pension level defined in such a way that demotion and part-time work at career end are not penalized. Some pension schemes, for instance, base the pension level on income at the age of fifty-five; other formulas are being discussed by various pension schemes.

9.4.2   The Efficiency of Old Age Income Provision

As regards efficiency, it is again the second pillar that is of greatest interest. The first pillar is organized simply as a general PAYGO scheme through the central government budget, and there is no debate about the costs of running it. The third pillar is open to full competitive pressures within the financial market sector.

For the greater part, the second pillar is run by pension funds. These are the responsibility of social partners (employers and employees, or their organizations); the government is not directly involved other than by defining the statutory context. Employers are obliged by law and general policy to participate in industry-wide funds whenever a branch of industry is defined; employees are obliged to participate in the employer's scheme. Given this situation, three elements are of specific relevance for the efficiency of pension funds: transparency and accountability, employers' scope for opting out, and financial supervision.

As an indication of the importance of second-pillar efficiency, it is illustrative to mention some recent computations by Ewijk et al. (2000). They found that a one percent lower pension fund return (keeping the general interest rate unchanged) would necessitate drastically higher pension contribution rates, and thus, through their tax deductibility, an additional raising of the annual government budget balance substantially greater than that already needed to cope with financing higher AOW and health care costs (see section 9.2).

Transparency and Accountability

Until a few years ago, pension funds were not obliged even to publish an annual report. Reporting requirements were introduced as of 1998, but the quality of pension fund reporting is still working toward a level customary for other financial institutions. Such transparency is important to enhance pressure on pension fund management and boards to deliver adequate performance. Several conditions need to be improved: No information is available on administrative costs; transparency requirements are less developed than those for life insurers; and employees are still not provided with comprehensive information about accrued rights and the costs at which benefits are being delivered.

As regards accountability, it is interesting to note that a great deal of attention is being paid in public debate to corporate governance in the Netherlands, stimulated in part by a more active role of pension funds as shareholders. The corporate governance of pension funds themselves, however, remains underdeveloped. In addition to transparency, the accountability of pension boards to their members with respect to key topics such as investment returns, administrative costs, and pension modalities offered will certainly be on the policy agenda in years to come.

Opting Out by Employers

Also as of 1998, some limited room has been created for companies to opt out of their industry pension funds when the funds' investment performance is significantly below the usual standards. The criteria for opting out are severe, and it remains to be seen to what extent opting out will be viable. Nevertheless, it is a positive effect that the investment performance of pension funds will now be measured and published on a comparable basis.[5]

Financial Supervision

Over the last few years several policy initiatives have been taken to align the quality of financial supervision of pension funds more fully with that of financial institutions in the market sector (especially that of life insurance companies). In one respect, the supervisory regime for pension funds in the Netherlands is quite amenable to efficient pension production: Modern ALM techniques are permitted and encouraged within a prudent-person approach, eschewing artificial quantitative restrictions (currency, financial instrument) on asset allocation. Dutch pension funds are free to invest their assets where and how they best see fit within a framework of modern prudential supervision (geared toward output in terms of risk versus return, rather than toward input in terms of asset restrictions)—and indeed they do, as witnessed by their worldwide investment presence. The share of pension assets invested abroad has risen quickly in recent years, from 25 percent in 1996 to 60 percent in 1999.[6] This undoubtedly reflects in part the introduction of the euro. Even outside the euro area, however, Dutch pension funds are quite active (in 1998, 25 percent of the total portfolio was invested outside the euro area; Verzekeringskamer 2000). In 1999, 57 percent of pension fund assets was invested in equity and real estate (William M. Mercer Company, April 2000). The portfolio structure per pension fund follows its chosen investment strategy, depending inter alia on the structure of liabilities (a fund with a younger population will

5. Systematic information on asset allocation and returns of Dutch pension funds is made available annually by the William M. Mercer Company; see, for example, *VB Contact* (1999 and previous years).
6. Source: CBS Webmagazine, 2 November 2000 [http://www.cbs.nl].

Table 9.4   **Pension Fund Asset Allocation (1998)**

	Percent of Total Assets
Under the prudent-person principle	
Ireland	76
United Kingdom	75
The Netherlands[a]	57
Belgium	53
Average	65
Under substantial quantitative investment restrictions	
Germany	22
Denmark	38
Average	30

Sources: Pragma Consulting, Brussels, and William M. Mercer Company.
[a] 1999; data from William M. Mercer Company (April 2000).

Table 9.5   **Pension Fund Asset Returns**

	Real Total Return[a]
Under the prudent-person principle	
Ireland	13
United States	11
United Kingdom	10
Belgium	10
The Netherlands	10
Average	11
Under substantial quantitative investment restrictions	
Germany	7
Denmark	6
Switzerland	5
Average	6

Sources: European Commission (1999, quoting European Federation for Retirement Provision [EFRP], OECD, and Pragma Consulting, Brussels).
[a] Annual average (1984–98) in local currency, expressed in percent.

typically invest more in equity, carrying more risk in the short term but more return in the longer term). The largest pension funds tend to diversify relatively more into equities and worldwide investments, also outside the euro area. An indication of asset allocation by Dutch pension funds in an international perspective is given in table 9.4.

Available evidence indicates that the freedom to invest optimally is an important element of pension efficiency (table 9.5). Against this background, it is of immediate importance to the Netherlands that the upcoming EU Pensions Directive be based (as announced) on the prudent-person principle.[7] The EC's proposal, published 11 October 2000 (see EC 2000) is consistent with this practice that has proved so successful in the Netherlands and elsewhere.

References

Boender, C. C. E., S. van Hoogdalem, R. M. A. Jansweijer, and E. van Lochem. 2000. "Intergenerationele solidariteit en individualiteit in de tweede pensioenpijler: Een scenario-analyse" (Intergenerational solidarity and individuality in the second pillar: A scenario analysis). *WRR Werkdocument* no. 114. The Hague: Wetenschappelijke Raad voor het Regeringsbeleid (WRR).

Centraal Bureau voor de Statistiek (CBS). 1999. *"Maandstatistiek van de bevolking"* (Monthly population statistics). The Hague: CBS, January.

Centraal Planbureau. 2000. *"Macro economische verkenning 2001"* (Macroeconomic outlook 2001), The Hague: Centraal Planbureau, September.

European Commission (EC). 1999. *Rebuilding pensions: Security, efficiency, affordability.* Brussels: European Commission.

———. 2000. *Proposal for a directive on the co-ordination of laws, regulations and administrative provisions relating to institutions for occupational retirement provisions.* COM (2000) 507 provisional. Brussels: European Commission, 11 October.

European Round Table of Industrialists. 2000. *European pensions: An appeal for reform.* Brussels: European Round Table of Industrialists.

Eurostat. 2000. *New national population baseline scenarios.* Luxembourg: Eurostat.

Ewijk, C. van, B. Kuipers, H. ter Rele, M. van de Ven, and E. Westerhout. 2000. *Ageing in the Netherlands.* The Hague: Netherlands Bureau for Economic Policy Analysis, August.

Kohl, R., and P. O'Brien. 1998. The macroeconomics of ageing, pensions and savings: A survey. OECD *Economics Department Working Paper* no. 200. Paris: Organization for Economic Cooperation and Development.

Kotlikoff, L. J., and W. Leibfritz. 1998. An international comparison of generational accounts. In *Generational accounting around the world,* ed. A. J. Auerbach, L. J. Kotlikoff, and W. Leibfritz, 73–101. Chicago: University of Chicago Press.

Kremers, J. J. M., and J. D. Flikweert. 1998. "Oudedagsvoorzieningen tussen keuze en collectief" (Old age provisions between choice and collective). *Economische Statistiche Berichten* 4152:392–97.

Kremers, J. J. M. , E. J. van Kempen, and J. A. de Groot. 1999. "Marktwerking en privacy in de sociale zekerheid" (Competition and privacy in social security). *Economische Statistiche Berichten* 4187:64–68.

Lutjens, E. 1999. *Een halve eeuw solidariteit* (Half a century of solidarity). Rijswijk: Vereniging Bedrijfspensioenfondsen.

Ministerie van Financiën. 2000. *Een verkenning van de schuldpolitiek op lange termijn* (A reconnaissance of debt policy for the long term). The Hague: Ministerie van Financiën.

---

7. See European Round Table of Industrialists (2000) for a succinct underpinning from the point of view of the European business sector.

Organization for Economic Cooperation and Development (OECD). 1995. Ageing populations, pension systems and government budgets: How do they affect saving? OECD *Economics Department Working Paper* no. 156. Paris: OECD.

————. 1998. *Maintaining prosperity in an ageing society.* Paris: OECD.

————. 1999. *Questionnaire on income distribution and poverty indicators.* Paris: OECD.

Stanton, D., and P. Whiteford. 1998. Pension systems and policy in the APEC economies. Report prepared for the Asian Development Bank. Canberra, Australia.

Tulfer, P. M. 1997. *Pensioenen, fondsen en verzekeraars* (Pensions, funds, and insurers). Deventer: Kluwer.

United Nations (UN). 1998. *World population prospects.* New York: United Nations.

VB Contact. 1999. "Rendementen pensioenfondsen over 1998" (Pension fund returns in 1998). Rijswijk: Uitgave van de Vereniging van Bedrijfspensioenfondsen, May.

Verzekeringskamer. 2000. *Pensioenmonitor, niet-financiële gegevens pensioenfondsen* (Pension monitor, non-financial facts about pension funds). Apeldoorn: Verzekeringskamer.

Vos, K. de, and R. J. M. Alessi. 1998. "Pensioenpreferenties: Hoe denken Nederlanders over hervormingen in pensioenregelingen?" (Pension preferences: What do Dutch citizens think about pension reform?) *Economische Statistiche Berichten* 4152:398–99.

Willemsen, M. 1999. "Pensioenen en EMU in het kader van vergrijzing" (Pensions and EMU in the context of population ageing). Finance Ministry of the Netherlands, *Staatscourant 1999* 150:2; 151:2; 152:2; 154:4; 157:2.

Comment   A. Lans Bovenberg

This paper provides an excellent overview of the Dutch pension system. Its main message is that, compared to other European countries, the Netherlands is well placed to cope with aging. This is mainly because the Netherlands features one of the most funded pension systems in the world. Because I did not find much to disagree with in the paper, I will provide some additional information about the Dutch pension system. I will also argue that even a country like the Netherlands, which is quite well placed compared to other countries, still has much work to do in order to address the aging problem adequately.

Early Retirement

My first point of concern in the Netherlands is the low effective retirement age (see table 9C.1). Three major routes facilitate early retirement:

A. Lans Bovenberg is professor of economics at CentER, Tilburg University, and a research fellow of the Centre for Economic Policy Research (CEPR), London.

Table 9C.1   Effective Retirement Age

	1950	1960	1970	1980	1990	1995
Males	66.4	66.1	63.8	61.4	59.3	58.8
Females	64.1	63.7	62.9	58.4	55.8	55.3

Source: CPB (1999).

Table 9C.2   Persons Aged 55–64 by Labor Market Status (1990)

	Men		Women	
Labor Market Status[a]	55–59	60–64	55–59	60–64
Employed	54.9	21.1	12.7	4.3
Disabled	31.3	37.7	10.5	10.8
Partly disabled/unemployed	1.8	1.0	0.4	0.3
Early retirement (VUT)	3.9	26.5	0.6	5.1
Social assistance	0.4	0.4	2.4	2.0
Unemployed	4.6	8.7	1.4	1.6

Source: CPB (1999).
[a]As a percentage of the population in that age category.

first, disability; second, occupational early retirement schemes; and third, unemployment benefits (see table 9C.2). Indeed, incentives to retire early are powerful. Empirical evidence reveals that the financial attractiveness of the three major routes to exit the labor force strongly affect the choice among these three alternatives.

Disability Benefits

The most popular public scheme for retiring early from the labor force is the disability program. At present, about a third of the males between the ages of fifty-five and sixty-four collect a disability benefit (see table 9C.2). As most of you probably know, the disability scheme is already extremely expensive in the Netherlands. Because the invalidity rates rise with age, aging makes the disability scheme even more expensive.

Early Retirement Benefits

Occupational early retirement schemes are the second most important route for early retirement. These so-called VUT (*Vervroegde Uittreding,* or early retirement) schemes are negotiated in collective bargaining among the social partners. At present, about a quarter of the men aged sixty to sixty-five collect early retirement benefits. There are two major differences with the occupational pensions that are provided after the statutory retirement age of sixty-five. First, in contrast to regular occupational pension benefits, early retirement benefits are financed on a pay-as-you-go

(PAYGO) basis. Second, one must completely withdraw from the labor market in order to be eligible for the benefits.

These schemes were introduced about twenty years ago, when unemployment was rising rapidly. At the present time, in contrast, the labor market is increasingly tight. In a number of collective labor agreements, early retirement provisions for the elderly are gradually being phased out and replaced by individual saving schemes for younger workers that are more actuarially fair. Hence, in the future, early retirement can be expected to be financed increasingly through funded rather than PAYGO schemes.

Unemployment Benefits

The unemployment scheme recently has become a more popular route for early retirement—due in part to recent measures making the disability scheme less attractive. Unemployment benefits are especially attractive for older people, for three reasons: First, the insurance character of unemployment benefits implies that elderly workers typically have accumulated substantial insurance rights. Indeed, most people aged sixty and older can expect to collect unemployment benefits equal to 70 percent of their previous earnings up to age sixty-five (in before-tax terms).

Second, another feature facilitating early retirement through the unemployment scheme is that unemployed workers older than 57.5 years need not apply for work in order to be eligible for unemployment benefits. Indeed, the number of people collecting unemployment benefits is more than twice as high as the number of people who are officially unemployed (i.e., are actively looking for work). This indicates that the unemployment scheme is in fact used as a route for early retirement.

Third, when laying off elderly workers, employers often provide supplementary severance payments to top-off the unemployment benefits. In this way, by providing relatively small supplementary benefits, employers can ensure that older, laid-off workers maintain their standards of living in early retirement. Because the public sector pays for most of the benefits, the employer does not internalize the full costs of early retirement.

One of the main challenges facing Dutch policy makers is to increase labor force participation—especially of elderly workers. The labor force participation rates of younger workers have increased during the past two decades, due mainly to a higher labor force participation of women. This can, in fact, be viewed as the other side of the coin of lower fertility. The participation rate of women between the ages of twenty and sixty-five, which has already risen rapidly during the past two decades, is expected to continue to rise further—from about 50 percent now to about 70 percent in 2020. Indeed, whereas two-earner households at present are about as common as households with one breadwinner and one nonparticipating partner, the two-earner family will become the norm in the next century.

In order to reduce the burden on the middle aged, who will be heavily burdened both by raising children and by caring for the older generations in an aging society, it will become extremely important to raise the labor force participation of elderly workers. Hence, the incentives to retire early should be phased out.

Public Pension System

I now turn to the three pillars of the Dutch pension system, beginning with the first. The pay-as-you-go public pension scheme (Algemene Ouderdoms Wet, or AOW) is quite vulnerable to aging, a problem that can be addressed by reducing benefits or by raising taxes or premiums.

Benefits

On the benefit side, the indexation mechanism is crucial. The flat public pension benefit is indexed to the minimum wage, which is in turn linked to contractual wages. Despite this effective indexation to contractual wages, the value of the public pension has declined compared to the average standard of living during the last two decades. There are two main reasons for this. First, the minimum wage was frozen during most of the 1980s in order to cut public spending. Second, contractual wages typically lag behind actual wages because of promotions and other supplementary earnings that are not included in collective wage contracts. Thus, the public pension does not grow in line with the average standard of living. This is a major reason that the costs of the public pensions (in terms of gross domestic product [GDP]) do not double between now and 2040, despite the doubling of the dependency rate during this period.

Most private occupational schemes (i.e., the second pillar) filled the gap left by the public scheme to ensure that the sum of occupational and public pension benefits stayed in line with the average standard of living. By reducing the generosity of the public scheme, the government has in fact privatized part of pension provision.

Contributions

Kremer's paper mentions two ways in which the government strengthens the financing of the public pension: first, by financing a larger part of the public pension out of general tax revenues, and second, by building up a temporary fund that will contain close to 20 percent of GDP by 2030. It is not clear, however, how effective these measures are. Financing a larger part out of general tax revenues implies that the elderly contribute more to the financing of public pensions because the wealthier elderly, who are exempted from paying public pension premiums on their supplementary incomes, *do* pay taxes on these incomes. By bringing the elderly within the tax net, the government in effect broadens the contribution base. However, the commitment of the government to do so is not very credible because the elderly are rather powerful politically. Indeed, despite earlier intentions, both the previous and the current government have increased the public pension premium in order to enhance the purchasing power of the elderly at the expense of the young.

In the same way, the prefunding of public pension benefits is not meaningful if it is not backed up by fiscal surpluses. Whether the fund for public pensions has any economic meaning will thus depend on future fiscal policy. Because the government has not yet committed itself to such a fiscal policy, the fund is largely symbolic at this stage. Moreover, even if the fund is filled by running fiscal surpluses, the fund does not seem to be large enough. Generational accounting exercises suggest that a sustainable fiscal policy requires fiscal surpluses larger than the inflows into the public pension fund—even if labor force participation rises substantially during the next two decades. In particular, these exercises assume that the trend toward higher labor force participation of women will continue, while the participation of males older than fifty-five will rise (in part due to lower invalidity rates; see, e.g., Bovenberg and ter Rele 2000 and CPB Netherlands Bureau for Economic Policy Analysis (CPB; 2000).

Occupational Pensions

Kremer's paper states that occupational pensions are fully funded. However, the defined benefit (DB) nature of these pensions, which are thus linked to wages rather than to rates of return on the capital market, imply that they also incorporate a PAYGO component on account of intergenerational risk sharing. Indeed, in order to be able to pay wage-linked benefits, the occupational schemes rely not only on the accumulation of financial assets but also on an implicit contract among the firm, its workers, and retirees. If returns are low and wage increases are substantial, the firm and its younger workers transfer resources to the retirees and older generations. If returns are high, in contrast, the transfer of resources goes the other way around.

Intergenerational risk sharing yields important advantages. The associated long-term horizon allows pension funds to take advantage of the risk premium on equity (the so-called equity premium). Indeed, Dutch pension funds are increasingly investing in equity. This facilitates the investment of pension saving in high-yield projects in the corporate sector, improves corporate governance, enhances capital mobility within the corporate sector, allows a higher expected return over a long horizon, and makes the return on pension saving less sensitive to unexpected inflation.

The price of intergenerational risk sharing is the compulsory nature of Dutch occupation schemes. This compulsion, however, is broadly supported by the Dutch population. Only about a quarter of the participants of these funds would prefer to have the discretion to choose a pension fund, which would undermine intergenerational risk sharing.

Challenges Facing Occupational Pensions

Several developments are putting severe pressures on the role of the second pillar in ensuring intergenerational risk sharing. First, aging makes the premiums levied by funded DB systems more sensitive to changes in the rate of return because aging, together with the maturing of these plans, reduces the premium base compared to the insured pension rights. Second, aging may depress the rate of return and raise wage growth, as it makes labor more scarce compared to capital.

Third, an increasingly competitive environment and higher labor mobility associated with a more flexible labor market are reducing the room for intergenerational risk sharing. Indeed, the DB schemes (which link pension benefits to wages rather than to the discounted value of individual premiums) back up the benefit promise not only by financial assets, but also by the market power of the firm and the commitment of future workers to the implicit contract between generations of workers. In particular, a firm can abide by the pension contract only if it earns enough rents to insure the elderly against low returns without being pushed out of the market by young firms that have no retired workers to care for. Exit barriers for young workers ensure that DB schemes can transfer resources away from younger workers to retirees and older workers. If young workers become mobile across firms, they cannot be forced to abide by the implicit contract with the retired and older workers in their new firms; if a firm attempted to tax its younger workers to transfer resources to its retirees, these workers would move to young firms without retirees and older workers. As competition intensifies in product, capital, and labor markets, occupational schemes are thus likely to acquire more features of defined contribution (DC) schemes. In particular, retirees will bear more risks. An important mechanism through which retirees absorb risk is through the conditional indexation of pension benefits. Whereas most retirees benefit from indexation of occupational benefits (to prices or even contractual wages), this indexation is not a regulatory requirement, but rather conditional on the financial health of a pension fund.

Shift to the Third Pillar

The paper correctly states that most occupation schemes aspire to a benefit level of 70 percent of the gross final wage (including the public benefit). However, even apart from the uncertainty about the indexation mechanism, many workers do not achieve the 70 percent final-wage aspiration level because of incomplete careers. Furthermore, even with full careers, many two-earner families and single-person households collect a collective pension of less than 70 percent of the final wage (in before-tax terms), because the occupational benefit typically assumes a public pension for a two-person family with a single earner of 100 percent of the minimum wage. Two-earner families and singles, however, receive public pensions of only 50 percent and 70 percent, respectively, of the minimum wage. Because two-earner families are becoming increasingly important, the ambition levels of collective pensions are falling. This increases the room for the third pillar.

Personal Pensions

The third pillar can be tailored to individual tastes with regard to the insurance level, but lacks intergenerational risk sharing. Interestingly enough, the paper does not discuss any reform measures for the third pillar. It states that "the third pillar is open to full competitive pressures within the financial market sector." Even so, the third pillar is ripe for reform. In particular, the market for personal pensions is neither very competitive nor transparent. Indeed, some observers maintain that insurance companies are able to capture a large part of the tax benefits of personal pensions. Intermediaries are paid by the insurance companies, and administrative costs are quite high.

Not only the second pillar, but also the third pillar, benefits from tax privileges. These tax benefits are in part due to the fact that the premium for public pensions is paid only by those younger than sixty-five years of age. Accordingly, individuals can reduce their tax liability by shifting their taxable income through pension saving toward retirement, when they do not pay the premium for the public pension.

I very much doubt whether tax benefits that are limited to pension saving are desirable in view of the need to raise labor force participation of the elderly—one of the main challenges facing the Dutch economy in years to come. Indeed, by stimulating pension saving, current tax benefits encourage early retirement. In my view, individuals should be allowed to take out some funds from tax-favored accounts before retirement age—to invest, for example, in their own human capital or that of their children (by caring for the children), or to start a business. Hence, individuals could save in the form of human capital and entrepreneurship. In this way, by investing early in life in human capital, individuals may be able to work longer.

To reduce reliance on public unemployment schemes that result in major disincentives to work, individuals could be allowed to draw on the tax-favored account during times of unemployment as well—in part, to invest in training to improve their positions on the labor market. In this way, these tax-favored accounts would facilitate a less rigid allocation of learning, working, caregiving, and enjoying leisure throughout the life cycle. Indeed, these accounts could be viewed as an instrument to insure against several human-capital risks (due not only to old age but also to unemployment and obsolescence of human capital during the working life). By increasing the flexibility in using tax-favored saving, the government may enhance human capital formation and stimulate entrepreneurship. Indeed, the main challenge facing the Dutch economy is not so much to increase financial saving, but rather to stimulate entrepreneurship and the accumulation of human capital.

References

Bovenberg A. L., and H. J. M. ter Rele. 2000. Generational accounts for the Netherlands: An update. *International Tax and Public Finance* 7 (4/5): 411–30.
CPB Netherlands Bureau for Economic Policy Analysis. 1999. *Challenging neighbours: Rethinking German and Dutch economic institutions.* Berlin: Springer Verlag.
———. 2000. *Aging in the Netherlands.* The Hague: Sdu Publishers.

Discussion Summary

Jeroen Kremers responded to the discussant that as far as early retirement as an exit from the active workforce is concerned, it is also relevant to add the element of demotion. The Netherlands are currently thinking of adjusting the final pay-related pension formula so that people are not penalized by a lower subsequent pension benefit if they stay in the labor force at a lower wage or as part-time workers. He agreed with the discussant's comments on the AOW budget fund and on transparency within the third pillar of the Dutch pension system. He reported that some aspects of intertemporal flexibility as mentioned by the discussant were included in the original tax reform package. However, they fell out in the last stage purely for budgetary reasons, and may return to the policy agenda.

Martin Feldstein inquired about the portability of pension claims if workers move from one sector to another. *Jeroen Kremers* reported that it is possible for a worker who moves between companies to take the accrued benefits along.

Eytan Sheshinski mentioned that there are three means for early retirement in the Netherlands: disability benefits, early retirement, or unemployment benefits. He asked about the benefit levels compared to each other and about the incentive effects of the three programs. *A. Lans Bovenberg* answered that the early retirement scheme is the most desirable of all three schemes, because there is no stigma attached to it, and it is used mainly by high-skilled workers. Low-skilled workers rely more on the disability scheme and the unemployment scheme. Of these two, the disability scheme is a bit more attractive because benefits are paid indefinitely, whereas the unemployment scheme only pays temporary benefits. Bovenberg emphasized that the major challenge for the Netherlands as well as for other European countries is to improve human capital of the low-skilled individuals to keep them employed without reducing their standard of living too greatly.

David A. Wise asked the discussant what he meant by his statement that tax benefits encourage early retirement. Wise pointed out that the employer-provided pensions give enormous incentives for early retirement, and he wondered how these incentives are related to each other. *A. Lans Bovenberg* responded that the Netherlands have large tax incentives to shift income within the life cycle from a younger age to an older age, so that the old have a great deal of accumulated wealth and may use that wealth for early retirement. To prevent early retirement, it might be wise to keep these tax benefits and allow individuals to use the benefits for education. According to Bovenberg, one of the main reasons for early retirement is that the workers do not have much human capital once they reach the age of around fifty-five. Wise also wanted to know more about the statement of the discussant that pensions are moving toward a defined contribution system.

Horst Siebert wondered why the comanagement of the second pillar by the social partners seems to work in the Netherlands, whereas in the case of France the point was made that the comanagement leads to high inflexibilities. *Jeroen Kremers* responded by mentioning that inflexibility of a comanaged pension system also means stability. Comparing the Netherlands with France, *Martin Feldstein* remarked that the relations between social partners are much less confrontational in the Netherlands than in France. *A. Lans Bovenberg* added that the attitude between social partners was more confrontational in the 1980s than it is now. Meanwhile, some good incentives for social partners to behave have been established. For example, the link between social benefits and the wage level is dependent on the ratio between the number of people on social insurance and the number of people in work.

Reijo Vanne asked how the increasing life expectancy is managed in the funded second pillar of the Dutch pension system.

Laurence J. Kotlikoff mentioned the high reliance of the Dutch system on the second pillar, the employer-defined-benefit (DB) plans. He wondered about the effects of administrative costs or insurance loads charged in these plans. He asked whether the Netherlands might consider the idea of opening up an account that is invested in a global index fund as an alternative to the defined benefit plan of the employers. *Jeroen Kremers* agreed that pension funds may have large administrative costs. For that reason, he reported, the Netherlands have begun policies to increase transparency and to give employers the possibility of leaving the pension fund. Although the conditions for opting out are so rigid that this may never happen, the performance of the different pension funds is now computed and published, and the issue has raised awareness in the public. Apart from that, standardization in pension funds may also have the effect of reducing costs. Nevertheless, in the near future there will probably be a gradual transition toward more room for the third pillar and less room for the second pillar.

Laurence J. Kotlikoff expressed his concern that the calculations of the future pension benefits by the employers may not necessarily be honest and reasonable. It may also be difficult for workers to compare their benefits with the benefits of workers in other firms. He referred to work by Kotlikoff and Wise that has shown that DB plans subsidize early retirement in their actuarial reduction factors. *Jeroen Kremers* responded that the employers also have a stake in the performance of the pension funds, because the pension premium is paid jointly by the employer and the employee. However, Kremers shared the skepticism of Kotlikoff concerning comparability of the different pension funds for the employees, but also mentioned that an increasing number of funds (including the largest, the civil servants' fund, or ABP) have begun to provide employees with easily understandable statements of accrued benefits.

Ignazio Visco asked about the involvement of the employees in the opting-out possibility that is given for the case where pension funds have returns below the average.

Assar Lindbeck noted that it was helpful for a country such as Ireland, New Zealand, Sweden, or Finland to have a serious enough crisis. He conjectured that the crisis in countries like France and Germany may not yet be severe enough.

10

The United Kingdom
Examining the Switch from Low Public Pensions to High-Cost Private Pensions

David Blake

10.1 Introduction

The United Kingdom is one of the few countries in Europe that is not facing a serious pensions crisis. The reasons for this are straightforward: Its state pensions (both in terms of the replacement ratio and as a proportion of average earnings) are among the lowest in Europe; it has a long-standing funded private pension sector; its population is aging less rapidly than elsewhere in Europe; and it governments have, since the beginning of the 1980s, taken measures to prevent the development of a pension crisis. These measures have involved making systematic cuts in unfunded state pension provisions and increasingly transferring the burden of providing pensions to the funded private sector. The United Kingdom is not entitled to be complacent, however, because there remain some serious and unresolved problems with private-sector provision.

This paper reviews the current system of pension provision in the United Kingdom, describes and analyzes defects in the Thatcher-Major governments' reforms that brought us to the present system, examines and assesses the reforms of the Blair government, and then identifies the problems that remain unresolved and how those problems might be addressed. The paper ends with an explanation of how the United Kingdom has been able to introduce changes relatively peacefully when attempts by continental European countries to reform their pension systems have frequently led to riots in the streets.

David Blake is professor of financial economics and director of the Pensions Institute at Birkbeck College, University of London.

I am very grateful for useful conversations with my discussant, Andrew A. Samwick.

10.2   The Current System of Pension Provision

A flat-rate, first-tier pension is provided by the state and is known as the Basic State Pension (BSP). Second-tier or supplementary pensions are provided by the state, employers, and private-sector financial institutions—the so-called three pillars of support in old age. The main choices are among (1) a state system that offers a pension that is low relative to average earnings but that is fully indexed to prices after retirement; (2) an occupational system that offers a relatively high level of pension (partially indexed to prices after retirement up to a maximum of 5 percent per annum), but that, as a result of poor transfer values between schemes on changing jobs,[1] is offered only to workers who spend most of their working lives with the same company; and (3) a personal pension system that offers fully portable (and partially indexed) pensions—although these are based on uncertain investment returns and are subject to very high setup and administration charges, often-inappropriate sales tactics, and very low paid-up values if contributions into the plans lapse prematurely.

Employees in the United Kingdom in receipt of earnings subject to National Insurance Contributions (NICs) will build up entitlement[2] both to the BSP[3] and, on "band earnings" between the Lower Earnings Limit and the Upper Earnings Limit,[4] to the pension provided by the State-Earnings-Related Pension Scheme (SERPS) and to its successor from April 2002, the (ultimately) flat-rate State Second Pension Scheme. These pensions are paid by the Department of Work and Pensions (as the Department of Social Security was renamed in June 2001) from State Pension Age, which is sixty-five for men and sixty for women.[5] The self-employed are also entitled to a BSP, but not to a SERPS pension. Employees with earnings in excess of the Lower Earnings Limit will automatically be members of SERPS, unless they belong to an employer's occupational pension scheme or to a personal pension scheme that has been contracted-out of SERPS. In such cases, both the individual and the employer who is contracting-out receive a rebate on their NICs (1.6 percent of earnings for the employee and 3.0 percent for the employer, unless it operates a COMPS [see

    1. Blake and Orszag (1997) estimated portability losses of 25–29 percent for typical workers in the United Kingdom, changing jobs an average of six times in a typical career.
    2. National Insurance Contributions also build up entitlement to health service, sickness, disability, and incapacity benefits and the job seeker's allowance.
    3. Worth £67.50 per week for a single person in 2000–01, while national average earnings were £415 per week, suggesting a replacement ratio of about 16 percent.
    4. The Lower Earnings Limit was £67 per week and the Upper Earnings Limit was £535 per week in 2000–01.
    5. The State Pension Age for women is being progressively raised to sixty-five over the period 2010–20.
    6. The non–contracted-out NIC rate in 2000–01 for employees was 10.0 percent of earnings between £76 per week and the Upper Earnings Limit, while for employers it was 12.2 percent on all earnings above £84 per week.

below], in which case the employer rebate is 0.6 percent[6]) and the individual gives up the right to receive a SERPS pension. However, there is no obligation on employers to operate their own pension schemes, nor, since 1988, has there been any contractual requirement for an employee to join the employer's scheme if it has one.

A wide range of private-sector pension schemes are open to individuals. One can join his or her employer's occupational pension scheme (if it has one), which can be any one of the following:

- Contracted-in salary-related scheme (CISRS)
- Contracted-in money purchase scheme (CIMPS)
- Contracted-out salary-related scheme (COSRS)
- Contracted-out money-purchase scheme (COMPS)
- Contracted-out mixed benefit scheme (COMBS)
- Contracted-out hybrid scheme (COHS)

A CISRS is a defined benefit (DB) scheme that has not been contracted-out of SERPS and thus provides a salary-related pension in addition to the SERPS pension. CIMPS provides a defined contribution (DC) supplement to the SERPS pension. COSRS must provide "requisite benefits" in order to contract out of SERPS—namely, a salary-related pension that is at least as good as the SERPS pension it replaced, whereas COMPS must have contributions no lower than the contracted-out rebate. COMBS can use a mixture of the requisite benefits and minimum contributions tests to contract out of SERPS; COHS can provide pensions using a combination of salary-related and money purchase elements. Individuals can also top off their schemes with Additional Voluntary Contributions or Free-Standing Additional Voluntary Contributions, up to limits permitted by the Inland Revenue.

As an alternative, individuals have the following personal pension choices that are independent of the employer's scheme:

- Personal pension scheme
- Group personal pension scheme (GPPS)
- Stakeholder pension scheme (SPS)

A PPS is divided into two components. The first is an Appropriate PPS, which is contracted out of SERPS and provides "protected rights" benefits that stand in place of SERPS benefits: They are also known as minimum contribution or rebate-only schemes because the only contributions permitted are the combined rebate on NICs with the employee's share of the rebate, grossed for basic rate tax relief (at 22 percent). The second is an additional scheme, also contracted out, that receives any additional contributions up to Inland Revenue limits. A Group PPS is a scheme that has been arranged by a small employer with only a few employees. It is essentially a collection of individual schemes, but with lower unit costs because of the savings on up-front marketing and administration costs.[7] Stakeholder pension schemes (SPS) are low-cost personal pension schemes introduced in April 2001.

In 1996, the U.K. workforce totaled 28.5 million people, of whom 3.3 million were self-employed (*Economic Trends Annual Supplement* 1999, table 3.2). The pension arrangements of these people were as follows (Department of Social Security 1998b, table 1.0; and estimates by the Government Actuary's Department):

- 7.5 million employees in SERPS
- 1.2 million employees in 110,000 contracted-in occupational schemes
- 9.3 million employees in 40,000 contracted-out occupational schemes (85 percent of such schemes are salary-related, although 85 percent of new schemes begun in 1998 were money purchase or hybrid)
- 5.5 million employees in personal pension schemes
- 1.7 million employees without a pension scheme apart from the BSP
- 1.5 million self-employed in personal pension schemes
- 1.8 million self-employed without a pension scheme apart from the BSP

These figures indicate that 72 percent of supplementary pension scheme members in 1996 were in SERPS or an occupational scheme and 28 percent were in personal pension schemes.[8]

Table 10.1 shows the aggregate values of the entitlements[9] in the four key types of pension scheme in 1994. The total value of entitlements in the BSP and in occupational plans amounted to more than 100 percent of gross domestic product (GDP) each, whereas the value of SERPS and personal pension plans amounted to 30 percent and 21 percent of GDP, respectively. Table 10.2 shows the sources of retirement income in 1997–98. A single person had total retirement income averaging 43 percent of national average earnings. Nearly two-thirds of this came from state benefits and another one-fourth from occupational pensions. Personal pensions provided only about 5 percent of total retirement income for the average person.[10]

7. Private pension schemes in the United Kingdom benefit from an EET system of tax breaks: the contributions into schemes are *e*xempt from tax, the investment returns (with the exception, since 1997, of dividend income on U.K. equities) are *e*xempt from tax, and the pension is *t*axed (with the exception of a tax-free lump sum equal to 1.5 times the final salary in the case of a DB scheme, and 25 percent of the accumulated pension fund in the case of a DC scheme).

8. For more details of the U.K. pension system, see Blake (1995, 1997), Fenton, Ham, and Sabel (1995), Pensions Provision Group (1998), and Reardon (2000).

9. By entitlements I mean either the expected discounted value of accrued rights in DB schemes (whether funded or unfunded) or the value of accumulated financial assets in funded DC schemes.

10. This is partly because personal pension schemes have been around only since 1988.

Table 10.1   **Aggregate Values of Pension Entitlements in 1994**

Type of Scheme	£billions	Percent of GDP
Basic State Pension (BSP)	703	104
State Earnings-Related Pension Scheme (SERPS)	202	30
Occupational pensions	743	110
Personal pensions	140	21

Source: Blake and Orszag (1999, table 12).

Table 10.2   **Sources of Retirement Income in 1997–98**

	Single Person			Married Couples		
Source	£ per Week	Percent of Total	Percent of NAE	£ per Week	Percent of Total	Percent of NAE
State benefits[a]	95	64	27	133	44	38
Occupational pensions	33	22	10	90	30	26
Investment income[b]	14	9	4	48	16	14
Earnings[c]	7	5	2	33	11	9
Total	149	100	43	304	100	87

Source: Department of Social Security (2000, table 1).

Note: NAE = national average earnings.

[a]Includes Incapacity Benefit, Housing Benefit, Council Tax Benefit, etc.

[b]Includes income from personal pensions.

[c]Women in the 60–65 age range and men in the 65–70 age range.

10.3   The Thatcher-Major Reforms to the Pension System

The Thatcher Conservative government that came into power in 1979 became the first government in the Western world to confront head-on the potential crisis in state pension provision. The reforms were continued by the succeeding Major government. These governments introduced the following measures:

1. Linked the growth rate in state pensions to prices rather than national average earnings, thereby saving about 2 percent per annum (Social Security Act 1980).

2. Raised the state pension age from sixty to sixty-five for women over the course of a ten-year period beginning in 2010, thereby reducing the cost of state pensions by £3 billion per annum (Pensions Act 1995).

3. Reduced the benefits accruing under SERPS (which had been set up in only 1978) in a number of ways: (a) The pension was to be reduced (over a ten-year transitional period beginning in April 1999) from 25 percent of

average revalued band earnings over the best twenty years to 20 percent of average revalued band earnings over the full career (Social Security Act 1986); (b) the spouse's pension was cut from 100 percent of the member's pension to 50 percent from October 2001 (Social Security Act 1986); (c) the revaluation factor for band earnings was reduced by about 2 percent per annum (Pensions Act 1995). The combined effect of all these changes was to reduce the value of SERPS benefits by around two-thirds.

4. Provided a "special bonus" in the form of an extra 2 percent National Insurance rebate for all PPSs contracting out of SERPS between April 1988 and April 1993 (Social Security Act 1986); provided an incentive from April 1993 in the form of a 1 percent age-related National Insurance rebate to members of contracted-out PPSs who were aged thirty or older, to discourage them from recontracting back into SERPS (Social Security Act 1993).

5. Relaxed the restriction on PPSs that an annuity had to be purchased on the retirement date, by introducing an income drawdown facility enabling an income (of between 35 and 100 percent of a single life annuity) to be drawn from the pension fund (which otherwise remains invested in earning assets) and delaying the obligation to purchase an annuity until age seventy-five (Finance Act 1995).

6. Enabled members of occupational pension schemes to join personal pension schemes (Social Security Act 1986).

7. Simplified the arrangements for occupational schemes to contract out of SERPS by abolishing the requirement for occupational schemes to provide Guaranteed Minimum Pensions (GMPs): since April 1997, COSRSs had to demonstrate only that they offer requisite benefits that are broadly equivalent to those obtainable from SERPS (Pensions Act 1995).

8. Ended its commitment to pay for part of the inflation indexation of occupational schemes (Pensions Act 1995). Until April 1997, COSRSs had to index the GMP up to an inflation level of 3 percent per annum, and any additional pension above the GMP up to an inflation level of 5 percent per annum. Since the GMP replaced the SERPS pension, which was itself fully indexed to inflation, the government increased an individual's state pension to compensate for any inflation on the GMP above 3 percent per annum. However, the 1995 act abolished the GMP altogether and required COSRSs to index the whole of the pension that they pay up to a maximum of 5 percent per annum.

9. Improved the security of the assets in private-sector schemes through the creation of a compensation fund operated by the Pensions Compensation Board, a Minimum Funding Requirement, and a Statement of Investment Principles (Pensions Act 1995).

10.3.1   Defects in the Thatcher-Major Reforms

The main defects of the Thatcher-Major reforms were as follows:

1. The removal of the requirement that membership of an occupational pension scheme could be made a condition of employment. Membership was made voluntary and new employees had to take the active decision of joining their employer's scheme; fewer than 50 percent of them did so.

2. The lack of a requirement to ensure that transferring from an occupational to a personal pension scheme was in the best interests of the employee, leading directly to the personal pensions misselling scandal that erupted in December 1993. Between 1988 and 1993, 500,000 members of occupational pension schemes had transferred their assets to personal pension schemes following high-pressure sales tactics by agents of PPS providers. As many as 90 percent of those who transferred had been given inappropriate advice. Miners, teachers, nurses, and police officers were among the main targets of the sales agents. Many of these people remained working for the same employer, but they switched from a good occupational pension scheme offering an index-linked pension into a PPS toward which the employer did not contribute and that took 25 percent of the transfer value in commissions and administration charges. An example reported in the press concerned a miner who transferred to a PPS in 1989 and retired in 1994 aged sixty. He received a lump sum of £2,576 and a pension of £734 by his new scheme. Had he remained in his occupational scheme, he would have received a lump sum of £5,125 and a pension of £1,791. As a result of a public outcry, PPS providers have had to compensate those who had been given inappropriate advice to the tune of £11 billion.

3. A lack of restriction on the charges that could be imposed in personal pension plans, under the hope that market forces alone would ensure that PPSs were competitively provided.

4. Giving personal pension scheme members the right to recontract back into SERPS. This option has turned out to be extremely expensive for the government because of the back-loading of benefits in DB pension schemes such as SERPS: Benefits accrue more heavily in the later years than the earlier years.[11] Despite the financial incentives given to contract out of SERPS into PPSs, it turned out to be advantageous for men over the age of forty-two and women over the age of thirty-four to contract back into SERPS once the period of the special bonus had ended in 1993. To discourage this from happening, the government has been forced to offer additional age-related rebates to PPS members over age thirty since 1993. Far from saving the government money, the net cost of PPSs during the first ten years was estimated by the National Audit Office to be about £10 billion.

---

11. Although the back-loading effect is lower in average salary schemes (such as SERPS) than in final salary schemes (such as a typical occupational scheme).

10.4   The Blair Reforms to the Pension System

The New Labour Blair government came into power in 1997 with a radical agenda for reforming the welfare state. During this time, Frank Field, appointed the first Minister for Welfare Reform at the Department of Social Security (DSS) and charged with the objective of "thinking the unthinkable," proved to be too radical for the traditional Old Labour wing of the Labour Party and was soon replaced. The eventual DSS Green Paper proposals, "A New Contract for Welfare: Partnership in Pensions" (DSS 1998), turned out to be much less radical than initially anticipated, but nevertheless continued with the Thatcher government's agenda of attempting to reduce the cost to the state of public pension provision and of transferring the burden of provision to the private sector through the introduction of stakeholder pension schemes. Nevertheless, there was much greater emphasis on redistributing resources to poorer members of society than was the case with the Conservatives. Shortly after the publication of the Green Paper, the treasury issued a consultation document on the type of investment vehicles in which stakeholder pension contributions might be invested. I will examine these proposals in turn.

10.4.1   The Department of Social Security Proposals

The key objectives of the DSS Green Paper were to:

1. Reduce the complexity of the U.K. pension system by abolishing SERPS.
2. Introduce a minimum income guarantee in retirement linked to increases in national average earnings on the grounds that people who work all their lives should not have to rely on means-tested benefits in retirement; the first-tier BSP will remain indexed to prices, however, and over time will become a relatively unimportant component of most pensions.
3. Provide more state help for those who cannot save for retirement, such as the low-paid (those on less than half median earnings), the disabled and carers (those who look after children, the disabled, or the elderly on a voluntary basis), via the unfunded state system.
4. Encourage those who are able to save what they can for retirement, via affordable and secure second-pillar pensions that are:
   a. provided by the state for those on modest incomes (via a new unfunded state second pension), and
   b. provided by the private sector for middle- and high-income earners, with the option of new low-cost DC stakeholder pensions, which are likely to replace high-cost personal pensions. However, there will be no extra compulsion to save for retirement at the second pillar and no additional incentives over those already existing at the second pillar.

The Green Paper proposals formed the basis of the Welfare Reform and Pensions Act, which received the Royal Assent in November 1999. The act deals with following issues.

State Pensions

1. A Minimum Income Guarantee (MIG) of £75 per week was introduced for pensioners in April 1999; it is means tested and indexed to earnings. In April 2003, the MIG will rise to £100 per week. In the same month, a pension credit will be introduced with the aim of rewarding thrift by providing additional cash at the rate of 60 pence for every pound of savings income, earnings, or second pension. An individual's total income entitlement will equal the MIG plus 60 percent of the income received from any second pension, any savings, or any part-time work. The total income entitlement will be capped at £135 per week.

2. SERPS was replaced by a new State Second Pension Scheme (S2P) in April 2002. The S2P was initially earnings related, but from April 2007 becomes a flat-rate benefit even though contributions are earnings related—a feature intended to provide strong incentives for middle- and high-income earners to contract out. The S2P

  a. Ensures that everyone with a complete work record receives combined pensions higher than the MIG;

  b. Gives low-paid individuals earning less than £9,500 per annum twice the SERPS pension given at £9,500 per annum (implying that the accrual rate is 40 percent of £9,500 rather than the 20 percent under SERPS);

  c. Gives a higher benefit than SERPS between £9,500 and £21,600 per annum (average earnings);

  d. Leaves those earning more than £21,600 per annum unaffected (with an accrual rate of 20 percent);

  e. Upgrades these thresholds in line with national average earnings; and

  f. Provides credits for carers (including parents with children under age five) and the disabled.

Stakeholder Pensions

1. New stakeholder pension schemes (SPSs) were introduced in April 2001, but are principally intended for middle-income earners (£9,500–21,600) with no existing private pension provision. They can be used to contract out of S2P.

2. They are collective arrangements, provided by:

  a. An employer,

  b. A representative or a membership or affinity organization, or

  c. A financial services company.

3. They are DC schemes, with the same restrictions as for personal pen-

sions—namely, that on the retirement date up to 25 percent of the accumulated fund may be taken as a tax-free lump sum; the remaining fund may be used to buy an annuity or to provide a pension income by way of a drawdown facility until age seventy-five,[12] when an annuity must be purchased with the remaining assets.

4. They have to meet minimum standards, known as "CAT" (charges-access-terms) marks concerning:

    a. The charging structure and level of charges (a maximum of 1 percent of fund value),

    b. Levels of contractual minimum contributions (£20), and

    c. Contribution flexibility and transferability (no penalties if contributions cease temporarily [for up to five years] or if the fund is transferred to another provider).

5. The main provisions of the 1995 Pensions Act apply to SPS, covering the annual report and accounts, the appointment of professional advisors, and the Statement of Investment Principles.

6. They are regulated principally by the Occupational Pensions Regulatory Authority, with the Pensions Ombudsman for redress and the selling of schemes and supervision of their investment managers by the Financial Services Authority.

7. Employers without an occupational scheme and with at least five staff members must offer access to one "nominated" SPS and must provide a payroll deduction facility.

8. There is a new integrated tax regime for all defined contribution pension plans. SPS, personal pension plans, and occupational DC plans will attract tax relief on contributions up to a maximum of 17.5 percent of earnings (below age thirty-six), rising to 40 percent (above age sixty-one). However, contributions up to £3,600 per annum can be made into any DC plan regardless of the size of net relevant earnings. Contributions in excess of £3,600 per annum may continue for up to five years after relevant earnings have ceased. Thereafter, contributions may not exceed £3,600 per annum. All contributions into DC plans will be made net of basic-rate tax, with providers recovering the tax from the Inland Revenue, and with higher-rate tax, if any, being recovered in the self-assessment tax return.

Occupational Pensions

1. Occupational schemes can contract out of the S2P.

2. Employers can again make membership of an occupational scheme a condition of employment, and employees are allowed to opt out only if they have signed a statement of rights being given up, certified that they have adequate alternative provision, and have taken advice that confirms that the alternative is at least as good as the S2P.

---

12. There are plans to raise this to age eighty.

3. The compensation scheme established by the 1995 Pensions Act was extended to cover 100 percent of the liabilities of pensioners and those within ten years of normal pension age.

Personal Pensions

1. PPS members may contract out of the S2P.
2. They receive protection in cases of the bankruptcy of the member.

10.4.2   HM Treasury Proposals

The treasury proposals were contained in "Helping to Deliver Stakeholder Pensions: Flexibility in Pension Investment" (HM Treasury 1999). They called for the introduction of more-flexible investment vehicles for managing pension contributions, not only those in the new stakeholder pension schemes, but also those in occupational and personal pension schemes. These investment vehicles were given the name Pooled Pension Investments (PPIs). The main PPIs are authorized unit trusts (open-ended mutual funds), investment trust companies (closed-ended mutual funds), and open-ended investment companies.

In comparison with the individual arrangements of existing personal pension schemes and the poor transferability of occupational pension schemes, PPIs offer:

- Lower charges, because collective investment vehicles have much lower overheads than individual investments, and
- Greater flexibility, because PPIs are easy to value and transfer between different stakeholder, personal, and occupational pension schemes. This flexibility allows employees to move jobs without having to change pension schemes, and thereby encourage greater labor market flexibility.

10.5   Assessment of the Blair Reforms

The Welfare Reform and Pensions Act, while containing some significant improvements on the existing system, does not fully meet the Green Paper's own objectives.

10.5.1   Reforms to State Pensions

Although the abolition of SERPS helped to simplify the United Kingdom's extremely complex pension system, the proposal to have a MIG (of £75 per week) that differed from the BSP (£67.50 per week) reintroduced substantial complexity at the starting point for state pension provision, especially when the difference between the two amounts (£7.50 per week) was initially so small. It would have been far simpler to set the MIG equal to the BSP and to link the latter to earnings. The government has explicitly rejected this on the grounds of both cost[13] and the fact that it would benefit the high-paid as well as the low-paid, whereas the government's emphasis was on helping the low-paid. However, the problem with keeping the BSP linked to prices rather than to earnings is that it will continue to fall relentlessly as a proportion of national average earnings: It is currently only 16 percent of national average earnings and will fall to well below 10 percent by 2025. Although the government admits that this will save substantial sums of money, it implies that the government is effectively abandoning the first pillar of support in old age and obliging everyone to rely on the second and third pillars or on means-tested benefits. The Green Paper talked about building on the BSP, but this implies building on a sinking ship.

If the government is genuinely concerned about security at the minimum level for all, it should consider funding the first pillar appropriately by establishing an explicit fund (like the Social Security Trust Fund in the United States) into which it places the NICs of those who are in work, while the government itself funds the contributions of the low-paid, carers and the disabled.[14] The contribution rate could be actuarially set to deliver the MIG for all when they retire. It could be a hypothecated part of NICs. In other words, the contributions would accrue "interest" equal to the growth rate in national average earnings. The state could explicitly issue national average earnings–indexed bonds, which the social security trust fund would buy. This is the only honest way of both preserving the value of and honoring the promises under the first pillar. The second and third pillars could then be formally integrated with the first pillar; that is, the second pillar could be used to deliver the tranche of pension between the MIG and the Inland Revenue limits, while the third pillar is used for voluntary arrangements above the Inland Revenue limits. If the first pillar remains unfunded, there is nothing to prevent future generations' reneging on an agreement that they are expected to keep but into which they did not voluntarily enter.

The fact that membership of pension schemes at the second pillar remains voluntary is highly worrying for reasons of myopia and moral hazard; compulsory contributions are seen as one way of dealing with these problems. Myopia arises because individuals do not recognize the need to make adequate provision for retirement when they are young, but regret

13. An additional £3 billion per year (*Daily Telegraph,* 31 July 1999).

14. In fact, the Conservative government in the United Kingdom announced in March 1997 plans to privatize the entire state pension system from the turn of the century and to end its unfunded nature. All individuals in work would receive rebates on their NICs, which would be invested in personalized pension accounts. The initial costs in terms of additional taxation were estimated to be £160 million in the first year, rising to a peak of £7 billion per year in 2040. However, the long-term savings to the taxpayer from the end of state pension provision were estimated to be £40 billion per year (all in 1997 prices). The proposals were put on hold as a result of the Conservative government's defeat in the May 1997 General Election (see *Basic Pension Plus,* Conservative Central Office, 5 March 1997).

this misjudgment when they are old, by which time it is too late to do anything about it. Moral hazard arises when individuals deliberately avoid saving for retirement when they are young because they calculate that the state will feel obliged not to let them live in dire poverty in retirement. Inevitably, this will lead to substantial means testing in retirement.

In short, although the Welfare Reform and Pensions Act has some good points, it fails three of Frank Field's tests for a good state pension system: It is not mandatory, it is not funded, and it remains means-tested (Field 1996a,b)

10.5.2 Reforms to Private Pensions

The government's proposal to have a maximum charge of 1 percent of fund value on SPSs will have two dramatic effects on private-sector pension provision, especially on PPSs.

The first is that it will help to force economies of scale in DC pension provision. This is because stakeholder pensions will be a retail product with wholesale charges. To deliver this product effectively providers will need to exploit massive economies of scale. The current charges for personal pension schemes, which average 1.4 percent and rise to as much as 2.2 percent of fund value for twenty-five-year policies (*Money Management,* October 1998); are much higher than the 1 percent CAT-marked limit on SPS. There may be a range of providers of SPS to begin with, but the only way for a provider to survive in the long run will be if it operates at low unit cost on a large scale. This will inevitably lead to mergers among providers and a final equilibrium with a small number of very large providers.

Existing personal pension providers and distribution channels face these challenges:

- Appropriate PPSs face massive competition from SPSs for future NIC rebates.
- SPSs could be better than PPSs for middle-income groups, leaving PPSs as a choice only for those on high incomes who require and are willing to pay for a bespoke product.
- New, affinity-based SPSs gateway organizations will link up with pension providers (e.g., Amalgamated Engineering and Electrical Union, which has 720,000 members, and Friends Provident).
- The treasury's proposed PPIs (see section 10.4.2) provide a low-cost alternative investment vehicle to the high-cost managed funds of most PPSs.
- Individual Savings Accounts (ISAs), introduced by the treasury in April 1999 to encourage greater personal-sector saving, also provide an important alternative to PPSs. Contributions into ISAs of up to £5,000 per annum are permitted, and the investment returns are free from income and capital gains tax. Although not intended as pension

saving vehicles (e.g., they do not attract tax relief on contributions, unlike standard pension saving products), ISAs can be used in retirement income planning because they enjoy the big advantage that they can be cashed in tax-free at any time, thereby avoiding the need to purchase a pension annuity on the retirement date.

The second benefit is that it will effectively force stakeholder pension funds to be managed passively, because active management would result in a charge higher than 1 percent. As demonstrated below, active fund managers have not demonstrated that they can systematically deliver the superior investment performance that justifies their higher charges. Furthermore, passively managed mutual funds (which are similar investment vehicles to PPIs) in the United States, such as Vanguard, have charges below 0.3 percent.

10.6   Unresolved Issues in Pension Scheme Design

Led by the United States, there has been an enormous growth in DC pension provision throughout the world: It seems that private pension provision in the future will be dominated by DC. The United Kingdom has had more than a decade of experience with DC provision, and much of this has been less than satisfactory. Various U.K. governments have attempted to deal with some of the problems that have been identified, but many issues have not been resolved. It is worthwhile explaining the key problems that the United Kingdom has experienced with its DC provision.

10.6.1   The Accumulation Phase of Defined Contribution
           Pension Schemes

The investment phase of DC schemes has experienced the following problems in the United Kingdom.

High and Confusing Charges

The charge structures of most existing personal pension scheme providers are high, complex, disguised, and front-loaded. Table 10.3 shows that the average personal pension scheme with a twenty-five-year investment horizon takes 19 percent of the fund value in charges, while the worst scheme takes nearly 30 percent.[15] On the one hand, such charge structures have the effect of confusing consumers to such an extent that they are unable to assess whether the schemes in which they are being invited to participate—for a significant period of time, and with a substantial commitment of resources—offer value for money. On the other hand, they give little incentive to the provider to offer value for money on a long-term basis. An examination of *Money Management's* annual *Personal Pensions*

15. More details on charges in personal pension schemes are contained in Blake and Board (2000).

Table 10.3   **Charges and Reductions in Yield in Personal Pension Plans (%)**

	5 Years	10 Years	15 Years	20 Years	25 Years
Charges as a percentage of fund value					
Best overall[a]	3.1	4.1	7.2	8.5	9.8
Best commission-loaded fund	4.0	4.1	7.4	8.9	10.6
Industry average	11.6	13.0	14.8	17.7	19.0
Worst fund	19.2	22.0	24.6	28.2	27.8
Reduction in yield					
Best overall[a]	1.26	0.79	0.90	0.76	0.68
Best commission-loaded fund	1.63	0.79	0.92	0.80	0.73
Industry average	4.91	2.65	1.93	1.68	1.39
Worst fund	8.47	4.76	3.43	2.88	2.16

Source: Money Management (October 1998).
Note: Regular-premium personal pension plan (£200/month).
[a] Lower of best commission-loaded and best commission-free.

publications (Walford 2000) also reveals that providers change their charge structures on a regular basis. This makes it very difficult to compare schemes over time and raises the question as to whether particular charge structures and changes to them are used to conceal the impact of costs, and thereby confuse consumers even more.

Furthermore, in order for consumers to compare products, it is important that they are aware of the full set of charges they face. It is frequently the case that some charges are disguised or hidden. One illustration of this concerns the treatment of paid-up policies (or PUPs; see Slade 1999, who reports a survey by AXA Sun Life). When policy holders move to a new pension scheme, they have the choice of taking a transfer value with them or leaving their assets in the original scheme, which is then converted into a PUP; the assets cannot be liquidated prior to retirement. Only 15 percent of policy holders take transfer values, whereas the rest leave PUPs. The regulator requires, however, that pension schemes disclose only transfer values and full maturity values. There is no obligation to disclose PUP maturity values, and, although schemes may do so if they wish, few actually do.

There is clearly a trade-off between high transfer values and high full maturity values: Schemes with front-loaded charges will quote low transfer values and high maturity values relative to schemes with level charges. Different providers compete on the basis of the transfer and full maturity values that they quote. However, PUP maturity values, which, in principle, should be related to transfer values, can turn out to be poor value for money. For example, the AXA Sun Life survey reports the case of one provider that quotes the highest transfer value among twelve leading providers, but ranks twelfth for its PUP maturity value quote. It appears that some schemes quote high transfer values to attract business, knowing that only 15 percent of those policy holders not going to full term are likely to take transfers, whereas the remaining 85 percent end up with low PUP maturity values.

Another example of hidden charges comes from a survey of fund management fees by Towers Perrin (1998): Some fund managers did not report their full sets of charges. The three key charges are for asset management, broking (i.e., transaction execution), and custody. There are also charges for reporting, accounting, and performance measurement. Some fund managers report the asset management fee (as some proportion of the value of the net assets under management) only *after* deducting the broking and custody fees. Some fund managers justify this on the grounds that both the portfolio transactions and the safekeeping are conducted by a third party independent of the fund manager, typically the global custodian. Other fund managers operate full "clean fees"; that is, they report full charges, including third party fees that are merely passed through to the client. Yet other fund managers add commissions to third party fees before passing them through. In some cases, however, the broker or custodian is related to the fund manager (e.g., is part of the same investment banking or insurance group). In such cases, it is more difficult to allocate charges appropriately.

The lack of transparency can also lead to incentive problems. Brokerage fees are related to turnover, which provides an incentive to churn (i.e., overtrade) the portfolio; this is especially so if the transactions are executed by an in-house broker and the brokerage fee is hidden from the client. Some fund managers, in contrast, use discount brokers to reduce the costs to the clients. Some clients impose turnover limits to reduce costs. However, the most effective means of keeping charges down is complete fee transparency, full disclosure for each fund management function, and benchmark-related performance measurement (where the impact of hidden fees is exposed through poor performance).

Low Persistency with Voluntary Arrangements

A regular-premium pension scheme involves a substantial commitment of time and resources by both the scheme's sponsor and its members if the desired objectives are to be achieved. Any significant front-loading of charges in schemes means that members suffer substantial detriment if their contributions lapse prematurely (as the discussion of PUP maturity values, above, indicates). As the Personal Investment Authority (the predecessor to the Financial Services Authority) argues, "if investors buy policies on the basis of good advice, they would not normally be expected to cancel premiums to their policies unless forced to do so by unexpected changes in their personal circumstances. This means that persistency is a powerful indicator of the quality of the selling process" (1998, 3).

The Personal Investment Authority shows that persistency rates after just four years of membership are between 57 and 68 percent (table 10.4). The persistency rate is higher for schemes arranged by independent finan-

Table 10.4   **Persistency Rates for Regular-Premium Personal Pension Plans (%)**

	Company Representatives				Independent Financial Advisors			
	After 1 Year	After 2 Years	After 3 Years	After 4 Years	After 1 Year	After 2 Years	After 3 Years	After 4 Years
1993	84.1	72.3	63.6	56.7	91.5	83.3	76.6	70.5
1994	83.7	72.8	64.4		91.3	82.1	74.5	
1995	85.5	75.0			90.8	81.6		
1996	86.6				90.2			

Source: Personal Investment Authority (1998, table 1).

cial advisors than by company representatives, suggesting that the clients of the former are generally more satisfied with their policies than those of the latter. Although only four years of data are available, the evidence suggests that very few personal pension scheme members (only about 16 percent) are likely to maintain their memberships in the scheme long enough to build up an adequate pension.

The Personal Investment Authority regards these persistency rates as "disturbing" (1998, 10) and offers a number of explanations: Members were missold pensions that were either unsuitable or too expensive; regular premium policies might be unsuitable for those with irregular earnings or uncertain long-term employment; a change of employment may lead to a member's joining an occupational scheme and abandoning his or her personal one; adverse general economic conditions could worsen persistency rates. The Personal Investment Authority also offers suggestions as to why the IFAs are more successful than company representatives. First, IFAs tend to advise clients who have higher incomes, and who are more likely to continue contributing; second, policies chosen by an IFA are likely to be from a wider range of policies than those offered by representatives of any single company, leading to a greater likelihood of the policy's closely matching the particular needs of the client.

Making membership in second-pillar pension schemes mandatory rather than voluntary would do much to deal with the problem of low persistency.

Below-Average Investment Performance

Investment performance as well as the costs of delivering that performance is critical in DC schemes. Research by Blake, Lehmann, and Timmermann (1999, 2000), Blake and Timmermann (1998), and Lunde, Timmermann, and Blake (1999) has shown the following.[16] On average, U.K. pension funds have underperformed the market in key asset classes (table

16. Similar results hold in the United States (see, e.g., Lakonishok, Shleifer, and Vishny 1992).

Table 10.5   **Performance of U.K. Managed Funds in Comparison with the Market, 1986–94**

	Average Portfolio Weight	Average Market Return	Average Pension Fund Return	Average Outperformance	Percentage Outperformers
U.K. equities	53.70	13.30	12.97	−0.33	44.80
International equities	19.50	11.11	11.23	0.12	39.80
U.K. bonds	7.60	10.35	10.76	0.41	77.30
International bonds	2.20	8.64	10.03	1.39	68.80
U.K. index bonds	2.70	8.22	8.12	−0.10	51.70
Cash and other investments	4.50	9.90	9.01	−0.89	59.50
U.K. property	8.90	9.00	9.52	0.52	39.10
Total	100.00	12.18	11.73	−0.45	42.80

Sources: Blake, Lehmann, and Timmermann (1999, 2000).
Notes: All numbers are percentages. International property is excluded because no market index was available.

10.5), and there has been a wide dispersion of performance by individual fund managers (table 10.6), with little evidence of funds' being able to generate superior (i.e., above average) performance consistently over extended periods. Poorly performing funds are eventually wound-up or merged into more successful funds, but it can take many years for this to happen, during which time policy holders experience consistently poor returns.

On top of this, the research found that fund managers have not been especially successful at active fund management. In particular, it found that 99.47 percent of the total return generated by U.K. fund managers can be explained by the strategic asset allocation—that is, by the long-run asset allocation specified by pension-scheme sponsors on the advice of their actuaries, following an asset-liability modeling exercise. This is the passive component of pension fund performance. The active components are security selection and market timing. The average pension fund was unsuccessful at market timing, generating a negative contribution to the total return of –1.64 percent. The average pension fund was, however, more successful in security selection, making a positive contribution to the total return of 2.68 percent. The overall contribution from active fund management, however, was just over 1 percent of the total return (or about 13 basis points per annum), which is *less than active fund managers' annual fees* (which range from 20 basis points for a £500 million fund to 75 basis points for a £10 million fund; *Pensions Management,* September 1998).

Virtually the same or better returns could have been generated if pension funds had invested passively in index funds. In addition, fund man-

Table 10.6   Fractiles of Total Returns by Asset Class for U.K. Managed Funds, 1986–94

	U.K. Equities	International Equities	U.K. Bonds	International Bonds	U.K. Index Bonds	Cash and Other Investments	U.K. Property	Total
Minimum	8.59	4.42	6.59	−0.64	5.59	2.67	3.05	7.22
5%	11.43	8.59	9.44	2.18	7.20	5.46	5.07	10.60
10%	11.85	9.03	9.95	7.56	7.81	7.60	6.58	10.96
25%	12.44	9.64	10.43	8.30	7.91	8.97	8.03	11.47
50%	13.13	10.65	10.79	11.37	8.22	10.25	8.75	12.06
75%	13.93	11.76	11.22	13.37	8.45	11.72	9.99	12.59
90%	14.81	12.52	11.70	14.55	8.80	14.20	10.84	13.13
95%	15.46	13.14	12.05	18.15	8.89	16.13	11.36	13.39
Maximum	17.39	14.68	17.23	26.34	10.07	19.73	13.53	15.03
Maximum − minimum	8.80	10.26	10.64	26.98	4.48	17.06	10.48	7.81

Sources: Blake, Lehmann, and Timmermann (2000, table 1).

Notes: The table shows the fractiles of the cross-sectional distribution of returns on individual asset classes as well as on the total portfolio. Amounts are average annualized percentages.

agement costs would have been lower and the dispersion in returns across fund managers would have been reduced. Alternatively, if fund managers believe that, despite all the evidence, they can generate superior investment performance, they should be willing to accept performance-related investment management fees that reward good ex post performance and penalize poor ex post performance.

Given the major weaknesses in the existing design of DC pension schemes in the United Kingdom, the above outcomes at the accumulation stage of high charges and fund management fees, low persistency of contribution payments, and poor and widely dispersed investment performance should come as no surprise.

10.6.2 Distribution Phase of Defined Contribution Pension Schemes

Stakeholder pensions are CAT-marked in an attempt to avoid the problems experienced with personal pensions. However, the CAT-marking applies only to the accumulation phase, the phase that the scheme member does not directly experience. Little or nothing has been said about the distribution phase, when the member discovers whether he or she will receive a good pension. The distribution phase for U.K. DC schemes involves the purchase of a life annuity. The provision of annuities involve the following risks.

Adverse Selection and Longevity Risk

This is the risk that the individuals most likely to purchase annuities on a voluntary basis are those who believe that they are likely to live longer than the average for the population of the same age. Individuals may have a good idea, on the basis of both their own personal medical and family histories, whether they are likely to experience lighter or heavier mortality than others in the population of similar age. Life insurance companies do not have access to this information with the same degree of reliability.

The insurance company is unable to differentiate between prospective purchasers who will experience heavier mortality (and so make a profit for the life insurance office) and those who will experience lighter mortality (and hence make a loss for the life insurance office); however, it realizes that those most likely to purchase annuities will come from the latter group rather than the former.

To hedge this risk, the life insurance office will base its annuity rates on the "select group" that is most likely to purchase annuities. Annuities will therefore be poor value for the money for members of the first group.

Underestimating Increases in Longevity

Longevity tends to increase over time and there can be severe financial consequences if insurance companies underestimate increases in longevity. Longevity forecast errors of up to 20 percent over intervals as short as ten years are not uncommon (MacDonald 1996).

Inflation Risk

This risk, faced by those purchasing level annuities, is that unanticipated high inflation rapidly reduces the real value of the pension.

Interest Rate Risk

Annuity rates vary substantially over time. They are related to the yields on government bonds of the same expected term; and because long-term yields vary by up to 100 percent, annuity rates will vary by the same order of magnitude (Credit Suisse First Boston 1999).

Reinvestment Risk

The risk faced by annuity providers that there are insufficient long-maturing matching assets (especially government bonds) available to make the annuity payments, with the consequence that the proceeds from maturing assets may have to be reinvested on less favorable terms or in less suitable assets.

Inefficient Allocation of Risks in Annuities Markets

These risks are currently allocated in the following way: The *state* assumes interest-rate and inflation risk after the annuity is purchased (because annuity providers purchase fixed-income and index-linked bonds from the government to generate the cash flows needed to meet their level and indexed annuity obligations). The *annuity provider* assumes mortality risk after the annuity is purchased (because it will incur losses if annuitants live longer than expected). The *annuitant* assumes interest rate risk before the annuity is purchased, and if he or she chooses to buy a level annuity, inflation risk after the annuity is purchased (because the annuitant can retire at a trough in interest rates and there could be unexpectedly high inflation after he or she takes out a level annuity).

Annuity providers add loadings of 10–14 percent (Finkelstein and Poterba 1999) to cover their costs and risks. Even loadings of this size, however, may be inadequate to cover the costs of failing to forecast mortality improvements accurately. Anecdotal evidence suggests that annuity providers in the United Kingdom have underestimated the life expectancy of their current annuity pool by about two years. Furthermore, since 1999, there has been a substantial shortage of new long-maturing government bonds (both fixed interest and index linked), and this has had the effect of introducing reinvestment risk into the U.K. annuity market for the first time in its history (Bishop 1999). From the annuitants' viewpoint, the falling annuity yields during the 1990s have shown that the interest rate risk they bear is substantial.

This allocation of risks is not efficient. Annuity providers could do more to promote products that help annuitants hedge interest rate risk (e.g., phased annuities, protected annuity funds in which the interest rate risk is hedged using derivatives, or investment-linked annuities). Similarly, the state could do more to help annuity providers hedge longevity risk. One way would be to make supplementary pensions mandatory, thereby bringing the longevity experience of annuitants closer to that of the whole population. Another would be to issue new types of bonds, known as Survivor Bonds (Blake and Burrows 2001). These are life annuity bonds whose coupon payments decline in direct proportion to the rate at which a cohort of sixty-five-year-olds on the issue date of the bond dies out, and with the coupons remaining in payment until this cohort had fully completed its life cycle. This would enable annuity providers to hedge both aggregate mortality risks and improvements in mortality, but leave specific mortality risks a commercial choice of the provider (e.g., the provider could target groups with lighter than average mortality [such as nonsmokers] and charge an additional premium, but that would be a commercial decision).

10.7   The Political Economy of Pension Reform

How has it been possible for U.K. governments to reduce the size of state pension provision without significant political protest, when similar attempts to do so on the Continent have led to street protests and strikes (e.g., in Italy in November 1994 and France in November 1995)?

Consider the SERPS pension. When it was first introduced in 1978, it offered a pension of 25 percent of the best twenty years' band earnings revalued to the retirement date by increases in NAE, with a 100 percent spouse's pension. Within a quarter-century, the value of these benefits had been reduced by two thirds before the scheme was abandoned altogether. How has this been achieved so peaceably? There are three main explanations. First, SERPS had been established only a few years before changes began to be made to it, so very few people were drawing the pension and little loyalty to the scheme had accumulated. Second, SERPS was an incredibly complex pension system that very few pension professionals have fully understand, let alone members of the general public. Although there was comment in the media at the time of these changes to SERPS, very little of it seemed to have permeated the consciousness of the mass of the population and the extent of the changes was little understood. Third, the changes were introduced with a lag of fifteen to twenty years, so it was easy for everyone to forget about them.

Even when changes were introduced immediately, such as the switch in the uprating of the state pension from earnings to prices, the immediate difference was relatively small and most people failed to realize how, over time, small differences can compound into large amounts.[17]

---

17. Had the indexation of the BSP been preserved to the growth rate in national average earnings since 1980, the BSP would have been £95 per week in 1999 rather than £66.75 (*Daily Telegraph,* 31 July 1999).

A final explanation lies in the fact that state pension provision is much less important for most people in the United Kingdom than on the Continent, and those for whom it is important (namely, the low-paid) have little political influence.

The situation on the Continent is rather different. State pensions there provide much higher replacement ratios than in the United Kingdom, and social solidarity appears to be a more important objective than it is in the United Kingdom. As a consequence, it is much more difficult to alter pension arrangements on the Continent, even if the political will to do so is strong—which it clearly is not.

10.8 Conclusion

Over the last twenty years, governments have had two major impacts on pension provision in the United Kingdom. First, they have reduced the cost of providing state pensions by reducing the level of benefits from the state schemes. Second, they have encouraged greater and more effective private-sector provision, although the Conservative and Labour governments have done this in quite different ways. The Thatcher-Major governments made private supplementary pension arrangements voluntary and used tax incentives to encourage consumers to join personal pension schemes; but they left it to the market to determine the structure and efficiency of these schemes. The result was schemes that exhibited very high front-loaded charges, because retail customers tend not to be skilled at assessing the cost-effectiveness of retail financial products (Office of Fair Trading 1997, 1999). In contrast, the Blair government, recognizing the market failure arising from poorly informed consumers, imposed restrictions on the structure of stakeholder pension schemes that helped to force economies of scale and hence lower charges.

Charges, however, constitute only one of the issues that must be resolved with DC pension schemes if such schemes are to provide effective long-term alternatives to state pensions. Other issues include persistency and investment performance during the accumulation phase, and longevity, inflation, and interest-rate and reinvestment risks during the distribution phase. With DB schemes, poor portability has been a perennial problem that neither the Conservative nor the Labour governments have tackled effectively.

The other countries of Europe would be wise to examine closely the situation in the United Kingdom, less for the way in which reforms to state provision were made (because there is no equivalent political will in Europe to match such reforms) than for the sometimes painful lessons that were learned in terms of private-sector provision.

References

Bishop, G. 1999. *Why are long gilts the richest bonds in the world, and getting richer?* London: SalomonSmithBarney.

Blake, D. 1995. *Pension schemes and pension funds in the United Kingdom.* Oxford: Oxford University Press.

———. 1997. Pensions choices and pensions policy in the United Kingdom. In *The economics of pensions: Principles, policies and international experience,* ed. S. Valdes-Prieto, 277–317. Cambridge: Cambridge University Press.

Blake, D., and Board, J. 2000. Measuring value added in the pensions industry. *Geneva Papers on Risk and Insurance: Issues and Practice* 25:539–67.

Blake, D., and W. Burrows. (2001). Survivor bonds: Helping to hedge mortality risk. *Journal of Risk and Insurance* 68:339–48.

Blake, D., B. Lehmann, and A. Timmermann. 1999. Asset allocation dynamics and pension fund performance. *Journal of Business* 72:429–62.

———. 2000. *Performance clustering and incentives in the UK pension fund industry.* London: Birkbeck College, Pensions Institute, Working Paper.

Blake, D., and J. M. Orszag. 1997. *Portability and preservation of pension rights in the UK.* Report of the director-general's inquiry into pensions, vol. 3. London: Office of Fair Trading, July.

———. 1999. Annual estimates of personal wealth holdings in the United Kingdom since 1948. *Applied Financial Economics* 9:397–421.

Blake, D., and A. Timmermann. 1998. Mutual fund performance: Evidence from the UK. *European Finance Review* 2:57–77.

Credit Suisse First Boston (CSFB). 1999. *Equity-gilt study.* London: CSFB.

Department of Social Security (DSS). 1998a. *A new contract for welfare: Partnership in pensions.* Command reference 4179. London: DSS, December.

———. 1998b. *Second tier pension provision 1995–96.* Newcastle upon Tyne: Analytical Services Division.

———. 2000. *The pensioners' income series 1997–98.* London: Analytical Services Division.

Fenton, J., R. Ham, and J. Sabel. 1995. *Pensions handbook.* Croydon: Tolley Publishing.

Field, F. 1996a. *How to pay for the future: Building a stakeholders' welfare.* London: Institute of Community Studies.

———. 1996b. *Stakeholder welfare.* Choice in Welfare Series no. 32. London: Institute of Economic Affairs.

Finkelstein, A., and J. Poterba. 1999. Selection effects in the market for individual annuities: New evidence from the United Kingdom. *Economic Journal* (forthcoming).

HM Treasury. 1999. *Helping to deliver stakeholder pensions: Flexibility in pension investment.* London: HM Treasury, February.

Lakonishok, J., A. Shleifer, and R. W. Vishny. 1992. The structure and performance of the money management industry. *Brookings Papers on Economic Activity, Microeconomics:* 339–79.

Lunde, A., A. Timmermann, and D. Blake. 1999. The hazards of mutual fund underperformance. *Journal of Empirical Finance* 6:121–52.

MacDonald, A. 1996. United Kingdom. In *The second actuarial study of mortality in Europe,* ed. A. MacDonald. Brussels: Groupe Consultatif des Associations D'Actuaires des Pays des Communautes Europeennes.

Office of Fair Trading. 1997. *Consumer detriment under conditions of imperfect information.* Research Paper no. 11, London: Office of Fair Trading.

————. 1999. *Vulnerable consumers and financial services.* Report no. 255. London: Office of Fair Trading.

Pensions Provision Group. 1998. *We all need pensions: Prospects for pension provision.* London: Stationery Office.

Personal Investment Authority. 1998. *Survey of persistency of life and pension policies.* London: Personal Investment Authority.

Reardon, A. M. 2000. *Pensions handbook.* London: Allied Dunbar.

Slade, P. 1999. Quote manipulation claims. *The Independent* (30 January).

Towers Perrin. 1998. *European active investment management charges.* London: Towers Perrin, August.

Walford, J. 2000. *Money management: Personal pensions.* London: Financial Times Business Publications.

Comment   Andrew A. Samwick

The system of public pensions in the United Kingdom is in many ways unique and, in particular, uniquely complicated to an outside observer. The author is to be commended for a clear and detailed discussion of what the U.K. system represents and how it has gotten to that point over the last twenty-five years. The main fact about the U.K. system is that it currently faces a substantially smaller financial problem than in other European countries. Less-rapid aging and a smaller pay-as-you-go (PAYGO) system bode well for the United Kingdom.

This fact tempts us to consider the United Kingdom to be a model for other European systems that now face financial crises. This would be misleading, since the United Kingdom is not in its current position because it emerged from a past financial crisis of the sort the Europe now faces. Instead, it achieved its enviable position directly, without the transition that other European countries must soon undertake. The distinction between the United Kingdom's being a model, rather than just an example, is critical in a discussion of the pension crisis now facing Europe. The general conclusion of my remarks is twofold. First, the system in the United Kingdom does not give us much guidance about the transition out of the pension crisis faced by countries with mature PAYGO systems. Second, the pension system in the United Kingdom is nonetheless quite informative about some of the pitfalls that may besiege other European countries once they have found their own ways to more funded systems.

It is not quite right to say that the United Kingdom is ahead of other European countries. Instead, it benefits from what can be described as a historical accident or a deliberate policy choice. In the postwar period, the United Kingdom adopted Beveridge's plan for public income support, in

Andrew A. Samwick is professor of economics at Dartmouth College and a research associate of the National Bureau of Economic Research.

which there was a basic fixed-rate pension set at a subsistence level. Prior to the implementation of the State Earnings-Related Pension Scheme (SERPS) in 1978, the United Kingdom had no comprehensive system of publicly funded earnings-related pensions.

As a result of this delay, SERPS has three defining characteristics that distinguish it from systems in other developed countries. First, SERPS was not very big, because it had to replace earnings only above the basic state pension and below an upper earnings limit. Second, it was easily scaled back in subsequent legislation during the mid-1980s. There were no vested interests in this system, because it had no large startup generation of pensioners to receive an enormous windfall. In the United States and other countries that currently have mature PAYGO public systems, there is always a generation dependent on Social Security for its current income, so that meaningful reform is politically unlikely (if not impossible) in the absence of a financial crisis. Third, by the time SERPS was established, there was a very well-developed employer-provided pension sector, and the public system was therefore designed to allow contracting out by suitable occupational and (later) personal pension schemes.

Public pension systems are intended to provide valuable services to their participants. Apart from issues of benefit levels, which will be discussed next, there are three economic reasons that countries establish public pension systems. The first is the standard problem of moral hazard. Societies implicitly, if not explicitly, provide a guarantee against poverty in old age. This insurance may give households an incentive to consume too much and to save too little while working. The second is the pooling of longevity risk. The possibility of slipping into poverty increases with longevity in the absence of an annuity, even if the moral hazard problem has been addressed in expected value. Because private annuity markets have always been incomplete, public systems have primarily paid benefits as indexed annuities. Making the "purchase" of the annuity mandatory for all beneficiaries overcomes the adverse selection problem that exists in private markets. Third, the goal of relieving poverty is close to uniform across all members of the population. The cost savings due to economies of scale in operating a single plan with centralized administration are enormous compared to the costs of a decentralized system operated by smaller private entities.

How well does the U.K. system address the goal of providing poverty relief among the elderly? This is the primary goal of the Basic State Pension (BSP), the first tier of the system. The BSP is a flat pension of £67.50 per week for a single person, an amount reported to be equal to about 17 percent of national average earnings. The first tier has much to recommend it. It is mandatory, centralized, and uniform, so it generates very little in the way of administrative or selection costs. It is also not very generous. This has the benefit of not distorting private saving decisions too much. However, the BSP seems quite low as a level of income to avoid poverty. A retiree receiving only the BSP would be eligible for additional poverty relief programs. Although these other programs may be run in a more discretionary manner than the BSP, their costs should still be included in an assessment of the overall public system to provide retirement income support.

Additionally, if the BSP does not provide poverty relief, then a case can be made for expanding it. In many countries, for example, the first tier of benefits is set at the level of the minimum wage. If the fiscal costs of expanding the BSP are deemed to be too high for an unfunded system, then the increase can be phased in gradually, thereby allowing for some prefunding of these new liabilities.

Importantly, most workers and beneficiaries are not covered by the BSP alone. Public policy goals typically extend to providing comfortable, more than just subsistence, levels of income in retirement. Having a comfortable retirement for most people requires earnings replacement. Furthermore, there is far more heterogeneity in a condition of comfort than in one of being "not impoverished." In particular, it is evident that there is considerable variation across households in their preferences to substitute consumption over time, leisure over time, and consumption for leisure during all periods of time. There is also variation in life-cycle earning experiences. This heterogeneity makes the need to implement a centrally managed, uniform system less imperative. Accommodating this heterogeneity makes the second-tier or earnings-related benefits far more complicated.

The U.K. system permits real choice in the way participants obtain their earnings-related benefits. The mechanism is "contracting out" of the state system (SERPS) on the condition that a privately provided substitute is available. Contracting out was initially simple, permitting a rebate only to occupational pension plans with defined benefits (DBs) comparable to SERPS benefits. It is now more complicated, in order to accommodate and promote innovation in the private pension sector. A pension can be eligible for a rebate if it provides similar benefits under a DB plan or uses the rebate to contribute to a defined contribution (DC) plan. Given the role played by contracting out, it would be nice to see more detailed information on both the time-series and cross-sectional aspects of contracting out. It is surprising that there not been more research on the economic effects of contracting out, particularly with respect to saving.[1]

The debate over social security reform in other European countries and the United States has included plans that look like a contracting-out rebate. In those plans, a new investment-based account is established for each person, into which a small contribution is made, perhaps 2 percent of payroll per year. In the future, the private account will replace some of

1. For an early example, see Samwick (1989).

the benefits that would otherwise be payable from the PAYGO system. If calibrated correctly, the amount of benefits replaced from the investment-based account can be enough to alleviate the entire fiscal burden that is generating the financial crisis today.[2]

If this investment account contribution is diverted from the existing PAYGO tax, then an equal-sized source of revenue must be found if current beneficiaries of the unfunded system are to be paid. Here is where the distinctive features of the U.K. system are important. In the United Kingdom, the contracting-out rebate was not "opting out" of paying the unfunded liability to past generations. It was entirely prospective—there were no such past generations. It was not a transition device to solve the problems currently confronting the rest of Europe or the United States, and it cannot be used as such in the absence of another revenue source. It is precisely the difficulty of finding this other revenue source in the political process—whether it is higher taxes or lower benefits in the pension system or elsewhere in the government budget—that keeps meaningful reform from being implemented.

Establishing provisions to allow contracting out was a sensible thing to do when starting a new system. Initially, these provisions could help keep costs low because they allowed existing occupational pension schemes to deliver the benefits that would otherwise have been required of the public systems. Over time, the system of contracting out has become more complicated in its implementation and underlying economics. In fact, the United Kingdom is sometimes used as an example of the heavy administrative costs that would occur if other countries allowed for private-sector implementation of the second tier of the pension system. The United Kingdom represents one possible system that mixes public and private components. Many of the same features exist in the United States in the part of the retirement system that is implemented through banks and employers but subsidized by the tax code—for example, Roth and traditional Individual Retirement Accounts, DB pension plans, DC and 401(k) plans, and Keogh plans for the self-employed. The amount of choice allowed in the U.K. system should be thought of as an upper bound on what would reasonably be expected in the rest of Europe. In other countries, there will be a greater emphasis on keeping costs low because administrative costs are in addition to the fiscal transition cost.

There is much to learn from the U.K. experience in that regard. Problems are generally the result of trying to manage a system with elements of both choice and insurance. Based on the early history of the U.K. experiment, several problems and some solutions can be offered. First, based on the numbers in the paper, 3.5 out of 28.5 million workers have only the

2. See Samwick (1999) for a complete discussion of the "Two Percent Plan" originally put forth in Feldstein and Samwick (1998).

BSP (before the new system). This suggests that one-eighth of the workforce is left out of the earnings-related system. Combined with the low level of the BSP, incomplete coverage is a recipe for elderly poverty.

Second, workers could initially contract in and out of SERPS several times over their working lives. Because SERPS was a DB plan, and DB plans tend to be back-loaded, the optimal strategy was for workers to contract back into SERPS late in their working lives.[3] One way this problem was addressed was to scale back the generosity of the public system, so the costs of this type of behavior are lessened. Another was to make the contracting-out rebate an increasing function of the worker's age to prevent this from occurring. Perhaps a better way should be established to prevent these sorts of switches through a longer-term commitment to being contracted out, or through a greater reliance on DC methods in the state system.

Third, establishing new administrative structures is costly, especially if they are organized as private financial market institutions in which turnover and aggressive selling tend to generate high initial costs. On the administrative side, private accounts generate additional transaction costs of processing payments into and out of the system. These costs can be minimized by relying on existing systems, such as the payroll and income tax systems, to process payments, perhaps with the assistance of a financial clearinghouse.[4] On the investment side, there have been dubious sales practices and worker confusion in the contracted-out market in the United Kingdom. Much of this has been due to new problems associated with widespread private management of DC schemes. Other parts of the problem relate to the aggressive selling of actively managed mutual funds, which, as the paper quite clearly shows, are seldom worth the extra management fees. When financial markets are used to achieve social objectives, and the government is therefore a residual claimant on the financial performance of the investments, then more regulation is optimal than may normally be the case. Limiting the range of investment options (particularly to passively managed funds) and imposing capitalization requirements on financial intermediaries are some of the ways in which this could occur. A default plan (like the treasury's proposed Pooled Pension Investments, or PPIs) may be useful when allowing choice in social insurance.[5]

One problem that the United Kingdom avoided was the issue of whether the financial investments should be managed in a central fund or in indi-

3. A pension plan is back-loaded when a disproportionate share of the benefit entitlement accrues in the later, rather than in the earlier, years of coverage.
4. See Goldberg and Graetz (2000) for a detailed discussion of such a system.
5. A formal plan along these lines is discussed in greater detail in Samwick (1999). A default plan has three important features. First, it sets the low-fee, low-service standard. Second, it provides an easy way to set a guarantee that is independent of individual investment choices. Third, it allows small accounts to incubate for several years before being transferred to a private financial institution.

vidual accounts. Because the private plans came first, the government was never in a position to own private securities directly. Not all countries are in a position to allow government-administered central funds as part of their transitions to more funded systems. For example, to close the funding gap in the United States will eventually require assets of about 60 percent of gross domestic product. Today, such a fund would be nearly $6 trillion (see Samwick 1999).

In summary, the current position in the United Kingdom is the result of favorable demographic and historical conditions. Delaying the introduction of earnings-related pensions, and then rescinding them shortly after implementing them, has helped keep the U.K. system out of dire fiscal straits. This is the feature of the public pension system that distinguishes the United Kingdom from the rest of Europe and the United States. Eventually, however, all countries will have to design institutions that blend insurance and choice in a way that provides poverty relief, earnings replacement, and income security for retirees. It is in this respect that the evolution of public pensions in the United Kingdom can provide guidance for other countries.

References

Feldstein, Martin S., and Andrew A. Samwick. 1998. Potential effects of two percent personal retirement accounts. *Tax Notes* 79:615–20.
Goldberg, Fred T., and Michael J. Graetz. 2000. Reforming Social Security: A practical and workable system of personal retirement accounts. In *Administrative aspects of Social Security reform;* ed. John B. Shoven, 9–37. Chicago: University of Chicago Press.
Samwick, Andrew A. 1989. Contracting out of the British social security system. Unpublished undergraduate thesis. Harvard University, Department of Economics, June.
———. 1999. Social Security reform in the United States. *National Tax Journal* 52 (December): 819–42.

Discussion Summary

David Blake agreed with the discussant that it was easy to get rid of the SERPS scheme because it had only just begun. Blake noted that the history of the United Kingdom in terms of social welfare protection is based on the Beveridge principle: maintaining the minimum safety net and giving the public responsibility for providing above that minimum safety net. The basic state pension does provide an extremely low pension in retirement, and it is not intended to provide a comfortable standard of living during retirement. Individuals without other resources would be able to receive additional welfare benefits, such as housing benefits or municipal tax relief.

Laurence J. Kotlikoff said that the speaker has done a great service in making clear the workings of the British pension system. In the view of Kotlikoff, the British pension reform (of introducing personal pension plans with their high charges) has generated an unmitigated disaster, with many people ending up with much lower pensions than if they had remained in their occupational plans and turning to the government for redress. As an alternative, he referred to a joint proposal for the United States by Kotlikoff, Sachs, and sixty-five other economists to put a portion of payroll tax contributions into private accounts with a matching contribution provided by the government on a progressive basis. These accounts are invested passively in a global index fund to provide an inflation-indexed pension. This proposal would lead to a collective low-cost pension system in which everyone gets the same return. *Axel Börsch-Supan,* responding to the Kotlikoff proposal, expressed his doubts that an index fund that carries about 64 percent of GDP can be passively managed.

David A. Wise asked about the difference between the United Kingdom and the United States concerning the institutional structure of personal pension plans. There is no evidence of high charges or fraud in the United States as are described in the paper for the United Kingdom. *David Blake* explained this difference between the countries by pointing out the different degrees of financial literacy among consumers. However, he regarded it unfair to speak of fraud. Instead, the problems in the United Kingdom are very high effective charges, which are disguised in the marketing literature. He said that British consumers lack the financial sophistication to make long-term decisions of this kind.

Axel Börsch-Supan noted that the contracting-out rebate is essentially a subsidy that leads to a significant fiscal burden. According to *David Blake,* the fiscal burden comes from the fact that the government must keep increasing national insurance rebate to discourage people from contracting back into SERPS.

11

Poland
Security through Diversity

Jerzy Hausner

The program for pension system reform launched at the beginning of 1997 in Poland was called by its authors "Security through Diversity" (Security 1997). This title emphasizes that pension reform—which is designed to guarantee security for the insured—must combine a first, pay-as-you-go (PAYGO) pillar; a second, mandatory, fully funded pillar; and a third, voluntary, funded pillar.

The beginnings of the pension system in Poland go back to the interwar period. It became a full-fledged universal PAYGO system in the 1950s. Since that time, the way it operates has not fundamentally changed. In the 1980s, the system came to cover the rural population as well. Each new measure, especially those adopted between the 1960s and the 1980s, involved granting additional privileges to different occupational groups. Nonetheless, until the end of the 1980s the system operated in relative financial equilibrium. This was possible due to—among other things—the gradual rise in the contribution rate. In the 1950s, it amounted to 15 percent of gross earnings, but by the end of the 1980s it had reached a level of 38 percent.

The financial insolvency of the PAYGO pension system in Poland is attributable to three sets of factors: those that are typical of modern societies in general and that are basically independent of the type of economic system; those that are specific to socialist and post-socialist societies; and those that are specific to Poland.

With respect to the first set of factors, society's aging, caused among other things by a fall in the birth rate and a rise in average life expectancy,

Jerzy Hausner is professor at Cracow University of Economics, former undersecretary of state for social security reform, and chief advisor to the deputy prime minister.

has increased pressure on the system. Demographic waves, caused by population losses in World War II and the postwar demographic boom, also have created growing difficulties over time.

The ratio of pensioners to the working population, that is, the demographic dependency ratio (DDR), stood at 20.6 percent in 1985. Since that time it has increased, reaching approximately 23.8 percent around the year 2000. In the years 2000–05, the situation will improve slightly as increasing numbers of children of parents born during the postwar demographic boom reach working age. The coefficient will fall as a result to 23.1 percent. Then, however, those born during the postwar baby boom will themselves reach retirement age, after which the demographic dependency ratio will rise sharply, reaching 33.9 percent in 2020. In 1990, for every one person of retirement age there were 2.2 working persons. In 2005 this figure will be 2.1, but in 2020 it will fall to 1.8.

What this shows is that, compared to Western European societies in particular, the pressure of demographic factors is for the moment neither a major cause of tension in the Polish pension system, nor a major reason for its reform.

The main problem inherited from the socialist system is the pressure of branch interest groups characteristic of such economies. It is often said that a PAYGO system is susceptible to political pressures and bargaining. In socialist systems, where certain occupational branch groups (mainly in mining and heavy industry) gain excessive influence, this problem is particularly acute.

Among the factors specific to Poland are protection of the purchasing power of pensions during the transitional recession; the policy of fighting unemployment by facilitating early retirement; and lax legislation and entitlement regulations for disability status. The effect of all the causal factors mentioned above has been an increase in the total number of persons receiving pension benefits in the 1990s. In 1996, this figure was nearly 30 percent higher than at the end of the 1980s. On the other hand, between 1989 and 1996, the number of people employed and paying contributions dropped by 14.4 percent (Müller 1999, 5).

As a result, the ratio of persons receiving social insurance benefits to persons paying insurance contributions (the system dependency ratio [SDR]) has steadily increased. In 1995, the value of the SDR exceeded the value of the DDR by close to 40 percent. Poland's pension system was thus under severe strain and contributions have risen. At the beginning of the 1990s, the contribution rate was raised to 45 percent (31 percent according to net calculation), which means that Poland has one of the highest rates in the world—a fact that, owing to the country's unusually high indirect labor costs, is undermining the competitiveness of the economy. Despite the huge level of contributions, the Polish pension system is charac-

Table 11.1   **Expenditure on Disability and Retirement Pensions in 1990–96, and State Subsidies to Social Insurance Funds (FUS, KRUS) (as a percentage of GDP)**

Item	1990	1991	1992	1993	1994	1995	1996
Retirement and disability pensions	8.6	12.6	14.6	14.2	15.8	15.6	15.2
Social Insurance Fund (FUS) subsidy	—	2.9	4.3	4.2	3.9	2.1	1.9
Farmers' Social Insurance Fund (KRUS) subsidy	—	1.7	2.0	2.0	2.2	2.1	2.2

Source: Author's calculations based on Hausner (1998), 25, and UNDP (1997), 132.
Notes: Long dashes in columns indicate that the funds were not subsidized during that year.

terized by an especially high implicit pension debt[1]: approximately 220 percent of gross domestic product (GDP), significantly higher than in other transition economies (James 1998).

The general financial effect of the causal factors discussed above has been a dramatic increase in expenditure on pension benefits as a share of GDP (table 11.1). In the years from 1989 to 1995, it more than doubled. This will, of course, prevent any major increase in spending on other social services and investment in human capital, particularly because—despite the rise in the contribution rate—the social insurance system began to record a considerable deficit in the 1990s, which must be financed from budget subsidies.

Since the beginning of the transition there has been a growing awareness among experts and politicians of the need to reform the social insurance system. The first plans for a radical overhaul of the PAYGO system and the introduction of a funded insurance component appeared in the early 1990s. At the time, however, politicians did not give these plans due consideration.

If, then, they have in the end embraced reform, it is because it has proved difficult, ineffective, and ultimately impossible to carry out short-term preventive measures.

The rapid growth in expenditure on pension benefits, as well as the need to subsidize them heavily, put pressure on decision makers. The mechanism of backward-looking wage indexation for these benefits meant that, periodically, financial pressure sharply increased. This was reflected, above all, in the inability to prepare a budget that would avoid the dramatic choice between a huge rise in the budget deficit—thus undermining macroeconomic stability and reversing disinflationary trends—and major cuts in expenditure on important social and economic goals. The success-

1. The present value of the pension promises that are owed to current pensioners and workers because of their participation in the old system (James 1998, 459).

ful defense of macroeconomic discipline by successive ministers of finance meant that in practice there was no choice. From time to time it became necessary to weaken the benefit indexation mechanism. With the help of supplementary budget legislation, it was technically possible to limit the expected rise in retirement and disability pensions.

Such a course of action was, of course, opposed by pensioners and their representatives; it accordingly became a major political burden. This also explains the sharp fall in support for the post-Solidarity governments, and their eventual collapse in 1993.

The post-communist opposition, which won the elections while promising, among other things, a return to "fair" benefits, faced not only the same difficulties as before, but also new ones: The public protests had been accompanied by formal appeals to the Constitutional Tribunal. On numerous occasions the tribunal ruled in favor of those who had questioned the amended regulations. The new parliamentary majority could have formally overruled the verdicts of the tribunal, but in most cases it did not, feeling bound by its election promises. Thus the verdicts of the tribunal came into force, which led to an increase in financial pressure. The state's unpaid debts to pensioners rapidly grew, and came to form a significant portion of public debt.

In its rulings, the Constitutional Tribunal consistently recognized as unconstitutional the practice of periodically and temporarily suspending a portion of the state's commitments to pensioners for fiscal reasons. At the same time, it clearly stressed that this did not preclude the possibility of a permanent systemic change in the regulations, provided that such a change was preceded by appropriate legislation.

Thus, it was only when legal and political factors prevented *ad hoc* manipulation of the pension system that the warnings of experts and the idea of major reform came to be taken seriously.

Under the circumstances, a radical program for pension system reform in Poland had to be devised and implemented. It was based on the following principles:

1. *Full security.* The program must provide all age groups—pensioners (the grandparents' generation), long-time employees (the parents' generation), and beginning or prospective employees (the children's generation)—with a guarantee of economic security on termination of their working lives or in the case of inability to work.

2. *Protection of acquired rights.* Benefits acquired prior to the moment the appropriate new legislation takes effect must retain their real value—under the conditions of economic growth—for the rest of the holders' lifetimes, and will be paid in accordance with previous principles. Thus, the reform does not apply to today's pensioners.

3. *Individual prudence.* One of the foundations of the system's security

will be individual prudence, manifested through deliberate investment in the form of appropriate social insurance contributions that will translate into one's own future pension or disability benefits.

4. *A multisegment structure of the pension system.* High security of the system of pensions and disability benefits will result from its being based on three main pillars: PAYGO, funded, and voluntary insurance.

5. *Maximum freedom of choice.* Payment of the insurance contribution will be mandatory, as it is now, but one will be able to choose the pension fund in which to entrust one's savings, and it will be relatively easy to transfer saving from one fund to another. In addition, one will be able to decide (within certain margins) about the date of one's retirement.

6. *Transparency.* This will be ensured by the introduction of a universal system of individual social insurance records and accounts. In addition, pension funds must be obliged by law to publish information about their financial results.

7. *An active (regulatory) role of the state.* By regulating the functioning of the capital market and, in particular, supervising the operation of pension funds, the state should guarantee full security of the pension system.

8. *Sustainable and balanced economic growth.* The new system of pensions will utilize mechanisms of secure investment of funds.

These principles formed the basis for the introduction of the relevant legislation, which was adopted in two packages by two politically different governments and parliaments. The first package, submitted to Parliament in April 1997 by the center-left coalition (SLD-PSL), comprised:[2]

1. The Law (of 28 August 1997) on the Organization and Operation of Pension Funds,

2. The Law (of 22 August 1997) on Employee Pension Programs, and

3. The Law (of 25 June 1997) on Applying the Revenues from Privatization of a Portion of State Treasury Assets for Purposes Connected with Reforming the Social Insurance System.

The package specifies how revenue from privatization will be used to bridge the growing financial gap that has appeared in the present PAYGO pension system. In addition, it initiates reform of this system, and launches a second (mandatory) and develops a third (voluntary) funded pillar of pension insurance. It also fully regulates the organization and operation of second-pillar pension funds as well as the state's administrative supervision of their activities. Moreover, it lays down the rules determining how employee pension schemes—an entirely new and prospectively dominant form of voluntary, fully funded insurance—are to be set up and run.

---

2. "SLD" is the *Soljusz Lewicy Demokratycznej,* or the Democratic Left Alliance Party; "PSL" is the *Polskie Stronnictwo Ludowe,* or Polish Peasants' Party. For a detailed analysis of the work on pension reform during the SLD-PSL government, see Hausner 1998.

The second legislative package, prepared and submitted to Parliament in April 1998 by the center-right coalition (AWS-UW),[3] comprised:

1. The Law (of 13 October 1998) on the Social Insurance System, and
2. The Law (of 18 December 1998) on the new PAYGO pensions from the Social Insurance Institution (ZUS).

These laws specify the operation of the new first pillar and the ZUS, as well as the transition path from the old to the new pension system.

The new pension system in Poland was introduced on 1 January 1999, with changes to the PAYGO pillar. The launching of the second pillar was postponed until 1 April 1999 for technical reasons. The first pillar (PAYGO) retains five-eighths of the obligatory pension contribution (12.22 percent of gross wages). Although it remains a repartition-based scheme, its operation is governed by the principle of *defined contribution* (DC). The remaining three-eighths (7.30 percent of gross wages) of the contribution goes to the second (fully funded) pillar, composed of privately managed pension funds and also based on the DC principle. These two pillars make up the mandatory segment of the general pension system and are closely interconnected. All participants in the general pension system have their contributions and benefits calculated in accordance with the same rules. The amount of benefit depends exclusively—in the first pillar—on the aggregate amount of one's contributions (recorded in the individual notional account of every participant), the uniform rules of indexation, and one's age at retirement; and—in the second pillar—on the aggregate amount of contributions (likewise entered into individual capital accounts) and the efficiency of the investment strategy of a given fund. Payment of a minimum pension is guaranteed by the state to all participants in the general system (this can be seen as a kind of "zero pillar"). Participation in the third (funded) pillar is voluntary. The law allows for a variety of organizational forms and types of pension schemes in this segment.

Participation in the new general pension system is mandatory for all employed persons born after 1969 (i.e., aged under thirty). Persons born between 1949 and 1969 (aged from thirty to fifty) could choose between the "old" (exclusively reformed PAYGO) and the "new" system. Persons over the age of fifty were not allowed such a choice and must continue under the old system. The rules for calculating benefits will be unchanged for those retiring through 2006 (Chlon, Góra, and Rutkowski 1999, 15). The new principles do not apply in any way to persons who acquired pension benefits before the reform was launched.

Entitlements to pension benefits acquired under the previous system will be converted—for all participants to whom the new arrangements apply—

3. "AWS" is the *Akcja Wyborcza Solidarność* (Solidarity Electoral Alliance); UW is the *Unia Wolności* (Freedom Union).

into an "initial capital" in the new system. Additional contributions are transferred from the state budget for periods of national military service, nursing a disabled child, and parental leave. The Labor Fund covers periods of unemployment. These transfers are estimated at a level of 0.2–0.3 percent of GDP annually (Chlon, Góra, and Rutkowski 1999, 19).

In order to relieve pressure on the first pillar caused by demographic waves, a demographic reserve fund has been established. It will encompass any surplus in the first pillar plus one percentage point of the wage bill (about 0.35 percent of GDP) transferred to the fund in years 2002–08. The demographic reserve fund will invest its resources, and any interest or extra revenues will be added to the fund. It is estimated that the fund will account for approximately 14 percent of GDP by the year 2020 (Chlon, Góra, and Rutkowski 1999, 24).

Persons under the age of thirty, for whom participation in the new system is mandatory, had to choose their pension funds (within the second pillar) by 30 September 1999. If they did not make a choice, pension funds were assigned to them randomly by the Pension Fund Supervisory Board. Persons aged thirty to fifty could chose whether to switch to the new system. If they did so, they had to select their pension funds by 31 December 1999.

According to initial estimates, between 6 and 7 million participants were to enter the new general system (first and second pillars). The total possible number of entrants was 11.5 million, including 3.8 million born after 1968 (aged under thirty) and 7.7 million born in the years 1949–68 (thirty- to fifty-year-olds). By the end of 1999, 10.5 million people had joined the system, each choosing one of the twenty-one registered pension funds. Certainly, some of the agreements signed will turn out to be invalid (double agreements, forged agreements, agreements signed with persons not entitled to sign them). It is estimated that, on average, 15 percent of the agreements in the portfolio of each pension fund may be invalid. This has not decreased the considerable level of public interest in joining pension funds or the perceived success of the reform.

However, the situation of the various pension funds is highly diverse. Three are clearly dominant on the market: Commercial Union, Nationale Nederlanden, and Złota Jesień–PZU (see table 11.2). These are funds managed by insurance companies that have existed on the Polish market for at least a few years and that had a large network of experienced canvassers the moment they began recruiting. The clear losers have been the banks, who, with no such network at their disposal, have tried to attract clients through their local branches.

Thus, after the initial formation period, the level of concentration on the pension fund market—measured by the number of members and assets—is very high. The number of actual funds is also large, but many are too small to survive. Therefore, the trend toward rapid consolidation

Table 11.2   Ranking of Pension Funds (end of 1999)

Rank by Value of Contributions (end of 1999)	Value of Assets (in millions of zlotys)	Market Share (%)	Number of Members (× 1,000)
1. Commercial Union	678.9	30.2	2 million 300
2. Nationale Nederlanden	478.2	21.3	1 million 600
3. Złota Jesień–PZU	360.2	16.0	1 million 900
4. AIG	178.6	8.0	850
5. Zurich Solidarni	96.9	4.3	455
6. Norwich Union	75.5	3.4	565
7. Bankowy	74.9	3.3	390
8. Skarbiec-Emerytura	58.1	2.6	390
9. Winterthur	50.7	2.3	300
10. Ego	34.4	1.5	286
11. Orzeł	32.3	1.4	328
12. Dom	31.8	1.4	250
13. Allianz	30.5	1.3	197
14. Pocztylion	27.9	1.2	393
15. Pioneer	13.9		150
16. Pekao Alliance	10.0		70
17. Arka-Invesco	5.2		80
18. Epoka	3.2		100
19. Polsat	2.9		160
20. Kredyt Bank	1.6		90
21. Rodzina	0.2		75

Source: Polityka (2000).

on the market seems only natural. The companies managing the pension funds are in favor of such consolidation, although it is opposed—for the moment, only informally—by the Pension Fund Supervisory Board (Urząd Nadzoru Funduszy Emerytalnych, or UNFE). The board has also stated publicly that in its opinion concentration on the market is excessive. At the beginning of 2000, it published a controversial report for the government, in which it gave a negative assessment of the situation on the pension fund market and suggested amendments to the legislation regulating pension funds. The purpose of this was to slow down the consolidation process and to enable the high level of concentration to be restricted through administrative means. The board's proposal was fiercely opposed by those responsible for preparing and implementing reform of the pension system as well as by the companies concerned. Its authors were accused of trying to steer the market manually and hinder the free interplay of market forces.

Pension funds (in the second pillar) are required by law to diversify their investment portfolios. The ceilings for particular types of investment are as follows: shares in companies quoted on the stock exchange, 40 percent; foreign assets, 5 percent; secondary market securities, 10 percent; National

Investment Funds, 10 percent; and bonds issued by local governments, 15 percent. The actual structure of pension fund assets at the beginning of 2000 is illustrated in table 11.3.

The pension companies that manage pension funds have strongly emphasized a need that investment discipline, imposed on them by legislators, be eased. They believe that this would ensure a significantly higher rate of return, and in future a higher level of pensions. Their demands usually concern raising the ceiling on foreign investment and allowing investment on the real estate market. Of the opposite opinion is the UNFE, which has suggested the complete elimination of foreign investment. UNFE representatives justify this primarily by the need to ensure market security and to protect the saving of members of pension funds.

It should be stressed that the clear motive for reform of the Polish system is a desire to reduce the very high replacement rate (over 60 percent;

Table 11.3   **The Structure of Pension Fund Assets (end of January 2000)**

Fund Name	Bonds Issued by Treasury and by National Bank of Poland	Bank Deposits and Securities	Assets at the end of January	National Investment Funds
AIG	66.76	3.11	24.99	
Allianz	79.10	0.30	18.40	
Arka-Invesco	70.00	0.26	29.57	
Bankowy	58.20	1.14	31.14	
Commercial Union	64.88		34.27	
DOM	53.66		37.39	6.98
Ego	71.53	4.46	21.21	1.39
Epoka	84.40		9.72	
Kredyt Banku	77.30	8.11	8.11	
Nationale-Nederlanden	64.41	4.96	30.43	
Norwich Union	74.06	0.22	23.03	
PBK Orzeł	64.98	1.81	25.98	
Pekao/Alliance	56.37	5.20	36.44	
Pioneer	49.92	1.80	38.69	9.43
Pocztylion	66.12	0.88	31.32	
Polsat	58.51	2.67	33.86	2.45
PZU Złota Jesień	65.66	0.20	33.42	
Rodzina	69.52	4.70	18.82	
Skarbiec-Emerytura	66.12	6.88	20.00	
Winterthur	66.37	0.35	28.85	
Zurich Solidarni	76.04	0.02	23.71	
Total		Weighted average: 30.50		

Source: Rzeczpospolita (2000).

Notes: All amounts are percentages. The funds' remaining assets comprise dues from the sale of securities, cash resources, and investments below 1 percent of the value of assets. In addition, the following funds have invested assets in enterprise shares: Bankowy, 0.30 percent; PBK Orzeł, 3.74 percent; Pekao/Alliance, 1.92 percent; and Winterthur, 4.34 percent.

see table 11.4). However, such a move would not serve to reduce pension purchasing power. If reform restores solvency to the pension system and increases and consolidates economic growth—both indirectly (instead of financing the deficit of the Social Insurance Institution, budgetary resources would be used for structural policy and the creation of new jobs) and directly (through greater savings, a better financial capital structure, and thus a higher level of investment)—then a lower replacement rate will in future guarantee higher benefits than at present.

Because the main cause of crisis in the majority of post-socialist countries is not (for the time being) demography but a poorly managed PAYGO system, it is important to ask whether this system can be prepared and radical reform avoided. Theoretically, this is possible. Rationalizing and regulating the PAYGO system would restore long-term financial stability to the system. The problem could thus be adequately solved by raising the retirement age, eliminating occupational privileges, and abolishing early retirement.

This is how things look from a strictly financial point of view. From a political perspective, however, implementing such a program does not seem possible, for two reasons. First, it would challenge the vested interests of major social groups—in Poland, proposals to rationalize the present system sparked serious social protest and became a highly sensitive political issue. Second, the PAYGO system is by nature susceptible to political manipulation—certain groups can be guaranteed privileges at the expense of others because the relationship between contributions and benefits is unclear and ambiguous. The social insurance contribution is a collective tax and not a form of individual saving. Few people are aware of being insured, and thus the system lacks an institutionalized social force that could defend the interests of the younger generation who are inconvenienced by privileges that politicians find it more expedient to grant to older generations. In such a situation, politicians will always be tempted by moral hazard and will secure the votes of the large and active pensioner electorate by granting them undue privileges.

Polish experience in this area furnishes one example that should serve as a warning. Despite the acceptance by Parliament and government of plans for a new and universal pension system, attempts to exclude two influential legal groups from this system—judges and procurators—failed under pressure of political and parliamentary lobbying. The legal lobby had created a dangerous precedent. A new privilege was introduced, which limited the possibility of cutting back on existing privileges.

If, however, for doctrinal, practical, and political reasons a mixed system with a large PAYGO pillar is introduced (as in Poland), then the system can be protected from its natural susceptibility to political manipulation by individualizing social insurance, such as through a notional defined contribution (NDC). Individualizing social insurance can prevent

Table 11.4   Projected Replacement Rates in the New System (% of last salary)

	Retirement Age										
Pillar	60	61	62	63	64	65	66	67	68	69	70
First	21.8	23.2	24.7	26.3	28.0	29.9	31.8	33.9	36.2	38.7	41.3
Second	22.9	24.5	26.2	28.0	30.0	32.2	34.5	37.0	39.7	42.6	45.9
Total	44.7	47.7	50.9	54.3	58.0	62.1	66.3	70.9	75.9	81.3	87.2

Source: Chlon, Góra, and Rutkowski (1999).

permanent decay of the PAYGO system. Moreover, for society at large individualization is both desirable and understandable.

A difficult problem that needs to be addressed is the size of the second, fully funded pillar. Because members of younger age groups transfer part of their contributions to individual accounts in pension funds, the deficit in the PAYGO system is increasing. From this point of view it would be sensible to limit the number of people obliged or entitled to participate in the second pillar and reduce the size of the contribution assigned to this pillar. On the other hand, the operation of the pension funds entails specific costs that are undoubtedly higher than in the case of the PAYGO system. If there is only a small number of participants in these funds and they must cover the costs, this will considerably limit the size of accumulated capital and benefit payments. From this point of view, it would be necessary to do the opposite: to increase the number of participants in the second pillar as well as the level of contributions transferred to pension funds.

The choice must depend on the method adopted to finance the additional gap that will appear in the PAYGO pillar when the fully funded pillar is launched. In Poland, this fiscal gap—which should not be confused with the costs of reform—will be covered from current privatization revenue.[4] This is still possible due to the large amount of suitable state treasury assets that have not yet been privatized. At the same time, the capital market is sufficiently advanced (i.e., relatively large and efficiently regulated) to increase the scope of privatization and secure appropriately high revenues.

The "delayed" privatization in Poland (due to societal resistance to this process) turns out to have brought a significant, although to some extent accidental, benefit: The state treasury assets can now be used to support the pension system reform. This also accounts for the altered social perception of privatization, which no longer stirs up much controversy and is approved of by the greater part of society.

Privatization revenues appear an ideal source from which to finance the additional transitional fiscal gap within the pension system caused by its reform (see fig. 11.1). The direct use of these funds to offset the current budget deficit has the disadvantage of concealing the actual public-finance imbalance and allowing excessive expenditure to continue. When this transient source of financing eventually runs dry and cuts short the additional

---

4. As a result of introducing the mandatory fully funded pillar, an additional gap in the social insurance funds will appear for a certain transitional period (lasting at least several dozen years). In an economic sense, however, this is not an additional item of expenditure or a new liability, but the replacement of one form of public debt (implicit debt) with another (explicit debt). Consequently, the problem of liquidity becomes temporarily more acute within the system, but additional costs do not emerge if this additional gap can be financed without increasing the current budget deficit.

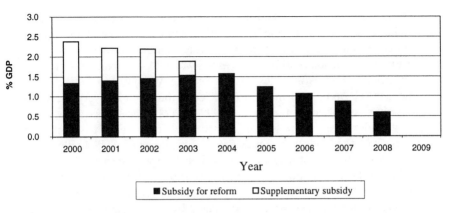

Fig. 11.1   Subsidy from the state budget to the social security fund (FUS)
Source: Chlon and Wóycicka (1999).

revenue stream, fiscal adjustment may prove extremely difficult and pain-ful. To put it bluntly, rather than spend privatization revenues on con-sumption, it is far more reasonable to use them to finance the historic pension reform.

Another important factor is whether the economy in question is en-joying economic growth. If it is not, it is difficult to imagine obtaining revenue from privatization, while the investments of pension funds might not be sufficiently effective to ensure an increase in the capital of the parti-cipants in investment funds.

It is evident from the above that multipillar pension reform cannot be treated as a binding blueprint or a universal remedy. It is thus appropriate only for those transition countries experiencing economic growth and hav-ing a well-regulated capital market, a relatively balanced economy, and controllable budget deficits. Such countries should also have at their dis-posal efficient administrations capable of developing computerized infor-mation systems to deal with individual insurance records and ensure the swift and cheap transfer of contributions to pension funds and between different kinds of insurance. Ideally, they should also possess a large amount of state assets suitable for privatization. It is only under such con-ditions that a fully funded pillar will function, and only under such condi-tions that its implementation will stimulate economic growth.

The opinions of economists vary on this issue, because empirical re-search does not unequivocally confirm that capital (funded) insurance re-sults in an increase in domestic saving. Even leaving aside arguments about the expected increase in domestic saving (which cannot be proved), it can be clearly shown that multipillar pension reform will accelerate eco-nomic growth as a result of changes in the capital structure. The establish-ment of pension funds is one of the relatively few fast-track methods of long-term capital development in transition economies. Their appearance on a large scale will undoubtedly help reduce interest rates and thus investment costs, and as a consequence accelerate economic growth.

Currently, pension funds manage assets worth $US 750 million. Increasingly, they are investing these assets on the Warsaw Stock Exchange, which, in the opinion of many experts, contributed to the very sharp increase in share prices at the turn of 1999 to 2000. The Warsaw Stock Exchange index easily surpassed its record level from 1994. It is estimated that by 2005 the funds will be managing resources worth $US 4 billion and will become the largest investors on the Polish capital market.

The legislative framework of pension reform in Poland is still awaiting completion. So far, no attempt has been made to reform the separate pension system for farmers, which is managed by the Farmers' Social Insurance Fund (KRUS). This system is subsidized almost entirely from the state budget, at a level of 2 percent of GDP, and encompasses more than 2 million people.

In addition, the government has been unable to complete the very difficult negotiations over bridging pensions, which relate to early retirement for those who work in special conditions that may adversely affect health, or who perform physically and psychologically demanding work of a special character in the interests of public safety. Bridging pensions should be granted for the period between the earlier age at which working career ends and the minimum retirement age. Also needed is an annuity companies law, and a national actuary law that would establish a national actuarial office to supervise the long-term solvency of all social insurance programs.

The legislation on employee pension programs is not working, in practice. There have been very few applications to establish such programs, and the UNFE has dealt with them in a drawn-out and bureaucratic manner. Experts believe that in the light of experience to date, the legislation on employee pension programs should be amended. A private member's bill to amend the law was submitted to Parliament in the spring of 1999, but it is still in the process of being examined by a parliamentary commission. In actual fact, therefore, one of the pillars of the new system has so far not begun to function. This is significant to the extent that the reform envisaged a reduction in the replacement rate within the mandatory pillars and the establishment of attractive possibilities for additional voluntary insurance, ensuring a significant increase in the replacement rate for persons with high and medium incomes.

The initial reform project assumed a significant change in the retirement age. Formally, this age is sixty for women and sixty-five for men; in practice, it is roughly fifty-five for women and fifty-nine for men. The project envisaged the introduction of an elastic retirement age, which would in fact have been standardized for men and women—sixty-two in each case.

The center-right AWS-UW coalition abandoned this proposal in fear of public protest and under pressure from its Catholic faction, which, for ideological reasons, primarily attributes a family-oriented role to women. However, the retirement-age issue will certainly be debated again soon, for an actuarially fair benefit formula increases incentives to postpone retirement decisions (Chlon, Góra, and Rutkowski 1999, 19). At the same time, the introduction of this formula and the maintenance of a lower retirement age for women will mean that the benefits received by women will be significantly lower than those received by men, which will be seen as discrimination.

Currently, the main problem with pension reform in Poland is the organizational inefficiency of the Social Insurance Institution (ZUS) and the fact that this institution has failed to set up a comprehensive, computerized information system. The first and second pillars cannot operate without such a system, for it is then impossible to maintain individual accounts. The pension companies estimate that by the end of 1999 the Social Insurance Institution had transferred barely 50 percent of contributions to them, and that about 40 percent of members' accounts are dormant (i.e., not a single contribution has been paid in). Clearly, the problems of the Social Insurance Institution will not be resolved quickly. The new head of ZUS, appointed at the end of 1999, believes that resolution will be possible at the end of 2000 at the earliest. The inefficiency of ZUS also led to a major decrease in the contribution collection rate in 1999. Consequently, ZUS has run up an additional large deficit, which for the moment has been financed from bank credits; sooner or later, however, the taxpayer will have to foot the bill.

The example of the Social Insurance Institution clearly shows the extent to which reform of the pension system is dependent on the efficiency of the public administration. In Poland, the efficiency of the administration is still very low and is further decreased by the practice of filling key public positions according to political (party) criteria. This practice is also responsible for the poor functioning of the Social Insurance Institution and the Pension Fund Supervisory Board, two key public institutions on whose efficiency the success of pension reform rests.

References

Chlon, A., M. Góra, and M. Rutkowski. 1999. Shaping pension reform in Poland: Security through diversity. Social Protection Discussion Paper no. 9923. Washington, D.C.: World Bank.

Chlon, A., and I. Wóycicka. 1999. *Social expenditures in the year 2000–2020* (in Polish). Warsaw: Gdańsk Institute for Market Economics.

Hausner, J. 1998. Security through diversity: Conditions for successful reform of the pension system in Poland. Collegium Budapest, Working Paper.

James, E. 1998. The political economy of social security reform: A cross-country review. *Annals of Public and Comparative Economics* 69 (4): 451–82.

Müller, K. 1999. The politics of pension reform in East-Central Europe. Contribution to the "Political Making of Socio-Economic Progress" workshop. 19–20 November, Humboldt University, Berlin. Mimeograph.

Polityka. 2000. Vol. 7, no. 2232 (12 February).

Rzeczpospolita. 2000. Vol. 31, no. 5501 (7 February).

Security. 1997. Security through diversity: Reform of the pension system in Poland. Warsaw: Office of the Government Plenipotentiary for Social Insurance Reform.

United Nations Development Program (UNDP). 1997. *National report on human development: The changing role of the state,* 132. Warsaw: UNDP.

The Hungarian Pension Reform
A Preliminary Assessment of the First Years of Implementation

Roberto Rocha and Dimitri Vittas

12.1 Introduction

In the summer of 1997, the Hungarian Parliament passed a proposal for a systemic reform to the pension system, involving substantive changes to the existing public pay-as-you-go (PAYGO) system and the introduction of a new pension system. The new system comprises a smaller public PAYGO system (the first pillar), and a new, funded, and privately managed system (the second pillar). A voluntary, funded, and privately managed pillar (the third pillar) already existed before the reform and continues to operate and grow.

The new pension system began operating in January 1998, and became mandatory for all new workers entering the labor force after July of that year. Workers with accrued rights in the old PAYGO pension system could choose to stay in the reformed PAYGO system or switch to the new multipillar system. At the end of September 1999 (the deadline for switching to the new system), more than two million workers accounting for half of the labor force had decided to switch to the new pension system. Although some workers are expected to switch back to the reformed PAYGO system until December 2002 (the extended deadline for switching back to the PAYGO), the large number of switchers reveals the popularity of the reform among workers, particularly workers under the age of forty, who account for more than 80 percent of the total number of switchers.

Roberto Rocha is head economist at the World Bank regional office for Central Europe, Budapest. Dimitri Vittas is head pension specialist in the research department at World Bank.

The authors are grateful to Patrick Wiese for performing the actuarial simulations, and to Zoltan Vajda, Judit Spat, Csaba Feher, and Tibor Parniczky for many fruitful discussions.

The Hungarian pension reform was the first systemic pension reform implemented in Central and Eastern Europe. Since then, a number of other countries have also implemented or are about to implement this type of reform, including Poland, Croatia, Latvia, Macedonia, and Kazakhstan. Multipillar systems are under preparation or consideration in several other countries of the region, as well. The facts that Hungary pioneered this type of reform in the region, and that three years of implementation have passed, raises a natural interest in the Hungarian reform experience, and in the lessons that may be identified for other countries.

The interest in the Hungarian reform experience may be enhanced by the fact that the center-right government that succeeded the reformist center-left government in mid-1998—after six months of reform implementation—demonstrated just a lukewarm support for the reform. The lack of initial support was revealed in numerous official statements, claiming that the reform had not been well prepared and that it had an adverse impact on the public finances. One clear evidence of the lukewarm support was the new Government's decision to maintain the contribution to the second pillar at 6 percent, instead of increasing it gradually to 8 percent, as originally planned and prescribed in the legislation. This measure may have important implications for some particular cohorts and for market participants, and raises a number of issues which are relevant for other reforming countries.

This paper reviews the main components and objectives of the Hungarian pension reform, and makes a preliminary assessment of the first years of its implementation. The paper is structured as follows. The second section provides some background material, examining briefly the performance of the pension system before the reform, and showing long-run projections of the system in the absence of reform. The third section describes the overall reform package, examines the switching results, and provides a number of long-run actuarial simulations of the new multipillar system. The fourth section examines the structure and performance of the private pillars in the early stages of implementation. Finally, the fifth section provides some conclusions and identifies possible lessons for other countries.

12.2   The Situation of the Pension System before the Reform

12.2.1   The Performance of the System in the Postwar Period

The Hungarian PAYGO system matured rapidly in the postwar period, as reflected in the rapid increase in the system dependency ratio (the ratio of pensioners to workers), and the increase in the average replacement ratio (the ratio of the average pension to the average net wage).[1] As shown

1. Section 12.2 draws on Palacios and Rocha (1998).

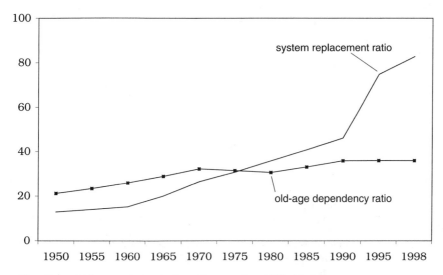

Fig. 12.1   Old age and system dependency ratios, 1950–98 (%)
Sources: Central Statistical Office; Pension Insurance Fund.

in figure 12.1, the system dependency ratio surpassed the old age dependency ratio in the mid-1970s, due primarily to the low retirement age for women, who comprised an increasing proportion of the pensioner population and whose life expectancy at retirement rose from twenty to thirty-three years in the last decades.

The average replacement ratio also increased steadily in the postwar period (figure 12.2), as a result not only of longer average contribution periods, but also of more generous benefits and more permissive eligibility rules. The increase in the number of pensioners and in the average benefit levels led to a steady increase in pension expenditures—from less than 5 percent in 1970s to more than 10 percent of gross domestic product (GDP) in 1990, requiring increasing contribution rates to balance the system. By the early 1990s, total contribution rates to the PAYGO system amounted to about 34.5 percent of gross wages, including 30.5 percent for old age and survivors and about 4.0 percent for underage disability pensions.

The Hungarian PAYGO scheme arrived in the 1990s with difficulty balancing expenditures and revenues, despite charging one of the highest contribution rates in the world (tables 12.1 and 12.2).[2] During the 1990s the PAYGO system was subject to further pressures, caused by a significant loss of revenues and a sharp increase in the system dependency ratio. As shown in tables 12.1 and 12.2, the loss of revenues amounted to almost 3

2. The PAYGO system is defined so as to include contribution revenues, the pension expenditures of the pension insurance fund, and the underage disability pensions of the health insurance fund. It is arbitrarily assumed that the underage disability expenditures are covered by equivalent revenue.

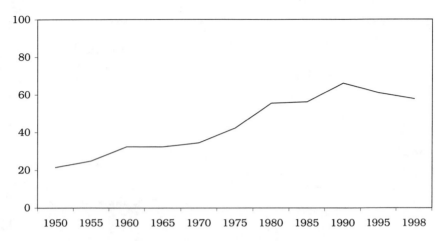

Fig. 12.2   Ratio of average pension to average net wage, 1950–98 (%)
Sources: Central Statistical Office; Pension Insurance Fund.

Table 12.1   Revenues, Expenditures, and Balance of the PAYGO System, 1991–99 (in % of GDP)

	1991	1995	1996	1997	1998	1999
Contribution revenues	11.0	8.9	8.4	8.3	8.2	7.8
Pension Fund	n.a.	7.5	7.1	7.0	7.0	6.8
Health Fund (disability)	n.a.	1.2	1.1	1.1	1.0	1.0
Pension expenditures	10.5	9.1	8.5	8.3	8.7	8.8
Old age	n.a.	6.8	6.3	6.2	6.4	6.4
Survivors'	n.a.	1.1	1.0	1.0	1.1	1.1
Disability	n.a.	1.2	1.1	1.1	1.2	1.3
PAYGO balance	0.5	−0.2	−0.1	0.0	−0.5	−1.0
Revenue loss to second pillar					0.3	0.6
Pure PAYGO balance	0.5	−0.2	−0.1	0.0	−0.2	−0.4

Sources: Central Statistical Office; Pension Insurance Fund.
Note: n.a. = not available.

Table 12.2   Base of Payroll Tax (% of GDP) and Contribution Rates, 1991–98

	1991	1995	1996	1997	1998	1999
Covered wage bill/GDP	30.9	23.6	22.2	22.4	22.1	22.3
Total contribution rates (%)	34.5	34.5	34.5	34.0	34.0	33.0
Pension Fund	30.5	30.5	30.5	30.0	31.0	30.0
Health Fund (notional)	4.0	4.0	4.0	4.0	3.0	3.0

Sources: Central Statistical Office; Pension Insurance Fund.

percent of GDP before the reform, due primarily to an erosion of the tax base (the covered wage bill). Such base erosion was due not only to problems of ceilings and exemptions, but also to increasing evasion of the heavy payroll tax. The increase in the system dependency ratio amounted to 66 percent during the 1990s, most of which occurred during the first half of the decade (figure 12.1). This dramatic increase in the dependency ratio was due to a reduction in labor force participation, increases in unemployment, and the maintenance of generous early retirement and disability schemes as a buffer against unemployment.

The sharp increase in the number of pensioners implied strong pressures on expenditures and, combined with the revenue loss, would have resulted in very large PAYGO deficits in the absence of other correcting measures. The main correction that took place involved the manipulation of indexation parameters in the benefit formula, which resulted in a significant drop of the average replacement ratio. A sharp real wage compression that took place in the mid-1990s (approximately 15 percent in 1995 and 1996) also contributed to the decline in real pensions, given the wage indexation of pensions. The final results of these measures were a drop in pension expenditures relative to GDP, and only modest PAYGO deficits in the early and mid-1990s.[3]

Although these corrections prevented the emergence of large deficits in the PAYGO system, they were perceived as arbitrary and unfair, diminishing the credibility of the PAYGO in the eyes of the population. Furthermore, the scope for additional ad hoc corrections narrowed severely, making the system even more vulnerable to the demographic shocks projected for the twenty-first century. As the consequences of a do-nothing scenario were more widely understood, it became increasingly apparent that the public pension system needed more fundamental reform. Before examining the long-run projections of the system, it must be noted that the PAYGO deficits have increased somewhat since 1997 (the year when the reform was passed); these deficits raise less concern, however, because they are partly due to the creation of a second pillar, and because the actuarial imbalances of the system were already being addressed by the reform.

12.2.2   The Future of the PAYGO System in the Absence of Reform

Along with the rest of Europe, Hungary will experience rapid population aging in the next few decades, a development that will submit the pension system to great pressures. The impact of these adverse demographic trends in the absence of reforms was assessed through the use of an actuarial model developed during the reform.[4] The base year used for

---

3. Palacios and Rocha (1998) provide a more detailed analysis of the performance of pension revenues and expenditures during the 1990s.
4. The actuarial model was developed by Patrick Wiese.

Table 12.3   Main Economic and Demographic Assumptions for Pension
               Simulations, 1997–2070

	1998	1999	2000–2030	2000–2070
Economic assumptions				
Real GDP growth	5.0	4.1	3.0	2.7
Real wage growth	3.5	3.5	3.0	3.0
Inflation rate	14.3	10.0	3.4	3.0
Unemployment rate	9.0	8.0	7.0	7.0
Demographic assumptions				
Population growth	−0.3	−0.3	−0.2	−0.3
Employment growth	1.4	1.1	0.0	−0.3
Life expectancy (men)	65.1	65.0	71.8	76.4
Life expectancy (women)	74.6	74.8	79.3	84.5

Notes: Actual figures for 1998 and 1999. GDP growth is derived from wage growth. The labor share is assumed to remain constant. Life expectancy is years at birth, based on current mortality.

the actuarial projections is 1997—the year preceding the implementation of the reform. The main economic and demographic assumptions used in the actuarial projections are shown in table 12.3.

The economic assumptions include a decline in inflation rates to Western European levels, a constant labor share in GDP, and a moderate decline in the unemployment rate. The demographic assumptions are the same as the baseline scenario developed by Hablicsek (1995), and imply a declining population and a significant increase in the old age dependency ratio. The system dependency ratio also increases as a result, although this increase is somewhat moderated by the assumption that labor force participation rates converge gradually to the levels prevailing in Western Europe. This implies a moderate increase in labor force participation rates from the current levels, especially for women.[5]

Under these demographic and economic assumptions, and in the absence of reforms, the Hungarian PAYGO system would generate growing deficits, as shown in figure 12.3. The deficits would grow to about 2.0 percent of GDP at the end of the first decade of the century, and would converge to about 6.5 percent of GDP in 2070, the end of the projection period. The result is essentially due to the assumption of a declining rate of inflation and to adverse demographic trends. The decline in the rate of inflation implies increasing real average pensions and replacement ratios, because of the full backward wage indexation rule (prevailing before the reforms), and also because of smaller inflation-related losses in entry-level

5. Labor force participation for women in their thirties and forties are assumed to increase from about 70 percent to about 75–83 percent. This assumption was adopted because labor force participation rates declined significantly during the early stages of the transition in the 1990s, from Hungary's historical levels and from the levels prevailing in most European countries.

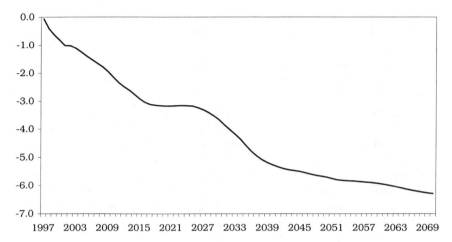

Fig. 12.3   Balances of the public pension scheme in the absence of reforms, 1997–2070 (% of GDP)

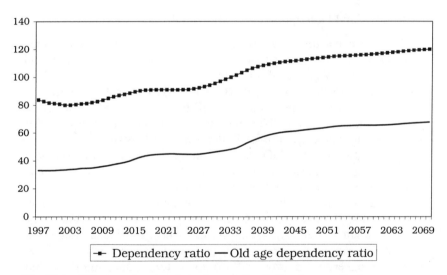

Dependency ratio ── Old age dependency ratio

Fig. 12.4   Old age and system dependency ratios in the absence of reforms, 1997–2070 (%)

pensions (the former benefit formula contained several indexation parameters that made entry-level pensions very sensitive to inflation).

Whereas the decline in inflation is the major cause of the early deficits, demographic factors dominate the results after the first decade. The projected fluctuations in the deficit closely mirror the old age and system dependency ratios, as shown in figure 12.4. Both ratios increase between 1995 and 2017, followed by a ten-year period of stability and then by another increase. The old age dependency ratio nearly doubles to 65 percent at the end of the projection period, while the system dependency ratio grows to 120 percent.

In the absence of reforms, balancing the pension system in 2070 would require increasing the contribution rate to more than 55 percent, or reducing the replacement ratio from about 60 percent to less than 35 percent. This would cause either greater distortions in the labor market or great dissatisfaction and unrest among future pensioners, or both. It is also clear that the absence of reforms would imply a massive burden on future generations, irrespective of whether the future imbalances were financed by higher contributions, lower replacement ratios, or general taxes. Recent calculations of generational accounts confirm that workers under thirty-eight years of age would be net contributors to the system, and that the net tax burden on future generations would be particularly heavy.[6]

12.3   The Hungarian Pension Reform

12.3.1   General Description of the Original Reform Package

The reform package gave workers the choice to stay in a reformed PAYGO system or to switch to a new, mixed pension system until the end of August 1999. Workers who initially opted for the new system will be able to return to the reformed PAYGO until December 2002. After that date, workers will be permanently affiliated with either the reformed PAYGO or the new system. New entrants in the labor force after July 1998 have been automatically enrolled in the new mixed system.

The reforms to the PAYGO system included the following main components: (1) a higher normal retirement age of sixty-two for both men and women (from sixty and fifty-five, respectively); (2) an increase in the number of years of service to be eligible for early retirement without penalties to forty years; (3) increases in the penalties for early retirement and in the rewards for late retirement; (4) changes in the benefit formula designed to eliminate its explicit redistributive elements (i.e., a correction factor that penalized higher-income workers); (5) a new tax regime; and (6) a shift from backward net wage indexation to a "Swiss" indexation formula consisting of a combination of contemporaneous price and wage indexation (50 percent net wages, 50 percent consumer prices).

The new legislation included detailed transition tables for the retirement age increase, the corresponding early retirement penalties, the minimum years of service for early retirement both without and with penalties, and

---

6. Auerbach, Kotlikoff, and Leibfritz (1999) provide a general methodology of generational accounts and empirical results for several countries. Gal, Simonovits, and Tarcali (2001) construct generational accounts for Hungary.

a new set of accrual rates that apply to gross rather than net wage history. The retirement age and the minimum years of service for early retirement began rising immediately, but do not reach their final state until the year 2009. The new legislation also included a transition period for the new indexation formula, specifying the maintenance of full backward wage indexation for 1998 and 1999, followed by a mixed 70–30 percent (wage-prices) contemporaneous indexation formula for 2000; and finally a contemporaneous Swiss formula for 2001 and subsequent years. The new benefit formula and tax regime will become effective by 2013.

Many of the changes reflected the government's position that redistribution should be removed from the pension scheme. This was based on the government's desire to tighten the link between contributions and benefits in order to improve compliance with and the insurance characteristics of the system. An element of intragenerational redistribution was maintained, but in the form of a minimum, top-up, means-tested pension benefit financed outside the pension system.

As summarized in table 12.4, workers deciding to remain in the reformed PAYGO system would pay a contribution rate of 30 percent of their gross wages, and would earn an accrual rate of 1.65 percent for each year of service.[7] Workers switching to the new system would have 22 percent of their gross wages channeled to the first (PAYGO) pillar, earning an annual accrual rate of 1.22 percent for each year of service. The switching workers would earn the same 1.22 percent accrual rate for every year of service before the switching date. The switching workers would also contribute 8 percent of their gross wages to their second-pillar accounts. This contribution rate structure would follow a two-year transitional period— the contribution to the second pillar would be 6 percent in 1998, 7 percent in 1999, and 8 percent from 2000 onward. The overall contribution rate would remain at 30 percent, and the contribution to the first pillar would be reduced accordingly.

The first pillar of the new multipillar system applies the same rules as the reformed PAYGO system, including higher retirement age, minimum years of service, and indexation arrangements. However, the benefit formula was scaled down in proportion to the size of the contribution rates. Therefore, the annual accrual rate in the new first pillar was reduced to 1.22 percent, or roughly 74 percent of the 1.65 percent accrual rate that applies to those workers who remain in the reformed PAYGO scheme. This corresponds to the ratio of the (1) the contribution rate to the PAYGO scheme paid by workers who pursue the multipillar scheme, to (2) the contribution rate paid by workers who do not switch; namely, 22–30. For

---

7. Workers remaining in the reformed PAYGO system may obtain additional coverage from the voluntary third pillar, which has been in existence since 1994. Vittas (1996) provides an early analysis of the Hungarian third pillar.

Table 12.4   Main Elements of the Reform Package

	PAYGO System		New System	
	Old	Reformed	First Pillar	Second Pillar
Contribution rate	30%	30%	24–23–22%	6–7–8%
Annual accrual rates	Nonlinear, equivalent to 2.00% of net wage	Linear, 1.65% of gross wage	Linear, 1.22% of gross wage	—
Pension base	Gradual increase to lifetime earnings	Gradual increase to lifetime earnings	Gradual increase to lifetime earnings	—
Redistribution factor	Yes	No	No	—
Normal retirement age	60 (men); 55 (women)	62 (men and women)	62 (men and women)	62 (men and women)
Early retirement rules	Low penalty rates and minimum service years for early retirement	Higher penalty rates and minimum service years for early retirement	Higher penalty rates and minimum service years for early retirement	—
Indexation of pensions	Backward net wage indexation	Contemporaneous Swiss	Contemporaneous Swiss	—

Note: Long dash indicates "not applicable."

those who switch to the new scheme, the 1.22 percent accrual rate applies for both past and future years of participation in the system, implying that anyone who switches is voluntarily forfeiting approximately one-fourth of his or her acquired rights in the process.

As discussed in greater detail in section 12.4, workers who switch to the new system and contribute for at least fifteen years to the new second pillar are guaranteed a minimum second-pillar benefit equal to 25 percent of the first-pillar pension. The guarantee is modest for new workers. However, the guarantee is equivalent to a minimum lifetime real return of more than 4 percent per annum for workers in their mid-forties, due to the shorter accumulation period. Therefore, the guarantee could be triggered for workers in their mid-forties who switched to the new scheme, although the amount required to meet this guarantee should not be significant.

12.3.2   Changes in the Reform by the New Government

The elections of May 1998 resulted in the departure of the government that designed and implemented the pension reform, and that consisted of a coalition of the Socialist Party (a center-Left party) and the Free Democrat Party (center-Right). Another coalition government, formed by the Young Democrats Party (center-Right) and the Small Shareholders Party (Right), won the elections by a narrow margin. The new government neither emphasized pension reform in its preelection program, nor mentioned its intention to modify the ongoing reform during the campaign period, but has expressed less than full support of the reform during its tenure.

One of the first measures announced by the new government was the decision to maintain the contribution rate to the second pillar at 6 percent in 1999, instead of increasing it to 7 and 8 percent, as originally planned. Another important measure involved changes in the transition indexation rules negotiated during the reform preparation. More specifically, instead of maintaining the backward wage indexation in 1999 (which would have resulted in nominal pension increases of 18 percent), the government announced an ad hoc increase of 14 percent. The announcement of these changes created uncertainty among workers and market participants, especially because they were not accompanied by an announcement of the policies that would be followed in 2000 and in future years. Some politicians in the new coalition raised the level of uncertainty further by announcing their intentions to introduce more fundamental changes and even to roll back the reform entirely.

Political factors may have motivated these initial sharp attacks on the reform. However, it also seems that some policy makers became concerned with the transitional deficits caused by the loss of revenues to the second pillar. Technical discussions both inside and outside the government showed that the size of the transitional deficit was moderate and that this deficit was, in any case, neutral from the point of view of macroeconomic stability (as discussed below). During the second half of 1999, the general attitude toward the reform improved somewhat and the attacks subsided, but the government still indicated that it would maintain the contribution to the second pillar at 6 percent until the end of its tenure (mid-2002). The government also extended the option for workers to switch back to the PAYGO scheme from December 2000 to December 2002.

12.3.3   The Actual Switching of Outcomes

The government that passed the reform initially considered a switching strategy that involved forcing all workers below the age of forty to switch to the new system, and all workers above that age to remain in the re-formed PAYGO system. However, it became increasingly apparent that a mandatory cut-off age could spark constitutional battles over accrued rights and prove too costly to implement. These problems led the government to make the reform mandatory for new entrants (after July 1998) and voluntary for anyone with a contribution history in the old system. Moreover, the government also decided to recognize accrued rights by making compensatory pension payments at the time of retirement, as practiced in Argentina, and not by recognition bonds, as practiced in Chile, Peru, and Colombia.

The rights earned under the old scheme are recognized by applying the accrual rates of the new first pillar. Because these accrual rates are lower than those implied by the old formula, workers who switch voluntarily forego part of their accrued rights. The new system is still attractive to most younger workers, because the higher expected returns in the second pillar result in higher pensions in the new system, under reasonable assumptions. Therefore, the valuation of past contributions in the context of a voluntary switch allowed the government a certain measure of control over the speed of the transition and the size of early transition deficits, as well as a reduction in the implicit pension debt.

As shown in figure 12.5, if the contribution rate to the second pillar were set at 8 percent, as in the original reform package, and under conservative assumptions on returns and costs (returns of 2 percent above wage growth, annuity rate equal to wage growth, and operating costs and charges amounting to 15 percent of contributions), workers below thirty-six years of age would tend to switch to the new system, whereas workers above that age would find it attractive to remained in the reformed PAYGO scheme. The higher replacement ratios of younger workers are essentially due to the effect of the compounding of interest over a longer number of years. This interest-accumulation effect outweighs the reduction in accrued rights for workers below thirty-six years of age, but is not sufficient for workers above that age.

Of course, these are rather conservative assumptions about pension fund returns. As shown in figure 12.6, the rate of return–wage growth differential in the 1980s and 1990s was higher than 2 percent in a sample of

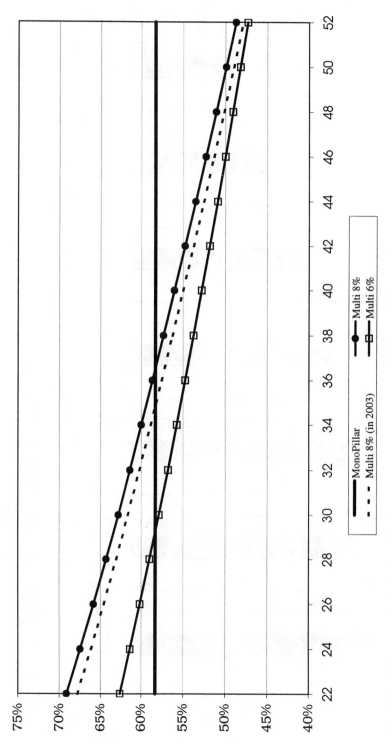

Fig. 12.5 Replacement ratios in the old and new systems for each cohort: Returns 2% above wage growth (gross pension/gross wage, in %)

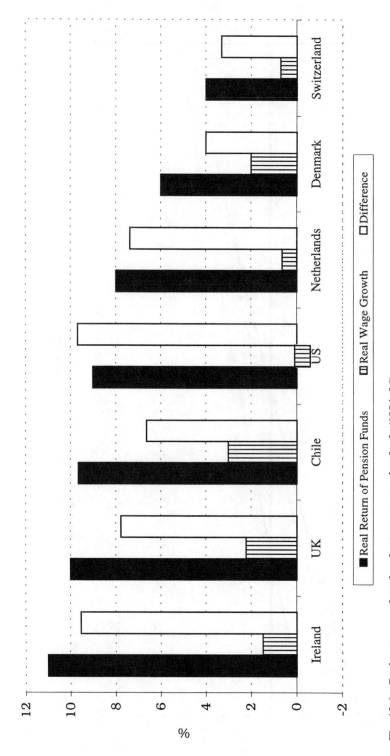

Fig. 12.6   Real wage growth and real returns on pension funds (1984–96)
Sources: European Federation of Retirement Provision (1996); Organization for Economic Cooperation and Development (OECD; 1998).

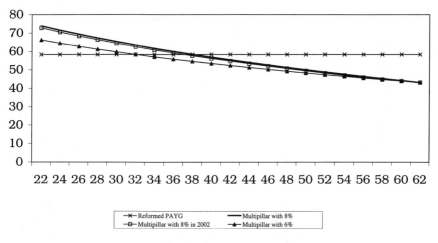

Fig. 12.7   Replacement ratios in the old and new systems for each cohort: Returns 3% above wage growth (gross pension/gross wage, in %)

countries with large funded systems, even in countries that imposed portfolio restrictions or followed very conservative portfolio strategies, such as Denmark and Switzerland. For the sake of illustration, assuming returns of 3 percent above wage growth, the equilibrium cut-off age would increase to thirty-eight years, as shown in figure 12.7. If returns were assumed to be as high as those shown in figure 12.6, the cut-off age would exceed forty years.[8]

The actual switching outcome was in line with other switching experiences and largely met initial expectations.[9] As shown in figures 12.8 and 12.9, the number of switchers was significant in the first few months of implementation, kept increasing throughout 1998 and 1999, and accelerated in the last two months before the final deadline for switching (September 1999), reaching approximately 2 million workers (nearly half of the labor force). At that point, more than 80 percent of switchers consisted of workers below forty years of age, and more than 80 percent of workers in their twenties and early thirties had switched to the new system. The increase in the number of switchers after that date reflects primarily the new

8. A positive difference between the return on capital and wage growth is also a condition of dynamic efficiency (see, e.g., Barro and Sala-i-Martin 1995). The returns on pension fund assets shown in figure 12.6 cannot be used as direct evidence of dynamic efficiency because they contain a risk premium on equity. However, see Feldstein (1995, 1997) for a discussion of the dynamic efficiency condition in the presence of risk for the U.S. case, and Kotcherlakota (1996) for a discussion of the equity risk premium.

9. See Disney and Whitehouse (1992) for an analysis of the opt-out experience in the case of the United Kingdom, Rofman (1995, 1996) for a description of the Argentine experience, and Palacios and Whitehouse (1998) for a comparison of switching outcomes in a sample of reforming countries.

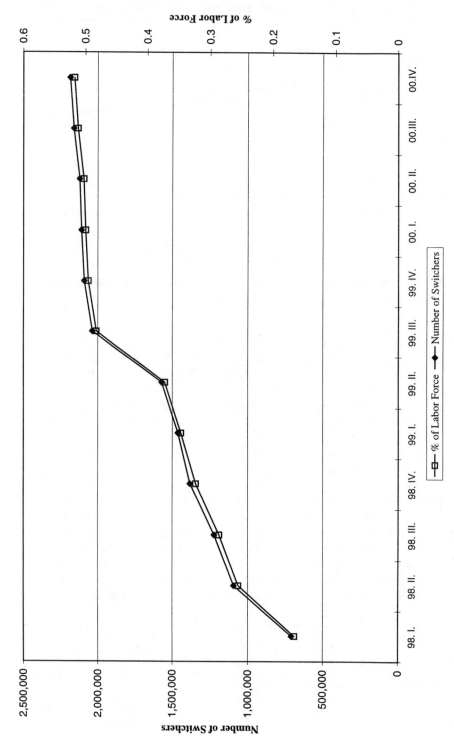

Fig. 12.8 Number of switchers to the new system (in absolute numbers and in % of labor force)

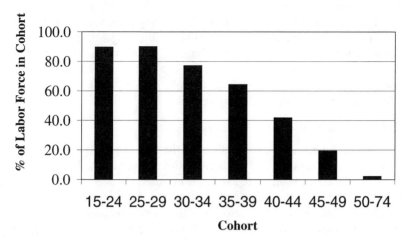

Fig. 12.9   **Actual switching outcome, December 2000 (as % of the labor force in each cohort)**

entrants to the labor force, which are mostly young workers. By December 2000, roughly 90 percent of workers in their twenties and early thirties were enrolled in the new system.

There may be a number of explanations of why workers continued switching despite the uncertainty caused by the absence of political support for the reform by the new government. One may be that the possibility to switch back to the reformed PAYGO scheme by the end of 2002 may have eliminated the perception of risk associated with early switching. In addition, some workers may have speculated that the originally envisaged contribution rate of 8 percent would sooner or later be restored. Indeed, if the contribution rate were increased to 8 percent in 2003 by either the same or a new government (after the 2002 elections), the equilibrium cutoff age would be only slightly reduced, as shown in figures 12.5 and 12.7.

Finally, workers switching to the new system may have assigned a great weight to the perceived political risk associated with the PAYGO scheme—a justified perception in view of the manipulation of the parameters of the Hungarian PAYGO benefit formula in the late 1980s and early 1990s (section 12.2). The decision of the new government to abandon the indexation formula that had been negotiated and agreed-upon for the period of transition (and established in the 1997 law), provides another example of how the parameters of a public PAYGO system may be easily changed by subsequent legal amendments.

It is noteworthy, however, that the failure to restore the original 8 percent contribution in the next few years could lead to a significant reduction in the equilibrium cut-off age. As shown in figures 12.5 and 12.7, maintaining the second-pillar contribution at 6 percent indefinitely would reduce the cut-off age to about twenty-eight to thirty-three years, depending on the assumption for pension fund returns in the long run. It is difficult to assess whether and when the contribution rate to the second pillar will be increased to 8 percent. However, it is clear that a few cohorts may be made better off by switching back to the reformed PAYGO scheme if the original contribution rate is not restored.

12.3.4   Simulating the PAYGO Reforms

It is useful to present the simulations of the reform in two stages. First, the various measures designed to improve the balance of the PAYGO system are examined and contrasted with the no reform scenario. Second, the direct fiscal impact of the introduction of the second pillar is examined, in combination with the PAYGO reforms. The macroeconomic assumptions used are the same as those in table 12.3, with the exception of a slightly higher growth rate of the labor force in the scenarios that include an increase in the retirement age (which also implies slightly higher rates of GDP growth, given the assumption of a constant labor share).

This section highlights the impact of the two major reform measures, namely, the increase in the retirement age and the shift toward mixed indexation. The changes in the benefit formula and the tax treatment have impacts on particular workers but little or no impact on the aggregate balance of the PAYGO scheme (Palacios and Rocha 1998). As shown in figure 12.10, the new retirement-age rules reduce significantly the projected deficits. This is due not only to the increase in the statutory normal retirement age over time, but also to the increase in the penalties for early retirement and in the minimum years of service for early retirement. Although it is difficult to predict retirement behavior in the face of the new penalties or the average number of contribution years, reasonable assumptions suggest an increase in the effective retirement age for men and women of roughly two and five years, respectively. The longer working period raises pensions and replacement ratios, given the accrual rates, but the higher pension is received for fewer years and some individuals continue to contribute to the scheme. The net effect is an average annual reduction in future deficits of about 1.5–2.0 percent of GDP.

Although the increase in retirement age has an important impact, it is only when the new indexation method is added to the reform package that the PAYGO scheme moves into an extended period of surplus. Figure 12.10 shows how these surpluses peak in 2013, which is the year when the baby boom cohorts begin to retire. Later, deficits reemerge when a second demographic shock hits the PAYGO scheme around 2035. With an increase in life expectancy of two years per decade assumed, the increase in retirement age to sixty-two years is insufficient to offset the demographic developments and to maintain a constant retirement duration in the long run.

These two major parametric reforms generate an average annual im-

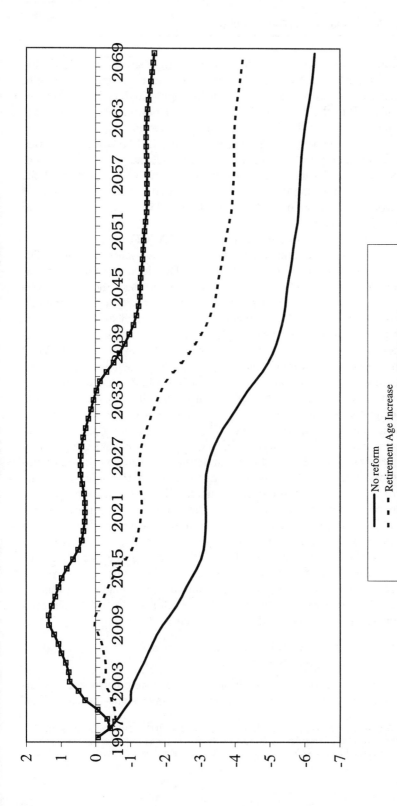

Fig. 12.10 Balances of the public pension scheme after PAYGO reforms, 1997–2070 (% of GDP)

provement in the PAYGO balance of more than 4 percent of GDP during the projection period. The implicit pension debt, measured according to an accrued benefit obligation (ABO) definition,[10] is reduced from 309 percent of GDP in the no reform scenario to 241 percent of GDP with the PAYGO reforms, a reduction of more than 20 percent.

The PAYGO reform measures shown in figure 12.10 provide the starting point for the analysis of the introduction of the second pillar. To this point, the package results in a significant improvement in the finances of the PAYGO scheme during the next decade, followed by a gradual erosion of the surpluses at the end of the following decade. The pension system would record deficits again at the end of the projection period, and the elimination of these deficits would require further PAYGO reforms, such as a further increase in retirement age (say, to sixty-five years, as in most Organization for Economic Cooperation and Development [OECD] countries) or the adoption of price indexation. Nevertheless, the reform measures achieve a significant reduction in future deficits and the implicit pension debt—in fact, the reforms produce some small surpluses.

Despite the presence of these surpluses, the government never gave serious consideration to a reform package limited to improving the PAYGO scheme because it saw four serious shortcomings in such a solution: First, the accumulation of surpluses in the PAYGO scheme would provide an easy opportunity to reverse the reforms through politically motivated benefit increases. Second, it would have created a new role for the public pension fund as an asset manager. There was little reason, from either historical Hungarian or international experience, to believe that such an arrangement would lead to efficient investment allocation or good corporate governance.[11] Third, this solution was unlikely to contribute to the type of capital market development that a multipillar package was capable of generating. Finally, the promise of higher returns in the private scheme, even after taking into account higher administrative costs, helped offset the benefit reductions in the PAYGO scheme and simultaneously diversified the workers' risk in the long run. This positive aspect of the overall package was instrumental in generating support, especially among younger voters. In view of these and other perceived advantages, the new system was designed to divert the saving generated by the reform to privately managed pension funds referred to as the second pillar.

12.3.5 Simulating the Multipillar Reform with a 6 Percent Contribution to the Second Pillar

The simulations of the full multipillar package were performed assuming initially that the number of switchers will stay roughly the same as of

10. The PAYGO scheme is assumed to be terminated in 1997 and the future pension obligations (accrued as of December 1997) are discounted at the rate of wage growth.
11. Iglesias and Palacios (2000) show that publicly managed pension funds have performed very poorly.

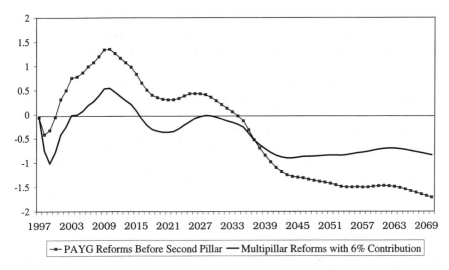

Fig. 12.11   PAYGO balances with 6% contribution to second pillar (% of GDP)

September 1999, and that the contribution rate to the second pillar will be maintained at 6 percent indefinitely. Figure 12.11 confirms the obvious fact that allowing workers who are switching to divert part of their contributions to the second pillar causes an immediate revenue loss to the PAYGO system. The revenue losses increase rapidly to about 0.8 percent of GDP in the first four to five years of the reform, then keep increasing at a more gradual pace to reach 1.4 percent of GDP in the third decade, when most of the active population will be enrolled in the new system. The PAYGO deficit would tend to increase at the same pace, but the PAYGO reforms described above more than offset the revenue loss, allowing a reduction in the deficit. The system is actually projected to generate small surpluses at the end of the decade, even considering the revenue losses, but returns to deficits again in the second decade, with the retirement of the baby boom generation.

The PAYGO deficit peaks around 2022 but then improves, as the first significant cohorts to receive first-pillar benefits in the new system (i.e., those in their mid-thirties in 1998) retire. The difference between the PAYGO balances with and without the chance to opt out to the second pillar increases until about that time, and narrows thereafter. By 2040, the deficit in the multipillar system is actually smaller than the PAYGO deficit had the second pillar not been introduced. These results are driven by two factors. First, the replacement ratio of the first pillar of the new system is about three-fourths of the replacement ratio in the reformed PAYGO scheme. Thus, the temporary imbalances between replacement ratios and contributions created by the opt-out begins to taper off after the cohorts in the mixed system begin to retire. Second, the reform involves a reduction of about one-fourth of the accrued rights of workers who opt for the new system. As a result, the valuation for the years of contribution under the old system are lower than would have been generated by the old benefit formula.

To determine the first-order impact of the reform on national saving, the public and private pension savings need to be combined, as shown in figure 12.12. The PAYGO balances with the second-pillar opt-out are reproduced in figure 12.12, together with the net private contributions to the second pillar (gross contributions plus interests minus redemptions), and the sum of the two balances. Total pension saving peaks around the year 2011 and decline thereafter, following the decline in the PAYGO balances, but increase again after 2020, when the first significant numbers of workers begin to retire in the new system. The contribution of the pension system to saving declines in the third decade, due to demographic aging. The private scheme begins maturing, with increasing redemptions and smaller net positive contributions, while the public scheme shifts into deficits. The net result is a decline in total pension saving to approximately 1 percent of GDP. In order to eliminate the public deficit and increase total saving, the authorities would have to increase further the retirement age or shift to price indexation (or both).

The final impact of the pension reform on national saving will depend on the reaction of voluntary private saving to the individual measures of the reform, and on the reaction of the government to the path of the PAYGO deficits and surpluses. The reaction of voluntary private saving to the reform is difficult to estimate numerically, although it is possible to identify some of the major changes that might occur. The increase in the retirement age could induce some decline in private saving, whereas the change in indexation would imply a decrease in expected retirement income, inducing some increase in private saving.[12] The expectations of higher returns on the contribution to the second pillar (relative to the PAYGO system) could have a positive or negative effect on voluntary saving, depending on the relative sizes of the income and substitution effects. Therefore, the net impact of all these factors on voluntary private saving is, in principle, ambiguous, and would in any case be dampened by the existence of liquidity constraints.

The reaction of the government to the path of future PAYGO deficits will be influenced primarily by Hungary's objective of joining the European Union (EU) by the year 2005. Meeting the objective of EU membership will require an effort to reduce the general government deficit from about 4.0–4.5 percent of GDP (the levels that prevailed in the late 1990s) to levels below the Maastricht ceiling of 3 percent of GDP. The expected reduction of the general government deficit to levels below 3 percent of

---

12. These are the responses predicted by the overlapping generations model. See, for example, Kotlikoff (1989).

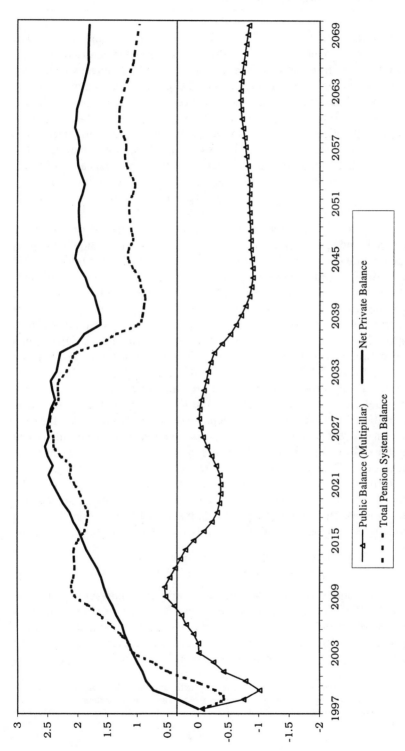

Fig. 12.12 Public, private, and total pension balances with 6% contribution to second pillar (% of GDP)

GDP suggests that the transition will be primarily tax financed and that saving effects might be stronger. However, additional increases in national saving arising from offsetting reductions in the government's deficit are likely to be moderate, because the general government deficit is already close to the Maastricht ceiling, the projected PAYGO deficits are moderate, and the actuarial projections even predict a period of PAYGO surpluses.

On the whole, there is no reason to believe that the direct impact of the reform on national saving would be substantially stronger than indicated in figure 12.12. Of course, to the extent that the reform has a positive impact on Hungary's growth performance, there could be additional indirect effects on saving as a result of endogenous interactions between saving and growth; these effects are not reflected in figure 12.12.[13]

The perception that the Hungarian transition would be primarily tax financed, due to the PAYGO reforms and the overall reduction in the general government deficit, led many observers to state that the reform would excessively benefit future generations to the detriment of current generations, who would be forced to "pay twice." However, although it is true that the reform package has significantly reduced the burden on future generations, it has not been sufficient to restore intergenerational balance entirely, given the severe initial bias against these generations. Calculations of generational accounts for Hungary indicate that the pension reform has reduced the net burden on future generation by roughly three fourths, but that future generations are expected to remain net contributors to the system (Gal, Simonovits, and Tarcali 2001). The reduction of the initial intergenerational imbalance has been achieved by slightly increasing the burden on current workers; older workers and pensioners have not been significantly affected by the reform and have remained net beneficiaries of the system. The calculations of generational accounts for Hungary also show that current workers would have incurred even greater losses if the second pillar had not been introduced. What the calculations do not capture, however, is the possible positive impact of the reform on Hungary's growth performance and on the welfare of current generations.

12.3.6   Simulating the Multipillar Reform with an 8 percent Contribution to the Second Pillar

The reluctance of the government to raise the contribution rate to 8 percent (allegedly because of the larger transitional deficit) raises the question of what would be the impact of this measure on the balances of the system and on the economy. This analysis is summarized in figures 12.13 and 12.14, where is it assumed that the contribution to the second pillar is

---

13. The interactions among pension reform, growth, and the welfare of different generations are examined in Kotlikoff (1995) and Corsetti and Schmidt-Hebel (1995). Loayza, Schmidt-Hebel, and Serven (2000) provide a recent survey of the empirical literature on savings.

raised to 8 percent in 2003. The number of switchers is assumed to be the same as in figures 12.11 and 12.12.

Figure 12.13 reveals the obvious fact that the increase in the second-pillar contribution from 6 to 8 percent would imply an additional loss of revenues to the PAYGO system and slightly larger PAYGO deficits. The difference between the two lines would be 0.3–0.4 percent of GDP in the

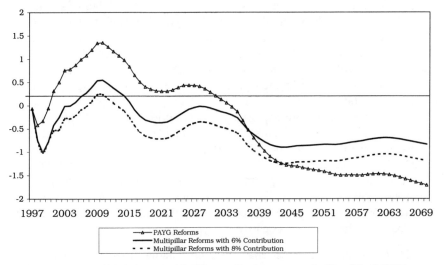

Fig. 12.13   PAYGO balances with 8% contribution to second pillar (% of GDP)

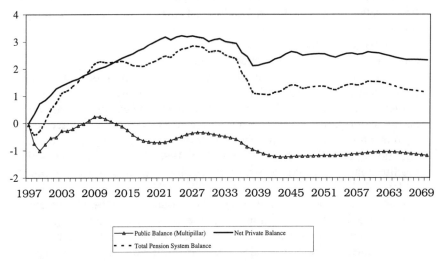

Fig. 12.14   Public, private, and total pension balances with 8% contribution of second pillar (% of GDP)

next decades. However, these larger deficits would be offset by larger private surpluses, leading essentially to the same overall pension balance as shown in figure 12.14 (by comparison with the overall balance in figure 12.12). Therefore, the increase in contribution rates to the second pillar would produce no adverse impact on key macroeconomic variables, such as inflation and the current account.

The difference between the two scenarios depicted in figures 12.11 and 12.14 is clearly artificial, because it assumes that the number of switchers is the same. If a large number of workers switches back to the PAYGO scheme, the scenario with a 6 percent contribution could actually prove worse, at the end of the projection period, than the scenario with an 8 percent contribution because it would imply a smaller reduction of accrued rights, a larger implicit pension debt, and possibly larger PAYGO deficits in the long run.

The failure to restore the original contribution rates could also imply some efficiency losses. A smaller second pillar implies a weaker link between contributions and benefits, with possible adverse effects in the labor market. A smaller second pillar also implies more limited capital market effects, due to the slower growth and smaller size of pension funds. It is very difficult to determine the long-term quantitative impacts of these two effects on economic performance with any degree of accuracy, but those impacts are bound to be negative.[14]

12.3.7 Simulations of Alternative (counterfactual) Reform Scenarios

As mentioned above, during the first stages of the reform the new system was criticized for various reasons, including the generation of a transitional deficit. Some of the critics in Hungary claimed that a system of notional defined contribution (NDC) accounts would have generated the same positive results without generating the deficits. To examine whether this criticism is valid, this section provides counterfactual simulations of an NDC-type reform, and compares them with the pure defined benefit (DB) reform and the multipillar reform examined above.

Figure 12.15 shows projections of the Hungarian pension system under all the major parametric reforms that have effectively been adopted (e.g., retirement-age increase and Swiss indexation), and the counterfactual adoption of an NDC scheme as of January 1998. Therefore, workers retiring after that date would receive a DB benefit based on their accrued rights under the old DB formula, and an NDC benefit based on their notional balances accumulated after that date. Two counterfactual NDC schemes are simulated, the first with a notional interest rate equal to GDP growth, and the second with an interest equal to GDP growth plus one percent. The schemes convert their notional balances into annuities, assuming the

---

14. See Levine and Zervos (1996) for an empirical analysis of capital market development and economic growth, and Holzman (1996) for an analysis of this effect in the Chilean case.

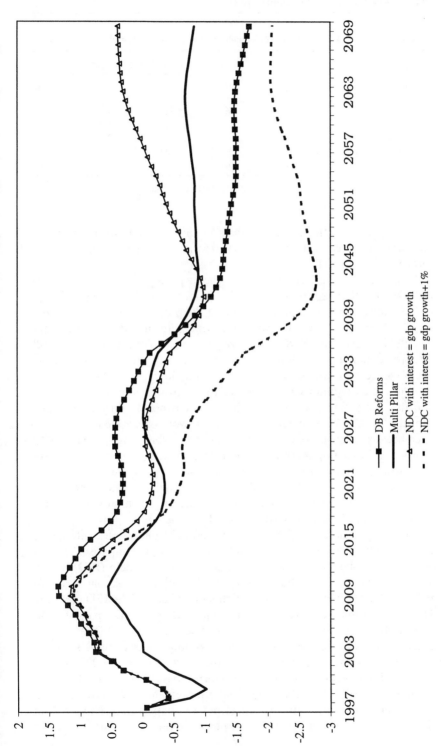

Fig. 12.15 NDC reforms × DB and multipillar reforms

DB Reforms
Multi Pillar
NDC with interest = gdp growth
NDC with interest = gdp growth+1%

Table 12.5   Implicit Pension Debt under Different Reform Scenarios (in % of GDP)

	Base Year			
Scenario	1997	2010	2020	2030
No reform	309	340	363	378
Pure DB reform	241	226	246	254
Multipillar reform	232	208	216	214
NDC with i = gdp growth	248	233	245	232
NDC with i = gdp growth + 1%	257	255	281	288

Notes: DB = defined benefit. NDC = notional defined contribution.

same respective notional interest rates in the payment period. The two lines are compared with the pure DB reform and the multipillar reform shown in figure 12.11.

As shown in figure 12.15, the NDC scheme paying an interest rate equal to GDP growth would produce smaller deficits than either the multipillar or the reformed DB systems at the end of the projection period, while the NDC scheme paying GDP growth plus one percent ends up with larger deficits. However, the NDC system paying only GDP growth would still fare worse than a pure DB reform for the first forty years. This is because the NDC scheme would "transform" the employment growth that happens in the early and middle stages of the transition into higher pension benefits, something that the DB scheme would not do. In the very long run, the NDC scheme paying GDP growth would generate a better balance because it would pay an interest rate lower than wage growth (GDP grows at a lower rate due to decline in employment). The multipillar reform would produce a higher deficit than an NDC paying GDP growth, but again, this is due to the partial diversion of contributions to the second pillar. The overall pension balances produced by the multipillar reform are better than those produced by the NDC schemes.

The computation of the implicit pension debt under these alternative reform scenarios provides another interesting tool for comparisons across scenarios. As shown in table 12.5, the implicit pension debt (IPD) falls in all the reform scenarios, but is lowest in the multipillar scenario, due to the voluntary reduction of accrued rights by switchers. The IPD of a pure DB reform is initially lower than that generated by an NDC paying GDP growth, because of initially lower replacement ratios. In the long run, the NDC paying a modest interest rate would produce a lower IPD, but again this is because the replacement ratios would drop under an NDC scheme paying GDP growth rates. A pure DB reform would also be capable of producing lower IPDs if accrual rates and replacement ratios were reduced.

The reforming government decided not to adopt a pure NDC reform for the same reasons it decided not to adopt a pure DB reform (e.g., the exclusion of a second pillar). The initial surpluses produced by a pure NDC reform could be depleted by politically motivated increases in pension benefits, by increases in the central budget deficit, or by political interference in the management of the assets that would lead to negative returns. Moreover, an NDC scheme would still be operated by the public sector on a PAYGO basis and would not have the risk-diversification properties of a mixed system. Finally, an NDC scheme would not contribute to the development of capital markets that Hungary and other transitional countries need in the current stage of their transformation.[15]

12.4 The Structure and Performance of the Funded Pillars

12.4.1 Evolution and Structure

Before the 1997 reform, Hungary already had a voluntary private pension scheme (the third pillar), which had begun operating in 1994. The concession of generous tax incentives led membership to increase to 1 million affiliates by 1999, the equivalent of 25 percent of the labor force. The average contribution has been about 5.0 percent of the average wage, and total assets reached 1.5 percent of GDP in 1999. Affiliates in the voluntary system tend to be middle- to high-income workers above thirty-five years of age and employed in larger enterprises. The industry was initially very fragmented, with a large number of very small and poorly managed funds, but a process of mergers and liquidations reduced the number of active voluntary funds from 270 in 1994 to 160 in 1999.

The pension funds in the mandatory (second) pillar were constructed as mutual associations, as in the third pillar. The system began operating in January 1998 with only thirty-eight licensed funds, as a result of stricter licensing criteria; the number of funds had already fallen to twenty-five by the end of 1999, as a result of mergers. Concentration in the second pillar is much higher than in the voluntary pillar—by mid-1999, the five largest funds accounted for 78 percent of all members and 73 percent of total assets, and only eight funds had fewer than 5,000 members.

Participation in the mandatory pillar increased rapidly to 2 million workers in September 1999, or the equivalent of 50 percent of the labor force, and will continue expanding in the future due to new entrants into the labor force. The total assets of second—pillar institutions rose at a rapid pace, reaching 0.9 percent of GDP in 1999, and are expected to

15. See Disney (1999) for a critical assessment of NDC schemes. However, most of the objections to NDC schemes (raised above) would not apply in the cases in which the NDC scheme is smaller and is only one part of a broader and truly mixed pension system, as in the cases of Latvia, Poland, and Sweden. See, for example, Lindeman, Rutkowski, and Sluchynsky (2000) for an updated account of recent reforms that include a first pillar built on NDC basis.

exceed the assets of the third pillar in less than three years' time due to the much larger membership (already twice as large as in the voluntary pillar) and the higher contribution rate.

12.4.2 The Regulatory Framework

The regulatory framework is generally sound and similar for both pillars, although it is more strict for the mandatory pension funds.[16] For example, voluntary pension funds can be established without any minimum capital or membership, even when they intend to offer annuities. In the mandatory pillar, there is a minimum size requirement of 2,000 members for a pension fund and 25,000 members for funds that offer annuities. In addition, an annuity-providing fund must create a capital reserve of 100 million, Hungarian forints (Ft).

The law stipulates that pension funds are separate legal entities and that their assets must be segregated from those of sponsoring employers or other founders. The funds are, in principle, governed by their members through their boards of directors, and the law contains detailed rules on fund governance that aim to preserve the independence of boards and management. In practice, however, most fund members do not exercise their voting rights or participate in general assemblies, making the pension funds more similar to mutual funds, which are effectively controlled by their sponsors. Switching across funds is allowed with few restrictions, and the possibility for fund members to leave poorly performing funds is expected to exert more discipline on fund managers than formal voting rights and board rules do.

Pension funds are required to employ the services of certified asset managers, accountants, auditors, actuaries, and custodians. A minimum capital requirement on external asset managers is imposed, amounting to Ft 100 million for small pension funds and Ft 500 million for pension funds with more than Ft 2 billion in assets. A pension fund must use a single-custodian institution, which is responsible for the safekeeping of assets and for ensuring compliance with asset allocation policies and prescribed investment limits.

To ensure asset diversification and limit the risk exposure of pension funds, investments are subject to quantitative limits both by asset class and by individual investments. No individual investment may exceed 10 percent of the assets of the fund (fund limit) or 10 percent of the equity of the issuer (issuer limit). The ceiling on equity holdings is 60 percent of the total asset portfolio; the ceiling on foreign assets was initially set at zero, but is scheduled to increase to 30 percent of the total portfolio by 2003. Quantitative investment limits on Hungarian pension funds appear rea-

---

16. Policy issues in pension fund regulation and supervision are discussed in Davis (1995), Demarco, Rofman, and Whitehouse (1998), Queisser (1998), Rocha, Gutierrez, and Hinz (1999) and Vittas (1997, 1998).

sonable and are unlikely to be binding and to affect marginal investment decisions, at least in their early years of operation. Investment restrictions are expected to be relaxed gradually, as the capital market develops and the country approaches the date of membership in the EU.

Although the regulatory framework is generally sound, some important weaknesses in both regulation and enforcement have yet to be corrected. Market valuation of assets is required only once per quarter, whereas declared interest is credited only once per year. This allows significant room for the creation of hidden reserves and the manipulation of reported investment returns. Pension funds are required to disclose their terms and conditions to new members and to send annual statements to all their members. They must also indicate clearly their returns and fees. However, the lack of more precise rules and guidelines for computing and disclosing costs and returns still creates room for different practices across funds and problems for comparing fund performance.

Two types of guarantees are offered in the second pillar. First, the second pillar-pension benefit may not be lower than 25 percent of the pension benefit from the first public pillar. This guarantee is backed by a central guarantee fund to which all pension funds contribute. Second, pension funds must make up any shortfalls in individual returns if investment performance falls below the return of a portfolio of long-term government bonds by more than 15 percent. The minimum return is backed by a minimum reserve equal to 0.5 percent of total member assets. Returns exceeding 40 percent of the benchmark are placed in reserve.

Although these guarantees have built support for the reform, they also present some complications. The first guarantee implies a lifetime real return guarantee of only 0 percent per annum for young workers, but a lifetime guarantee of about 4 percent per annum for workers in their forties. The probability that this guarantee will be called for these older workers is not negligible, especially if the contribution is kept at 6 percent indefinitely. The second guarantee was expected to complement the first and to improve capital protection, but contains some flaws in design: Using a bond index as a benchmark for the second guarantee seems to have distorted pension fund investments in favor of bonds. More important, the excess reserves are imposed at the level of the pension fund, not of the asset manager.[17] The two guarantees together imply access to a central guarantee fund without first putting the capital of the asset manager at risk, raising the issue of moral hazard in the behavior of asset managers.

12.4.3 Performance

Unfortunately, good data on the operating fees and costs and on the investment returns of the private pension funds are not readily available.

---

17. Rocha, Gutierrez, and Hinz (1999) and Vittas (1998) examine in more detail the problems in designing pension guarantees.

Operating fees have absorbed between 5.5 and 7.5 percent of contributions in voluntary funds and between 7.5 and 11.0 percent in mandatory funds. These rates are lower than those reported for Latin American pension funds, the operating fees for which frequently amounted to more than 25 percent of contributions in the first years of operation. Three reasons may account for this difference. First, in Hungary, asset management and external administration involve additional changes, which seem to add 50–100 basis points for most funds. Second, sponsors of pension funds in Hungary may have absorbed a higher proportion of operating costs. It is reported that employer-sponsored funds, in particular, subsidize the operations of pension funds by providing rent-free premises and by not charging for the time of staff who are involved in the administration of pension funds. Third, Hungarian pension funds seem to spend less on marketing and on sales commissions than their Latin American counterparts.

Data on investment returns are even less satisfactory. Although most pension funds publish some data, the numbers seem to include neither unrealized capital gains or losses, nor accrued but not-yet-received dividends and interest. To shed some light on the performance of pension funds, investment returns were simulated by using average quarterly asset allocations of pension funds for 1998 and 1999, and the total market returns on bank deposits, bonds, and equities. Assuming a quarterly investment horizon, gross investment returns in 1998 amounted to 17 percent for the mandatory funds and to 14 percent for the voluntary funds against a 14 percent annual inflation rate. For the first three quarters of 1999, annualized investment returns were 13.4 and 12.8 percent, respectively, for the mandatory and voluntary funds, against an inflation rate of 10 percent. Allowing for asset management and custodial fees, it is likely that real returns on individual accounts have been positive in real terms, although not much above zero.

The returns of pension funds in 1998 and 1999 were low in real terms, primarily as a result of the financial crises of recent years—particularly the collapse of Russian markets, which led to a sharp increase in short-term interest rates and capital outflows, and a sharp decline in the return on equity and bonds during 1998. Equity prices recovered in 1999, but in view of the overall volatility of world capital markets, pension fund managers decided to maintain low shares of equity in their portfolios (less than 10 percent in the case of mandatory funds), and did not benefit from the recovery in equity prices. Real returns are expected to increase to higher levels in future years, in line with the expected increase in the share of domestic and foreign equities in portfolios.

13.5 Conclusions and Possible Lessons to Other Countries

Despite the initial lukewarm support from the government succeeding the reforming government and the poor initial performance of capital markets due to the Russia crisis of 1998, Hungary's multipillar pension reform has entered its fourth year of implementation and has proved popular among workers. Approximately half of the labor force has joined the new system voluntarily. Most of the switchers are workers below forty years of age, and the young workers who switched account for more than 80 percent of the labor force in their age group.

The decision to switch was motivated by a number of factors, the most important being the better risk-diversification properties of the new system. The credibility of the PAYGO system had been severely damaged by repeated manipulation of its parameters, and the PAYGO system clearly offered a low return on contributions. The new system is still predominantly a PAYGO system, because the first pillar accounts for more than two-thirds of the total contribution, but the new system also contains a new second pillar that offers the prospects of higher average returns on contributions. Most workers probably understood intuitively the risk and return characteristics of both a pure PAYGO system and a mixed system, including the capital market risk in the second pillar and the political risk in the PAYGO scheme. The new system offers better prospects of long-term, risk-adjusted returns for young workers, and most young workers effectively opted for the new system. However, some overselling of the new system probably occurred as well, making older workers switch even though they would ultimately have fared better by staying in the reformed PAYGO system.

The government has decided thus far not to increase the contribution to the second pillar from 6 to 8 percent as it had originally planned, alleging that such an increase would increase the size of the transitional deficit and possibly produce macroeconomic imbalances. However, the increase in the contribution to the second pillar would have no adverse impact on the economy, because the increase in the PAYGO deficit would amount to only 0.3–0.4 percent of GDP and would, in any case, be offset by larger private saving levels. This decision has also violated the objectives and the internal consistency of the original reform package, in which contribution rates and accrual rates were jointly calculated to produce an equilibrium cut-off age around thirty-five to forty years. Clearly, many workers who have switched are counting on a higher contribution rate; if the 8 percent original contribution is not restored in the next few years, some of these workers will be in worse positions than before the switch. The failure to restore the original contribution rates may also produce smaller efficiency gains in labor and capital markets than originally anticipated.

The PAYGO system is still projected to produce deficits in the long run, despite the PAYGO reforms. Addressing these projected deficits will require additional future adjustments, such as further increases in the retirement age and a shift to price indexation. Such adjustments are bound to result in some reduction in net benefits for future generations. Independent calculations of generational accounts for Hungary suggest a similar outcome—the reform package has reduced sharply the severe initial bias against future generations, but has not eliminated the bias entirely. Future generations remain net contributors to the pension system, even after the reform. Therefore, the criticism frequently voiced in Hungary—that the reform had excessively benefited future generations to the detriment of current generations—seems unjustified.

A more ambitious reform package would have involved larger initial surpluses (and smaller deficits in the steady state) and a significant reduction in the high contribution rates, with stronger positive effects on saving and on the labor market. However, the erosion in the tax base that occurred in the 1990s ruled out any ambitious plan to reduce contribution rates, and the additional PAYGO reforms that could have allowed larger initial surpluses or reductions in contribution rates (e.g., a direct move toward price indexation) were ruled out for political reasons.

Despite these shortcomings, any preliminary assessment of the Hungarian pension reform would be likely to conclude that the reform has been successful, especially considering the severe constraints imposed by initial conditions (e.g., large fiscal deficits, high contribution rates, high tax rates, very adverse demographic trends). The reform has reduced significantly the imbalances of the PAYGO system and the implicit pension debt, while also introducing a mandatory, funded, and privately managed pillar that seems to be operating fairly well, despite the initial problems in the payment and registration system and some weaknesses in the regulatory framework. Moreover, the current shortcomings can be corrected during the next few years by the restoration of the original 8 percent contribution rate to the second pillar and the strengthening of the regulatory framework.

The Hungarian reform also suggests that a voluntary switching strategy achieves essentially the same outcome as a forced switch based on an arbitrary cutoff age, while avoiding legal problems and contributing to the reduction of the implicit pension debt. The disadvantage of this strategy is that it leaves a few individuals worse off relative to their best options. A well-designed public information campaign may minimize the occurrence of these cases. The implementation of the new second pillar met difficulties at first because its information, registration, and payments systems had not been yet fully developed. These difficulties caused some initial discomfort and, although the technical problems were eventually solved, they show that more attention to practical and technical aspects of implementation is required from policy makers. Finally, the Hungarian reform would benefit from a stronger regulatory and supervisory framework, including several aspects of asset valuation and disclosure. Although no major problems have been reported, and these areas of the regulatory framework are expected to be improved in the near future, a stronger regulatory framework could have been introduced at the beginning of the program without major technical difficulties.

References

Auerbach, A., L. Kotlikoff, and W. Leibfritz. 1999. *Generational accounts around the world.* Chicago: University of Chicago Press.

Barro, R., and X. Sala-I-Martin. 1995. *Economic growth.* New York: McGraw-Hill.

Corsetti, C., and K. Schmidt-Hebel. 1995. Pension reform and growth. World Bank Policy Research Working Paper no. 1471. Washington, D.C.: World Bank.

Davis, E. P. 1995. *Pension funds, retirement-income security, and capital markets: An international perspective.* Oxford, U.K.: Clarendon Press.

Demarco. G., R. Rofman, and E. Whitehouse. 1998. Supervising mandatory funded pension systems: Issues and challenges. Washington, D.C.: World Bank. Unpublished manuscript, January.

Disney, R. 1999. Notional accounts as a pension reform strategy: An evaluation. Social Protection Discussion Paper no. 9928. Washington, D.C.: World Bank.

Disney, R., and E. Whitehouse. 1992. *The personal pensions stamped.* London: Institute for Fiscal Studies.

European Federation of Retirement Provision (EFRP). 1996. *European pension funds: Their impact on European capital markets and competition.* London: EFRP.

Feldstein, M. 1995. Would privatizing social security raise economic welfare? NBER Working Paper no. 5281. Cambridge, Mass.: National Bureau of Economic Research, September.

———. 1997. The missing piece in policy analysis: Social security reform. NBER *Working Paper* no. 5413. Cambridge, Mass.: National Bureau of Economic Research, July.

Gal, R., A. Simonovits, and G. Tarcali. 2001. Generational accounting and the Hungarian pension reform. Budapest: TARKI. Unpublished manuscript.

Hablicsek. 1995. *Long-term demographic scenarios: Hungary 1995–2000.* Budapest: KSH Nepessegtudomayi Intezet.

Holzmann, R. 1996. Pension reform, financial market development and economic growth: Preliminary evidence for Chile. IMF Working Paper no. WP96/90. Washington, D.C.: International Monetary Fund.

Iglesias, A., and R. Palacios. 2000. Managing public pension reserves: Evidence from the international experience. Social Protection Discussion Paper no. 0003. Washington, D.C.: World Bank.

Kotcherlakota, N. 1996. The equity premium: It's still a puzzle. *Journal of Economic Literature.* 34 (1): 42–71.

Kotlikoff, L. 1989. *What determines savings?* Cambridge, Mass.: MIT Press.

———. 1995. Privatization of social security: How it works and why it matters. NBER *Working Paper* no. 5330. Cambridge, Mass.: National Bureau of Economic Research, October.

Levine, R., and S. Zervos. 1998. Stock markets, banks, and economic growth. *American Economic Review* 88 (3): 537–58.

Lindeman, D., M. Rutkowski, and O. Sluchynsky. 2000. The evolution of pension systems in Eastern Europe and Central Asia: Opportunities, constraints, dilemmas, and emerging best practices. Washington, D.C.: World Bank. Unpublished manuscript.

Loayza, N., K. Schmidt-Hebel, and L. Serven. 2000. Savings in developing countries: An overview. *World Bank Economic Review* 14 (3): 393–414.

Organization for Economic Cooperation and Development (OECD). 1998. *Maintaining prosperity in an ageing society.* Paris: OECD.

Palacios, R., and R. Rocha. 1998. The Hungarian pension system in transition. Social Protection Discussion Paper no. 9805. Washington, D.C.: World Bank, April.

Palacios, R., and E. Whitehouse. 1998. The role of choice in the transition to a funded pension system. Social Protection Discussion Paper no. 9812. Washington, D.C.: World Bank, September.

Queisser, M. 1998. Regulation and supervision of pension funds: Principles and practices. *OECD Development Centre, International Social Security Review* 51 (April-June): 1–21.

Rocha, R., J. Gutierrez, and R. Hinz. 2001. Improving the regulation and supervision of pension funds: Are there lessons from the banking sector? In *New Ideas in Social Security Reform,* eds. R. Holzman and J. Stiglitz, Washington, D.C.: World Bank.

Rofman, R. 1995. Moving social security toward fully funded schemes: Who pays the cost? Buenos Aires, Argentina. Unpublished manuscript.

———. 1996. "Crisis de la seguridad social y reforma provisional en Argentina: Un analisis de sus causas y consecuencias." Buenos Aires, Argentina.

Vittas, D. 1996. Private pension funds in Hungary: Early performance and regulatory issues. Policy Research Working Paper no. 1638. Washington, D.C.: World Bank.

———. 1997. Investment rules and state guarantees for mandatory private pension funds. Washington, D.C.: World Bank. Unpublished manuscript.

———. 1998. Regulatory controversies of private pension funds. Washington, D.C.: World Bank. Unpublished manuscript.

Romania's Pension System
From Crisis to Reform

Georges de Menil and Eytan Sheshinski

13.1 Introduction

Romania, a country of 23 million people strategically located at the mouth of the Danube, is the largest country in Southeastern Europe. When communism collapsed in Europe, the leadership of the Romanian Communist Party ousted the dictator Nicolae Ceausescu in a bloody coup, and set the country on a course of slow transition to the market. In November 1996, a coalition of democratic parties defeated the reformed communists in legislative and presidential elections and launched a new program of radical reforms. Pension reform become a key feature of this program.

This paper describes pension reform in Romania. Sections 13.2 through 13.3 review the prereform situation, focusing on initial economic and dem-

Georges de Menil is professor of economics at the Ecole de Hautes Etudes en Sciences Sociales, Paris. From 1997 to 2000 he was economic advisor to the prime minister of Romania and codirector with Eytan Sheshinski of the private pension reform task force of the Ministry of Labor in Bucharest. Eytan Sheshinski is professor of economics at Hebrew University of Jerusalem. The project team consisted of Mihai Seitan, Yacob Antler, Iain Batty, Cristina Brinzan, Elena Diaconu, Hermann von Gersdorff, Stephane Hamayon, Catalina Marcu, Tudor Moldovan, Lena Zezulin, and the authors.

The authors are deeply indebted to Alexandru Athanasiu, Minister of Labor and Social Protection from November 1996 through December 1999, and to Smaranda Dobrescu, Minister from December 1999 to September 2000, for their direction and support. Much of the work was done under a contract between the Ministry and the Pro Democratica Foundation, financed by the World Bank. The authors are also grateful for grants to the Ministry from George Soros, the Pro Democratia, and the International Finance Corporation. In addition, this summary has benefited extensively from conversations with Rodrigo Acuna, Suzannah Carr, Francois Ettori, Robert Holzmann, Augusto Iglesias Palau, John Innes, Valentin Lazea, Michal Rutkowski, Peter Temin, and Emil Tesliuc; and from the administrative and secretarial support of Mihaela Grigorescu, and the assistance of Geomina Turlea and Raluca Miron. The authors are solely responsible.

ographic conditions and on the characteristics of the social security system in 1996. Section 13.4 describes the political economy of the process. Sections 13.5 through 13.7 sketch the architecture of the new public and private systems. Sections 13.8, 13.9, and 13.10 analyze the budgetary, economic, and financial effects of transition to the new system. Section 13.11 concludes.

13.2   Initial Conditions: The Economy

Economically, Romania lies near the poorest end of the spectrum of the transition economies of Eastern Europe and the former Soviet Union. In 1998, its gross domestic product (GDP) per capita ($1,696) was well below that of the Czech Republic ($5,479) and of Hungary ($4,694), and close to that of Russia ($1,882). Official output was still 25 percent below the level of that during the last communist year; its declines in the first postcommunist years had not yet been erased by a sustained period of recovery, as they had in Poland and Hungary. On the other hand, output had not dropped as far (40 percent) as it had in Russia (see Vienna Institute for International Economic Studies [WIIW] 2000). In its level of cumulative liberalization since the end of communism, Romania was substantially behind Poland and the Czech Republic.

13.3   Initial Conditions: The Pension System

The public pension system Romania inherited from the Ceausescu regime was a loose collection of separate systems for the main industrial workforce, farmers, artisans and craftsmen, church officials, and other categories. The principal pensions, those of former industrial workers, were financed by social security contributions that formally passed through a social insurance fund to the budget. The provisions of the system as it existed in 1989 were unsustainable. To survive the transition to a decentralized (even if only slightly privatized) economy, the social security system inherited from Ceausescu would have required radical consolidation and a comprehensive tightening of the rules.

The successive governments between 1990 and 1996 chose to go in exactly the opposite direction, increasing the number of beneficiaries and multiplying special retirement provisions. At the same time, a general migration from the formal to the informal economy—to which social security taxation contributed, but of which it was not the only cause—melted away the contributor base.

Sections 13.3.3 and 13.3.4 summarize the way in which a decade of unsustainable relaxation of benefit criteria and of growing tax evasion left the public pension system in deep crisis as the century closed. We begin, however, with brief descriptions of the imbalances inherited from the previous regime (section 13.3.1) and of subsequent demographic and economic trends (section 13.3.2), both of which were unfavorable.

13.3.1   The Pension Legacy of the Ceausescu Regime

In 1989, 3.5 times as many contributors as beneficiaries were covered by the basic state pension system. The balance would have seemed able to support a reasonable pay-as-you-go (PAYGO) system; however, two fatal flaws rendered the system unviable: The benefit formulas were too generous, and the state provided pensions to many retirees outside the system, who made no contributions.

Benefit Formulas

The rules regulating the regime's pension system, many of which had been enacted in 1977, provided that a new retiree was entitled to a pension equal to about 75 percent of the average wage earned in the five best consecutive of the previous ten years. This implied a replacement ratio of about 65 percent, possibly higher. With a ratio of contributors to beneficiaries of 3.5, such a generous replacement ratio would have required a social security tax of 18.6 percent; the actual tax was 14 percent. Clearly, an adjustment was needed.

Another imbalance characterized a supplementary pension scheme, which had been operating since 1968. Whereas contributions to the basic pension scheme were paid by employers, contributions to the supplementary scheme were paid entirely by employees. The contribution rate was 3 percent. The problem was that this entitled the worker to a supplementary pension of 8 percent of the average of the five best of the previous ten years' wages, after he or she had worked five years. The addition to the replacement rate increased to 16 percent after twenty-five years of work. Given the ratio of contributors to beneficiaries, the additional contribution rate required for balance at maturity was 4.6 percent.

During the introductory years of this system, while workers were making contributions but not receiving benefits, the system was obviously in surplus. However, the parameters were such that once it reached full maturity, it would have been sustainable only with a contribution-beneficiary ratio of 5. 3. Again, something had to give.

Uncovered Beneficiaries: Farmers and Others

The largest category of uncovered beneficiaries was farmers, many of whom were employees of cooperative farms. The cooperatives were dissolved in 1990. Two years later, the farmers' contributions to their special pension system became optional; only a small portion of them (approximately 80,000 in 1999—less than 5 percent of potential contributors) agreed to pay the 7 percent contribution rate. To cover the farmers' pension payments, the government introduced a special tax on companies involved with food and agricultural products.

In summary, the average replacement ratio implied by the written and implicit rules of the Ceausescu pension system was many times the average contribution rate. The ratio of the former to the latter far exceeded the adjusted real ratio of contributors to beneficiaries. Had the Ceausescu pension system not, in fact, been run by a state that commanded the entire economy, it would have collapsed.

13.3.2   Demographic and Economic Fundamentals

Adverse demographic developments made a relatively modest contribution to Romania's pension squeeze during the 1990s. The population above the age of sixty did increase by 14 percent from the beginning to the end of the decade as well-populated cohorts aged. The prime working-age population (fifteen to sixty years), however, remained stable at about 14.1 million.[1]

Declining output and an even greater reduction of real wages—which were half their 1990 levels by the end of the decade—did reduce the potential base in the real economy for the funding of a PAYGO system. However, distortions attributable to the system itself were the greatest contributors to its increasing imbalances.

13.3.3   System Effects: A Growing Number of Beneficiaries

Throughout the region, there was a tendency for both postcommunist and reformed communist administrations to undermine the solvency of the PAYGO systems they inherited from the Soviet period. In order to solidify popular support, they tended to grant liberal advantages to special interest groups; common among these were special early retirement arrangements and other pension provisions. In Romania, this granting of privileges and exemptions led to a rate of increase in the number of retirees far higher than that observed in any other country in Eastern Europe (see Rutkowski 1999, fig. 1). Average benefits per retiree were also ratcheted up at sensitive moments, even if they would subsequently be allowed to become eroded by inflation.

The first big increase in entitlements came within months of the fall of Ceausescu, when five years of early retirement with full pensions were granted to individuals who had worked longer than thirty years (for men) or twenty-five years (for women). This provision caused the number of retirees with full benefits to jump by almost 400,000 persons, from 1.068

1. Ceausescu's promotion of population growth (abortion was outlawed in 1967) did not, as might have been expected, result in an increase of the prime working-age population in the 1990s. Many of the additional young people born in the 1970s and 1980s appear either to have died or to have emigrated right after the fall of the regime. See National Commission of Statistics (various years).

million at the end of 1990 to 1.423 million at the end of 1991. (This increase accounts for most of the increase in the total number of pensioners of all categories, which is reported in table 13.1.) Because both numbers are year-end figures, it can be fairly said that the immediate effect of the decree was to create a one-year flow of new entrants into retirement equal to half of the existing stock.

Eligibility for early retirement was subsequently extended for workers in "hardship" categories. Workers in "difficult" and "very difficult" occupations (working groups II and I) could reduce their ages of retirement with full benefits to fifty-five years for men and fifty for women (group II) and to fifty years for men and forty-five for women (group I). The definition of hardship was lax. At the end of 1989, the number of employees in working groups I and II was about 300,000; by the end of 1992, this number has risen to 3 million (see Ministry of Labor and Social Reform 1993). These and other relaxations of retirement criteria caused the total stock of retirees in all categories under the state system (not including farmers and some other categories) to rise to 3.9 million by 1998, an increase of sixty-five percent over the 1990 level.

13.3.4   System Effects: The Collapse of the Number of Contributors

The decade was also marked by a dramatic decline in the number of contributors to the state pension system. (See table 13.1.) Between 1990 and 1998, the number of contributors fell by almost 3 million. Of this number, 1 million[2] (about one-third of the decrease) corresponded to a significant rise in unemployment. By the end of 1998, the unemployed constituted 10 percent of the number of active persons. Under the prereform system in Romania, unemployed persons did not make social security contributions. Each additional unemployed person reduced the contributor base—a classic example of the way in which unemployment strains a social security system.

The increase in unemployment was not the only source of contributor-base erosion during the decade. The number of active persons dropped by 1 million, although the working-age population (aged fifteen to sixty) remained constant. The implication is that the number of inactive persons grew by about 1 million. Furthermore, the number of employed persons who were not wage earners (farmers, other self-employed, part-time workers, etc.) grew by about 1 million to a total of 3,612,000 in 1998—this, at a time when the farming population is known to have remained stable.

Thus, a total of about 2 million persons—twice as many as the number unemployed by the transition—moved out of active labor market status

---

2. These data are for the registered unemployed, many of whom continue to be employed. Unemployment by International Labor Organization (ILO) measures is three-fourths of this number.

Table 13.1 Basic Facts of Romania's State Pension System

Demographic and Economic Trends	1990	1991	1992	1993	1994	1995	1996	1997	1998
Total population	23,206,720	23,185,084	22,788,969	22,755,260	22,730,622	22,680,951	22,607,620	22,545,925	22,513,233
Population aged 15–60 years	14,105,078	14,148,184	13,908,563	13,965,275	14,026,502	14,075,541	14,098,705	14,101,632	14,094,720
Population aged 60 years and older	3,632,966	3,708,780	3,778,153	3,842,518	3,901,357	3,960,969	4,009,166	4,068,500	4,130,225
Ratio of population over age 60 to population aged 15–60 (%)	25.76	26.21	27.16	27.51	27.81	28.14	28.44	28.85	29.30
Indices of real economy-wide net wage (%; 1989 wage = 100)	104.6	84.9	73.2	61.7	61.8	69.1	75.5	58.6	55.6
Beneficiaries									
Average number of pensioners (all categories)	2,380,038	2,816,629	2,996,419	3,174,128	3,358,925	3,518,932	3,651,728	3,782,304	3,923,721
Ratio of beneficiaries to population aged 15–60 years (%)	16.87	19.90	21.54	22.73	23.94	25.00	25.90	26.82	27.83
Contributors									
Number of active persons	10,840,000	11,123,440	11,387,019	11,226,705	11,234,925	10,491,432	10,036,564	9,904,475	9,837,100
Number of employed	10,840,000	10,786,000	10,458,000	10,062,000	10,011,000	9,493,000	9,379,000	9,023,000	8,812,000
Number of unemployed	n.a.	337,440	929,019	1,164,705	1,223,925	998,432	657,564	881,435	1,025,100
Number of Wage Earners (Contributors)	8,156,000	7,574,000	6,888,000	6,672,000	6,438,000	6,160,000	5,939,000	5,597,000	5,200,000
Ratio of contributors to population aged 15–60 years (%)	57.82	53.53	49.52	47.77	45.90	43.76	42.12	39.69	36.90
Imbalance									
Dependency ratio (number of wage earners/number of pensioners)	3.43	2.69	2.17	2.10	1.91	1.75	1.63	1.48	1.32
Indices of real average pension benefits (%)	100.0	77.5	63.7	56.5	55.3	61.2	62.8	49.7	48.5
Replacement ratio (ratio of average pension to average net wage; %)	44.69	45.05	43.64	45.20	43.27	40.78	38.60	40.33	39.13

Sources: Calculations by Pro Democratia Foundation and the Ministry of Labor and Social Protection.

Notes: Numbers of beneficiaries and contributors refer only to those in the basic state system. They exclude farmers, self-employed persons, and other categories with special pension systems, and do not take account of contributors to or benefits received from the supplementary pension system. Numbers of the employed are end-of-year data from the *Statistical Yearbook* for 1990–97 period. Data for 1998 are from the National Commission of Statistics (NCS) labor force balance. According to the NCS methodology, the employed include all persons who, during the reference year, carried out socioeconomically profitable activities, excepting military staff and employees of similar political and community organizations, and convicts. The unemployed are those who were registered unemployed at the end of the year, as published in the NCS 1998 yearbook and monthly bulletins from 1998 to 1999. The number of active persons is the sum of employed and unemployed persons. The number of wage earners is the average number of employees. n.a. = not available.

and wage reporting jobs during this period. Many of these probably went into the informal economy. Relative to the original contributor base (8,156,000 wage earners in 1990) this represents a decline of 24 percent. The loss of the contributor base to unemployment corresponds to an additional decline of 13 percent. The total reduction of the contributor base was thus 37 percent.

Explanations for the erosion of the official contribution-paying workforce are not difficult to find. There were both a demand and a supply for tax evasion. On the side of demand, the incentive not to declare was substantial: Taxes on wages increased dramatically throughout this decade. By 1999, the total tax rate for the top income bracket—which began at the equivalent of $500 per month—was 118 percent: 58 percent for various social contributions, and 60 percent for the wage tax.

At the same time, the declining enforcement capacity of the state in many areas generated an increasing number of opportunities to evade taxes. The demise of the command economy, decentralization, and the relatively more rapid growth of private wages than civil service wages all combined to produce opportunities for bribes, and to reduce the effectiveness of tax collection in general.

Whatever the explanation, a loss of 37 percent of the contributor base, combined with a 65 percent increase in the number of beneficiaries, inevitably magnified the imbalance of the system.

13.3.5   The Resulting Imbalance

The unsustainability of the Ceausescu pension system was not immediately apparent because benefits were paid directly from the state budget. As we have seen, some of the first actions of the new government went in the direction of widening it.

From 1990 to 1992, the government responded to the growing imbalances in the system by progressively raising the basic tax rate for social security contributions from 14.0 percent to 25.5 percent, an increase of 82 percent, in a little over two years. The resulting increase in revenues collected was surprisingly low: Real revenues actually fell by 8 percent in 1992. Nonpayment of taxes, particularly by large state enterprises, became a common practice at that time.

For the remainder of the period, through 1996, inflation remained the principal mechanism for controlling the growing imbalances in the system. The commitment to replace the average wages of the best five of the previous ten years referred to the *nominal* value of those past wages. Inflation reduced the real value of that commitment.

Pensions were not eradicated by inflation, as they were in Russia, where they did not keep pace with prices at all. The government arbitrarily increased existing nominal pensions each year. These operations were called "indexations", but they fell far short of compensating for price increases.

The real value of wages similarly declined, but pensions were generally adjusted to a lesser degree than wages, and, as a consequence, the replacement ratio tended to decline, falling from a high of 45.2 in 1993 to a low of 38.6 in 1996 (a drop of 15 percent).

In 1996, the Vacaroiu government partially released even the inflation break. Government Decision 595/96 provided that the wage history of new retirees would no longer be based on historical, nominal net wages, but would be indexed to equivalent, current wages. This resulted in roughly a 20 percent increase in the pensions that would be due to all future new retirees. The public pension system entered a period of terminal crisis at that point; the basic system was constantly in deficit from 1995 through the end of the century.

The last attempt to balance the old system, in January 1999, was an increase in the combined, basic-plus-supplementary tax rate, from 28.5 percent to 37.5 percent. This time, an effort had been made to enforce greater compliance; nonetheless, real revenues rose by only 4 percent. Fortunately, a complete overhaul of the Romanian pension system was, at that point, underway.

13.4   The Political Economy of Pension Reform

The fact that Romania did not join the first wave of rapid reformers in Eastern Europe between 1990 and 1992 had long-lasting implications for the country.

Romania lost the potential benefit of a period of "exceptional politics," such as Balcerowicz (1994) has described, in which the society was prepared to accept a broad program of democratization and liberalization. Instead it followed during the first seven years, a self-styled gradualist strategy, and postponed many major structural changes. Three successive International Monetary Fund (IMF) standby agreements were signed and shortly thereafter broken. The cumulative pressure of the resulting imbalances eventually bred conditions of crisis in which reform became inevitable. It was thus that in the time leading up to the elections of November 1996, an incipient budgetary and balance-of-payments crisis created the conditions that made the newly elected democratic coalition government's program of liberalization, convertibility, and stabilization a necessity. Similarly, the cumulative imbalances of the pension system also made comprehensive reform inevitable.

As the new prime minister, Victor Ciorbea, moved to free the exchange rate and prices and to eliminate subsidies, the new minister of labor and social protection, Alexandru Athanasiu, resumed work on a stalled public-pension reform act designed to correct the major imbalances. The liberalization and stabilization programs were imbedded in agreements with the IMF for a new standby loan, and with the World Bank for a resumption of private-sector and agricultural-sector adjustment loans (which had been suspended a year earlier). The World Bank made the approval and passage of public pension reform a performance criterion for its revived private-sector adjustment loan.

The upshot was that in Romania, proposals for a comprehensive reform of the public system (the first pillar) were the first pension reform proposals to be approved by government and sent to Parliament (September 1998), and the first to be passed by Parliament (December 1999). At the initiative and insistence of Minister Athanasiu, a proposal for the creation of a mandatory system of private, funded pensions (the second pillar) was submitted to Parliament in January 1999, four months after submission of the first-pillar law. Political conflict led to procedural delays, and it took eighteen months for the draft law to clear the budgetary and labor commissions of the Chamber of Deputies (June 2000). By then, the governing coalition had weathered the second of two internal crises that marked its term, a new government had been formed, and legislative elections were five months away (November 2000). The new prime minister, Mugar Isarescu (previously the governor of the central bank) and the new minister of labor, Smaranda Dobrescu, were both forceful advocates of a fully funded and privately managed second pillar. The prime minister had supported the project as central-bank governor, because it promised to raise domestic saving and to redress the growing imbalance between dependent beneficiaries and working contributors. Minister Dobrescu was committed to the project as a fiscally responsible, medium-term answer to the impoverished state of pensioners. Together they tried to accelerate the legislative process. The prime minister submitted the draft law for review to the Economic and Social Commission, a consultative body with important union and employer representation. After intensive but rapid deliberations, the commission approved the project, and the government promulgated the law (modified to take account of some of the observations of the commission) as an emergency ordinance.[3] The government's expectation was that the consensual nature of the project would permit the new legislature—which, by necessity, would have to approve or modify the ordinance—to deliberate more efficiently and rapidly.

In point of fact, the new government that formed after the elections in December 2000 included second-pillar reform as a legislative priority in the program, on the basis of which it obtained parliamentary confirmation. It nonetheless cancelled the emergency ordinance, and mandated a new special commission to review pension reform strategy. Legislation has also been drafted to regulate voluntary private pension funds (the third pillar) and is awaiting consideration by the government.

---

3. By then, Minister Dobrescu had left the government and been replaced by Lucian Albu, an economist, who was also a strong advocate of the project.

The sequence in which reform has advanced in Romania is the logical one from an economic point of view. When there is a threat of insolvency of the public system, the overriding economic priority is to rationalize it in order to avoid the crisis. Moreover, if the eventual intention is to create a mixed system, reform of the first pillar can, through the savings it produces, wholly or partly finance the revenue shortfall associated with the introduction of the second pillar. Finally, if private pension funds are initially almost nonexistent (as in the case of Romania), their regulation, although important, can wait for completion of reform of the first two pillars.

Politically, however, the order in which these three related reforms are being addressed in Romania involves placing the most unpopular measures first, and the least controversial, last.

13.5   The Reformed Public System

The new public law passed by Parliament in December 1999, after more than a year of debate, reflects major substantive changes.[4] Political compromises had to be made in some areas to achieve passage. The law puts a halt to the most egregiously unsound practices of the prereform system, and moderately tightens others. Some of the improvements in financial sustainability will take the form of additional revenue; others, of reduced expenditure.

Most of the previous special regimes—notably, that pertaining to farmers—are integrated into the basic social security system. Two million self-employed persons, including farmers, are required to join the basic system. The biggest effect of this change is on the revenue side. The self-employed are required to declare their incomes, and to make social security contributions at the standard employer-plus-employee rate (35 percent) for normal categories of work. The income declared by a self-employed person cannot be less than 25 percent of the economy-wide average wage. If the self-employed declare, on average, 50 percent of the economy-wide wage, the potential increase in contributors is equivalent to an additional 1 million wage earners at the average wage.

Benefits are no longer an entitlement divorced from contributions. A new point system—modeled on the German system—replaces the old, open-ended benefit formulas. Workers accumulate points for each full year worked at the average economy-wide wage.[5] At retirement, the value of

4. The description that follows corresponds to the law that was passed in December 1999, and does not take into account subsequent modifications.
5. The system has a built-in ceiling. A worker may not accumulate more than 3 points per year, no matter how high his or her wage is. Contributors are similarly capped above three times the average wage.

the new retiree's points is determined according to a formula that ensures that a worker who has worked a standard full term of years at the average wage will receive a pension equal to 45 percent of the going average gross wage in the year of his or her retirement.[6]

The point system eliminates the excesses of the previous formula, which was based on the best, recent five-year average. It also replaces the financially unsound provisions of the prereform supplementary pension system, which is merged into the general system and, by and large, disappears as a separate calculation.

Expenditures will also be reduced by phased increases in the retirement age and a restriction of the conditions under which a worker is entitled to early retirement at full pension. In both areas, the final legislation reflects compromises between the government's more stringent proposals and parliamentary pressure to retain former privileges. The legal retirement age (sixty-two for men and fifty-seven for women in the prereform system) is raised by small increments over the course of thirteen years to sixty-five for men and sixty for women.[7] Furthermore, provisions for early retirement with full pension are moderately tightened, but continue to depend on the presumed difficulty of working conditions. The new law limits the right of workers in normal working conditions and in conditions of "particular difficulty" to retire early with full pension. The principal difference between the old and the new law is that there is a large reclassification of jobs, intended to reduce the proportion of workers in "special difficulty" and "particular difficulty" jobs.[8] The combined effect of these changes will reduce the minimum retirement age for new retirees by two years.

Provisions for invalidity benefits are also made moderately more rigorous. Beneficiaries of pensions for persons who are unable to work but who can take care of themselves—a category whose numbers had swollen in the previous decade—are required to be examined every six or twelve months, with a possible view to discontinuation.

The new law also created a new, public, autonomous body to collect contributions and distribute pensions. This is the National House of Social Insurance, a body governed by a board with representatives from unions, employer associations, retiree associations, and government, and run by a president appointed to a seven-year term by the prime minister. This effectively makes the social partners coresponsible with government for the operation of the public pension system.

6. When the system is mature, a standard work history will be thirty-five years for men and thirty for women.
7. The minimum work history required for full pension is also raised in increments, from twenty-five and thirty years (for women and men, respectively) to thirty and thirty-five years.
8. Many jobs in heavy industry—notably, steel making and metallurgy—are reclassified from the most difficult category to the intermediate category.

13.6   Universal Pension Funds

Four months after the new public law was introduced in Parliament, the government introduced a second pension law, the purpose of which is to establish a new mandatory system of private, individual pension accounts.[9] The Universal Pension Fund Law mandates that 10 percent of every worker's wage—roughly one-third of the average social security contribution—be reallocated to a personal account in the worker's name in a privately managed Universal Pension Fund. The worker's total contribution remains the same, but a portion of it is diverted to his or her personal account. The principal entity in the proposed system is the Universal Pension Fund, a civil company to which individuals adhere as members. It cannot have profits, declare bankruptcy, or otherwise act as a commercial entity. The purpose of the fund is to invest its members' contributions collectively, distributing all profits back to participants.

The law stipulates that each fund will contract a profit-making commercial entity—the Universal Pension Fund management company (fund manager)—which will invest the pension fund's assets and will derive a profit from this activity. In order to assure continuity and stability, the relationship between a fund and a fund manager will not be terminated on short notice. Thus the law provides for a close relationship between the Universal Pension Fund and the fund manager. The fund manager's investments are subject to close regulation and supervision by a special agency (below).

The fund manager will not actually hold the assets of participants. Instead, participants will have contracts with specially licensed depositories that will keep custody of the assets and serve as additional guarantees of securities. Depositories will have the legal duty to report immediately all transactions to the pension regulator. Although the fund manager and the Universal Pension Fund may have a significant link between themselves, the depository will be allowed no financial links with either.

The funds are based on a defined contribution (DC) principle. Thus, each member will have an account. The assets accumulated consist of mandatory contributions and of investment income attributable to those contributions. Participants select their initial preferred pension funds and may later switch, with some limitations, to other funds. This potential mobility and competition for members among funds is regarded as a major disciplinary measure. Because of the DC nature of the funds, no particular annual rate of return is guaranteed. However, the government assures that over the course of a lifetime of saving, participants will be provided upon

---

9. This section describes the provisions of the law as it was originally submitted to Parliament. Some provisions were changed in the emergency ordinance, but the structure remained essentially as it had been originally proposed.

retirement no less than their accumulated real contributions (i.e., a zero real rate of return). We discuss below in some detail the possible effects of this guarantee, and compare it with other forms of guarantees in different countries.

Upon retirement, the participant will deposit his or her accumulated saving in a licensed annuity company, which will convert the saving into annually paid retirement benefits. The specific terms of these (indexed) annuities will be determined by the regulator. Because the reform is designed to produce in one decade the first retirees who will receive benefits from their contributions to private funds, there is time to refine the necessary regulatory framework for annuity companies.

13.6.1   Identifying the Risks of Universal Pension Funds

The risks of privately managed DC pension funds can be classified as (1) portfolio and investment risk, (2) agency risk, and (3) systemic risk.[10]

Portfolio risk contains unsystematic or diversifiable risk and systematic or market risk. Rules pertaining to portfolio diversification should reduce the unsystematic risk and, to a lesser extent, the market risk (by diversification into other markets, including foreign ones). The principal objective of regulation is to ensure that *some* very risky and illiquid assets are eliminated from the range of eligible investment. The exposure to market risk (i.e., business cycles, episodes of asset price fluctuations, and inflation) can also be reduced by proper diversification, including investments in foreign markets; but some risk does remain.

Agency risk occurs when the interests of fund administrators and asset managers are not fully aligned with the interest of fund members. Asymmetric information between fund managers and fund members with regard to portfolio strategies as well as the low levels of financial sophistication of these members may lead to inefficiency and abuse. These risks depend in good part, as Rocha, Gutierrez, and Hinz (1999) point out, on the legal and governance structures of the pension funds.

In addition to the obvious risks of misfeasance, malfeasance, and theft of assets, there are more intricate risks of investments that reduce the return to members: investment in related companies, directed fee arrangements, kickbacks, and inflated overhead changes, for example. Transparency is a problem because of the multiplicity of fees, netting against investment returns, or bundling with other services.

Concerning systemic risks, although pension funds (unlike banks) do not confront short-term liquidity problems (such as runs on banks), they may be affected by a banking crisis that leads to a collapse of asset prices and the insolvency of some banks. There may also be negative spillovers from the insurance industry.

---

10. See Rocha, Gutierrez, and Hinz (1999).

13.6.2   Supervisory Authority: Pension Control Commission

A Pension Control Commission will be established as an autonomous public institution, the purpose of which will be to grant and withdraw authorizations and licenses (see below) and issue investment regulations. It will work in conjunction with the National Bank of Romania (BNR), the stock market supervision authority (CNVM), the insurance supervisor, and the National House of Social Insurance (the first pillar). The establishment of a new autonomous pension authority, instead of an enlargement of the supervisory jurisdiction of the above institutions to cover private pension funds, was preferred because of the unique aspects of these funds (e.g., long-term investments and annuitization) and the apparent weaknesses of some existing regulatory agencies.

The president of Romania shall appoint the chairman of the Pension Control Commission to a seven-year renewable term. Strict provisions ensure the independence of the chairman, and removal from office is restricted to extreme cases of dereliction of duty.

An important role of the Pension Control Commission is the monitoring and inspection of the funds, including review of financial reports and on-site reviews. Supervisors are required to monitor portfolio composition and other structural requirements in real time, and to provide financial data to members. The Pension Control Commission has authority to impose remedial and punitive sanctions, remove fund managers, and impose fines.

13.7   The Regulation of Private Pension Funds

The regulation of the private pension funds aims to ensure the security, stability, cost minimization, transparency, and sound investment decisions of these funds. Because pension funds typically are concerned with a larger portion of lower-income groups than are other financial institutions, a major crisis may lead to the creation of pockets of poverty among the elderly and to a demand for support and intervention by the government. This explains the motivation for tight prudential regulations and supervision of these funds.

The main components of the regulation of universal pension funds by the supervisory authority, as set in the law, are the following (see also Rocha, Gutierrez, and Hinz 1999):

- Licensing (authorization) criteria
- Governance rules
- Independent custodianship rules
- Disclosure requirements
- External audit/actuary requirements

- Investment regulations
- Guarantees
- Minimum capital and reserve requirements
- Regulations on costs and fees

Licensing (authorization) Criteria

The Pension Control Commission will grant and withdraw licenses for pension funds and fund managers. Regulations focus on the capital and professional credentials of the management company (which includes the professional standing of the parent bank or insurance company). Extensive capital and reserve requirements are imposed in order to limit entry to a relatively small number of entities, making in-depth oversight practical.

Governance Rules

Each pension management company must be exclusively dedicated to the management of one pension fund; it cannot delegate or subcontract its management functions. The quality of governance is addressed by rules on self-dealing, conflicts of interest, and the responsibilities and credentials of board members.

Independent Custodianship Rules

The independent depositary for assets described above are aimed at limiting agency risks. The fund manager does not directly hold legal title to the assets of the pension fund, limiting the opportunity for fraud.

Disclosure Requirements

These rules include methods of asset valuations (mark to market), the frequency of those valuations, and the distribution of information to fund members and to the general public. Thus, account statements are made available to members every quarter, and the Pension Control Commission will publish extensive and detailed information on the industry. Regulators have wide authority to verify the accuracy of financial statements issued by pension funds. Disclosure requirements enable participants to make informed choices and place competitive pressure on fund managers, although some argue that switching across funds in other countries was driven mainly by marketing efforts (Vittas 1998).

External Audit/Actuary Requirements

Auditors are required to report any problem to the control commission and are legally liable for failure to do so.

Investment Regulations

These rules aim at minimizing portfolio risks and, to an extent, market and agency risks. The law stipulates ceilings on the holding of several limited classes of assets, with emphasis on bank deposits, state bonds, publicly listed shares in Romania, and to a lesser extent, bonds and shares listed in major stock exchanges around the world. Regulations also place ceilings on holdings by the issuer, thereby disallowing a controlling interest by any pension fund.

Restrictions imposed on pension fund investments in certain asset classes have generated controversy. Some Organization for Economic Cooperation and Development (OECD) countries do not impose restrictions by asset class and follow the "prudent-person" rule, which requires that investment decisions be diligent and satisfy the goal of risk diversification. Rocha, Gutierrez, and Hinz (1999) cite evidence that real returns of pension funds in prudent-person environments were higher than those of funds operating under quantitative restrictions on asset classes. The similarity of investment portfolios of pension funds in Chile, which restrict member choice, was cited by Feldstein as one reason for their high costs.

It seems, however, that tight quantitative investment restrictions in Romania—a transition economy with underdeveloped markets and regulatory structures—are justified, at least initially. The quantitative approach (termed "draconian" by some) is simple, easy to police, and greatly reduces uncertainty for all parties. These restrictions can be relaxed over time as markets and the legal framework improve.

The same argument applies to the rule against multiple portfolios. Although a single portfolio significantly reduces the degree of choice among the risk-return combinations, which typically differ across age groups, the additional costs associated with multiple portfolios seem to outweigh the benefits in countries such as Romania, the bulk of whose citizens cannot be expected to make informed decisions on the compositions of their portfolios.

Guarantees

Like some other countries that have introduced a second mandatory pillar, Romania offers participants a zero real rate of return on their contributions. This is similar to Hungary (which offered a zero real rate of return to workers below the age of forty and a 4 percent real rate of return for other workers) or to Switzerland (which guarantees a 4 percent *nominal*—about a 2 percent real—rate of return). This guarantee is backed by required minimum reserves and equity imposed on the pension manager and by a central guarantee fund. In case of insolvency of the manager and the central guarantee fund, there is an explicit guarantee from the government budget.

The provision of guarantees raises two basic questions. First, what is the probability that the guarantee will be called, and is the capital backing adequate for this purpose? Second, to what extent does the guarantee introduce a moral-hazard problem (i.e., distortions of the fund managers' investment decisions)?

In Latin America and Central Europe, most countries have provided guarantees in the form of annual minimum returns, expressed in relative terms. Thus, a minimum return is defined relative to the average return of all pension funds, or relative to a broader market benchmark. The benchmark is expressed in either real or nominal terms. In Chile, for example, each fund must achieve a minimum return equal to 50 percent of the average real rate of return of the industry. In Argentina, funds must achieve 70 percent of the average nominal return of the industry (Vittas 1998). These relative guarantees attempt to deal primarily with inefficient (or fraudulent) fund managers. They induce, however, a visible moral hazard in the form of a "herding" effect. That is, portfolios tend to cluster around the portfolios of the large and leading funds. As a result, the choices available to members are further limited (in addition to the limits imposed by ceilings on asset classes).

A related moral hazard concerns the extent to which private capital is put at risk in relation to the guarantees. If the assets of the fund manager (or the parent company) are not affected *before* the government guarantee is called, a negative agency risk is introduced. Although calculations indicate that this is not a serious problem (see below), it is an issue on which Romanian law may have to be modified.

Absolute guarantees, such as in Romania (or Switzerland and Hungary), defined as a minimum return over the working lifetime of members, introduce a measure of *intergenerational pooling* similar to that found in defined benefit (DB) systems. This seems to be a major advantage of the Romanian system.

The guarantee of a zero real return is based on detailed calculations and simulations. Baseline calculations assume an 8 or 10 percent contribution rate to the second pillar. With a zero-return benchmark, annuity benefits as percent of GDP will rise from 0.03 percent in 2025 to 0.77 percent in 2040 for an 8 percent contribution rate; and from 0.04 percent to 0.96 percent for a 10 percent contribution rate. To evaluate the risks entailed by the guarantees, calculations have used time series data on equity and bond returns in France from 1870 to 1998. Obviously, application of French time series to a transition economy such as Romania's requires caution. Emerging economies are considered to have higher risks and higher expected returns than mature economies. For cumulative processes over long periods, such as lifetime investment returns, the higher returns can be expected to dominate the higher short-term risks. Thus, we believe that our calculations are, on the whole, conservative.

The average annual return on equities in France since 1870 has been 4.5 percent (standard error 14.6 percent). The average annual real return on bonds since 1950 has been 2.1 percent (standard error 5.3 percent). Simulations have shown that the probability of exceeding a zero real rate of return on equities over a twenty-year holding period is 91 percent, and over a thirty-year period (approximately) 100 percent. The numbers for bonds are similar.

Statistical tests show that the time series of returns on equities and bonds are stationary and have zero serial correlation. Consequently, a large number of samples have been constituted from random time series of returns with the appropriate parameters. The simulations are based on a 50–50 portfolio of equities and bonds. The difference between each sample's outcome and the baseline (zero real return) provided the gains or losses that must be covered according to the guarantees.

Figure 13.1 displays one such calculation of gains and losses as a percentage of GDP (in 1996). The heavy line (Hamayon 1998, 6) gives the baseline of zero return.

Each line represents a different possible growth scenario, reflecting successive drawings from the underlying distribution of returns. It is seen that an overwhelming number of runs (samples) exceed the baseline (i.e. the guaranteed zero return). Figures 13.2 and 13.3 provide estimates of bypassing the guaranteed threshold. They display a histogram of the excess (shortage) over the guaranteed zero return, as a percentage of GDP (fig. 13.2) or of the rate of return (fig. 13.3), of sample returns. The right-hand axis applies to the cumulative probability represented by the downward-

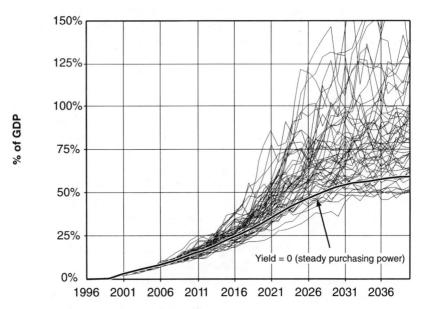

Fig. 13.1   The variability of the growth of private pension funds as a percentage of GDP (normal conditions)

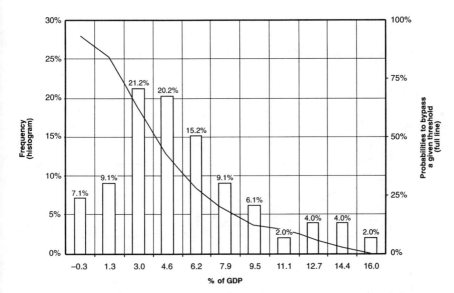

Fig. 13.2 Distribution of actualized gains and losses from 2025 to 2040 (10% contributions to private funds)

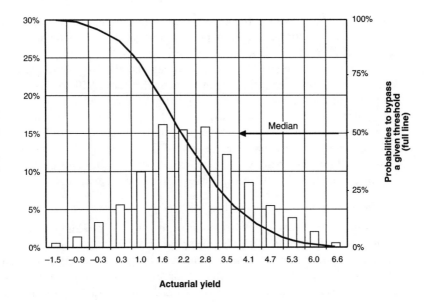

Fig. 13.3 Distribution of generations' actuarial yields of (10% contribution to private funds)

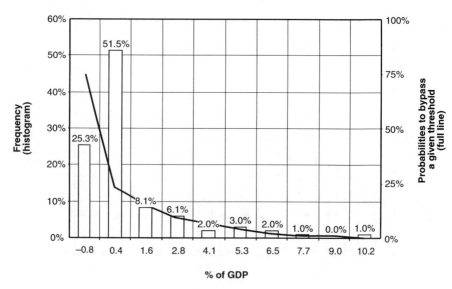

Fig. 13.4   Effects of ten-year crash (beginning in 2010) on distribution of
actualized gains and losses from 2025 to 2040 (10% of contributions)

sloping line. Thus, with a 10 percent contribution rate, about 90 percent
of the 100 simulations yielded a positive return, and 50 percent of the
samples gave a return higher than 2.2 percent.

A more severe scenario has also been calculated. Discarding the zero
serial correlation assumption, returns from the year 2010 to 2020 have
been sampled from only the *negative* portion of the frequency of returns,
reflecting a market-crash scenario lasting for ten years. Under these circumstances there is a 25 percent chance that the guarantee will be called,
although it will be less than one percent of GDP (see figs. 13.4 and 13.5).
Based on these calculations, it seems reasonable that the central risk fund
will be adequate to back even extremely adverse circumstances.

Minimum Capital and Reserve Requirements

A significant share capital (10 million euros) is required and may not be
encumbered. A portion of the share capital (5 million euros) must be kept
permanently in cash in Romania. Fund managers shall be required in addition to contribute to the National Guarantee Fund. These capital requirements seem excessive. In DC funds, there is no rationale for holding
capital at these levels, and such a requirement imposes a significant cost
that will be shifted to members. Presumably, the capital requirement has
been introduced as a screening device to reduce agency risks associated
with unreliable fund managers.

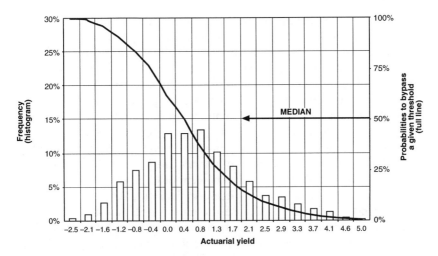

Fig. 13.5   Effects of ten-year crash (beginning in 2010) on distribution of generations' actuarial yields (10% of contribution)

Regulations on Costs and Fees

Two types of commissions are allowed: a percentage of contributions (front-load) or of the value of net assets. A ceiling (1.0 percent) has been imposed on the latter type, whereas the former is expected to be set competitively. The restrictions imposed, although they tend to cluster expenses at the allowable maximum, were intended to protect relatively uninformed members who are unable to evaluate alternative multidimensional pricing schemes.

13.8   The Budgetary Implications of the Public and Private Reforms

13.8.1   The Saving Generated by First-Pillar Reform

A move from a PAYGO system to a funded system, whether partial or complete, necessarily entails a transitional deficit while existing liabilities under the previous system are progressively paid off. How that deficit is financed has a major influence on the economic effect of the reform.

In the Romanian case, the principal source of financing for the transitional deficit is expected to be saving from the reform of the public system. We shall evaluate this source, then report projections of the net effect on the budget of public reform and private funding.

Our analysis begins with an estimate of the saving to be expected from tightening the conditions for early retirement, tightening benefit formulas, and increasing the retirement age. We measure these in a succinct way by comparing the present discounted value of the liabilities—to persons who were alive in 1999—of the old and the new public system.

The computation adds up the expected lifetime payments to which persons alive in 1999 were entitled at that point. It does not include future entitlements that young persons in 1999 could have expected to accumulate during the remaining years of their working lives; nor does it include the possible entitlements of future entrants to the workforce.[11]

Table 13.2 tells the basic story. In 1999, the total implicit liabilities of the prereform public system, discounted at 5 percent, were 140 percent of GDP. The total implicit liabilities of the reformed system, had it gone into effect in 2000, would have been 106 percent of GDP at the same discount rate, or 24 percent less than the prereform liabilities.

It is worth noting that, because the reform does not alter the state's liabilities to existing retirees (who have already taken advantage of whatever formulas and provisions were available), the entire amount of those savings must come from a reduction of liabilities to working people. One can see from table 13.2 that the discounted total liabilities to working men and women went from 67 percent of GDP to 38 percent of GDP. Tightening reduced those liabilities by a factor of 43 percent.

The reform is also expected to increase the number of contributors paying social security taxes. One important source of the increase is the incorporation of an estimated 2 million farmers and other self-employed persons into the basic system. If one assumes that the average new contributor declares half of the average wage, the enlargement is equivalent to an increase of 1 million contributors at the average wage, or 19 percent of the 5.2 million contributors in the system at the end of 1998. It is estimated that it will take four years for these new contributors to integrate fully into the system. Eventually, the new contributors also become new beneficiaries; the fact that they enter first as contributors implies that there is an increase in the present discounted value of revenue into the system.

In addition, the combination of the first- and second-pillar laws creates strong incentives for compliance on the part of the population at large. The first-pillar law establishes a direct link, which previously did not exist, between future pension benefits and lifetime contributions. The second-pillar law expands on this by treating social security tax payments and contributions to each worker's individual account symmetrically. If the tax is not paid, the corresponding individual account is not credited. It is expected that a worker will feel a sense of ownership of his or her individual

---

11. To the extent that workers could be expected to continue accumulating entitlements beyond 1999, the computation underestimates the total effective liabilities of both systems. What is important for our purposes is that we measure the implicit liabilities of the pre- and postreform systems in a comparable matter. Simulations from 1999 forward with the Hamayon, Legros (1998) model are used to estimate the implicit debt of the old and new systems. See de Menil, Hamayon, and Seitan (1999) for further details.

Table 13.2   Implicit Debt as Percentage of GDP of the Prereform and Postreform Public Pension System, 1999 (5% real discount rate)

| | Men | | | Women | | | | | |
	Already Retired	Working	Total	Already Retired	Working	Total	Survivors	Disability	Grand Total
Prereform	19	30	49	31	37	68	11	12	140
Postreform	19	17	36	31	21	52	9	9	106

Sources: de Menil, Hamayon, and Seitan (1999) and Hamayon (1999).

account, and will therefore pressure his or her employer to pay on time. It is reasonable to assume that these two changes together will, over time, reduce evasion and further increase the ratio of the contributor base to the active population. We estimate that Romania's currently high evasion rate will converge slowly to the European Union (EU) average, thus bringing about a gradual increase in both the contributor base and the number of beneficiaries.

13.8.2   Simulations of the Net Budgetary Implications of the Combined Reforms

The replacement ratio for full pensions mandated by the new pension law is 45 percent of the gross wage (which is high, but well below the potential replacement rate, under conditions of full indexation, of the old system). The equivalent average replacement ratio for all pensions is 35 percent (including survivors and disability). We have estimated that at the end of 1999 the ratio of contributors to beneficiaries (including farmers) was roughly 1. Under those conditions, a 35 percent (including farmers) replacement ratio would require a 35 percent social security tax on net wages. The actual effective average tax at the end of 1999 was 34 percent. The integration of the farmers and other self-employed persons should, in a few years, bring the ratio of contributors to beneficiaries to 1.22. If one adds to that measure the reduction in the number of beneficiaries through early retirement that the tightening of retirement provisions is expected to produce, as well as a reasonable reduction of the evasion rate, it seems clear that the provisions of the new public law should, in time, produce enough saving to ensure its medium-term sustainability on a stand-alone basis.[12] This begs the next question, however: Is the additional saving enough, and is it realized quickly enough, to finance the introduction of the second pillar? The answer to this question has been sought in a series of simulations of combined first- and second-pillar reform, under various economic, demographic, and policy assumptions.

Model and Assumptions

The model used for these simulations is a medium-term model developed by Stephane Hamayon and the Quantix consulting firm (Hamayon and Legros 1998), which focuses on the relationships between demographic trends and the rules and provisions of the public retirement system. It approximates the age distribution of the working-age population with density functions that can be projected many years forward, and modified to take account of changes in the birth rate and life expectancy.

---

12. The increase in the earliest possible legal retirement age is expected temporarily to freeze new entries into retirement. Even if this effect is partially compensated by some retirements in anticipation of the law, the effective number of beneficiaries could fall by 100,000 in the first two years. The reduction of evasion is likely to be modest, if first-pillar reform is not accompanied by second-pillar reform.

Entry into retirement is modeled according to the provisions of the public law in effect. The benefit formulas of the law are used to relate retirement benefits to past wage histories. Economic production, the movement of real wages, and the evolution of the evasion rate are exogenous inputs into the model.[13]

The model is used to examine the short- and medium-term effects of joint implementation of the government's public and private pension reforms, beginning in January 2001. The following economic and demographic assumptions are made: The life expectancy of men and women is assumed to continue rising at a slow rate. The net reproduction rate is assumed to reach a low of 1.7. Real output and real wages begin flat, and converge at a 4 percent rate of growth. Evasion converges slowly to West-European levels. Our focus will be on the resulting simulations of the growth of the private pension funds, on the one hand, and the budget of the public pension system, on the other.

The crucial policy parameters in these simulations are the provisions of the reformed public system, the magnitude of the diversion to private funds, and the nature of the phasing-in of this diversion. We examine the implications of a switch to the new public law, as described above, and of a 10 percent diversion, which is mandatory for all workers with more than twenty years until retirement and optional for workers with ten to twenty years until retirement. We assume that 35 percent of the workers given the option choose the diversion.[14]

Table 13.3 documents the magnitude of the flows into private pensions. They begin in 2001 at 0.57 percent of GDP, and rise over twenty-five years (as contributions progressively become mandatory for the entire workforce) to 3.56 percent. Twelve years after the reform, the accumulated contributions and compounded growth raise the total assets of these funds to 20 percent of GDP. Total assets eventually level off at 72 percent of GDP.

There is a modest transitional deficit, but it ends, and becomes a surplus after four years. It begins at 1.91 percent of GDP in the first year and diminishes progressively. In the first year, it is greater than the amount of the funds being diverted to private accounts. This is a reflection of the unbalanced initial conditions prior to the reform, and the fact that the saving introduced in the first pillar materialize only progressively.[15] The saving continues beyond the point, in the fourth year, at which it entirely

---

13. The simulations thus do not take account of potentially important feedbacks from the reforms themselves to real economic evolutions. For a description of the model, see Hamayon and Legros (1998).

14. Hungarian and Polish experiences suggest that this is a reasonable number.

15. In the first instance, the provisions of the new law that reduce the number of new retirees and limit their pensions affect only marginally the total volume of payments to all outstanding retirees. On the other hand, the provision that makes indexation of existing pensions to the consumer price level mandatory immediately eliminates what had previously been a constant annual source of erosion. On the revenue side, the integration of farmers and other self-employed persons takes four years to become complete.

Table 13.3   Accumulation of Private Pension Funds, and the Effect on the Social Security Budget of the Simultaneous Reform of the Public Pension System and Introduction of Private Pension Funds

Date	Net Flows into Private Funds	Capitalization of Private Funds	Surplus/Deficit of Social Security Budget (% of GDP)
2001	0.57	0.57	−1.91
2002	1.26	1.84	−1.65
2003	1.41	3.25	−0.87
2004	1.59	4.83	0.05
2005	1.74	6.55	0.74
2006	1.92	8.43	1.49
2007	2.11	10.50	2.29
2008	2.31	12.75	3.00
2009	2.46	15.15	3.59
2010	2.60	17.67	4.07
2015	3.03	31.47	5.02
2020	3.32	45.29	4.64
2030	3.56	68.11	3.95
2040	3.55	71.83	2.39

Source: Simulations with the Hamayon and Legros (1998) model.
Notes: Ten percent of wages allocated to personal accounts, participation mandatory for workers with fewer than twenty years to retirement, optional for those with fewer than ten years.

pays for the diversion of contributions to the second pillar. Saving generates a positive surplus in the social security fund that lasts for the full fifty years of the simulation. It rises to 5 percent of GDP in the fifteenth year of the reform, and then slowly declines.

In summary, saving in the public pension law over time more than pays for the diversion to private pensions. The saving does not become operative immediately, however. There is an initial three-year period during which the budgetary costs of diversion to the private system are added to the residual deficit of the public system. These results are not very sensitive to changes in demographic assumptions or to reasonable changes in the speed of reduction of evasion. They are affected significantly by the rate of growth, the rate of return, the magnitude of the draw-down to private accounts, and the timing of its introduction.

13.9   The Economic Effects of Pension Reform

13.9.1   Reduced Labor Market Distortions and Evasion

A major argument for a fully funded, mandatory pension system as a second pillar for retirement income is that it will have a positive effect on efficiency and growth. This effect can be achieved by a reduction in labor market distortions created by the first pillar of mandatory, PAYGO, defined benefits, and through an increase in the national saving rate and the capital stock, and consequently in income per capita. Which of these economic effects can Romania's joint first- and second-pillar reforms be expected to produce?

In the Romanian case, the labor market effect is qualitatively different from what it is in other countries. The simulations in table 13.3 show that, after four years, the 1999 reform of Romania's public pension system more than pays for the permanent diversion of 10 percent of wages to individual private accounts. If existing workers view their contributions to private accounts as benefits rather than as taxes, the combination of the two reforms can be said to reduce the effective tax on wages of existing contributors by 10 percent. We have shown above, however, that the Romanian reforms include the integration of a substantial number of new contributors—largely farmers—who were previously paying very little tax. The net result of the reforms from the point of view of taxes is that they equalize the effective tax on existing and new contributors at a 25 percent rate. The average tax rate is unchanged, but a distortionary difference between the two is removed.[16] There is presumably a gain in efficiency, but it is difficult to estimate, and is qualitatively different from the efficiency gains of across-the-board reductions in wage taxes estimated in other studies.

A further remark is in order. The simulation in table 13.3 shows that the combined reforms produce a rising surplus in the public pension fund after the third year. If that surplus were used to pay for an across-the-board reduction in Romania's very high social security taxes, additional efficiency gains would likely result.[17]

The simulation in table 13.3 assumes that the percentage of the population covered by social security in Romania will increase from the current 63 percent to 90 percent, due to the introduction of the point system and the creation of the private pension system. Clearly, funded DC plans are less likely to be evaded because they closely link benefits to contributions. The magnitude of this effect, however, is difficult to estimate. If workers are myopic (contrary to the preceding discussion), they may continue to evade contributions because they will be unable to access their mandatory saving for many years. When investment returns are low, workers may es-

16. Existing contributors, who were paying 35 percent on average before the two reforms, perceive that their social security tax has been reduced to 25 percent. New contributors, who were previously paying roughly zero, perceive that their social security taxes have been increased to 25 percent (the new 35 percent contribution, minus the 10 percent diversion to a private account).

17. Feldstein and Samwick (1996) have estimated that a 10.4 percentage point reduction in the U.S. payroll tax increases steady state GDP by one percent annually. Kotlikoff (1996) finds that a similar reform leads to a 4 percent gain in consumption. Comparable tax reductions might be expected to lead to a greater decrease in dead-weight loss in Romania, because of its higher effective tax rates.

pecially be tempted to evade, preferring to consume an investment in housing or durables. On the other hand, the relatively low coverage rate in Romania is, at least in part, due to legal avoidance rather than evasion. (The use of civil contracts is an example.) This is why we think the Hamayon estimates are realistic.

13.9.2   Augmented Retirement Age

Another source of inefficiency of PAYGO, DB systems is that political considerations (particularly during periods of unemployment) lead to excessively early retirement ages with generous benefits (high replacement rates). One can expect that fully funded DC plans will mitigate this effect, because if the worker retires early the costs are internalized via a reduced pension. Thus, for example, if Romania's reforms eventually lead workers to raise their retirement ages by at least four years, and if leisure is worth, on average, half the wage during that period, then the supply of labor and GDP (assuming constant marginal productivity of labor) are both raised by almost 10 percent and welfare by 5 percent.

13.9.3   Increased National Saving

Perhaps the most important economic effect of a pension reform program like that of Romania is its effect on national saving. It is well known that the effect on national saving of a switch—partial or total—from a PAYGO, DB system to a private, funded DC system depends on how the change is financed. If it is completely deficit financed, the introduction of the funded system has no effect on national saving because the additional saving going into the private system is offset by additional dissaving in the state budget. We have shown above that, in the Romanian case, the transitional deficit is fully financed, after the first three years, by saving realized in the public system. It follows that, in our case, once the first three years have passed, mandatory, national saving is increased by the full amount of flows into the private funds.[18]

Of course, mandatory saving may not increase total national saving if individuals find ways to offset it against other voluntary saving. One may speculate about the size of this "crowding-out" effect, but presumably it is quite small in a transition economy such as that of Romania, where opportunities to accumulate capital and information about them are limited for a substantial part of the population.

According to the simulation reported in table 13.3, the capital stock accumulated in the funded system is about 70 percent of GDP after forty years. Using standard calculations of the contribution of capital and labor

18. We have seen in the Hamayon simulations that the combination of public and private reform generates a surplus in the state's social security fund. If that surplus is allowed to accumulate, it constitutes additional national saving. We assume here that it is used to finance future reductions in social security taxes.

to the growth rate of GDP, we have shown elsewhere that the establishment of a funded pension system in Romania will increase the growth rate of output by almost one percent per year.[19]

13.10   Universal Pension Funds and the Capital Markets

A major concern regarding the implementation of a mandatory, fully funded pension system in Romania is the ability of the system to provide stable and adequate retirement benefits to covered workers. Critics of the pension reform have argued that because of the volatility of equity and bond markets and the repeated episodes of high inflation, there is concern that a catastrophic collapse of capital markets might wipe out the real value of accumulated balances and leave retiring workers with inadequate income.

In response to this criticism it should first be pointed out that the exposure of retirees to market risk depends on the relative sizes of the first (public) and the second (private) pillars. Contributions to the first pillar are only weakly correlated with market returns, and the second pillar is expected to provide at maturity 30–50 percent of total benefits. Thus, the multipillar structure tends to dilute the impact of market risks.

The experience from similar reforms around the world provides some confidence in the successful establishment of multipillar structures in economies similar to Romania's. After Chile's abolition of the first pillar (1981), several Latin American countries implemented multipillar reforms: Argentina (1994), Colombia (1994), Bolivia (1997), El Salvador (1998), Mexico (1997), Peru (1993), and Uruguay (1996). More recently, several transition economies—led by Hungary and Poland—have successfully implemented mandatory, fully funded, privately managed pension funds complementing a public, PAYGO first pillar. Risks can be further reduced by allowing investment abroad.

The introduction of a private second pillar in a country such as Romania can be expected to have significant positive externalities on capital markets. The establishment of an independent, pro active pension supervision authority with wide jurisdiction should have, if properly implemented, positive effects on other existing regulatory agencies (e.g., in banking, insurance, and the stock market).

The establishment of privately managed pension funds can be expected to lead to the entry of major global insurance firms and investment banks into Romania, as was the experience in Poland. These firms have a reputation for following solid investment and auditing practices, which will positively affect the practices of local firms.

---

19. See de Menil and Sheshinski (1998). This calculation assumes that there is no crowding-out of voluntary private saving. Some of the issues addressed throughout section 13.9 are discussed in de Menil (2000).

13.11   Conclusion

Throughout Eastern Europe, the collapse of communism revealed an incipient crisis in the provision of social security. Actuarially unsound retirement systems that were incapable of surviving in other than a command economy were threatened with collapse. Both the critical condition of retirees and the burden of pension payments on state budgets made fundamental changes in the existing PAYGO systems a priority for reform. In a number of countries, a desire to balance the promises of a state redistributive system with the potential benefits of the growth of capital markets led to the design of mixed, multipillar systems with private, funded components. The combination of the saving achieved through the tightening of the public system and the impetus to capital markets of the introduction from private pension funds was expected to raise growth and improve economic efficiency.

Romania, the second largest country in the region, is poorer than its neighbors, and has been slower to reform. Although its benefits were less (both in absolute terms and as a percentage of GDP) than elsewhere, its pension system was equally as bankrupt. For the first seven years after 1989, instead of tightening the provisions inherited from Ceausescu, successive governments relaxed controls on benefits and responded to the melting-away of the contributor base by raising taxes. By 1996, the pension system was in full crisis. The government formed by the parties that won the elections at the end of that year made pension reform a priority. It focused first where the need was most critical: closing the deficit by fundamentally restructuring the PAYGO system. After a three-year process of debate and negotiations, Parliament passed a new law that scaled back the present discounted value of the entitlements of existing workers by 43 percent, and legislated a 19 percent increase in the contributor base. Several months later (November 2000), the government passed, by emergency ordinance, legislation to create a mandatory, second-pillar system of private, funded pensions. The government that emerged from the elections later that month withdrew the emergency ordinance and set up a commission to review its pension reform strategy. At the present writing, it is unclear what the next step will be.

The second-pillar design imbedded in the emergency ordinance passed in Romania in November 2000 is notable for some distinguishing characteristics. For instance, the state guarantee that is built into the system is extended to the individual beneficiary, not to the fund; thus it entails less moral hazard.

The success and safety of any future system depend critically on a central institution, the Pension Supervisory Commission. The authority and effectiveness of this independent, autonomous professional body, responsible for licensing and regulating private fund managers, is decisive. If the commission succeeds in remaining above politics and enforces the prudential regulations imbedded in the law, private funds can increase future retirement benefits and enhance the liquidity, transparency, and safety of Romanian capital markets.

References

Balcerowicz, L. 1994. Common fallacies regarding economic reform. *Economic Policy* 19S.

De Melo, M., C. Denitzer, and A. Gelb. 1994. From plan to market: Patterns of transition. Policy Research Department Working Paper no. 1564. Washington, D.C.: World Bank.

de Menil, G. 2000. A comment on the place of funded pensions in transition economies. *International Tax and Public Finance* 7:431–44.

de Menil, G., S. Hamayon, and M. Seitan. 1999. Romania's pension system: The weight of the past. Paper presented for CASE Workshop, "The Medium and Long-Term Fiscal Adjustment of Selected Central European Countries," 12 June, Warsaw, Poland.

de Menil, G., and E. Sheshinski. 1998. Growth and income effects of the proposed establishment of a second pillar funded pension system in Romania. Bucharest: Pro Democratia Foundation. Unpublished manuscript, 7 October.

Feldstein, M., and A. Samwick. 1996. The transition path to social security. NBER Discussion Paper no. 5761. Cambridge, Mass.: National Bureau of Economic Research.

Hamayon, S. 1998. Estimates of the probability costs of pension fund guarantees. Bucharest: Pro Democratia Foundation. Unpublished manuscript.

———. 1999. Implicit debt under new public law conditions. Bucharest: Pro Democratia Foundation. Unpublished manuscript.

Hamayon, S., and F. Legros. 1998. A simulation model of pension reform in Romania. Bucharest: Pro Democratia Foundation. Unpublished manuscript.

Heindl Rondanelli, E. 1996. Chilean pension reform and its impact on saving. Chile: Universidad Gabriela Mistral.

Holzmann, Robert. 2000. The World Bank approach to pension reform. *International Social Security Review,* no. 1.

Kotlikoff, L. J. 1996. Privatizing social security at home and abroad. *American Economic Review* 86:368–72.

Ministry of Labor and Social Protection. 1993. *White paper on social insurance and pension reform.* Bucharest: Government of Romania.

National Commission of Statistics. Various years. *Statistical yearbook.* Bucharest: Government of Romania.

Parniczky, T. 1999. *Case study of the three-pillar pension system in Hungary.* Hungary: State Private Funds Supervision.

Pro Democratia Foundation. 1997. *White book regarding the implementation of a national system of capitalized, privately managed pension funds.* Bucharest: Pro Democratia Foundation.

Rocha, R., J. Gutierrez, and R. Hinz. 1999. Improving the regulation and supervision of pension funds: Are there lessons from the banking sector? Policy Research Department Working Paper no. 9929. Washington, D.C.: World Bank.

Rutkowski, M. 2001. Restoring hope, rewarding work: Pension reforms in post-communist economies. In *Transition and growth in post-communist countries,* ed. L. T. Orlowski, 243–69. Cheltenham, UK: Edward Elgar.

Vienna Institute for International Economic Studies (WIIW). 2000. *WIIW handbook of statistics: Countries in transition 1999.* Vienna: WIIW.

Vittas, D. 1993. The white paper on social insurance and pension reform. Romania: Government of Romania, Ministry of Labor and Social Protection.

———. 1996. Private pension funds in Hungary: Early performance and regulatory issues. Policy Research Department Working Paper no. 1638. Washington, D.C.: World Bank.

———. 1998. Regulatory controversies of private pension funds. Policy Research Department Working Paper no. 1893. Washington, D.C.: World Bank.

Comment on chapters 11, 12, and 13   John McHale

Over the last decade, reforming politicians in post-communist countries have often said their goal is to "return to Europe," meaning, I suppose, that they wish to adopt the economic institutions and policies of the successful countries to their west and eventually join the European Union (EU). Reading these excellent papers on fundamental pension reform in three post-communist countries, one cannot help but be struck by the fact that in this area, all three are leapfrogging their established market-economy neighbors. On this question, we are looking east to see what we can learn.

With three countries and limited space, I will not try to comment in any detail on the individual papers. Instead I will briefly reflect on the information given that helps answer three big questions: What did these countries do in the area of pension reform? Will the reforms be to their overall benefit? and, How, politically, did they manage to implement the reforms?

Although there are important differences in the details, it is striking that each of the three countries has adopted or plans to adopt a version of the three-pillared retirement income system that has been advocated by the World Bank. The first pillar is a restructured pay-as-you-go (PAYGO), defined benefit (DB) pension, with substantially reduced costs and tighter links between contributions and benefits. The second pillar is based on the diversion of a portion of contributions to individual investment accounts. The third pillar is voluntary (tax-favored) saving. Not surprisingly, it is the second, Chilean-style pillar that is receiving the most attention, because it involves the most radical break with the past. Although it involves only part of the total mandatory contributions, the shares of covered wages flowing into the second pillar are (or will be) significant: 7.3 percent in Poland, 6–8 percent in Hungary, and a planned 10 percent in Romania.

It is worth emphasizing that changes to the *first pillar* have also been

John McHale is associate professor of economics at Harvard University.

quite radical, with each country attempting to make contributions seem less like taxes by strengthening the links between contributions and benefits. Poland appears to have gone the farthest along this dimension, adopting a Swedish-style notional defined contribution (NDC) system (but without a flexible retirement age). The Hungarian reforms "gradually eliminate some of the redistributive elements in the formula," although the details are not spelled out in chapter 12. Finally, Romania (chap. 13) has moved to a German-style points system, in which "workers accumulate points for each full year worked at the average wage," instead of a system with a benefit based on the best five earning years in the ten years prior to retirement.

Will the reforms make these countries better off? The answer to this question depends, of course, on complex judgments about equity between and within generations; but it is helpful to look for evidence provided in these papers on two important sub-questions: Will the reforms increase economic efficiency? and, How will the reforms affect retirement income security?

Reforms to the first and second pillars are likely to have a significant impact on labor market distortions. Exceptionally high labor tax rates,[1] weak links between taxes and benefits, low average returns on PAYGO contributions, and extensive opportunities for (low-productivity) informal-sector work, all indicate that the distortions created by the old system were large. Working-age labor supply was distorted, unemployment rates were pushed up by large tax wedges and high net replacement rates,[2] and there was a strong bias toward early retirement. Elementary economics suggests that, given the initial conditions, even modest reforms should lead to large efficiency improvements.

The impact of second-pillar reforms on capital market distortions is less obvious. A reasonable starting assumption is that national saving is inefficiently low (say, because of capital income taxation), so that a second-pillar induced increase in saving will lead to a net gain. In other words, the decreased consumption today is more than offset in present value terms by the increase in output (and thus consumption) in the future. However, will adding a funded pillar actually increase saving? The well-known problem is that the diversion of contributions to individual accounts leaves a revenue shortfall for funding the pensions of the presently retired. If this shortfall is made up by domestic borrowing, then saving will not increase.

The direct impact on saving of diverting contributions to the second pillar is considered most explicitly in the papers on Hungary and Roma-

1. Just prior to the reforms, contributions to the pension system alone accounted for 45.0 percent of covered wages in Poland, 33.0 percent in Hungary, and 37.5 percent in Romania (having risen from 28.5 percent in January 1999).

2. The three countries had similar unemployment rates in 1998: 10.4 percent in Poland, 9.1 percent in Hungary, and 10.3 percent in Romania.

nia, both of which include informative simulation evidence. In Hungary the early increase in the PAYGO deficit is about 0.8 percent of gross domestic product (GDP), which is quite low given that 50 percent of the labor force are diverting 6 percent of covered wages. Rocha and Vittas provide simulation information on the net (direct) impact of the combined reforms on saving over time, adding together the deficit in the first pillar and the increased net saving in the second pillar; this reaches about 2 percent by the end of the decade. This is not quite the right calculation, however, because what matters for the impact on saving is the *increase* in the first-pillar deficit, not its absolute size.

The Romanian case is interesting in that the previous PAYGO system cuts are sufficiently large, and that the overall balance is projected to be in surplus by 2004. Again we must ask if this is the right number to examine. Without a diversion to the second pillar, the PAYGO pillar would turn to surplus even earlier. On the other hand, large cuts to first-pillar spending might not have been feasible without the promise to introduce a second pillar.

The Polish solution to transitional funding is to use privatization revenues. It must be remembered, however, that those privatization revenues could have been used to bring down the budget deficit and boost national saving directly. There is (to use the jargon) an opportunity cost to using privatization revenues to cover the transition. Thus privatization revenues, although politically useful in filling the gap, do not remove the need to raise taxes or cut spending if saving is to rise over the transition relative to the no-reform benchmark.[3]

A second, often-discussed (but difficult to quantify) benefit of introducing a funded pillar is that it will spur the development of capital markets, in part because it forces the government to establish carefully a system of prudential regulation for financial intermediaries. A more well-developed financial system should increase saving by raising expected return,[4] lead to a better allocation of capital, and reduce the vulnerability of the economy to domestic-banking and foreign-funding shocks. This effect is probably quite important for countries in which financial markets are poorly developed, a category that surely includes all of the post-communist economies. There is a danger, however, that the political perception of governmental responsibility for the performance of the funded pillar that it created— and the fact the government is offering limited investment return guarantees—will lead to an overly heavy regulatory hand. As described in the

3. From a national-saving point of view, a free giveaway of ownership stakes in former state enterprises would be even worse, because recipients will probably raise their consumption in response to this windfall.
4. More developed financial markets can also reduce saving if they reduce liquidity constraints by making it easier to borrow.

papers, the regulatory systems are still very much works in progress. It is not self-evident that all the induced regulation will be for the best.

Next, I turn to the impact of reform on the security of retirement income. Overall, my judgment is that the multipillared system does make retirement income more secure—there is "security in diversity." Of course, the diversion of contributions to the second pillar exposes workers to investment risk and charges, which eat into returns. Against that, however, must be weighed the very high political risk in the unreformed PAYGO systems: that is, the risk that the parameters of the retirement benefit and contribution formulas will be altered by politicians. Even the limited reforms to benefit formulas pursued thus far by the major industrial economies have usually had quite large impacts on the present value of an average worker's expected stream of benefits. The risk of benefit cuts is high when current benefits are costly, when the system is in deficit, and when demographic trends will raise the overall cost (and deficit) under existing rules. As outlined in the three papers, the old systems have faced all these problems to varying degrees. On balance, then, the diversification advantages provided by the multisource provision of retirement income, especially when combined with sensible regulation and limited guarantees for the funded pillar, should allow workers to look forward to more secure retirements.

This brings me to the last of the three questions: How were these countries able to push through such radical reforms? Although politics of reform differed among the three countries, it seems that the perception of political risk under the old system was a common element. Workers simply did not believe that they would receive the benefits that were being promised under the old DB rules. During the 1990s, they saw how benefit formulas could be made more austere through formula changes and limited inflation protection—dramatically so in Romania. This made them receptive to alternatives, especially when the alternatives involved having the concrete ownership of individual accounts that would be difficult for politicians to take away. The perception of political risk was sufficiently high that it allowed reformers to overcome the usual obstacles of the transition cost and the distributional churning of fundamental reform. (The refusal of the new government in Hungary to follow through with the planned increase in the contribution to the second pillar is a reminder, however, that political risk is not entirely absent in a funded system, either.)

A remarkable feature of the reforms in Hungary and Poland is that participation in the funded pillar was voluntary for large sections of the population. Essentially, workers are offered a type of asset swap: They can exchange part of their eligibility in the DB system for the right to divert part of their contributions to the funded pillar. By appropriately choosing the terms of the swap, the government can take advantage both of the higher return in an investment-based system and of any perceptions of political risk. In Hungary, for example, switching leads to the loss of approximately one-fourth of already acquired rights. Nevertheless, half the Hungarian labor force has made the switch. (In Poland, 10.5 million of the eligible 11.5 million have switched). Voluntary diversion also allows the government to take advantage of a free rider problem for those being offered the opt-out. The lost revenues to the PAYGO system by the diversions will probably have to be made up by tax increases or spending cuts, which will hurt current working generations. The burden of these fiscal adjustments will fall broadly, however, landing on both those who do and those who do not take the partial opt-out. Thus, members of the transition generations might be collectively disadvantaged by the asset swap, but still find it individually advantageous to accept.

What do the accounts of fundamental reform in these countries tell us about the probability of similar reforms in Western Europe? Encouragingly for advocates of reform, the stories told in these papers show that it is possible to have radical change even when there is a large implicit pension debt. The Polish and Hungarian cases, in particular, show how reform can come through voluntary choice rather than through politically difficult benefit cutting. In each of the three countries, however, the present value of *expected* accrued benefits based on past contributions was probably much less than the face value of the implicit debt. Ironically, reform in Western Europe is made more difficult by the greater credibility of its pension promises.

Discussion Summary for Chapters 11, 12, and 13

Laurence J. Kotlikoff commented on the reform proposal for Romania. He criticized the notion that a country may develop by mobilizing domestic saving to invest, because all the countries that have developed quickly— such as Korea, Singapore, Malaysia, or more recently, China—have done so with massive amounts of foreign investments. In his view, the Romanians will end up investing in government debt because there are no domestic alternatives to invest. The government will use that borrowing to spend more and in the end will be unable to repay the debt. *Eytan Sheshinski* responded by noting that 90 percent of China's investments are financed by local saving and that China has done reasonably well with that. Sheshinski said that, in general, there is a trade-off between the tightness of regulations and the degree of competition in the pension system. He reported that when the Romanians had to weigh the security of the new system against the degree of competition, they adhered to the cautious side. He noted that the support for moving to a funded system is very fragile in Romania, and a fund's going under once or twice could be disastrous for the whole system. As examples of the cautious approach taken in Romania, Sheshinski mentioned fee regulations, regulations with respect to the portfolio structure, and pension guarantees.

Axel Börsch-Supan asked about the assumptions made in the paper by Rocha and Vittas with respect to the crowding out of savings. *Roberto Rocha* answered that the paper does not contain estimates for overall private savings, but only for pension savings. The total effect of the pension reform on voluntary private saving is unclear in the view of Rocha, because different reform parameters have contradictory influences on private saving.

Börsch-Supan noted that a conversion to a notional defined contribution (NDC) plan does not change the economics of the pension system. Rocha responded that Hungary did not undertake an NDC reform but a defined benefit (DB) reform. He said that the simulations of NDC reforms in the paper are counterfactual, because they show what the effects of an NDC reform would have been. With respect to the growth effects of pensions, Rocha called the literature on growth schizophrenic: The empirical literature on growth shows a powerful and robust capital market effect on growth, whereas in the pensions and growth literature this effect does not exist. *Ignazio Visco* remarked that the capital market effects quoted by Rocha may depend on some extreme observations.

Referring to the paper by de Menil and Sheshinski, *Axel Börsch-Supan* asked how the surplus that accrues to the government in a pay-as-you-go system is transferred to private accounts. *Eytan Sheshinski* answered that the collection of contributions is performed by the public system for reasons of returns to scale. The diversion to the private funds is performed through the government on the basis of membership. Sheshinski called this the most efficient and secure method of collecting and distributing the contributions. Börsch-Supan expressed his opinion that the important goal is not to increase saving but to increase capital productivity.

Sheshinski noted that the terms concerning the annuitization of the pension funds have not been determined yet in the transition economies. He called this a real weakness of the reforms in these countries. Sheshinski finally emphasized that the structure of the regulatory authority is of utmost importance for the success of the reforms. For Romania the decision was to establish a new regulatory authority detached as much as possible from the political arm.

Roberto Rocha noted that the first pillar that has been introduced in the central and eastern European countries is not the first pillar the World Bank has advocated. The World Bank has advocated a redistributive first pillar, whereas the first pillar in the central and eastern European countries is less redistributive, and redistribution has been shifted outside the pension system. Regarding the question of the discussant as to why the transition numbers for Hungary look reasonable, Rocha mentioned the erosion of the tax base that preceded the reform. If a country had already suffered a massive erosion of the tax base before a reform, the revenue losses from the introduction of a second pillar after the reform are much smaller.

Jerzy Hausner said that even if one cannot prove that a pension reform will raise domestic saving, one advantage is obvious: A pension reform will change the proportions in the capital market, because domestic long-term capital could not be created in any other way.

14

Recent Developments in Old Age Pension Systems
An International Overview

Klaus-Jürgen Gern

14.1 Introduction and Summary

The reform of public pension systems has become an increasingly urgent topic on the political agenda in most Organization for Economic Cooperation and Development (OECD) countries, because during recent years it has become more and more evident that, given the progressive aging of the population, existing pension plans are fiscally unsustainable under prevailing rules—albeit to differing degrees (see OECD 1995a; Noord and Herd 1993; Chand and Jaeger 1996). Against that background, the purpose of this paper is to give an account of the present state of the matter in an international perspective, centering on the industrial countries. The remainder of this section summarizes the main findings of the country-by-country analysis that follows in subsequent sections. Section 14.2 briefly sketches the main characteristics of the pension systems of seventeen industrial countries and gives information on recent reforms. In section 14.3, developments in other parts of the world (namely in Central and Eastern Europe, East Asia, and Latin America) are covered, although in a much more general way.[1] The paper ends with some concluding remarks.

Klaus-Jürgen Gern is head of the international business cycle research department at the Kiel Institute of World Economics.

The author would like to thank Alfred Boss, Jan Gottschalk, and Marcus Schlie. The author himself, not the Kiel Institute of World Economics, is solely responsible for the contents and distribution of each Kiel Working Paper.

1. For more extensive discussions of Argentina, Australia, Chile, Mexico, and the United Kingdom, see Cottani and Demarco (1998), Edey and Simon (1998), Edwards (1998), Sales-Sarrapy, Solis-Soberón, and Villagómez-Amezcua (1998), and Budd and Campbell (1998).

14.1.1   Institutional Design Differs across Countries

Generally, retirement income can be provided from three sources: public pension schemes, privately managed (but usually government-regulated) occupational pension schemes, and individual (retirement) saving. Across countries, there is a great deal of variation in the relative importance of these three sources of income as well as in the institutional organization of each of them. Differences in the organization of the pension systems are one reason behind the fact that the problems facing pension systems for the future are more serious in some countries than in others.[2]

Table 14.1 summarizes facts over a number of dimensions of the institutional design of old age pension systems in seventeen OECD countries. The relative importance of public pension schemes is to some extent reflected in the level of public pension expenditure relative to gross domestic product (GDP), and is related to the ratio of average pensions to average wages (the implicit replacement rate). According to these indicators, the role of the public sector is especially prominent in continental Europe (with the Netherlands, Switzerland, and Denmark as the exceptions) and tends to be less pronounced in the Anglo-Saxon countries.[3] The present value of uncovered future liabilities in the public-sector pension system as a percentage of GDP may give an indication of the extent to which reforms are necessary. As a measure of the relative weight of occupational pensions in the overall old age security system, the percentage of employees covered can be misleading when occupational pension plans are designed to provide only a marginal addition to other (public) pensions. This is the case, for example, in Germany. Therefore, the importance of occupational pension plans may be better reflected in the value of accumulated assets measured as a proportion of GDP.[4]

In most industrial countries, a mandatory public pension plan is at the heart of the old age security system. Formal arrangements, however, can differ in a number of ways. Pension schemes may have either redistribution or saving and insurance as dominant objectives. They may specify either their benefits in advance (defined benefit type), or their contributions and pay benefits according to the return on the contributions (defined contribution type). They may be financed on a pay-as-you-go basis (from general tax revenues or from social security contributions), or on a largely funded basis.

---

2. Of course, the differing degree of population aging is another important factor.

3. For Japan and New Zealand, the assessment is somewhat unclear because a relatively low share of GDP spent on public pensions combines with a relatively high implicit replacement rate.

4. Mandatory occupational pension schemes that work (primarily) on a PAYGO basis are included in the public sector even if private-sector institutions are involved in the management of the system. Such arrangements can be found in Finland and France.

Table 14.1   Synoptic Overview of Old Age Pension Systems in Industrial Countries

Country	Public Pension System					Occupational Pensions			Recent Reforms of Significance
	Type of Benefits and Financing	Pension Expenditure (% of GDP)[a]	Implicit Replacement Rate[b]	Assets of the System (% of GDP)[a]	Net Unfunded Liabilities (% of GDP)[c]	Type	Coverage (% of employed)[d]	Assets (% of GDP)[d]	
Australia	MTF, TF	2.6	30	n.a.	96.7[e]	compulsory	92	45	Introduction of a pattern of mandatory, fully funded occupational pensions (since 1986).
Austria	CR, CF[f]	8.8	40	n.a.	92.5	voluntary	10	n.a.	Change of indexation from gross to net wages (1993); reduction of preferential treatment of public-sector employees (1997).
Belgium	CR, CF[f]	10.4	63	n.a.	152.6	voluntary	31	10	
Canada	UF/MTF/CR, TF/CF	5.2	33	7	100.7	voluntary	48	25	Increased prefunding of the earnings-related scheme through advanced contribution hikes, improved investment rules, lower benefits (1997). Revision of the basic scheme (2001).
Denmark	UF/MTF/CR, TF/CF	6.8	40	n.a.	234.5[e]	quasi-compulsory	80	21	Extension of coverage of occupational pension schemes through collective bargaining (early 1990s).
Finland	UF/CR, TF/CF	11.5	65	41.0[f]	64.8	voluntary[g]	n.a.	0.5	Increase of actuarial fairness, increase in the period of reference earnings, change in reference index, gradual increased in means testing on the basic pension (1993–96).
France	CR, CF[f]	10.6	56	−0.5	102.1	voluntary[g]	n.a.	3	Change of indexation from gross to net wages (1984) to CPI (1988); private-sector scheme only: increase in the period of reference earnings, transfer of noncontributory pension rights to a tax-financed "solidarity fund" (1993).

(continued)

Table 14.1 (continued)

Country	Public Pension System					Occupational Pensions			Recent Reforms of Significance
	Type of Benefits and Financing	Pension Expenditure (% of GDP)[a]	Implicit Replacement Rate[b]	Assets of the System (% of GDP)[a]	Net Unfunded Liabilities (% of GDP)[c]	Type	Coverage (% of employed)[d]	Assets (% of GDP)[d]	
Germany	CR, CF[f]	11.1	46	1.1	61.6	voluntary	42	6	Change of indexation from gross to net wages; reduction of benefits for early reitrees, gradual increase in the normal retirement age for women (1992); introduction of a demographic factor into the benefit formula (1999).
Italy	CR, CF[f]	13.3	49	nil	59.7	voluntary	5	4	Suspension of indexation to gross wages (1992); shoft toward a more uniform, contribution-based system with improved actuarial fairness and an effective reduction in average benefits (1995). Introduction of tax incentives for individual retirement saving.
Japan	CR, CF[f]	6.6	54	26.5	70.0	voluntary	50	18	Gradual increase of the retirement age to sixty-five between 2001 and 2018, change of indexation from gross to net wages, increase in the contribution rate by 2.5 percentage points every five years (1994).
Netherlands	CR, CF	6.0	39	n.a.	53.3	voluntary	83	85	Calculation of benefits in occupational pension schemes on the basis of lifetime rather than last earnings (underway).
New Zealand	UF, TF	5.9	51	n.a.	212.8[e]	voluntary	22	n.a.	Gradual increase of the statutory retirement age from sixty to sixty-five (1992–2001).
Spain	CR, CF	10.0	34	n.a.	108.6	voluntary	15	2	Introduction of private pension funds (1988); increase of the reference period for earnings, increased actuarial fairness (1995).

Sweden	UF/CR, TF/CF	11.8	54	25.8	132.3	partly compulsory	90	16	Improved actuarial fairness, increased means testing of basic pension, introduction of a growth factor into indexation, increased prefunding through individual accounts (1998).
Switzerland	CR, CF[f]	6.7	n.a.	6.6	n.a.	compulsory	90	70	Funded occupational pensions made mandatory (1985); only minor changes to public system.
United Kingdom	CR, CF	4.5	23	−0.2	23.8	voluntary	75[b]	82	Introduction of personal pensions as an option to contract out of the public scheme (1987); measures to increase the attractiveness to opt out (1986, 1995); increase in the statutory retirement age of women to sixty-five between 2010 and 2020.
United States	CR, CF[f]	4.1	30	7.0	23.0	voluntary	46	72	Increased pre-funding through accumulation in a trust fund, increase of the retirement age to sixty-seven from 2000 onward (1983); increased prefunding through individual accounts, increase of the retirement age to seventy by 2029 (underway).

Sources: World Bank 1994 (tables A6, A7); Chand and Jaeger 1996 (table 7); OECD 1996b (table 2.2), 1997 (table 16); Davis 1996 (table 1); Thomas 1997 (table 1); and author's own tabulations.

Notes: MTF = means-tested flat benefit. TF = tax financed. CR = contributions-related benefit. CF = contributions financed. UF = universal flat benefit.

[a]As of 1995.

[b]Calculated as the ratio of average pensions to average wages.

[c]As of 1994.

[d]As of 1993.

[e]Net liabilities are equal to gross liabilities, because pensions are tax-financed.

[f]In these countries there is a significant subsidy from the government budget, ranging from about 10 percent of expenditures in France and the United States to about 33 percent in Japan.

[g]Because of their PAYGO character in the cases of Finland and France, the mandatory occupational pensions are included in the public pension system.

[h]Including personal pensions (25 percentage points).

In reality, we find basically two different approaches to public pension schemes. The first is the social insurance approach, which can be found in most continental countries of western Europe, in the United States, and in Japan. Here, the working generation is required to contribute to the system a certain percentage of a relevant income, and benefits are related to contributions or earnings (or both). The countries that have public pension schemes at work according to the social insurance approach again differ significantly with respect to the arrangements in detail—for example, the degree of redistribution inherent in the system, the coverage of the population, and the proportion of retirement income that is supplied by the system. Another difference concerns funding. Although financing is, in principle, pay-as-you-go (PAYGO) across the board, in some countries (such as the United States or Japan) it works effectively on a partially funded basis because contribution rates, having been deliberately set beyond what is needed to finance current pension expenditure, allow the accumulation of funds that can be used in the years when the strong cohorts are to retire.

The other approach to social security dominates in the Anglo-Saxon countries (with the major exception of the United States) and in Scandinavia. The public pension in this approach, originally designed as a flat-rate benefit that provides a floor for old age income, is financed by flat-rate contributions or general tax revenues. Retirement income exceeding this basic benefit should, in principle, be provided privately. Over time, however, an earnings-related part has usually been added. This has led to an increased importance of the public pension schemes for the overall old age security system and has reduced the actual difference between the two approaches to some extent.

As concerns the second important source of retirement income, occupational pensions, countries differ in a number of aspects, including the arrangement as defined benefit (DB) or defined contribution (DC) plans, the adjustment for inflation, regulations on investment (which affect risk and return), and relevant rules in the tax code, which make it more or less attractive for a firm to offer a pension fund. Of particular importance for the outcome in terms of coverage is that in some countries, namely in Australia, Switzerland, and increasingly Denmark, the enrollment in occupational pension schemes is mandatory, whereas it is voluntary in the other countries. An additional factor is whether it is possible to contract out of public earnings-related schemes; this is the case in the United Kingdom and in Japan. The relative role of occupational pensions as a source of retirement income is found to be dependent on the scale of public pension provision, especially if there is generous provision for individuals with higher income levels (Davis 1998). The replacement of a rather high share of earnings through the public pension system for medium- and high-income earners, as is the case for example in Germany, France, and Italy, tends to reduce incentives to provide for additional sources of retirement income. By contrast, the role for additional pillars is likely to increase, when the replacement rate of public pensions decreases strongly with rising income so that the pensions are more like flat benefits, which is the case, for example, in the Netherlands or in Switzerland.

With respect to the third pillar of retirement income—individual voluntary saving—there is lack of data that can to some extent be traced to the fact that it is difficult to discriminate between saving for retirement and other saving. It seems safe to say, however, that the extent of voluntary retirement saving is negatively influenced by the amount of saving that is already "forced" by the arrangements in the first and second pillars.[5] Another influence is the tax treatment of income saved for retirement.

14.1.2   Recent Reforms in Industrial Countries

Recent reforms[6] made to adjust to the pressures of the changing economic and demographic environment have essentially proceeded along three routes: (1) redressing the public pension systems; (2) strengthening the role of funded occupational pension schemes; and (3) increasing incentives for voluntary retirement saving.

Almost every country surveyed has made public pension reforms of some significance to improve the financial prospects of the system. One direction of reform was effectively reducing the level of benefits through a number of measures: The period of earnings referred to in the calculation of benefits has been increased (Belgium, Finland, France, Netherlands, Spain); basic benefits have increasingly been made subject to an income test (Canada, Finland, Sweden); and indexation rules have been changed (Austria, Finland, France, Germany, Italy, Japan, Sweden). As a further measure to contain the rise in pension expenditure, the statutory retirement age will gradually be raised in a number of countries (Germany, Italy, Japan, New Zealand, the United Kingdom, the US,), and eligibility rules for early retirement have been tightened in most countries. In addition, sometimes as part of a general tendency to strengthen the link between contributions and benefits and improve actuarial fairness, steps have been taken to reduce the attractiveness of early retirement and reward a longer working life. Another direction that has been followed by a number of countries is to increase prefunding of future pension expenditure. In some countries, a gradual increase in the rate of contribution has been legislated beyond what would have been necessary to immediately balance the system's finances in order to partially fund future liabilities (the United States, Japan, Canada). Other countries have decided to divert a certain share of contributions into funds (Finland, Sweden), which in the case of Sweden

---

5. Voluntary saving will be affected less when the promised pension benefits implicit in current rules are not credible.

6. A sketchy overview of reform measures is given in the last column of table 14.1

(and in the future, according to recent plans, in the United States) are personal accounts. In Germany, private pension funds will be integrated into the public pension system, but on a voluntary basis.

A second route of reform has been to increase the importance of fully funded, privately managed occupational pensions. One way to achieve this is to reduce the generosity of public pension benefits, and hence, to reduce the attractiveness of these schemes. There have also been important changes in the regulations concerning occupational pensions. In several cases (Australia, Denmark, Switzerland), occupational pensions have been made compulsory. Other countries enable individuals to opt out of part of their social security contributions (the United Kingdom, Japan). A further direction has been to allow additional types of pension schemes to be operated. In particular, there has been a tendency to favor the establishment of DC over DB plans (Australia, Denmark, Switzerland, the United Kingdom, the United States) in order to make occupational pension schemes more attractive, especially for smaller firms, and to reduce the problem of portability.[7] On the investment side, there is a clear tendency to ease restrictions on investment of funds, which are now recognized to contribute to increasing risk by limiting the possibility of diversification rather than to foster "prudent" investment behavior. Particularly, the allowed share of equity in the portfolio has been increased, and restrictions on cross-border investments have been eased in countries such as Australia, Canada, Denmark, Germany, Japan, and Sweden. External funding of liabilities is increasingly the rule, with Japan, for example, reducing the tax benefits to book reserve funding relative to external funding.

As for the third pillar of retirement income, the tax treatment of retirement saving has been improved in some countries. In Italy and Spain, in particular, tax incentives have rather recently been introduced.

14.1.3   More Radical Reforms in Middle-Income Countries

Although reforms in the industrial countries have been rather gradual in most cases (as will be the impact of these changes), an increasing number of middle-income countries have, in the face of a more imminent pressure to reform, resorted to a more radical transition toward a multipillar system involving a major funded element. In Latin America in recent years, countries such as Argentina, Bolivia, Colombia, Mexico, and Uruguay have followed the pioneering example of Chile. Others are engaged in serious discussions. More countries that are about to implement pension reforms along similar lines can be found in Central and Eastern Europe, including Estonia, Hungary, Latvia, and Poland. The experiences of these countries lead to the conclusion that at some stage a radical approach to reform may be more feasible than gradual adjustment. The considerable

---

7. Another reason to favor DC plans may have been the risk of default that is inherent in DB plans.

variation in the details of the pension systems that are to be established as well as in the details of the transition can be explained in part by country-to-country differences with respect to objectives, history, and current circumstances, particularly the relative strengths of redistributive and saving goals, financial market development, and taxing and regulatory capacities (James 1997). However, comparative evaluation of the pension reforms in these countries can be expected to give further empirical evidence on the shape of a well-designed pension reform.

14.1.4 Summary: Toward Increased Funding

There is a clear tendency toward reforms that increase the degree of prefunding of pension obligations. Numerous countries have proceeded significantly along that route, be it through stronger funding in the public pension schemes (Canada, Finland, Sweden, the United States) or through strengthening the role of private occupational pensions (Australia, Denmark, the Netherlands, Switzerland, the United Kingdom). Measures such as these that tend to lessen the burden on future generations have resulted in a current burden somewhat higher than it would have been without such reforms—despite the fact that measures to restrain expenditure were also taken. In some countries, contribution rates are raised beyond what would have been necessary without increased funding; in other countries, subsidies to the system from general tax revenues are increased. To this end, it can be said that the consolidation of general government finances (excluding social security) can greatly contribute to the viability of a major switch to funded pensions. This can be also concluded from the experience of the increasing number of middle-income countries that have implemented rather sweeping reforms. Other industrial counties have confined their reforms mainly to more or less significant adjustments to the prevailing PAYGO systems, without increasing the funded element (Austria, Belgium, France, Germany, Italy, Japan, New Zealand, Spain). The capacity of the conventional measures to redress these systems in order to balance their finances in the long term, however, seems limited.

14.2 Pension Systems and Pension Reforms in Industrial Countries

14.2.1 Australia

The Australian government has introduced a three-pillar system very similar to that recommended by the World Bank (1994; Bateman and Piggott 1997). It consists of a basic, tax-financed state pension (age pension), which is means tested.[8] The pension for an individual is a flat 25 percent

---

8. Since the Age Pension was introduced in 1909, it was subject to income or property tests that changed over time. In the 1970s, the means test was abolished for those over the age of seventy, but during the 1980s an income test for all age pensions was reintroduced in combination with an asset test (Knox 1995, 107).

of average weekly earnings, and the cost to the federal budget is currently around 3 percent of GDP (Edey 1997, 169). The eligibility age is sixty-five for men and sixty for women, and the pension is indexed to consumer prices (Rosenman and Warburton 1996).

Since 1986, Australia has been gradually introducing a second pillar, an obligatory (since 1992) private insurance that is fully funded and financed primarily from employer contributions, which are scheduled to reach 9 percent of wages in the year 2002. In addition, employee contributions will be 3 percent in the year 2000. The contributions are paid into an individual account that belongs to the employee and are tax deductible. Low-wage earners' contributions are supplemented by the state. A third pillar is voluntary saving or voluntary occupational pension schemes, which also receive some preferential tax treatment.

One main reason for the move of the Australian government toward a compulsory superannuation was the desire for a wider coverage of occupational old age insurance, because occupational pension schemes have traditionally been an important source of retirement income. Since the introduction of the scheme, private-sector coverage has risen from about 30 percent to some 90 percent of employees. The transition has been relatively easy because many of the features of the superannuation industry remain as they were when coverage was voluntary,[9] and the transition has not been complicated by the existence of a contributory public-sector pension scheme with unfunded liabilities.

One problem with the Australian system is that it has produced substantial uncertainty because, although it was established only recently, there have been frequent changes to the provisions of the system and to the tax treatment of both contributions and benefits (Knox 1995). An additional problem is the integration of the various pillars in a rational, equitable, and sustainable way. Specifically, the question of means-tested versus universal basic pension benefits has so far been resolved in Australia in favor of a means test. However, the retirement age of the compulsory superannuation has not been aligned with the pension age, nor is it required to take the superannuation entitlement in the form of a pension. Thus, incentives remain to retire early and become eligible for the age pension after dissipatation of some of the individual's superannuation benefit.

14.2.2   Austria

The Austrian old age pension system closely resembles the German system. It is basically earnings related and does not provide a minimum pension, although the principle of contribution equivalency has been weak-

---

9. Most of the older (voluntary) plans that remain in existence have been of the DB type, whereas the newer plans introduced in response to government requirement are of the DC type.

ened by various provisions that introduce a rather strong redistributionary element into the system. One-fourth of expenditures are covered by general tax revenues to compensate for expenditures that result from such redistribution. The financing is PAYGO, and pensions are indexed to net wages, although the increase of consumer prices serves as a bottom limit. The statutory retirement age is at sixty-five for men and sixty for women.

Austria's public pension payments represent more than 15 percent of GDP—the highest number among the industrialized countries (World Bank 1994)—mainly because of a relatively high benefits level; the replacement rate is at 76 percent on average, with significantly higher numbers for some groups of workers (Guger 1998). The contribution rate paid by employers and employees (with the exception of civil servants) is 22.8 percent with a maximum contribution threshold.

The future problems for the system due to the aging of the population are particularly alarming. One reason is that the demographic developments are slightly more unfavorable than on average in the OECD countries. A second problem is that the present burden of the system on the economy is already relatively large. Balancing the system by the year 2045 would require a contribution rate of more than 35 percent, a reduction of the replacement rate to less than 50 percent, an increase in the retirement age by more than ten years, or a combination of these. A significant reform has not yet been implemented, although the pension reform of 1993 included the change of indexation from gross to net wages. Recently, there has been some discussion on further steps to secure the viability of the system, but proposals are mainly restricted to adjustments within the system (Rürup 1997). Measures have concentrated on reducing the preferential treatment of public-sector employees but have not been convincing (Lenhardt 1997). Recently, the increased incidence of early retirement came into focus. There was an increase in the number of years used to calculate the pension in the case of early retirement, from the last fifteen to the last eighteen years. The pension reform decided upon in 2000, which otherwise contains only minor changes, went further in reducing the incentives for early retirement.

14.2.3   Belgium

The Belgian public pension[10] system is on a PAYGO basis. It consists of four major schemes: one for civil servants, one for wage earners, and one for the self-employed, as well as a guaranteed minimum-income scheme. There is a supplementary pillar of occupational pensions, which is of limited significance although some 30 percent of the workforce are covered; accumulated assets amount to about 10 percent of GDP (OECD 1994c). Private retirement insurance is available but has so far been limited in size.

---

10. This section draws on de Callatay and Turtelboom (1997).

The pension scheme for private-sector wage earners is funded through social security contributions of 16.36 percent of gross income (7.50 percent by the employee another 8.86 percent by the employer), plus a government subsidy amounting to about one percent of GDP. The level of pensions paid depends on the individual's salary during his or her entire career (with an imputed salary used for periods of illness, unemployment, etc.), the length of the career, and the individual's marital status when retired. Pensions are indexed to the consumer price index (CPI). Although there is a ceiling on earnings used to calculate the pension, there is no ceiling on contributions. Because the ceiling on pensionable income is rather low—about 20 percent above the average wage—the tax component of the social security contributions is rather large. Because the ceiling is indexed to the CPI and real wage growth is not accounted for, the pension scheme is gradually moving toward a flat basic pension scheme.

Pensions for public-sector employees are paid from the general government budget. Retirement age is sixty to sixty-five years. The retirement pension depends on the reference salary, the career length, and the replacement rate (which is dependent on the career length), and is subject to a maximum. There is also a minimum pension differentiated according to household structure. The pension scheme for the public sector is more generous than the private-sector scheme because, for one reason, pensions are effectively indexed to wages rather than to CPI.

A minor reform undertaken in 1996 will raise, over the course of the next fifteen years, the career length necessary for women to receive the full pension benefit from forty to forty-five years—the minimum career already effective for men. Retirement age at which the full pension can be drawn is between sixty and sixty-five, provided that the required number of years has been worked.[11]

14.2.4 Canada

The Canadian public pension system has two tiers. The first is financed from tax revenues and is designed to put a floor on old age income. It consists of a basic universal grant (Old Age Security [OAS]) and income-tested supplements (the Guaranteed Income Supplement [GIS] and Spouse's Allowance [SPA]). The benefits are indexed to CPI and are not taxable. They are payable from the age of sixty-five (and from the age of sixty to sixty-five for widows of OAS pensions in the case of SPA). The second tier is an earnings-related pension scheme (Canada and Quebec Pension Plans), which are PAYGO financed[12] by compulsory contributions

11. Before 1991 it was sixty-five years of age for men and sixty for women, and the pension was reduced by 5 percent for each year of retirement before reaching this statutory retirement age.
12. The Canada Pension Plan has in the past accumulated a fund amounting to roughly 7 percent of GDP.

from employers, employees, and the self-employed. The contribution rate is presently at 6.1 percent of covered earnings, split equally between employees and employers.[13] Benefits replace 25 percent of average lifetime earnings, but combined with the OAS, the benefit schedule is steeply progressive (i.e., the replacement ratio declines strongly with increasing earnings). Benefits are taxable and indexed to consumer prices. The statutory retirement age is sixty-five, but it is possible to retire as early as age sixty with an actuarial reduction of the benefit. In addition, there are tax incentives to engage in registered private pension plans, which are a relatively important source of retirement income in Canada. In 1992, 47.5 percent of workers were covered by occupational pensions (Gruber 1997, 13).

At 5 percent of GDP, public pension expenditure at present is relatively modest in international comparison; one reason is that public pensions replace a relatively small share of working-age income. The expenditure ratio has doubled over the past 25 years, however, and is projected to rise to more than 9 percent of GDP by 2030, partly as a result of a particularly steep rise in the old age dependency ratio.[14] Although expenditure on the first tier of the public pension system currently represents about one-half of total outlays, the debate has focused on the second tier because the increase in expenditure stems mainly from this part of the public pension system. It is expected that contribution rates will have to triple in the absence of reforms to keep the Canada Pension Plan (CPP) in balance.

In order to keep the CPP solvent, increases in the contribution rate to 7.9 percent in 2005 and to 9.9 percent in 2025 have already been legislated (Kramer and Li 1997, 7), but this will be insufficient without further reform. In 1997, a reform proposal was drafted that consisted of increased prefunding through an increase of the contribution rate to 9.9 percent as early as 2003. Further measures included a revision of the regulations on the investment of social security funds to raise the rate of return on these funds, a tightening of eligibility criteria, and lower benefits. The combination of these measures is projected to allow the contribution rate to be held constant after the year 2003.

Other important changes relate to the first-tier benefits (OAS, GIS, and SPA). It is envisaged to replace these benefits through a single Seniors Benefit from the year 2001. The essential feature of the Seniors Benefit is that it is more targeted than the old system, while at the same time it increases the guaranteed minimum income for pensioners (OECD 1996c,

---

13. There is both a basic exemption and an upper limit to pensionable earnings.

14. Of the difference between the contribution rate that had been projected for the year 2030 at the time of the introduction of the 1966 Canada Pension Plan—5.5 percent—and the currently expected 14.5 percent, only 30 percent is attributable to demographic developments. Another 25 percent is attributable to revisions in the underlying macroeconomic assumptions. The remainder can be attributed to the enrichment of benefits and to higher disability benefits (OECD 1996c, 126).

142). As for the transition, all Canadians aged sixty by the end of 1995 can choose either the new Seniors Benefit or the old system for the rest of their lives (Battle 1996).

14.2.5 Denmark

The Danish pension system consists of a tax-financed general basic pension replacing about 38 percent of an average wage (Danish Ministry of Economic Affairs 2000; Barnes 1997). The amount can be supplemented subject to an income test. Adding to the basic old age pension is a compulsory national pension scheme, *Arbejdsmarkedets Tillaegspension* (ATP), which is fully funded and of a DC type. Contributions are based on hours worked, but are fairly low,[15] so that the share of the ATP pension in retirement income will be fairly low when the system that was established in 1964 first matures in the early years of the next century.

In addition to the public pension schemes, most salaried employees contribute to fully funded DC pension plans established through the collective bargaining system.[16] In the beginning of the 1990s, employers and trade unions agreed to extend the coverage to virtually all workers. Contributions will gradually rise to about 9 percent of gross wages. The collective saving schemes are legally independent of the companies whose employees are covered, and the saving belongs to the individuals.

To promote further individual provision for retirement income there is a tax deduction for saving in private pension plans. However, a tax of 40 percent is levied when this saving is withdrawn. Despite this fact, individual pension plans are a popular form of saving (Barnes 1997).

With a major part of the pension system organized in fully funded DC schemes, the threat of an aging population is less pronounced in Denmark than in other countries. Recent reforms have been concerned with extending the coverage of occupational pension schemes. In 1999, the early retirement allowance scheme was changed to reduce incentives for early retirement. At the same time, the retirement age in the basic pension scheme was reduced from sixty-seven to sixty-five years. Discussion about a reform of the tax-financed basic pension involves in particular the question of introducing an income test (Gamillscheg 1997).

14.2.6 Finland

The Finnish public pension system consists of two pillars (OECD 1997e, 67ff). One is a basic pension (national pension), which is comparatively low (and supplemented from general tax revenues in the event of no other income); the other is a compulsory employment scheme granting earnings-

---

15. In 1995, the contribution for a full-time worker was 2,332 Danish krone a year, or a little more than one percent of an ordinary annual income (Barnes 1995).

16. Some central government civil-service pension schemes still work on a PAYGO basis, but they are being discontinued.

related benefits. The basic pension scheme is nationally administered and financed by contributions on a PAYGO basis; although the employment scheme is managed by more than sixty private pension institutions. The employment scheme is also financed by contributions, but it is partially funded: Financial assets cover roughly one-third of the present pension obligations (Noord 1997). The national pension tends to decrease as the occupational pension increases; except for low-wage earners, the combination of both replaces a maximum of 60 percent of pensionable income. The statutory retirement age is sixty-five years, but the average retirement age is only fifty-eight years due to disability or early-retirement schemes. Due to the generous benefit levels and a virtually universal coverage of the population by the public pension system, the market share of voluntary pension insurance has until recently been very small.

Against the background of pronounced population aging, relatively generous benefits, a low effective retirement age, and a general erosion of the tax base due to the recession in the early 1990s, a relatively far-reaching reform of the system was implemented in several steps during recent years. Without changes, the pension expenditure had been estimated to reach nearly 18 percent of GDP by the year 2030—a level exceeded only in Italy (OECD 1996b).

The main objectives of the pension reform were to promote longer working careers, to reduce benefits, and to improve the management of the pension funds, all the while maintaining the basic features of the system: its two-tier approach, its mixture of funding and PAYGO financing, its pronounced redistribution, and the strong involvement of private insurers in the management of the system.

The major components of reform have been the following (OECD 1997e, 76ff; Noord 1997):

- Discontinuation of preferential treatment for public-sector employees (1993).
- Measures to improve the pensions of older workers who remain active relative to those of workers who retire early (1994 and 1996).
- Increase in the number of years on which the calculation of pensions is based, from the last four years to the last ten years (1996).
- Change in the indexation of earnings-related pensions to a weighted average of CPI (80 percent) and earnings index (20 percent). National (basic) pensions remain indexed to CPI (1996).
- Decision gradually to abolish the flat rate component of national pensions by the end of the decade. Future national pensions will be fully offset against employment pensions.
- Adjustment of the funding method of the employment pensions, since 1993; also since 1993, employees contribute to the system. Roughly three-fifths of the contributions are used to finance current pension

expenditure. The remainder enters the account of the pension institutions. A number of measures aim at raising the efficiency of the financing of the system.

As a result of these reforms, the rise in contributions necessary to balance the system is now expected to be contained at roughly 26 percent of earnings (from 21.4 percent currently), compared to an estimated 38 percent under prereform rules. Current policies concentrate on increasing the effective retirement age. To this end, a National Program on Aging Workers for the years 1998–2002 was designed, and in 2000 the lower age limit for individual early retirement pensions was raised from fifty-eight to sixty years.

14.2.7   France

In France, the pension system (OECD 1994a) comprises a large number of PAYGO schemes (about 120 basic schemes and 400 supplementary ones). The system differentiates between private-sector and public-sector employees (including some categories of workers such as railway workers, miners, Electricité de France employees, etc.). The private sector consists of a two-level system—the general and the supplementary levels—whereas the public-sector pensions are usually one-level. Retirement age, contribution rates, and calculation of benefits may vary considerably between different schemes (Kaufmann 1997). The ordinary retirement age, introduced in 1982, is sixty. Funded pension schemes play only a very minor role.

In 1993, the first major effort to reform the public pension system aimed at the method of calculating pensions in the general scheme of the private sector (Darnant 1997). It included

- An increase in the contribution period necessary to receive the full-rate pension from 37.5 years to 40.0 years;
- An increase in the number of years used to calculate the reference wage, from ten to twenty-five;
- A change in indexation from wage growth to CPI; and
- Creation of a separate fund to finance noncontributory old age benefits resulting from national solidarity.

The effect of the 1993 reform is rather limited. Although it improves financial prospects until 2005, it leaves many questions unresolved, particularly the sustainability of the public-sector "special schemes." A proposal aimed at reforming public-sector pensions had to be withdrawn in 1995 following strikes in the public sector. Given that demographic developments are relatively beneficial until 2005 but worsen progressively afterward, the main problems are still to be solved.

In 1997, a law passed the National Assembly that would have allowed employers and employees to contribute to fully funded private pension schemes to top off their state retirement incomes. The level of payment was voluntary, but there were generous fiscal incentives to contribute up to a certain level. The aim was to strengthen the role of privately managed, capital funded pension schemes. However, after the change of government, legislation came to a halt and the law never went into effect.

Recently, the discussion centered on increasing the retirement age to sixty-five, following the publication of a report on the long-term prospects of the pension system commissioned by the government (the so-called Charpin Report). A peculiarity of the French situation is that despite the obvious demographic developments and a worldwide trend toward increasing the retirement age, there used to be a strong demand to go in the opposite direction and to decrease further the retirement age—which already is among the lowest in the world—to fifty-five. This attitude in the public, however, may be about to change with the recent pronounced decline of unemployment.

14.2.8   Germany

The provision of old age pensions in Germany is dominated by the public system, which provides roughly 85 percent of pensions. Voluntary occupational pension schemes, although they cover some 50 percent of employees, provide only 5 percent of pensions. About 10 percent of pensions come from life insurance (OECD 1996d). Old age insurance in the public pension scheme (*Gesetzliche Rentenversicherung,* or GRV) is compulsory for employees other than civil servants, whose pensions are paid out of general tax revenue, and voluntary for the self-employed. The system is PAYGO financed by contributions levied on gross wages at the rate of 19.1 percent (2001), and a transfer from the federal budget that currently covers about one-fourth of pension outlays. The statutory retirement age is sixty-five, but employees may retire earlier if they have long contribution records (at the age of sixty-three), if they are handicapped (at the age of sixty), or if they are unemployed prior to retirement (at the age of sixty). Women also may retire at age sixty if they fulfill certain eligibility criteria. As a result of these rules, more than half of the work force retires before the statutory retirement age.

A major adjustment to the system was made in 1992 to cope with the financial burden of a rising old age dependency ratio (SVR 1991, 142). In particular, the retirement age for women will be raised gradually to sixty-five from 2001, and benefits for pensioners who retire early were reduced.[17] Most importantly, the adjustment of pensions was changed from indexation to *gross* wages to indexation to *net* wages. Pension benefits are calculated according to a formula that is designed to replace 70.1 percent of

---

17. The 1992 pension reform has diminished (but not abolished) the incentives for early retirement (Börsch-Supan 1998).

average net wages during a forty-five-year working career (67.8 percent in East Germany).

Despite the reform of 1992, the public pension system's viability remained in doubt due to the progressive aging of the population. To combat the expected increase in pension expenditure (from slightly more than 11 percent of GDP in 1995 to almost 19 percent of GDP in 2035; OECD 1996d, 71), which, without other changes, would require an increase in the contribution rate to nearly 30 percent in 2030, a further reform package was legislated to take effect in 1999 (Verband Deutscher Rentenversicherungsträger [VDR] 1997). The main feature of the 1999 reform act was to reduce the ratio of pensions to net wages gradually, according to a demographic factor reflecting the increase in life expectancy of new retirees. A ratio of 64 percent was projected to be reached in about three decades. The reform package, which included additional measures to increase the effective retirement age, lay in the general direction outlined by the Council of Economic Advisors (SVR 1996, 227), but it responded to the need for reform to only a limited extent (SVR 1997, 98). More importantly, it was rejected by the opposition parties as being distributionally unacceptable and dismissed after the change in government before taking effect.

The new center-Left government's first measures toward pensions were of a stop-gap nature, aimed at reducing the contribution rate while at the same time improving the state of public finances. They consisted of increasing the federal subsidy with funds raised from a stepwise increase in energy taxes (the so-called ecological tax reform) and of an exceptional adjustment of pensions in line with consumer price inflation rather than net wages in 2000 and 2001, which will result in a decline of the replacement ratio by nearly 2 percentage points.

A major pension reform geared at coping with the long-term challenges was presented in 2000 and becomes effective in 2002. The basic idea of the reform is to reduce the replacement ratio of the public pension scheme over the years to 68 percent of wages,[18] and at the same time to introduce a funded private pillar that, when in its mature phase, is expected to supply an additional 6 percent of wages. The contribution rate to the private pension funds will be 1 percent in the first year, and will be increased by 1 percentage point every two years to reach a final 4 percent in 2008. The contributions are to be financed exclusively by employees. Although contributing to the private pillar is not compulsory, the contributions will lower the net wage and enter the calculation of pension rights in any event. The pension funds can be integrated with occupational or individual

---

18. It should be noted that the reform includes a change in the definition of the net wage. The positive effect of tax reductions—such as those legislated to take effect in 2005—on net wages will be excluded in the calculation of this new synthetic net wage. As a result, the pension level relative to the actual net wages will decline more strongly, to around 64 percent.

schemes. In order to stimulate participation in private pension insurance, a federal subsidy will be granted.

The reform is projected to keep the contribution rate to the public pension scheme below 20 percent until 2020, and below 22 percent until 2030. Including the contributions to the new private pillar, the contribution rate will reach 26 percent by 2030, which is a rate similar to the rate expected without reform, albeit at a somewhat higher level of pensions. Hence, the reform has only partly succeeded in reducing the burden of the aging population and balancing the finances of the public pension system in the long term. Proposals for other kinds of reform that include an increase of the retirement age to seventy years, or an indexation of pensions to consumer prices rather than wages, are refused at the moment. Furthermore, a more pronounced shift toward a funded system as discussed in Siebert (1998) or Börsch-Supan (1998) is currently opposed in the political arena.

14.2.9   Italy

The Italian pension system is the most expensive old age security system, in terms of GDP, among OECD countries and has expanded rapidly over the last thirty years. Although the average pension benefit relative to per capita income is broadly in line with those of other EU countries, there is a disproportionate number of pensions relative to population. This, in turn, reflects the relatively high proportion of persons over the age of sixty; the use of pensions to substitute for passive income support to the unemployed; and favorable access to early retirement through seniority pensions (until recently, workers could retire after thirty-five years of work irrespective of age; in the public sector, even earlier). Institutionally, the Italian pension system is extremely fragmented, administered by funds differentiated for professional categories (Klammer 1997). This translates into significant inequalities across groups, particularly with more favorable treatment for public-sector employees and the self-employed.

In the early 1990s, a number of minor reforms were undertaken; the most important was probably the suspension of the link between nominal wage growth and pension benefits (1992). In August 1995, however, a major reform package passed Parliament (the Dini reform); it provided the following (OECD 2000c; Reynaud and Hege 1996):

- A shift from an earnings-based system to a contributions-based system, with contributions over a lifetime period capitalized on the basis of nominal GDP growth;
- A flexible retirement age (fifty-seven to sixty-five years), with a link between benefits and residual life expectancy at retirement age;
- A phased increase in contributions required for a seniority pension from thirty-five to forty years;

- A ceiling on pensionable income; and
- Fiscal incentives for stimulating the growth of private pension funds.

As to the implementation of this major institutional reform, there is a transition period in which the old system and the new system coexist. New entrants into the labor market fall under the new system, and workers with more than eighteen years of contributions remain in the old one. To the intermediate group applies a weighted average of the old and the new formulas.

Although the 1995 reform represents an important improvement toward a more uniform and financially viable system, there remains a significant shortfall between benefits and contributions. In order to achieve the short-term goal of stabilizing pension spending as a percentage of GDP, the so-called Prodi amendments were introduced in November 1997. These included an acceleration of the harmonization of the public and private pension regimes and of the rules for a number of special schemes; a tightening of the conditions governing access to seniority pensions; and a gradual increase in the contribution rates for the self-employed from 16 to 19 percent of earnings by 2014. Despite significant progress in reform in the 1990s, the worsening of the situation over the coming thirty years is mitigated only to a limited extent. This is partly due to the long transition period; and the retirement age remains among the lowest in the OECD.

14.2.10   Japan

The Japanese pension system (OECD 1997d, 121ff.) consists of a major pillar of funded occupational pension schemes; 90 percent of private enterprises provide some form of occupational benefits at retirement, whether in form of lump-sum payments or in form of pensions. The public pension system is PAYGO financed although it has been held in surplus over an extended period of time, which resulted in the accumulation of assets amounting to some 30 percent of GDP. The system consists of two tiers. The first is a flat rate system that covers, in principle, all residents between the ages of twenty and sixty (the National Pension) Benefits are proportional to the number of years of contributions (minimum twenty-five years, maximum forty years). In the second tier, contributions and pensions are related to earnings (the Employees Pension). It is possible to contract out into certain occupational pension plans. Pensions are indexed to net wages, and the statutory retirement age is sixty years.

Against the background of the extremely rapid aging of the Japanese population, a massive deterioration of the fiscal balance of the public pension system (or a drastic increase of contribution rates to approximately 35 percent from 17.35 percent today) was to be expected. As a reaction to the deteriorating prospects of the system, the pension system was revised in 1994 (Kihara 1998; Takayama 1995).

- The retirement age at which the full amount of the pension is payable will be raised from sixty to sixty-five over the period from 2001 to 2013 for men and over the period from 2006 to 2018 for women.[19]
- The indexation was changed from gross wages to net wages.
- A one percent special contribution rate was applied to the semi-annual bonus payments, which had not been subject to contributions before.
- The increase in the contribution rate, which is scheduled to take place every five years, was increased from 2.2 percentage points to 2.5 percentage points.
- Various measures aimed at promoting delayed retirement were introduced.

As a result of these measures, it was expected that the contribution rate from the year 2025 onward could be lowered from 35 percent to 30 percent. However, a revision in underlying assumptions about birth rates and life expectancy resulted in a revised estimate of the contribution rate necessary to balance the system in the long term—an estimate that is very close to the 35 percent estimated before the reform (Kihara 1998).

A further reform package, the 1999 reform plan, was enacted in March 2000 (OECD 2000a). The bill aims to cut benefits by 20 percent when the measures are fully effective; these measures include the following:

- A reduction of Employees Pension benefits by 5 percent,
- A switch to inflation indexation for benefits from the National and Employees Pensions for those aged sixty-five or older,
- A stepwise increase in the retirement age from sixty to sixty-five for the Employees Pension, and
- The introduction of contributions on wage income for those aged sixty-five to seventy and a partial cut of their benefits according to their earned incomes.

In addition, the financial resources of the National Pension will be strengthened by a rise in the share of the government subsidy from one-third to one-half by 2004.

Despite this second major reform in five years, benefits remain largely underfunded given current rates of contribution; further reform is necessary to avoid a sizeable increase in the contribution rate. Many proposals have already been advanced, but there is strong opposition in the political arena to the introduction of funded elements.

14.2.11   The Netherlands

The Dutch pension system consists of a PAYGO financed public pension scheme that secures a universal basic pension; an extremely well-

---

19. For details of the rules concerning retirement age, see Takayama (1995, 52).

developed occupational pension sector; and, in addition, voluntary retirement saving. The public old age pension (*Algemeene Onderdomswet,* or AOW) is part of a broader social security scheme that also insures against nursing care and disability. To those who have reached the age of sixty-five it pays a flat rate pension benefit set at 70 percent (100 percent for a married couple) of the statutory minimum wage. The full rate is contingent on forty years of contributions. The benefit is reduced by 2 percent for each full year a person was not insured (Bedee et al. 1995, 268). The AOW pension benefits amounted to 5.5 percent of GDP in 1996 (Hetzel 1997), and they are PAYGO financed by contributions that are levied on the first income bracket of the tax code at the rate of 15.4 percent (1997).

The second pillar consists of funded occupational pension schemes that have developed over a long period. Probably as a consequence (in part) of the fact that the replacement rate under the public pension scheme falls sharply with increasing income, the second pillar covers virtually the entire labor force (83 percent). This is highly unusual because provision is voluntary. In most countries where provision is voluntary, coverage of occupational pension schemes tends to peak at around 50 percent (Davis 1996). Most pension plans are of the DB type, usually designed to replace 70 percent of final salary at the age of sixty-five together with the public pension, and 90 percent of pensioners receive inflation protection.[20] To increase labor mobility, there is implemented a kind of clearinghouse that makes transfers between DB plans straightforward. The occupational pension funds have accumulated a huge amount of assets representing nearly 100 percent of GDP. Additional individual retirement saving is of relatively little importance, although there are quite significant tax incentives.

In the recent discussions on reforming social security, the main focus in the Netherlands has been on cutting down on expenditures for disability insurance that, due to extremely generous rules, had virtually exploded during the 1980s (OECD 1991), with the result that 15 percent of the labor force received disability benefits at the beginning of the 1990s (Neue Zürcher Zeitung [NZZ] 1993). In 1993, disability benefits were reduced and eligibility criteria tightened.

With respect to old age pensions, there recently have been only minor changes. Notwithstanding, contribution rates to the public scheme are planned to be held at around 15 percent. The government counts on improved macroeconomic performance in general and on an increase of the labor force participation ratio (which is extremely low by international standards) in particular, in order to finance the expected rising pension expenditure due to the aging of the population. Moreover, the benefit lev-

---

20. This is also unusual. In most countries with DB plans, inflation protection is incomplete or partial, and as a result, pensions often fall sharply in real terms over time (Davis 1996, 2).

els of the basic pension may be gradually lowered relative to the incomes of the active generations, because statutory minimum wages are expected to lag behind average incomes. Any resulting deficit in the public pension scheme is planned to be covered by tax revenues. As for the occupational pension schemes, benefit calculations are envisaged to replace 70 percent of average incomes over the whole career rather than 70 percent of the last earned wage. The main objective of recent reforms has been to improve the portability of pensions in order to increase labor mobility.

14.2.12   New Zealand

In New Zealand, public pensions are flat rate benefits that are not means tested and that are paid from general tax revenues. The system works under the label "New Zealand Superannuation." Since 1994, benefits have been differentiated according to household and marital status (NZZ 1994). In order to raise revenues in the process of fiscal consolidation, a surtax of 20 percent had been introduced in 1985 on additional retirement income exceeding a certain limit. In 1992, the surtax rate was increased to 25 percent and the limit was nearly halved, which aggravated the detrimental incentive effects implied by this rule. The tax surcharge was removed in 1997. From 1990 to 1993, the benefits that are normally adjusted for inflation remained nominally unchanged with the result of a real decrease in the benefit levels.

Despite a relatively low level of benefits at present (public pension benefits in 1994 amounted to 5 percent of GDP in 1997, well below the OECD average), the rapid aging of the population will put a considerable strain on public finances. As one reaction, a gradual increase in the statutory retirement age from sixty to sixty-five years over the 1992–2001 period has been legislated.

In 1997, a major reform proposal was voted down by an overwhelming majority of 92.4 percent of the voters (Hall 1997). The reform essentially planned to replace the state pension with a compulsory private insurance scheme, in which 8 percent of taxable income would have been set aside in individual long-term saving accounts until a target sum (NZ$ 120,000) was reached in order to buy an annuity on retirement. The government would have supplemented the amount if the target was not met, but there would have been neither government guarantees nor indexation. The result would have been a decrease in government pension outlays to 2 percent of GDP in the long run. However, with the old system now remaining in place, an increase to 12 percent of GDP is still to be expected (*The Economist* 1997).

14.2.13   Spain

The public pension system in Spain is part of a more general social security scheme that also includes support for survivors, the disabled, health care, and social services. Contributions amount to 28.3 percent of wages, of which 4.7 percent is paid by employees. The share of contributions that goes to old-age pensions is not published separately. The system is extremely generous (OECD 1996a, 87): It delivers the highest income replacement ratio in the EU after Greece (nearly 100 percent after contributions and taxes). Pensions are indexed to consumer prices.

Fiscal imbalances have led to subsequent reforms that partially rectified the problems for a limited period of time (OECD 1997c, 70). In the second half of the 1980s, benefit criteria were tightened with an increase in the minimum contribution period from ten to fifteen years, and pensions began to be assessed on the last eight rather than the last two years' earnings. Since 1988, old age pensions (in addition to the public pension system) can be obtained through participation in private pension funds, an arrangement promoted by the tax code. Because they have been introduced only recently, pension funds are still relatively spare, although they are growing rapidly (Stapf 1996; OECD 1996a, 79). The volume of assets amounts to approximately 5 percent of GDP.

In 1995, a reform concept known as the Toledo Pact envisaged only minor changes (Engler 1997), including an institutional separation of the different branches of social security; an increase in the number of years on which the calculation of pensions is based, from eight to fifteen; and a change in the pattern of the accrual rate over the time of contribution, a (minor) step toward a more actuarially fair scheme that also reduces incentives to retire early.[21] Another important change is that the financing of noncontributory pensions is no longer to be made from contributions but from general tax revenues by the year 2000. Any resulting surplus in the social security system shall be used to build up a reserve fund.

14.2.14   Sweden

The Swedish public pension system[22] consists of two pillars, a flat rate basic pension and an income-related supplementary pension (ATP). The system works primarily on a PAYGO basis, although there have been surpluses accumulated in the past amounting to some 35 percent of GDP (by 1994). Discussions about the reform of the system are old. In 1994, a major reform proposal was principally agreed upon, although the specific details of the report had not been decided at that time; and it was only at the beginning of that year that the government and opposition parties agreed on the introduction of the new system (Handelsblatt 1998; *Frankfurter Allegemeine Zeitung* [FAZ] 1998). The dominant feature of the 1994 proposal was the improvement of actuarial fairness (only 25 percent of the

21. An increase in the minimum pension in 2000, however, works in the opposite direction (OECD 2000b).

22. This section draws on OECD (1995b, 1997b) and Persson (1998).

contribution can be regarded as an [actuarial] insurance premium under the old system). The new system is to be phased-in over a period of twenty years. Its main features are the following:

- The flat rate basic pension is gradually reeled in as the earnings-related pension exceeds a certain threshold.
- Earnings-related pensions are based on lifetime income rather than on the best fifteen years' income, which was the case under the old system.
- Pensions are indexed to inflation, with a reduction in the indexing factor when real GDP growth is below a certain norm (1.6 percent) and an increase when growth exceeds that norm.
- The official retirement age remains sixty-five, but earlier retirement from the age of sixty-one onward and later retirement (with no upper age limit) is possible with an actuarial adjustment of the pension.
- Pensions will be linked to life expectancy at retirement.
- The funded element of the system will be strengthened: 2.5 percentage points of the contribution rate (which is 18.5 percent of wages) will be put into individual accounts, to be managed upon the guidelines of the contributor.
- Contributions that formerly were paid by employers only (since 1995, employees have contributed at a rate of 1 percent) are shared equally between employers and employees in the new system. The extra burden on workers is compensated by income tax reductions.

14.2.15   Switzerland

In Switzerland, the three-pillar system of old age income provision has a long tradition. The system consists of a government-run old age insurance program, Alters- und Hinterlassen enversicherung (AHV), which is financed on a PAYGO basis;[23] obligatory occupational pension schemes on a funded basis; and voluntary saving promoted by preferential tax treatment.

The public pension, AHV, is financed by contributions by every person over eighteen years of age at a rate of 4.2 percent of all earned income. Contributions are paid equally by employees and employers. Since 1998, spouses who are not in the labor force have also had to contribute and are, from the year 2005 onward, entitled to a pension at the age of sixty-four. There is also a contribution from the federal budget amounting to about 20 percent of expenditures (Rechsteiner 1996, 376).

A minimum contribution is set at 390 francs (Fr) per year; an upper limit does not exist. By contrast, for the resulting benefits there is an upper

---

23. The AHV consists of assets amounting to one year of expenditure (*Ausgleichsfonds*), however (Günthardt 1997).

limit at Fr 1,990 in 1997 for single persons and Fr 2,985 for couples. The minimum pensions are Fr 995 and Fr 1,493, respectively (Ahfeldt 1997). Pensions are adjusted according to the average of a wage index and the consumer price index. The statutory retirement age is sixty-five for men and, since recently, for women as well (Berger 1997).

Because the public pension system is designed to provide only a floor to retirement income, the second pillar was made compulsory after a 1985 referendum. It requires employers to insure their employees with a pension scheme and to pay at least half of the contributions, which amount to 10 percent of the wage bill (Brestel 1998). Although occupational pensions before the introduction of the obligatory second pillar were often lost when the employer was changed, the contributions are now paid into personal accounts that belong to the individual worker. The funds collected in the second-pillar pension schemes amounted to roughly 90 percent of GDP in 1995 and are increasing rapidly.

Due to the enormous funded part of the old age pension system, the problems with the aging of the population are limited compared to other OECD countries. However, the AHV, which is PAYGO financed, will run progressively into a deficit and needs additional financing in the medium to long term (NZZ 1998) in the absence of other reform measures. A recent reform proposal includes, most importantly, restrictions on benefits for survivors; the harmonization of the retirement ages for men and women by the year 2009 combined with a general increase in flexibility of the retirement age; and an increase in subsidies from general tax revenues (NZZ 2000).

14.2.16   United Kingdom

The public pension system in the United Kingdom originates from the Beveridgean idea of a comprehensive National Insurance (providing both a basic flat rate benefit in the case of unemployment, sickness, or disability, and an old age pension) that is financed by flat rate contributions (Disney and Johnson 1998). Additional private insurance would be left to the individual's choice. In the decades after World War II, a system developed in which flat rate benefits were combined with earnings-related contributions, which eventually led to the demand for an earnings-related component of pensions. As a result, in 1978 the State Earnings-Related Pension Scheme (SERPS) was introduced. An essential feature of the arrangement was the contracting-out principle, which allows one to opt for contributing to an approved company pension scheme in exchange for a reduction in the contribution rate to the National Insurance. This should be viewed against the background of the time of introduction of SERPS, when half of the workforce was already covered by occupational pension schemes.

Further reforms, mainly the return to consumer price indexation (1979) and a downgrading of SERPS benefits (1986), made the public pension scheme less attractive (and much less expensive for the budget in the long run). In addition, the range of pension plans entitled to the contracted-out status was expanded to include DC plans in order to make occupational pension schemes more attractive, especially for smaller companies. Moreover, the possibility of opting for individual retirement saving accounts (Personal Pensions) was introduced. As a result, since the mid-1980s the number of persons remaining in SERPS has declined to about one-fourth of the workforce.

The problem for the government with this development has been that contributions to the PAYGO system were reduced through increased contracting-out. An estimated 2 percentage points of the increase in National Insurance contributions that was necessary to finance the current expenditure on SERPS pensions can be attributed to this factor (Disney and Johnson 1998).[24]

In 1995, a reform bill was designed primarily to tighten the regulation of occupational pension plans, but contained some notable components relevant to the future prospects of the public pension system as well. First, the pensionable age of women will be raised gradually between the years 2010 and 2020 to equal that of men, at sixty-five. Second, a technical reform of the calculation of SERPS benefits and the abolition of a guaranteed minimum pension will produce a large amount of saving in future government expenditures.

Due to (a) the relatively small market share of PAYGO financed public pensions, which consist of the relatively low basic pensions and provide about 15 percent of average earnings for an individual (Dilnot et al. 1994), (b) a small and declining portion of earnings-related pensions; and (c) a relatively benign demographic structure (compared to that of other countries), the problems of the public pension schemes in the United Kingdom are projected to be minor. Provided that the basic state pension continues to be indexed to prices, no increase in contribution rates will be necessary (OECD 1994b).

Recent reforms by the Blair government have concentrated on distributional aspects and on restoring public confidence in private pension schemes. Much of that confidence had been lost due to high management costs and to the inappropriate sales tactics of some of the providers, who lured financially unsophisticated workers into unsuitable pension schemes. A minimum income guarantee was introduced in April 1999 that is means tested and linked to earnings. From April 2002, SERPS will be replaced by a new State Second Pension (S2P), which will be more generous to low-income earners and will be changed into a flat rate benefit in April 2007. As concerns the funded pillar, a new kind of standardized individual DC

---

24. At the same time, the obligations in the future—and hence the future contribution rates—decreased.

schemes, so-called stakeholder pension schemes, will be introduced in April 2001.

14.2.17   United States

In the United States, the central part of the public pension system is the Old Age, Survivors, and Disability Insurance (OASDI), which is known as Social Security. This is a DB pension scheme financed by a payroll tax of currently 12.4 percent on a PAYGO basis. The system covers, in principle, every person in employment (except part of the public sector and domestics with incomes of less than $1,000 per year). There is an upper limit to average monthly earnings subject to the payroll tax. Benefits are calculated on the basis of the best thirty-five years of the career and are indexed to the consumer price index. The benefits formula contains a quite significant element of redistribution, so that low-income wage earners receive a retirement return on their Social Security taxes at more than triple the rate of high-income wage earners (Kuttner 1998).

The OASDI is required to be financially balanced over a period of seventy-five years. In 1983, after a commission chaired by Alan Greenspan testified to a severe long-term financial disequilibrium, a reform was carried out that included a slight cut in the inflation adjustment formula, an increase in the taxable income base, a gradual raising of the statutory retirement age by two years to sixty-seven beginning in the year 2000, and the taxation of Social Security benefits to retirees with abundant other incomes. Incentives to retire early were also reduced and obstacles to working longer years removed (Lumsdaine and Wise 1994, 21). In addition, the Social Security tax rate was gradually raised from 10.8 to 12.4 percent.

In combination, these measures not only restored the short-term solvency of the system but generated a surplus of contributions and a return on assets of the system higher than pension outlays. As a result, assets are accumulated in a trust fund, the volume of which is expected to peak in the year 2021 (Kijakazi, Primus, and Greenstein 1998).[25] From that year on, expenditures on Social Security benefits will surpass revenues so that the trust fund assets will progressively be run down from the year 2032 onward, until (according to recent projections) the system becomes (partially) insolvent. In contrast to the assessment of the Greenspan commission, the 1983 reforms have apparently not been sufficient to stabilize the system. There is still a significant deficit diagnosed when finances are calculated over the next seventy-five years.[26]

25. The amount of assets at the peak is estimated at around $3 trillion, about 35 percent of GDP in 1998 (*The Economist* 1998a).

26. The unfunded obligations of OASDI are an estimated $9 trillion, 106 percent of this year's GDP (Mitchell 1998). The main reason for the revision has been unanticipated weak wage growth in the decade between 1983 and 1993. It must be noted that the calculations are now based on assumptions about real growth in the economy that are extremely moderate

As a reaction to the perception of a high level of unfunded liabilities implicit in current rules, an Advisory Council was formed to evaluate the situation and possible reforms of the system. The committee came up with a number of reform proposals (Gramlich 1998), ranging from minor changes in benefit schedules and contribution rates (the financial balance would be restored mainly through improved investment of Social Security funds) to a wide-ranging reform in which the present DB system would be replaced with a large-scale DC scheme, similar to the Chilean model.

Entering the discussion very recently has been the proposal of a bipartisan working group, which essentially plans to divert 2.0 percentage points of the current 12.4 percent payroll tax into individual saving accounts (*The Economist* 1998b). To secure the system's solvency despite the reduced contributions that finance current pension expenditure, the retirement age would rise to seventy by 2029, and the early retirement age (at which a reduced pension can be received) would rise to sixty-five by 2017. In addition, some of the expected surplus in the federal budget could be used to finance the transition. As a result, the transition to a system comprising a significant funded pillar could be managed without a (Social Security) tax hike.

Although a major overhaul of the public pension scheme has not yet been decided, the administration has progressively increased incentives to save for retirement on a voluntary basis (Eckhardt 1998). Contributions to individual retirement accounts are tax deductible up to a certain limit (currently $2,000 per year). So-called 401(k) accounts (named after the respective paragraph in the income tax code) are tax-favored saving accounts for which the amount of individual saving is matched by an employer contribution.

14.3 Other Parts of the World

14.3.1 Central and Eastern Europe

The formerly centrally planned economies of Central and Eastern Europe inherited a comprehensive unfunded pension system. Pension expenditure in percent of GDP has been quite high in many countries and has increased rapidly during the early years of transition, partly due to the fact that the necessary reduction of the workforce often took place through early retirement. High pension expenditure is reflected in high rates of social security contributions, often at about 50 percent of gross wages (Holzmann 1997).[27]

(1.6 percent annual real GDP growth, compared to about 3.0 percent over the last seventy-five years).

27. In most countries, the lion's share (if not all) of the contributions is paid by the employer.

The prevailing old age pension scheme in Central and Eastern Europe was characterized by relatively low statutory retirement ages (Cichon, Hagemejer, and Ruck 1997, 16): Men generally were entitled to receive pensions at the age of sixty, women at the age of fifty-five (except in Poland, where retirement ages were sixty-five and sixty, respectively). Typical qualifying conditions were twenty-five years of contributions for men and twenty for women. Benefit formulas normally used a fixed percentage of reference income for the required minimum number of years, plus an increment for additional years of contributions. Actual replacement rates were usually relatively high and could reach 75 percent of the reference income for persons with forty years of contributions and fifty percent for as little as twenty years of contributions. In the early years of transition, however, due to incomplete indexation, the real value of pensions declined markedly in a number of countries, with the result that despite high pension expenditure in terms of GDP, a significant share of pensioners receive income below the official poverty lines (Holzmann 1997, 16).

Initial reform considerations were geared toward a financial redressing of the unfunded schemes and an elimination of the main distortions found in the traditional measures. These considerations included an increase in the statutory retirement age, an extension of the reference period on which benefits are calculated, a reduction in the replacement rate, higher deaccrual factors for early retirement, price instead of wage indexation, elimination of group privileges, and consistent tax treatment of contributions and benefits.

However, none of the reform countries has successfully implemented a consistent reform package along these lines that would have put the public pension scheme on sound financial footing in the short and medium terms. In most countries, only minor adjustments or discretionary changes have been made.[28]

Although progress in reforming the PAYGO financed pension systems along traditional lines proved to be difficult, given that such measures necessarily mean a cutback on acquired rights for important segments of the population, the focus increasingly shifted toward the possibility of a major systemic reform. In particular, a move toward funded schemes through the introduction of a multipillar pension system as proposed by the World Bank (1994) has gained popularity. In a number of countries, pension reform plans that include (partial) shifts to funded pension schemes have been proposed, and in an increasing number of them—including Estonia, Latvia, Hungary, and Poland, among others—the implementation is prepared in earnest or has even already begun. The preparation of reform plans has been assisted by the World Bank (Eesti Pank 1998), which has

---

28. For a country-by-country overview of pension reforms undertaken or under discussion, see Cichon, Hagemejer, and Ruck (1997, 22).

also granted financial assistance in the implementation (*Financial Times* 1998). In the remainder of this section, recent developments in the three major countries of the region are described in more detail.

Czech Republic

The main pillar of the Czech pension system is a public PAYGO financed system comprising (since 1996) flat-rate and earnings-related components. In order to provide additional retirement income, the establishment of private pension funds (for which pensioners' investment decisions are restricted) was made possible as early as 1993. Participation in private insurance schemes is voluntary but is supported by state contributions. Although public pension expenditure is relatively modest (compared to that of other Central European countries): at 9 percent of GDP (OECD 1996e), the rate of contribution to the public pension scheme at 26 percent is still high by international standards and is expected to increase due to a deteriorating depending ratio. In reaction to this fact, it was decided in a 1995 reform bill that the retirement age would gradually be increased from sixty to sixty-two years for men, and for women, from the original fifty-three-to fifty-seven-year range (based on the number of children) to a range of fifty-seven to sixty-one years by the year 2006. Additional measures include a gradual increase (from ten to thirty) in the number of active years on which the calculation of benefits is based, the introduction of more formal indexing rules,[29] and perhaps most importantly, the strengthening of the link between contributions and benefits. The pension reform debate has recently begun again, and focuses on the introduction of an additional mandatory, fully funded tier.

Hungary

In Hungary,[30] the National Pension Fund established in 1991 provided pensions on a PAYGO basis. A second voluntary tier, introduced in 1995, was based on mutual funds. The aging of the population, declining employment rates, and a large and rising share of the workforce in early retirement and disability pensions has inclined the government to make a number of reforms in recent years. These reforms have included a broadening of the contribution base and the raising of the statutory retirement age from the original sixty and fifty-five for men and women, respectively, to a uniform sixty-two years by 2009. The latest reform package also changes

29. Contributions are indexed to average wages and benefits to the consumer price index and wages. The adjustment of pensions to developments in prices still has a significant discretionary element. According to the reform bill, pensions are to be adjusted when consumer price increases have accumulated to 5 percent, and increases in wages are to be taken into account. In order to generate saving in government expenditures in the face of a deteriorating economic environment, however, it was decided that pensions not be raised before a rise in prices of at least 10 percent occurred (Lodahl and Schrooten 1998, 109).

30. This section draws on OECD (1997, 136) and Cichon, Hagemejer, and Ruck (1997, 23).

the indexation method from a wage-based system to a combination of wages and consumer prices (the so-called Swiss index).

The above changes in the PAYGO scheme are expected to lead to a significant surplus in the finances of the system at today's contribution rate (30 percent) in the short to medium term (although a deficit after the year 2030 is still to be expected). These use of these surpluses is planned to help finance the transition to a more equitable and financially sustainable three-tier system, which was begun at the beginning of 1998. The new system consists of a scaled-down PAYGO scheme, complemented by a compulsory, privately managed, fully funded second tier and a voluntary, fully funded third tier.

In the new system, the PAYGO tier will be DB and earnings related, providing a replacement rate of 40 percent after thirty-five years of contributions. It will be financed by three-fourths of the total present contributions. The remaining fourth will be paid into the individual retirement saving scheme. The new system will be compulsory for new entrants into the labor market, whereas existing employees below forty-seven years of age can opt for either the new multitier system or the modified old pension system.

Poland

The Polish public pension system underwent a major revision in 1993, when the system was split into two tiers (Heinrich et al. 1996, 87). One tier provides a basic flat-rate pension amounting to 24 percent of the average gross wage; the second tier pays a benefit related to the individual's years of contribution and his or her earnings in the five best of the fourteen years preceding retirement. Pension benefits are taxable. Together with the reform of the institutional characteristics of the pension system, the benefits level was raised in order to compensate for incomplete indexation in the preceding years, and a regular adjustment to changes in average wages was introduced. Currently, public pensions are (on average) as high as 70 percent of the average wage. As a result of the combination of a high benefits level and a rising number of pensioners,[31] public pension expenditure has increased strongly and has reached 16 percent of GDP, compared to an average of 10 percent in the OECD countries.

The high financial burden of the existing pension system and the mounting doubts about its viability in the future led to persistent demand for further reform. Recently, a rather sweeping reform[32] has been legislated

---

31. Although the statutory retirement ages of sixty-five and sixty for men and women, respectively, are relatively high compared to those of other Central European countries, the actual retirement age is much lower due to early retirement.

32. For a detailed description of the reform and its rationale, see World Bank (1997, 72) and Loboda and Szalkiewicz-Zaradzka (1998).

and is scheduled to become effective in 1999 (Woycicka 1998). It aims gradually to replace the present social security system with a system consisting of two mandatory pillars: the first financed on a PAYGO, DC basis (as has been introduced recently in Latvia), and the second fully funded and privately managed. In addition, retirement income is to be supplied by voluntary individual saving. As for the first pillar, benefits are calculated according to past contributions and the life expectancy at retirement, which effectively corrects for early or late retirement. In light of experience in Latvia, however, the statutory retirement ages will be kept at present levels. Twenty percent of the current social security contributions (9 percent of wages) will be paid into the second tier of the system, which consists of individual accounts in privately managed but regulated pension funds.

The system will be introduced gradually. Workers over age fifty remain in the old system, workers under age thirty will contribute to the new system, and workers between the ages of thirty and fifty may contribute to the second tier of the new system on a voluntary basis. A deficit in the current pension scheme, which results from the effective 20 percent reduction in contributions from younger workers to the PAYGO system, is planned to be financed from the general budget using receipts from privatization.

14.3.2   East Asia

East Asia is both the most rapidly aging and the most rapidly growing region (James 1997, 362). In many countries the aging of the population combines with the erosion of the extended family, and their governments will have to act quickly to meet these challenges. Currently, public pension schemes based on the principle of PAYGO financing are virtually nonexistent in East Asia. Although in some countries (such as Singapore and Malaysia) retirement saving is mandatory, and in the Philippines, there is a relatively well-developed two-pillar pension system (Asher 1998), most countries (including China and Indonesia) still must build up formal universal pension schemes. Recent steps have been dominated by efforts to extend the coverage of occupational pension schemes on a DC basis (Piazolo 1998). A special case that deserves particular attention is China, where the problems of the pension system interlink with the challenge of structural adjustments in the state-enterprise sector (World Bank 1997).

14.3.3   Latin America

Public pension systems in Latin America have traditionally been financed on a PAYGO basis. These systems have fared particularly bad in an international comparison. They did not deliver what they had promised, and although there had been cuts in benefits and rising contribution rates, financial disequilibrium increased. The Argentine public pension system, for example, was virtually bankrupt in 1991 (Queisser 1998).

In view of the deteriorating performance of the PAYGO schemes and the prospects for a further worsening of the situation, an increasing number of Latin American governments decided to implement major systemic reforms, partly along the lines of the Chilean model and partly in accordance with the World Bank's three-pillar approach. In any case, the introduction of a significant element of pension prefunding was at the heart of the reforms.

The Chilean reform of 1981 is both well known and well documented (e.g., Edwards 1998; Vittas 1995). Essentially, the reform meant to privatize old age pensions. The former PAYGO system—which was inefficient, distributively unjust, and basically insolvent—was replaced with a mandatory system based on individual capitalization, fully funded, privately managed, and operating on a DC basis. The government guarantees a minimum pension that is defined relative to the average yield of the pension funds. Pension claims that had been accumulated under the old system were recognized by issuance of government bonds.

Although some weaknesses have been identified, including a lack of coverage, problems of moral hazard among low-wage workers, and high administrative costs, the Chilean reform has been widely judged a success. This may have contributed to the spread of the idea among an increasing number of Latin American countries that public pension system reforms should tend toward more funding. Major reforms were undertaken or are still underway in Argentina (1994), Bolivia (underway), Colombia (1994), Mexico (1992, 1995), and Uruguay (1996). Other countries, including Brazil, Costa Rica, Ecuador, El Salvador, Honduras, and Paraguay, are engaged in serious discussions. In all cases the reforms involved setting up a fully funded saving plan while continuing to pay the pensions of retirees and of workers who do not switch, and issuing bonds recognizing the accrued entitlements of workers who do switch (James 1997, 363). However, the reforms in the individual countries differ significantly in a number of key respects,[33] including the character of the funded pillar (mandatory or voluntary), the mode of financing of the new system, the size of any remaining PAYGO pillar, the existence and level of a guaranteed minimum pension, the size and financing of the transition obligation, and the details of the regulatory framework. The variations in recent approaches to old age pension reform in Latin America will give an opportunity to gain further empirical evidence on the shape of a well-designed pension reform.

---

33. For a more detailed discussion of the characteristics of the reforms and of problems associated with the various pension systems, see Aiyer (1997) and Mitchell and Barreto (1997).

14.4   Concluding Remarks

There is a clear tendency toward reforms that increase the degree of prefunding of pension obligations. Many countries have proceeded significantly along that route, whether through stronger funding of the public pension schemes (Canada, Finland, Sweden, the United States) or through strengthening the role of private occupational pensions (Australia, Denmark, the Netherlands, Switzerland, the United Kingdom). These measures, which tend to lessen the burden on future generations, have resulted in a burden today that is somewhat higher than it might have been without such reforms, despite the fact that measures to restrain expenditure were also taken. In some countries, contribution rates are raised beyond what would be necessary, without increased funding; in other countries, subsidies to the system from general tax revenues are increased. Another set of industrial countries have confined their reforms mainly to more-or-less significant adjustments to the prevailing PAYGO systems, without increasing their funded elements (Austria, Belgium, France, Germany, Italy, Japan, New Zealand, Spain). The capacity of the conventional measures to redress these systems in order to balance their finances in the long term seems limited, however, for the following reasons:

- The increase in revenues through higher contribution rates or taxes is obviously about to reach a ceiling in a number of countries, due to the associated excess burdens caused by such policies and to rising international tax competition.
- Lowering other public expenditures (e.g., on education or defense) can contribute only partially, given the scope of the task.
- A marked increase in the retirement age can contribute significantly, but is politically difficult to implement—especially in cases in which high unemployment is effectively pressing actual retirement age into the opposite direction.
- The reduction in the benefit level per retiree through lower pension benefits, lower indexation, higher taxing, or enhanced means testing has been applied in recent reforms in various countries, but these measures can only mitigate some of the problems and are unlikely to put the pension schemes on sound long-term fiscal footing.

Because an early move to increase funding can significantly reduce the burden that is to be borne when the strong cohorts retire, pension reform in that direction should be part of a strategy to cope with the problems of an aging population. The majority of Euro area countries in particular have been lagging behind in that area until now. By increasing the capacity to finance the transition, further consolidation of the general government finances (excluding social security) can greatly contribute to the viability of a major switch to funded pensions. Rectifying existing PAYGO schemes (raising the retirement age, eliminating rewards for early retirement, downsizing benefits) can be seen as the first step toward developing a system with a major funded pillar, and is needed to reduce the uncovered liabilities and increase the relative attractiveness of a new system. Perhaps the examples of more radical reforms in some future member countries of the European Union in Central Europe can stimulate the discussion on more decisive reforms within the Union itself.

References

Ahfeldt, H. 1997. "Umlagesystem dient nur der Sicherung der Existenz" (Pay-as-you-go system is only to provide for basic needs). *Handelsblat* 11 (December): 4.

Aiyer, S.-R. 1997. Pension reform in Latin America: Quick fixes or sustainable reform? World Bank Policy Research Working Paper no. 1865. Washington, D.C.: World Bank.

Asher, M. G. 1998. "Die Zukunft der Altersversorung in Südostasien" (The future of old age pensions in Southeast Asia). *Internationale Revue für Soziale Sicherheit* 51 (1): 3–34.

Barnes, H. 1995. Security for elderly. *Financial Times,* 29 March.

———. 1997. The Danes will be growing old gracefully. *Financial Times,* 9 April.

Bateman, H., and J. Piggott. 1997. Mandatory retirement saving: Australia and Malaysia compared. In *Economics of pensions,* ed. M. S. Valdés-Prieto, 318–48. Cambridge: Cambridge University Press.

Battle, K. 1996. A new old-age pension. In *Reform of retirement income policy,* ed. K. G. Banking and R. Boadway, 135–90. Kingston, Ontario: School of Policy Studies.

Bedee, H., W. D'haese, V. Peitry, and A. J. Rompelman, eds. 1995. *The international guide to social security.* The Hague: Kluwer Law International.

Berger, A. 1997. "Die AHV von 1948 his heute" (The AHV from 1948 until today). *Neue Zürcher Zeitung* 30 (June): 65.

Börsch-Supan, A. 1998. Germany: A social security system on the verge of collapse. In *Redesigning social security,* ed. H. Siebert, 129–59. Tübingen, Germany: Mohr Siebeck.

Brestel, H. 1998. "400 Milliarden Franken Zwangsersparnisse in der Schweiz" (400 Billion franken forced savings in Switzerland). *Blick durch die Wirtschaft,* 12 March, 1.

Budd, A., and N. Campbell. 1998. The roles of the public and private sectors in the U.K. pension system. In *Privatizing social security,* ed. M. Feldstein, 99–127. Chicago: University of Chicago Press.

de Callatay, E., and B. Turtelboom. 1997. Pension reform in Belgium. *Cahiers Economiques de Bruxelles* 156: 373–412.

Chand, Sheetal K., and Albert Jaeger. 1996. Aging populations and public pension schemes. IMF Occasional Paper no. 147. Washington, D.C.: International Monetary Fund.

Cichon, M., K. Hagemejer, and M. Ruck. 1997. Social protection and pension systems in Central and Eastern Europe. ILO-CEET Working Paper no. 21. International Labor Organization—Central and Eastern European Team.

Cottani, J., and G. Demarco. 1998. The shift to a funded social security system: The case of Argentina. In *Privatizing social security,* ed. M. Feldstein, 177–206. Chicago: University of Chicago Press.

Danish Ministry of Economic Affairs. 2000. A sustainable pension system. Copenhagen: Danish Ministry of Economic Affairs.

Darnant, N. 1997. Reform of the social security system in France: Challenges and prospects. *European Economy, Reports and Studies* 4:193–236.

Davis, E. P. 1996. International experience of pension fund reform and its applicability to the Netherlands. Pensions Institute Discussion Paper no. 9611. London: Pensions Institute.

———. 1998. Pensions in the corporate sector. In *Redesigning social security,* ed. H. Siebert, 93–116. Tübingen, Germany: Mohr Siebeck.

Dilnot, A. W., R. Disney, P. Johnson, and E. Whitehouse. 1994. *Pension policy in the U.K.: An economic analysis.* London: Institute for Fiscal Studies.

Disney, R., and P. Johnson. 1998. The United Kingdom: A working system of minimum pensions? In *Reforming social security,* ed. H. Siebert, 207–32. Tübingen, Germany: Mohr Siebeck.

Eckhardt, J. 1998. "Privat vorsorgen oder kurztreten" (Make provisions privately or pull back). *Handelsblatt,* 2 June, 10.

The Economist. 1997. When pay stops. 19 July, 55.

———. 1998a. Social security, star of the show. 31 January, 50.

———. 1998b. And the work goes on. 23 May, 46–47.

Edey, M. L. 1997. Retirement income policy in Australia. In *Social security reform,* eds. S. A. Sass and R. K. Triest, 168–73. Federal Reserve Bank of Boston conference series no. 41. Boston: Federal Reserve Bank of Boston.

———. 1998. Australia's retirement income system. In *Privatizing social security,* ed. M. Feldstein, 63–89. Chicago: University of Chicago Press.

Edey, M., and J. Simon. 1998. Australia's retirement income system. In *Privatizing social security,* ed. M. Feldstein, 63–89. Chicago: University of Chicago Press.

Edwards, S. 1998. Chile: Radical change towards a funded pension system. In *Redesigning social security,* ed. H. Siebert, 233–63. Tübingen, Germany: Mohr Siebeck.

———. 1998. The Chilean pension reform: A pioneering program. In *Privatizing social security,* ed. M. Feldstein, 33–57. Chicago: University of Chicago Press.

Eesti Pank. 1998. Republic of Estonia memorandum of economic policies. Available at [http://www.ee/epbe/en/release/memorandum.html].

Engler, A. 1997. "Renten in Spanien auf weichem Fundament" (Pensions in Spain on weak foundations). *Börsen-Zeitung,* 12 March, 3.

Frankfurter Allegemeine Zeitung (FAZ). 1998. "In Schweden gibt es eine Einigung über die große Rentenreform" (In Sweden there is an agreement on the great pension reform). *Frankfurter Allgemeine Zeitung,* 14 January, 16.

Financial Times. 1998. Hungary to reform pensions. 30 January, 2.

Gamillscheg, H. 1997. "Volkspension auf dem Prüfstand" (The people's pension in the test house). *Frankfurter Rundschau,* 17 January, 9.

Gramlich, E. M. 1998. The United States: How to deal with uncovered future Social Security liabilities. In *Reforming social security,* ed. H. Siebert, 161–68. Tübingen, Germany: Mohr Siebeck.

Gruber, J. 1997. Social security and retirement in Canada. NBER Working Paper no. 6308. Cambridge, Mass.: National Bureau of Economic Research.

Guger, A. 1998. Austria's pension system in an international comparison. *Austrian Economic Quarterly* 1 (1): 31–42.

Günthardt, W. 1997. "Offene Generationsrechnung bei der AHV" (Open generational account at the AHV). *Neue Zürcher Zeitung,* 30 June, B5.

Hall, T. 1997. NZ coalition in doubt after referendum defeat. *The Financial Times,* 30 September, 8.

Handelsblatt. 1998. "Parteien einigen sich zähem Ringen auf Rentenreform" (Parties agree on pension reform after tough struggle). 12 January, 8.

Heinrich, R. P., et al. 1996. "Sozialpolitik im Transformationsprozeß Mittel- und Osteuropas" (Social policy in the Central and Eastern European transformation process). *Kieler Studien,* vol. 273. Tübingen, Germany: Mohr Siebeck.

Hetzel, H. 1997. "Pensionfonds federn vieles ab" (Pension funds cushion much). *Börsen-Zeitung,* 5 April, 3.

Holzmann, R. 1997. Pension reform in Central and Eastern Europe: Necessity, approaches and open questions. *Serie Financiamento del Desarollo* no. 45. Santiago, Chile: Economic Commission for Latin America and the Caribbean.

James, E. 1997. Public pension plans in an international perspective. In *The economics of pensions,* ed. M. S. Valdés-Prieto, 350–70. Cambridge: Cambridge University Press.

Kaufmann, O. 1997. "Alterssicherung in den französischen Sondersystemen" (Old age security in the French special systems). *Die Angestelltenversicherung* 44 (9): 430–42.

Kihara, S. 1998. How should Japan's public pension system be revised? *Japan Research Quarterly* 7 (1): 64–113.

Kijazaki, K., W. Primus, and R. Greenstein. 1998. Understanding the financial status of the social security system in light of the 1998 trustees' report. Available at [http://www.cbpp.org/424socsec.html].

Klammer, U. 1997. *Alterssicherung in der Europäischen Union II: Alterssicherung in Italien* (Old age social security in the European Union. Part II: Old age social security in Italy). Berlin: Duncker & Humblot.

Knox, David M. 1995. The age pension: Means tested or universal? *Australian Economic Review* 3:107–10.

Kramer, C., and Y. Li. 1997. Reform of the Canada pension plan: Analytical considerations. IMF Working Paper no. 97/141. Washington, D.C.: International Monetary Fund.

Kuttner, R. 1998. Rampant bull. *The American Prospect* 39 (July-August): 30–36.

Lenhardt, P. 1997. "Die gescheiterte Reform" (The failed reform). *Die Presse,* 6 November, 11.

Loboda, A., and L. Szalkiewicz-Zaradka. 1998. "Zur Reform des Rentenversicherungssystems in Polen" (On the reform of the pension system in Poland). *Wirtschaft und Recht in Osteuropa* 7 (4): 128–30.

Lodahl, M., and M. Schrooten. 1998. "Probleme der Rentenversicherung in Osteuropa" (Problems of pension systems in Eastern Europe). *Soziale Sicherheit* 47 (3): 104–10.

Lumsdaine, R. L., and D. A. Wise. 1994. Aging and labor force participation: A review of trends and explanations. In *Aging in the United States and Japan,* ed. Y. Noguchi and D. A. Wise, 7–41. Chicago: University of Chicago Press.

Mitchell, O. S. 1998. Developments in pensions. *NBER Reporter,* Spring: 12–14.

Mitchell, O. S., and F. A. Barreto. 1997. After Chile, what? Second-round pension reforms in Latin America. NBER Working Paper no. 6316. Cambridge, Mass.: National Bureau of Economic Research.

Neue Zürcher Zeitung (NZZ). 1993. "Niederländische Rentenreform verabschiedet" (Dutch pension reform passed). *Neue Zürcher Zeitung,* 8 July, 11.

———. 1994. "Pensionsfragen im pazifischen Raum" (Pension questions in the Pacific region). *Neue Zürcher Zeitung,* 11 February, 13.

———. 1996. "Staatszuschuß zur niederländischen Altersrente" (Government subsidy for the Dutch old age pension). *Neue Zürcher Zeitung,* 18 September, 11.

————. 2000. "Unverändertes Gerüst der 11 AHV-Revision" (Unchanged scaffolding of the eleventh AHV revision). 3 February, 25.

Noord, P. van den. 1997. Finland: Reforming the pension system. *OECD Observer* 207 (October/November): 34–35.

Noord, P. van den, and R. Herd. 1993. Pension liabilities in the seven major economies. OECD Working Paper no. 5. Paris: Organization for Economic Cooperation and Development.

Organization for Economic Cooperation and Development (OECD). 1991. *Economic Surveys: Netherlands.* Paris: OECD.

————. 1994a. *Economic Surveys: France.* Paris: OECD.

————. 1994b. *Economic Surveys: United Kingdom.* Paris: OECD.

————. 1994c. *Economic Surveys: Belgium/Luxembourg.* Paris: OECD.

————. 1995a. *Economic Outlook* 57 (June). Paris: OECD.

————. 1995b. *Economic Surveys: Sweden.* Paris: OECD.

————. 1996a. *Economic Surveys: Spain.* Paris: OECD.

————. 1996b. Aging in OECD-countries: A clinical policy challenge. *OECD Social Policy Studies,* no. 20. Paris: OECD.

————. 1996c. *Economic Surveys: Canada.* Paris: OECD.

————. 1996d. *Economic Surveys: Germany.* Paris: OECD.

————. 1996e. *Economic Surveys: The Czech Republic.* Paris: OECD.

————. 1997a. *Economic Surveys: Italy.* Paris: OECD.

————. 1997b. *Economic Surveys: Sweden.* Paris: OECD.

————. 1997c. *Economic Surveys: Spain.* Paris: OECD.

————. 1997d. *Economic Surveys: Japan.* Paris: OECD.

————. 1997e. *Economic Surveys: Finland.* Paris: OECD.

————. 1997f. *Economic Surveys: Hungary.* Paris: OECD.

————. 2000a. *Economic Surveys: Japan.* Paris: OECD.

————. 2000b. *Economic Surveys: Spain.* Paris: OECD.

————. 2000c. *Economic Surveys: Italy.* Paris: OECD.

Persson, M. 1998. Reforming social security in Sweden. In *Redesigning social security,* ed. H. Siebert, 169–85. Tübingen, Germany: Mohr Siebeck.

Piazolo, M. 1998. "Alterssicherungssysteme in Asien: Reformbedarf und neuste Entwicklungen" (Old-age pension systems in Asia: Reform needs and recent developments). *Asien* 66 (January): 5–22.

Queisser, Monika. 1998. *The second generation pension reforms in Latin America.* Development Centre Studies. Paris: OECD.

Rechsteiner, R. 1996. "Neugestaltung der schweizerischen Alterssicherung: Flexibler, funktioneller und sozialer" (Reform of the Swiss old age social security: More flexible, more functional, and more social). *Schweizerische Zeitschrift für Sozialversicherung* 40 (5): 372–98.

Reynaud, E., and A. Hege. 1996. "Italien: Grundlegende Umgestaltung der Altersversorgung" (Italy: Sweeping reform of old age social security). *Internationale Revue für Soziale Sicherheit* 49 (3): 75–86.

Rosenman, L., and J. Warburton. 1996. "Umgestaltung der australischen Altersversorgung: Veränderungen in den Arbeits- und Ruhestandsstrukturen und ihre Auswirkungen" (Reform of the Australian old age social security: Changes in the work and retirement structures and their effect). *Internationale Revue für Soziale Sicherheit* 49 (4): 5–27.

Rürup, B. 1997. "Perspektiven der Pensionsversicherung in Österreich" (Perspectives on the pension system in Austria). Study commissioned by the Federal Ministry of Labor, Health, and Social Affairs. Vienna-Darmstadt: Technische Hochschule Darmstadt.

Sales-Sarrapy, C., F. Solis-Soberón, and A. Villagómez-Amezcua. 1998. Pension system reform: The Mexican case. In *Privatizing social security,* ed. M. Feldstein, 135–72. Chicago: University of Chicago Press.

Siebert, H. 1998. Pay-as-you-go versus capital-funded pension systems: The issues. In *Redesigning social security,* ed. H. Siebert, 3–33. Tübingen, Germany: Mohr Siebeck.

SVR (Sachverständigenrat zur Begutachtung der gesamtwirtschaftlichen Entwicklung [Council of economic advisors]). 1991. *Die wirtschaftliche Integration in Deutschland. Perspektiven—Wege—Risiken.* Jahresgutachten 1991/92. Stuttgart: Metzler-Poesche.

———. 1996. *Reformen voranbringen.* Jahresgutachten 1996/97. Stuttgart: Metzler-Poesche.

———. 1997. *Wachstum, Beschäftigung, Währungsunion—Orientierungen für die Zukunft.* Jahresgutachten 1997/98. Stuttgart: Metzler-Poesche.

Takayama, N. 1995. "Der Gesetzentwurf von 1994 zur Reform der öffentlichen Renten in Japan: Hauptinhalt und Erörterung" (The 1994 act on the reform of public pensions in Japan: Main topics and discussion). *Internationale Revue für Soziale Sicherheit* 48 (1): 51–73.

Vittas, Dimitri. 1995. *Strengths and weaknesses of the Chilean pension reform.* Washington, D.C.: World Bank.

Verband Deutscher Rentenversicherungsträger (VDR). 1997. *Die Rentenreform 1999* (The 1999 pension reform). Frankfurt: VDR.

World Bank. 1994. *Averting the old-age crisis.* Oxford: Oxford University Press.

———. 1997a. *Old age security: Pension reform in China.* Washington, D.C.: World Bank.

———. 1997b. *Poland country economic memorandum.* Washington, D.C.: World Bank.

Woycicka, I. 1998. "Dreisäulenmodell soll Rentensystem vor dem Kollaps retten" (Three-pillar model will save pension system from collapse). *Handelsblatt,* 2 June, 10.

Appendix

OECD Statistical and Analytical Information on Aging

In recent years, the Organization for Economic Cooperation and Development (OECD) has published a wide range of analyses examining the demographic forces in and likely economic and social impacts of aging societies, and has evaluated the policy options and responses.[1] The following tables and figures are largely taken from these studies. They are grouped around four broad themes: the demographic, labor-market, social-spending, and institutional features of pension systems. The OECD has also examined financial market issues connected with changing trends in the way individuals and societies provide for retirement, although this information is not presented here.[2]

The demographic data in this information pack are sourced from the United Nations' (UN's) 1998 revision of world population prospects, which was released in 1999.[3] For European Union (EU) countries they differ from those compiled by Eurostat, due in part to different assumptions concerning fertility and net immigration rates. As a consequence, derived measures such as the dependency ratio can be very different depending on the source used for demographic data, especially as the projection period is extended.

The data on social spending and the labor market are compiled partly from the OECD labor force statistics and social-spending databases, and partly from analytical studies. The cutoff date for information varies de-

1. This work was synthesized in OECD (1998a).
2. Information of this kind is available in OECD (1998b).
3. The next revision to the UN demographic projections, the highlights of which were published in early 2001, will be released in mid-2001.

pending on the source, but in most cases it is 1997. Special care, in particular, needs to be taken when one uses the information contained in the tables and figures summarizing the institutional features of pension systems. These data were collected in 1997 and verified in 1998, and therefore characterize the situation as it was three years ago. For the most part, the tables remain broadly up to date; but there are exceptions. In Italy, for example, measures (the Prodi agreement) were taken in late 1997 and effected in 1998 to phase in more rapidly the increase in the early retirement age, to bring forward the harmonization of public and private pension regimes, and to increase pension contributions paid by the self-employed. Furthermore, since 1997, ten other OECD countries, including Japan, Spain, and the United Kingdom, have implemented or are in the process of implementing reforms that are also expected to increase the amount of time spent in employment and reduce the amount of time spent in retirement. Another six countries, including Korea and the Netherlands, are actively considering such polices. However, the impact and specific nature of measures adopted since 1997 vary widely. Some countries have opted to increase the official retirement age, others effectively to lower the level of benefit if taken early, and others to tighten the eligibility criteria.[4]

Data are posted at *http://www.nber.org/pensioncrisis.*

OECD Tables and Figures on Aging

Tables

I. Demographic
   1. Total population growth estimates and projections in OECD countries
   2. Total population estimates and projections in OECD countries
   3. Elderly population growth estimates and projections in OECD countries
   4. Elderly population estimates and projections in OECD countries
   5. Population growth estimates and projections for the fifteen- to sixty-four-year-old age group in OECD countries
   6. Population estimates and projections for the fifteen- to sixty-four-year-old age group in OECD countries
   7. Median age estimates and projections in OECD countries
   8. Female fertility rate estimates and projections in OECD countries
   9. UN net migration rate estimates and projections in OECD countries

---

4. For a report summarizing recent progress in implementing reforms in OECD countries, see OECD (2000).

6. Average implicit tax rates and average retirement ages
7. Expected number of years in and out of employment in OECD and G7 countries
III. Social Spending
8. Trends in and composition of total social expenditures in G7 countries
9. Proportion of GDP spent on old age pensions in OECD countries, 1997
IV. Institutional
10. Estimates of the average age of retirement (by sex) in OECD countries
11. Countries taking policy action in retirement incomes, as a proportion of countries surveyed

References

Organization for Economic Cooperation and Development (OECD). 1998a. *OECD proceedings: Institutional investors in the new financial landscape.* Paris: OECD.
———. 1998b. *Maintaining prosperity in an ageing society.* Paris: OECD.
———. 2000. *Reforms for an ageing society: Social issues.* Paris: OECD.

Contributors

David Blake
Birkbeck College
University of London
7-15 Gresse Street
London WIT ILL
United Kingdom

Didier Blanchet
INSEE
18 Bd Adolphe Pinard
75675 Paris Cedex 14
France

Axel Börsch-Supan
Department of Economics
University of Mannheim
D-68131 Mannheim
Germany

A. Lans Bovenberg
Faculty of Economics and Business
    Administration
Tilburg University
PO Box 90153
NL-5000 LE Tilburg
The Netherlands

Michael Burda
Institut für Wirtschaftstheorie
Humboldt-Universität zu Berlin
Spandauer Str. 1
D-10178 Berlin
Germany

Martine Durand
OECD
Economics Department
2 rue André Pascal
75016 Paris
France

Martin Feldstein
National Bureau of Economic
    Research
1050 Massachusetts Avenue
Cambridge, MA 02138

Daniele Franco
Research Department
Banca d'Italia
Via Nazionale, 91
00184 Roma
Italy

Klaus-Jürgen Gern
Kiel Institute of World Economics
Düsternbrooker Weg 120
D-24105 Kiel
Germany

Jonathan Gruber
Department of Economics, E52-355
Massachusetts Institute of Technology
50 Memorial Drive
Cambridge, MA 02142-1347

Jerzy Hausner
Cracow University of Economics
ul. Kakowicka 27
31-510 Krakow
Poland

Herbert Hax
Institut für Betriebswirtschaftslehre
Universität Wien
Bruenner Str. 72
A-1210 Wien
Austria

Alain Jousten
Faculté d'Économie, de Gestion,
    et de Sciences Sociales
Université de Liège
Boulevard du Rectorat, 7
4000 Liège
Belgium

Laurence J. Kotlikoff
Department of Economics
Boston University
270 Bay State Road
Boston, MA 02215

Jeroen J. M. Kremers
Ministry of Finance of the
    Netherlands
Korte Voorhout 7
PO Box 20201
2500 EE The Hague
The Netherlands

Jukka Lassila
ETLA–The Research Institute of the
    Finnish Economy
Lönnrotinkatu 4 B
FIN 00120 Helsinki
Finland

Florence Legros
CERPEM
University of Paris IX-Dauphine
Place du marechal de Lattre de
    Tassigny
75775 Paris Cedex 16
France

Assar Lindbeck
Institute for International Economic
    Studies
Stockholm University
S-106 91 Stockholm
Sweden

John McHale
Department of Economics
Harvard University
Littauer Center 230
Cambridge, MA 02138

Georges de Menil
École des Hautes Études en Sciences
    Sociales
54, Boulevard Raspail
75006 Paris
France

Edward Palmer
Head of Division for Research and
    Evaluation
National Social Insurance Board
Adolf Fredriks Kyrkogata 8
103 51 Stockholm
Sweden

Franco Peracchi
Faculty of Economics
Tor Vergata University
I-00133 Rome
Italy

Pierre Pestieu
Faculté d'Économie, de Gestion,
    et de Sciences Sociales
Université de Liège
Boulevard du Rectorat, 7
4000 Liège
Belgium

Roberto Rocha
Lead Economist, ECSPF
The World Bank
1818 H Street, NW
Washington DC, 20433

Bert Rürup
Institut für Volkswirtschaftslehre
FG Finanz- und Wirschaftspolitik
Technische Universität Darmstadt
Residenzschloß
D-64283 Darmstadt
Germany

Andrew A. Samwick
Dartmouth College
Department of Economics
6106 Rockefeller Hall
Hanover, NH 03755

Eytan Sheshinski
Department of Economics
Hebrew University of Jerusalem
Mount Scopus
Jerusalem 91905
Israel

Horst Siebert
Kiel Institute for World Economics
Düsternbrooker Weg 120
24105 Kiel
Germany

Tarmo Valkonen
ETLA–The Research Institute of the
    Finnish Economy
Lönnrotinkatu 4B
FIN 00120 Helsinki
Finland

Reijo Vanne
Research Department
Central Pension Security Institute
Kirjurinkatu 3
00065 ELÄÄKETURVAKESKUS
Helsinki
Finland

Dimitri Vittas
Development Research Group
The World Bank
1818 H Street NW
Washington, DC 20433

David A. Wise
John F. Kennedy School of
    Government, Harvard University
and National Bureau of Economic
    Research
1050 Massachusetts Avenue
Cambridge, MA 02138-5398

Author Index

Subject Index